HUMAN
RIGHTS
WATCH
WORLD
REPORT
1 9 9 5

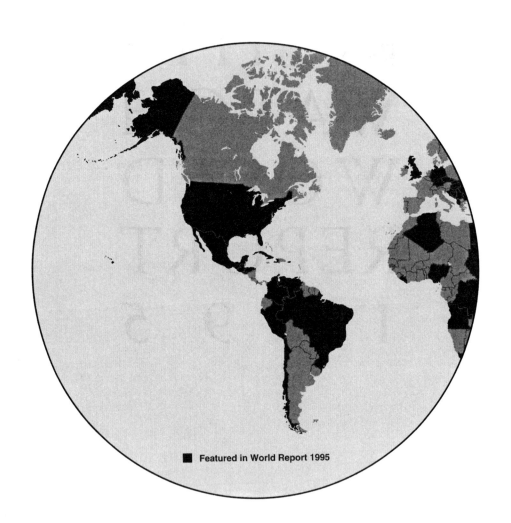
Featured in World Report 1995

Featured in World Report 1995

HUMAN RIGHTS WATCH WORLD REPORT 1995

Events of 1994

New York · Washington
Los Angeles · London · Brussels

ISBN 0-300-06363-6
ISSN 1054-948X

Human Rights Watch
485 Fifth Avenue
New York, NY 10017-6104
Tel: (212) 972-8400
Fax: (212) 972-0905
E-mail: hrwatchnyc@igc.apc.org

Human Rights Watch
1522 K Street, N.W., Suite 910
Washington, DC 20005-1202
Tel: (202) 371-6592
Fax: (202) 371-0124
E-mail: hrwatchdc@igc.apc.org

Human Rights Watch
10951 West Pico Blvd., Suite 203
Los Angeles, CA 90064-2126
Tel: (310) 475-3070
Fax: (310) 475-5613
E-mail: hrwatchla@igc.apc.org

Human Rights Watch
33 Islington High Street
N1 9LH London
United Kingdom
Tel: (71) 713-1995
Fax: (71) 713-1800
E-mail: hrwatchuk@gn.apc.org

Human Rights Watch
15 Rue Van Campenhout
1040 Brussels, Belgium
Tel: (2) 732-2009
Fax: (2) 732-0471
E-mail: hrwatcheu@gn.apc.org

HUMAN RIGHTS WATCH

Human Rights Watch conducts regular, systematic investigations of human rights abuses in some seventy countries around the world. It addresses the human rights practices of governments of all political stripes, of all geopolitical alignments, and of all ethnic and religious persuasions. In internal wars it documents violations by both governments and rebel groups. Human Rights Watch defends freedom of thought and expression, due process and equal protection of the law; it documents and denounces murders, disappearances, torture, arbitrary imprisonment, exile, censorship and other abuses of internationally recognized human rights.

Human Rights Watch began in 1978 with the founding of its Helsinki division. Today, it includes five divisions covering Africa, the Americas, Asia, the Middle East, as well as the signatories of the Helsinki accords. It also includes five collaborative projects on arms transfers, children's rights, free expression, prison conditions, and women's rights. It maintains offices in New York, Washington, Los Angeles, London, Brussels, Moscow, Belgrade, Zagreb, Dushanbe, and Hong Kong. Human Rights Watch is an independent, nongovernmental organization, supported by contributions from private individuals and foundations worldwide. It accepts no government funds, directly or indirectly.

The staff includes Kenneth Roth, executive director; Cynthia Brown, program director; Holly J. Burkhalter, advocacy director; Gara LaMarche, associate director; Juan Méndez, general counsel; Susan Osnos, communications director; and Derrick Wong, finance and administration director.

The regional directors of Human Rights Watch are Abdullahi An-Na'im, Africa; José Miguel Vivanco, Americas; Sidney Jones, Asia; Jeri Laber, Helsinki; and Christopher E. George, Middle East. The project directors are Joost R. Hiltermann, Arms Project; Lois Whitman, Children's Rights Project; Gara LaMarche, Free Expression Project; Joanna Weschler, Prison Project; and Dorothy Q. Thomas, Women's Rights Project.

The members of the board of directors are Robert L. Bernstein, chair; Adrian W. DeWind, vice chair; Roland Algrant, Lisa Anderson, Peter D. Bell, Alice L. Brown, William Carmichael, Dorothy Cullman, Irene Diamond, Edith Everett, Jonathan Fanton, Alan Finberg, Jack Greenberg, Alice H. Henkin, Harold Hongju Koh, Stephen L. Kass, Marina Pinto Kaufman, Alexander MacGregor, Josh Mailman, Peter Osnos, Kathleen Peratis, Bruce Rabb, Orville Schell, Gary G. Sick, Malcolm Smith, Nahid Toubia, Maureen White, and Rosalind C. Whitehead.

ACKNOWLEDGMENTS

A compilation of this magnitude requires contributions from a large number of people, including the entire Human Rights Watch staff. The contributors were:

Bess Abraham, Fred Abrahams, Aziz Abu-Hamad, Patricia Gossman, Marcia Allina, Abdullahi An Nai'm, Cynthia J. Arnson, Michelle Baird, Ann Beeson, Kathleen Bleakley, Sebastian Brett, Cynthia Brown, Holly Burkhalter, Bruni Burres, Holly Cartner, Jim Cavallaro, Diana Tai-Feng Cheng, Allyson Collins, Steven Crandall, Melissa Crow, Erika Dailey, Rafael de la Dehesa, Rachel Denber, Richard Dicker, Janet Fleischman, Alison Des Forges, Christopher George, Mark Girouard, Eric Goldstein, Stephen Goose, Patricia Gossman, Sasha Greenawalt, Jeannine Guthrie, Heather Harding, Elahé S. Hicks, Giselda Hidalgo, Joost Hilterman, David Holiday, Suzanne Howard, Jennifer Hyman, LaShawn Jefferson, Mike Jendrzejczyk, Vanessa Jimenez, Sidney Jones, Jasminka Kalajdzic, Farhad Karim, Robin Kirk, Anne Kuper, Gara La Marche, Jeri Laber, Sarah Lai, Zunetta Liddell, Ivan Lupis, Anne Manuel, Michael McClintock, Joanne Mariner, Zeljka Maekic, Aliya Mawani, Kimberly Mazyck, Evelyn Miah, Vlatka Mihelic, Loren K. Miller, Aung Myo Min, Robin Munro, Ivana Nizich, Binaifer Nowrojee, Brian Owsley, Christopher Panico, Magaly Pérez, Alexander Petrov, Dinah PoKempner, Regan Ralph, Jemera Rone, Virginia Sherry, Karen Sorensen, Mickey Spiegel, Gretta Tovar Siebentritt, Lee Tucker, Alex Vines, José-Miguel Vivanco, Marti Weithman, Joanna Weschler, Lois Whitman, Berhane Woldegabriel, Fatemeh Ziai.

Cynthia Brown and Michael McClintock edited the report, Robert Kimzey designed and proofread it, and Nandi Rodrigo assisted throughout the editing and production process. Holly Burkhalter and Lotte Leicht reviewed sections on policy.

CONTENTS

Helsinki Watch

Middle East Watch

Human Rights Watch

INTRODUCTION

The will to uphold human rights failed dismally in 1994. Having bound and shelved the volume of high-sounding pronouncements made the year before at the World Conference on Human Rights, the major powers led a wholesale retreat from their implementation. These governments shrank from the year's most urgent challenge—preventing genocide in Rwanda. And they allowed a growing mercantilism to dominate their foreign policy and undermine the vigorous protection of human rights. Increasingly, the duty to ensure respect for the most basic human values gave way to a vision that equated economic self-interest with the common good.

In Washington, the year opened on a bright note, with the Clinton administration having linked trade benefits for China and Indonesia to human rights improvements and conditioned the lifting of sanctions against Serbia on its cooperation with international efforts to investigate and prosecute war criminals. The year closed with an abandonment of trade linkages in favor of "commercial diplomacy" and a weakening of sanctions against Serbia without any commitment from Belgrade to support the quest for justice.

Throughout the year, President Clinton rarely showed the moral leadership needed to build public support for a tough human rights policy. Typical was his role during the debate about using Most Favored Nation (MFN) trade status to improve China's abysmal human rights record. Rather than personally emphasizing the importance of ending systematic torture and political imprisonment among U.S. trading partners, he left the task of defending his policy to the State Department while allowing the Treasury and Commerce Departments publicly to oppose it.

When the killing broke out in Rwanda, the President never made the case for ending genocide. Instead of pressing for safe havens that might have saved countless lives, his administration issued a laundry list of objections to U.N. action. Only when televised pictures of desperate Rwandan refugees provoked public outrage did the administration mount a relief operation in Zaire, but by then the genocide in Rwanda was largely complete.

Haiti was a notable exception to this passivity. President Clinton was ahead of American public opinion in insisting on an end to the military's reign of terror and the return of elected President Jean-Bertrand Aristide. But even the Haitian crisis was aggravated by his administration's initial sixteen months of indifference, when it downplayed atrocities and forcibly returned those who fled.

The Clinton administration continued the U.S. government's reluctance to subject itself to international human rights law and mechanisms. While it actively supported adding Rwanda to the jurisdiction of the international tribunal for the former Yugoslavia, it resisted the creation of a permanent international tribunal that would have jurisdiction worldwide, including for the United States. And although it belatedly acquiesced to international law by ending the summary repatriation of Haitians, it tacitly encouraged the Cuban government to violate that law by prosecuting those who exercised their international right to flee.

The European Union and some of its key member states shared in this retreat from human rights values. Bonn led the charge for Asian contracts, to the neglect of Asian human rights victims. Paris financed arms purchases by a ruthless government in Rwanda, intervened at the height of the genocide only to let the killers escape, weapons in hand, and then used the Rwandan crisis to rehabilitate Zairean despot Mobutu Sese Seko. London and Paris championed the U.N.'s practice of accommodating the Bosnian Serbs, espoused a vision of ethnically pure enclaves in Bosnia-Hercegovina that was incompatible with basic human rights norms, and ensured that the occasional defense of civilians in Security Council-declared "safe areas" never ventured beyond the token.

A similar moral vacuum filled the halls of the United Nations. Secretary-General Boutros Boutros-Ghali acknowledged the difficulty of upholding human rights while maintaining a posture of neutrality between murderer and victim, but then opted for neutrality. This failure of leadership, eagerly abetted by the Security Council's permanent members, led to a squandering of the U.N.'s unique capacity on the global stage to articulate fundamental human rights values and to legitimize their enforcement. The loss in 1994 was felt most deeply in Bosnia and Rwanda.

There were positive developments in the past year. The steps taken, however haltingly, toward building an international system of justice for the worst human rights criminals were of extraordinary importance. These had parallels at the national level in several countries. The end of the apartheid regime in South Africa and the inauguration of freely elected President Nelson Mandela were milestones for the human rights movement. Consolidation of respect for human rights continued in parts of Eastern Europe and Latin America. Overall, however, these positive trends were overshadowed by the disturbing withdrawal of the major powers from the human rights arena.

The Mercantilist Threat

In 1993, as the World Conference on Human Rights approached, several Asian governments stepped up their promotion of an "Asian concept of human rights." They maintained that Asians sought economic development before political liberty, valued communal obligations over individual rights, and supported national rather than universal human rights standards. The argument was a convenient justification for the political status quo. Asian nongovernmental organizations, when they had the opportunity to speak freely, forcefully rejected it. Their defense of universal human rights was joined by a broad range of governments worldwide, including the United States, Japan and many European governments.

This year, while the major economic powers continued to give lip-service to universality, their rhetoric suggested increasing acceptance of the "Asian concept" that economic growth by itself would improve human rights. The pursuit of trade and investment came to dominate their foreign policy, and they justified this new mercantilism in part as a defense of human rights.

In Washington, the reorientation could be seen in the heightened prominence of the U.S. Commerce Department in formulating and implementing U.S. foreign policy. Commerce Secretary Ron Brown led delegations of American corporate leaders from Brazil to China, hawking trade and investment deals while relegating human rights to the ineffectual realm of private diplomacy. The administration's position on India exemplified the shift. Its refreshing but short-lived public criticism of Indian abuses in Kashmir was replaced by the eager promotion of India as an "emerging market" where public discussion of human rights was taboo. So thoroughly did the quest for foreign markets eclipse human rights that Secretary Brown made the audacious claim, without presidential contradiction, that promoting trade *is* a human rights policy, and that the public stigmatization of abusive regimes that for over two decades has been indispensable to the defense of human rights is a mere "feel-good policy" that accomplishes nothing.

To be sure, trade and economic engagement, as part of a broader vision, can be beneficial. But the unbridled pursuit of economic development in the absence of the vigorous promotion of human rights is, in the words of Burmese Nobel Laureate Aung San Suu Kyi, a "recipe for disaster." Proponents of "commercial diplomacy" sometimes argue that boosting trade advances human rights by creating a middle class that ultimately will demand a greater political voice. Yet for every liberalizing Taiwan or South Korea, there is a Singapore, Indonesia, China or Peru where economic growth simply bolsters an authoritarian regime. Indeed, even if economic development could be correlated in the long term with improved respect for human rights—an unproved proposition—that would offer little solace to those who are imprisoned or tortured today. Moreover, repression can often have devastating consequences for the economically underprivileged, by denying them the opportunity to speak out and organize themselves in order to seek better wages, avert impending famine, combat environmental hazards, or defend against arbitrary deprivation of their property.

It is ironic that the argument for "commercial diplomacy" was heard in the year in which a long-term commitment to trade sanctions and public stigmatization, not business as usual, contributed to President Mandela's triumph over apartheid in South Africa. And that it coincided with the five-year anniversary of the fall of the Berlin Wall, symbol of the yearning for freedom that public criticism and economic pressure helped unleash. In recent years, coordinated economic pressure, involving bilateral donors as well as the World Bank, contributed to multiparty elections in Kenya and Malawi, and the release of some 2,000 political prisoners in Burma and the opening of a dialogue between the Burmese military and opposition leader Aung San Suu Kyi. Indeed, even the Asian governments that the Clinton administration so assiduously solicited have been responsive, in small but significant ways, to sustained public criticism and economic pressure on human rights. But as this pressure gave way to "commercial diplomacy," the Chinese leadership tightened the noose on all forms of dissident activity, deaths in custody mounted at the hands of Indian troops in Kashmir, and Indonesia's government arrested and imprisoned independent labor organizers.

East and South Asia were not the only sites of this fixation on trade and investment. Fearing the consequences for the recently approved NAFTA agreement, the Clinton administration took nearly a month to acknowledge publicly that the Mexican army had committed serious abuses in quelling the Chiapas uprising in January, and then expressed unjustified confidence in the Mexican government's willingness to account fully for them. Commerce Secretary Brown's delegation of corporate leaders toured Latin America without any public effort to address the region's human rights problems. Administration officials pursued construction contracts and military sales in Kuwait and Saudi Arabia, but President Clinton and a host of other senior officials found no occasion during their visits to protest publicly the governments' crackdown on legitimate dissent and systematic discrimination against women. In the newly independent states of the former Soviet Union, the prospect of tapping resources defined U.S. relations with such countries as Turkmenistan and Uzbekistan, with little concern shown for persistent authoritarian practices.

Other governments joined Washington in emphasizing trade over human rights. Germany, France, Canada and Australia all vied for Chinese commercial contracts, with waning interest in Chinese repression. France, driven by geopolitical designs and commercial motives, led the charge to embrace Iraq's genocidal regime. The European Union, having concluded a cooperation agreement with India in 1993 conditioned on respect for human rights, lapsed into silence on the atrocities in Kashmir in 1994. The governments of the Association of Southeast Asian Nations (ASEAN), themselves beneficiaries of diminished attention to their oppressive records, pursued trade and tourism through a policy of "constructive engagement" with the Burmese military junta. National leaders convened for the Asia Pacific Economic Cooperation forum in Jakarta and planned the Summit of the Americas in Miami without any serious attention to human rights.

For all their emphasis on commerce as a human rights policy, the industrialized powers should at least have supported human rights initiatives by corporations based in their countries. As it de-linked MFN from Beijing's appalling human rights record, the U.S. administration promised a voluntary set of principles for corporate investment and trade in China. By year's end, the effort appeared moribund. During the MFN debate, many corporate leaders (with a few notable exceptions) touted unimpeded investment in China as the best way to enhance human rights. Later, when it came time to subscribe to human rights principles governing operations in China, some of the same business interests denied they could have a meaningful impact. President Clinton might have shown moral leadership by highlighting the duty of corporations to avoid direct complicity in abuse, at least by ensuring that their plants and those of their suppliers remain free of political repression and discriminatory treatment. Instead, he said nothing publicly to discourage Americans from building prosperity on the oppression of others.

The administration did maintain a periodic human rights dialogue with abusive governments. But with no commitment in Washington to back up these conversations with meaningful pressure, the dialogue was increasingly empty. With the President usually trumpeting trade and whispering about rights, victims worldwide were regularly abandoned.

A Few Positive Exceptions

There were exceptions to this disturbing trend. The Clinton administration played a highly constructive role in selecting a prosecutor for the international tribunal for the former Yugoslavia and extending its jurisdiction to Rwanda. Washington maintained strong pressure on the Nigerian military to relinquish power, including the continued suspension of all but humanitarian aid and the presumptive denial of licenses for commercial arms sales. The U.S. Congress conditioned 10 percent of U.S. military aid to Turkey on human rights progress—a welcome and unprecedented, if still inadequate, response to Turkish security forces' routine use of torture and their brutal campaign against a Kurdish insurgency. Congress, echoing administration policy, also restricted certain arms transfers to Indonesia with human rights conditions focused on East Timor.

In Peru, despite ongoing anti-narcotics assistance to a police force that tortures, the State Department pressed for an end to the trial of civilians before military "faceless" courts and helped convince the Peruvian government to establish a Central Registry for Detainees in Lima, which contributed to a decrease in the number of forced disappearances.

The administration continued to give strong rhetorical support to combatting violence and discrimination against women, including expanding its treatment of women's rights in the State Department's annual *Country Reports on Human Rights Practices for 1993* and supporting the successful effort to appoint the first U.N. special rapporteur on violence against women. However, the administration lagged in implementing this general commitment in particular countries, such as when it sought to discredit evidence of systematic rape by the Haitian military. In Congress, opposition from the Senate Foreign Relations Committee undermined efforts to ratify the Convention on the Elimination of All Forms of Discrimination Against Women. (While several other human rights treaties still await ratification, the administration did obtain ratification of the International Convention on the Elimination of All Forms of Racial Discrimination.)

As for the European Union, it attempted to strike a more appropriate balance between trade and human rights in its policy toward Vietnam. Through protracted negotiations to overcome Vietnamese objections, the E.U. insisted that a proposed trade and cooperation agreement include a standard human rights clause. Senior officials from Sweden, Britain, the Netherlands, and the E.U. also raised human rights during visits to Vietnam.

By contrast, Japanese Prime Minister Tomiichi Murayana found no occasion to mention human rights during his stay in Vietnam, despite the obvious leverage of $640 million in Official Development Assistance (ODA). Japan did on human rights grounds cut all but humanitarian assistance to Sudan, Sierra Leone, Nigeria and, until the governments changed, Haiti and Malawi. But Burma was the only Asian government to face restrictions on ODA funds. Aid continued unimpeded to such abusive regimes as China, Indonesia, and India, where the Japanese preferred "quiet and continuous démarches" on human rights.

Misguided Neutrality at the United Nations

The past year highlighted an increasingly apparent conflict among the different roles that the United Nations has been asked to assume. On the one hand, the U.N. was called on to mediate conflicts and deliver humanitarian supplies. On the other hand, it was requested to prevent the slaughter of innocent civilians. The first required strict impartiality. The second demanded siding with the victims of abuse. To choose impartiality when both tasks must be performed is to signal a moral equivalence between victim and victimizer. Yet to choose the defense of human rights compromises the U.N.'s role as mediator and risks retaliation against U.N. personnel involved in delivering humanitarian aid.

The conflict was most apparent in Bosnia. The U.N. showed some signs in 1994 of a determination to protect civilians. A February mortar attack on an open-air market in Sarajevo led to a U.N.-authorized NATO ultimatum that Serb forces withdraw their heavy weaponry. The near fall of Gorazde to Serbian troops in April led NATO to vow to use air power to defend all six Security Council-declared "safe areas."

But Yasushi Akashi, the senior U.N. representative in the former Yugoslavia, repeatedly vetoed efforts to protect civilians in the "safe areas" and, in his public pronouncements, regularly sought to equate abuses by Serbian and Muslim/Croat forces, despite far greater Serbian culpability. On the few occasions when "safe areas" were defended, the main contribution was to introduce the concept of "pinprick" bombing into our lexicon to denote the token nature of the action. Backed by Britain, France and U.N. Secretary-General Boutros-Ghali, Akashi's concerns were maintaining the neutrality needed to protect U.N. personnel on the ground, negotiate the delivery of humanitarian supplies and, ultimately, he hoped, arrange an end to the conflict. What emerged was a policy of endless compromise, which placed accommodation with the killers above protection of their prey. Squandered was the opportunity to play a forceful role in protecting Bosnian civilians from ethnic slaughter and expulsion.

A similar conflict arose in Rwanda. The U.N. was painfully slow to recognize that the neutrality it maintained between the two warring parties was no longer appropriate once the war became a sideshow to orchestrated genocide. The Security Council's April 21 decision to reduce the U.N. peacekeepers to a skeletal presence was the classic response of a neutral peacekeeper to the breakdown of peace. But a full two weeks after the massacre of civilians had begun, the decision was a virtual invitation to extend the slaughter. Then, to avoid the legal obligation to stop the killing, the Security Council took another three months before venturing to call it genocide.

The Clinton administration, which deserves much of the blame for abandoning Rwanda, saw the crisis as a test case of its new cautious policy toward peacekeeping. To avoid "another Somalia," it developed a checklist of potential problems, but contributed little to their solution. The lesson evidently drawn from Somalia was the importance of not taking sides in a conflict. But it is one thing to choose favorites among abusive military leaders, as the U.N. and the U.S. did in Somalia, and quite another to be partisan on behalf of helpless victims. Washington's passivity toward the Rwandan slaughter was particularly inexcusable because, with its active support, the U.N. could have saved countless lives simply by creating safe havens, without entering the war on behalf of government or rebel forces. (Indeed, if the goal of protecting human rights had been fairly and evenly applied in Somalia—as part of a strategy to marginalize all abusive warlords whenever possible—the

U.N. might have attracted the broad support among Somalis that was a prerequisite for success. That strategy, at the very least, should have included efforts to document and publicize the warlords' atrocities and to ensure that any contact with these killers avoided legitimizing them.)

At the height of the Cold War, when the world was divided into two nuclear-armed blocs, neutrality may have been the United Nations' only option. But in today's multi-polar world of smaller conflicts, the choice is less clear. There are many seasoned diplomats who might play the part of mediator without U.N. affiliation. And there are humanitarian agencies outside the U.N. that, given comparable resources, might deliver humanitarian aid, using the same methods of negotiation that the U.N. now favors. But the U.N. is unique in its capacity to legitimize force in the most extreme circumstances to uphold human rights. Even if in recognition of its limited operational capacities it hands off the running of enforcement operations to regional bodies, the U.N.'s unequaled ability to identify when force might legitimately be used should make it hesitant to set impartiality as its highest aspiration. Faced with genocide and mass slaughter, neutrality should not be the ultimate value.

One might have looked to the first occupant of the newly created post of U.N. High Commissioner for Human Rights, José Ayala Lasso, to protest this disturbing trend in U.N. human rights protection. But his voice was not heard on the major human rights questions of the day, be it stopping "ethnic cleansing" in Bosnia, reversing the mercantilist abandonment of human rights in Asia, integrating human rights into U.N. military operations, building an international system of justice, or even encouraging specific governments to cooperate with the U.N.'s traditional human rights machinery. For his first three official trips, he chose Switzerland, Austria and Denmark. When he did address more pressing problems, such as the desperate need for monitors in Rwanda and Burundi, his efforts were undermined by the failure to develop country-specific expertise at the U.N.'s Centre for Human Rights and by inadequate funding from U.N. headquarters in New York. On his few high-profile visits with oppressive governments, he opted for quiet persuasion, what he called "human rights diplomacy." During his November visit to Cuba, for example, he offered no public comment on the government's repressive human rights record or even its refusal to allow a visit by the U.N.'s special rapporteur on Cuba, who would have reported his own findings publicly. By pointedly refraining from public criticism, the High Commissioner squandered his unique capacity to stigmatize abusive conduct and abandoned his most powerful weapon to defend human rights.

The U.N.'s tendency to underestimate the importance of human rights to war and peace was paralleled worldwide by mediators who acted as if human rights were an irrelevant irritant. The attitude was evident in signals emanating from Paris, London and Moscow that the territorial division of Bosnia was more important than the cessation of "ethnic cleansing" and accountability for war crimes and crimes against humanity. It was seen in the Clinton administration's silence on human rights violations by the Israeli government, justified on the grounds that contentious issues should now be left to negotiations between Israel and the Palestine Liberation Organization, and in its indifference to political restrictions imposed by the Palestinian authority, which boded ill for the region's democratic future. It was apparent in Washington's selection of a peace envoy for Sudan who was precluded from publicly voicing human rights concerns. And it was visible in the administration's muted criticism of human rights abuses in Angola, Guatemala, Lebanon and Syria in the name of not jeopardizing ongoing peace talks. Until the protection of human rights is seen as an essential component of peace, wars are likely to be prolonged and suffering magnified.

Ethnic Hatred and Communal Violence

As in 1993, hatred and violence along ethnic and religious lines continued to pose the paramount threat to human rights worldwide. The genocide in Rwanda was only the most horrendous example of a phenomenon that ranged from "ethnic cleansing" in Bosnia and similar atrocities in Nagorno-Karabakh to increasing xenophobia and anti-immigrant hysteria in parts of the West.

Preventive diplomacy, much touted these days in U.N. circles, is ideally suited to combatting communal violence, since the precursors of such bloodshed are well known. Without stimulation by opportunistic governmental leaders, communal tensions rarely rise to large-scale violence. Recent evidence of the governmental origins of such violence includes the state-orchestrated genocide in Rwanda, the security-force involvement in past political violence in South Africa (as confirmed this year by the Goldstone Commission), and the role of governmental restrictions on Kurdish political and cultural freedoms in stoking the devastating war in southeastern Turkey.

Yet in 1994, the international community showed little inclination to heed these early signs of disaster. One positive example was the successful effort to diffuse a potentially inflammatory situation by convincing the Latvian government to drop proposed restrictions on citizenship for ethnic Russians. Unfortunately, the international failure to impede the brewing tragedy in Rwanda was more characteristic. Human Rights Watch and others had issued repeated warnings that officials with a demonstrated propensity for ethnic slaughter were training and arming militia, with notable French help. Yet no one acted to halt this ominous trend while genocide might have been averted. As the year ends, renewed slaughter is once more threatening Rwanda as these same armed killers regroup in Zairean refugee camps and discipline among largely Tutsi troops in Rwanda wears thin. Neighboring Burundi stands poised to join the butchery as militias are armed, impunity for past killing reigns, and hatred is spewed over the government-controlled media. Yet despite urgent need, the deployment of international monitors, the building of viable justice systems, and the demobilization and quarantine of armed murderers proceed at a snail's pace.

Early warning of ethnic or religious strife might also be found in the hardening of divisions between northern and southern Nigeria caused by the military's suppression of democracy advocates, the ethnic tensions heightened by the government's restrictions on political competition in Ethiopia, the Cambodian government's continued refusal to provide legal protection to long-term ethnic Vietnamese residents, continued Serbian repression of the Albanian majority in Kosovo, the Indian government's failure to prosecute police for participating in attacks on Muslims, and the Russian government's selective attention to the rights of Russian-speakers in the "near abroad" while neglecting the rights of minorities within Russia itself.

In similar fashion, violence by Islamist movements was aggravated by Middle Eastern governments' denial of political freedoms. The raging violence in Algeria, a legacy of three decades of one-party rule which culminated in the 1992 decision to halt the electoral process, illustrated the consequences of closing off legitimate avenues of dissent. In 1994, the Egyptian government, backed by U.S. aid, persisted in barring the Muslim Brotherhood from participating in the political process in its own name, and continued to use incommunicado detention, torture, and excessive deadly force to combat Islamist militants. The militants, in turn, intensified their political violence against members of the security forces and civilians, including foreigners. The Israeli government, also supported with U.S. aid, announced a toughening of permissible interrogation methods, which already constituted torture, to battle Islamist militant groups that had attacked Israeli soldiers and civilians.

Some governments abetted violence by ignoring or endorsing it when directed by fundamentalist religious groups against secular activities. In Bangladesh, the government failed to denounce, investigate or punish violence by militant Islamist groups against minorities, journalists and those seen to promote women's rights. Instead, it capitulated to the demands of these groups by banning books and issuing arrest warrants for writers. In Pakistan, the government succumbed to pressure from religious parties by postponing amendment of the country's "blasphemy" laws, which have been used primarily against religious minorities. In Mauritius, where the author of a book on sexual violence against women faced violent threats by Hindu militants, the government compounded her danger by accusing her of offending Hindu morality.

European and North American governments showed their own ambivalence toward ethnic and religious diversity as they responded to mounting xenophobia at home by restricting asylum. In Bosnia as well, they offered a peace plan that divided the country along ethnic lines with little meaningful guarantee of minority rights—an ethnic partition that is antithetical to the respect for individual difference that is a core human rights value. The "ethnic cleansing" that continued during 1994 in the Bosanska Krajina and Bijeljina regions—Serb-held areas of Bosnia that were far from any war zone—illustrated the likely fate of ethnic minorities under such a peace.

The Brightening Prospects
for International Justice

Perhaps the year's most important positive human rights development was the progress made toward building an international system of justice for the worst human rights criminals. Traditionally, apart from rare military ventures, public stigmatization and economic pressure were the sole tools available to defend human rights. During 1994, it seemed increasingly possible that there would be a new tool: an international judicial system to ensure that those responsible for genocide, war crimes and crimes against humanity are held accountable. For the first time since the Nuremberg and Tokyo tribunals, such a system would promise justice for the victims of extreme abuse and deterrence for those tempted to repeat such crimes.

The two largest steps toward this goal were the appointment of Judge Richard Goldstone as chief prosecutor for the international tribunal for the former Yugoslavia and the addition of Rwanda to the jurisdiction of that court. Both received the strong, public support of the Clinton administration. Hans Corell, U.N. under secretary-general for legal affairs, played an important role in breaking the Security Council's deadlock over the choice of prosecutor.

The creation of a tribunal for Rwanda reflected growing international awareness that the rule of law must be established to break the cycle of violence and retribution that has plagued that country. Some of those who survived the genocide will predictably resort to summary revenge and further killing unless they can see justice done lawfully. Judge Goldstone, who built a reputation for investigating the South African government's role in political violence, vowed to pursue to the very top those who directed the killing in Rwanda as well as Bosnia and Croatia. But the allocation of resources—both to the international prosecutors and to the Rwandan legal system—remains a test of the international community's will to see justice done. The record for 1994 leaves cause for concern.

The idea of an International Criminal Court, having been debated for decades, was taken up seriously in 1994 by the U.N. General Assembly. This court, too, would handle the gravest human rights crimes, and possibly other offenses as well. One of the greatest impediments to its establishment was Washington, which insisted that the Security Council approve on a case-by-case basis any episode to be considered by the court.

The Clinton administration alleged it was motivated only by a desire to prevent overloading the court's docket and to ensure for prosecutors the political backing of the Security Council. But Washington's motives were suspect in light of its traditional unwillingness to subject itself to international human rights mechanisms. Evidently informing its position was the desire to avoid criminal prosecution of American pilots or soldiers. Theoretically, the U.S. government could indulge this parochial view by simply refusing to accept the court's general jurisdiction. But because that could prove politically embarrassing, the administration wanted instead to be able to embrace the court...sort of, by retaining the option of exercising its Security Council veto over any category of prosecutions. That stance threatened to undermine a fundamental premise of justice, that it should apply even-handedly to all.

Human Rights Law for Others Only

Washington's position on the International Criminal Court reflected its attitude toward international human rights law more generally—that it is meant only for other people, not for Americans. The perspective could be seen in the continued failure to grant Americans a judicial remedy for violations of the International Covenant on Civil and Political Rights. Although the U.S. government ratified the covenant in 1992, its declaration that the Covenant was "non-self-executing" and its failure to enact implementing legislation rendered ratification a cosmetic gesture for external consumption rather than a genuine effort to provide international human rights guarantees at home.

This distrust of international human rights mechanisms could not be attributed simply to the Senate Foreign Relations Committee, whether before or after the shift in power following the U.S. elections in November. It was also evident in the State Department's first-ever assessment of U.S. compliance with the covenant, submitted to the U.N. Human Rights Committee in July. The report ignored the range of concrete human rights problems in the United States, from the Border Patrol's abuse of undocumented migrants to the arbitrary use of inhumane supermaximum security prisons, from the federal government's abdication of its role in fighting police abuse to its summary repatriation of Haitian refugees. Instead, the report's 213 pages consisted of dry analysis of judicial decisions and constitutional and statutory provisions, divorced from the reality of their implementation. Concrete human rights problems, such as racial discrimination and the legacy of slavery, were mentioned in the report's introduction, but only as history, to herald the U.S. government's stated success in overcoming them. A reader could search in vain for acknowledgment that Americans, too, might benefit from the right to rely on international human rights standards.

The Persistent Threat of Amnesty

Another impediment to the international quest for justice, particularly in Bosnia, was the international community's uncertain commitment to it as an essential element of lasting peace. A time is likely to come when Bosnian Serb leaders offer a cease-fire in return for amnesty for their war crimes (or its functional equivalent, a pledge that each party will try its own abusers). Madeleine Albright, U.S. ambassador to the U.N., led the defense against this ploy by affirming, as recently as January, Washington's opposition to the lifting of sanctions against Serbia if Belgrade failed to cooperate with the international war crimes tribunal, including extraditing indicted war criminals. The vow seemed to reflect recognition in Washington that the former Yugoslavia would not emerge from its cycle of retaliatory killings until impunity for atrocities ended and the rule of law was established.

Yet as the year progressed, the commitment to justice seemed in jeopardy, as Washington appeared increasingly willing to reward Serbia for political steps despite Belgrade's persistent failure to cooperate with international human rights investigators. Following the initiative of London, Paris and Moscow, Washington endorsed the lifting of some sanctions in return for Belgrade's agreement to permit the placement of 140 civilian observers along its border with Bosnia to deter military aid from reaching Bosnian Serb forces. But Belgrade persisted in denying admittance to the U.N. special rapporteur for the former Yugoslavia, Tadeusz Mazowiecki, and to monitors from the Conference on Security and Cooperation in Europe. It also continued to withhold cooperation with international prosecutors while denouncing the international tribunal as discriminatory.

The quest for justice in Bosnia and Rwanda was also undermined by the Clinton administration's position on the same issue in Haiti. Throughout his three years of forced exile, Haitian President Aristide resisted Washington's pressure for an amnesty for the thousands of murders committed by the Haitian military and its allies. While President Aristide offered amnesty for crimes against the state such as the act of rebellion, he refused to grant amnesty for crimes against individuals such as murder, rape and torture. Yet with U.S. troops about to be deployed, the Clinton administration's envoys, including former U.S. President Jimmy Carter, offered these killers a general amnesty as a last inducement to step down. While President Aristide and the Haitian parliament ultimately rejected a blanket amnesty, the episode left the U.S. government open to accusations that it insists on justice for human rights crimes only when its own troops are not at risk and its own shores do not face a massive refugee influx.

Washington was not alone in finding it periodically convenient to countenance impunity for murder and other atrocities. Latin America's much-hailed democratic trend continued to be marred by the same phenomenon.

Outgoing Colombian President César Gaviria (now secretary-general of the Organization of American States) vetoed a bill that would have treated forced disappearance as a common crime exempt from military court jurisdiction and the defense of obedience to orders. He contended that this crime against humanity was an "act of [military] service." Typical of the result of such impunity was the report from Colombia's leading trade union that 1,542 of its members had been killed since 1986, without a single killer having been convicted.

The Guatemalan military fended off efforts to investigate its abusive conduct by selectively killing police officers and judges. A proposed truth commission was denied the right to name the names of those responsible for atrocities, while the military tried to preclude U.N. human rights monitors from conducting investigations.

Eleven months after the Chiapas uprising, no one from the Mexican army had been prosecuted for any of the documented acts of abuse committed in the course of suppressing the rebellion. Government investigators seemed more intent on exonerating the army than investigating its crimes.

President Alberto Fujimori's purge of the Peruvian judiciary and his decision not to allow the courts to be independent meant a continued lack of control over a highly abusive military.

Local police continued to engage in "social cleansing" killings of street children and other "undesirables" in Colombia and Brazil without fear of punishment.

In Latin America and elsewhere, however, there were some advances in the effort to hold abusive forces accountable for their crimes.

In Ethiopia, trials were set to begin of 1,315 former officials of the Derg regime for their alleged role in the "Red Terror." While it was inexcusable that these officials had been held for some three years in detention without formal charges, the Ethiopian government appeared willing to embark on a serious effort to bring them to justice lawfully.

In Honduras, National Commissioner for Human Rights Leo Valladares issued a report representing the first official acknowledgment of governmental complicity in disappearances during the 1980s. President Carlos Roberto Reina dissolved the military's infamously abusive Dirección Nacional de Investigaciones and transferred investigative powers to a civilian-controlled agency.

In Chile, judges in two cases against a former secret police official endorsed the view that crimes committed in violation of international law were not subject to a national amnesty decreed in 1978. Sixteen officers accused of the post-amnesty murder of three Communists—the so-called *degollados* case—were also convicted.

In Argentina, a court ordered Admirals Massera and Lambruschini, former leaders of the military dictatorship, to pay damages for their role in the disappearance of the Tarnopolsky family. The government began paying reparations to people who had been held under the dictatorship in administrative detention without trial, and the Congress was contemplating a bill to pay reparations to all other victims of the "dirty war." For the second year in a row, public outcry forced the Congress to deny promotions to two notorious members of the Navy's ESMA "task force," which had been responsible for thousands of disappearances.

In Nicaragua, a new military code required members of the armed forces who were accused of common crimes to be tried in civilian rather than military courts.

South Africa presented a mixed case on the issue of accountability for human rights crimes. Although the African National Congress (ANC), the dominant party in the new government of national unity, supported a truth commission to investigate the crimes of the past, it was forced to water down its commitment under pressure from the security forces and the outgoing National Party. After long negotiations, the interim constitution mandated amnesty legislation. Subsequent draft legislation called for individuals to apply for amnesty and disclose the acts to be covered, but did not require public amnesty hearings as proposed by the ANC. Moreover, in the waning days of the old government, then President F.W. de Klerk granted amnesty under existing legislation to a number of notorious security force members without disclosure of any kind.

Similarly in Russia, a human rights committee established by President Boris Yeltsin issued a highly critical report on the government's troubling human rights record in 1993. But the report made no mention of serious violations of the laws of war committed by members of Russia's armed forces during conflicts in 1992-93 in Georgia, Moldova, and Tajikistan. Nor were steps taken to identify or punish those responsible.

Civilians as the Target of War

Some of the most severe abuses of 1994 took place in the course of armed conflicts. As in recent years, civilians were less the incidental victims of warfare than its targets. The purpose of military action in many corners of the world went well beyond defeating an opposing army to include eradicating its civilian sympathizers or even expelling a civilian population. While war is horrendous under any circumstances, the suffering only escalated as the scope of conflict widened. International law sets clear rules to minimize the impact of war on those who do not take up arms. Yet these rules were regularly flouted in 1994.

The Bosnian conflict remained the paradigmatic war on civilians, with the principal point being the acquisition of territory by expelling members of the "wrong" ethnic group.

In Angola, both government and rebel UNITA troops spent much of the year indiscriminately attacking and starving besieged cities, where tens of thousands died. UNITA also attacked relief convoys, compounding the misery.

In southeastern Turkey, the military continued to force ethnic Kurds to become "village guards" against the rebel Workers Party of Kurdistan (PKK) which, in turn, retaliated brutally against anyone who cooperated with the government. Hundreds of thousands of civilians, mostly ethnic Kurds, have been displaced in the ten years of fighting.

Radical Islamist groups in Algeria made good on death threats to civilians accused of supporting the government or acting contrary to their notions of Islam. The government, with substantial credit and loan guarantees from France and the United States as well as aid from other European countries and Japan, also targeted relatives of suspected Islamists, suspected sympathizers, and the local population where armed groups were active.

Armenian troops forcibly expelled some 50,000 Azeri civilians from their homes in areas surrounding Nagorno-Karabakh, adding to the 450,000 who had been displaced the previous year.

All factions in the Liberian civil war targeted civilians. Throughout the five-year conflict, far more civilians have been killed than combatants.

The Sudanese government indiscriminately bombed civilians in the southern part of the country, adding to the hundreds of thousands who have been displaced in the country's eleven-year war.

During a two-month war against separatists, the Yemeni government placed half a million civilian residents of Aden under siege, bombarding them and cutting off their water.

The civilian population in Guatemala and Peru continued to bear the brunt of the armies' counterinsurgency efforts.

The Khmer Rouge in Cambodia and the government in Burma frequently abducted civilians to use as forced porters.

Rebel groups in Colombia and Guatemala continued to exact "war taxes" by kidnapping civilians for ransom.

Foreign powers contributed to this high civilian toll by flooding many of these conflicts with weapons. Once the product of geopolitical machinations, these arms sales today derive increasingly from commercial motives. The impact can be devastating. As ruthless as the Haitian military was during its three-year rule that ended with President Aristide's return, its capacity to exact terror was limited by its modest supply of arms. But Haiti was more the exception than the rule. In Angola, Afghanistan, Nagorno-Karabakh, Rwanda, and Somalia, the slaughter was made immeasurably worse by external governments supplying abusive forces with the weapons of war.

Symptomatic was the continued proliferation of landmines. Even as de-mining operations were underway in Cambodia, where an estimated four to seven million landmines are buried, these deadly weapons continued to be deployed. Thousands more mines have been laid in Angola since fighting resumed in 1992, contributing to an estimated 70,000 mine amputees nationwide. In Mozambique, the site of some two million mines, hundreds of civilians have been killed or maimed since the 1992 peace accord was signed. Globally, landmines claim some 15,000 victims each year, most of them civilians. In 1994, a moratorium on the export of antipersonnel mines, originally declared by Belgium, France, the Netherlands, and the United States, was joined by Argentina, the Czech Republic, Germany, Greece, Israel, Italy, Poland, the Slovak Republic, South Africa, Spain, Sweden, Switzerland, and (for some mines) the United Kingdom. President Clinton pledged to seek the eventual elimination of all anti-personnel landmines.

However, the Pentagon and other militaries continued to resist this trend. They cited various legitimate uses of landmines and proposed new restrictions on use short of abolition, such as mandating the deployment of self-destructing mines. But these restrictions will inevitably be flouted, just as the current regulatory regime has been, and the civilian toll will again undoubtedly far exceed the legitimate military benefits. Only when the use, possession, manufacture and transfer of all mines are banned and stigmatized will these dangerous weapons cease to exact such civilian suffering. Whether the international community has the courage to act on this fact will be seen when an international conference convenes in 1995 to consider tightening the current weak restrictions on landmine use.

The Right to Monitor Human Rights Practices

Twenty-four human rights monitors are known to have been killed or disappeared in the past year, more than double the toll for 1993. The genocide in Rwanda took the largest number, eleven. Among those slaughtered were Patrick Gahizi, Joseph Habarugira, Fidele Kanyabugoyi, Father Chrysologue

Mahame, S.J., Sylvestre Nkubili, Abbé Augustin Ntagara, Ignace Ruhatana, Augustin Ruzindana, Charles Shamukiga, and Matthieu Uwizeye. The government-allied Radio Mille Collines also singled out as "enemies" or "traitors" who "deserved to die" such human rights activists as Monique Mujawamariya, executive director of the Rwandan Association for Human Rights and Public Freedoms, who narrowly escaped with her life. In addition, in May, the Rwandan Patriotic Front killed Charles Mbabajende.

Elsewhere, thirteen monitors were killed or disappeared, including three in Turkey and two each in Brazil and South Africa.

Muhsin Melik, Ikram Mihyas, and Mehmet Sen, all members of the Turkish Human Rights Association, were killed by unknown assailants.

In Brazil, Reinaldo Guedes Miranda and Hermógenes da Silva Almeida Filho, advisors to a Workers Party city council-woman in Rio de Janeiro, were killed, evidently for their role in investigating the Candelária and Vigario Geral massacres, in which military police were suspects. Both monitors had received numerous death threats.

In South Africa, two "peace monitors" of the political violence in Natal, Isaac Shandu and Petras Mphathekhaleni Mbokazi, both members of the Inkatha political party, were shot by unidentified assassins as they left a meeting of monitors.

María Lucía León Nuñez, a human rights activist with the Commission on Human Rights in El Salvador, was murdered in Chalatenango. A warrant was issued for two suspects, one of whom she had been investigating in connection with a rape case, but as of mid-November, no one had been arrested.

The president of the Algerian League of Human Rights, Youcef Fathallah, was assassinated by unknown assailants. He had been a critic of both government and opposition abuses.

José Sucunú Panjol, an active member of the Guatemalan human rights group CERJ, disappeared. Military commissioners and civil patrollers in his village had repeatedly questioned him about his human rights activities.

In India's Punjab, human rights lawyer Sukhwinder Singh Bhatti disappeared after being abducted by armed men thought to be police.

Jairo Barahona, a Colombian human rights activist and long-time target of harassment and intimidation by security forces, disappeared in September at the hands of men who identified themselves as members of the Anti-Extortion and Kidnapping Unit of the National Police.

Former Libyan diplomat Mansour Kikhia, a founding member and board director of the Arab Organization for Human Rights and a prominent member of the Libyan political opposition, disappeared from his Cairo hotel room in December 1993. The Libyan government was widely believed responsible.

Violence short of murder was used in several cases. Unidentified attackers sprayed bullets at the house of Clement Nwankwo, one of Nigeria's leading human rights monitors. Sara Poroj Vásquez, a Guatemalan monitor, was stabbed and seriously wounded by unidentified men. The five-year-old daughter of an employee of a U.N. human rights worker in Cambodia was abducted and shot in the leg. Monitors from Cuba, Turkmenistan, and Uzbekistan were beaten, as were women's rights activists in Kenya. Death threats were issued to monitors in Brazil, Colombia, Guatemala, Honduras, Peru, Haiti under the military regime, Mexico, Pakistan, and Venezuela. Threats of rape were used against women's rights activists in military-dominated Haiti.

A variety of other techniques were employed to prevent human rights reporting. Monitors were detained or imprisoned in Angola, Burma, China, Cuba, Egypt, India, Lebanon, Mexico, Saudi Arabia, Syria, Tajikistan, Tunisia, Turkey, and Uzbekistan. Libel suits were brought in Mexico and Colombia. Egypt refused to register the Egyptian Organization for Human Rights, impeded its investigators, and blocked distribution of its annual report. Indonesia published a draft decree that would justify dissolving human rights groups if they acted against an undefined "national interest" or provided assistance to "foreign parties" (presumably the international press and international human rights organizations) that was in any way "damaging to Indonesia's foreign policy." China issued a new state security law that widened the basis for restricting peaceful dissent and independent organization, and imprisoned members of the Shanghai Association for Human Rights while setting up its own China Society for Human Rights Studies, whose statements were indistinguishable from government policy.

Turkey harassed several human rights groups in its Kurdish region, and confiscated *File of Torture*, a report by the Turkish Human Rights Foundation. A Chilean human rights lawyer was charged with sedition. Ethiopia denied a license to its only national human rights organization on the grounds that it was "political." Uzbekistan also refused to register its only independent human rights group. Kuwait, having refused to license its local human rights groups, closed them down for being unlicensed. Sudan continued to outlaw its leading human rights organization.

Open monitoring by local human rights activists continued to be impossible or extremely restricted in Brunei, Burma, China, Cuba, Iran, government-controlled Iraq, Kuwait, Libya, North Korea, Saudi Arabia, Singapore, Sudan, Syria, eastern Turkey, Turkmenistan, Uzbekistan, and Vietnam.

Human Rights Watch

At Human Rights Watch, we took significant steps in 1994 to internationalize our strategies for change. While our concerns have always been broadly international—we regularly work in some seventy countries, investigating human rights conditions, reporting our findings, and generating international pressure to curb abuses—our advocacy traditionally has been centered on Washington and the U.S. press. Today, however, we recognize the need to extend the scope of our advocacy to other fora and major powers. We believe that only such a multilateral approach, with pressure coming from multiple sources, will ensure that abusive governments feel compelled to reform.

Applying this strategy, in May we opened an office in Brussels to facilitate our efforts to monitor and influence the human rights policies of the European Union and its member governments. In November, we created our first full-time staff position to scrutinize human rights policy at the United Nations. Over the year, we began transforming our Moscow office from a center for launching field investigations to one that also addressed Russian foreign policy. Through visits and regular exchanges of information, we intensified our efforts to influence Japanese foreign policy. And we undertook more systematic efforts to infuse our information and views into decision-making at the World Bank.

As "commercial diplomacy" spread among the major economic powers, we also began to focus on multinational corporations, with the purpose of enlisting their influence on behalf of human rights. Our goal was to ensure that, at minimum, they do not become complicit in repression and, more positively, to encourage them to use their presence to promote human rights actively. With respect to China, we developed a draft set of principles that seeks to prevent workplace restrictions on expression, association and religious belief and to promote the monitoring of compliance with these principles by company-owned factories and their suppliers. We also began a dialogue with American companies on their prospective role in addressing human rights problems in Indonesia and Vietnam.

While seeking to encourage voluntary measures in support of human rights, we also publicly criticized corporations that ignored human rights in the conduct of their or their suppliers' operations. Cases of concern in 1994 included the suspension of a religious dissident (later reinstated) from a Chrysler joint venture in China, the use of excessive violence against ethnic Ogoni protesters by

Nigerian security forces called in by Shell Oil, and the forced repatriation from Thailand to Burma of ethnic Mon refugees just days before a consortium of companies, including Total of France and Unocal of the United States, announced plans to build a natural-gas pipeline near the camp that the refugees had occupied.

As we expanded the reach of our advocacy, we continued to build our capacity to investigate and expose human rights abuses. To facilitate this core part of our work, we added offices in 1994 in Dushanbe, Tajikistan, and Rio de Janeiro, Brazil. At the same time, we recognized that in many parts of the world it is not enough simply to publish information about human rights abuses. The expanded scope of our advocacy efforts allowed us to link this information to the policy decisions of governments and institutions with influence in the countries in question. By demonstrating the concrete steps that major powers can take to promote respect for human rights, we exerted pressure on these bodies to take action while helping to undercut the sense of despair and hopelessness that the mere publication of information about abuses can engender.

The past year saw the addition of our fifth thematic project, on children's rights. The project reflected our awareness of a class of victims who tend to fall outside the classic paradigm of political persecution but who nonetheless merit the attention of the human rights movement. While Human Rights Watch has long defended child victims of abuse, we felt the need to institutionalize our commitment through the creation of a special project. Its initial focus will be the use of child soldiers, a particularly common phenomenon in conflicts in Angola, Liberia, Sudan and elsewhere. Children suffer special psychological harm when forced to witness or participate in violence that they lack the maturity to comprehend. In addition, because of their diminished judgment, child soldiers are particularly prone to abuse others. Current international law permits the use of child soldiers as young as fifteen. We began a campaign to promote international efforts to raise the age to eighteen.

What follows is a review of human rights in sixty-five countries. The report covers events from December 1993 to November 1994. For each country examined, we discuss some of the major human rights developments of the year, and our own strategy and work toward improving human rights conditions. Reflecting the increasingly international focus of our advocacy efforts, our traditional discussion of U.S. policy is often combined with an analysis of the broader international community's response. We also examine restrictions on human rights monitoring in the country.

This is our fifth report that describes human rights developments worldwide, and our twelfth that examines U.S. human rights policy. This volume does not include a chapter on every country where we worked. Nor does it discuss every issue of importance. The countries and issues treated reflect the focus of our work in 1994, which in turn was determined by the seriousness of abuses, our access to information about them, our ability to influence abusive practices, and our desire to balance our work across various political and other divides.

HUMAN RIGHTS WATCH WORLD REPORT 1995

HUMAN RIGHTS WATCH /AFRICA

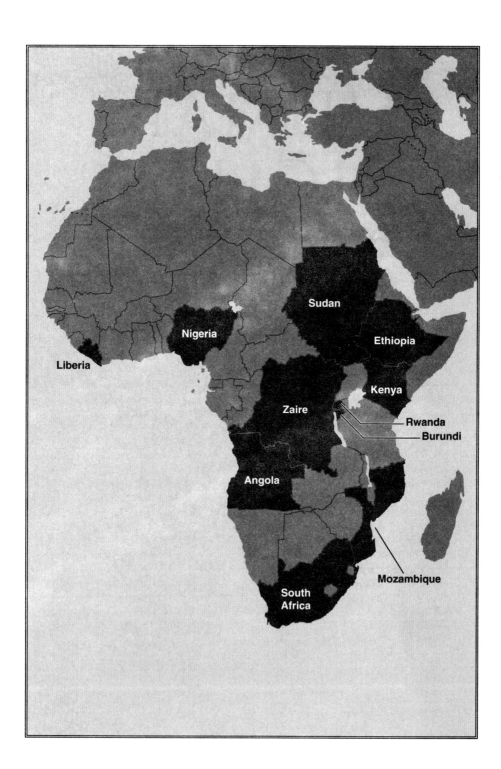

HUMAN RIGHTS WATCH/AFRICA OVERVIEW

Human Rights Developments

The ground-breaking democratic advances in South Africa and the genocide in Rwanda were at the extremes of Africa's human rights developments. In between these poles, African states experienced the perpetuation of one-man-no-vote rule and military regimes, varying forms of communal violence, civil war, and near disintegration. Half a continent apart, South Africa and Rwanda provide instructive human rights and humanitarian law lessons. In South Africa, fears of endless and destructive civil war have not materialized as political and social change is taking the form of a dramatic democratic transformation. To the north, between 500,000 and a million Rwandans were killed before a one-party genocidal government was swept away in a whirlwind of its own creation. Rwanda remains in a state of precarious peace with most fundamental issues of political and social change awaiting urgent resolution.

The transition to democratic rule in South Africa represents the magnificent outcome of the long and costly struggle of the South Africans themselves, but also reflects the value of the support and assistance given them by many throughout the world, from both civil society and governmental quarters. Although it was slow in coming, and not as consistent and sustained as it might have been, international support to the cause of democracy and human rights in South Africa did make a contribution, not least through the imposition of sanctions and effective isolation of the offending apartheid regime.

Despite the clear victory of their cause, and the powerful and visionary leadership provided by President Nelson Mandela and his colleagues, the people of South Africa must nevertheless maintain the vigil and struggle to protect and enhance their hard-won liberty. Close monitoring and activism must continue in order to keep the present democratic government in conformity with its obligations to protect and promote human rights for all the people of South Africa. To this end, the country's human rights community must adapt to the demands of the new situation, and make the necessary conceptual and methodological adjustments. During this next and indefinite stage of sustaining and consolidating past achievements, the international community also has a role to play in supporting the local human rights community as well as engaging in its own monitoring and advocacy efforts.

One of the benefits of the dramatic transformation in South Africa is that it is no longer expected to play the disruptive and destabilizing role it did in the past. South Africa when under apartheid rule secretly armed the single-party Habyarimana regime in Rwanda as it prepared its army and militia for genocide (others who provided arms during this crucial period included France, Belgium, and Egypt). The arming of Rwanda was the subject of a Human Rights Watch/Africa and Human Rights Arms Project report published four months before the genocide began. In addition to its domination of Namibia for decades, in defiance of the international community, South Africa also actively participated in the decades-long wars in Angola and Mozambique. With Namibia now one of Africa's examples of democratic government, and Mozambique seemingly on its way to stability and democratic rule after holding national elections under international supervision, one can hope that South Africa will now play a positive role in promoting an end to the war in Angola and a transition to democratic government there as well.

South Africa is also now expected to provide leadership and support for human rights efforts throughout the continent. It is true that other Africans should not have unrealistic expectations of South Africa, and must make due allowance for the competing domestic priorities of the South African government and civil societies. Nevertheless, there is much that the country can and should share with the rest of Africa.

As shown in this report, one of the main lessons of the genocide in Rwanda is the need to appreciate and address the role of the state in promoting and manipulating ethnic tensions. Another conclusion to draw from that catastrophe of untold proportions is that the international community must take its obligations to prevent and punish the crime of genocide seriously. The fact that the U.N. Security Council voted on April 21, 1994 to reduce the U.N. peace-keeping force (UNAMIR) to a skeletal presence in Rwanda soon after the mass killings started appears to have been interpreted as a license to commit genocide with impunity. The lengthy, though expected, delay in reinforcing the U.N. presence contributed to the loss of hundreds of thousands of Rwandan lives, most of them identified as Tutsis and moderate Hutus, and to the subsequent flight of millions of Hutu refugees into Tanzania and Zaire upon the defeat of the former government by the Rwandan Patriotic Front (RPF). A fraction of the effort and costs of humanitarian assistance provided for the refugees could have prevented most of the mass killings and the flight of civilians in the first place. Only 5,200 of the 6,800 troops approved on May 17 were on the ground by the time of writing in November 1994.

The continuing crisis in Rwanda also merits two further conclusions. First, evidence of violations of human rights and humanitarian law by the present government, installed after the RPF military victory in early July 1994, clearly show that victims can turn victimizers. Unfortunately, genocide and civil war diminish and inhibit the ability of local and international non-governmental organizations to monitor and advocate for the protection of human rights. Local Rwandan groups in particular suffered not only from the killing of their own members, but also, for the survivors, from the society-wide loss of trust across the ethnic divide as allegations of partiality to one side or the other become the norm.

Second, while accountability for previous and current violations should be seen as integral to, indeed essential for, national reconciliation and reconstruction, this is too often sacrificed to political expedience. The tendency of local and international actors is to rush to some sort of "peaceful settlement" that includes the premature granting of amnesty or immunity from prosecution to human rights violators. In the case of Rwanda, there appears to be a commitment to accountability by the present government under its own domestic jurisdiction, but the international community does not seem to be willing to provide necessary assistance in this regard. Given the collapse of the country's judicial system, and the many competing priorities facing the government, the lack of substantial international assistance can in effect mean impunity for the perpetrators of genocide.

An international tribunal for genocide, crimes against humanity, and other grave breaches of humanitarian law can provide another important avenue through which to establish accountability. Although the Security Council has determined to create an International Tribunal on Rwanda, the success of the initiative will ultimately depend upon the cooperation of the international community in the pursuit of those responsible for the genocide and in surrendering these individuals to the custody of the tribunal. The effective work of the tribunal in particular requires action to apprehend those who are now living abroad—notably within the large refugee populations in Zaire and Tanzania, and the few key leaders believed to be in France and elsewhere in Europe.

The flight of refugees from Rwanda to Zaire and Tanzania, followed by the army and militia of the former government, has created an extremely dangerous situation for the whole central African region. The refugees continue to suffer serious abuses in the camps from elements of the army and Hutu militias who effectively control the camps. Yet, at the time of writing, the international community is doing nothing to protect the refugees or to address and defuse the situation as a whole. Preparations by the well-armed former army to return in force to Rwanda, with a stated intention to "finish" the genocide of that nation's Tutsi minority, have been met with the seeming indifference, if not complicity, of some of the governments with a special capacity to make a difference in the region.

The conclusions and lessons of South Africa and Rwanda clearly apply to other crises involving severe violations of human rights and humanitarian law in Africa today, whether it is a "failed state" situation like Somalia and Liberia, a horrendous civil war as in Angola and Sudan, a state of collapse and political deadlock as in Zaire, or massive repression by a military regime as in Nigeria. From a human rights point of view, the question for the international community should always be how to empower and protect local human rights groups in their monitoring and advocacy efforts, and how to pressure offending governments into compliance with their human rights and humanitarian law obligations. That challenge should not be evaded by claiming that killing and torture and other violations cannot be helped because they are the result of age-old "tribal" hatreds. Governments and ruling elites must be held accountable for their role in promoting and manipulating existing communal and other tensions.

The Right to Monitor
Opportunities for African human rights monitors and activists continue to grow, and so does the struggle with governments over the right to monitor as well as the frustrations of limited resources. There is a vibrant and robust human rights community in all parts of the continent. But human rights workers are continuously detained, intimidated and otherwise harassed in violation of national constitutional and legal systems, and of international human rights law. Some human rights monitors have been tortured or killed. All suffer from the lack of resources and other limitations on their practical ability to monitor and advocate human rights.

Although there is a role for the international community to play in protecting and promoting the right to monitor, the primary responsibility must lie with African civil society in general, and African human rights activists and organizations in particular. In looking for local monitors to support, however, international human rights and development nongovernmental organizations and aid agencies should not confine themselves to preconceived models of what an NGO is supposed to look like or be. African forms and processes of civil society must be accepted for what they are and supported on their own terms in their work for human rights, whether they are informal groups of elders, associations of women market-traders or, Western style, formally constituted NGOs.

U.S. Policy
In the case of Rwanda, the U.S. hung back from effective engagement in part because of fears of becoming involved in "another Somalia." But even beyond the difficult issues of how best to deploy U.N. peacekeeping forces in Rwanda, the United States failed to take the lead diplomatically, deferring instead to Rwanda's former European patrons, France and Belgium. This deference to France, in particular, was also characteristic of U.S. policy towards other African countries, such as Zaire. For the United States to have a more effective policy in Francophone Africa, the Clinton administration should come out from behind France's shadow, articulate its own human rights policy, and encourage the French government too, to introduce objective human rights criteria into its policy in Africa.

Elsewhere on the African continent, where the United States has not insisted upon taking a back seat to other governments, human rights policy has been more vigorous. In the case of Nigeria, for example, the United States responded strongly to President Ibrahim Babangida's disruption of the democratic electoral process and the subsequent military coup by General Sani Abacha, imposing economic sanctions and sharply condemning the human rights abuses that accompanied the political upheaval. Similarly, a strong human rights stance on Malawi, adopted in cooperation with Malawi's other donors, played a key role in persuading the Banda regime to submit to demands for multi-party elections. In South Africa, U.S. involvement in the tense period preceding the elections was useful in encouraging the Inkatha Freedom Party to participate, and in helping minimize the threat of violence. Significant political and economic support for the new South African government, and a high-level delegation at President Mandela's inauguration, sent a welcome signal that multi-racial democracy in South Africa is of deep interest to the United States.

The cases of Nigeria, Malawi, and South Africa suggest that the Clinton administration does have the capacity to support human rights and democracy vigorously on the African continent. But the administration has failed to devote the political and diplomatic resources required to the continent's human rights disasters, particularly Angola, Sudan, Rwanda, Somalia, and Liberia. In Angola, for example, the United States has been engaged in the peace process (and appointed a special envoy to add weight to diplomatic efforts), but the action comes only after over 100,000 Angolans lost their lives in the resumption of hostilities that followed the aborted elections of 1992.

Clearly, the United States' bitter experience in Somalia is the key factor in the Clinton administration's disinterest in humanitarian engagement elsewhere on the African continent. Yet a retreat from leadership in some of the worst human rights crises of our time is the wrong lesson to be drawn from Somalia. In fact, the United Nations' ill-fated experiment in "peace enforcement" in Somalia points to the need to incorporate human rights protection into humanitarian operations, and to limit those operations to the protection of civilians.

Throughout the Cold War, U.S. involvement with Africa was largely determined by support for anti-communist regimes and forces opposing regimes considered to fall into the Soviet camp. In the 1980s, for example, the top recipients of American assistance were the governments of Sudan, Somalia, Kenya, Zaire, Liberia—and Jonas Savimbi's UNITA in Angola. In each of these cases, political, economic and military and security assistance contributed considerably to gross abuses of human rights. Today, anti-communism is no longer the single overriding principle guiding such assistance, and the U.S. has largely abandoned its associates of the recent past. Yet it is not clear that another framework for U.S. relations with Africa has taken its place. Consequently, events in Africa seldom receive the attention they deserve, and the Clinton administration appears disinclined to commit the political, economic, and diplomatic resources needed to help resolve the continent's most intractable human rights disasters.

The Work of
Human Rights Watch/Africa

Throughout 1994, Human Rights Watch/Africa continued its work of close monitoring and documentation of the human rights situation in twelve countries in Africa, while following developments in the continent as a whole. Central Africa was a primary concern, with the aftermath of the attempted coup in Burundi, genocide, and massive abuses in Rwanda, and the situation of refugees in Zaire requiring particular attention. A report on Rwanda issued in January provided documentary evidence of the formation and arming of the government's Hutu militias, and the series of killings by them that proved the immediate antecedents of the genocide to come.

Continuing with a theme underscored throughout 1993, it focused on the role of governments and associated elites in promoting and manipulating communal tensions for their own political ends. This theme is emphasized in several of the country sections that follow.

During 1994, it collaborated with four of the specialized projects within Human Rights Watch, namely, the Arms, Children's,

Prison, and Women's Rights Projects, in monitoring and advocacy efforts in relation to Angola, Botswana, Liberia, South Africa, Sudan, and Zaire. The work concerned landmines in Mozambique, the arms trade and violations of the laws of war since the 1992 elections in Angola, prison conditions in South Africa and Zaire, and discrimination against women with respect to the citizenship of children born in Botswana. Details of that work can be found in the respective sections of this report concerning those projects of Human Rights Watch. The newest project, the Children's Rights Project, worked with Human Rights Watch/Africa to address the issue of child soldiers in Liberia and in southern Sudan.

ANGOLA

Human Rights Developments

Angola's civil war continued. The human cost of the war in 1994 was impossible to determine with precision, but the United Nations estimated that more than 100,000 people have died. In October 1993, 250 child deaths were reported each day in the besieged government-held city of Malanje alone. In September 1994, the U.N. Secretary-General reported that there had been a 10 percent increase in the number of people severely affected by the war since February 1994, and that nearly 3.7 million Angolans, mostly displaced and other victims of conflict, were in need of emergency supplies, including essential medicines, vaccines and food aid.

The appalling levels of death and destruction were in large part consequences of the widespread and systematic violations of the laws of war for which this conflict has been notable. Both the government and the rebels, the National Union for the Total Independence of Angola (Uniao Nacional para a Independencia Total de Angola, UNITA) have been responsible for these violations. In particular, indiscriminate shelling of besieged cities by UNITA resulted in massive destruction of property and the death of untold numbers of civilians. Indiscriminate bombing by the government took a high civilian toll. As noted by an Africa expert from the U.S. Department of Defense, "This type of warfare bears mainly, cruelly and disproportionately on the populace, which is caught between the warring parties." If the human cost is staggering, so is the lack of international attention. Angola has earned the sobriquet of "the forgotten war."

Thousands of civilians were killed or injured in the indiscriminate government bombing of population centers in UNITA-controlled zones during 1994. The government also actively recruited child soldiers. Human Rights Watch witnessed and photographed the recruitment of minors in May and June, and interviewed some of the child recruits. Foreign nationals, including Katangans under the protection of the United Nations High Commissioner for Refugees, were also illegally conscripted by the government into its army.

UNITA laid siege to a number of cities and towns in 1994, most notably Malanje and Kuito. UNITA sieges caused widespread starvation of the civilian population. UNITA attacks on humanitarian relief operations were numerous and well-documented. On June 21 UNITA attacked a relief convoy between Lobito and Bocoio with mortar and small arms fire, destroying fifteen World Food Program (WFP) vehicles. Two WFP workers were wounded.

Reports about the torture of prisoners at the Ministry of Interior's high-security interrogation facility, Central de Criminalistica, known as the "Laboratorio" at Catete road, Luanda, continue. Extrajudicial executions also continued in the Luanda area on a reduced scale. In May 1994, Human Rights Watch interviewed a family in Samba suburb who claimed that their son was killed by the police because he came from central Angola. The International Committee of the Red Cross (ICRC) estimated that there were some 1,100 UNITA detainees in Luanda from the 1992 purge of the city. Many of these were free to move around the city, but could not leave it.

UNITA held large numbers of government prisoners in 1994. It provided ICRC some access to these prisoners. In May 1994, the ICRC for the first time visited government prisoners held by UNITA in Huambo. While in Huambo, Human Rights Watch/Africa was told that these prisoners were held there as an interim measure before being sent to "re-education camps," where captured soldiers were prepared to work for UNITA as porters. UNITA also continued to abduct foreign nationals. On August 26, UNITA soldiers seized two Africare employees north of Porto Amboim.

Mine warfare intensified after hostilities resumed following the September 1992 elections, with thousands of new mines being laid by the government and UNITA to obstruct roads and bridges, to encircle besieged towns with mine belts up to three kilometers wide and to despoil agricultural lands. There were an estimated nine to fifteen million mines laid throughout the country. The U.N. estimated that the number of amputees as a result of mines injury will reach 70,000 in 1994.

But the balance on the battlefield began to change in August 1993, with government forces recapturing from UNITA large tracts of Benguela, Huila, and Bengo provinces. The government made further gains in 1994. Between March and July, the area dominated by UNITA was reduced from 60 percent to 40 percent of national territory. Several strategic centers, such as Ndalatando (Cuanza Norte province), Cafunfo (Lunda Norte), and several occupied wards of Kuito, were recaptured by the government. The loss of Cafunfo, a key diamond area, was particularly hard on UNITA. UNITA was financing its military campaign, including arms imports in breach of U.N. arms embargo, with Angola's diamond wealth.

In response to its greater isolation and battlefield losses, UNITA increased its forcible recruitment of the local population in its war effort. Underage conscription also significantly increased since mid-1994, especially in the UNITA-controlled city of Huambo.

The renewed conflict, and accompanying human rights abuses and violations of laws of war, were being fueled by new flows of arms into the country. In 1993 the government repudiated the "Triple Zero" arms embargo clause of the 1992 Bicesse cease-fire agreement, and went on an international spending spree, buying more than $3.5 billion worth of weapons in 1993 and 1994. Weapons procurement reached record levels. The government of Angola was unquestionably the largest arms purchaser in sub-Saharan Africa during the past two years. Some analysts believed that Angola has mortgaged the next seven years of oil production to finance arms purchases, even though its current oil reserves are estimated to last only fifteen years.

The Angolan government was buying weapons from numerous governmental sources in Europe, Africa, Asia, and Latin America, although much of the weaponry was purchased from private international arms dealers. Russia was the largest supplier to Angola. Other countries apparently involved in arming and training the government's forces included Brazil, Ukraine, Bulgaria, the Czech Republic, Uzbekistan, North Korea, Portugal, and Spain. By supplying arms, Portugal and Russia undermined their role as members of the official "Observing Troika" for the peace process.

A private South African "security consultant" firm, Executive Outcomes, apparently provided armed personnel to assist both government forces and UNITA, and at the time of writing had a multi-million dollar contract with the Angolan government.

UNITA was purchasing large amounts of weapons from foreign sources, as well. Such purchases violated both the 1991 Bicesse Accords and the international arms and oil embargo against UNITA imposed by the U.N. in September 1993. UNITA was effective in "sanctions-busting" through neighboring countries, especially South Africa, Namibia, and Zaire. UNITA appeared to obtain much of its weaponry from private sources, rather than foreign governments, although there was some evidence that Russia, Zaire, and others provided arms. Zaire became the most important source of support for UNITA, becoming a transit area and conduit for diamond sales and weapons transfers.

The Right to Monitor

The sole functioning human rights group in Angola, the Luanda-based Angolan Association of Human Rights (Associacao Angolana dos Direitos do Homen), experienced police harassment and, in May and June the detention and imprisonment of its members, including its Secretary General Lourenco Agostinho and William Tonet. The detentions followed immediately after the publication of a critical report about prison conditions, which blamed the Ministry of the Interior for corruption and breaches of international human rights standards.

Incidents of harassment of journalists increased in mid-1994 with several detentions. Attempts to publish articles about corruption in the military were also censored on several occasions and access to war zones remained restricted.

UNITA continued to tightly control its zones. Although some journalists in early 1994 were able to move freely in Huambo, this ended by mid-1994 as UNITA tightened its control again.

Angolan journalists have been trying to set up a human rights training project to improve the quality and focus of their reporting.

U.S. and U.N. Policy

With the exception of the official recognition of the government in 1993, U.S. policy under the Clinton administration changed little from U.S. policy at the end of the Bush administration. Only at the urging of key members of Congress did the administration in late 1993 appoint a special envoy to assist U.N. peace efforts and attend the talks.

U.S. policy in Angola during 1994 focused on the slow and tortuous peace talks taking place in Lusaka, Zambia. In an attempt to push the process forward, President Clinton, on advice from Paul Hare, special representative to the Angolan Peace Process, sent two letters, in April and in May to President dos Santos. The letters urged the Angolan president to accept proposals put forward by the mediators. President dos Santos replied on May 27, agreeing to the proposals but also adding a list of his government's conditions. These details were also discussed by the Angolan president with a delegation of U.S. senators, led by Senator Paul Simon, chair of the Senate Foreign Relations Subcommittee on Africa, who were on a fact-finding visit at the time. President Clinton sent a letter in early June to UNITA head Jonas Savimbi urging him to accept the Angolan government's offer of positions in central, provincial, and local administrations.

Apparently fearing that public attention to human rights abuses by the government and UNITA might jeopardize the peace process, the State Department largely kept silent about human rights in Angola. Testimony before Congress over the past year concentrated on developments in the peace process and humanitarian concerns, but there was little public censure of the warring parties for violations against noncombatants. Growing government confidence on the battlefield led to a growing coolness between the U.S. and the government as Luanda appeared to be increasingly critical of international mediation efforts.

The Lusaka peace talks, which started on November 15, 1993, were the focus of U.N. mediation attempts. Chaired by U.N. Special Representative Alionne Blondin Beye, with the participation of Hare and observers from Russia and Portugal, the talks have taken place behind closed doors. The negotiations included a timetable for a cease-fire and UNITA troop demobilization, and a formula for national reconciliation between the two parties. Following clear progress on military issues in the peace talks, on December 13 the government presented to Beye its proposal for a national reconciliation government.

Soon thereafter, the Lusaka talks broke for consultations in the wake of allegations that the government had bombed Kuito, where it was rumored Savimbi was attending a soccer match. Talks resumed in January 1994, with the government and UNITA negotiators agreeing on January 31 on the composition of both the police and anti-riot units. The talks progressed slowly, with the pace determined by calculations on each side on the basis of the situation in the battlefield.

Despite this appearance of progress the talks bogged down in discussions on power-sharing. In late April the U.S. intervened with President Clinton sending letters to both sides. By June the outstanding issue became who would gain the governorship of Huambo. Finally, on September 5, following military set-backs across the country, UNITA compromised by accepting the complete set of U.N. proposals on national reconciliation put forth during the talks, thereby avoiding also a further package of sanctions.

The Lusaka Protocol was finally initialled by both sides on October 31 and the signing of the cease-fire agreement should follow. However, fighting also increased across the country with both sides trying to grab territory to strengthen their territorial positions before any cease-fire is signed. By the middle of November, government troops had recaptured the second city of Huambo from UNITA, and continued military activity appeared to be delaying the signing of an agreement.

Compromise was the U.N. strategy in Lusaka. Accountability for, or discussion about human rights abuses or future monitoring of human rights observance did not play a prominent role in the negotiations. Human Rights Watch urged that it should be integral to any agreement that a contingent of full-time U.N. human rights monitors be deployed to observe, investigate, and publicize violations of human rights and humanitarian law by all parties.

The Work of
Human Rights Watch/Africa
Human Rights Watch/Africa conducted a joint mission with the Arms Project to Angola in May/June. This mission included the first ever Human Rights Watch visit into UNITA zones. In September a second mission to South Africa provided further information. In November, *Angola: Arms Trade And Violations of The Laws of War Since the 1992 Elections*, was published. It was timed to focus attention on continued weapons flows to the country and to press for the prioritization of human rights monitoring in the future U.N. mission following the reaching of a lasting peace agreement.

Human Rights Watch/Africa was actively engaged in the promotion of measures to address human rights concerns on Angola with the U.S. Congress, the U.N's Department of Humanitarian Affairs and various European and southern African governments, conducting briefings, and highlighting the nature and scale of humanitarian concerns. In addition, Human Rights Watch/Africa gave frequent radio, television and press interviews with U.S., African, and European journalists, and presented its findings on Angola in several academic forums, such as the April "Why Angola Matters" conference at the University of Cambridge, England.

BURUNDI

Human Rights Development
Burundi began 1994 still reeling from months of violence that had followed the assassination of its first democratically elected president the previous October. In the last two months of 1993 between 30,000 and 50,000 people had been killed. The population of Burundi, like that of its northern neighbor, Rwanda, is predominantly composed of Hutu, who make up about 85 percent, and Tutsi, who represent about 15 percent of the total. As in Rwanda, there is also a very small number of a third people, the Twa.

Tutsi dominated political, economic and military life in Burundi until the early 1990s. Following internal and foreign pressure for reform, the elite permitted the establishment of a multi-party electoral system. In June 1993, the first Hutu president of Burundi, Melchior Ndadaye, was elected, but he was assassinated on October 21 in the course of a coup attempt by the largely Tutsi army. Within hours of the beginning of the coup, Hutu in the northern, central and eastern parts of the country began barring the roads to prevent troops from reaching their communities. In many of these communities they also launched attacks on Tutsi civilians, sometimes under the direction of local government authorities who were Hutu. The army responded with excessive and often indiscriminate force and attacked Hutu communities, including those where there had been no previous disorder. During the worst weeks of violence, hundreds of thousands of people fled to swamps and forests, to safer regions elsewhere in Burundi or across the frontiers to Tanzania, Rwanda, or Zaire. At the beginning of 1994, thousands—mostly Hutu—remained abroad while thousands of others—mostly Tutsi—clustered in camps or in urban centers, where they could count on ready protection by soldiers or police.

The attempted coup, which collapsed within two days, touched off a constitutional crisis. Both the officials designated by the constitution to succeed the slain president had also been assassinated, leaving a weak caretaker government in power. The crisis continued until January 1994 when the National Assembly designated Cyprien Ntaryamira to serve the remainder of Ndadaye's term as president. Ntaryamira, in turn, was killed two months after his installation in the same April plane crash that killed President Habyarimana of Rwanda. Sylvestre Ntibatunganya, then President of the National Assembly, succeeded him as interim President of Burundi for three months. According to the constitution, a national election should have been held to choose the President who would fulfill the remainder of the five-year term. But given the general insecurity in the country, with thousands of people in displaced persons' camps or abroad, such an election was impossible. Faced with the refusal of the political parties to find a

mutually acceptable candidate for the presidency, the constitutional court extended the interim authority of Ntibatunganya. In September the parties finally agreed to install Ntibatunganya for the remainder of the five-year term originally won by Ndadaye in June 1993.

Extremists on both sides increased their bases of support during the eleven months of instability between the assassination of Ndadaye and the installation of Ntibatunganya. Each side used threats and actual violence against the other and against moderates who sought to craft a compromise between the two.

Splinter groups of extremist Tutsi sought to achieve their objectives, such as representation in the cabinet, by "dead city" demonstrations. In February, April, and August, they shut down the capital by barricades, threats, and attacks on those who dared to move around Bujumbura. Each such demonstration resulted in several dozen people dead or injured. Army and police rarely intervened to restore order in these incidents and actually participated in some of them.

Extremist Hutu began training and arming underground militia groups. Throughout the year they staged ambushes and small attacks on soldiers and on camps where displaced Tutsi were housed. In early May, for example, they killed three soldiers in an ambush in the northern province of Ngozi and in June two more were killed in the section of the capital, Bujumbura, known as Kamenga. The army responded to those attacks, killing Hutu indiscriminately. In March, April, and September troops raided predominantly Hutu sections of Bujumbura, such as Kamenga, to search for arms. The operation in April, the most violent of the three, involved encircling and bombarding the neighborhood after most of the inhabitants had been evacuated. The government acknowledged that six hundred people were killed at this time. Several hundred people died in the other attacks. In connection with the September disarmament operation, 385 people were arrested on the orders of the

Military Auditor General, Lieutenant-Colonel Janvier Baribwegure. Thirteen of these prisoners subsequently disappeared, apparently the victims of summary execution: their bodies were found several days later just outside the city.

Both Hutu and Tutsi suffered from violence in the countryside as well. Every month there were attacks from one side or the other, particularly in the northern and central provinces. Tutsi from the displaced persons' camps attacked Hutu in adjacent areas, often with the assistance of soldiers. Some of the killing was in reprisal for earlier massacres of Tutsi in the same communities, but other cases of violence were related to the struggle over the control of land and other property. Hutu also attacked Tutsi, such as in Tangara commune, Ngozi province, where thirty-two Tutsi were killed in February, and in Muramvya, where six Tutsi were killed in late June.

The influx of thousands of Rwandan refugees after the genocide began in their country in early April heightened tensions, particularly in those parts of northern Burundi near the frontier. In the province of Kirundi, Rwandan Tutsi, who had sought refuge in Burundi some time previously, killed dozens of Rwandan Hutu refugees who had just arrived in Burundi. In late July Tutsi killed more than forty Hutu refugees from Rwanda in the province of Kayanza.

Tutsi extremists also assassinated a number of officials or important political leaders, including the administrators of Vumbi commune and Kiremba commune, Kirundo province, and the parliamentary representative from Ngozi province Sylvestre Mfayokurera, who also headed the militia of the FRODEBU (Front for Democracy in Burundi) political party. Assassins also targeted but failed to kill the Governor of Ngozi province in July and killed an expatriate agent of the United Nations High Commission for Refugees in Kirundo province in mid-August.

Increasingly, extremist rhetoric contributed to the atmosphere of insecurity. In June, a Hutu pirate radio station, called Radio Rutomorangiro, or Radio Truth, began broadcasting calls to violence from a mobile transmitter that shifted between Rwanda and Zaire. In late July the parliamentary leader Christian Sendegeya was forced to resign after accusations that he had circulated a tape recording inciting Hutu to hatred and violence. A number of apparently random incidents of violence, such as bomb and grenade explosions in markets and buses, increased the fear of ordinary citizens.

By threats and attacks on houses, Tutsi extremists have forced Hutu to move out of sections of the capital that were predominantly Tutsi. Meanwhile, Hutu have pushed Tutsi out of neighborhoods where they were the minority. This forcible separation of the city into hostile, virtually mono-ethnic zones extended the general separation of the groups that had occurred in some regions of the interior following the violence of late 1993.

The Burundi authorities have made no effective response to halt the continuing violence. The first governmental commission named to investigate the assassination and the attempted coup d'etat of October 1993 and the ensuing killings accomplished nothing. In September new commissions were established at the level of the provinces to gather information about the events. There have been no trials of any of the authors of the coup or the subsequent massacres. Francois Ngeze, implicated in the execution of the coup, was under house arrest for the first six months of the year, but was released in June. The administrator of the commune of Ryansoro was arrested on charges of having directed the killing of Tutsi in his commune but he was released after three months of detention without ever having been brought to trial. When organizers of street violence were arrested in Bujumbura in August, Mathias Hitimana, head of the Party for the Reconciliation of the People, a small extremist party, led students in clashes with the police to force their release. He was subsequently arrested himself but the authorities liberated Hitimana and the other detainees after a "dead city" demonstration left some twenty people dead.

The Right to Monitor

Most civilian and military authorities cooperated with the International Commission of human rights experts who arrived in January 1994 to investigate the 1993 coup and its aftermath. After the departure of the commission, however, and particularly after the publication of its report critical of both civilian and military authorities, Burundi human rights activists who had assisted the commission were subjected to threats and harassment. Two of them found it necessary to flee the country. The human rights league ITEKA was subjected to intimidation by authorities during the month of September following its effort to press for investigations into disappearances and summary executions.

The Role of the
International Community

The international community responded rapidly and effectively to the 1993 attempted coup. Its unanimous rejection of the military take-over was important in convincing the troops to return to the barracks. It was less effective, however, in the weeks of violence that followed and paid relatively little attention to the massacres of Hutu and Tutsi that continued for some weeks. In early 1994, international concern with bringing to justice the authors of the coup and the massacres produced no real results. A three person investigatory commission was dispatched by the United Nations Security Council in March. Its report, presumably submitted to the Secretary-General not long after, has never been published nor even made available to members of the Security Council.

The Secretary-General of the United Nations, Boutros Boutros-Ghali, sent a special representative to Burundi after the October violence. He served as a useful mediator between the various factions, helped keep international attention focused on Burundi, and provided balanced assessments of events to correct distorted accounts circulated by extremists. In the face of the catastrophe in neighboring Rwanda, international concern with preventing a similar disaster in Burundi increased. The Organization of African Unity

deployed a military observation mission of several hundred soldiers over the course of several months in the spring. They continued to monitor the situation throughout the country until the end of the year. The United Nations High Commissioner for Human Rights visited Burundi in May and called for international attention to the critical situation there. The U.N. then launched a human rights program, focusing largely on long term efforts to improve the judicial system and to educate people about human rights.

A series of international observers visited Burundi including the former African heads of state Sekou Toure and Obasanjo, sent by the Organization of African Unity, a delegation of members of the U.N. Security Council, and a high-level delegation representing President Clinton. African presidents Ali Hassan Mwinyi, Yoweri Museveni, and Frederick Chiluba met in August to seek a solution to the political conflict in Burundi and the Security Council continued to follow developments there throughout the year. The United States has played a constructive role in pressing for political dialogue, judicial reform, and the prosecution of those accused of assassination and mass killings.

International attention has not been sufficient to eliminate the continuing violence nor to bring those guilty of the massacres to justice, but it has helped to prevent a recurrence of killings on the scale of the previous year.

The Work of
Human Rights Watch/Africa

Immediately after the assassination of President Ndadaye and the onset of the massacres, Human Rights Watch/Africa responded to a call from the local human rights league to investigate massive human rights abuses in Burundi. In cooperation with the International Federation of Human Rights (Paris), The Great Lakes League for the Defense of Human Rights (Kigali), and SOS Torture (Geneva), Human Rights Watch/Africa carried out this inquiry in late January and early February. The thirteen researchers from eight countries, known as the International Commission to Investigate Human Rights Abuse in Burundi, published a 200-page report in July, which concluded that the majority of the armed forces in Burundi participated in the attempted coup d'etat and assassination or did nothing to stop these crimes. The report also concluded that members of the administration participated in the subsequent killings of civilians in a number of communes and that the armed forces repressed the violence in these communes, often with the use of excessive force. In some places, the army attacked civilians who had not previously been involved in the disorder and killings. The most pressing recommendation of Human Rights Watch/Africa and other members of the International Commission was to bring those responsible for the assassination and the other massacres to justice immediately.

Through advocacy at the United Nations, with U.S. officials and with authorities of other governments, and through publication and interviews, Human Rights Watch/Africa worked to secure international pressure on the Burundian authorities for the arrest and trial of those accused of participation in these massive human rights violations. It pressed for measures to make the Burundi courts more effective, including the temporary recruitment of foreign jurists and prosecutors. Human Rights Watch/Africa also kept decision-makers, the press and the public informed about current developments in Burundi, helping to provide factually-based assessments of developments in an atmosphere rife with propaganda.

ETHIOPIA

Human Rights Developments

The Transitional Government of Ethiopia (TGE) has brought about significant improvements in the human rights situation in the country since the overthrow of the government of Colonel Mengistu Haile Mariam in May 1991 ended seventeen years of the rule of the Dergue. However, after three years in power, the TGE was still dominated by the Ethiopian People's Revolutionary Democratic Front (EPRDF), the party whose military forces, together with those of the Eritrean People's Liberation Front, defeated the Dergue. The EPRDF held thirty-two out of the sixty-four seats in the Council of Representatives; its army served as the national army of the country, as members of the other forces who fought against the Dergue had yet to be integrated into it. The army of the Dergue government was dissolved and all its members dispersed.

In its early days the TGE adopted a Transitional Charter ("the Charter") which guaranteed basic human rights. A Constitutional Commission was established to draft a new constitution, and a National Electoral Board was created to conduct elections in the country. The government ratified major international human rights instruments and permitted the emergence of more political parties and other associations than ever before in the history of Ethiopia. On the basis of the Freedom of the Press Proclamation (Proclamation No. 34/1992) about two hundred licenses were issued for independent journals and newspapers.

In addition, the TGE took initial steps to support the rehabilitation of former refugees returning from neighboring countries, as well as the hundreds of thousands of former soldiers of the disbanded army who were left without means of support. The government also acted effectively through its Relief and Rehabilitation Commission to avert the imminent famine which threatened an estimated 6.7 million people in 1994.

The systematic "disappearances" and massive extrajudicial executions that characterized the Dergue regime were no longer part of the general human rights situation in Ethiopia. However, the human rights situation was far from satisfactory, as arrests and detention of members of opposition political parties and journalists, and some killings in disputed circumstances, continued to occur. There were increasing allegations of human rights abuses, often involving intimidation of leaders of members of parties and groups that were competing with the EPRDF in the political process. These political opposition parties and groups included the Oromo Liberation Front (OLF), the Sidama Liberation Movement (SLM), the Coalition of Ethiopian Democratic Forces (COEDF), the Ogadeni National Liberation Front (ONLF), Ethiopian Democratic Union Party (EDUP), the All Amhara People's Organization (AAPO), and the Council of Alternative forces for Peace and Democracy in Ethiopia (CAFPDE). The government appeared reluctant to hand over power to a democratically elected government in the event of its losing in the forthcoming March 1995 general election, when the period of rule by transitional government should come to an end. Unlike the economy, which was doing relatively well, the political situation in Ethiopia appeared to be deteriorating, and tension was mounting.

Members of the opposition parties suffered intimidation, harassment, and other abuses, particularly at the hands of local officials. In many areas, political opponents, despite the freedom to organize, found administrative obstacles to freedom of expression and association insurmountable. The Peaceful Demonstration and Public Political Meeting Proclamation (Proclamation No. 3/1991), which guarantees the right to peaceful demonstration and public political meetings, was largely ignored or misinterpreted, depending on the region in which an application is made.

Although the law does not require political parties to obtain permission to hold public meetings, permits were nevertheless generally required. Furthermore, permission was often refused or delayed to such an extent that parties such as the EDUP, AAPO, and CAFPDE did not have the time to organize effectively or to inform the public of their activities. Some political parties found their meetings surrounded by security personnel who could be seen in the streets advising people not to attend.

The harassment of political opponents extended to personal intimidation and harassment of party members and officials. In Addis Ababa, Ato Aberra Yemane Ab, of the COEDF, was arrested in December 1993 when he arrived in the country for a peace conference, and was still in prison at the time of this writing. Though charges against Mr. Aberra at the time of his initial arrest were dismissed by the courts in April 1994, he was detained indefinitely by virtue of a fresh order by a lower court without formal charge or trial. Members of the SLM, ONLF, and AAPO were also arrested and detained without charge or trial.

Those killed by EPRDF security in 1994 include more than a dozen officials and alleged members of the ONLF in the Somali region, as well as six AAPO members in the Amhara region and five SLM members and officials in and around Awasa town in the Sidamo district. Some of these killings occurred during armed clashes, but others occurred in disputed circumstances in which there was reason to believe killings were arbitrary.

One hundred and fifty-eight supporters of AAPO were detained in September, on charges of staging an illegal demonstration, but released twelve days later on October 2, 1994. They were among the hundreds of AAPO members and supporters who had congregated at the court's compound when the President of the organization, Professor Asrat Woldeyes, already imprisoned on a previous occasion, went on trial on another charge in September. At least fourteen members of AAPO were held at Alem Bekagne (World's End) the central prison in Addis Ababa on different charges and without bail.

At least two hundred of the estimated 20,000 members and supporters of the Oromo Liberation Front (OLF), the main organization which helped the EPRDF form the transitional government in 1991, were still detained in Hurso, Eastern Ethiopia. In September 1994 alone, 194 members of the Sidama Liberation Movement (commonly known as SLM1 to distinguish it from the pro-government SLM2) were arrested and held in Awasa prison. The chair of SLM1, a very outspoken ex-member of the Council of Representatives, Ato Woldeamanuel Dubale, fled to the United Kingdom after escaping an assassination attempt attributed to EPRDF security in Awassa town in 1992.

More than thirty-seven alleged supporters of the OLF were also arrested on September 3, 1994, in the town of Ambo when they gathered to give condolences to the family of Ato Darara Kafana, a sixty-year-old Oromo businessman, killed by uniformed men in Ambo. Among those arrested was sixty-four-year-old Olli Atomsa.

Outside Addis Ababa and a few other major cities, political activities were subjected to more arbitrary control, and in some regions the local chiefs did not abide by formal guidelines on freedom of association. Supporters of opposition parties were often regarded as enemies of the government. In the Tigray region, members of the Ethiopian Democratic Union Party (EDUP) complained of intimidation and harassment by local authorities belonging to the Tigray People's Liberation Front (TPLF).

Unequal access to the mass media was another major concern in the democratization process, although unfairness was vehemently denied by the head of the Ethiopian News Agency, Ato Amare Aregawi, the most powerful person in the Ministry of Information. Technically, all of the twenty-five or more political parties that were legally registered in May 1994 were to be given regular access to television and radio air time, by a decision of the Council of Representatives. In practice, the allocation was still arbitrary, and liable to be abused. There was a perception of unfair competition among political parties. The Ministry of Information assisted the few parties that needed help to prepare programs for broadcasting. Every other party was entitled only to "campaign time" (available only during the campaign period). Prior to the June 1994 election of the constituent assembly, some parties were specifically denied air time because the Council alleged that this privilege had been abused to "insult other organizations" rather than promote a political program.

The fairness of the political process continued to be a cause for concern. It be-came increasingly difficult to distinguish between the EPRDF as a political party and the EPRDF as the government in power. Opposition parties lacked equal opportunities and facilities to compete effectively with the government. In some regions the government administrative building also housed EPRDF party offices, which were guarded by security men in military uniform.

On June 5, 1994, elections were held for the Constituent Assembly, the body responsible for debating and enacting the draft constitution. However, the major opposition political parties all boycotted the elections for the Assembly on the grounds that they had been excluded from participation in the drafting of the constitution. Consequently, of the entire 548 seats, 464 (84.7 percent) were won by candidates representing the EPRDF.

The government's ongoing suppression of freedom of the press heightened the feeling of anxiety, fear, and confusion in the country. In the first six months of 1994 twenty-three journalists were detained or subjected to fines because of their critical writings. This had a profound impact on the fledgling independent press, and a number of private newspapers shut down as a result. At the time of writing, there were eight journalists in prison. Keleme Bogale and Tewodros Kebede, both working for *Zog*, an Amharic weekly, were arrested in the second week of October 1994. Other journalists who were also detained, and released on bail, were Tefera Asmare, Daniel Kifle, Girma Endrias, Habtamu Belete, Ezeddin Mohammed, Girma Lemma, Melaku Tsefaye, and Tsefaye Tadesse.

A number of factors contributed to the press's current problems, including the provisions of the press law itself and the government's apparent disposition to secrecy. The press law (Press Proclamation No. 34 of October 21, 1992) uses such vague and ambiguous language in regulating the content of what journalists may write—as can be found in article 2.4(c)—that it can easily be abused and manipulated in harassing journalists by bringing criminal charges against them if they are critical of government policies or action, and setting bail too high for them to be discharged awaiting trial.

The presence of soldiers in large numbers moving about in civilian communities caused insecurity, although their number was decreasing. The national army, which was in effect and composition the armed wing of the EPRDF, was not restricted to the borders, or those areas presenting high security risks, as stipulated in the Deployment of the State "Defense Army of the Central Transitional Government" Proclamation. These soldiers were in most cases fully armed, often without any form of identification and not in full military uniform. EPRDF soldiers were generally reported to be more responsible than soldiers during the Dergue regime, but reliable accounts of intimidation, harassment, and other forms of abuse nevertheless abounded. A good number of the soldiers did not speak the language of the community where they were billeted, which led to increased tension, fear, abuse, and misunderstanding.

The government's policies on regionalization, ethnicity and language continued to have profound effects on human rights in the country. The TGE created fourteen self-governing regions divided along ethnic lines. The Charter guaranteed the right of every nation (defined as a people living in the same geographic area with a common language and identity) to self-determination. Each region had the added right to adopt its own language.

Though ethnic-based hostilities decreased in intensity and frequency after the adoption of this new policy, they nevertheless continued. This was largely due to failure, on the government's part, to expressly provide for the protection of minorities and ethnic groups dwelling outside their home regions. Inflammatory remarks by the government and local officials, including allusion to Amhara as "neftegna" (meaning "musketeers," a reference to the sort of weapons they used to carry in the past), particularly in Oromo areas dominated by the Oromo People's Democratic Organization, and as

"the oppressors" by the troops of the Tigray People's Liberation Front stationed in the South, continued to perpetuate ethnic tensions and hostilities in the country.

The ongoing struggle for secession in the ethnic Somali area of the Ogaden (now known as Region Five) resulted in continuing bloodshed and threatened future peace and stability in the country. It also provided a disturbing picture of the problems which could face the country in the future if the issue of secession is not settled. The Charter guarantees a right to secession of a people if they are "convinced that their rights are denied, abridged or abrogated." It remained unclear how secession can be peacefully accomplished in Ethiopia under the new policy.

The government had yet to review its policies on land and language, which have contributed to loss of life and enhanced ethnic tensions in the country. Nor had the government adopted specific policies to protect ethnic minorities, to define the rights of ethnic groups in divided communities or to provide specific protection for dispersed groups and persons living outside their ethnic base.

Since the EPRDF assumed powers in Ethiopia in 1991, about 1,300 officials and others associated with the former Dergue regime have been in detention for their alleged involvement in various atrocities committed by the regime. While most of the detainees were held in Addis Ababa, others were held in detention centers in other parts of the country. For more than three years, the detainees were held without charge as investigations continued and a new judicial system was established. The Office of the Special Prosecutor (SPO) created to handle prosecutions attributed the delay in bringing charges and initiating the trial process to difficulties in gathering evidence. On October 25, a range of charges were presented against sixty-six senior officials of the Dergue regime. Some of the accused, including Mengistu, were to be tried *in absentia* since their extradition could not be secured.

Attempts to extradite Mengistu from

Zimbabwe failed, despite a formal request in February and the visit of the Ethiopian Minister of Foreign Affairs, Ato Seyoum Mesfin, in August 1994. An extradition treaty was signed, however, with Djibouti in September 1994, which should help in bringing some of the accused to trial in Ethiopia.

The Right to Monitor

A key factor in establishing confidence is the right of human rights organizations to monitor. The transitional government was generally very open to monitoring by human rights organizations based outside the country. Human rights monitoring by local human rights groups was more restricted, however. Several local human rights and development organizations existed in Ethiopia but were required to obtain permits subject to annual renewal. Some were denied permission to operate or experienced extensive delays in obtaining permits.

Two human rights organizations, the Ethiopian Human Rights Council and *Gadado* (an Oromo word meaning "agony"), were actively involved in receiving complaints, documenting abuses, and publishing their findings. The government denied both organizations formal registration, thereby severely restricting their ability to operate. Professor Mesfin Woldemariam, Chair of the Ethiopian Human Rights Council, was taking the government to court for denying his organization a license, and to contest its claims that the Human Rights Council was "a political organization," that "sides with the opposition," was "ethnically oriented," or engaged in inaccurate reporting. Woldemariam had previously been the target of verbal attacks by the government. Detained in 1993 and since released on bail, he had yet to be charged or tried with any crime.

U.S. Policy

The U.S. moved from unequivocal support of the transitional government, to more cautious expressions of solidarity and support, but stopped short of seriously, publicly criticizing the government on human rights. Gen-

erally, the United States appeared reluctant to stigmatize the government that it helped to set up, or to deal with mounting complaints by opposition parties.

This failure by the U.S. to publicly identify with the human rights cause encouraged misrepresentation of U.S. policy by the Ethiopian government. For example, following his meeting with President Clinton in August 1994, according to the BBC summary of world broadcasts (September 6, 1994), President Meles said that U.S. officials considered attacks on the transitional government by the opposition to be "hooliganism." Human rights concerns were reportedly raised by the State Department and the White House at every meeting with Meles. State Department officials told Human Rights Watch/Africa that Assistant Secretary of State for African Affairs George Moose discussed concerns about press freedom, detention without trial and free association, particularly in the context of next year's elections. While in the U.S., President Meles also met briefly with President Clinton and with Defense Secretary William Perry, Secretary of State Warren Christopher, and AID Director Atwood. The meeting with the Department of Defense was said to focus on Ethiopia's leadership in the talks on Sudan within the framework of the Inter-governmental Authority on Drought and Development (IGADD), and for the participation of Ethiopian forces in international peacekeeping.

The U.S. government has provided significant foreign assistance to Ethiopia, and should use that leverage to encourage human rights improvements. After South Africa, Ethiopia is the largest recipient of U.S. aid in sub-Saharan Africa. In fiscal year 1994, the U.S. provided $135.69 million in economic aid ($37.31 million in the Development Fund for Africa; under PL480, $55.80 million under Title II and $42.50 million under Title III), and under others items.

The U.S. Embassy in Addis Ababa was not a forceful public proponent of human rights, and refrained from criticizing the government for its human rights record. The former U.S. ambassador to Ethiopia, Marc

Baas, noted in a May 1994 interview with *The Ethiopian Herald*, a government-owned English-language daily, that the U.S. was concerned about the number of people detained without charge, but he went on to applaud the government for some recent releases and said that he thought that a large part of the problem was that no infrastructure existed for the processing of persons suspected of crimes. He also stated that he remained concerned about the unintentional signal that the transitional government might be sending by arresting and prosecuting journalists.

Similar, cautious approaches were used by the State Department. In February 1994, Assistant Secretary of State George Moose gave an interview to *The Ethiopian Herald* in which he was asked about the state of human rights in Ethiopia. His response was that he recognized that were still improvements to be made and that the U.S. government intended to continue making its views known, as in the State Department's annual *Country Reports on Human Rights Practices for 1993* and in ongoing discussions with Ethiopian authorities.

U.S. officials did give rhetorical support to the need for respect for human rights. In a press conference in December 1993, Ambassador Marc Baas stated that support for democratization was the keystone of U.S. policy toward Ethiopia, in addition to promotion and respect for human rights and the development of economic reform.

The Work of Human Rights Watch/Africa

Representatives of Human Rights Watch/Africa traveled to Ethiopia in the spring of 1994 to investigate issues of accountability for human rights violations by officials of the previous regime, and questions of freedom of association and press under the present government. Some of the findings of this mission were published in *Human Rights in Africa and U.S. Policy*, a special report by Human Rights Watch/Africa for the White House Conference on Africa held June 26-27, 1994.

On July 27, 1994, the executive director of Human Rights Watch/Africa testified before the Subcommittee on Africa of the House Foreign Affairs Committee, highlighting various concerns arising from the findings of the mission and subsequent follow-up monitoring, including rising ethnic tensions in Ethiopia. A report on accountability issues was due to be published before the end of 1994.

KENYA

Human Rights Developments

During 1994 government intolerance of criticism continued to threaten Kenya's shaky return to a multiparty system. Opposition supporters were required to obtain licenses to hold meetings, but were routinely denied such licenses and arrested if meetings were held without them. Political trials were held of several prominent figures, and mysterious attacks took place on opposition Members of Parliament's (MP) private homes. The right to freedom of expression was threatened by the arrest and charging of a number of journalists in connection with articles critical of the government. The government was particularly sensitive to allegations of involvement in rural violence in Rift Valley Province and continued to deny access to journalists or human rights monitors to the affected areas. Despite plans announced in June 1993 by Attorney General Amos Wako to look into the need for law reform, no attempt was made to amend or repeal repressive legislation. The lack of an independent judiciary remained a serious problem in political cases.

The Kenyan opposition remained divided between two factions of the Forum for the Restoration of Democracy (FORD), FORD-Kenya, and FORD-Asili, and a third party, the Democratic Party (DP), largely along ethnic or regional lines. Although the death in January of Oginga Odinga, leader of FORD-Kenya and member of the group that led Kenya to independence, ended a period of rapprochement between FORD-Kenya and the government, it did not lead to greater union in the opposition. Several unsuccessful efforts were made during the year to set up cross-party or cross-regional alliances; and pledges not to run competing candidates at bye-elections, made at the launch of the short-lived "United Democratic Alliance" in June, were not honored. The ruling Kenya African National Union (KANU) of President Daniel arap Moi successfully won over several MPs representing opposition parties, allegedly with significant financial inducements, and increased its majority in parliament.

Opposition MPs were regularly harassed during the year. Under Kenyan law, the organizer of a meeting must apply in advance for a license from the district commissioner of the area in which the meeting is to be held. Licenses to hold meetings in their constituencies were denied to many MPs during the year, and a number of gatherings that were held were forcibly broken up by police. In March the home of FORD-Kenya MP Anyang' Nyong'o was attacked by armed men, killing his uncle. In other cases, the government continued to use the justice system to silence critics and punish political opponents. A number of MPs were detained for short periods and in some cases charged with political crimes such as subversion. Former MP and political prisoner Koigi wa Wamwere, an outspoken critic of Moi's government, was brought to trial in April with three others, on charges of attempted robbery with violence. Wamwere was alleged to have taken part in a raid on a police station in November 1993, but claimed to have witnesses that he was several hundred miles away at the time the raid occurred. An observer attending the trial on behalf of the International Bar Association concluded that "procedural anomalies" would result in a "miscarriage of justice." The trial is continuing.

A number of other political trials took place in 1994 involving political leaders, journalists and other government critics. In March charges of contempt of court were brought against prominent lawyer and former chair of the Law Society of Kenya G.B.M. Kariuki, and Bedan Mbugua the editor of *The People* (a weekly newspaper owned by Kenneth Matiba, the leader of FORD-Asili), together with the company publishing *The People* and David Makali, a journalist at the newspaper. The charges were brought in connection with an article in which Kariuki was quoted describing a decision of the court of appeal as a "judicial lynching." In June 1994 the defendants were collectively fined the equivalent of approximately $25,000. Fines were paid on behalf of Kariuki and the publishing company, but the two journalists served prison sentences of four and five months.

Four journalists with the *Standard* newspaper were charged with sedition in March, after publication of an article alleging that several people had died in renewed "tribal" violence in Rift Valley Province. The charges were later dropped. Journalists with the *Daily Nation* newspaper were also regularly harassed: in April charges of sedition, later dropped, were brought against the news editor in connection with an article about the violence; and in July the Australian training editor at Nation Newspapers was ordered to leave the country. *Society* and *Finance* magazines, two of the most prominent critics of the government during 1993, were silenced in 1994 as a result of multiple court cases (both criminal and civil), attacks on their printers, and the impounding of controversial editions.

Allegations of torture and ill-treatment in police custody continued to be routine in 1994. In September, following his release from prison, David Makali of *The People* announced that he intended to sue the state in connection with assaults on him by prison wardens. The accused in the Wamwere case similarly complained of ill-treatment. The killing of several street children by police reservists in Nairobi in July and August led to a public outcry; encouragingly and unusually, charges were made against the policeman responsible.

Two cases illustrated the lack of freedom

of association in Kenya. University lecturers at Kenya's four universities continued the strike action begun in November 1993, in protest against infringements of academic freedom and the government's failure to allow registration of the University Academic Staff Union. Twenty-three lecturers were dismissed in January 1994 and evicted from staff housing. A court case for their reinstatement was dismissed following several public statements by President Moi attacking the lecturers. Clashes between students and police took place at various campuses, as students demanded the reinstatement of lecturers. Three thousand doctors at state-run hospitals went on strike in June, also in protest against the failure to register a union. They were fired in August and evicted from their housing, leaving hospitals without staff.

Although fewer serious incidents were reported than in 1993, political violence in the rural areas in the west of the country remained a serious problem. In late 1993 Human Rights Watch/Africa estimated that approximately 1,500 Kenyans were killed and perhaps as many as 300,000 internally displaced since the clashes began. Allegations of government promotion of violence between government-allied members of the Kalenjin or Maasai ethnic groups and members of the numerically dominant Kikuyu and Luo groups, verified in September 1992 by the report of a parliamentary committee made up of KANU members, continued to be made. The existence of several "security operation zones" (established in September 1993), where emergency-type regulations promulgated under the Preservation of Public Security Act gave the government extraordinary powers to limit access to outsiders and to enforce law and order. These measure prevented independent monitoring of security force behavior and did not prevent the outbreak of renewed clashes in late March 1994 in Burnt Forest and in September 1994 in Molo. Eyewitness reports described members of the security forces standing by while homes were attacked. No effort was made to investigate these allegations.

Although no further major outbreaks of violence took place during the year, individual attacks continued and the security situation remained precarious in many areas.

The great majority of relief to the victims of the violence was carried out by church groups, principally the National Council of Churches of Kenya (NCCK) and the Catholic church. Church members engaged in relief efforts or reporting on conditions in the clash areas were subject to official harassment. In January 1994 government officials ordered the demolition of a camp of 30,000 displaced people driven from their land by Maasais. Maasai local government minister William ole Ntimama warned of "war" in July if the 10,000 remaining at the camp were resettled on "Maasai" land. There was no public censure of his remarks. In September 1994 the United Nations Development Programme (UNDP) reportedly stated that one third of an estimated total of 260,000 displaced had been resettled during the nine months of a joint UNDP/Kenyan government project. The UNDP also commended the Kenyan government for its efforts to halt the violence. Following a public outcry in which local relief organizations disputed these figures and challenged the assessment of the government's performance, UNDP accussed reporters of taking its statements out of context. The National Council of Churches estimated that no more than 5 percent of those estimated by UNDP to have returned to their homes had actually returned.

Political violence also affected Kenya's coastal cities, where the Islamic Party of Kenya (IPK), denied permission to register as a party for the December 1992 elections, clashed both with police and with a rival party, the United Muslims of Africa (UMA), set up by pro-KANU politicians apparently in an attempt to divide the allegedly Arab IPK from Muslims of African descent. In September the UMA declared a *fatwa* against IPK leader Sheikh Khalid Balala.

The situation in Kenya's North East province, along the border with Somalia, remained unstable. Local Somali-Kenyan bandits known as *shiftas* and Somali fighters continue to operate throughout the region, preying on local residents, refugees, and relief workers. The incidence of rape among Somali women living in refugee camps—the subject of critical reports from Human Rights Watch/Africa and African Rights—fell during the year after increased security measures were taken at the camps by the UNHCR, with the aid of funding from several sources, including the U.S. and the E.U.

The Right to Monitor

Although several Kenyan nongovernmental organizations engaged in monitoring human rights in Kenya operated during 1994, their members as well as individual lawyers defending those accused of political offenses were subject to official harassment. The security operation zones in which clashes occurred effectively prevented independent monitoring of security force behavior in preventing or instigating violence.

The charges against Koigi wa Wamwere appeared to be motivated by his activities in founding the National Democratic and Human Rights Organization in 1993 and in monitoring violence in the Rift Valley. Paul Muite, a prominent FORD-Kenya MP and lawyer acting for Wamwere, complained officially to the Director of State Intelligence and Security in June of constant security police surveillance. The government did permit several international human rights organizations, including Amnesty International and the Robert F. Kennedy Memorial Center for Human Rights, as well as the International Bar Association and the Norwegian Bar Association, to attend the trial of Koigi wa Wamwere as international observers.

In September, Minister for Information and Broadcasting Johnstone Makau cautioned foreign correspondents based in Nairobi against publishing articles that negatively portrayed Kenya.

U.S. and International Policy

During 1994 U.S. policy toward Kenya continued to de-emphasize human rights concerns. Public statements by Ambassador Aurelia Brazeal and by visiting U.S. officials did not highlight abuses by the Kenyan government, in contrast to the outspoken criticism voiced by previous ambassador, Smith Hempstone.

The U.S. Department of State's *Country Reports on Human Rights Practices for 1993*, in its section on Kenya, released in February 1994, reported the "substantial evidence" of the complicity of high-level government officials in instigating the clashes, yet the ambassador or other senior officials did not publicly call for investigation of these allegations. On April 7, 1994, the day following the announcement of a curfew in one of the security operation zones, Assistant Secretary of State for African Affairs, George Moose, visiting Kenya at that time, commended President Moi for taking "decisive steps...to curb the resurgence of ethnic violence" and failed to raise other serious concerns. In June 1994, after returning from a visit to the U.S. and a few days after the decision in the Kariuki case mentioned above, Ambassador Brazeal praised political and economic reforms, though "regretting" that permits to hold meetings were still being denied to some political groups and leaders. Brian Atwood, the head of the U.S. Agency for International Development (USAID), visiting Kenya in June, stated publicly that he was concerned about harassment of the opposition and ethnic clashes in the Rift Valley.

In November 1991 the consultative group of bilateral donors to Kenya suspended balance of payments support on governance, economic, and human rights grounds. This suspension was lifted at a consultative group meeting in November 1993, when $850 million of new aid was pledged in recognition of the "significant efforts of the government to reestablish an appropriate macroeconomic framework and initiate structural reforms." However, the aid was to be released in tranches, and the joint press release issued following the meeting called for the Kenyan government to take action to end the ethnic clashes and to show respect for basic freedoms of assembly and expression. In June 1994 the consultative group met again to review progress. Although further tranches of aid were released by bilateral donors, continuing concern was expressed at corruption, continuing ethnic violence, and restrictions on freedom of expression and assembly.

The U.S. took part in the decision to suspend balance of payments support in November 1991, though it continued to provide development aid, totaling about $18 million a year, to nongovernmental organizations working in Kenya. USAID announced in April 1994 that it had programmed $20.2 million, including emergency food aid, in assistance during fiscal year 1994, for the relief of "clash" victims and to alleviate the effects of drought.

The Work of
Human Rights Watch/Africa

Several detailed letters were sent to President Moi throughout the year, protesting violations of due process in political trials and threats to the rights of freedom of expression and association. In June Human Rights Watch/Africa issued a special report to coincide with the White House conference on Africa. The report addressed human rights conditions and U.S. policy in ten countries, including Kenya, and made policy recommendations to the Clinton administration. In July, a report was issued on continuing rural violence and restrictions on freedom of speech and assembly, to coincide with the meeting of the consultative group of donors. In September, a researcher traveled to refugee camps in North East Province, to investigate progress made by the UNHCR since the 1993 issue of a report on rape of Somali refugees.

LIBERIA

Human Rights Developments

Liberia remains a divided country plagued by the proliferation of warring factions. All the factions are responsible for serious human rights abuses against the civilian population, sometimes based on the civilians' ethnic affiliation or their perceived support for another faction, but often simply as a means of sowing terror. A characteristic of the Liberian civil war has been that civilians suffer the most, and are killed in far greater numbers than combatants. The lack of protection for civilians from abuses by all sides and the profound distrust among the warring factions remain obstacles to lasting peace.

There was considerable fragmentation and inter-factional fighting during 1994. The Liberian National Transitional Government (LNTG), a coalition government, was formed on March 7, 1994, replacing the Interim Government of National Unity (IGNU); it governed the capital, Monrovia, backed by the West African peacekeeping force (ECOMOG). Two of the principal rebel factions represented in the coalition continue to dominate much of the country. Charles Taylor's National Patriotic Front of Liberia (NPFL), claimed to control 60 percent of the country prior to its split in August. The United Liberation Movement for Democracy in Liberia (ULIMO), made up primarily of soldiers from former President Samuel Doe's army, the Armed Forces of Liberia (AFL), controlled at least three western counties, but it also split along ethnic lines in March, pitting the Krahns against the Mandingos. A new faction, the Liberian Peace Council (LPC), comprising former AFL soldiers from the Krahn ethnic group, controlled areas of the southeast.

A peace agreement signed in July 1993, known as the Cotonou accord, was believed to be Liberia's last, best hope. The accord stipulated that concomitant with disarmament, a five-person Council of State elected by all the factions would take power from the interim government until elections were held. A thirty-five-member transitional parliament would include thirteen members from the NPFL and the interim government, and nine from ULIMO. Between August 1993 and February 1994, political wrangling prevented the LNTG from being seated. In February

1994, it was agreed that David Kpomakpor, a lawyer representing IGNU, would chair the LNTG, with Dexter Tahyor of ULIMO and Isaac Mussah of the NPFL as vice chairs. Finally, in mid-May, Dorothy Musuleng Cooper was named Foreign Minister.

An important element of the plan involved the creation of a U.N. Observer Mission in Liberia (UNOMIL) to help supervise and monitor the agreement, in conjunction with ECOMOG. The plan also provided for an expanded ECOMOG force, under the auspices of the Organization of African Unity (OAU), to be composed of African troops from outside the West African region. By early 1994, some 800 Tanzanians were deployed in Kakata, and 900 Ugandans were in Buchanan.

In early August, the AFL demanded the right to join the LNTG, saying it should replace the defunct IGNU as the third signatory to the Cotonou accord. The next day, a six-point "statement of intent," calling for an end to hostilities and for cooperation with international peacekeeping efforts, was signed by the AFL, the ULIMO Krahn faction, the LPC, and the LDF, and Tom Woewiyu of the NPFL, but not the main NPFL faction.

On September 12, a supplementary agreement to the Cotonou Agreement was signed in Akosombo, Ghana, that allies the AFL with the NPFL and ULIMO in a new ruling council charged with disarming the warring factions and leading the country to elections in October 1995. The new council replaces the previous Council of State. The agreement was widely criticized by various members of Liberian civil society as giving too much control to the warring factions. At this writing, no progress has been made in its implementation.

On September 15, a coup attempt was made by troops under the leadership of former AFL chief Charles Julue, who briefly took over administrative offices but were forced out by ECOMOG forces. Julue and some eighty others were taken into custody by ECOMOG. Approximately twenty-eight are being charged with various offenses; seven-teen, including Julue, are being charged with treason and are expected to stand trial beginning in late November.

Human rights abuses continued throughout the country by all the warring factions. By mid-September, renewed fighting and attacks on relief workers and other noncombatants, including the capture by NPFL forces of forty-three U.N. observers and six NGO staff who were later released, had forced all relief organizations to recall their staff members to Monrovia. All the fighters continued to act with impunity in their territory, subjecting civilians to a range of abuses, from harassment and detention to arbitrary execution. For its part, the NPFL attacked civilians in its war against the LPC in the southeast, and in the inter-faction fighting that broke out in August. In October, UNICEF reported that about 500 orphaned children, who had been housed in the NPFL capital of Gbarnga, had been moved to Totota, near the battlefront, and were "starving and in grave danger."

ULIMO also engaged in attacks on civilians, looting, and executions. On December 23, 1993, ULIMO attacked the United Nations base in Vahun in Lofa County: U.N. and nongovernmental organizations' vehicles were stolen, and their warehouses were looted. The U.N. was forced to evacuate all its staff, as well as eighty-two orphans. In March 1994, ULIMO split into two factions, Krahn versus Mandingo. The fighting in the western counties has been fierce, with civilians being targeted by both sides. On May 27, the Mandingo faction of ULIMO captured sixteen Nigerian ECOMOG soldiers, blaming them for cooperating with the Krahn faction; they were later released. On June 28, the Krahn faction of ULIMO held five UNOMIL observers hostage and subjected them to humiliating mistreatment. ULIMO is also believed to have been responsible for cross-border attacks on Liberian refugees in Guinea.

Late 1993 witnessed the emergence of the LPC, which demanded a seat on the LNTG. The LPC is largely Krahn and was created by former AFL soldiers to fight the

NPFL. There are confirmed reports of AFL soldiers fighting alongside the LPC; the AFL soldiers regularly travel through ECOMOG checkpoints into LPC territory, often carrying weapons. The LPC is responsible for serious human rights abuses against the civilian population, especially those the LPC considers to have supported the NPFL. Its abuses include extrajudicial executions, arbitrary arrest and detention, torture, rape, and looting. In late May, the LPC abducted ten soldiers from the Ugandan contingent of ECOMOG, but they were released the following day.

There have been consistent reports that members of the Nigerian contingent of ECOMOG—not the Ugandans or the Ghanaians, who are also stationed in the Buchanan area—are aiding the LPC. Reports indicate that the Nigerians are supplying arms and ammunition to the LPC as a way to weaken the NPFL while profiteering on the side. This allegation has serious implications, even though it is not clear what level of authority in the Nigerian contingent is responsible for the collaboration.

A disturbing characteristic of the Liberian war has been the use of child soldiers. International law, notably the Protocols of the Geneva Conventions and the United Nations Convention on the Rights of the Child, forbids the use of children under the age of fifteen as soldiers in armed conflict. The African Charter on the Rights of the Child has a higher threshold, stating that no one under the age of eighteen can serve in armed hostilities. In spite of these clear provisions, thousands of children are being used as soldiers in Liberia. There are no precise figures on the number of child soldiers in Liberia; even the total number of combatants in all the factions is unknown, but estimates range between 40,000 and 60,000 combatants. UNICEF estimates that approximately 10 percent of the fighters are under the age of fifteen. The NPFL and ULIMO have consistently used children under the age of eighteen, including thousands of children under fifteen.

The situation of the displaced civilians, estimated at anywhere from half a million to a million, and others resident in many parts of Liberia became increasingly desperate in 1994. Some 200,000 civilians were uprooted in the fighting after August. Relief assistance to these areas had been effectively cut off after the October 1994 offensive, although some food and medicine continued to flow through the Ivory Coast border.

The renewed fighting since August created a new outflow of between 120,000 and 130,000 refugees to Ivory Coast and Guinea. As of November, the total number of Liberian refugees in the neighboring countries was believed to exceed 800,000: 500,000 were reported in Guinea, 318,000 in the Ivory Coast, 20,000 in Ghana, 6,000 in Sierra Leone, and 4,000 in Nigeria. The war also displaced some 400,000 Sierra Leoneans, 170,000 of whom went to Guinea and 100,000 to Liberia. The issue of repatriation of the refugees remained contingent upon progress on the political front and the resolution of security concerns. As of November, refugees had not returned in significant numbers.

The Right to Monitor

A number of human rights organizations were able to function in Monrovia without interference from the LNTG or ECOMOG, and the local press often reports on human rights issues. The principal domestic human rights organizations include: The Catholic Peace and Justice Commission, The Center for Law and Human Rights Education, The Liberian Human Rights Chapter, The Association of Human Rights Promoters, and Liberia Watch for Human Rights. However, it was very difficult for these groups to travel outside Monrovia to document abuses. There were no known human rights organizations operating in NPFL, ULIMO, or LPC territory.

Similarly, international human rights organizations, including Human Rights Watch/Africa and Amnesty International, were permitted to visit Monrovia in 1994, but had problems in obtaining permission to travel to other parts of the country.

The Role of the
International Community

U.S. Policy

The main tenets of U.S. policy toward Liberia are to support and promote conflict resolution efforts by ECOWAS (the organization of West African States that sponsors ECOMOG) and the U.N., to withhold recognition of any government in Liberia until free and fair elections lead to a representative government, and to promote ECOWAS and its peace plan. By the end of 1993, the conflict resolution efforts had gained new momentum: On September 30, 1993, the U.S. obligated $19.83 million ($13 million in Economic Support Funds and the rest in Foreign Military Financing) to the U.N. Trust Fund for peacekeeping in Liberia. The money would be used by ECOMOG and the OAU to help finance the deployment of further ECOMOG troops from ouside West Africa, but not for lethal assistance. On December 20, 1993, the U.S. allocated an additional $11 million in support for the UN-monitored African peacekeeping operation in Liberia.

The U.S. was the leading donor to the victims of the war: since the beginning of the conflict, the U.S. had provided some $320 million in humanitarian assistance to victims of the conflict, including more than $57 million in fiscal year 1994. An additional $28.7 million had been provided since April 1991 to assist the ECOWAS-led peace process.

On three occasions in 1994, the U.S. sent senior officials to Liberia: in January, Deputy Assistant Secretary of State for African Affairs Prudence Bushnell; in February, Assistant Secretary of State for African Affairs George Moose; and in June, when Ms. Bushnell returned. All these visits involved meetings with representatives of the main warring factions and were meant to deliver a message that the U.S. had limited patience, and that the factions had to move forward on the peace process. Shortly after the first two visits, the factions announced their agreement about the seating of the LNTG.

Bushnell returned to Liberia in June, and delivered a stronger message to the factions, warning them that if there was no visible progress in the peace process, the U.S. was going to examine its options, and that those factions leaders considered to be obstructing the peace process might no longer be allowed access to the United States. This message was meant to resonate particularly with George Boley, the LPC head, who owns a home in Maryland. However, General Hezekiah Bowen, chief of staff of the AFL, received a U.S. visa and travelled to the U.S. in July, despite that organization's human rights record and its links with the LPC.

On May 9, acting State Department spokesperson Christine Shelly expressed the U.S.'s increasing concern about human rights abuses in Liberia, especially those involving the LPC: "We have received numerous credible reports of gross human rights violations—including murder, rape, mutilation and torture—committed by the LPC against unarmed civilians. The LPC's aggressive military activities have displaced tens of thousands of Liberians and threaten to plunge the country back into full-scale war." The statement also criticized human rights abuses by both factions of ULIMO and the NPFL. U.S. concern over human rights abuses by all sides to the conflict is welcome.

On May 18, Assistant Secretary Moose testified about Liberia before the House Subcommittee on Africa, and articulated U.S. policy as follows: "We seek a negotiated settlement of the conflict with the assistance of the U.N. and Liberia's neighbors in ECOWAS. We believe such a settlement should include provisions for full disarmament of all Liberian warring factions, the return home of more than a million Liberian refugees and displaced persons, credible democratic elections, and the establishment of a unified government based on respect for human rights, democratic principles, and economic accountability." That formulation of U.S. policy remained unchanged for the rest of 1994.

Finally, in late October, Deputy Secretary of State Strobe Talbott, accompanied by Assistant Secretary Moose, travelled to

Ghana and the Ivory Coast as part of a week-long African tour, where the issue of the Liberian conflict was discussed with local officials. The talks focused on what the U.S. could do to strengthen the conflict resolution efforts of the West African states.

The U.N. Role

After the U.N. addressed the Liberian crisis in November 1992 by imposing an arms embargo (Security Council Resolution 788), Secretary-General Boutros Boutros-Ghali dispatched his special representative, Trevor Gordon-Somers, to investigate the situation. Human rights concerns have been notably absent from the Secretary-General's statements on Liberia, and he has missed many opportunities to insert provisions for human rights protection into the peace process. The UNOMIL observer mission was created by Security Council resolution 866 in September 1993, and the first contingent of observers arrived in Liberia by year's end.

In April 1994, the U.N. Security Council extended UNOMIL's mandate to October 22, 1994. This was, however, strictly limited: in practice, it has meant that UNOMIL has not reported publicly on either the violations of the cease-fire or violations of human rights and humanitarian law, although apparently reports are being sent to U.N. headquarters in New York. UNOMIL is also restricted in its movements, and has not been able to conduct investigations into reported violations due to practical obstacles as well as the lack of a clear human rights component in its own mandate. However, by avoiding the human rights issues, the U.N. is failing to discharge its mandate in Liberia.

On June 24, Boutros-Ghali submitted his fifth progress report on Liberia to the Security Council. The report included a section on the protection of human rights, which highlighted the continuing "disregard for human life" and even noted abuses attributed to the LPC. However, in a clear indication of the U.N.'s failure to carry out its own human rights monitoring and documentation responsibilities, the report stated that "widespread allegations of human rights vio-lations have not as yet been transformed into verifiable data by either international human rights groups or the four main Liberian voluntary human rights organizations."

In a statement on July 13, the U.N. Security Council described "limited progress" in the peace negotiations, and called for a "substantial acceleration of the disarmament process" as a prerequisite for free and fair elections. It also called on the LNTG to convene a meeting of all the warring factions to formulate realistic plans for resuming disarmament. The statement condemned "all those who initiate fighting and who violate international humanitarian law," but did not identify any of the violators.

In a report to the Security Council on August 29, the Secretary-General noted that the situation had "further seriously deteriorated." He withheld recommendations pending a report by a U.N. fact-finding team headed by Special Envoy Lakhdar Brahimi, a former Algerian foreign minister.

On October 18, Boutros-Ghali recommended a two-month extension of UNOMIL, pending recommendations by another investigative team who will consult the ECOWAS chair, President Jerry Rawlings of Ghana, about the role and responsibilities of the ECOMOG forces and U.N. observers. The Secretary-General also said that because of recent attacks on U.N. observers, their number was being reduced to about ninety.

The U.N. mission in Liberia constitutes one of the only means of exerting pressure on the warring factions, as well as on the Nigerians, to halt this downward spiral. The U.N. must implement its mandate: U.N. observers should be required to report on violations of the cease-fire and of human rights and humanitarian law, and they must protest publicly when they are restricted in their movements. The appointment of a human rights officer for UNOMIL should be a step forward to this end, but the officer must engage in active human rights monitoring, drawing upon all available resources so that human rights and humanitarian law violations can effectively be documented and their perpetrators identified.

The Work of
Human Rights Watch/Africa

In April and May, Human Rights Watch/ Africa and the Human Rights Watch Children's Rights Project conducted a fact- finding mission to investigate the use of child soldiers by the warring factions. The mission to Liberia also investigated the hu- man rights abuses associated with the ongo- ing fighting, including extensive abuses at- tributed to the Liberian Peace Council.

Two publications resulted from the mission. In May, Human Rights Watch/Af- rica issued *Human Rights Abuses by the Liberian Peace Council and the Need for International Oversight*, which documented abuses by the LPC as well their links with elements of the Nigerian contingent of ECOMOG. In July, *Easy Prey: Child Sol- diers in Liberia*, was published by Human Rights Watch/Africa and the Children's Rights Project. The report focused on the use of child soldiers by the two main warring factions—ULIMO and the NPFL, and noted that many had been killed in the conflict and many had been forced to take part in killing, maiming, and rape of civilians.

Throughout the year, Human Rights Watch/Africa was involved in extensive ad- vocacy for human rights in Liberia, includ- ing briefings for Congressional staff and administration officials, numerous radio and newspaper interviews, and cooperation with nongovernmental organizations working on Liberia. On May 18, Human Rights Watch/ Africa testified before the Africa Subcom- mittee of the U.S. House Foreign Affairs Committee about human rights in Liberia.

MOZAMBIQUE

Human Rights Developments

In its second year of peace, following the October 4, 1992 General Peace Accord, the overall human rights situation continued to improve and culminated in Mozambique's first multi-party election. Restricted free- dom of movement and expression in some areas controlled by the former rebel Mozambique National Resistance (RENAMO) and appalling prison conditions and intimidation in some areas of RENAMO supporters by the paramilitary Rapid Inter- vention Police were the main concerns.

The first ever democratic elections were held on October 27-29, with voter turnout above 85 percent despite RENAMO's abor- tive and short-lived day-long boycott of the first day of voting. With 95 percent of the votes counted at time of writing the ruling Front for the Liberation of Mozambique (FRELIMO) took 45 percent in the parlia- mentary elections, giving it 129 out of 250 seats. RENAMO got 38 percent, gaining 112 seats. The Democratic Union, a rightest op- position party won nine seats. Joaquim Chissano, the current president was the win- ner in the presidential race, with 54 percent of the vote (compared to 34 percent for RENAMO leader Alfonso Dhlakama). On November 14, Dhlakama phoned U.N. Sec- retary-General Boutros Boutros-Ghali to ac- cept the election results and announced that he was prepared to cooperate with the gov- ernment in the post-election era.

The election campaign began officially on September 22 and over 5.2 million people registered to vote. It saw little violence and a low key campaign was conducted by both sides, although there was some intimidation by both in their stronghold areas. The south and far north voted for Chissano and FRELIMO while the central provinces of Manica and Sofala for RENAMO. The re- sults in the strategic provinces of Nampula and Zambezia, where 41 percent of the elec- torate were registered, were close, neighbor- ing villages often voting for opposing candi- dates.

The war and experience of human rights abuses played a role in the electoral out- come. In northern Mozambique, RENAMO campaigned to politicize villagers and in some areas sought to make amends for past brutalities. In some districts of Zambezi prov- ince RENAMO transferred a number of of- ficers with particularly brutal reputations out of the vicinity, and apologized for past brutalities. In the far south, the scene of many massacres by RENAMO in the 1980s, the electorate overwhelmingly rejected the former rebels, to the extent that even RENAMO controlled zones voted for Chissano and FRELIMO.

Human rights protection remained a low priority at official levels and will probably not feature highly in the policies of the new government. Some sort of accommodation between the two main contending parties is likely and past records of human rights abuses are being ignored. There are no plans for a "Truth Commission," or accountability for past human rights abuses.

The appointment on April 6 of Lieutenant General Lagos Lidimo (by the government) and Lieutenant General Mateus Ngonhamo (by RENAMO) as joint heads of the new Armed Defense Forces of Mozambique (FADM) army is a good indication of this approach. Lagos Lidimo in particular has a reputation for brutality in the late 1980s in operations against RENAMO in Zambezia province.

The official demobilization process for former combatants has been completed, although there are still former soldiers who failed to register. The forty-nine U.N.-run assembly points closed their doors to new arrivals on August 15. ONUMOZ, United Nations Operations in Mozambique, had registered 64,130 government troops and 18,227 RENAMO soldiers. Of these, 7,774 troops have moved to the training camps for the FADM. The total of the new army may reach 12,000, but this is far less than the 30,000 strong army envisaged in the 1992 GPA. Most notable is that the majority of soldiers from both sides wanted to be demobilized and appeared to have no interest in being in the future army.

A notable development in 1994 was the collapse of discipline amongst rank and file RENAMO soldiers toward their leadership, reflected in a significant increase in mutinies and in beatings of their senior military leaders. For example on June 1, RENAMO's Brigadier General Raul Dick was badly beaten by his men in Mocubela Assembly Area when he tried to mediate a dispute about poor conditions. In June and July there were over thirty incidents of soldiers mutinying, often by setting up road blocks and holding civilians hostage until their demands were heard.

Re-integration into civilian society of these demobilized soldiers was one of the greatest challenges for the new post-election government. There was widespread concern that a lack of employment prospects will result in economic and socially induced banditry.

During his first ever U.S. visit in June, RENAMO leader Dhlakama admitted for the first time that RENAMO had in the past recruited child combatants. There were over 2,000 child soldiers known to international nongovernmental organizations in May. According to a UNICEF survey of the problem at this time "these children are under military supervision, kept in tightly guarded bases within RENAMO's strongest military zones." By September RENAMO had began to fully assist in permitting these children to leave. These children have been problematic for RENAMO, not least because there have been several incidents in which they went on strike demanding benefits equal to those of adult soldiers. Human Rights Watch interviewed several child soldiers in October just after the elections. Having already lost their families, they also felt betrayed by RENAMO, which they said had "dropped" them. Child combatants have been regarded as unassembled troops by the U.N. and are not eligible for the same sort of benefits that assembled soldiers receive.

The government has continued to build up its paramilitary police force, the Rapid Intervention Police. This force is some 2,000 strong, made up of former army and security personnel, and has a reputation for intimidation and heavy-handed tactics. On October 23 Human Rights Watch witnessed the Rapid Intervention Police use excessive violence against civilians in unrest following the end of a RENAMO electoral rally at Xai Xai.

There remain large quantities of arms cached across the country. A typical arms cache seen by Human Rights Watch in October included six AK-47s, six hand grenades, one RPG-7, and two PMN anti-personnel mines. These had been stored in greased cloth. ONUMOZ officials admit that there are literally millions of guns still in circulation and that both sides have been stockpiling their better weaponry. In September there was a stand-off between the government and ONUMOZ when the U.N. established that there was a massive arsenal of undeclared weaponry, including hundreds of landmines, in storage under the Ministry of Interior in Maputo. After some tense discussions, the U.N. allowed the government to register the arsenal.

Reports of appalling prison conditions and detention without trial continue to be received. There is currently a two year backlog in court hearings that is stalling the judicial process. U.N. Civilian Police monitors (Civpol), whose mandate includes prison visits, spoke of poor conditions, cases of forced labor and incidents of rape by police of inmates in the prisons visited. RENAMO continued to deny complete free movement in its zones, although this situation had gradually improved throughout 1994. In October several informants told Human Rights Watch that they had recently joined RENAMO in exchange for gaining the freedom of their relatives.

The Right to Monitor

The Mozambican "Human Rights League" attempted to visit RENAMO areas, including its headquarters at Maringue, without success, despite several public invitations by RENAMO leadership to human rights groups to visit its areas. Human Rights Watch/Africa had travelled in RENAMO zones in June and July 1993 when researching its report *Landmines in Mozambique.*

International human rights groups visited government areas in Mozambique throughout 1994 without hinderance and the London-based organization Article 19 conducted a successful media-monitoring project during the election campaign.

U.S. and U.N. Policy

The Clinton administration played an important role in the build-up to the elections. U.S. AID continued to invest in the peace process including in several civil education programs. The administration was also anxious that the elections be held in the fall. U.S. permanent representative to the U.N. Madeleine Albright in March warned against any further delay in holding elections. The administration has also pushed for greater accountability of government, including concern for human rights. Following the April appointment of Lagos Lidimo by the Mozambican government as joint head of the new Armed Defense Forces of Mozambique, the administration called the Mozambican Ambassador to the State Department to request an explanation for the appointment of a man with a poor human rights record to such a senior post.

The administration also played a constructive role in May in putting pressure on RENAMO to permit UNICEF access to its child combatants and speed up efforts to reunite these children with their families. RENAMO leader Dhlakama was told that such actions would facilitate his June visit to the U.S. During Dhlakama's visit to the U.S. he met with the Acting Secretary of State for African Affairs at the State Department and Department of Defense officials. He also called upon U.N. Secretary-General Boutros Boutros Ghali in New York.

The U.S. administration presented two critical "non-papers," on May 23 and on October 11 to the Mozambican government. In May the U.S. administration expressed particular concern about the government's efforts to withhold key combat units such as the Sixth Tank Brigade and the Nyanga Brigade from demobilization, by declaring them "non-assembly areas" in violation of the GPA. The new U.S. ambassador to Maputo, Dennis Jett, used his July 4 speech to follow up on those issues, in addition to pushing for a Government of National Unity (GUN) power-sharing agreement. U.S. Assistant Secretary of State for African Affairs, George Moose visited Mozambique for six hours on August 9 and held talks with Foreign Minister Pascoal Mocumbi and RENAMO leader Dhlakama. In these meetings Moose pushed for both sides to meet the demobilization and election schedules.

The October "non-paper" was even more hard hitting, threatening to "re-evaluate our future development assistance program in Mozambique" unless the government assisted on five key areas, including access to regional arms depots and payment of the salary and subsistence requirements of electoral officials.

The growing costs of nation-wide peacekeeping have made the international community more determined than ever to secure a U.N. withdrawal from Mozambique quickly following the elections. In early May the U.N. Security Council extended the mandate of the United Nations Operation in Mozambique (ONUMOZ) to November 15 and ordered the closing down of the mission by January 31, 1995. In November, the mandate was extended to mid-December, the date when a new government is to be sworn into office. It also authorized the establishment of a police component, Civpol, comprising 1,144 officers, while cutting back the 6,200 member military peacekeeping force to avoid additional costs on top of the annual $210 million per year already budgeted. In September the U.N. obtained funds from the U.S. to retain a reduced Civpol presence in Mozambique past January 31, 1995. ONUMOZ currently costs $26,900,000 per month, or about $900,000 per day.

The Civpol contingent has been ineffectual in some areas. In October Human Rights Watch witnessed Civpol officers consciously avoid investigating reports of human rights abuses. We were told that it would be "too much work," although this was their job.

Beginning in September U.N. priorities focused on a successful outcome of the elections and symbolic actions, such as military and police patrols, increased, pro-active investigation in reports of human rights abuses and the search and destruction of arms depots and caches declined. Only following

international pressure, including from the U.S., was the issue of arms caches made a priority in October.

In December 1993 and January 1994 Italian members of the U.N. were accused of child abuse in Sofala province by an alliance of U.S., British, and Norwegian Save the Children Fund organizations. Soldiers from the now withdrawn Italian battalion Albatroz, which had been responsible for guarding the Beira corridor, were accused of repeated abuses of young girls for sexual purposes. In 1993 Human Rights Watch witnessed Italian soldiers solicit attention from a seemingly underage girl in Chimoio. Internal U.N. investigations have produced no official results on the charges.

The Work of
Human Rights Watch/Africa

In March, Human Rights Watch/Africa and the Arms Project published *Landmines in Mozambique*, a 136-page report documenting the serious landmines problem. The report demonstrated how most combatant forces, including those of the Mozambican government, RENAMO the former Rhodesia, South Africa, Tanzania, and Portugal have been responsible for laying landmines, especially antipersonnel mines. At least fifteen countries, most notably the former Soviet Union, have manufactured more than fifty different types of mines used in the Mozambican conflict.

Most of the mines were laid without markings or warnings to the civilian population. A large proportion were laid in such a way that their victims could not be other than civilians. More than 8,000 civilians are amputees as a result of landmines.

Professional mine clearance only began in mid-1994. Although the U.N. is responsible for coordinating initiatives, its plans were delayed by government and RENAMO political fighting, as well as the U.N.'s own bureaucracy. The U.N. has also engaged in "double dipping," giving clearance contracts to mines manufacturers, an action that Human Rights Watch vigorously opposed. The tragedy in Mozambique caused by landmines demonstrated once again that the 1980 Landmines Protocol had been wholly ineffective.

Human Rights Watch/Africa visited Mozambique in September and October and is preparing an updated Portuguese translation of *Landmines in Mozambique*. Following the government's appointment of Lagos Lidimo as joint head of the new army, the organization actively lobbied against the appointment on the grounds of his poor human rights record. In September Human Rights Watch/Africa met with Raul Domingos, the Head of RENAMO's Political Affairs Department to discuss human rights issues. It also engaged in other forms of advocacy, focused on informing politicians and diplomats on the current human rights situation. Human Rights Watch/Africa participated in several academic forums and conducted numerous press interviews about human rights in Mozambique.

NIGERIA

Human Rights Development

Nigeria edged closer to political chaos in 1994, after the brutal suppression of a broadly supported campaign to remove the military from political office. At the end of 1994, the country was further from the goal of its pro-democracy movement than it had been the previous year. A major concern in the ongoing crisis was the rise of ethnic and regional tension. The government's brutal way of dealing with pro-democracy strikes and demonstrations hardened the separation between north and south and increased the likelihood of more serious outbreaks of violence. During 1994, hundreds of critics of the military regime were arbitrarily detained, and many were killed or wounded as protests and demonstrations were attacked with military force.

General Sani Abacha, who seized power in November 1993, proved unwilling to try to peacefully resolve the political crisis that began in June 1993, when results of a presidential election were annulled by Abacha's

military predecessor, General Ibrahim Babangida. Protests over the cancellation of the election forced Babangida out of office in late August 1993, and his hand-picked civilian successor, industrialist Ernest Shonekan, was deposed in November by General Abacha, Babangida's defense minister.

Upon seizing power, General Abacha disbanded the national and state legislatures, removed the elected civilian governors, and banned all political activity, while, at the same time, avowing his intention to return the country to democracy.

In January 1994 the government announced that a constitutional conference, controlled by the military, would be held to decide Nigeria's future form of government. This announcement was greeted with scorn by pro-democracy leaders, who viewed it as yet another attempt to prolong the military's stay in power and refused to participate in the military's scheme.

In early May, Moshood Abiola, widely believed to be the winner of the 1993 presidential election, announced his intention to form a "government of national unity." The following week, the formation of the National Democratic Coalition (NADECO) was announced. The group, made up of politicians, retired military officials, and pro-democracy figures, was formed in an effort to coordinate and focus the various pro-democracy factions around four main demands: (1) the military must leave political office; (2) Abiola must be installed as president; (3) a sovereign national conference must be held to debate the country's future; and (4) the country must be restructured along truly federal lines. NADECO immediately called on the government to install Abiola as president before the end of May, and called for a boycott of the Constitutional Conference elections, the first of which was to be held on May 23.

Elections to select 273 of the 369 delegates to the Constitutional Conference (the remainder of whom were government appointees) were largely boycotted in the Yoruba-dominated southwest, the home region of Abiola. On the day of the elections, approximately fifteen human rights and pro-democracy activists were arrested, allegedly for trying to disrupt the elections. They were later released.

In late May and early June, members of Nigeria's disbanded legislature met secretly and issued statements calling on Abacha to surrender power to Abiola. On June 1, Ameh Ebute, the former senate president, publicly announced the senators' decision to reconvene. Ebute was arrested the following day. Many more arrests of former senators, former members of the House of Representatives, former governors, and others quickly followed. Many of those arrested were detained without charge for days or weeks. At least thirteen, however, were charged with treason and held for nearly two months before being released on bail. They included six senators, several governors, and several members of NADECO. The six senators were granted bail when they appeared in court on July 27, but their passports were impounded on court orders and they were put under surveillance. Some have been detained again; others have gone into hiding.

On June 11, Chief Abiola declared himself president. He was arrested on June 23 and held incommunicado until his first court appearance on July 5, when, at a Federal High Court in Abuja that had been set up especially for his trial, he was charged with various counts of treason. He was initially refused bail for several months, but the judge ordered that he be given access to his doctor, lawyers, and family members. Abiola's charges were later amended to five counts. According to these charges, Abiola "levied war against the State," "form[ed] an intention to remove or overawe otherwise than by constitutional means the Head of State," "conspired to do an illegal or treasonable act," and "represent[ed] him]self to be the President and Commander-in-Chief of the Armed Forces of the Federal Republic of Nigeria."

Abiola's health has deteriorated dramatically while in detention. Early in September, the Nigerian Medical Association, whose representatives had been allowed to examine him in the presidential clinic, said that Abiola was critically ill, suffering from high blood pressure and a painful neurological condition that was affecting the use of one leg. Although he was granted bail on November 4, government officials reportedly indicated that Abiola would be freed only if he renounced his claim to the presidency.

The Constitutional Conference convened on June 28. The outcome of the conference, which is supposed to serve as the basis for next year's political program, was to be summarized in a November report; however, in November the delegates announced that they would not finish their work until January 1995. The lifting of a ban on political activities, which was supposed to take effect in January 1995, was also expected to be delayed. No date has been set for the military regime's departure from political office.

A strike was announced on June 27 by the National Union of Petroleum and Gas Workers (NUPENG), which included among its demands recognition of the results of the June 1993 election. Although the government declared it illegal, the strike began on July 4, as planned. A week later, NUPENG's white-collar sister union, the Petroleum and Natural Gas Senior Staff Association of Nigeria (PENGASSAN), joined. Although the strike did not initially affect oil exports, it had an immediate effect on domestic fuel supplies, sparking riots and protests. By August, the strike had seriously eroded oil export earnings as well.

In attempting to break the strike, Abacha resorted to bribes, threats, arrests, and eventually, when these methods failed, in mid-August dissolved the leadership of the oil unions and ordered workers back to work. Frank Kokori, NUPENG general secretary, was arrested on August 20 by agents of the State Security Services (SSS) in Lagos. Other NUPENG and PENGASSAN officials were also arrested, including the NUPENG president, Wariebi Agamene, who was arrested in mid-September by the SSS. Other oil union representatives have also been arrested. By early September, it became clear that the strike had been broken.

Many other unions, including the National Union of Banking and Financial Institutions, the National Union of Air Transport Services Employment, and the National Union of Local Government Employees, also joined the oil workers strike in early July and stayed out for much of the duration of the strike.

The National Union of Teachers also joined the strike in early July. The Academic Staff Union of Universities (ASUU), the national academic union, embarked on a strike on August 22, which is still in effect at this writing. Many universities had closed down even before the ASUU strike because of protests or school administrators' fear of such protests.

The national leadership of the Nigerian Labor Congress (NLC), the national federation of labor unions, initially did not take a strong stand against the government. However, various state branches joined the strike in July. The national NLC finally went on strike on August 3–5, but it was not observed in the northern states. On August 17, the NLC executive was dissolved along with the oil unions' executives.

Attacks on pro-democracy activists have been ongoing throughout the crisis. Some activists have been killed; others have had their homes and offices bombed. Hundreds have been detained for periods ranging from several hours to several months. A number have been deprived of their passports.

Following the announcement of the oil union strike in late June and continuing through August, police and soldiers were unleashed on pro-democracy demonstrators with tear gas and live ammunition. An unknown number were killed, mainly in the Yoruba areas. Many of the killings occurred during suppression of peaceful protests, although in some demonstrations, especially in Lagos, violent thugs known as "area boys" took part in anti-military protests that were then suppressed with police gunfire. Violent police and military attacks on universities took place in the south; students were killed, beaten, raped, and arbitrarily detained.

Beginning in late August, there was a new trend in the increased level of lawlessness and terror: firebomb attacks on the homes of dissidents. Although none of the perpetrators of these attacks can be conclusively identified, the government's other abuses against members of the pro-democracy movement created the impression that the government was behind the attacks. Residences of pro-government figures were also destroyed, and a bomb was set off at the premises of the government-owned Radio Nigeria and Nigerian Television Authority in Kaduna, in northern Nigeria.

The detention of opposition figures has been common throughout the crisis. Among the well-known political detainees were Anthony Enahoro, the NADECO vice chair and a statesman who was at the forefront of the struggle for Nigerian independence. Many other politicians and human rights activists were also detained or went into hiding.

Also detained were members of the Ogoni ethnic group, who have protested the environmental degradation of their land by international oil companies, particularly Shell. The leader of the Ogoni movement, Ken Saro-Wiwa, has been detained without charge since May 23 and is currently believed to be very ill. He has been denied medical attention. In November, government-controlled media announced that he and other Ogoni leaders would be tried by a special tribunal in connection with the killing of four Ogoni leaders in May. Past trials before similar tribunals have not respected internationally accepted standards for fair trials.

The authorities also resorted to a variety of other tactics to harass and intimidate the opposition. Meetings were prevented or broken up by armed policemen. Pro-democracy leaders were placed under heavy surveillance. Passports were seized. Human Rights Watch/Africa is aware of at least thirteen passport seizures since July 1994; none has been returned. Those whose passports have been confiscated include Nobel

Laureate Wole Soyinka.

The independent press was targeted throughout the crisis, as it was during the political crisis immediately following the annulment of the election in 1993. Newspapers were shut down; reporters attacked and arrested. On June 11, the Concord group of publications (owned by Abiola) and the Punch group of publications were shut by police. Both publishers sued for wrongful closure, but damages awarded by the courts were never paid. *Punch* began publishing again during the first week of August before it was finally sealed off on September 7, 1994. On August 15, the Guardian group of publications was closed down.

Five photographers were assaulted by security forces and their cameras either confiscated or destroyed at a protest in Abuja on July 28, in which five people were killed during a court appearance by Abiola. The photographers were beaten with horse-whips, batons, and guns.

The News/Tempo has continually angered authorities since it began publishing in 1993. Its staff was targeted on several recent occasions. Bayo Onanuga, editor-in-chief, was arrested and detained briefly in August and September. Deputy editor-in-chief Dapo Olorunyomi was arrested twice after August. Journalists at *Punch* and *The Guardian* were also arrested in August. On August 26, two CNN reporters were forced to leave the country without explanation. Their expulsion occurred on the same day that CNN aired their report, which included interviews with two opposition leaders whose homes were firebombed the previous night.

On September 5, it was announced that General Abacha had promulgated a series of harsh new decrees targeting the press, the trade unions, and the judiciary. The decrees sanction the closure of the publications of the Concord group, the Punch group, and the Guardian group for six months from the time of their closures. The premises of all three publishers were to remain sealed-up during this period.

Other decrees dissolved the executive councils of the NLC, NUPENG, and PENGASSAN. The decrees, which were retroactively dated to August 18, 1994, forbid any court from inquiring into any actions taken pursuant to the decrees. They also suspended the constitutional protections of fundamental human rights for the purposes of the decree.

Another decree amended Nigeria's infamous administrative detention law, Decree 2, to allow persons who are deemed to present a security risk to be detained for three months without charge on orders either of the chief of general staff of the armed forces or the inspector-general of police. After three months, the detention order may be renewed. Previously, Decree 2 had allowed detentions for renewable six-week periods and only on orders of the chief of general staff. The amendment was made effective from August 18, just before a round-up of government opponents who remain in detention.

Another decree referred to Abacha's coup as a "military revolution," and stipulated that no "act, matter or thing done or purported to be done under or pursuant to any Decree or Edict" may be challenged in court.

On September 6, Attorney-General and Justice Minister Olu Onagoruwa called a news conference to distance himself from the decrees and threatened to resign if they were not rescinded. He was fired on September 12; no reason was given.

One of the most severe forms of human rights abuse in Nigeria was the repression of the Ogoni ethnic group in the oil-producing Niger delta region. Oil drilling has been responsible for the destruction of the environment in Ogoniland, which led to protests by the Ogonis and, in turn, resulted in their persecution. Oil companies, particularly Shell, have on occasion asked the government to intervene forcibly to suppress Ogoni protests, and their requests have been answered with military action. Hundreds of Ogonis were killed in attacks in 1993. On April 21, 1994, the Rivers State Commissioner of Police ordered an operation involving the military and police to "restore and maintain law and order in Ogoniland." Following the announcement, more villages were attacked, and more than forty Ogonis were killed. Many women and girls were reportedly raped, and villages were looted and burned to the ground. Hundreds of Ogonis were arrested and detained in military camps in the area; most were later released. Visitors to Ogoniland, both Nigerian and foreign, were prevented from conducting investigations into the Ogonis' complaints.

The Right to Monitor

Nigerian human rights groups were permitted to operate in 1994, but their work became increasingly difficult and dangerous. The abuses endured by groups such as the Civil Liberties Organization (CLO), the Committee for the Defense of Human Rights (CDHR), and the Constitutional Rights Project (CRP) included physical attacks, which could not be definitively tied to any particular group, but were believed to be connected to the government. For example, in August 1994, the home of Clement Nwankwo, head of the CRP, was sprayed with bullets. Similarly, a firebomb was thrown at the headquarters shared by the Campaign for Democracy (CD) and CDHR, also in August.

Human rights monitors were detained on several occasions. Dr. Beko Ransome-Kuti, head of the CD and CDHR, was arrested on June 9, charged with treason, but later released. He was re-arrested on September 14 and released a week later, after being charged with sending "threatening letters to oil company heads." Many members of the CLO, CD, and CDHR were arrested throughout the south in connection with pro-democracy protests.

Meetings and press conferences were routinely prevented or broken up by police, including a press conference on July 18 at the headquarters of the CD and CDHR that was taken over by about fifty armed policemen. Again, on September 10, more than fifty policemen invaded CD headquarters at about 5:00 a.m. and stayed until about 10:00 p.m., during which time they harassed CD personnel and visitors. This attack was believed to be related to a meeting of the CD National Coordinating Council scheduled for that day.

U.S. and E.U. Policy

The U.S. has been the most outspoken member of the international community advocating for democracy and human rights in Nigeria. Limited steps were taken to press for reform after the annulment of the June 1993 elections, including the cancellation of all but humanitarian aid. Military relations between the two countries were also reduced. In July 1993, the U.S. announced that commercial military sales would be reviewed on a case-by-case basis with the presumption of denial. After Abacha's coup in November, a White House proclamation was announced "suspending the entry into the United States of immigrants and nonimmigrants who formulate or implement policies impeding a transition to democracy in Nigeria or who benefit from such policies, and the immediate families of such persons." These steps have all been maintained to the present.

In April 1994, relations between the two governments cooled even further when President Clinton added Nigeria to the annual list of countries making insufficient efforts to combat illegal drug production. This precludes Nigeria from receiving U.S. aid and from receiving U.S. support for loans from international lending institutions.

On July 27, Jesse Jackson arrived in Nigeria as President Clinton's special envoy and met with General Abacha, Chief Abiola, and members of the human rights community. He failed to make any progress in easing the deadlock and stated upon his return home that the U.S. and other countries should begin "assertive, aggressive diplomacy" to prevent civil war.

In late July, the House of Representatives passed a resolution condemning human rights abuses and calling on the Clinton administration to consider additional means of encouraging a return to democracy. On July 28, four U.S. congressmen, William Jefferson, Donald Payne, Lucien Blackwell, and Craig A. Washington, who were planning to visit Nigeria to investigate political developments and lend support to the pro-democracy movement, were denied visas by the Nigerian embassy in Washington. Nigerian ambassador Alhaji Zubair Kazaure later denied that they were prevented from visiting Nigeria.

Following the annulment of the June 1993 election, the European Political Cooperation (the foreign ministers of the European Community), issued a statement in which "the Community and its member States" decided to adopt the following measures: suspension of co-operation in the military sphere; restrictions on visas for members of the military or the security forces and their families; suspension of visits by members of the military; and suspension of any further cooperation aid. These policies have not, however, been stringently followed. The U.K. has permitted unofficial visits by members of the government. Former military strongman Ibrahim Babangida, who maintains strong ties to the present government, is reportedly living in Hamburg.

Some statements condemning human rights abuses in Nigeria have been made by European governments. Following the dissolution of the trade unions, the U.K. said it "deeply regretted the turn of events" in Nigeria, and called the banning of the trade union leadership "a further regressive act." On August 26, the E.U. urged the Nigerian government to halt a campaign against political opponents. The statement was released by Germany, which held the rotating E.U. presidency. The statement said it "deeply regret[ted]" the shutting down of newspapers, the dissolution of the boards of the labor unions and the NLC and called on the government "to reverse these trends and to move rapidly to restore Nigeria to a civil democracy to which all Nigerians, including the present regime, have pledged their support."

Weapons shipments have reportedly continued from some European countries. The U.K. has reportedly recently shipped 150 tanks that were ordered in 1992, according to *The Economist* (September 9, 1994). In both the U.K. and Germany, commercial sales of weapons are licensed by the government, allowing those governments the opportunity to stop the sales on human rights grounds.

The Work of
Human Rights Watch/Africa

Human Rights Watch/Africa continued to pay close attention to human rights abuses in Nigeria. A letter to General Abacha in June raised the issues of the attacks on the Ogonis and the arrests of pro-democracy activists. In July, Human Rights Watch protested the continuing detention of activists and press closures. A letter in August protested the abusive treatment of Ken Saro-Wiwa.

A press release in August detailed the killings and other abuses directed against members of the opposition. *"The Dawn of a New Dark Age": Human Rights Abuses Rampant as Nigerian Military Declares Absolute Power*, a report on human rights abuses relating to the pro-democracy protests, was published in October.

Human Rights Watch/Africa participated in a briefing for congressional aides on the Ogoni issue in July. Throughout the political crisis, it conducted radio interviews with the U.S. and foreign media.

Human Rights Watch/Africa and the Human Rights Watch Women's Rights Project conducted two missions to Nigeria in 1994 to investigate human rights abuses directed against women, focusing on abuses against widows in the southern part of the country and the plight of child brides in the north. A report on these matters will be published in 1995.

RWANDA

Human Rights Developments

The Genocide
On April 6, 1994 Hutu extremists bent on retaining control over the Rwandan state launched a campaign of genocide against the Tutsi, a minority who made up about 15 percent of the approximately 7.2 million

people living there in early 1994. A plane crash of suspicious origin that killed President Juvenal Habyarimana triggered the massacres, but the campaign to eliminate the Tutsi had been planned for months as a way to upset a peace agreement that reduced the extremists' hold over power. The international community beat a hasty retreat from the killing fields, where between one half million and one million persons were slaughtered before mid-July.

The Rwandan Patriotic Front, a predominantly Tutsi exile force, brought an end to the massacres by defeating the forces of the government responsible for the genocide. The defeated government and its armed forces and militia fled to Zaire, ordering Rwandans under its authority to follow it into exile. The resulting catastrophic exodus to Goma and Bukavu cost thousands of lives as Rwandans died of disease, starvation, and lack of water. The authorities responsible for the genocide rapidly re-established their rule over the refugees, using control over the humanitarian supplies of food, water, and medicine to force compliance with their orders. By the end of the year, the guilty authorities were proclaiming their intention to return to Rwanda "to finish the work" of killing Tutsi, and their army and militia, nourished for months by the international community, were preparing for incursions into Rwanda.

In August 1993 the Rwandan government had signed the Arusha Accords, formally ending its three-year old war with the Rwandan Patriotic Front. An important group of Hutu leaders, however, were determined never to implement the agreement, which would have required them to share power with the RPF and to integrate the RPF's guerrilla force into the army. As President Habyarimana repeatedly postponed installation of a transitional government, preparations continued for a massive attack on Tutsi and those Hutu members of the political opposition willing to cooperate with them. A campaign of broadcast propaganda prepared the ground by inciting the Hutu majority to violence against the Tutsi—and against those Hutu who supported reconciliation between the two groups and a power-sharing arrangement in government. In August 1993 a radio station owned by members of Habyarimana's inner circle, *Radio Télévision Libre des Mille Collines*, had begun broadcasting ever more dramatic incitements to hatred and killing. They targeted by name leading members of the opposition and civil society, as well as the Tutsi minority as a group.

In late 1993 and early 1994, the Hutu extremist political parties (the National Republican Movement for Democracy, MRND, and the Coalition for the Defense of the Republic, the CDR) recruited increasing numbers of unemployed young men to swell the ranks of exclusively Hutu militias. The militia members were trained by soldiers of the Rwandan Armed Forces, particularly by members of the elite Presidential Guard, and arms were distributed to militia members throughout the country. In February militia members killed a moderate Hutu cabinet minister, Emmanuel Gatabazi, who was likely to have opposed Habyarimana in a presidential election, along with several dozen others in the capital. Supporters of Gatabazi then assassinated the president of the CDR party, whom they held responsible for Gatabazi's death.

Arms for the army and militia flowed into the country in considerable quantities in the two years before the genocide from South Africa and Egypt, while advisory assistance was provided by a French military mission. In January, the Human Rights Watch Arms Project issued *Arming Rwanda: The Arms Trade and Human Rights Abuses in the Rwandan War*, a report that documents the arming both of the government forces and the RPF. The report includes as an appendix a secret Rwandan government document setting out the organizational structure of the Hutu militias that were to play such a crucial role in the genocide, including details of their arms requirements and their place in the government's command and control structure.

The preparations for slaughter were well

known to the resident expatriate community, including diplomats as well as representatives of nongovernmental organizations. The special representative of the Secretary-General of the United Nations and the commander of a United Nations peace-keeping force (UNAMIR), present to facilitate the execution of the Arusha Accords, were also informed about these threatening developments. The U.N. commander even apparently sought authorization from New York for some form of preventive action. But no effective measures were taken. By March 1994 tensions were so great within Kigali that Rwandan human rights activists had sent their children out of the city. When the president's plane crashed on April 6, the armed forces command seized the opportunity to set in motion a plan of genocide that had developed over months. Within thirty minutes of the plane crash, military, police, and civilian militia set up roadblocks around the city, and the killing began.

Members of the army's presidential guard were initially dispatched to the homes of moderates within the government. Among the earliest victims were Prime Minister Agathe Uwilingiyimana, a progressive Hutu from an opposition party; Lando Ndasingwa, a Tutsi cabinet minister in the Habyarimana transition government, who was executed along with his Canadian wife, their two children, and his mother; President of the Supreme Court Joseph Kavaruganda; and numerous human rights activists. The presidential guard also tortured and executed ten Belgian soldiers from UNAMIR who had attempted to protect Prime Minister Uwilingiyimana.

The presidential guard was soon joined by the party militias. Together, they killed an estimated 20,000 people in Kigali and its immediate environs within a week. Shortly after the crash and the beginning of the massacres, a group of politicians close to Habyarimana and backed by the military proclaimed themselves the new government. The RPF resumed the civil war on April 8, with an immediate objective the rescue of its troops in Kigali and in an attempt to stop the massacres. On April 12 Belgium announced its intent to withdraw its 400-person UNAMIR contingent. Emboldened by the evacuation of Belgian troops and the failure of the remaining UNAMIR forces to respond, the leaders of the genocide extended its scope outside the capital to the east and the southwest by April 15.

In communities where the killing was not proceeding rapidly or thoroughly, outside elements, usually militia members, were imported to spur the slaughter. In the southern prefecture of Butare, it was both militia and members of the presidential guard who were brought in to execute massive killings in a region in which local people had largely resisted carrying out the genocide of their Tutsi neighbors. In such cases, local people were often given the choice of kill or be killed. Faced with such a choice, most agreed to join in the slaughter.

In most communities, local government officials organized and personally directed the murders. Eyewitnesses in several places reported that the killers arrived under the direction of local officials to begin their "work" at 8 a.m. and to finish at 4 p.m. The assailants then returned home singing, to come back the next morning and begin the slaughter once more. In most communities, the repeated attacks continued until all the Tutsi were killed: clearly the goal was complete elimination of the minority rather than its simple defeat.

Barriers on all roads and paths prevented victims from fleeing massacre sites. All Rwandans were required to carry identity cards which specify their ethnic group. Tutsi who sought to pass the barriers were selected on the basis of these identity cards and killed on the spot. When people sought shelter in neighborhood churches, hospitals, or schools, they were killed all the more efficiently, often through the use of grenades. Survivors were finished off with machetes, clubs, or guns. At such sites as Kibungo, Cyahinda, and Shangi, thousands of people were executed in a matter of hours.

By mid-May, militia leaders were calling upon their members to finish "cleaning up" (*nettoyer*) Tutsi and members of the Hutu opposition who had escaped death up to that point. In the months that followed, militia backed by the military made nightly visits to other locations where people at risk had taken refuge and removed groups of people to be executed. Anyone who was educated or had shown capacity for leadership was targeted first to ensure that the mass of victims would be left disorganized and unresisting for later slaughter. A substantial number of Catholic clergy were among the victims. The RTLM radio urged attackers not to repeat the mistake of sparing children, as had been done in previous massacres. The killers, some of whom had a radio in one hand and a machete in the other, heeded the advice and slaughtered children as well as adults.

Reliable accounts describe the heroism of some Rwandan authorities, both civilian and military, who sought to prevent or halt the slaughter in their regions. Unfortunately, their efforts proved futile in most cases. Military officers who tried to maintain order or to save threatened civilians were themselves killed. The systematic murder of the Tutsi population continued even as forces of the RPF engaged the military in an advance on Kigali.

Although representatives of the RPF and the Rwandan army reportedly agreed to a cease-fire on June 14, the agreement never took effect. In tandem with the genocide, but quite distinct from it, the active fighting continued throughout the month of June. On July 4 the RPF took control of Kigali, prompting a mass exodus of Hutu soldiers and civilians to Zaire, Burundi, and Tanzania. In late October there were an estimated 1.2 million Rwandan refugees in Zaire, 270,000 in Burundi, and over 500,000 in Tanzania.

By the end of 1994, soldiers of the former Rwandan army and members of the militia were terrorizing the refugee camps, particularly in Zaire. Unrestrained either by authorities of the former Rwandan government or by authorities of the local government, they were murdering, raping, and stealing at will. They systematically intimidated any refugees who might have wanted to return to Rwanda and in several cases killed those who appeared ready to leave the camps. One of the most serious incidents occurred in late August in Kibumba camp where several hundred refugees awaiting transport were attacked by militia members. Thirty Rwandan boy scouts in Katale camp, who had been charged with organizing security and helping with food distribution, vanished in late September, apparently murdered because they had represented an obstacle to full militia control of the camp. Militia members also threatened expatriate members of the relief community in late 1994.

Soldiers in Zaire continued to be paid by the former Rwandan government and, as the year ended, were preparing to resume the war against the new government of Rwanda. At the end of October, these soldiers were apparently the assailants responsible for killing thirty-six civilians in an early morning raid in the northwestern prefecture of Gisenyi.

The New Government of Rwanda

The new government of Rwanda, headed by President Pasteur Bizimungu and Prime Minister Faustin Twagiramungu, was installed on July 21. Although the cabinet includes representatives from all the parties that signed the Arusha Accords except the MRND, the party responsible for the genocide, the new government is clearly dominated by the victorious Rwandan Patriotic Front. Speaking for the new authorities, the Minister of Justice announced plans to prosecute all those accused of having participated in the genocide. He disposed of absolutely no resources, however, to carry out the enormous task of bringing to justice thousands of killers

The former government had taken along all bank funds, vehicles, computers and other movable property in its retreat to Zaire. The Ministry of Justice, like other branches of the new government, had no funds to draw upon for salaries or equipment as it struggled to begin operations. The Minister appealed for international assistance, both in the form of seconded personnel—judges and prosecutors—and in the form of funds. As of early November, no significant international assistance had begun, either to the Justice Ministry or other parts of the government.

Findings of an investigation by Human Rights Watch/Africa indicate that the RPF troops killed hundreds of civilians as they advanced south and west through Rwanda prior to and just after the cease-fire in mid-July. They executed these unresisting civilians in groups ranging in size from several dozen to several hundred, often in regions where Tutsi had been massacred in large number. The victims, some of whom included Tutsi, were killed indiscriminately and were not interrogated before being killed. In an incident in late October, approximately forty persons were killed in the commune of Gisovu, and in early November, nine others were killed and thirteen wounded at Musebeya in the prefecture of Gikongoro.

RPF soldiers were also responsible for the removal of thousands of other persons, individuals, and small groups who were accused of having played a role in the genocide. Human Rights Watch/Africa documented several cases in which the accused were subject to interrogation and then summarily executed. Further investigation was needed to establish the number of such victims, but it was clearly at least in the hundreds. Thousands of those who disappeared could have in fact have been alive in detention, but given the initial absence of an administrative capacity to register and keep track of prisoners, it was impossible to know for sure who was in custody and who had been killed.

Approximately 10,000 of the people accused of involvement in the killings were detained in civilian prisons at the beginning of November. Thousands of others were imprisoned in irregular conditions at military camps, communal lockups, private houses, latrines, and shipping containers. Conditions in the regular prisons were deplorable, largely as a result of overcrowding and lack of resources. Sanitary conditions were lamentable, and dysentery was a major problem. Between two and seven prisoners

died daily from this and other diseases at Kigali Central Prison. Prisoners at the regular prisons counted themselves lucky, however, because they were not subject to beatings or torture, as were those less fortunate persons who were detained in irregular facilities. About 20 percent of the prisoners in Kigali Prison had had some kind of preliminary hearing by early November. Some have been in detention since August, but the lack of personnel in the courts posed major obstacles to rapid processing of cases. Hundreds of persons were arrested every week and, given the paralysis of the judicial system, there was little prospect for speedy trials of the accused.

Various government authorities have repeatedly asserted that reprisal killings of those accused of genocide would be severely punished, and the government has in fact arrested several dozen of its own soldiers on charges that they killed civilians. To bring an end to reprisal killings, the government must have the resources to make its judicial system operational so that the accusations of participation in the genocide can be dealt with in an orderly fashion.

In the absence of a police force, the maintenance of order remained in the hands of the army, creating widespread fear. An atmosphere of insecurity was also heightened by frequent and bitter disputes over property. Refugees who left Rwanda decades ago had returned and appropriated property, including a large number of the houses and businesses in the capital. Authorities insisted that the original proprietors would be able to reclaim their property but, in many cases, those who tried to do so ended up being arrested, accused of having participated in the genocide by those who wished to keep their property. In some cases, property owners seeking to reclaim their houses were attacked outright by the squatters, who often have the support of local military forces.

The Right to Monitor
Until April, Rwandan human rights organizations were permitted to function—albeit in the face of growing threats. Numerous

members of the human rights community, including Charles Shamukiga, Fidele Kanyabugoyi, Ignace Ruhatana, Patrick Gahizi, Father Chrysologue Mahame, S.J., and Abbé Augustin Ntagara, were massacred by the presidential guard immediately after the plane crash on April 6. Subsequently, Matthieu Uwizeye, a human rights activist and judge, was killed by Hutu extremists, as were Joseph Habarugira, Augustin Ruzindana, and Sylvestre Nkubili. Charles Mbabajende, permanent secretary of the human rights league LIPREDHOR, was executed by the RPF in Byumba. Among those singled out by *Radio Mille Collines* as "enemies" or "traitors" who "deserved to die" was human rights activist Monique Mujawamariya, executive director of the Rwandan Association for Human Rights and Public Freedoms, who narrowly escaped with her life.

Following the organization of a new government by the RPF, local human rights organizations resumed their activities and organized teams which have begun documenting the genocide. Although the new government agreed to allow U.N. human rights monitors to be posted inside Rwanda and professed to be open to investigations by local and international human rights organizations, the new government sometimes restricted access to particular areas. For example, the representative of the U.N. special rapporteur on Rwanda was refused permission to visit Butare Veterinary School. A representative of Human Rights Watch/Africa, who was investigating reports of abuses by the current Rwandan government, was intercepted by soldiers and discouraged from continuing her research. Out on the hills densely occupied by soldiers, many people were afraid to talk about abuses.

The Role of the International Community

The international community, satisfied with the success of the Arusha Accords in August 1993, found itself faced with a terrible defeat nine months later. Following the plane crash, the beginning of the massacres, and the resumption of the civil war, the U.N. and the U.S. initially reacted with retreat, confusion, and lethargy. This apparent indifference, combined with the lack of any reaction by the international community to the massacres in Burundi in October and November 1993, made the Rwandan Hutu extremists think that they too could kill with impunity.

U.N. Policy

The Rwandan tragedy should have come as no surprise to the international community. Repeated warnings by human rights activists, as well as sources within the Habyarimana government, combined with the broadcasts by *Radio Mille Collines*, sent a clear signal that a crisis was imminent. But neither the U.N. nor any individual nation took any effective action to avert the disaster. When the massacres began, UNAMIR troops did not even draw their guns to defend themselves—a result of their limited mandate which extended only to monitoring, as well as insufficient arms and equipment. If UNAMIR had intervened rapidly and firmly in the first week, the massacres might not have turned into genocide. On April 21 when the U.N. Security Council withdrew all but a token number of UNAMIR troops, the de facto authorities were encouraged to extend the scope of the killings.

Even in the face of convincing proof of the true nature of the massacres, a few Security Council members refused to acknowledge that they constituted genocide. Part of the reason may have been that Jacques Roger Booh-Booh, the Special Representative of the U.N. Secretary-General in Rwanda, who appears to have been sympathetic to the self-proclaimed regime throughout his tenure, repeatedly characterized the slaughter as free-for-all fighting between the RPF and the army. Finally, after eight hours of discussion, the Council adopted a declaration on April 30 that used all the terminology of the International Convention on the Prevention and Punishment of the Crime of Genocide, but paradoxically rejected the usage of the term "genocide" itself. The members of the Council apparently wanted to avoid the obligation to act under the terms of the Convention, which requires its signatories to "prevent and punish" this crime against humanity.

Faced with the horror in central Rwanda and the mass exodus of refugees to Tanzania on April 29, delegates from the Czech Republic, New Zealand, Spain, and Argentina took steps to persuade the other states represented on the Security Council to send more troops to Rwanda with an expanded mandate. On May 17 the Council finally authorized the deployment of UNAMIR II, with up to 6,800 soldiers, including ninety police, to defend displaced persons, refugees, and civilians in danger. However, internal U.N. conflicts and bureaucracy caused further delays. The poor countries that had agreed to provide troops and the rich countries that had agreed to provide equipment continuously begged each other to deliver what they had promised. Moreover, the key actors seemed unwilling to expedite their normal decision-making processes. In late June a contingent of French troops entered Rwanda and established a peacekeeping zone in the southwestern region of the country. The Security Council welcomed the French intervention, which lessened pressure on the U.N. for speedy action. As of early November, only 5,254 UNAMIR II soldiers were in place; their numbers included only thirty police.

Shamefully absent at the moment of the killings, the international community is now moving slowly to bring those guilty to justice. On July 1 the Security Council voted to establish a Commission of Experts to examine crimes against humanity perpetrated in Rwanda since April 6 and to advise on the desirability of further proceedings through an international tribunal. After several months of study, the Commission recommended establishment of an international tribunal to try those accused of these crimes. In early November the Security Council established the International Criminal Tribunal for Rwanda to consider genocide, crimes against humanity and other violations of international humanitarian law. The Tribunal will be expanded by the addition of two trial chambers. The Tribunal will share an appeals chamber with the tribunal for the former Yugoslavia, and will be served by the same chief prosecutor, South African jurist Richard Goldstone. Rwanda, which has a seat on the Security Council, voted against the resolution—largely because the International Tribunal would not have the power to order the death penalty. The government of Rwanda did agree, however, to cooperate with the Tribunal.

In an extraordinary session held in May, the U.N. Commission for Human Rights recommended that a special rapporteur and human rights field officers be sent to investigate the genocide in Rwanda. In reports published in June and July, Special Rapporteur René Degni-Ségui documented the genocide and other human rights violations. The first U.N. human rights field officer arrived in Rwanda on June 10 but received none of the personnel or resources needed to carry out her important charge. In August the U.N. High Commissioner for Human Rights promised 147 observers, but only fifty-two were in place by early November. They received almost no training and had great difficulty obtaining vehicles and communication equipment.

U.N. human rights monitoring efforts were further undermined by a conflict between U.N. departments. In September the UNHCR published a report charging the RPF with systematic revenge killings and suspended further repatriation of refugees. U.N. authorities in Kigali, including UNAMIR and representatives of the U.N. Center for Human Rights, publicly challenged the validity of the report. They subsequently investigated the charges in a cursory fashion before declaring them unfounded.

U.S. Policy
From the beginning of the Rwandan civil war on October 1, 1990, the U.S. tried to play the role of "honest broker" between the Rwandan government and the RPF. This strategy, reasonable at the beginning of the conflict, appeared to have attained its great-

est success with the signing of the Arusha Accords in August 1993.

Aware of the Rwandans' preparations in anticipation of the resumption of civil war and shocked by the extent of the killings, the executive branch responded by setting up, in the first week of the crisis, an inter-agency working group, which included among its members representatives from the Pentagon, the State Department, the National Security Council, and the Central Intelligence Agency. According to one of the participants, this working group asked all the necessary questions but never formulated effective answers.

The U.S. remained constrained by its earlier interpretation of the situation as a civil war and failed to confront the genocide that was launched as part of a strategy for winning the war. The priority of the U.S. was to achieve a cease-fire and a return to the terms of the Arusha Accords. When this misplaced strategy proved unsuccessful, the U.S. had no alternative plan of action. Certain White House officials counseled that military intervention would be useless because they believed that the war resulted from deeply rooted "tribal hatreds" which, "because they had always existed," would continue forever. A few weeks after the massacres had begun, when it had long been evident that genocide was taking place, a senior member of the Clinton administration ordered officials not to speak of "genocide" because the use of this term could increase the moral pressure on the President and force him to act. Only in mid-June, in the face of Congressional outrage and a rash of critical articles in the press, did Secretary of State Warren Christopher finally invoke the term.

Focused on the combat between armies, the U.S. failed to deal with the massacres of civilians—which were clearly more than simple and inevitable consequences of the war. American officials refused to consider asking the Pentagon to jam broadcasts of *Radio Mille Collines* through which the murder squads were directed, as human rights activists and members of Congress had asked. They likewise refused to organize the international community to condemn the massa-

cres and to isolate the de facto government for its having been established on the basis of genocide. The rump genocidal regime was permitted to operate out of the Rwandan Embassy in Washington and to represent Rwanda at the U.N.

Members of Congress expressed their concern about the massacres and pressured the administration for more action. On April 26 the Senate passed a resolution condemning the systematic massacre of civilians in Rwanda. The House Subcommittee on African Affairs held hearings on the subject on May 4, and the Senate held hearings in July. These efforts had little effect due to the American public's lack of interest. Public pressure on President Clinton to act developed only later, after the mass exodus of refugees to Goma.

The decision of the U.S. to restrict its role in Rwanda to traditional diplomacy was most significant for its impact on U.N. policy in the crisis. The U.S. supported the formation of UNAMIR in October 1993, even though the vote in the Security Council took place on the day after eighteen American soldiers were killed in Somalia. By April 1994, however, the specter of U.S. troop losses in Somalia had come to haunt Washington, and U.S. officials sought only to limit U.N. peacekeeping in Rwanda.

Rwanda was the first case to be treated under Presidential Decision Directive 25 (PDD 25), which dictated that the U.S. would provide military or financial support only to peacekeeping operations that met certain criteria: well-defined objectives and a plan to attain them, a detailed budget, a cease-fire between belligerents and their agreement to the presence of U.N. forces, a relatively fixed date for the termination of the operation, and an indication of countries that would make soldiers available.

Given the weak roles played by Belgium—because of the prior withdrawal of its soldiers—and France—because of its close relationship with Habyarimana's government, the U.S. played a key role in the U.N.'s decision to withdraw the majority of UNAMIR forces in late April. The long delay in deploying UNAMIR II was also largely a result of U.S. intransigence.

To its credit, the U.S. government actively encouraged the U.N. High Commissioner for Human Rights, José Ayala Lasso, to become involved in investigating and condemning the mass slaughter. Only a few days after meeting with John Shattuck, the State Department's Assistant Secretary for Human Rights, in mid-May, Ayala Lasso called for the appointment of a special rapporteur on Rwanda and convened a special session of the U.N. Human Rights Commission.

Following the French entry into Rwanda ,in late June, the U.S. government deferred to the French. The U.S. did not call upon the French to jam the radios and arrest persons involved in genocide. Nor did the U.S. speak to the need for other governments, such as Tanzania and Zaire, to arrest suspected mass murderers who had fled to refugee camps there or provide the means to help them do it. Meanwhile, the deployment of a proposed African UNAMIR enhancement stalled, with no additional men made available for want of equipment from the West.

Only after the RPF had taken over all of Rwanda except the French zone and announced the formation of a national government did the Clinton administration take its first actions to stigmatize and denounce those who had committed genocide. On July 14 President Clinton announced that he would close the Rwandan Embassy in Washington. D.C. and freeze the assets of Rwandans in the U.S. The U.S. government also announced that it would seek the expulsion of the rump government from Rwanda's seat at the U.N.

In late July the U.S. stepped up its relief efforts in Rwanda. The U.S. contributed over $237,000,000 in emergency assistance to Rwanda between April and mid-November 1994. Like the rest of the international community, the U.S. conditioned direct bilateral assistance on the new government's human rights record.

The Work of Human Rights Watch/Africa

Before the Rwandan genocide began, Human Rights Watch/Africa attempted to alert the international community to the imminent crisis and to assist Rwandan human rights groups in monitoring an increasingly dangerous situation. Following the April 6 attacks on Tutsi and members of Rwandan civil society, the organization tried to protect its colleagues and to facilitate evacuation, where possible. It also focused on persuading decision makers and the press to call the killing "genocide" instead of labeling it "tribal bloodletting" and worked to get a new and enlarged U.N. force with a broader mandate sent back to Rwanda to halt the massacres. In addition, it lobbied the U.N. Human Rights Commission to send a special rapporteur to investigate the situation and prepared documentation for his inquiries.

At the height of the genocide, Human Rights Watch/Africa published a report entitled *Genocide in Rwanda: April-May 1994* as well as numerous news releases, articles, and editorials denouncing the genocide and demanding an international response. In May the organization brought a lawsuit in U.S. federal district court on behalf of Tutsi Rwandans living in the United States against the head of the CDR for his role in inciting the genocide.

Human Rights Watch/Africa undertook missions in mid-August and again in October to gather documentation on the genocide and to monitor the human rights situation.

The organization is currently attempting to ensure that those individuals guilty of genocide and crimes against humanity are brought to justice in an orderly fashion. To this end, it welcomed the establishment of the international tribunal and urged governments to contribute funds, equipment, services, and expert personnel and to collaborate in apprehending former Rwandan leaders. Human Rights Watch/Africa is also advocating for increased international assistance to the Rwandan judiciary.

The organization continues to report on and seek to deter abuses, including vengeance killings, by or with the acquiescence of the new government. It is assisting Rwandan colleagues in rebuilding the human rights movement, encouraging them to remain representative of the entire spectrum of ethnic and political groups in the country.

SOUTH AFRICA

Human Rights Developments

South Africa's first all-race elections, held from April 26 to 29, 1994, opened a new era in the country's history. A new interim constitution came into effect on the first day of voting, under which all South Africans will have for the first time the protection of a bill of rights enforced by a constitutional court. At the same time, the ten ethnically determined "homelands," the foundation of the apartheid system, were dissolved and were incorporated into nine new administrative regions. In a landslide victory, the African National Congress (ANC) won 62.6 percent of the national vote, and on May 10, Nelson Mandela, the president of the ANC, was inaugurated as State President. A five-year government of national unity (GNU) was installed, in which both the National Party (NP), led by outgoing president F.W. de Klerk, and Chief Mangosuthu Gatsha Buthelezi's Zulu-dominated Inkatha Freedom Party (IFP) were represented in the cabinet. The new national assembly, in which women as well as black South Africans were substantially represented for the first time, was empowered to draw up and adopt by a two-thirds majority a final constitution for South Africa. In October, during a visit to the U.N., President Mandela signed the International Covenants on Civil and Political Rights and on Economic, Social and Cultural Rights.

Although ultimately certified as "free and fair" by the Independent Electoral Commission (IEC), which was charged with the conduct of the election, serious concerns were raised during the election campaign and the days of voting, particularly in Natal,

the stronghold of the IFP. The IFP, together with several right wing parties and the homeland "governments" of KwaZulu (where Buthelezi was chief minister), Ciskei, and Bophuthatswana had withdrawn from multiparty negotiation in August 1993. Until one week before the poll, the IFP maintained it would boycott the vote. On April 19, 1994, well after all nominal deadlines had passed, Buthelezi announced that the IFP would after all participate. Although the criticisms of the IEC are mostly centered on lack of planning and disorganization rather than fraud or deliberate sabotage, there were allegations of ballot-stuffing, intimidation, and even of "pirate" voting stations in rural KwaZulu, where independent monitoring proved difficult to arrange at such short notice. With 50.3 percent of the regional vote, Inkatha received much greater support than had been predicted by opinion polls, although the IEC stated that it was satisfied that the final result had not been significantly affected by any irregularities in the poll.

The administrations of the homelands of Bophuthatswana and Ciskei, both hostile to the elections, collapsed in the weeks before the vote. In Bophuthatswana, a wave of mass strikes and protests by civil servants provoked a crisis in the second week in March in which the homeland president, Lucas Mangope, was deposed. Several thousand members of the extreme right-wing Afrikaner Resistance Movement (AWB) invaded the homeland in support of the government, but were eventually escorted back to South Africa by South African troops. At least twenty-seven black civilians were killed in the course of the disturbances, many of them in drive-by shootings by the AWB, others by Bophuthatswana security forces as civilians engaged in looting. Following an exchange of fire with Bophuthatswana security forces in which one AWB member was killed, two others were summarily executed. In Ciskei, which had for some months shown signs of weakening in its resistance to the elections, civil servants strikes led the government to invite South African intervention and voluntarily step down. Administrators were appointed by the government to take over responsibility for each homeland for the period leading up to the elections.

Political violence, which had been the principal threat to the transition process and was expected to disrupt voting in Natal and on the East Rand near Johannesburg, did not affect the election days themselves, which were amongst the most peaceful in several years. However, it was difficult to assess the effect that violence prior to the election had on voting behavior. During the last two weeks of March and first two weeks of April, 429 people were recorded killed in political violence in Natal/KwaZulu, the worst affected area, largely in clashes between supporters of the ANC and IFP. In an attempt to contain the crisis, the government declared a regional state of emergency on March 31. Levels of violence decreased dramatically after Chief Buthelezi announced that the IFP would contest the elections, and continued to decrease over the following months. The Natal state of emergency was lifted in August. By the end of October 1994, 2,480 people had died in political violence during the year, according to the Human Rights Committee of South Africa (HRC), a nongovernmental monitoring organization based in Johannesburg. One thousand six hundred thirty-one of these died before the election.

Long-standing allegations that political violence had been perpetrated and deliberately provoked by "third force" elements within the security forces and members of extreme right wing parties and paramilitary groups, were confirmed during the election campaign, by the investigations of a standing commission of inquiry headed by Justice Richard Goldstone. On December 6, 1993, the Goldstone Commission's fourth interim report concluded that there was a "high probability" that at least one "hit" squad had been operating in the KwaZulu Police (KZP). On March 18, 1994, the Goldstone Commission published a report which finally confirmed that senior South African Police (SAP) officials had been involved in supplying Inkatha with weapons and financial support. On March 22, 1994, a task force appointed by the Transitional Executive Council (TEC) to carry out the investigation into the operation of security force hit squads concluded that hit squad activity was responsible for the killing of "a significant proportion of those who have died in political violence in Natal/KwaZulu." In July, the retiring commissioner of the KZP stated that he was convinced of the existence of hit squads and called for a thorough investigation. On May 18, 1994, the task group issued a further report concluding that paramilitary training camps set up by Inkatha in KwaZulu in 1993 and 1994 were illegal and "may have provided elements within the IFP and KwaZulu government with the capacity for large scale insurrection." A third report, leaked to the press, linked the minister of police in the new KwaZulu/Natal administration, to allegations of gun running for Inkatha. Several individuals implicated in the allegations were elected as IFP members of the new national or regional assemblies.

The white right wing, which had posed a potentially serious threat to the elections, was split into more moderate and hardline wings by the failed AWB "invasion" of Bophuthatswana. Although the hardliners continued to boycott the elections, ex-General Constand Viljoen contested the elections as leader of a new party, the Freedom Front, which won 2.2 percent of the national vote, and nine seats in the new national assembly. A right-wing bombing campaign culminated in several massive blasts which killed at least twenty-one people in and around the greater Johannesburg metropolitan area in the days immediately preceding the election. Thirty-four members of extreme right-wing organizations opposed to the elections were arrested during the next few days and charged with murder and attempted murder. However, although the Freedom Front continued to call for an "Afrikaner homeland," the threat of widespread white violence in resistance to a black government receded.

Reforms by the National Party government since 1990 or by the TEC, the body charged by the multiparty negotiating forum with facilitating the transition to a democratic order in South Africa, were accelerated by the new government. Amongst the most significant measures were a Police Bill, for the reform of the police force; a new child welfare program, to provide health care, primary education and promising that all children would be removed from South Africa's prisons; and a Restitution of Land Rights Bill, to establish procedures for the investigation and adjudication of claims by communities dispossessed by apartheid. The day before the election, following weeks of controversial debate within the TEC, President de Klerk signed a declaration abolishing the principal provision of security legislation allowing detention without trial. However, legislation allowing detention without trial in some cases remained in force, though subject to new guarantees of due process under the bill of rights.

Unrest in prisons was a feature during the entire negotiations process, in connection with disputes over the release of political prisoners and the extension of the franchise to prisoners, and continued to be a serious problem. Riots affected many prisons both before and after the elections; on June 10, Mandela announced a six month reduction in all prison sentences in an effort to quell the latest disturbances, and in August a program of new prison building to relieve overcrowding. A judicial commission of inquiry was appointed to investigate unrest in prisons over the election period. Several hundred people were still on death row at the end of September although a moratorium on executions remained in effect, some sentences were commuted and the ANC reaffirmed its opposition to the death penalty. In October, the constitutional court announced that its first case would be to decide the constitutionality of the death penalty.

The question of accountability for past abuses was one of the first issues to be addressed by the new government. The Minister of Justice, Dullah Omar, a longtime human rights activist, announced that amnesty legislation would be enacted for politi-

cal crimes—as required by the interim constitution. Each person seeking immunity from prosecution would have to make a separate and public application, and amnesty would be linked to the operation of a truth commission, to be appointed to record the crimes of apartheid. However, the detailed terms of the truth commission and amnesty were the subject of intense negotiation within the GNU. Draft legislation was released in October, but without the agreement of the NP and the IFP. In the meantime, little was done to bring known human rights abusers to justice. In the last days of the old government, President de Klerk controversially granted amnesty under existing legislation to a number of security force members. Agreed draft legislation was finally released in November, which reflected NP pressure by providing for the amnesty hearings to be in secret. Despite the findings of the Goldstone Commission in regard to covert support for hit squads and for Inkatha, no high ranking officials were indicted and most remained in office. One prosecution was mounted against the commander of a unit and his subordinates found to have been involved in illegal covert operations near Johannesburg. However, the trial was postponed, after the principal accused indicated that he intended to apply for amnesty if he were eligible under the new legislation.

The Right to Monitor

With the installation of a new government, all official restrictions on monitoring human rights abuses in South Africa were lifted, although violence in the townships remained a serious threat to media reporters and human rights monitors alike during the lead up to elections: in January, a freelance photographer was killed in the East Rand township of Katlehong. Large numbers of international and local observers monitored the conduct of the election, with the agreement or under the control of the IEC. The ANC also indicated its intention of introducing a much more open style of government; for example, by establishing standing committees of the national assembly to monitor the performance of the executive branch and proposing a new freedom of information act.

International and U.S. Policy

Following the election, South Africa completed a process of reintegration into the international community begun under the previous government. In ceremonies over the next months it was readmitted to the Commonwealth and joined the Organization of African Unity and Southern African Development Community (SADC). In October, Nelson Mandela became the first South African head of state to address the General Assembly of the U.N. Presidents François Mitterrand of France and Robert Mugabe of Zimbabwe were the first heads of state to be received by the new government; British Prime Minister John Major visited South Africa in September, announcing a $160 million aid package from the U.K. British officers were retained to assist in the integration of ANC cadres into the new South African army. The European Union, South Africa's largest donor, announced the inclusion of South Africa within its Generalized System of Preferences, and authorized $350 million worth of loans from the European Investment Bank. Crises in the small enclave state of Lesotho, in January and in August, saw high level representatives of the old and new governments meeting for the first time with the leaders of Botswana and Zimbabwe to discuss a common approach.

In May 1994, the U.N. Security Council finally lifted the arms embargo in force against South Africa since 1977, opening the alarming possibility of South Africa becoming a major weapons supplier to the rest of Africa. The chief executive of Armscor, the procurement agency for the South African army and the armaments industry's marketing organization, announced that he expected South Africa to double arms exports as a result—and to gain 25,000 jobs in arms manufactures. South Africa participated in several major arms exhibitions throughout the year. However, the new government stated that South Africa would contribute to the U.N. conventional arms registers, an-

nounced a ban on the export of landmines, and stated that South Africa would not export arms to countries that abused human rights or were divided by civil war. In November, a commission of inquiry appointed by the new government held hearings into illegal arms trading by Armscor both before and after the election. Inquiries focused on an October shipment of AK-47 rifles, supposedly bound for Lebanon, that had attempted to offload in Yemen and been returned to South Africa. Armscor admitted that, provided an end-user certificate was provided, it made little effort to verify the final destination of weapons. Due to outstanding criminal proceedings against Armscor in a Philadelphia court, in connection with violations of arms sanctions during the 1980s, U.S. arms sales to South Africa remained embargoed after the new government was installed.

Nelson Mandela was the only African leader invited to President Clinton's inauguration; although Clinton did not himself attend Mandela's own inauguration, a high level delegation headed by Vice-President Al Gore and First Lady Hillary Rodham Clinton represented the U.S. at the ceremony. The Vice-President spoke of the "beginning of a new partnership" between the U.S. and South Africa, at both government and commercial levels. In October, President Mandela visited the U.S.

In May 1994, President Clinton announced that U.S. assistance would be increased to $600 million over three years; including a doubling of U.S. AID's contribution to $166 million for 1994. Although continuing to support the nongovernmental sector, U.S. agencies would for the first time work directly with the South African government. In addition to previously announced investment guarantees by the Overseas Private Investment Corporation (OPIC), other components of the aid package included trade promotion services by the Commerce Department; a 30 percent increase, to $3.4 million, in the U.S. Information Agency budget for South Africa; a $100,000 Department of Defense training program for the

South African military; and negotiation of a double taxation treaty. During Mandela's October visit, AID committed a further $150 million in loan guarantees for housing and electrification programs, as well as a $100 million enterprise fund for the southern Africa region. OPIC announced two equity funds, totaling $150 million, designed to generate about $1.3 billion in new investment.

Legislation lifting the ban on U.S. support for IMF and World Bank loans to South Africa, and removing all conditions on Export-Import Bank guarantees, was passed through Congress shortly after the formal lifting of U.N. sanctions in September 1993. In June 1994, the U.S. Information Agency hosted a two-day conference for representatives from the business, government and nonprofit sectors of both South Africa and the U.S., to stimulate ties between the two countries. In October, a new cooperative commission was announced, chaired by Vice-President Gore and South African Deputy President Thabo Mbeki, to promote joint initiatives in energy, education, and economic development.

The Work of
Human Rights Watch/Africa

A representative of Human Rights Watch/Africa traveled to South Africa in January and February, following up previous work by investigating violence in Natal and abuses of freedom of expression and association in Bophuthatswana. A report based on the research, *Impunity for Human Rights Abuses in Two Homelands: Reports on KwaZulu and Bophuthatswana*, was published in March 1994. In February, a report on prison conditions in South Africa was published, based on research carried out in 1992 and 1993.

Two representatives of Human Rights Watch attended a conference in South Africa in February examining the question of accountability for past abuses, and a detailed letter urging respect for the need for truth and justice was sent to President Mandela in June. Beginning in October, a representa-tive of Human Rights Watch/Africa was currently based in Pretoria.

SUDAN

Human Rights Developments

The military-National Islamic Front (NIF) government is in its sixth year of power, continuing to dismantle civil society and to enforce laws and policies which discriminate against non-Muslims and women. Civil and political rights even for Muslim men are not recognized, suspended by a draconian set of emergency rules established when the junta seized power in 1989. Political parties and independent trade unions remain banned, with no prospects, under the present regime, for freedom of association or expression. Torture and arbitrary detention continue to be prominent features of the human rights picture in Sudan.

The civil war, waged mostly in the southern third of the country and in the Nuba Mountains in the central region known as the transition zone, remains beyond military solution as the parties to the conflict continue to inflict extreme hardship on the southern and Nuban population. Massive and expensive humanitarian assistance by the world community has been required to prevent starvation of hundreds of thousands of civilians. Negotiations to end the armed conflict petered out in 1994, despite international encouragement.

Sudan, the largest country in Africa and with a population of about twenty-five million, is ethnically and religiously diverse, although the current government seems determined to impose one mold, of Arabism and militant Islam, on the population. An aspect of this has been to impose its contested version of Islamic *shari'a* law on both Muslim and non-Muslim segments of the population. The government has also embarked on urban clearance programs to remove the large non-Muslim population with war-displaced southern and Nuban people from the greater Khartoum area to isolated sites far from urban areas. With little or no notice, the displaced, who have fled for safety and work in the north, have seen their homes destroyed without compensation as a result of this clearance program. In the first seven months of 1994, at least 160,000 were newly displaced in this manner, according to Médecins Sans Frontières (MSF). An estimated 800,000 southerners displaced by the war are presently sheltered in the outskirts and slums of Khartoum.

Sudanese security forces clashed with protesting squatters in Omdurman on October 15, 1994. The security forces killed at least five and severely injured fourteen squatters who protested the government's attempts to destroy their settlements and remove them to primitive sites in the desert far outside Khartoum.

Children among the southern displaced have suffered in particular. Young southern boys have been picked up by the government from the streets and markets of Khartoum and sent to remote indoctrination camps without notice to their families. The program flouts child welfare laws and procedures, although it is presented as a measure to deal with "street children." Boys are given Muslim names and religious instruction in Islam regardless of the fact that most do not come from Muslim families. Boys who have escaped from the camps say that camp officials tell them they will be inducted into the government militia (for the war in the south) when they reach fifteen.

The northern political opposition, which formerly found expression in political parties, remains severely repressed. Not only are parties banned, but the leaders and activists who have remained in the country are periodically arrested, often without charges, and frequently mistreated or tortured. Those who are released sometimes have been put under daily obligation to report to the security forces, where they are made to wait until nightfall. This harassment continues for months in some cases; the authorities may see this as a means to avoid international criticism of long-term detentions.

In 1993 retired Brigadier Mohamed Ahmed al-Rayah al-Faki, imprisoned in 1991, complained in writing to the authorities of having been severely tortured over an eighteen-month period. He said he was raped, subjected to electric shock, beaten, doused in hot and cold water, and held in chains over long periods. Although al-Faki named his torturers and gave details of the torture, the complaint has not been addressed by the authorities.

When defendants accused of conspiring to cause acts of sabotage testified at their trial in early 1994 that they had been tortured, court-ordered medical examinations confirmed torture. The only remedy offered by the court, however, was to advise the victims to file a complaint with the police. The accused were convicted and sentenced to long terms of imprisonment on the basis of confessions obtained through torture.

Arrests of political activists continued in 1994. The top leaders still in the country of the two largest Sudanese political parties, now banned, were both arrested, as were many of their followers. Sadiq al-Madhi, elected prime minister in 1986 and overthrown in 1989, who is the head of the Umma Party, was kept in a "ghosthouse"— an unofficial place of detention—for ten days; many of his followers were jailed for longer periods of time, some of them more than once. Sid Ahmad al-Hussein, the secretary general of the Democratic Unionist Party, was also detained and tortured several times. Several members of the Communist Party were arrested; and others remain long-term political detainees without charge or trial.

Independent trade unions remain banned, and government-sponsored unions are being established, but union activists continue to press for improvement in working conditions. Many were arrested in 1994, including those who organized a campaign in Sennar to require government agencies to pay long overdue wages to their employees.

All of the independent press was banned after the 1989 coup, but the government introduced a new, allegedly more liberal press law in late 1993. The first and only independent newspaper to try to operate under this law, *al-Soudani al-Doulia*, was stifled in early 1994, despite the fact that it was owned and operated by a leading NIF party member. Because of its rather independent line, this newspaper was raided and its publication stopped for two days in February, and the news editor was arrested and held for almost two months. In April, as the result of reporting on corruption and other matters critical of the government, two journalists and the owner-editor were arrested. This time the newspaper was closed and its assets confiscated. The journalists and owner were eventually released.

During this process, the new press law was not invoked; the newspaper was banned under the emergency law "for raising doubts about the purpose and struggle of the armed forces and People's Defense Forces" and having the aim of "destroying the revolution."

In the war in the south and Nuba Mountains, the government made military gains against the rebel forces of the Sudan People's Liberation Army (SPLA)-Mainstream, headed by Commander John Garang. Formerly rebel-held towns and areas in Equatoria province were captured by the government, using means which included indiscriminate bombing of civilian areas. Kajo Keji, an important town on the Ugandan border, fell to the government.

Much of the large civilian population living in these areas was evacuated prior to government advances, in particular the three displaced persons camps known as the "Triple A" camps. Located on the east bank of the White Nile, these camps sheltered about 100,000 people.

In the evacuation some 60,000 fled to Laboni, a remote site near the Ugandan border, which was only accessed with difficulty by relief agencies who had been assisting the displaced at the "Triple A" camps. At first, access was almost blocked because of the poor condition of the roads. Later in the year, however, relief agencies using the roads in northern Uganda to truck food into southern Sudan were faced with sharply increased problems of banditry and landmines on those roads, apparently placed by Ugandan rebel groups. As a result, deliveries to the two camps of Laboni and Mughale (together sheltering about 97,000 people) were often suspended for safety reasons.

The source of the landmines in Uganda's border areas is unclear, although the beneficiary of this activity is most certainly the Sudanese government, which has long viewed all relief efforts in southern Sudan as plots to aid the SPLA. Ugandan rebel activity by the Lord's Resistance Army against the Ugandan government resulted in a clash in August near the border in Gulu, Uganda, where U.N. and nongovernmental relief staff were located, forcing their evacuation for several weeks. Also in August, Norwegian Church Aid's compound and the Catholic mission in Pakele, Uganda, which ministers to Sudanese refugees, were attacked by armed men, killing three and abducting five, including two nuns and a priest.

Mundri in Sudan's Western Equatoria province was bombed by the government of Sudan for several days in early October. Fighting was reported between the government of Sudan and the SPLA-United (renamed South Sudan Independence Army, SSIA, on September 27, 1994) around Bentiu in September and October; there had previously been no clashes between the government and SPLA-United since Malakal was attacked in late 1992.

In another development related to the war, an epidemic of Kala Azar, a disease transmitted by sand flies, was reported by MSF to have claimed some 200,000 victims, many in Bahr el Ghazal; access to the area for medical teams and supplies was frequently thwarted by fighting by the government and SPLA factions.

The southern Sudanese rebel movement continued to be split. The SPLA-Mainstream and the SSIA (led by Commander Riek Machar) continued to differ over personalities and program, SSIA being in favor of a sovereign south. But open warfare between the two factions was greatly reduced from the level of 1993, when together they were responsible for probably tens of thousands of civilian casualties due to indiscriminate attacks, raiding, asset destruction, and war-related diseases.

Clashes between the two factions were reported in the Ikotos area of Eastern Equatoria in February 1994. In mid-1994 faction fighting again disrupted life in Lafon village of Eastern Equatoria; there were faction clashes there in early 1993 when Lafon was burned to the ground with dozens of civilian casualties. In 1994 the Pari community of Lafon complained of military occupation and food aid abuses by SSIA.

In the period July to September 1994. there was serious faction fighting in and around Mayen Abun, Bahr el Ghazal. SPLA-United commanders Faustino and Kerubino (both formerly long-term political prisoners of SPLA-Mainstream, who escaped in late 1992) attacked SPLA-Mainstream's Mayen Abun, then departed after ten days. The town was thoroughly looted by both sides. Heavy fighting took place in the villages, with an estimated 1,000 dead, mostly civilians, some of whom drowned trying to cross the Lol river fleeing the attackers. Nearby Akon. where MSF had warned in April of a serious rate of malnutrition, remained insecure, however, making resumption of assistance difficult.

Further south in Bahr el Ghazal, in Akot, an attack by SSIA on this SPLA-Mainstream town on October 22 resulted in an estimated 106 deaths (only twenty were SPLA soldiers) and eighty-nine wounded (only eighteen of them SPLA soldiers). Some of the killed were patients in the Akot hospital. The town, including the hospital, the church and relief organization compounds. was heavily looted, and about 35,000 civilians were displaced.

The SSIA by late 1993 reversed its year-long refusal to permit unaccompanied boys to be reunited with their families by U.N. agencies, which was a step forward in the solution of the problem of thousands of boys segregated from their families for SPLA military purposes (which began in the mid-1980s). The SPLA-Mainstream, however, made no move in the direction of recogniz-

ing that this was even a problem, and continued to have under its jurisdiction several thousand boys whom it had separated from their families and who when not obliged to perform military duties were receiving grossly inadequate care.

The Right to Monitor

Both the Sudan Human Rights Organization (SHRO) and the Bar Association were effective Sudanese human rights monitors prior to the 1989 coup. Since then, the SHRO has been banned, and in 1993 the Bar Association was taken over by government supporters. The Bar Association no longer serves as an independent human rights voice.

The U.N. special rapporteur on Sudan, Dr. Gáspár Biró, visited Sudan twice in 1993. He published an interim report in November 1993 and a final report in February 1994. The government took umbrage at his finding that *hudud* and *gisas* punishments were contrary to international human rights law binding on Sudan. Some hudud offenses, sometimes referred to as "absolute crimes" in Islamic law, are punishable either with death or amputation or flogging. Armed robbery, for example, is punishable by death or death and crucifixion, or amputation of the right hand and left foot. Children who have not attained puberty may be whipped by way of discipline instead of being subjected to other corporal punishments or death. Gisas is the institution of retribution, whereby a premeditated offense is punished by inflicting the same act which was committed—an eye for an eye. As a result of these critical reports, the government has refused to allow the U.N. special rappporteur to return to Sudan, thus making even more difficult his mandated duty of human rights monitoring.

The government of Sudan in mid-1993 rescinded an earlier invitation to Human Rights Watch/Africa to visit Sudan. After publication of the report, *Civilian Devastation: Abuses by All Parties in the War in Southern Sudan*, in July 1994, the government renewed its invitation to Human Rights Watch/Africa. It has responded that it would like to make this visit in early 1995.

The Role of the International Community

The U.S. government condemned human rights violations by both the government and the SPLA factions in the State Department's *Country Reports on Human Rights Practices for 1993.* Ambassador Melissa Wells (a strong human rights advocate who was U.S. ambassador to Mozambique when a peace agreement was negotiated) was appointed in May as special envoy for Sudan. Her brief, which was specifically on the peace process and humanitarian matters, did not include public criticism of human rights concerns, which remained in the purview of U.S. Ambassador Donald Pettersen, based in Khartoum. Ambassador Pettersen continued his visits to the southern war zones in 1994, including Nimule in February 1994.

The U.S. government issued statements during 1994 condemning various human rights violations; on February 8, 1994, it expressed concern over the indiscriminate bombing of civilians in the south by the government, and in October it condemned the riot police in Khartoum for shooting into a crowd of unarmed displaced persons and squatters protesting forcible resettlement. In November it strongly condemned the South Sudan Independence Army's killing of more than one hundred residents in the town of Akot in southern Sudan in October.

In mid-1994, the Sudanese authorities turned over accused terrorist Ilich Ramirez Sanchez, known as "Carlos the Jackal," to the French government. This cooperation did not, however, result in the lifting of the 1993 U.S. listing of Sudan as a state sponsor of international terrorism. Some asserted that the French, however, supported Sudan in its negotiations with the International Monetary Fund (IMF), and that as a result the IMF did not proceed with its threatened expulsion of Sudan from the IMF.

The European Union condemned the February 1994 bombings by the Sudanese Air Force in Equatoria, which harmed the civilian population and caused a mass exodus to Uganda. On October 31 the E.U. condemned the use of violence by the government to repress demonstrators in Omdurman who protested the razing of their homes. The E.U. called upon the government of Sudan to halt its violent campaign against the inhabitants of squatter settlements, and to compensate these victims.

Peace talks in Nairobi, Kenya between the government and the SPLA factions were sponsored by the Inter-Governmental Agency on Drought and Development (IGADD), an East African agency comprising Eritrea, Ethiopia, Kenya, and Uganda. Other countries such as the U.S. also encouraged the peace negotiations. Human rights were not specifically included in the talks that IGADD facilitated, and in September 1994 the talks foundered over the issues of autonomy for southern Sudan and the role of shari'a law.

The U.N. continues to maintain Operation Lifeline Sudan (Southern Sector), a large relief operation for the needy war-affected population of southern Sudan, operating from bases in Uganda and Kenya. Aside from the appointment of a special rapporteur on human rights, the U.N. has taken no other steps to increase its monitoring of human rights in Sudan, such as a program of human rights monitors. The U.N. has also failed to press the Sudan government to rescind its decision to prevent the special rapporteur from revisiting the country.

The Work of Human Rights Watch/Africa

Human Rights Watch/Africa has kept up the pressure on the government of Sudan by publishing and widely disseminating a series of reports on human rights abuses in the war zones and in the north, and by advocating a program of U.N. human rights monitors to promptly investigate and intervene with the government and the rebels on human rights issues. We have also advocated that the Security Council impose an arms embargo on all sides to the conflict, based on the indiscriminate use of weapons by all parties. The international community is urged to vote against any further disbursements or loans to Sudan until its human rights performance is substantially improved.

The reports were the book-length *Civilian Devastation: Abuses by All Parties in the War in Southern Sudan* (July 1994) and *In the Name of God: Repression Continues in Northern Sudan* (October 1994). In addition, the Children's Rights Project of Human Rights Watch reissued the chapter on child soldiers and children in the custody of the SPLA factions from *Civilian Devastation* to bring additional attention to this special worldwide problem, with a view to raising the minimum age of recruitment from fifteen to eighteen in all conflicts, and to encouraging the family reunification efforts undertaken by the U.N. in Sudan. This report is entitled *Lost Boys: Child Soldiers and Unaccompanied Boys in Southern Sudan.*

ZAIRE

Human Rights Developments

The human rights situation in Zaire continued to deteriorate during 1994, with widespread abuses against a population with no recourse to the rule of law. Extrajudicial execution, arbitrary arrest, illegal detention, torture, rape, looting by government troops, and rampant corruption were the hallmarks of government in President Mobutu Sese Seko's twenty-ninth year in power. The massive influx of Rwandan refugees into Zaire in July and August further complicated Zaire's human rights picture.

An economic crisis, characterized by soaring inflation (estimated at 13,000 percent in Kinshasa), massive unemployment (estimated at 80 percent), nonpayment of civil servants, paralysis of the commercial banking system, and the collapse of the country's copper mining industry, produced starvation, malnutrition, and disease. Shortages of food and medicine were also the result of frequent rioting and massive looting by rampaging troops of the army. Lines of communication broke down, and roads

ceased to exist. In urban areas throughout the country, vulnerable populations including children, the elderly, and the handicapped were especially at risk. The World Bank closed its office in Zaire in January 1994 due to the country's failure to pay its debts.

Faced with the breakdown of government services, communications, and the economy, the nongovernmental sector took on many essential functions. Nongovernmental organizations (NGOs) were active in providing health care and education, organizing feeding centers and development projects, and performing a range of other services. This active civil society, which included human rights groups, was one of the only bright spots in Zaire in 1994.

For most of 1994, the general atmosphere of insecurity was intensified by the ongoing political stalemate between President Mobutu and the opposition coalition known as the Sacred Union, headed by former Prime Minister Etienne Tshisekedi, who was elected by the Sovereign National Conference in 1992. Mobutu repeatedly undermined prospects for a transition to multiparty democracy, which he promised to support in April 1990. As long as the army's elite troops and the treasury remain under his personal control, Mobutu may be able to maintain power.

A report on the human rights situation in Zaire by United Nations Secretary-General Boutros Boutros-Ghali, published on December 23, 1993, described human rights violations by the security forces as well as their interference in the transition process. The report stated that "[t]he virtual impunity apparently enjoyed by the security forces would seem to indicate that they commit human rights violations with the consent of the highest authorities."

Between late 1993 and early January 1994, an agreement was forged between Mobutu's Political Forces of the Conclave and the Sacred Union, which was to lead to the dissolution of their rival parliaments. On January 14, however, Mobutu unilaterally merged Tshisekedi's transitional parliament, the High Council of the Republic (HCR), with his own National Assembly. Mobutu called the new parliament, which was given the authority to select a new prime minister, the HCR-Parliament of Transition (HCR-PT). The opposition considered this move a "constitutional coup" and on January 19 called for a nationwide strike, which was observed throughout the country.

A new constitution designed to govern the country during the transition period was promulgated by Mobutu on April 9. The transition was supposed to last fifteen months, culminating in presidential and legislative elections.

The battle subsequently focused on the process of selecting a new prime minister under Article 78 of the transitional constitution. The opposition split and did not put forward a consensus candidate. Tshisekedi refused to resubmit his candidacy on the theory that he had already been elected prime minister by the national conference. The HCR-PT proceeded to validate seven other candidates.

On June 14 Kengo Wa Dondo, a former prime minister and businessman, was appointed prime minister by the HCR-PT; he was installed on July 11. The opposition Union for Democracy and Social Progress (UDPS) protested this, maintaining that Tshisekedi remained the lawful prime minister; the UDPS subsequently refused to accept three ministerial posts offered by Kengo and threatened to boycott the upcoming general and presidential elections. On August 5 Kengo announced his intention to abide by the transition schedule fixed by the constitution.

As of this writing, the voting majority in the transitional assembly was in the hands of Mobutu supporters. Eighteen out of the twenty-eight most significant ministers, including the Minister of Defense, were also close allies of Mobutu. Moreover, the Zairian armed forces and the national economy remained largely outside the control of the new prime minister. Human rights violations continued; civilians were continually subjected to a range of abuses by the military,

including rounds of pillaging, arbitrary arrests, ill-treatment, and murder.

Independent journalists and opposition politicians were particularly targeted in 1994. In March security forces detained the outspoken Zairian journalist Kalala Mbenga Kalao for eighteen hours and confiscated his possessions before permitting him to leave for the United States, where he was granted political asylum. In June the mutilated corpse of Pierre Kabeya, a journalist with the weekly *Kin-Matin*, was found near the Loano military camp in Kinshasa. On the previous evening, Kabeya had reportedly submitted for publication an article regarding the 1991 trial that followed the killings of students in Lubumbashi in May 1990 in which security forces were implicated. Other journalists affiliated with newspapers close to the opposition, including Ipakala Abeyi Mobito, editor of *La Référence Plus*, and Wilfried Owandjankoi, publisher of *La Tempête des Tropiques*, were arrested and detained by the authorities. A further crackdown on the press was expected from a warning issued by the government in late September, which specified that all writers, publishers, or printers committing a press offense would be tried and eventually sentenced according to the laws of the Republic.

Political opposition members were harassed as well. Joseph Olenghankoy, a member of the High Council of the Republic and a leader of the Radical Opposition Renovation Force, was arrested on June 10 by Mobutu's Special Presidential Division (DSP), detained incommunicado, and reportedly beaten and interrogated about his political activities. He was released on June 22. The elite army troops of the DSP ransacked Olenghankoy's house on September 13 and October 4, reportedly in retaliation against Olenghankoy's organization of a protest against the government.

On June 12 Tshisekedi was arrested by the DSP and detained for ten hours. The DSP also arrested and detained Denis Bazinga, one of Tshisekedi's counselors, stripped him of his clothing, and released him in a cemetery the following day. Troops opened fire on civilians in front of the home of Frederic Kibassa Maliba, President of the UDPS, on June 13. On June 27 an opposition meeting at the UDPS headquarters in Mbuji Mayi was broken up. Lambert Mende, a UDPS spokesman, was arrested and released shortly afterward.

On July 5 the Civil Guard, the paramilitary police force, arrested Léon Muntuntu Kadima, a member of the National Secretariat of the UDPS and one of Tshisekedi's counselors, after he denounced Kengo's election. Muntutu was detained incommunicado and without charge until September 16. While in detention, he was tortured.

Members of the Civil Guard and the DSP opened fire on Tshisekedi's compound on July 11, killing his bodyguard and wounding at least five other people. At least six people are reported to have been taken to Makala Central Prison in Kinshasa, notwithstanding their injuries. Tshisekedi's home and office were ransacked. Some observers say that this raid was intended as a reprisal for a violent confrontation that had occurred on the morning of the same day between UDPS activists and soldiers around Tshisekedi's house, in which four soldiers had been seriously injured.

Soon after Kengo's appointment, the new prime minister reportedly issued an order forbidding all opposition leaders to travel outside the capital, whether abroad or within Zaire. A group of soldiers led by Kengo's brother reportedly seized and beat Lambert Mende so that he was unable to leave as planned on a flight to Brussels on August 25. The Kengo government also restricted access by opposition activists to the broadcast media.

Shaba, Zaire's mineral rich province, continued to offer the clearest case of the government's manipulation of ethnic and regional divisions. A government-inspired campaign of terror that began in August 1992 caused approximately 500,000 Shaba residents to be displaced from their homes in the neighboring region of Kasai. While Kengo denounced the expulsion of Kasaians from their homes, he had taken no action to facili-

tate their return as of November 1994.

The influx of between 800,000 and 1,400,000 Rwandan refugees into eastern Zaire in mid-July significantly heightened the level of instability in this region. Public infrastructure grew even more overburdened, and cholera and dysentery became widespread. The arrival of thousands of Hutus, many of whom were heavily armed, in the North Kivu region reportedly exacerbated pre-existing tensions between local Zairians and villagers of Rwandan origin (Banyarwanda). Aid agencies estimated that 250 villagers died in ethnic clashes and 32,500 villagers fled their homes between September and November.

The security situation in the refugee camps in Goma, Zaire became increasingly volatile by the end of 1994 due to the activities of former Rwandan army troops and militia members, most of whom were still armed; the failure of the Zairian military to exert control over the refugees, the involvement of Zairian troops in widespread violence and extortion in the camps, and banditry. Members of the defeated Rwandan army and Hutu militia intimidated other refugees through control of the system of distribution of food relief and access to shelter and terrorized those who wanted to return home. Those suspected of seeking to return or of opposing the former government were murdered. One of the most severe incidents occurred in late August in Kibumba camp, where a group of 200 to 300 refugees awaiting transport were attacked by Hutu militia members. Thirty Rwandan boy scouts in Katale camp, who had been charged with organizing security and helping with food distribution, were either murdered or vanished in late September. Militia members also threatened foreign members of the relief community in late 1994. The situation deteriorated so much that by early November international humanitarian groups were threatening to withdraw from the camps. Units of the former army and Hutu militias were reported to have carried out armed incursions into Rwandan border areas and to be training and rearming for military operations on a large scale.

In October the Zairian government prohibited the enrollment of Rwandan children in local schools in an effort to encourage repatriation. The Zairian and Rwandan prime ministers and the United Nations High Commissioner for Refugees signed a tripartite agreement setting out a framework for repatriation, which will be implemented when security conditions improve and it can be ensured that returning refugees will not be victimized by the new Rwandan authorities.

Zairian soldiers, sent to Goma after the mass influx of refugees in July, looted from both refugees and Zairian residents and were reportedly responsible for a number of killings of civilians in Goma. They committed such abuses with apparent impunity.

The Right to Monitor

The human rights community in Zaire was amazingly vibrant. Recognizing that they have a crucial role to play in the democratization process, Zairian NGOs were planning major initiatives to prepare the terrain for elections. Other activities included education and consciousness-raising efforts relating to human rights and democracy.

The principal human rights groups in Kinshasa included Amos, which emphasized the link between human rights and Christian values; the Association for the Promotion of Responsible and Democratic Broadcasting (APARD); the Zairian Association for the Defense of Human Rights (AZADHO); the Black Robes; the Zairian Human Rights League (LIZADHO); the Voice of the Voiceless for Human Rights (VSV); and Human Rights Now, a coalition of human rights organizations. There were also specialized groups, including the Association of Prison Professionals, the Christian Service for Women's Rights, and the Zairian League of Voters.

Other new human rights groups emerged in various regions. In South Kivu, these included the Association for the Promotion of Human Rights (APDH), the Office of Legal Assistance (BAJ), the Union of Young Democrats for Reconstruction, Heirs of Jus-

tice, and the Justice and Peace Commission of South Kivu. In North Kivu, they included the Advice and Support Group for the Realization of Internal Development, the Justice and Peace Commission of North Kivu, Muungano, and the Training Center for the Promotion of Human Rights. In Upper Zaire, Justice and Liberation, the umbrella group of which all the functioning human rights groups in Kisangani are members, was the most active organization. In Shaba, the primary groups were the Center for Human Rights and Humanitarian Law, the Justice and Peace Commission, and the local branch of LIZADHO.

As in past years, Zairian human rights activists were subject to harassment by the Zairian government and security forces in 1994. At the beginning of the year, Muile Kayembe, who headed the Black Robes, an organization of young lawyers that investigates prison conditions and focuses attention on important court cases, was interrogated by security forces following the distribution of materials claiming that all citizens, from the *caporal* (a low-ranking soldier) to the *maréchal* (a clear reference to President Mobutu) were equal before the law. Guillaume Ngefa Atondoko, the President of AZADHO, was reportedly pulled aside by agents of the National Intelligence Service at Ndjili Airport. The authorities confiscated all the AZADHO publications that he was carrying and permitted him to leave the country to attend a human rights seminar only after a week of discussions. Reverend Placide Tshisump Tshiakatumba, the chair of the International Society for Human Rights, was reportedly threatened by the Zairian government in March and has since gone into hiding.

U.S. and E.U. Policy

Since early 1992 the U.S., France, and Belgium have periodically collaborated to support the transition process begun by the National Conference and pursued by Prime Minister Tshisekedi until his ouster by President Mobutu's supporters. These three countries have repeatedly called on the opposition and the Mobutu regime to proceed with the transition.

In 1994 most contacts with the authorities were made privately by the U.S., France, and Belgium. Prior to the appointment of Prime Minister Kengo in June, the U.S. and its allies expressed concern about the deteriorating situation and supported the mediation efforts of Archbishop Monsengwo. Much of their energy was directed toward pressuring the opposition to compromise and urging Tshisekedi to rejoin the government.

The Clinton administration's policy on Zaire, which exemplifies its deference to the French with regard to Francophone Africa, was virtually indistinguishable from that of the Bush administration. Prior to Kengo's appointment, U.S. support for Tshisekedi was lukewarm. As in the past, U.S. policy seemed to turn on the perception that while Mobutu may be the main obstacle to the transition, he must play a crucial role in that process, although senior U.S. officials made statements publicly distancing themselves from Mobutu and criticizing human rights abuses.

The U.S., France, and Belgium viewed the appointment of Prime Minister Kengo with cautious optimism. All three countries issued carefully worded statements implicitly recognizing his appointment and received Kengo in their capitals in late 1994. They announced, however, that they would not renew bilateral aid to Zaire until Kengo demonstrated control of the economy and the security forces, as well as an improved human rights record. A realistic calendar for free and fair elections was also of central concern to the U.S. and its allies.

In the wake of the Rwandan crisis, Mobutu portrayed himself as a regional mediator, and the French government appeared willing to help him assume that role. In return for allowing French troops to operate out of the Zairian border town of Goma, senior French officials reportedly promised to end Mobutu's diplomatic isolation. The French government subsequently invited Mobutu to the Franco-African summit in

November. Mobutu also sought to play on the world's fears that the Rwandan tragedy could be replicated in Zaire and that only he could prevent it. Even had it wished to, the U.S. was too disengaged from Zaire to mount any effective challenge to these efforts to rehabilitate Mobutu.

The U.N.'s involvement in Zaire focused on the provision of humanitarian assistance in the refugee camps on the Rwandan border. Special envoy Lakhdar Brahimi conducted an investigatory mission to Zaire from July 31 to August 8. In July Roberto Garreton was appointed special rapporteur on Zaire, and he was scheduled to visit in November.

Zaire's voting rights were suspended at the IMF on June 1, as a result of its failure to pay debt arrears of approximately $315 million. The U.S. strongly supported the suspension; France abstained in the vote. This move had little practical effect since the IMF had already cut off funding to Zaire, but it was symbolically important.

The US provided approximately $6.5 million in humanitarian aid to Zaire in fiscal year 1993 and approximately $11 million in fiscal year 1994, in addition to funds for relief assistance. The last U.S. military forces involved in emergency relief operations for Rwandan refugees pulled out of Zaire on October 1. In late October the U.S. was considering sending an ambassador to Zaire; the last American ambassador was withdrawn in March 1993. U.S. State Department officials were also discussing the possibility of assisting in training the Zairian armed forces to perform a peacekeeping role in the refugee camps on the Rwandan border.

By the end of the year, France had undertaken to increase its humanitarian aid to Zaire in the health, education, and transport sectors. There were indications that the French government might begin providing limited bilateral assistance after the IMF and the World Bank had approved Kengo's program. Like the U.S., Belgium opted to provide humanitarian aid but refused to resume direct assistance. The U.S., France, and Belgium appeared inclined to support

Kengo before the multilateral lending institutions.

The Work of
Human Rights Watch/Africa

In January Human Rights Watch/Africa and the Human Rights Watch Prison Project issued *Prison Conditions in Zaire*. The report, based on a mission to Zaire in 1993, examines all aspects of Zairian prisons, where the already decrepit and overcrowded system has virtually collapsed under the weight of neglect and corruption. The prisons reflect and magnify the general devastation of Zairian society.

In June Human Rights Watch/Africa issued a special report to coincide with the White House conference on Africa. The report addressed human rights conditions and U.S. policy in ten countries, including Zaire, and made policy recommendations to the Clinton administration.

Human Rights Watch/Africa also engaged in campaigns to raise awareness about human rights in Zaire and to advocate needed remedies, working to attract governmental, congressional, and press attention to the ongoing crisis.

HUMAN
RIGHTS
WATCH
/AMERICAS

HUMAN RIGHTS WATCH/AMERICAS OVERVIEW

Human Rights Developments

During 1994, the crises of Cuba and Haiti dominated international news from the Americas. The repression facing Cubans and Haitians at home was widely documented and condemned, as were the erratic immigration policies of the United States, which turned back tens of thousands of refugees in violation of international refugee law. The untold story of the region, however, was the persistence of the egregious, systematic human rights violations in countries with institutional democracies.

In many Latin American nations, even where civilian governments appeared firmly established, respect for human rights had not emerged as a central, functioning component of "democracy" and had failed to bring either political tolerance or the rule of law. Torture, police abuse, assassinations of political activists and "disposable people," electoral irregularities, and threats against the press coexisted with nominally democratic governments and were tolerated by them. Particularly abusive was the civilian government of Alberto Fujimori in Peru, which turned the nation's judicial system into a tool of repression and showed open contempt for human rights precepts. But torture was commonplace throughout the region: in Brazil, Colombia, Peru, and El Salvador, among others. Elsewhere, as in Honduras and Nicaragua, despite some positive efforts by the governments, the military and police continued to have sufficient independence from civilian control to carry out abuses frequently and with impunity.

The closely watched democratic transition in Haiti after the return of President Jean-Bertrand Aristide in October was unique in many ways, but also reflected some of the challenges facing other recently established civilian governments in the region. Like Haiti, a large number of Latin American governments faced the pressing need to establish an independent judiciary, to replace notoriously abusive security forces, and to ensure accountability for past human rights violations. Throughout the hemisphere the institutions of democracy have to some degree opened space for the emergence of an active civil society, which has expanded political debate and empowered previously marginalized members of society. Nevertheless, the process of transition has created new human rights concerns. So long-established a democracy as Venezuela struggled with a nearly complete incapacitation of its judicial system; El Salvador and Chile continued to confront the need for the replacement of abusive officials and for prosecutions in human rights cases from their military pasts.

Some governments made notable efforts to increase the effectiveness of human rights monitoring and protection. In Nicaragua, a new military code passed in August, mandating that members of the armed forces accused of common crimes be tried in civilian rather than military courts. In Honduras, the government of President Carlos Roberto Reina fulfilled an earlier initiative to establish civilian control over the police forces by dissolving the military-controlled Dirección Nacional de Investigaciones (DNI), infamous for its human rights abuses, and transferring investigative powers to the civilian-controlled Criminal Investigating Bureau.

Other countries took several steps to address crimes committed under former military regimes. The judiciary in both Paraguay and Chile actively pursued cases against former human rights abusers. In Argentina, the government began paying compensation to victims of arbitrary detention under its military regime, and the Argentine Congress was studying a law to compensate the families of the "disappeared."

Despite these efforts, state security forces, even under elected governments, acted with impunity and were among the principal perpetrators of human rights violations, as they had been in the past. The targets of these violations were not only political suspects, but criminals, prisoners, and other groups marginalized by society. In Colombia, paramilitary squads often linked to the military continued campaigns of "social cleansing," targeting street children, homosexuals, beggars, and other so-called disposable people. These violations persisted because too often, investigations of state agents in Latin America did not occur, and when they did, the exercise of military jurisdiction usually guaranteed acquittals. Deep social and economic cleavages, which ensure certain individuals' marginalization, also contributed to the lack of justice in cases of abuses committed against them.

Frequently, these abuses were committed in the name of internal security. In Peru and Colombia, the ongoing internal war between the military and insurgent armies resulted in violations of international humanitarian law on both sides. In Mexico, during its suppression of a rebellion that erupted on January 1 in the southern state of Chiapas by the previously unknown Ejército Zapatista de Liberación Nacional (EZLN), the army was responsible for numerous human rights violations, including serious cases of extrajudicial executions and extensive use of torture. In Venezuela, President Rafael Caldera cited the country's economic crisis as reason to declare a state of emergency on June 27. While officially justified as an economic necessity, grounds which are not consistent with international law, the state of emergency provided a pretext to detain without due process grass-roots leaders, opposition politicians, and socially and economically marginalized individuals.

In 1994, accountability for human rights abuses suffered serious setbacks in both Colombia and Guatemala. On July 7, Colombian President César Gaviria vetoed a proposed "Disappearance Law." By establishing the crime of "forced disappearance of persons," the law would have placed perpetrators under civilian jurisdiction and ended the impunity with which disappearances are committed. It would also have eliminated the "due obedience" defense by which military personnel have been routinely exonerated for crimes committed following superior orders. In Guatemala, the administration of President Ramiro de León Carpio backtracked from its commitment to demilitarize the National Police, firing key reformers in the government and permitting several individuals linked to the army once again to infiltrate the agency. As a result, there was a marked increase in violence by police and military agents in 1994.

At the same time, in Peru and Colombia, "faceless courts," in which the identities of the judges and witnesses were concealed, arbitrarily convicted thousands of civilians often relying strictly on evidence provided by state agents or the testimony of a single witness.

Another problem endemic to Latin America's judicial system was the excessive use of pre-trial detention. Many prisoners interviewed by Human Rights Watch/Americas in Venezuela's Sabaneta Prison, for example, were jailed and awaiting trial for periods longer than the maximum sentences which they were facing. The overcrowding that resulted was a central cause of the January riot and fire in Sabaneta, which led to more than one hundred deaths as guards looked on. In Honduras, only 12 percent of the country's 6,100 prisoners had been tried and sentenced. Besides violating the rights of those being detained, the situation of excessive pre-trial detention exacerbated conditions of overcrowding, filth, lack of food, and violence, which already existed in many of the region's prison systems. In October, unsanitary conditions and systematic abuses in Argentine prisons led to massive hunger strikes by inmates in several penal institutions.

Unelected governments, at the same time, committed human rights violations as state policy while rejecting even the pretense of democratic institutions. Until its demise in September, upon arrival of the U.S.-led occupation force, Haiti's military regime conducted an intensive campaign throughout 1994 to eliminate supporters of exiled President Aristide. The government of General Raoul Cédras employed extrajudicial execution, disappearance, and torture to crush political opposition and create a climate of terror. Rape was used as a tool of state terror by police, soldiers, and armed civilian auxiliaries (known as *attachés*) to punish women thought to support Aristide. The multinational, U.S.-led intervention ultimately returned Aristide to Haiti and created hope for the beginnings of democratic participation for the long-abused Haitian people. This was only after tightening repression on the island cost thousands of lives and forced tens of thousands to flee the island and seek refuge in the U.S. state of Florida.

Like Haiti, Cuba contributed to the flood of refugees landing in Florida. The exodus of Cuban rafters focused attention on the country's law prohibiting "illegal exit," a violation of the right to freedom of movement, and an unprecedented riot on August 5 in Havana underscored the growing discontent on the island. After the riot, the Cuban government briefly suspended enforcement of the illegal exit law but reimposed it in September as part of an agreement with the United States. On the island, the government maintained its repression of political and civil rights and cracked down further on political dissidents.

The involvement of the Organization of American States and the United Nations in the region produced mixed results for human rights during the year. The OAS continued to avoid condemning systemic human rights violations by elected civilian governments in certain countries. On the other hand, individual cases of human rights violations brought before the Inter-American Commission on Human Rights and the Inter-American Court of Human Rights underscored the abuses that routinely occurred in these countries.

In Haiti, the U.N.'s performance, like that of the Clinton administration, shifted dramatically and was notably weak in early 1994. Early in the year, despite the Cédras regime's abrogation of the Governor's Island Accord, U.N. Special Envoy to Haiti Dante Caputo pressed Aristide to make addi-

tional concessions to the military rulers. The U.N. also failed to renew the mandate of the U.N./OAS Civilian Mission, opening its staff to the harassment of state security forces. Later, at U.S. urging, the U.N. took several steps to tighten the economic embargo on the island and on July 31, passed Resolution 940, which permitted the use of any means to ensure the departure of the military leaders, in effect sanctioning a U.S.-led invasion of the island.

The U.N. also played a central role in monitoring human rights violations in El Salvador and pressing negotiations between the government and guerrillas in Guatemala. In Guatemala, while the political will to enforce human rights protections established by the negotiations seemed absent, the peace process provided the U.N. a tool to press for greater political will.

Overall, the trend in Latin America toward consolidation of civilian governments did not—in many countries—guarantee that vulnerable members of society, dissenters, labor organizers, the press, or voters could confidently exercise their rights. In this context, Latin American governments increasingly focused on achieving economic success through such partnerships as NAFTA and Mercosur, the subregional pact which includes Brazil, Argentina, Paraguay, and Uruguay. At the Rio Group Summit held in Rio de Janeiro in September, regional leaders supported the creation of a South American Free Trade Agreement (SAFTA), to create a region-wide free trade zone which would make the region's products more competitive in the world economy. But these plans proceeded without addressing a crucial precondition for balanced, sustainable economic development—respect for human rights.

United States Commerce Secretary Ron Brown explained to reporters in November, "Our strategy of commercial engagement, we believe is the most effective strategy to have a positive impact on labor rights and human rights." The concept that trade is a conduit for respect for human rights, echoed by other officials in the Clinton administration as well as leaders from the rest of the hemisphere, was disproved by the experiences of several countries in Latin America where free market policies, like the formal institutions of democracy, coexisted with gross human rights violations. The disassociation of civilian government and economic planning from a human rights agenda was of grave concern to Human Rights Watch/Americas. To the extent that free trade agreements define a community of nations, governments should insist that the community be founded on the shared fundamental values of respect for the rights of the individual. As such, it would be important that such agreements include an explicit commitment to respect and enforce the human rights standards enshrined in the American Convention on Human Rights and that they include a mechanism for the adjudication of individual complaints of human rights violations that may arise in the context of the commercial relations permitted under the agreement.

The Right to Monitor

The institutions of democracy, which have mushroomed throughout the hemisphere, have in part contributed to the remarkable growth of civil society in Latin America. During 1994, human rights organizations and groups with common goals ranging from labor unions to indigenous groups to women's organizations participated actively in civil society and sought to expand democratic guarantees. An active press served both as a watchdog to monitor abuses of power and as an effective medium for expressing alternative views. In many countries, however, such activism was still dangerous, as human rights monitors, political dissidents, and journalists covering governmental abuses faced threats to their freedom, their security, and their lives.

In Cuba and under the Cédras regime in Haiti, human rights monitors continued documenting abuses despite ever-present threats to their safety. Between January and its expulsion from the country in July, the U.N./OAS human rights mission was briefly al-

lowed to return to Haiti, during which time it was able to document 1,400 cases of human rights violations despite severe restrictions on its movements. Domestic groups documented numerous other cases despite continued threats to their safety. In Cuba, human rights monitors and members of so-called illegal organizations continued to be the targets of arbitrary arrest, physical violence, and intimidation, particularly after the August 5 riot in Havana, which prompted the government to tighten its repression on the island's growing dissident movement.

In other countries as well, human rights monitors continued to face intimidation. In Mexico and Colombia, human rights activists faced arbitrary detention, surveillance, illegal searches, and death threats.

In Guatemala, the government made it apparent that it would seek to limit the role of the United Nations in monitoring human rights in the country. On the one hand, the government was seeking to terminate the mandate of the United Nations Human Rights Commission's independent expert once the U.N. Verification Mission to Guatemala (MINUGUA) was installed. On the other hand, it was attempting to restrict MINUGUA's mandate to the point of undermining its mission by denying authorization to investigate human rights cases and only permitting the mission to "strengthen domestic institutions."

U.S. Policy

On September 19, U.S. troops occupied Haiti in what the Clinton administration termed "a semi-permissive environment," after a delegation constituted by former President Jimmy Carter, Senator Sam Nunn, and General Colin Powell negotiated with the Haitian military high command. The operation, which sought to restore deposed President Aristide to power, seemed to put into practice the administration's stated policy goal of "enlargement," the expansion and strengthening of democracy, set forth by National Security Advisor Anthony Lake as the thematic successor to the Cold War policy of containment.

The intervention also marked a radical shift from the considerably less critical United States policy toward the Haitian military at the beginning of the year. Despite ample evidence of massive human rights abuses early in 1994, United States officials consistently downplayed the situation, even suggesting that human rights violations were being exaggerated and manipulated by Aristide supporters for political reasons.

The underlying motivation for the administration's policy was the fear that Florida shores would be flooded by masses of Haitians fleeing the island. In response to the refugees, the United States first assumed a policy of forcible return, in violation of the international prohibition on *refoulement*, and later shifted to a policy of safe haven, transferring Haitians intercepted at sea to the U.S. naval base at Guantánamo Bay, Cuba.

When the United States did intervene, its troops landed on the island with the conflicting objectives of returning Aristide and democracy to Haiti and of maintaining the existing Haitian armed forces as the interim police force and scaled-down army. During the first days of U.S. occupation, a series of incidents, including an attack on unarmed demonstrators by heavily armed Haitian police officers, which left two dead as U.S. troops watched and did nothing, made it obvious that the two goals were irreconcilable. Responding to these contradictions, the Clinton administration shifted policy in a positive direction, changing the rules of engagement so that U.S. soldiers could respond to such incidents. Nonetheless, the United States' reliance on the existing security forces to maintain order, the lack of an adequate plan to screen human rights abusers out of the new police force, and the reluctance to disarm all members of paramilitary forces, represented possible threats to the establishment of democracy. While outcome could not be predicted at this writing, by early December the Clinton administration had the opportunity to help foster a true democratic opening on the island and thus send an important message in support of human rights to the rest of the hemisphere.

The shifting U.S. policy toward human rights violations in Haiti over the year reflected the inconsistency in human rights policy toward the continent as a whole. While democratic ideals were invariably incorporated into political discourse, these ideals were frequently overshadowed by other considerations, most notably trade and immigration. As was previously mentioned, when faced with a second refugee crisis, this time from the neighboring island of Cuba, the United States reached an agreement with the Cuban government requiring Cuba to take measures to stop the refugee flow. This accord essentially made the United States an accomplice in the violation of the fundamental guarantee of freedom of movement, including the right to leave one's own country, by encouraging Cuba to criminalize emigration.

It was not immigration but trade considerations that explained the Clinton administration's notably weak response to the human rights violations committed by the Mexican army in suppressing the EZLN uprising in Chiapas. Fearing the implications for the recently approved NAFTA agreement, the Clinton administration took nearly a month to publicly acknowledge that human rights abuses had been committed by the Mexican army. The administration proved equally passive regarding the labor rights mechanisms incorporated into the NAFTA treaty. In 1994, Secretary of Labor Robert Reich refused to pursue two cases presented for consideration, both of which charged that Mexico had failed to enforce labor organizing rights.

Human rights concerns should also have played a more central role in determining U.S. aid to Latin America. Despite its abysmal record on human rights, Colombia was the second largest recipient of U.S. military aid in the hemisphere. Meanwhile Honduras, a country flooded with U.S. aid during a period of horrendous human rights abuses, in 1994 received little assistance from Washington as the reformist government of President Carlos Roberto Reina strove to build a new civilian police force.

The Summit of the Americas, scheduled to begin December 9, offers President Clinton an ideal opportunity to remind the hemispheric leaders gathering in Miami that even after the days of brutal dictators, serious human rights problems endure. Unfortunately, human rights issues have been entirely absent from the Summit's agenda, despite the apparently coincidental timing of the meeting on International Human Rights Day, December 10. Instead, plans for the Summit focused almost entirely on proposals for a hemisphere-wide free trade zone, with business leaders welcome at the conference and nongovernmental organizations politely excluded.

The Work of
Human Rights Watch/Americas

In 1994, accountability for human rights violations continued to be a central objective of Human Rights Watch/Americas's efforts. The obligation of the state to prevent and investigate human rights violations; prosecute and punish their perpetrators; and to safeguard the right of the victim to seek justice is the only guarantee that the institutions of democracy will foster a truly democratic society.

Human Rights Watch/Americas was encouraged that the newly restored Haitian parliament resisted diplomatic pressures to enact a broad amnesty that would have included human rights abuses committed by the former Haitian military rulers, opting instead for a narrow amnesty, covering only political crimes: that is, the military coup. Human Rights Watch/Americas had pressed the Aristide government in exile, the United States government, and the United Nations to reject a blanket amnesty. It also pressed for the establishment of an autonomous and vigorous truth commission to investigate human rights abuses and of independent courts to try those responsible.

In pressing for greater accountability, Human Rights Watch/Americas also continued to use the human rights mechanisms of the Organization of American States to focus international attention on individual cases of impunity. Human Rights Watch/Americas presented numerous cases, together with the Center for Justice and International Law (CEJIL), before the Inter-American Commission on Human Rights. In 1994, a friendly settlement was reached in the case of Guillermo Maqueda, from Argentina, who had been unjustly sentenced to ten years in prison for alleged participation in a failed takeover of a military installation in 1989. By the terms of the settlement, the President of Argentina commuted Maqueda's sentence, resulting in his immediate release. This marked the first time that a case was presented before the Inter-American Court for human rights violations in Argentina, which, as in other cases brought before the Commission, was cooperative with the Inter-American system. In another case petitioned by Human Rights Watch/Americas, the Court ordered provisional measures to protect witnesses and human rights monitors in Colotenango, Guatemala. In the aftermath of the slaying of a human rights activist by members of the military-organized civil patrols there, patrollers beat and threatened several witnesses and monitors who had pursued the case in court. Although a judge ordered the patrollers arrested, the police refused to carry out the order, leaving witnesses and monitors totally unprotected.

In 1994, we continued to focus international attention on political rights and fair elections. Prior to the elections in El Salvador and Mexico, we published reports documenting cases of electoral irregularities and political violence. We also urged President Joaquín Balaguer of the Dominican Republic to investigate reported incidents of fraud in that country's elections.

With the shift away from military dictatorships in Latin America, Human Rights Watch/Americas also focused increasing attention on human rights violations that were directed not at a political enemy but at certain sectors of society such as slum dwellers, prison inmates, and detainees. These violations, perhaps because they were committed under the guise of democracy, did not receive the international attention that their prevalence would warrant. In 1994, we investigated cases of torture and killings of street children in Brazil and, with the Human Rights Watch Children's Rights Project, carried out a similar investigation in Colombia and documented the abysmal penal conditions in which minors are detained in Jamaica. Of particular concern, too, were human rights violations specifically targeting women. In 1994, Human Rights Watch/Americas released, with Human Rights Watch Women's Rights Project, a report documenting the politically motivated rape of women in Haiti. We also conducted an investigation into the forced prostitution of women and girls in Brazil. In all of these efforts, we maintained close and productive relations with human rights colleagues throughout the hemisphere.

If Latin America and the Caribbean has seen substantial progress over the last decade in building the institutions for civilian government, transitions to democracy will nevertheless remain incomplete unless human rights are incorporated as central to the process and impunity for violations is ended. The continued prevalence of torture, including rape, extrajudicial executions, arbitrary detention, intimidation, and violations of due process and the freedom of expression indicate the gulf between these democratic ideals and reality in the region.

BRAZIL

Human Rights Developments

On October 3, 1994, Brazilians went to the polls to elect a president, twenty-seven governors, state legislators, the full complement of the lower house of the national legislature, and two-thirds of the nation's senators. These elections, which produced the greatest overhaul in public officials since Brazil's return to civilian rule in 1985, proceeded under relatively open and fair conditions. Yet despite this democratic achievement, Brazil continued to be plagued by severe human rights violations in areas ranging from labor conditions approaching slavery to the killing of children and adolescents by off-duty police officers.

Following a presidential campaign replete with controversy and scandal, Fernando Henrique Cardoso emerged triumphant, garnering an absolute majority in the first round, in a field of eight candidates. Given Cardoso's long-term commitment to democratic values and his broad popular mandate, 1994 ended with high hopes for improvement of Brazil's human rights record.

As we reported in previous years, the Brazilian human rights landscape was characterized by official and extraofficial violence committed against persons at the margin of mainstream society. These victims and their representatives found that the protections guaranteed them by Brazilian law were rarely applied, effectively denying them recourse for abuses suffered.

Perhaps the clearest example of the vast distance between legal theory and practice concerned the plight of Brazil's children. Although the recently drafted Children's and Adolescents' Statute guaranteed minors a panoply of rights matched by few countries, the better part of the statute's protections are simply ignored. In 1994, as in previous years, children and adolescents that lived or worked on the streets continued to be subject to severe acts of violence, including homicide. According to statistics summarized by the Gabinete de Assessoria as Organizações Populares (GAJOP), the number of minors killed in the first six months of 1994 in the northeastern state of Pernambuco, one of four states analyzed by Human Rights Watch/Americas in its report *Final Justice: Police and Death Squad Homicides of Adolescents in Brazil* increased by 94 percent as compared to the same period in 1993: from thirty to fifty-eight. Rio de Janeiro exhibited a similar, though less dramatic increase. According to official figures, 318 minors were homicide victims in the first half of 1994, compared to 298 during the same period of 1993. Those responsible for the crimes, including many former and off-duty policemen, were rarely convicted.

One troubling development in Brazil's major cities has been the increasingly common use of deadly raids on slums (*favelas*) to attack suspected drug traffickers. In October, after an attack on police which injured three officers, a group of over 120 Civil Police officers stormed the Rio de Janeiro favela of Nova Brasília, killing thirteen alleged drug traffickers. Despite indications that the operation was designed as a lethal assault and later revelations that ten of the thirteen victims had no prior criminal record, Governor Nilo Batista waited a month before labeling the operation a massacre, and shortly thereafter the operation's commander was promoted.

In the aftermath of this attack, in the face of popular demand for aggressive official action, Rio de Janeiro Governor Nilo Batista reached an agreement with President Itamar Franco on October 31 by which the military would direct the operations of local authorities to combat the wave of violence afflicting Rio. In letters to government authorities, Human Rights Watch/Americas expressed its concern that operations to combat criminal violence be effectuated with respect for the basic human rights of suspects.

Although police violence continued to plague several of Brazil's major cities, 1994 witnessed a continued reduction in official violence in São Paulo, at least according to official statistics. While São Paulo military police killed an astounding 1,470 civilians in 1992, after the outcry following the October 1992 Casa de Detenção prison massacre the number fell to 409 in 1993, demonstrating that clear reductions in the incidence of abusive police conduct were possible given the political will. Partial statistics for the first half of 1994 indicated that the São Paulo military police killed roughly as many civilians as in the first half of 1993. Although a spokesman for the São Paulo military police informed Human Rights Watch/Americas that they were taking concrete steps to reduce official violence, such as establishing special investigative units, little was being done to prosecute those responsible for homicides in the past.

The human rights situation in rural Brazil continued to be dominated by the targeted assassinations of rural union leaders, and by land conflicts that often ended in fatal violence. According to the annual report of the Pastoral Land Commission (Comissão Pastoral da Terra, CPT), there were fifty-two killings in rural conflicts in 1993, nearly 50 percent more than in 1992. Although the number of land disputes remained the same (361 in each year), the number of persons involved increased significantly, from 154,223 in 1992 to 252,236 in 1993. Partial figures for 1994 indicated that the level of violence remained high. One worrisome trend in 1994 was the nearly ten-fold increase in the number of people forcibly evicted.

Also on the rise were the number of persons reportedly involved in forced labor, the practice in which rural laborers are lured by false promises of high wages and good working conditions to work sites with conditions tantamount to slavery. The laborers were maintained against their will either by force, or through the manipulation of debts. According to the CPT, while 1992 witnessed eighteen cases involving 16,442 victims, 1993 presented twenty-seven cases involving 19,940 persons. Although federal government officials openly recognized the existence of the practice, little was done to combat it. As of November, no one had ever been convicted in Brazil on forced labor charges.

One particularly gruesome aspect of forced labor in Brazil was the booming trade in women. According to the Ministry of Social Welfare, 300,000 to 500,000 minors worked as prostitutes. According to a parliamentary report released in September 1994, those who recruited girls to work as prostitutes often relied on the complicity of local police and the failure of the justice system. The report noted one case in which, after an extensive exposé by the newspaper *Zero Hora* on the trafficking of girls in southern Brazil, sixty-two criminal complaints were filed. However, the parliamentary report noted, after being opened, there was no significant progress in any of the cases.

Alarming reports surfaced in 1994 about the operation of *"grupos de exterminio"* or death squads, often composed of former or off-duty police, in rural areas. In September, press accounts indicated that a death squad known as the Mission had been responsible for the killing of nearly one hundred persons in the northeastern state of Sergipe. The group, which apparently began as a vigilante organization formed to eliminate cattle thieves, reportedly turned its sights on journalists who have worked to expose it. Apparently, the Mission included shock troops of the state military police, and had significant official support.

In mid- and late 1994, the CPT released information indicating that a "hit list" of roughly forty persons had been circulating in the municipality of Xinguara, in the south of Pará state. By November, five of those on the list had been killed, two injured, and one kidnapped, beaten, and released.

One of those whose names appeared on the list was Father Ricardo Rezende. Rezende, who had defended the rights of the rural poor for the CPT since 1979, had suffered repeated death threats related to his work in the Amazon frontier town of Rio Maria, Pará in the previous several years. For his work in rural Brazil, Human Rights Watch named Rezende as one of the monitors to be honored in its 1994 annual ceremony marking December 10.

One of the suspects in the case, *fazendeiro* (rancher) Jerônimo Alves de Amorim, had been implicated in the murders of several rural activists in the region, including that of Expedito Ribeiro de Souza, then president of the Rural Laborers Union of Rio Maria. On November 3, the *Folha de São Paulo* reported that the civil police had been authorized to enter four ranches in the area and arrest the suspects. Due to the publicity afforded the planned action, local human rights groups did not expect that any of the suspects would be arrested. Their lack of confidence was reenforced by reports that the civil police investigation charged one of

those on the hit list, CPT human rights lawyer Father Henri des Roziers, with aiding in the planning of fazendeiro Fábio de Abreu Vieira's assassination. Weeks earlier, Father des Roziers, a French national, had been awarded the Legion of Honor by French President François Mitterand for his work in defense of human rights.

Particularly disturbing were reports that torture continued to be practiced on a routine basis by police authorities in rural Brazil. In January, the CPT reported that police in the town of Couto Magalhães in the northern state of Tocantins, brutally beat and tortured six workers accused of killing a councilman. In September, two organizers of the landless or *sem terra* movement were arrested in Paraupebas. The two men stated that during their detention they were threatened with death, beaten, whipped and kicked to the point of vomiting blood.

Legal proceedings began in the case of Adão Pereira de Souza, tortured to death by seven police officers in the precinct of São Félix do Xingu, in the state of Pará in May 1993. The torture and murder of Pereira de Souza were witnessed by at least four persons in the police station who were willing to testify. The flagrant nature of the killing of Pereira de Souza and the numerous denunciations by Church-based groups in São Félix indicate that torture continued to be a common practice.

In a potentially positive development, in August and September, after eight years as fugitives, several of those presumed to be responsible for the 1986 murder of human rights activist Father Jósimo Morais Tavares were arrested after one of the gunmen disclosed their whereabouts to police. Though detained, the men's conviction was far from assured as of this writing.

Ranchers and their hired gunmen, gold miners and others seeking to appropriate or exploit the lands belonging to indigenous peoples, continued to commit violent acts against Indian communities in 1994. This violence was facilitated by the failure of the federal government to demarcate Indian lands. By October 1993, the end of the five-year period established by the 1988 Constitution to complete demarcation, only 260 of the 519 identified areas had been set aside as protected areas.

According to statistics of the Indianist Missionaries Council (CIMI), forty-three Indians were murdered in 1993, up from twenty-four the previous year. In 1993, 600 Indians received death threats, twenty Indians were violently beaten by the police and eighteen others were illegally arrested. CIMI's partial data for 1994 indicated that the level of violence against indigenous populations continued to be high, as did mortality rates from disease and suicide. During a mission conducted in March and April 1994, Human Rights Watch/Americas documented severe abuses including mass arrests and police brutality suffered by the Wapixana and Macuxi Indian populations, and the government's failure adequately to protect their rights.

Typical of the failure of the government to prosecute those who violated the rights of indigenous peoples was the utter lack of progress in the investigation of the notorious massacre of sixteen Yanomami Indians near the Brazil-Venezuela border in July 1993. According to CIMI, more than one year after the killings, the two men initially arrested had been released, and none of the miners responsible for the killings had been found.

Although quite varied, this array of human rights abuse was tied together by one critical factor: impunity. Impunity was virtually assured to those who committed offenses against victims considered socially undesirable. As a result, those responsible for grave human rights violations continued to abuse the rights of others. For example, the fazendeiro allegedly responsible for organizing the Xinguara hit list had been indicted, though never successfully prosecuted, for the murder of other rural activists.

The Right to Monitor

The Brazilian government imposed no formal obstacles to human rights monitoring, and Brazil had a well developed network of nongovernmental organizations that promoted the rights of women, children, indigenous groups, workers, prisoners and other victims of human rights violations. Nonetheless, incidents of threat, intimidation and physical violence against those engaged in such monitoring were not uncommon.

Reinaldo Guedes Miranda and Hermógenes da Silva Almeida Filho, two advisors to Workers Party City Councilwoman Jurema Batista were found dead on June 17, murdered execution style, in the Cachumbi area of Rio de Janeiro. The two men were active in Brazil's African consciousness movement and were also investigating the highly publicized Candelária and Vigário Geral massacres for the Rio de Janeiro City Council's human rights commission. Both men had reported receiving death threats. According to Batista's office, police intentionally delayed responding to a critical lead, thus allowing important evidence to be destroyed.

Over the course of 1994, CIMI documented numerous incidents of death threats against those who defended the interests of indigenous peoples. Similarly, the CPT in several states reported that its workers had been subjected to death threats, including those directed against Fathers Rezende and des Roziers in southern Pará. Similarly, Dr. Luiz Mott, president of Grupo Gay da Bahia, who had documented 1,260 cases of assassinations of gays and lesbians in Brazil since 1980 of which only 10 percent had resulted in convictions, often with minimal sentences, continued to be the target of attacks and threats in 1994.

Often, government officials that investigated the kinds of human rights abuses outlined above did so at great personal risk. In September, Human Rights Watch/Americas publicly denounced the death threats that two military prosecutors in São Paulo, Dr. Stella Kuhlman and Dr. Marco Antônio Ferreira Lima, had been receiving for almost two years. Rather than intensifying their investigation into the threats, the São Paulo Military Police brought an administrative action against Ferreira Lima when he denounced corruption in that organization, ultimately forcing his resignation.

U.S. Policy

Despite the United States' close economic and political ties with Brazil, the Clinton administration, following the pattern established by previous administrations, failed to use its considerable influence to press for improvements in Brazil's human rights record. Although the U.S. was Brazil's most important trading partner, and thus could exert significant influence, the administration chose to remain silent publicly. In testimony before Congress on May 10, Assistant Secretary of State for Democracy, Human Rights and Labor John Shattuck stated that human rights concerns were raised in private bilateral discussions between Brazil and the United States. However, the Brazil desk officer at the State Department was unaware of any human rights statement made by the State Department or the U.S. Embassy in Brasília during the year, with the exception of the Brazil section of the annual *Country Reports on Human Rights Practices for 1993*.

Although the State Department's country report portrayed the grave human rights situation in Brazil with a high degree of accuracy, that document was largely irrelevant to U.S. policy toward Brazil. The U.S. missed several key opportunities to criticize Brazil's human rights record publicly. In March, Vice President Al Gore visited Brazil to sign a pact expanding an earlier agreement on scientific and technological cooperation, meeting with President Itamar Franco and Foreign Minister Celso Amorim. In June, Secretary of Commerce Ron Brown spent three days in Brazil as the head of a delegation of twenty-two U.S. business executives visiting Brazil, Argentina, and Chile. Through these meetings and other initiatives, the U.S. sought to increase trade with Brazil. Unfortunately, the administration failed to link closer trade relations to human rights progress.

In 1994 direct U.S. assistance to Brazil continued to be relatively low. For fiscal year 1995, the administration requested $100,000 for direct training (through the International Military Education and Training Program, IMET). Although the administration's request for funding noted serious human rights problems in Brazil such as "'death squad' activities and killings of Indians," it erroneously asserted that Brazilian authorities were aggressively investigating these cases.

Brazil's growing role in the international drug trade, particularly as a center for money laundering and cocaine processing, prompted the administration to request $1 million in anti-narcotics assistance. The anti-narcotics strategy vis-à-vis Brazil consisted primarily of providing assistance for the drug interdiction efforts of the Federal Police. Unfortunately, the United States failed to seize the opportunity presented by this aid grant to the Federal Police to press that force to respond to severe human rights abuses within its competence. For example, despite the Brazilian government's recognition that slave labor was practiced in various parts of the country, the Federal Police consistently failed to investigate adequately credible reports by local human rights groups.

The Work of
Human Rights Watch/Americas

In 1994, Human Rights Watch/Americas continued to focus attention on human rights abuses committed against marginalized groups in Brazilian society. In January, Human Rights Watch/Americas released *Final Justice: Death Squad Homicides of Adolescents in Brazil*. The report was released in Brazil in February, receiving significant coverage in the major national print and television media. That report called for a series of actions by Brazilian authorities to respond to the urgent problem of homicides of children and adolescents in four of Brazil's largest cities. These included increasing the federal government's role in investigating and prosecuting the abuses, closer monitoring of private security firms, which often serve as fronts for death squads, and administrative dismissal of abusive police officers.

In light of the increase in violence against indigenous peoples in Brazil, and in particular those residing in the Raposa Serra do Sol area, Human Rights Watch/Americas dispatched a researcher to Brazil in March to investigate this situation. Human Rights Watch/Americas investigated the violence directed at the Macuxi and Wapixana indigenous peoples, met with federal prosecutors and other officials in Brasília to pressure them to ensure these groups adequate protection, and in June, released *Violence Against the Macuxi and Wapixana Indians in Raposa Serra do Sol and Northern Roraima from 1988 to 1994*

In August and September, an Human Rights Watch/Americas representative visited Brazil to participate in a conference on forced labor and to update research on police and death squad violence against children. During the conference on forced labor, Human Rights Watch/Americas met with attorneys from the federal attorney general's office and top ranking police officials to express the organization's concerns about the continuing problem of forced labor and the government's failure to prosecute those responsible despite its recognition of the widespread nature of the problem.

Human Rights Watch/Americas continued to use international mechanisms to focus attention on human rights violations in Brazil. In February, in conjunction with the Center for Justice and International Law (CEJIL), the organization submitted petitions in seven cases to the Inter-American Commission on Human Rights. Those cases focused on four areas of concern: extrajudicial killings of minors by police; abusive prison conditions, including two notorious massacres in the São Paulo prison system; rural violence; and forced labor. In February and September, representatives of Human Rights Watch/Americas and CEJIL appeared before the Inter-American Commission to inform that body of the endemic human rights problems which Brazil faces and the status of the eight cases pending on Brazil. In November, Human Rights Watch/Americas and CEJIL filed a petition with the commission to denounce the lack of effective action by the Brazilian government to respond to the death threats against Fathers Rezende and des Roziers.

Finally, Human Rights Watch/Americas planned to open a permanent office in Brazil in early December 1994. Having a representative in Brazil would allow us to monitor the complex, diverse human rights situation and follow cases that Human Rights Watch/Americas and CEJIL jointly litigate in the inter-American system.

CHILE

Human Rights Developments

On December 11, 1993, in a significant step for the consolidation of democracy, Chile held its first presidential elections since the end of military rule. Eduardo Frei Ruiz-Tagle was elected President as the candidate of the center-left Concertación de Partidos por la Democracia, the governing coalition under then-President Patricio Aylwin.

Under Aylwin's leadership, Chile had made notable progress in reinstituting democracy and reestablishing respect for human rights, a trend that continued under Frei. In marked contrast to the wholesale violence of the Pinochet dictatorship, the Chilean government did not engage in a consistent pattern of gross human rights violations. Nonetheless, its record of respect for human rights remained flawed, in large part due to the legacy of the former military regime. Most obviously, the amnesty law decreed under military rule has continued to pose an enormous obstacle to the investigation and prosecution of abuses committed between 1973 and 1978. In addition, many members of the judiciary were appointed by the military; their continuing authority, and in particular their presence on the Supreme Court, contributed to impunity. An even more serious obstacle to justice was the broad jurisdiction of military courts over crimes committed by members of the armed forces, including police, in which civilians were victims. Finally, the limitations on civilian legal jurisdiction were mirrored by restrictions on institutional accountability: specifically, the elected authorities still lacked control over appointments to the armed forces and the police.

To some extent, the Frei administration, like its predecessor, was restricted in its ability to remove the remaining obstacles to justice and respect for human rights. Because of military appointees in the Senate and a "binomial" voting system that favors minority parties, the opposition had disproportionate strength in Congress, including a Senate majority. Although Frei submitted reform legislation targeting some of these undemocratic aspects, its passage through Congress—in light of rightist opposition and the super-majority required for constitutional amendment—was expected to be difficult at best.

The National Corporation of Reparation and Reconciliation, which succeeded the truth commission that had worked from 1990-1991 ("the Rettig Commission"), continued investigating human rights abuses that occurred under the former military regime. In 1994 it revised upward its estimate of the number of people murdered for political reasons during that period to 3,129. The exhumation of bodies also continued, although, in one notable case, the head of the army Subofficials School in Rinconada de Maipú squarely blocked judicially mandated exhumations on its property.

While the record was mixed, there were some important breakthroughs in prosecutions for human rights violations during military rule, notably in the trial and appellate courts. The most important case involved the prosecution of two DINA (former secret police) officers charged with being the "intellectual authors" of the 1976 Letelier-Moffitt murders. On November 12, 1993, the two offenders were convicted and sentenced to six- and seven-year prison terms for their part in the murders. (Largely due to intense U.S. pressure stemming from the fact that the murders occurred in Washington, D.C. and Moffitt was an American citizen,

the prosecutions had been exempted from a 1978 amnesty.)

Two other potentially historic cases from this period were decided by different chambers of the Santiago Appeals Court in September. The Third Chamber reopened the prosecution of DINA agent Osvaldo Romo for the 1974 abduction and murder of Lumi Videla, holding that crimes committed in violation of international law are not subject to national amnesty. The Eighth Chamber issued a similar ruling a few days later in another case involving Romo. Although both cases were on appeal to the Supreme Court at this writing, they represented significant developments in the jurisprudence on amnesty.

In what might be a hopeful indicator for these appeals, the Supreme Court in April reopened the judicial inquiry into the 1976 murder of Carmelo Soria, a United Nations official who was killed by DINA agents. Based on the amnesty law, the investigation had been closed, after a number of procedural complications, when DINA's involvement was established. On appeal, however, the Supreme Court credited the plaintiffs' argument that application of the amnesty would violate Chile's international obligations, specifically, the Vienna Convention on crimes against international civil servants and diplomats.

Judicial investigations into human rights crimes post-dating the amnesty continued as well. These resulted in a few convictions, the most dramatic of which involved sixteen former police officers belonging to a secret agency known as DICOMCAR, who abducted three communists in 1985, tortured them, and killed them by cutting their throats. On March 31, the officers accused in this case—known as the *degollados* case—were convicted of kidnapping, murder and terrorist conspiracy.

Institutional restrictions marring even human rights successes such as this became apparent, however, when the first political crisis of Frei's administration exploded. Besides the degollados convictions, seven highranking police officers including General

Rodolfo Stange, the head of the Carabineros, Chile's police force, were accused of dereliction of duty for failing to prevent or investigate the murders. The Frei government, which lacked the power to dismiss Stange, requested that he resign, unsuccessfully. A highly public political standoff ensued, finally resulting in Stange's "vacation," but he returned to his post in July after the courts ruled his conduct not criminal. The Frei administration, unable to act, simply issued its "regrets" about Stange's return.

The dangers of police autonomy from civilian control have been graphically illustrated by recent cases of abuse of detainees and excessive force. The Committee for the Defense of the Rights of the People (CODEPU), which monitors police treatment of detainees, lodged nineteen lawsuits involving torture and physical abuse between October 1993 and September 1994. The police also came under heavy criticism for their alleged "shoot first, ask questions later" policy, demonstrated most notoriously in the Las Condes incident of October 21, 1993, in which seven people were killed when police fired indiscriminately on a bus carrying civilian passengers as well as members of an armed opposition group.

Besides ill-treatment, security-related detainees were likely to face prolonged incommunicado detention and denial of their due process rights. Such abuses were rarely questioned by the courts. In what was thus an unusual ruling, the first chamber of the Santiago Appeals Court overturned the convictions of eleven alleged armed opposition group members in October. The court found that, besides being tortured, some of the prisoners had been held incommunicado for twenty days during questioning, and forced to incriminate themselves in order to secure the release of their illegally detained relatives.

Existing laws, though enforced less intensively than previously, still permitted gross infringements on the right to free expression. For example, two journalists who criticized the Supreme Court's decision to relinquish jurisdiction over an important disappearance case were prosecuted for insults, libel and defamation under the Law of State Security, receiving suspended prison sentences in June; other of their controversial writings led to indictments for "inciting sedition," presently pending in military courts. Another example was the November confiscation of a day's issue of the newspaper La Epoca for allegedly violating the reporting ban on a human rights case. La Epoca's editorial response to this action—that "the reporting ban was used as an extension of the amnesty . . . [restricting] the public's right to be informed"—was, in the view of Human Rights Watch/Americas, persuasive.

The Right to Monitor

Overlapping with restrictions on free expression was the legal harassment of human rights lawyers, which, besides curbing their speech, hindered their ability to litigate on behalf of victims of abuses. The close encounter with military justice endured by Héctor Salazar Ardiles, lawyer for the relatives of the degollados victims, was indicative of the phenomenon. In April, he was charged with sedition by a military prosecutor for comments critical of the police high command, detained, and then released on bail; in June, his indictment was upheld by a military appeals court; in August, finally, the Supreme Court overturned his indictment and put a stop to the prosecution.

U.S. Policy

Chile removed an important impediment to good relations with the United States by sentencing the offenders in the Letelier-Moffitt assassination case, facilitating the current emphasis on commercial relations between the two countries. With that ruling, human rights issues were dropped from the U.S. agenda vis-a-vis Chile; the Clinton administration did not, in fact, even comment on the ruling or make any other public statements regarding human rights during the year.

Having strengthened commercial ties with Canada and Mexico by ratifying the

North American Free Trade Agreement (NAFTA), the United States—prompted by a decade of uninterrupted growth in the Chilean economy—looked to Chile in 1994 as the locus for further trade liberalization. U.S. interest in signing a free trade agreement with Chile was signaled in March when U.S. Trade Representative Mickey Kantor attended President Frei's inauguration, and in May when the Clinton administration approached Congress seeking fast-track authority for the proposed negotiations. Trade negotiations had not formally begun by year's end, however.

Besides the proposed trade agreement, there was little U.S. action relevant to human rights in Chile, except for the grant of $100,000 in fiscal year 1994 for Defense Training (formerly International Military Education and Training), an amount that was due to be matched in fiscal year 1995. The focus of the training, according to the State Department, was to "emphasiz[e] the proper role of the military in a democracy."

The Work of
Human Rights Watch/Americas

In the view of Human Rights Watch/Americas, the current impetus toward a free trade agreement between the United States and Chile provided a two-fold opportunity for human rights advocacy. First, in assessing Chile's suitability as a close trading partner the United States should, as a threshold matter, inquire into its record of respect for human rights. Second, a free trade agreement might—and should, in our opinion—incorporate institutional mechanisms for preventing human rights abuses and remedying any abuses that occur.

In light of the first consideration, Human Rights Watch/Americas maintained a representative in Santiago whose work monitoring events and conditions led to the release of a comprehensive report on the state of human rights during the final period of the Aylwin government. The report, titled *Unfinished Business: Human Rights in Chile at the Start of the Frei Presidency*, was issued in May, together with an open letter to President Frei summarizing our concerns regarding human rights in Chile. In addition to wide coverage in the Chilean press, we received a positive response from the deputy minister of foreign relations, who alluded to constitutional and legal obstacles that impede the Chilean Congress from effecting the legal changes necessary to resolve certain of Chile's human rights problems.

In August, after preliminary free trade negotiations had begun, we wrote an open letter to U.S. Trade Representative Mickey Kantor urging attention to human rights in the negotiation and drafting of a free trade agreement. We pressed two recommendations in particular: first, that the proposed agreement contain each country's explicit commitment to respect the rights articulated in the American Convention on Human Rights, with the strength of these commitments to be monitored through the submission and review of yearly compliance reports; and second, that the agreement contain a mechanism for the adjudication of individual complaints of human rights violations that arise in the context of the commercial relations permitted by the agreement.

Finally, Human Rights Watch/Americas continued litigating on behalf of relatives of the disappeared before the Inter-American Commission for Human Rights (IACHR), seeking reparations and condemnation of the former military regime's egregious violations of the American Convention on Human Rights. Together with the Center for Justice and International Law (CEJIL), we submitted briefs to the IACHR in a case involving seventy disappearances carried out by state security forces in the mid-1970s.

COLOMBIA

Human Rights Developments

After taking office in August, President Ernesto Samper affirmed that human rights in Colombia was "not a question of image, but reality." But while the actions of the

Colombian government in 1994 bespoke an overriding concern for image, they resulted in little substantive progress in resolving chronic problems of political violence, "social cleansing," torture, and impunity. While President Samper did take some positive initial steps, like creating an office of human rights within the Defense Ministry, the record left by his predecessor, OAS General Secretary César Gaviria, was abysmal.

The clearest evidence of this was the presidential veto of the Disappearances Law, passed by Congress with the strong support of human rights groups, which reported forty-three unresolved disappearances in the first nine months of 1994.

Then-President Gaviria vetoed the bill on July 7, arguing that it was unconstitutional because it abolished military court jurisdiction over members of the security forces accused of carrying out disappearances and because it penalized not only those who participated in the violations, but also those who gave the orders. Disappearances, government officials claimed in defending the veto, were "act[s] of [military] service." Both the Procuraduría, the oversight branch of government, and the Public Ombudsman (Defensoría) strongly objected to the veto.

Attacks on leftists, peasant leaders, trade unionists, indigenous activists, and community organizers continued. The Centro de Investigación y Educación Popular (CINEP), a leading human rights group, registered 177 extrajudicial executions by state agents in the first nine months of the year. One of the most prominent was the killing on August 9 of Manuel Cepeda Vargas, the sole remaining Senate representative of the coalition between the Communist Party and the Patriotic Union (PCC-UP) political parties. Cepeda, who had months earlier informed government authorities that he believed members of the military were planning to kill him and other UP leaders, was murdered by armed men as he drove to work in Bogotá. The day of Cepeda's murder, a paramilitary group calling itself Death To Colombian Guerrillas (MACOGUE) claimed responsibility and released death threats against

twenty-five others, including political and Church leaders.

The military's direct involvement in human rights violations had been underscored eight months earlier, when two Navy officers testified before the public prosecutor's office about how Navy intelligence planned, participated in, and paid for over one hundred murders in the Middle Magdalena region since 1991. According to their testimony, Navy officers and a band of hired killers under the command of Colonel Rodrigo Quiñonez Cárdenas, systematically hunted down and shot people they considered enemies, among them two members of the Barrancabermeja-based Regional Committee for Human Rights (CREDHOS).

Human rights groups remained highly concerned about the rural operations of army Mobile Brigades, elite counterinsurgency units which continued to be implicated in extrajudicial execution, torture, arbitrary detention, and threats. Children were prime targets, viewed as potential informants on their parents. In June, for example, a group attached to Mobile Brigade II was accused by peasants in Yondó, Antioquia, of torturing five children, one of whom was four years old. In addition, during the same attack, the group apparently tortured local youths, and said that they would be killed "if the guerrillas keep attacking us."

In one of the most serious incidents, a paramilitary group with alleged ties to Mobile Brigade II was implicated in the extrajudicial executions of nine men, including seventy-year-old Adriano Portillo, a resident of Norean, Cesar. On July 29, armed and hooded men in civilian clothing reportedly forced Norean villagers to assemble, then stole their watches, money, and jewelery, even though a military checkpoint and a provisional post of Mobile Brigade II were located in the village. The men shot and killed Portillo in his house, reportedly for failing to assemble quickly enough. Two other men were executed in front of the crowd, which was warned not to report the killings. Two days later, a group of similarly hooded and armed men executed six villagers in nearby Minas.

In a September article in a Colombian magazine, paramilitary leader Fidel Castaño asserted that his private army, linked to a grisly string of massacres and assassinations, was initially recruited and trained by state security forces. Even though there was an outstanding warrant for Castaño's arrest and he had admitted helping plan the 1990 murder of UP presidential candidate Bernardo Jaramillo, he was apparently free to travel between his Córdoba ranches and Paris home. underscoring the official impunity many paramilitary leaders continued to enjoy.

The Comisión Intercongregacional de Justicia y Paz reported in August that families living in Aguamieluda, Santander, were forced to attend a meeting called jointly by paramilitaries and local Army officers. There. they were told to collaborate. leave. or be killed. Several families apparently lost their farms to paramilitary agents who decided to use their property as a base.

Trade unionists were hard hit by paramilitary killings. According to the Unified Central of Workers (CUT). between January and mid-October, 123 trade unionists were murdered in Colombia, most in incidents tied to paramilitary groups. In Medellín. a group calling itself COLSINGUE (Colombia Without Guerrillas) took responsibility for the murders of three trade unionists in July, including Guillermo Marín. a leader of the Antioquia Unified Federation of Workers (FUTRAN). Two months later, heavily armed men forced their way into FUTRAN offices and shot the union's complaints secretary, Hugo Zapata, who was killed. and its human rights secretary. Carlos Posada. who was seriously injured.

So-called social cleansing killings— the murder of street people. often children— continued to occur in urban areas. A report released by CINEP registered 1.926 "social cleansing" killings between 1988 and 1993. with an additional 256 for the first nine months of 1994. The security forces either participated directly or turned a blind eye when these killings occured.

Torture remains a daily reality for de-tainees throughout the country. A study carried out by three human rights groups in the city of Barrancabermeja found that of the 183 individuals detained by state security forces between January 1993 and June 1994, 170 were tortured. Both physical torture— beatings. electric shocks, and near-drowning—and psychological torture—death threats. mock executions, sleep deprivation, and threats against family members—were employed. Over one-third of these incidents of torture occurred in the Nueva Granada army barracks. Despite the frequency of torture, most cases reported to the authorities went unpunished.

Impunity remained the rule for members of the security forces implicated in human rights violations. Although investigations were undertaken in some instances, leading to the identification of the guilty parties, it was truly the exceptional case in which the offenders were punished. For example. the CUT reported that 1,542 trade unionists had been killed since the union was founded in 1986, yet not one of the murders had led to a conviction.

The case of two persons arrested and brutally interrogated during a May Day march was typical. When the officer and two agents of the judicial police (SIJIN) accused of torturing the marchers were absolved by an internal police investigation, Police Commissioner Adolfo Salamanca, a civilian, called for a review. However, the commissioner had no power to punish offenders, a critical weakness that contributed to impunity. The second police investigation again found no faults. arguing that one of the detainees was probably wounded "in a fight during the march . . . or as the result of his work in construction."

Some headway was made by the Procuraduría. however. In April, it denied the appeal of an officer whose dismissal had been ordered for having directed indiscriminate shooting during the retaking of the Palace of Justice, which was violently occupied in 1985 by the M-19 guerrilla group, taking hostage the Supreme Court and many judicial employees. The Procuraduría concluded that General Jesús Arias Cabrales, who led the attack, had ordered his men to dynamite a wall and shoot indiscriminately into a room containing over sixty guerrillas and hostages. Although the decision represented an important step toward curbing impunity, it was mitigated by the fact that Arias was apparently acting on orders from superiors who were not charged. Meanwhile, a military court acquitted Arias of any wrongdoing.

In August, the Procuraduría released a report confirming that soldiers had executed two guerrillas who had been negotiating an amnesty with the government. Evelio Antonio Bolaño and Carlos Prada, leaders of the Corriente de Renovación Socialista, were ambushed by the army on September 22, 1993. The Procuraduría accused four army officers and four soldiers with abuse of authority and negligence, among other charges. However, by mid-November there was no indication that they were punished.

Colombia's justice system remained seriously deficient. Delays caused by inefficiency and corruption prompted President Gaviria to resort to emergency legislation to keep detainees in jail past the six-month limit for specifying charges. Meanwhile, "faceless" courts—which employed judges and witnesses whose identities were concealed, withheld evidence from the defense, relied on evidence gathered by the military, and used prolonged pre-trial detention—continued to violate the right to a fair trial. Although these courts were defended as necessary for prosecuting drug traffickers and insurgents, they were often deployed against other targets, such as peasants and nonviolent protesters.

Measures that further restricted justice were enacted in June under the State of Exception Law, which created broad powers typically used to give the security forces greater latitude in investigating, making arrests, and prohibiting nonviolent protest. The Constitutional Court did, however, strike down some of the law's more egregious provisions. In July, the court disallowed the use of states of exception to keep uncharged

detainees in jail, holding that the measure violated due process. Three months later, the court also struck down the ban on the media dissemination of interviews and press releases from armed insurgents.

In an effort to salvage the country's human rights record, the government proposed adopting Protocol II Additional to the Geneva Conventions of 1949. Nevertheless, the Gaviria administration added three reservations to the protocol, including one allowing the government to determine what constitutes a legitimate military target, robbing the document of much of its value. President Gaviria also inaugurated a cabinet-level committee in June to consider reforms to the military court system, which included creating a separate Attorney General's Office within the military to investigate reports of abuse and transferring jurisdiction over the military courts from the Joint Chiefs of Staff to the Defense Ministry, currently run by a civilian. Like the government's other efforts to address human rights violations, however, this one failed to compensate for the military courts' inherent lack of impartiality.

For their part, guerrillas continued to violate international humanitarian law by engaging in murder, indiscriminate attacks, kidnapping, and the mining of civilian areas. The most egregious incident occurred in January, when hooded guerrillas apparently under the command of the Fifth Front of the Fuerzas Armadas Revolucionarias de Colombia (FARC) attacked a local fundraising party in the La Chinita neighborhood of Apartadó, Antioquia, killing thirty-five. The FARC was also blamed for the July murder of Manuel Humberto Cárdenas Vélez, the mayor of Fusagasugá, Cundinamarca.

In May, militants of the Ejército Nacional de Liberación (ELN) detained a group of forty municipal officials near Aguachica, Cesar. The body of municipal council president Oswaldo Pájaro was found abandoned on a soccer field two days later. A second man, also a community activist, remains missing. The others were released. Four months later, ELN guerrillas claimed responsibility for assassinating Chamber of

Representatives member Arlen Uribe Márquez and his driver, who were shot in the parking lot of the University of Medellín. where Uribe taught law.

Among the 221 individuals kidnapped by guerrillas in the first nine months of 1994 were members of Congress, municipal and government authorities, and seven foreigners. As of October 1994, five American missionaries and a scientist remained missing. Besides targeting missionaries, ELN guerrillas also bombed Mormon and Protestant churches, seen as tied to the U.S.

Although the government claimed to have made significant progress against guerrillas and drug traffickers, especially with the killing of Pablo Escobar in December 1993, private violence nonetheless increased. According to the Defense Ministry. 30,050 people were murdered in the year prior to July 20, 1994, a marked increased over the previous year. A National Planning investigation found that only 3 percent of the crimes committed in Colombia ever reached a judicial verdict, an astonishing two verdicts per month for the entire country.

The Right To Monitor

Groups and individuals who spoke up about Colombia's human rights problems continued to be targets of persecution, with activists in rural areas being particularly at risk. For example, Jairo Barahona, a human rights activist in Pailitas, Cesar, was disappeared in September by men who identified themselves as members of the Anti-Extortion and Kidnapping Unit (UNASE) of the National Police. For several years prior to his disappearance, Barahona had been the target of harassment and intimidation by security forces.

During the congressional debate over the Disappearances Law, Yanette Bautista and Gloria Herney Galíndez, leaders of the Asociación de Familiares de Detenidos-Desaparecidos, reported being followed by unidentified men and receiving telephone death threats. Hernando Valencia Villa, the deputy *procurador* for human rights and one of the key individuals responsible for investigating and sanctioning official abuses, was accused by one senator of being a guerrilla supporter, which jeopardized Valencia's safety. The basis for the accusation was Valencia's public criticism of the reservations attached to Protocol II by the government, as well as his strong defense of the Disappearances Law.

Government ministers and some pro-government media outlets also accused leading members of the Catholic church who support respect for human rights, of having guerrilla sympathies. In March, Attorney General Gustavo de Grieff publicly accused four bishops, including Bishop Dario Castrillón of Bucaramanga, of collaborating with the guerrillas. Castrillón, who has said that he believes that the military executes some of its detainees, was also sued for "slander and harm" by the armed forces.

Lawyers, too, were threatened due to their advocacy on behalf of victims of abuses. Carlos Alberto Ruíz, who has represented internally displaced people seeking reparations from the state, was one of the lawyers mentioned during the interrogations by the SIJIN of the May Day marchers. Later, Ruíz began receiving telephone death threats from callers who said he would have to "account for his work."

U.S. Policy

A series of controversies led one Clinton administration official to describe relations between the U.S. and Colombia as "strained." After initial, shared euphoria over the death of Pablo Escobar, problems arose regarding the U.S. perception that top Colombian officials were not doing enough to convict surviving drug kingpins. A highly publicized dispute over the sharing of intelligence between the two countries, allegations about newly-elected President Samper's connections to the Cali cartel, and the characterization of Colombia as a "narco-democracy" by the outgoing head of the Drug Enforcement Administration all contributed to increased tensions.

Human rights remained a secondary issue, overshadowed by the drug war and trade negotiations. Even as serious abuses by the Colombian armed forces continued, the U.S. Embassy in Bogotá maintained a virtual silence on human rights. In a positive move, incoming Ambassador Myles Frechette broke this silence once, in a July speech to military officers completing a U.S.-sponsored course on military justice in support of human rights.

But despite U.S. budget cuts in foreign assistance, Colombia remained a priority because of the drug war, with its police in particular receiving a relatively large amount, $18.2 million in fiscal year 1994, with a similar amount requested for fiscal year 1995. By contrast, Colombia's poor record prompted Germany, a weapons supplier, to suspend sales of guns and helicopter parts and bar certain Colombian military officers from entering the country.

Congress included some restrictions on aid to Colombia in the foreign aid appropriations bill for fiscal year 1995. The legislation required the Clinton administration to provide notification prior to disbursement of funds for Colombia and added a certification to verify that security assistance was being used "primarily" for counternarcotics, not counterinsurgency activities. These requirements stemmed from reports from human rights groups and the General Accounting Office demonstrating that the administration had failed to ensure that those involved in abuses were not receiving aid.

In August, the administration submitted a letter of notification, requesting that the fiscal year 1994 appropriation of $7.7 million in security assistance to the armed forces be released. Congress agreed to the request, most of which was slated for the Navy and Air Force for counternarcotics efforts. According to the fiscal year 1995 request for $16.5 million for the military's counternarcotics support efforts, the assistance would be used for "targeting narco-guerrilla activities, occupying seized real estate, and controlling remote areas." Due to budgetary constraints, the military was expected to receive approximately half of the amount requested for fiscal year 1995.

In addition to generous amounts of security assistance, Colombia acquired $57 million in U.S. governmental and commercial arms purchases in 1993, more than any other country in Latin America. In fiscal year 1994, sales to Colombia were expected to top $73 million. The U.S. continued to make or approve arms sales to Colombia despite human rights conditions that should have been applied.

During the year, the administration claimed to have implemented end-use monitoring, although specific details were not revealed. As State Department officials acknowledged, there were no units in the Colombian military devoted exclusively to counternarcotics activities, making definitive prohibitions on aid for other activities impossible, even with enhanced oversight. Documents obtained by Human Rights Watch through the Freedom of Information Act demonstrated that much of the equipment provided to Colombia under the guise of the "war on drugs" was designed for counterinsurgency.

In response to congressional concerns, the U.S. Embassy in Bogotá prepared a confidential document identifying recipients of U.S. assistance and describing the allegations against them. The document reportedly included information about investigations conducted by Colombian officials and measures taken against abusive members of the armed forces. Unfortunately, the administration chose to classify the document, and it remained unavailable to human rights groups.

The Agency for International Development (AID) continued its funding of a $36 million Administration of Justice program during the year. AID officials assured Human Rights Watch/Americas that U.S. assistance was no longer provided for the controversial "public order courts." In past years, Human Rights Watch/Americas had objected to U.S. support for these courts because of their inherent due process violations and the misuse of this jurisdiction to quell legal protest.

The State Department's annual *Coun-*

try Reports on Human Rights Practices for 1993 continued to characterize violations by state security agencies and nongovernmental forces as equal, even though human rights groups agreed that abuses by the military, police, and their paramilitary clients far outnumbered violations of the laws of war by insurgents. Indeed, the report lumped together insurgents and drug traffickers, overestimating the degree to which they collaborated.

The Work of
Human Rights Watch/Americas

Human Rights Watch/Americas sought to bring the issue of human rights to the forefront of any discussion of Colombia.

We registered frequent protests with the Colombian government regarding human rights abuses, and urged the guerrillas to cease violating international humanitarian law. Together with the Andean Commission of Jurists-Colombian Section and the Center for Justice and International Law (CEJIL), we represented victims of abuses before the Inter-American Commission on Human Rights. In December 1993, we issued *State of War: Political Violence and Counterinsurgency in Colombia*; a Spanish translation was released in 1994. Also during 1994, Human Rights Watch/Americas sent two missions to Colombia, where our representatives met with senior U.S. and Colombian government officials in Washington and Bogotá, and with the representatives of human rights groups and humanitarian organizations. Finally, in cooperation with the Human Rights Watch Children's Rights Project, we issued *Generation Under Fire: Children and Violence in Colombia* in November, a report on government responsibility for the murders of children.

In the U.S. Congress, we were at the forefront of efforts to give human rights a central role in U.S.-Colombia relations while urging greater accountability regarding the Colombian security forces' use of U.S. aid. We were especially concerned that military and police aid received by Colombia in the name of anti-narcotics operations not be used for counterinsurgency efforts or other operations in which human rights were violated. With the help of key committee members, we insisted on stricter end-use monitoring of aid, particularly lethal aid sent as part of the "drug war."

CUBA

Human Rights Developments

Popular dissatisfaction with the Castro regime deepened in 1994 in the face of continuing political repression and an ever-worsening economic crisis. Increasing numbers of people fled the island by raft and boat, and a spontaneous demonstration by the Havana harbor on August 5 was the largest expression of anti-government sentiment since the 1959 revolution brought Castro to power. During the ensuing weeks more than 30,000 people left the country, taking advantage of Castro's decision to temporarily allow departures. This move was calculated to bring the U.S. to the negotiating table and was partially successful in that regard. On September 9, the United States and Cuba reached an agreement on emigration whereby 20,000 Cubans would be allowed into the U.S. each year. In exchange for this concession, Castro once again clamped down on those attempting to leave the island through informal channels. Meanwhile, more than 32,000 Cubans, picked up at sea by the U.S. Coast Guard and prohibited from entering the United States, continued to be held under U.S. authority at Guantánamo Bay naval base and in Panama.

With the exception of this month-long exodus, Cuba continued to violate its citizens' right to freedom of movement through application of its "illegal exit" laws, which forbid Cubans from leaving the country without government permission. In the past three decades, thousands of Cubans have been arrested and imprisoned on this charge. In 1994, the maximum punishment was three years. Related crimes included the use of violence, intimidation or force while attempting to leave the country (punishable by three to eight years in prison); organizing, promoting or inciting illegal exit (two to five years in prison); and lending material aid or information facilitating illegal exit (one to three years in prison). Exact numbers were unavailable, but illegal exit prisoners were thought to constitute the largest category of political prisoners in Cuba.

Enforcement of the illegal exit law had eased somewhat in recent years, with the trend increasingly to fine first-time offenders and incarcerate only repeat offenders. Despite this overall softening of enforcement, cases of shootings or prosecution for illegal exit were not uncommon. In June 1994, coastal authorities from the port of La Fe, in the municipality of Guane, shot dead José Inesio Pedraza Izquierdo when he tried to set to sea for the United States. This was followed one month later by the most prominent case in 1994, the sinking of the hijacked state-owned tugboat, the *13 de Marzo*. The boat, carrying seventy-two passengers, was intercepted by three government boats a few miles out from the Havana harbor early on the morning of July 13. The Cuban authorities sprayed the *13 de Marzo* with high-pressure water cannons, reportedly sweeping several passengers off its deck and into the ocean. According to survivors, the boat's path was then cut off, and one of the pursuing tugs deliberately rammed the *13 de Marzo*, causing it to sink. At least thirty-seven people died, including many children who had sought refuge from the water cannons in the hold of the vessel.

Despite these restrictions, the long-standing political repression and deepening economic crisis prompted more and more people to abandon the island. The numbers leaving by boat and small raft have steadily grown and, with increasing frequency, Cubans have fled in stolen or hijacked vessels, despite the serious penalties these crimes carry. Word of successful escapes during the summer of 1994 encouraged a surge of attempts. Eventually, rumors spread in Havana that emigration by boat was to be officially permitted, and it was those rumors that

led to the unprecedented clash on August 5 between thousands of would-be emigrants and Cuban authorities near the mouth of the Havana harbor. When police officers attempted to prevent a group of Cubans from launching a raft, hostile crowds turned on them, seizing their weapons. Two officers were killed and a third seriously injured. Thousands of people joined in the fracas, and a spontaneous riot ensued in the downtown commercial area of the Cuban capital.

The next day Fidel Castro made a public speech in which he criticized the U.S. for encouraging illegal emigration while simultaneously refusing to admit substantial numbers of Cubans through legal channels. Castro declared that the government would no longer detain those who sought to leave on their own rafts.

At the same time, Cuban authorities embarked on a crackdown on dissidents and opposition groups, despite the fact that there was no indication that the August 5 riot was an organized or premeditated event. Several hundred people, including dozens of human rights and pro-democracy activists, were detained in subsequent days. Some were released after a few days of interrogation and detention in crowded and dilapidated jails. Others were held for longer periods of time, and at least two of these—Gloria Bravo of the Association of Mothers for Dignity (AMAD) and Carlos Ríos of Cambio 2000—were severely beaten while in detention. Still others remained incarcerated as of October, including 162 people who were transferred on September 17 to the maximum security prison Kilo-7 in Camagüey.

Most of the dissidents released after one or two days of detention reported ongoing harassment after their release, including random assaults and beatings on the street. In some cases activists were picked up for yet another period of detention without charge.

In addition, the Castro regime used the chaos of the August exodus to attempt to force many dissidents and activists out of the country via boats or rafts. At least twenty people were reported to have been forced to leave because of their political activities. In these cases, government agents approached the dissidents, either directly or via an intermediary or family member, and told them that the government had information regarding their "illegal activities" and that, consequently, it would be in their "best interests" to take advantage of the opportunity to leave the country.

The Right to Monitor

Human rights monitoring was illegal in Cuba and the government refused to grant legal status to opposition or pro-democracy groups. Free expression and association continued to be severely restricted, and state security forces maintained close surveillance of activists and dissidents. Persecution took a variety of forms, including frequent harassment, intimidation, and arrests. Pro-democracy and human rights workers were imprisoned on vague and malleable political charges that violated basic political and civil rights. Typical charges included "illicit association," "clandestine printing," and "disrespect to the head of state." After completing their sentences, dissidents might be kept in prison under the commonly used provision of "high dangerousness," which could add as much as four years to the original period of incarceration. "Spreading enemy propaganda," one of the most common political charges, carried prison sentences that frequently reached ten years.

In addition to lengthy prison terms, the government relied increasingly on other patterns of intimidation, including seemingly random acts of violence by anonymous assailants and short-term interrogations and detentions in municipal jail cells that were often crowded, airless and overflowing with excrement.

Human rights activists detained or harassed in 1994 included René del Pozo Pozo, a prominent member of the Cuban Commission for Human Rights and National Reconciliation (CCDHRN), who was detained four times in the chaotic weeks of the exodus and its aftermath. Early on the morning of August 6, five uniformed and two plainclothes police officers came to his house with a search warrant authorizing seizure of "illicit materials." They searched the house and removed personal items, including all of del Pozo's working papers and materials. His telephones were ripped from the walls, and he and his family were insulted and verbally assaulted. After several hours of this treatment, the police arrested del Pozo, his aunt, and his cousin, and took them to a local police station. Del Pozo's aunt and cousin were released later that night.

Del Pozo was charged with illegal possession of goods (*receptación*), for having in his possession three cases of beer left over from his May 1994 wedding party. The following day authorities transferred him to another police station and charged him with spreading enemy propaganda; three days later he was released. His beer was returned to him, but his papers and other working materials were not.

Del Pozo was picked up and detained again on August 23, together with CCDHRN member Vladimiro Roca. Taken to a local police station, Del Pozo was threatened with a lengthy imprisonment if he refused to sign a statement denouncing the pro-democracy Democratic Socialist Current group and his own prior statements, critical of the Cuban government, that had been broadcast on Radio Martí. He signed the statement under duress.

On August 26, del Pozo was picked up a third time and taken in for a "chat." He was told not to talk to foreigners or to go to the U.S. Interest Section (the only U.S. diplomatic presence in Cuba). He was told that if he wished to leave Cuba by boat the government would not stand in the way.

On October 12, del Pozo was detained yet again and held by the National Police in Havana. He was released after several days.

In addition to these short-term detentions and harassment, del Pozo received a threatening telephone call on August 30, and was assaulted on the street by a lone assailant, who beat him with brass knuckles. The blows were strategically placed and caused ongoing neurological damage.

The harassment directed against del

Pozo was representative of the experience of dozens of activists. Elizardo Sánchez, one of Cuba's best-known dissidents, was under virtual house arrest from July to December, the result of a questionable conviction for "illegal possession of goods" (he had a key to a house where gasoline was stored). Labor activist Lázaro Corp, president of the National Commission of Independent Unions (CONSI), was arrested on June 22, 1994 after paying visits to the Belgium and German embassies and interrogated repeatedly before his release the next day. He estimated this to be his eighth detention by state security forces in the past three years. On August 2, Corp and his son were attacked by three unknown assailants near their home and beaten with fists and sticks on their heads and shoulders. Three days later a group of men attacked their house with rocks and bottles. In addition, twice in 1994 cars deliberately knocked Corp off of his bicycle. Other activists reported similar attacks and beatings.

Francisco Chaviano González, president of the National Council for Civil Rights in Cuba (CNDCC) and signatory to an April 1994 petition seeking amnesty for and official recognition of human rights groups in Cuba, was arrested on May 7. Prior to this arrest, Chaviano had been subjected to steadily mounting harassment, including frequent surveillance and acts of vandalism and graffiti against his house. His arrest on May 7 was preceded by an odd early morning visit from a stranger, who gave Chaviano an envelope containing mysterious documents. As Chaviano was looking through these papers, state security agents rushed in, arrested Chaviano and ransacked his house and belongings. The initial charge against him, "illegal possession of goods," was later increased to "possession of state secrets, " a reference to the documents planted on him shortly before the police raid.

Chaviano was jailed in Villa Marista, a state security prison outside of Havana. As of this writing he had not been tried, and his lawyer had not been permitted to see him or the indictment sheet listing the charges against him. In addition to Chaviano, four other members of the CNDCC had been arrested and imprisoned since May 1994.

While Cuba maintained its refusal to recognize internal dissident groups, Foreign Minister Roberto Robaina met with three leaders of the Cuban exile opposition in September and announced an intention to hold subsequent meetings. In addition, the Cuban government invited the recently appointed United Nations high commissioner for human rights, Ambassador José Ayala Lasso, to visit the country and conduct a human rights investigation. This was a marked departure from Cuba's ongoing refusal to admit the U.N. Human Rights Commission's designated special rapporteur on Cuba, Ambassador Carl-Johan Groth.

U.S. Policy

The U.S. government's response to the Cuban exodus was two-fold: alarm at the prospect of high numbers of refugees and dismay with Castro for permitting them to leave. Hoping to discourage would-be rafters, on August 19 the Clinton administration announced that it was reversing U.S. policy on Cubans picked up at sea. From that day forward, Cubans rescued or apprehended in international or U.S. territorial waters would not gain automatic entry into the United States, but would instead be detained at the Guantánamo naval base, together with the 14,000 Haitian boat people already being held there. In addition, the new policy declared that Cubans picked up at sea would not be eligible to enter the United States without first returning to Cuba for in-country processing, whether as refugees or immigrants.

On August 26, the Clinton administration announced additional policy changes, intended to punish Castro for the exodus by further tightening the already stringent economic embargo against Cuba. The administration revoked the general licenses for family visits to Cuba by Cuban-Americans, for professional research in Cuba, and for news-gathering on the island, requiring people seeking to travel under one of these three categories to apply for a specific license from the Treasury Department. The new policy required Cuban-Americans wishing to visit family members in Cuba to demonstrate a compelling humanitarian need, such as the grave illness of a family member. The class of journalists permitted to travel to Cuba on a general license was reduced to professional, full-time journalists; free-lance journalists were required to obtain special permission. These restrictions reduced the number of U.S. travelers to Cuba by approximately 90 percent. In addition, the administration prohibited Cuban-Americans from giving money to any Cuban national, regardless of the reason—reversing existing policy which had permitted Cuban-Americans to make annual cash gifts of up to $1200 to their families on the island. This draconian new policy was criticized on humanitarian grounds.

In addition to humanitarian concerns, U.S. policy toward Cuba raised several human rights concerns. Primary among these was the detention of Cubans by U.S. authorities in "safe haven" camps, a practice that violated Article 9 of the International Covenant on Civil and Political Rights (ICCPR), which prohibits arbitrary detention. As of November 1994, Cuban detainees had a "choice" of either returning to Cuba or remaining indefinitely detained. They were categorically denied the possibility of entering the United States and no third country had agreed to admit them, nor were they provided an opportunity to demonstrate the legitimacy of their fear of persecution and thus qualify as legally-recognized refugees.

Another area of serious concern was the U.S. insistence that Cuba prevent its citizens from leaving the country outside of official channels, which by themselves offered very limited opportunities for exit. Article 12 of the ICCPR protects the right "to be free to leave any country, including [one's] own." The September 9 agreement between the two countries, in which Cuba agreed to clamp down on extralegal exits in exchange for increased flows of legal immigration, rendered the U.S. complicit in Cuba's ongoing violation of this right to free movement.

Finally, the tighter restrictions on travel curbed the flow of people and information between Cuba and the U.S., in violation of both the First Amendment of the United States Constitution and Article 19 of the ICCPR, which protects the right to freedom of expression, defined as including the "freedom to seek, receive, and impart information and ideas of all kinds, regardless of frontiers."

The Work of
Human Rights Watch/Americas

Human Rights Watch/Americas has long worked to focus international attention on Cuba's persecution of those who attempt to flee the island. After the sinking of the *13 de Marzo* in July, Human Rights Watch/Americas wrote to President Castro expressing concern over the sinking of the ship and resultant loss of life and requesting permission for a Human Rights Watch representative to visit the island to investigate the incident. As of mid-November, we had received no reply. (Despite repeated requests over the years, Cuban authorities have never granted Human Rights Watch permission to visit Cuba and monitor human rights conditions.)

On August 31, Human Rights Watch wrote to President Clinton, criticizing the administration for urging President Castro to prevent flight from Cuba and calling on the U.S. president to publicly recognize the right to free movement. Our letter and the media coverage it engendered prompted debate over this aspect of the policy, which had previously been ignored.

In October, Human Rights Watch/Americas released a report focused on Cuba's response to "illegal exit," the human rights implications of U.S. policy regarding Cuba and Cuban detainees in Guantánamo and Panama, and Cuba's continuing violation of its citizens' basic civil and political rights.

EL SALVADOR

Human Rights Developments

In 1994, the human rights situation in El Salvador showed some improvement over the political violence that was seen at the end of 1993. Important advances were made in the development of a new civilian police force and in the administration of justice. Still, impunity for political violence remained the norm and questions persisted about the hotly contested "election of the century," held in March.

For the first time since the signing of the historic 1992 peace accords, the former rebels of the Frente Farabundo Martí para la Liberación Nacional (FMLN) participated as a legal political party in March's presidential, legislative, and municipal elections. The governing ARENA party won the presidency and the vast majority of municipalities, and fell just short of a majority in the Legislative Assembly, where the FMLN became the second political force. In an April run-off for the presidency, San Salvador Mayor Armando Calderón Sol easily beat the candidate of a FMLN-led leftist coalition Rubén Zamora by a two-to-one margin.

The elections were monitored by the United Nations Observer Mission to El Salvador (ONUSAL), which declared them "acceptable." Nevertheless, ONUSAL and other international observers noted that electoral irregularities ranging from incomplete voter lists to failures in distributing voter cards prevented many people from casting a ballot. The relatively low voter turnout in the elections, furthermore, underscored the alienation from the political process felt by broad sectors of the country's citizens.

On May 19, the FMLN and the outgoing government of President Alfredo Cristiani agreed on the "re-calendarization" of the still unfulfilled aspects of the peace accords. Most importantly, this included a reinvigorated role for ONUSAL in the monitoring of the new National Civilian Police (PNC) and police academy. The PNC comprised prima-

rily civilians who did not participate in the twelve-year civil war but also included former members of the FMLN and the National Police.

In 1994, serious human rights concerns continued to be raised about the new force and in particular about its deputy director, Oscar Peña Durán, a former army captain who had directed the anti-narcotics police unit. Peña Durán was responsible for the rupture of the PNC's close working relationship with ONUSAL, which had been providing key technical assistance to the new police force during its initial deployment. Reports of the PNC's militarization were substantiated by the increased number of abuses being reported and by the privileged position given former anti-narcotics officers who had not attended the new police academy. A dramatic example of PNC abuses was a series of large-scale and aggressive round-ups of supposed "delinquents" in early 1994, operations which captured few criminals but violated the civil rights of many innocent bystanders. ONUSAL received 147 complaints against the PNC between November 1993 and June 1994, from which it confirmed that fifty-eight violations had occurred, including cases of arbitrary detentions, lack of due process, and torture. In May, before the change of presidential leadership, Peña Durán resigned his post, as did PNC Director José María Monterrey.

Several appointments made by President Calderón Sol, who was sworn in on June 1, raised hopes that the new administration might be more responsive to human rights concerns surrounding the PNC. Among these appointments was that of Hugo Barrera as vice-minister of public security and of Rodrigo Avila as PNC director. In response to criticism of former anti-narcotics and criminal investigations officers who had been transferred into the PNC in early 1993 without having attended the new academy, Barrera and Avila agreed to transfer some of these members out of the agency and to send others to the police academy. Avila was the object of several armed attacks, possibly related to his commitment to a more professional public security force. One encouraging sign of change was that unlike security forces in the past, the PNC went to great lengths to punish agents accused of violations and regularly made such cases known to the public.

Also addressing the problem of political violence in El Salvador was the Joint Group for the Investigation of Illegal Armed Groups with Political Motivation in El Salvador, known as the Grupo Conjunto. The group was established in December 1993 in response both to a recommendation of the United Nations-sponsored Truth Commission and to the upsurge in death-squad assassinations in late 1993.

After eight months of work, the Grupo Conjunto published its findings on July 28, reporting on violent conditions in four separate areas of El Salvador (Guazapa, Morazán, San Miguel and Usulután) as well as on four specific cases of murders and attacks. Contradicting the Cristiani administration's repeated denials of the existence of death squads, the Grupo Conjunto report described how the classic structures of the death squads had undergone a process of "mutation and atomization" in recent years and explained that political violence now "moves within and mimics the underworld of organized crime and delinquency." Finally, the Grupo Conjunto noted that some of these clandestine groups' activities, while not a part of official state policy, "are directed, supported, covered up or tolerated by members of the military and police institutions, and the judicial and municipal organs."

Although the information published by the Grupo Conjunto differed little in content or analysis from that released in ONUSAL's reports, the findings were important because they were well received by President Calderón Sol and some conservative sectors of society. Calling the group's work "patriotic," he pledged to carry out its recommendations, which included the creation of a special PNC unit to look into the cases cited, as well as the writing of new laws that would facilitate the prosecution of cases involving political violence or organized crime.

Another positive development in 1994 was the long-awaited selection in July of a new Supreme Court. All of the justices on the previous court had been asked to resign by the Truth Commission, a recommendation which was ignored. Nevertheless, it had so stigmatized the magistrates that not one was reelected.

The new justices were widely accepted as a great improvement, and immediately began to exercise the kind of independence and professionalism which the previous court lacked. Shortly after taking office, the new court appointed a competent director to the Institute of Legal Medicine, responsible for the judicial branch's forensic work.

The new court also began to tackle the problem of impunity in Salvadoran courts by implementing a review of all judges, which it hoped to complete by the end of 1994. In its eleventh report, released in July, ONUSAL found that between November 1992 and February 1994, in the seventy-five most serious cases of violations of the right to life, including arbitrary executions, attempted executions, and death threats, no one had been tried or sentenced. An important but incomplete list of constitutional reforms relating to the judicial system was approved by the outgoing Assembly on April 29 and was due to be ratified sometime during the current Assembly's three-year term. These reforms included expanded access to constitutional guarantees such as *habeas corpus* and invalidation of all extrajudicial confessions. In addition, pending legislative proposals for a new criminal code and criminal procedure code would outlaw extrajudicial confessions.

The dire situation of the country's prison system came to the forefront in 1993-94 as several riots broke out, resulting in dozens of deaths and injuries. ONUSAL provided mediation in all of these instances, in which prisoners generally demanded better prison conditions. The fact that some 80 percent of inmates had not been tried and sentenced, also contributed to the volatile situation. In response to this situation, the new Supreme Court proposed a review of the legal situation of all inmates and a new penitentiary law was brought up for consideration in the Assembly.

Finally, one of the most potentially destabilizing aspects of the post-war political situation involved the plight of demobilized military and security forces. In both July and September, former soldiers took over the Assembly building, in the second instance holding more than two dozen deputies hostage for over two days. In both cases, the assailants demanded indemnization they claimed was due them by the government for their service during the war. Both takeovers were resolved peacefully, and although no amnesty was granted, the government urged that no legal action be taken against those responsible. Some of the deputies held hostage filed charges anyway. Following the September episode, the government agreed to review each case individually and expand the possible number of beneficiaries to include some former civil defense members and others who were not previously eligible. Again ONUSAL played an important role as mediator.

The Right to Monitor

Despite some cases of intimidation and political violence, human rights groups generally felt few limitations in carrying out their activities in 1994.

ONUSAL continued to take complaints from citizens through its offices in Santa Ana, San Salvador, Chalatenango, San Vicente, San Miguel, and Usulután, although it planned to scale back significantly by the end of 1994 in preparation for a withdrawal early next year.

By mid-year, the human rights division of ONUSAL began a closer working relationship with the Office of the Human Rights Ombudsman, which had grown to eight regional offices. The ombudsman, a three-year post, which was due to come up for re-election in February 1995, improved its operations somewhat during 1994, but still lacked trained personnel, financial resources, and the confidence of the Salvadoran citizenry needed to do its job effectively.

U.S. Policy

The U.S. government continued to be supportive of the peace process in 1994. In addition to providing financial support for the work of Grupo Conjunto, the U.S. (along with Spain) was a major contributor to the National Civilian Police and the National Academy for Public Security, providing training and technical assistance as well as material resources. U.S. aid also helped resolve a potentially explosive problem early in the year by providing funds to the Land Bank, which was required to help resolve the transfer of properties in the former conflict zones.

In July, the U.S. Trade Representative removed El Salvador from the list of countries under examination for labor rights violations, allowing it to be fully eligible for trade benefits under the Generalized System of Preferences.

Addressing recent human rights violations, the State Department twice expressed concern about attacks on FMLN leader Deputy Nidia Díaz which occurred in February and May. The U.S. also, after some hesitation, pressed for the removal of PNC Deputy Director Peña Durán; although this position was slow in evolving due to the resistance of Peña's former benefactors in the Drug Enforcement Agency.

The Work of Human Rights Watch/Americas

In 1994, Human Rights Watch/Americas was principally concerned that human rights considerations should remain an integral part of the peace process. In pursuing this goal, we made clear our support of the human rights organizations working in the country. Human Rights Watch/Americas wrote a letter to U.N. Secretary-General Boutros Boutros-Ghali expressing support for the work done by ONUSAL and underscoring its continued importance. We also supported the work of the Grupo Conjunto by providing documentation on cases of human rights violations in the country.

Also important in maintaining the centrality of human rights in the transition process, Human Rights Watch/Americas continued focusing international public attention on current human rights violations. In March 1994, Human Rights Watch/Americas published a report on the eve of the elections which emphasized continuing human rights problems at a particularly critical juncture in El Salvador, underscoring the need for free and fair elections. We also continued to bring individual cases of human rights abuses to the attention of United States lawmakers in order to continue diplomatic pressure for change.

GUATEMALA

Human Rights Developments

The human rights situation in Guatemala deteriorated in several important respects during 1994, even while the promised installation of a United Nations verification mission raised hopes for significant improvement. The government and guerrillas made important human rights commitments with the signing of a comprehensive human rights accord on March 29, 1994, but then proceeded to violate these commitments flagrantly. And although the accord called for the establishment of a U.N. mission to monitor human rights "at the earliest possible date," the U.N. did not formally approve financing for the mission until September 1994, and the mission was not expected to be fully staffed and operational until late November.

The peace process created the impression that Guatemala is a society in transition, embodying hopes for an end to the cycle of human rights violations and impunity that had produced tens of thousands of disappearances and extrajudicial executions in the last three decades. Besides the human rights accord signed in March, the government and the URNG guerrillas also reached an agreement regarding the resettlement of refugees and displaced persons, and the establishment of a truth commission to document human rights violations and violations of the laws of war by both parties during the thirty years of armed conflict. Unlike the human rights accord, however, these last two agreements were designed to go into effect only upon the signing of a final accord between the two sides. Several difficult issues remained to be negotiated before the final accord would be reached, including indigenous rights, land reform, and the strengthening of civilian control over the military. Moreover, the record in 1994, in which the government shrank from all meaningful reforms that threatened the army's power, suggested that the signing of agreements might not in itself fundamentally change the human rights situation in Guatemala.

During the eight-month delay between the signing of the human rights accord and the establishment of the U.N. mission, human rights violations surged, yet the government showed no sign of undertaking serious efforts to investigate and prosecute those responsible. According to the statistics of the government's own human rights ombudsman, there were 109 extrajudicial executions and sixteen forced disappearances between the signing of the human rights accord on March 29 and the end of July. Press reports and statistics compiled by the Human Rights Office of the Archbishop of Guatemala also indicated a continued high level of killings in August and September. Meanwhile, a series of violent attacks and threats against judges known for their integrity and independence dimmed prospects for building an independent judiciary capable of prosecuting human rights violations, which is fundamental to bringing those violations to an end.

Also victims of violent attack were trade unionists, journalists, and human rights monitors. Violence against street children intensified, after a relative lull during the first months of the new government.

Much of the deterioration in the human rights situation could be traced to the government's retreat from the series of reforms undertaken shortly after the June 1993 inauguration of President Ramiro de León Carpio, the former human rights ombudsman. During his first months in office, de

León Carpio sought to bring Guatemala into compliance with the recommendations of U.N. Independent Expert Christian Tomuschat and his successor Mónica Pinto by thoroughly demilitarizing the National Police, and placing civilians committed to police reform in key positions; these efforts were, however, abandoned early in 1994. The sacking of reformist Interior Minister Arnoldo Ortiz Moscoso and National Police Director Mario René Cifuentes was followed by renewed infiltration of police ranks by elements connected to the army, an upsurge in police violence, and an end to what had been a brief period in which the police genuinely sought to investigate human rights abuses. Moreover, the October 14 murder of a high-ranking police officer, César Augusto Medina, prompted the new interior minister to suggest that several thousand members of the military be assigned to the police. If carried out, such a move would bury hopes for investigations into human rights violations and dramatically enhance the army's power.

Two cases spoke volumes about the change in behavior of the police since the reformers were ousted. One was the August attack by riot police on workers occupying the San Juan del Horizonte farm in Coatepeque. The second was the reaction of the police to the kidnapping of a National Police agent assigned to protect a judge whose life had been threatened.

On August 24, several hundred riot police stormed the San Juan del Horizonte farm to arrest workers who had occupied the property in a work protest. Although the government, through the executive branch human rights commission COPREDEH, claimed that heavily armed workers fired at the police, all independent investigations, including those by Human Rights Watch/ Americas, the Catholic church, and the human rights ombudsman (an independent government official elected by the Congress), concluded that the workers were not armed, except with machetes. During the assault, the riot police shot fifteen workers, savagely beating and kicking several of them as they lay injured on the ground. One of the workers, Basilio Guzmán Juárez, died on the farm, and another, Efraín Recinos Gómez, died en route to the hospital. A third worker, Diego Orozco García, was captured by the police and taken to an undisclosed location. His body was found the next day some sixty kilometers away with a gunshot wound and signs of torture. Two of the riot police were treated for minor injuries at the hospital in Coatepeque and three others in Guatemala City. No charges had been filed against police agents for this brutal attack as of this writing.

Not only was the attack notable for its brutality, it also demonstrated the government's sharp departure from practices developed during the first eight months of the de León Carpio government when Ortiz Moscoso was interior minister. Under Ortiz Moscoso, the Interior Ministry routinely invited the human rights ombudsman to send a representative to any police action with the potential for violence. The presence of the ombudsman was an important element in avoiding violence. As a result, there were no deaths during this kind of police action during Ortiz Moscoso's tenure. However, his successor, Danilo Parrinello Blanco, abandoned cooperation with the human rights ombudsman, a factor which undoubtedly contributed to the tragic events of August 24.

A second case that illustrated the changes in the police was the kidnapping of police agent Miguel Manolo Pacheco. Pacheco had been assigned to provide security for appeals court judge María Eugenia Villaseñor after she received several death threats. On the evening of August 29, Pacheco left the judge's house for what he expected to be a quick trip to a store nearby. As he approached the store, however, three armed men, two of them with the closely cropped hair typical of soldiers, grabbed him and forced him into the cab of a pickup truck. The men drove Pacheco around, beating him and interrogating him about the judge's activities as well as those of Helen Mack, sister of slain anthropologist Myrna Mack. When they released Pacheco, they warned him not to talk about his experience or they would kill him. They also told him to stay away from the judge's residence, because they were going to kill her and her roommate, Helen Mack's attorney.

Despite this serious threat to the life of a police agent for carrying out official police duties, the authorities did not open a serious investigation. Instead, they insisted that agent Pacheco was an epileptic, and most likely invented the story of his kidnapping out of embarrassment for having hurt himself in an epileptic seizure. Pacheco told Human Rights Watch/Americas that he does not suffer from epilepsy. His doctor confirmed this to the Archbishop's Human Rights Office.

Judge Villaseñor was known for her independence and integrity; she had been closely identified with the struggle for justice in the Myrna Mack case, which she handled at several points both as a district court judge and later from the appeals court. Villaseñor had also written a book about the courts' handling of the case. The kidnapping of her police bodyguard was most likely a warning to her and others pressing for prosecution of the intellectual authors of that crime.

In another notorious incident, gunmen shot dead Constitutional Court President Epaminondas González Dubón on April 1. Although the government interpreted the case as a common crime, this theory appeared highly unlikely. Attorney General Ramsés Cuestas told Human Rights Watch/Americas that the magistrate was killed by a gang who wanted to steal his car, but had no explanation for why the gang made no attempt to steal the car after killing the judge.

The Constitutional Court had several controversial cases pending at the time of González Dubón's slaying, including one involving an imminent criminal investigation into senior military officers thought to have ordered the September 1990 murder of anthropologist Myrna Mack, and another involving the extradition of a powerful ex-army officer wanted in the United States for cocaine trafficking. Shortly before González

Dubón was killed, the court had also ruled that changes in the electoral law proposed by the Congress were unconstitutional. Notwithstanding the highly controversial nature of the court's caseload, the attorney general's office failed to investigate the possibility that the murder was related to González Dubón's work on the court.

On August 20, Judge Elías Ogaldez, of the Chimaltenango district court, was gunned down execution-style outside the University of San Carlos in Guatemala City. He had recently ordered the detention of an army officer and a civil patrol chief in connection with two separate murder cases. Judge Yolanda Pérez Ruiz, also from the district court in Chimaltenango, consistently faced threats, harassment, and legal action after she sought to execute a writ of *habeas corpus* on behalf of a young man detained in the Chimaltenango military base in February.

Given the violent attacks on those judges who had the courage to make decisions that defied army interests, it was no surprise that there was only one prosecution in a human rights case during 1994, the conviction of a police officer for the murder of a student in Chiquimula. In other human rights cases, judges faced obstruction by the police and army. In several important cases, the police simply ignored the arrest warrants that judges issued for civil patrollers or police officers wanted for human rights violations. For example, the police continued to ignore the warrants for the arrest of eleven civil patrollers wanted for the murder in August 1993 of human rights activist Juan Chonay Pablo of Colotenango, even though the orders were issued in September 1993. Moreover, when the judge presiding over this case held a public hearing on charges against two civil patrollers who had been detained, the army brought dozens of civil patrollers to the courthouse in Huehuetenango to demonstrate for their freedom. The chief of staff of the armed forces stated in a letter to Human Rights Watch/Americas that the patrollers rented private vehicles to arrive at the demonstration. Nonetheless, witnesses saw the patrollers arrive in two army trucks. Not surprisingly, the judge freed the civil patrollers a few days later.

For their part, the guerrillas were responsible for several operations which violated the laws of war applicable to internal armed conflicts. On March 11, 1994, guerrillas fired on a truck filled with civilians on the road between Nebaj and Chajul in the northern Quiché department, injuring a nineteen-year-old boy. On August 22, guerrillas launched a surprise attack on the military base at Chupol, on the inter-American highway. In the attack, the rebels stopped civilian vehicles on the highway to block traffic and fired on several that refused to halt. One civilian was slain and several more wounded when the insurgents opened fire, according to the Human Rights Office of the Archbishop of Guatemala. Besides violating the applicable international laws of war, these attacks on civilians also violated the commitments made by the guerrillas in the March 29 human rights accord. Finally, the archbishop's office documented the September murder by the guerrillas of an army officer in Chimaltenango after his capture in violation of the absolute prohibition on attacks on captured combatants contained in Article 3 common to the Geneva Conventions.

The government, too, honored the human rights accord only in the breach. Among the commitments undertaken and then ignored by the government was the commitment to "combat any manifestation" of "clandestine security machinery." Yet the government made no effort to investigate the continued pattern of killings, abductions, threats and harassment of members of popular organizations, trade unionists, human rights monitors, and journalists, although many of these abuses were perpetuated by armed men in plainclothes, often driving vehicles with no license plates.

The government also vowed to cease using press-gang methods to round up youths for military service, and to end the discriminatory practice of recruiting exclusively indigenous or poor *ladino* (mixed race) youths in this forcible manner. During the months of May, June, and July, however, the army launched a massive recruitment campaign, rounding up hundreds of indigenous and poor ladino youths without previous citation or family notification, and disregarding completely required exemptions for those who were the sole support of their families or under draft age. After facing a hailstorm of criticism from human rights groups and the press for this abusive campaign, the defense minister, General Mario Enríquez Morales, admitted to "errors" in the recruitment process. The human rights ombudsman, Jorge Mario García Laguardia, obtained the release of 333 youths who had been illegally recruited, including 148 minors.

The repatriation of Guatemalan refugees from Mexican camps proceeded at a snail's pace due to governmental delays in facilitating land acquisition and credit. Approximately 5,900 refugees had returned as of November, and two thousand more were tentatively scheduled to return before the end of the year. Over 40,000 officially recognized refugees, and perhaps as many unrecognized, continued to face uncertainty in conflictive southern Mexico. Refugee communities and church sources reported ongoing tensions in return sites inside Guatemala, including army attempts to foment local opposition to returnees. One repatriate, Manuel Lopez, was found murdered on October 27 in Centro Veracruz in the Ixcán, and as of this writing, no official inquiry into the death had been undertaken.

The Right to Monitor

The persecution of human rights activists in Guatemala by the army and its agents since the formation of the first rights organization in 1984 has been so severe that a special section of the human rights accord signed by the government and guerrillas was dedicated to their protection. In the accord, the government committed itself to "take special measures to protect" human rights monitors; nonetheless, the army and civil patrols, as well as unidentified individuals, continued to persecute them with impunity. José Sucunú Pajol, an active member of the human rights group CERJ, disappeared on October 29 in Guatemala City. He had been repeatedly interrogated by civil patrollers and military commissioners about his human rights activism. On June 22, a leader of the Mutual Support Group (GAM), Guatemala's oldest human rights organization, Sara Poroj Vásquez, was stabbed and seriously wounded by unidentified men in the capital. Poroj, like other GAM leaders, had received death threats and come under surveillance after the group's office was raided by unidentified men in October 1993. In January and April, the commander of army troops stationed in Chel, a village in the municipality of Chajul, threatened to kill members of a human rights commission. Dozens of civil patrollers in San Pedro Jocopilas burst into a parish meeting of a local human rights commission on May 27, accusing the participants of engaging in guerrilla activities and threatening to kill them. Rosalina Tuyuc, the leader of the National Coordinating Committee of Widows of Guatemala, suffered several incidents of intimidation by the army, as did members of her family. On at least two occasions in 1994, army officials publicly accused Tuyuc of being a guerrilla commander, without offering any evidence to support the charge, but with the clear intention of intimidating her. Meanwhile, neighbors and family members of victims of disappearances committed in the early 1980s in villages near Rabinal faced threats and intimidation from the second in command of the Salamá army base after they helped a forensic team exhume the remains of hundreds of victims of army and civil patrol massacres in the area.

U.S. Policy

The United States was active in the so-called Group of Friends, six countries working to support the United Nations-mediated peace process in Guatemala, and as such was deeply involved in diplomatic efforts to get the military and guerrillas to sign a final accord. Certainly these efforts were important contributions to future improvements in the human rights situation. Nonetheless, at times,

the desire to keep the army committed to the peace process caused the Clinton administration to remain mute on human rights issues when its leadership would have been constructive. For example, the administration resisted calls from human rights groups to take a position on the establishment of a truth commission, a critical element in the effort to account for the horrendous human rights violations committed during thirty years of armed conflict. The administration refused to publicly condemn the army's disappearance after capture of Efraín Bámaca Velásquez, a guerrilla commander married to U.S. citizen Jennifer Harbury, even after she fasted for thirty-two days demanding an explanation of his fate. Similarly, late in the year, the administration appeared reluctant to support the renewal of the mandate of the U.N. independent expert on human rights, an issue due to be reconsidered in Geneva in early 1995.

The government of Guatemala was eager to end the mandate of the independent expert, who was named by the U.N. Human Rights Commission and was not part of the U.N.'s effort to mediate between the government and the guerrillas. It was, however, precisely that independence from the U.N.'s diplomatic efforts in Guatemala which made the expert's continued work so important. Although Guatemala was expected to have a large body of international monitors stationed in the country at least through 1995, those monitors would inevitably be less free to publicly denounce abuses and structural problems than would the independent expert. Because of the tremendous influence that the United States wields in the U.N. Human Rights Commission, the mandate of the independent expert was unlikely to be renewed without U.S. support.

U.S. military assistance had been suspended since December 1990 because of human rights abuses, but the administration announced in 1994 that approximately $4.6 million that had been frozen would be transferred to a "peace fund" once a final peace accord was signed, a move Human Rights Watch/Americas supported. Nonetheless, military training continued, as did joint exercises between the U.S. National Guard and the Guatemalan army. Those exercises boosted the image of the Guatemalan army in rural areas where its power remained excessive and where memories of the scorched-earth policies of the 1980s had not faded.

The administration also spent $36,000 providing military training to the army in fiscal year 1994; it requested $125,000 for fiscal year 1995. Human Rights Watch/ Americas urged the administration to use this continued assistance to the army, albeit limited to training and exercises, as a vehicle for raising human rights concerns, in particular regarding cases that directly involved the army. For example, we urged the administration to press the army regarding the failure of the military police to act on arrest warrants issued by the judge in the Colotenango case, described above, before agreeing to bring army officers to the U.S. for training in 1994. Although the U.S. Embassy told us that it had raised this case several times with army officials, the army still failed to act on these warrants, which had been issued more than a year previously against civil patrollers who worked directly with the army. Because diplomatic pressure was fruitless, we believe the Clinton administration should publicly condemn the army's obstruction of justice in this case.

In fiscal year 1994, the adminstration provided the de León Carpio government with $11.5 in economic support funds, which had been suspended because of human rights violations during the previous government, but were released as a sign of confidence in the new government's first steps. The administration requested $2 million dollars in this category of assistance in fiscal year 1995.

Meanwhile, a decision by the United States Trade Representative regarding lifting or extending the review of Guatemala's labor rights practices, a review that was mandated as a condition for benefits under the Generalized System of Preferences, was pending as of this writing. Human Rights Watch/Americas urged the administration to extend the review and thereby continue to pressure the government, because of persecution of trade unionists over the last few years, including the police assault on the workers at San Juan del Horizonte described above.

On the positive side, the U.S. Embassy remained accessible to human rights monitors and was quick to intercede privately with the authorities over specific cases of human rights abuse.

The Work of Human Rights Watch/Americas

Human Rights Watch/Americas sought through frequent visits and publications to take advantage of the unique opportunity offered by the inauguration of a former human rights ombudsman as president of Guatemala and by the continued peace negotiations, to encourage the government to address fundamental human rights issues. At the same time, we continued to press for action on individual cases by mobilizing interest in the U.S. Congress and by presenting cases to the Inter-American Commission on Human Rights of the Organization of American States.

In June, we issued a comprehensive report titled *Human Rights in Guatemala During President De León Carpio's First Year*. In September, we released the book in translation in Guatemala City. In November, we led a delegation pressing for an explanation of the fate of U.S. citizen Jennifer Harbury's disappeared husband, Efraín Bámaca Velásquez, described above.

Through the Inter-American Commission on Human Rights (IACHR), we successfully requested the Inter-American Court of Human Rights to issue an injunction requiring the government of Guatemala to protect several human rights activists and witnesses to the murder of Juan Chonay Pablo after they were threatened or physically attacked by civil patrollers in the Colotenango area. With the injunction, the level of intimidation dropped significantly. We also successfully lobbied the IACHR to press the government to protect the life and guarantee the freedom of expression of a Claretian priest, Father Daniel Vogt, who had been falsely accused of sedition and threatened with death or expulsion from his parish, and to protect the lives of witnesses in the case of Jorge Carpio Nicolle, murdered with three companions, by elements connected to the army in July 1993. In September, we formally asked the commission to submit the notorious "white van case" for trial at the Inter-American Court, a case that we had pressed through the inter-American system for over five years. The case involved the abduction, torture, and murder of university students by Treasury Police agents during the late 1980s.

In May, we publicly called for the release of four peasants who had spent ten months in pre-trial detention, falsely accused of the Carpio murder. Within days of our press release, the peasants were freed; weeks later, a group of civil patrollers and military commissioners who had been implicated in the crime were detained and charged. (They were later granted provisional liberty.)

In June, we wrote to U.S. Trade Representative Mickey Kantor calling for an extension of the review of labor rights practices in Guatemala; that review was extended for an additional three months.

HAITI

Human Rights Developments

Human rights violations in Haiti mounted in 1994 as the military regime increasingly turned to terror tactics in its effort to eliminate all vestiges of support for elected President Jean-Bertrand Aristide. During the first half of the year, as international efforts to restore democracy foundered, the army joined forces with paramilitary thugs in a marathon of gross human rights violations.

In May, the Clinton administration stepped up pressure on the regime through stiffer international sanctions and threaten-ing the use of force. In September, a last-minute agreement with the regime led to the unopposed occupation of Haiti by a U.S.-led multinational force. Within weeks, the coup leaders had stepped down and President Aristide returned on October 15. The U.S. deployment interrupted the regime's campaign of brutality, although violent incidents continued to occur.

Violations previously less common in Haiti emerged as patterns during the first months of the year. These included forced disappearances, rapes, and grotesque murders, crimes calculated to terrorize the population at large. These acts were increasingly directed against the relatives and neighbors of activists.

The army used armed civilian adjuncts, or *attachés*, to crush civil society. The army-backed paramilitary group calling itself the Front for the Advancement and Progress of Haiti (FRAPH) continued to be implicated in countless human rights crimes. Composed of well-armed neo-Duvalierists and attachés, FRAPH opened offices around the country and established informer networks in numerous communities, recruiting members through bribery and terror.

On December 27, 1993, FRAPH agents with police protection torched a section of Cité Soleil, a Port-au-Prince shantytown, killing at least thirty-six, and leaving thousands homeless. The massacre became the blueprint for systematic attacks on poor neighborhoods that, though indiscriminate in their choice of victims, comprised a broader strategy to neutralize opposition to the regime.

On April 23, the army and FRAPH massacred at least fifteen residents of Raboteau, a poor neighborhood of Gonaives that had already suffered numerous army incursions. Hundreds of residents fled the area in the aftermath of the massacre. Similar attacks in the vicinity of Le Borgne were reported, although the army prevented journalists and human rights activists from entering the besieged area. While the army typically justified these operations with the pretext that it was looking for weapons or routing suspected guerrillas, there was no evidence that the scores of victims of these assaults were guerrillas or were armed.

The United Nations/Organization of American States International Civilian Mission investigated over two hundred reports of extrajudicial executions from February to July, adding to the estimated death toll of 3,000-4,000 people since the September 1991 *coup d'etat*. More than fifty-three cases of forced disappearances were also reported. In most of these cases the victims never reappeared or were found dead, while victims found alive reported that they had been held at clandestine detention sites and tortured.

Rape became a frequent tool used with impunity by state agents to repress women activists and women relatives of activists. The U.N./OAS Mission documented sixty-six cases of politically motivated rape in the first half of 1994; other cases were documented by Human Rights Watch, the National Coalition for Haitian Refugees, and the Inter-American Commission on Human Rights. Victims fearing retaliation by their army-backed assailants, effectively were prevented from reporting the attacks, seeking medical attention, or obtaining legal redress.

The army and FRAPH conducted innumerable warrantless arrests of suspected activists whom they routinely tortured, and usually released only after extorting large sums of money from their families. Other detainees were imprisoned for indefinite periods, without charges, trial, or sentence. In Les Cayes, U.S. soldiers occupying the army barracks found approximately forty emaciated prisoners, some bearing marks of torture; one later died.

In May, the army installed former Supreme Court Justice Emile Jonaissant as *de facto* president, albeit unrecognized by the international community. In August, he declared a state of emergency which redundantly accorded sweeping powers to the military. Throughout the year basic freedoms were suppressed: journalists continued to be threatened and harassed, meetings were banned, and all expressions of opposition quelled.

An estimated 300,000 Haitians were forced into hiding under the coup regime. Soldiers and paramilitary agents frequently attacked the families of activists already in hiding. As one appalling indication of this practice, forty human rights violations against children were documented by the U.N./O.A.S. Mission during the first half of the year.

Thousands of Haitians continued to flee by sea. In May, de facto President Jonaissant ordered the army to deter boat departures, invoking an arguably illegal 1980 decree that prohibited "clandestine voyages." During the following months, hundreds of Haitians preparing to depart by sea were violently assaulted and arrested by the Haitian army.

The army rampage against Haitian civil society was halted by the U.S. intervention. Human rights violations continued, however, in the form of bloody attacks on exultant pro-Aristide demonstrators. Dozens of people were murdered by the Haitian army and FRAPH around the country during the first weeks of the occupation.

The Right To Monitor

To their credit, Haitian human rights monitors continued to document and report human rights violations, often at great personal risk. The murder of a prominent priest, and death threats received by members of the Haitian Human Rights Platform, signaled a recrudescence in repression that forced many of them into hiding in August.

The U.N./OAS International Civilian Mission returned to Haiti on January 31 for the first time since its 200-strong observer staff was evacuated in October 1993. Seventy mission observers in Port-au-Prince conducted thorough investigations of reported violations. Disappointingly, the United Nations failed to renew the mission's expired mandate, leaving it vulnerable to the whims of the army regime. In March, mission observers visiting Hinche were harassed and chased out of town by well-armed FRAPH members with army cooperation.

On July 11, Jonaissant ordered the mission to leave the country, which it did on July 13.

The Inter-American Commission on Human Rights made two trips to Haiti during the year. During its second visit in October, the commission urged the Haitian government to investigate past violations and hold the perpetrators accountable.

The Role of the International Community

The Clinton administration made a sharp reversal in Haiti policy midway through the year, transforming its failed approach of accommodating the military regime into a face-off that resulted in the September intervention. Throughout the year, however, the administration was consistent in failing to promote accountability for human rights violations or to insist on safeguards to prevent their recurrence.

During the first half of 1994, U.S. officials actively promoted a blanket amnesty for human rights violations committed since the coup, in addition to the amnesty for crimes associated with the coup itself already decreed by President Aristide. Even after the U.S.-led occupation of Haiti, the administration consistently failed to oppose a broad amnesty that would deny victims of human rights crimes their internationally guaranteed right to a legal remedy.

Until April, the administration responded to the army's failure to comply with the July 1993 Governors Island accord by pressing President Aristide to accept a power-sharing arrangement with elements of the military regime. During the first months of the year, U.S. Special Envoy Lawrence Pezzullo and U.N. Envoy Dante Caputo backed initiatives which required additional concessions by President Aristide without insisting that the coup leaders comply with their previous commitments.

Consistent with its pursuit of a power-sharing arrangement, the administration downplayed human rights abuses committed by the Haitian armed forces and its supporters, choosing not to condemn publicly serious abuses or to attribute responsibility for them to the military regime. The Haiti entry of the Department of State *Country Reports on Human Rights Practices for 1993*, released in February 1994, was characterized by serious omissions and errors of content and analysis. But by far the most damning manifestation was an April 12 confidential U.S. Embassy cablegram, signed by Ambassador William Swing, that was leaked to the press in early May. While admitting that violence was high, the embassy's cablegram exhibited more concern that Aristide supporters were using the human rights situation to their political advantage than for the victims of violations: "The Haitian Left manipulates and fabricates human rights abuses as a propaganda tool, wittingly or unwittingly assisted in this effort by human rights NGOs and by the ICM [U.N./OAS International Civilian Mission]." The cablegram provoked an international furor and deepened the schism between the embassy and Haitian and international human rights monitors that would prove difficult to bridge.

During the first half of the year, U.S. Coast Guard cutters continued to interdict and forcibly repatriate Haitians fleeing by sea, according them no prior hearing to determine their eligibility for recognition as refugees. Scores of these repatriates were detained by the Haitian army upon return. In at least two cases, a repatriated Haitian was assaulted in the presence of U.S. officials.

Asylum-seekers were referred to the U.S. Embassy's in-country processing program, which remained chronically unfair in processing claims. With an inexcusable lack of foresight, the U.S. allowed 2,000 approved refugees to become stranded for months in Haiti after the June suspension of commercial flights. In June, an approved refugee in hiding was kidnapped and left for dead by paramilitary attachés.

Clinton reversed his policy of forced repatriation in early May. In June, thousands of fleeing Haitians quickly overwhelmed an ill-conceived shipboard screening program. On July 6, all interdicted Haitians were interred at the U.S. naval base at Guantánamo Bay, Cuba, where they were offered a choice between voluntary repatriation or indefinite detention. While the new policy effectively ended the illegal practice of summary repatriation, it did little to uphold the right of Haitians to seek asylum. By late October, all but 6,000 of a total population of 20,000 detained since July had repatriated.

In April, with international efforts to restore democracy stymied and outrage over U.S. refugee policy and serious human rights violations mounting domestically, President Clinton overhauled his Haiti policy. Special Envoy Lawrence Pezzullo resigned in late April, and was replaced by a former congressman, United Negro College Fund president William Gray, III.

The U.S. also successfully sought a U.N. resolution upgrading the oil and arms embargo to a full-fledged trade embargo with stronger enforcement mechanisms. The lists of Haitian military and civilian coup supporters targeted for the freezing of assets and visa denials was expanded and adopted universally under the U.N. resolution.

On July 31, the U.N. Security Council passed Resolution 940, which invoked Chapter VII of the U.N. Charter and allowed the U.S. to form a multinational force "to use all necessary means to facilitate the departure from Haiti of the military leadership." The defiant Haitian military responded by levying charges of treason against President Aristide, while Lt. General Cédras made a show of training civilian militias who would attack the invading troops.

On September 13, the State Department rectified its past indifference by issuing a strong condemnation of human rights abuses in Haiti. Two days later, President Clinton addressed the nation with an emotional description of the regime's brutality as a principal rationale for invading Haiti. Of course, after months of misleading the U.S. public on human rights and tolerating unfounded CIA attacks on Aristide's fitness for the presidency, Clinton had difficulties convincing a skeptical Congress and public that restoring Aristide to Haiti merited risking the lives of U.S. soldiers.

In a last-ditch effort to avoid an un-popular hostile intervention, President Clinton authorized former President Jimmy Carter, Senator Sam Nunn, and General (Retired) Colin Powell to negotiate with the Haitian army's high command. On September 18, with war planes en route to Haiti, the Carter delegation produced an accord, signed by de facto president Emile Jonaissant, under which the top three coup leaders would step down by October 15, the Parliament would pass a general amnesty, and international sanctions would be lifted. U.N. Special Envoy Caputo resigned in protest over the lack of consultation during the last-minute negotiations.

The Carter agreement allowed U.S. army soldiers and marines to enter the "semi-permissive environment" of Haiti on September 19 without firing a single shot. The U.S. troops were then joined by personnel from other countries, constituting a 16,000 strong multinational force. The mission of the U.S.-led force was to create a "secure environment" which would enable the U.S. to turn the operation over to a U.N. peace-keeping force in early 1995.

While the Carter agreement provided for a bloodless entry into Haiti, U.S. forces were left in the position of working in cooperation with the Haitian army. On September 20, American soldiers watched Haitian police beat two men to death, prompting a reevaluation of the rules of engagement that enabled the troops to intervene to protect Haitian lives. On September 24, an altercation between U.S. soldiers and Haitian policemen in Cap Haitien left ten Haitian police dead and a U.S. army interpreter slightly wounded. Thereafter, a significant portion of the Haitian military, including police, simply deserted to avoid contending with the American troops and an accusing population.

Reluctant to become entangled in internal matters such as law enforcement, the Clinton administration unwisely looked to the Haitian army as the only institution capable of maintaining order pending the creation of a new civilian police force. Alarmingly, in spite of months of preparation, the

U.S. plan did not include adequate mechanisms for the meticulous screening of the army to purge it of human rights violators.

An all-military Haitian commission was charged with selecting 3,000 police recruits from its own ranks for an interim force. The army lists were then reviewed by the U.S. Embassy with information it had compiled on known human rights violators. This cursory screening process lacked essential investigative capability, transparency, and Haitian civilian involvement. Those selected received a six-day course from U.S. police trainers, were issued sidearms, and were redeployed under the same army command structure. These soldiers were expected either to qualify for admission into the new police acadamy or be retained as part of a smaller, reformed army. About 1,000 former refugees from Guantánamo also recruited for the interim force were likely to be unarmed and assigned to administrative duties.

While disarmament would be essential to ending the violence in the short and long term, the U.S. had no plans for the systematic recovery of weapons held by paramilitary groups. Although U.S. officials reported in November that 14,000 weapons had been recovered, many thousands remained in the hands of soldiers, attachés and FRAPH members still at large. The concentration of international troops in major cities and towns, moreover, had left vast rural areas unprotected.

· Press reports in October presented credible evidence of Central Intelligence Agency funding of notorious FRAPH leader Emmanuel Constant, which continued until early 1994. After the intervention, the U.S. maintained close contact with Constant, raising concerns about the U.S. commitment to dismantling the most vicious of the paramilitary groups.

Aristide supporters occasionally turned to violence in efforts to seek retribution for the abuses they had suffered at the hands of state agents. More often, however, they detained and disarmed alleged abusers and turned them over to the multi-national forces. The latter usually released them, to the frustration of their accusers. Clearly, one central requirement was U.S. support for lawful mechanisms to provide justice for serious crimes in part to prevent the recurrence of such crimes in the future and in part to prevent the spread of popular retaliatory violence.

On October 15, President Aristide returned to Haiti and was welcomed by jubilant crowds. After naming a new prime minister and government, he faced the enormous tasks of repairing the ravaged national economy, establishing a permanent, civilian police force answerable to civilian authority, and rehabilitating a crippled judiciary. He was also responsible for establishing a climate favorable to holding parliamentary and local government elections, tentatively scheduled for early in 1995. Most importantly, with financial and technical assistance of the international community, he would have to break the cycle of violence that has plagued Haiti for decades by assuring accountability for thousands of crimes committed under the coup regime.

The Work of Human Rights Watch/Americas

Human Rights Watch/Americas continued to work closely with the National Coalition for Haitian Refugees (NCHR) to press the Clinton administration to make accountability for human rights violations a centerpiece of its efforts to restore democracy to Haiti. A principal goal of our work was to articulate why the U.S. should not promote a broad amnesty excusing human rights crimes. A week after the U.S. intervention, a Human Rights Watch and NCHR delegation arrived in Haiti to raise the profile of accountability issues. Our concern about the amnesty then under consideration by the Haitian parliament was consistent with the views of broad sectors of Haitian society, and was reflected in the limited scope of the amnesty eventually passed.

We also advocated for the establishment of a truth commission, not as a substitute for legal justice, but as a mechanism to investigate past abuses and encourage national debate about the appropriate ways to establish justice and foster reconciliation.

We continued to insist on an end to the U.S. policy of forcibly repatriating Haitians fleeing by sea without a refugee status determination. The halting of summary repatriations in June was a partial victory, yet we continued to assert that the camp established at Guantánamo Bay should be only a temporary measure, and that no Haitian should be returned involuntarily without a full and fair hearing of his or her asylum claim.

We published three reports during the year based on a February mission to Haiti, and the ongoing research of Human Rights Watch's Americas division and Women's Rights Project, and the NCHR. Each of these reports documented the mounting repression and devastation of Haitian society during the first half of the year: *Terror Prevails in Haiti: Human Rights Violations and Failed Diplomacy* (Human Rights Watch and the NCHR, April 1994); *Rape in Haiti: A Weapon of Terror* (Human Rights Watch and the NCHR, July 1994); and *Fugitives from Injustice: The Crisis of Internal Displacement in Haiti* (Human Rights Watch, the NCHR and Jesuit Refugee Service/USA, August 1994).

Jean Claude Jean, the Secretary-General of the Haitian Human Rights Platform, a consortium of nine human rights groups, was invited to participate in Human Rights Watch's annual event honoring selected human rights monitors from around the world.

Throughout the year, we urged the administration to incorporate effective mechanisms for meticulous human rights screening of recruits for the interim and permanent police forces. A mission in late October focused on the issue of police and the dismantling of paramilitary structures of repression, both essential to the credibility of elections due to be held in early 1995, and to the success of Haiti's efforts to build a democracy from the ashes of a dictatorship.

HONDURAS

Human Rights Developments

The past year was one of transition for human rights in Honduras. The fair and free election of noted human rights defender, Carlos Roberto Reina, in November 1993 reaffirmed the stability of democratic processes in Honduras. The new administration made several efforts to guarantee constitutional rights and establish civilian authority over the security forces. Despite the Reina government's apparent interest in respecting human rights, violations continued to occur. Although a systematic campaign of abuse was not evident, forced disappearances, extrajudicial executions, and torture persisted. Illegal detention and abuse of authority by the police and military continued to be common practices, and justice remained a scarce commodity in the inefficient and corrupt criminal justice system.

On December 29, 1993, the national commissioner for human rights, Leo Valladares Lanza, presented *The Facts Speak for Themselves: The Preliminary Report on Disappearances of the National Commissioner for the Protection of Human Rights in Honduras*, a landmark report surveying the disappearances of over 180 Hondurans and foreigners during the 1980s. The Valladares report was the first government acknowledgement of official responsibility for the pattern of disappearances of the previous decade. It cited members of the Honduran military and Nicaraguan insurgents operating in Honduras as responsible for the disappearances, and noted that Argentine and U.S. intelligence units were instrumental in training those responsible. The report also included a controversial military document that named the current chief of the armed forces, General Luis Alonzo Discua, as the commander in 1984 of Battalion 3-16, the infamous army intelligence division condemned by the Inter-American Court on Human Rights for its heinous acts. The Reina government promised to prosecute those responsible, assigning investigation of these cases to the Public Ministry's newly created special prosecutor for human rights.

On June 11, the new administration moved to establish civilian control over the security forces by dissolving the military-run National Investigations Directorate (DNI), notorious for its human rights abuses, and replacing it with the civilian Department of Criminal Investigation (DIC). The DIC's lack of economic resources and qualified recruits, however, delayed its functioning until the end of 1994, leaving the country without an investigative police unit. Most former DNI detectives, including many implicated in human rights abuses, were incorporated directly into the main police force (Fuerzas de Seguridad Publica, FUSEP), which remained under military control. Although initial steps were also taken to transfer the merchant marine, immigration service, and anti-narcotics operations to civilian authority, little attention was devoted to removing FUSEP from military command and creating a professional, civilian force.

The armed forces not only retained control of the police, but also secured a sizable budget increase for 1995 and continued to promote former members of Battalion 3-16 implicated in disappearances and torture, despite public protest.

The Reina administration gained a moral victory with Congress's initial approval in May to suspend the military's brutal practice of forced recruitment, replacing obligatory service with a "voluntary, educational, social, humane, and democratic" corps. Recruitment had not yet been abolished by year's end, however, pending Congressional ratification in 1995. Meanwhile, the military announced its plans to conduct another nationwide campaign to conscript young men in October 1994, which most expected to be abusive.

Self-proclaimed death squads reappeared in 1994 for the first time in recent years. As common crime increased, FUSEP played an increasingly minor role in combating delinquency, in what some saw as a deliberate attempt to destabilize the Reina administration. In this context, vigilante groups, such as the self-styled Civilian Squadron to Execute Thieves, claimed responsibility for the assassinations of several suspected criminals.

A clandestine cemetery containing six bodies was discovered in Jacaleapa, El Paraíso, in March, corroborating the Valladares report's conclusions on the disappearances of the 1980s and the existence of makeshift graves. The government, at the insistence of human rights organizations, invited foreign forensic specialists to conduct the exhumation. Although initial speculation by Committee of Families of the Detained and Disappeared in Honduras (COFADEH) and others that the bodies corresponded to victims of the military's systematic campaign of disappearances during the 1980s proved incorrect, the bodies bore signs of torture and summary execution. General Discua admitted the existence of additional clandestine cemeteries along the Nicaraguan border, claiming that the victims were casualties of the *contra* war. Another cemetery was discovered in July in El Paraíso, Copán, near the Guatemala border. At the time of this report the exhumation process had been interrupted awaiting the arrival of international forensic experts.

The weakness, inefficiency, and corruption inherent in the criminal justice system remained the largest obstacles to establishing the rule of law in Honduras. The Honduran government in December 1993 created the Public Ministry under the guidance of a civilian attorney general and a corps of special prosecutors in the areas of human rights, consumers' rights, women's rights, children's rights, ethnic affairs, the environment, and anti-corruption efforts. The Public Ministry, however, remained in the organizational stages almost a year after its establishment, lacking economic resources and qualified lawyers to staff its offices. Rather than diminishing, the judicial backlog grew as the National Human Rights Commission and other human rights groups referred cases to the Public Ministry for investigation and prosecution.

Judicial reform was attempted including the replacement of incompetent, untrained judges (*jueces de paz*) with those educated in the law (*jueces de letras*); the removal of corrupt judges; and the depoliticization of the judiciary. Little progress, however, was actually made during the year.

Likewise, a commission of Supreme Court justices, members of congress, and attorneys from the Public Ministry undertook an overhaul of the antiquated Code of Criminal Procedure. A final draft of the reform, however, was unlikely to be presented to Congress for debate until the beginning of 1995, at the earliest. Human Rights Watch/Americas pressed for completion and ratification of the new legal code to improve the currently inefficient criminal justice system.

One of the most pervasive violations of basic human rights in Honduras was the blatant denial of justice for the thousands of prisoners trapped in the inefficient and unjust Honduran penal system. Of the more than 6,100 prisoners throughout the country, fewer than 700, or 12 percent, had been sentenced. Additionally, hundreds of prisoners had not even been registered or otherwise officially recognized.

Two exceptionally appalling cases demonstrated the deplorable inefficiency of the Honduran judicial system during 1994. Gustavo Adolfo Sierra, arrested in 1975 for theft and acquitted six months after his detention, spent seventeen years in prison because his release order (*carta de libertad*) was never processed. A government commission "discovered" him in April 1994 and subsequently secured his release. Hector Antonio Mendoza spent four years in the Central Penitentiary awaiting trial. Once his case was heard, he was deemed innocent of all charges. In the interim, Mendoza contracted the AIDS virus in prison.

The past year also saw developments in earlier cases of human rights violations. On February 2, 1994, the Inter-American Commission on Human Rights condemned Honduras for the 1988 double murder of Miguel Angel Pavón Salazar and Moisés Landaverde Recarte. (Pavón provided cru-

cial testimony to the Inter-American Court on Human Rights against Honduras in the reknowned *Angel Manfredo Velásquez* and *Saúl Godínez* trials.) The commission instructed the Honduran government to conduct a thorough and impartial investigation to resolve the case, which had languished in a San Pedro Sula court for five years. More than five years after its condemnation by the Inter-American Court in the *Velásquez* and *Godínez* cases, the Honduran government had still not paid the full indemnizations owed the victims' families.

The 1993 headline trial of the rape and murder of Riccy Mabel Martínez, in which Colonel Angel Castillo Maradiaga became the first high-ranking officer in Honduras convicted of human rights abuses, was revisited in 1994. On April 4, an appeals court, citing irregularities and "procedural errors," annulled Castillo Maradiaga's sixteen-year sentence. After reviewing the evidence and correcting inconsistencies, the lower court reconfirmed the original sentence. The case returned to the appeals court for a final review.

FUSEP was implicated in numerous cases of human rights violations in 1994, underscoring the need for a professionally trained, independent police force. The case of Nicaraguan Juan Pablo Laguna Cruz demonstrated that forced disappearance by security forces was not exclusively an historical phenomenon. On December 11, 1993, seven FUSEP and DNI agents kidnapped and murdered Laguna Cruz, who was carrying U.S. $15,900 in transit to El Salvador, in El Paraíso in southern Honduras. Following an intensive investigation carried out by the Committee for the Defense of Human Rights in Honduras (CODEH) that made their continued denial implausible, the police, on January 19, 1994, finally admitted complicity in the robbery and murder.

In another disturbing incident in Puerto Lempira, Gracias a Dios, FUSEP agents detained Fernando Flores Salgado on August 11, 1994, for possession of a firearm. The agents then proceeded to torture him for three days, disfiguring his face with acid and attempting to drown him in a river. The local district attorney managed to free Salgado and presented the case before a criminal court in Puerto Lempira, where it remained pending at the time of this writing.

The torture of minors, and their illegal detention with adults, continued throughout 1994. In November 1993, five DNI agents illegally detained and mistreated three minors — Denis David Osorto, Edwin Bonilla, and Iván Antonio Ponce — for eight days at DNI headquarters in Tegucigalpa. On July 10, 1994, eight members of FUSEP illegally imprisoned the minor Mario René Enamorado Lara with adults at the First Squadron police station in Tegucigalpa where he was beaten by both the police and other prisoners. In one week in October 1994, FUSEP illegally detained and tortured at least twelve minors, as young as ten years old, jailing them with adults for periods exceeding twenty-four hours.

The extrajudicial execution of two former activists in late 1993 suggested the resurgence of political assassinations aimed at members of the Honduran left. Roger David Torres Vásquez, alias "Raulito," an ex-guerrilla with the Cinchonero Popular Liberation Movement, was shot six times at point-blank range by an unidentified assailant in a bus in San Pedro Sula. Rigoberto Quezada Figueroa, a former member of the Honduran Communist Party, was shot eleven times by two unidentified gunmen while stopped at a traffic light in a San Pedro intersection. In both cases, the gunmen took no possessions, discounting robbery as a motive.

Attacks on the indigenous population continued in 1994, with the murders in February and May of Dionisio Martínez and Rutilio Matute, eyewitnesses in the 1991 murder of Xicaque leader, Vicente Matute. In July over 3,000 members of the Honduran indigenous communities marched on the capital Tegucigalpa to demand respect for their rights. Ethnic leaders signed an historic accord with President Reina which promised among other points the investigation of the murders of twenty-three indigenous leaders.

As of this writing, however, investigations had stalled and no one had been arrested for the Matute and Martínez murders, nor any of the previous cases.

The Right to Monitor

Human rights organizations in Honduras were permitted to organize legally and operate freely. The continued functioning and expansion of the official National Commission for Human Rights demonstrated the government's interest in human rights protection. Members from various human rights groups, however, suffered intimidation in 1993 and 1994. Beginning in October 1993, National Commissioner for Human Rights Leo Valladares Lanza, and his assistant, Jorge Valladares Valladares (no relation), received death threats on numerous occasions in connection with their work on *The Facts Speak for Themselves*. COFADEH was also targeted for intimidation. Death threats were left in the group's offices, its members were surreptitiously followed, and an unidentified man threatened Berta Oliva de Nativí, its director, and her children.

U.S. Policy

After the end of hostilities in the region in 1990-91, U.S. policy in Honduras shifted dramatically. While U.S. policy in the 1980s focused on bolstering the government through massive military aid, despite its flagrant human rights violations, policy in the 1990s sought to strengthen existing democratic institutions. Current goals include subordination of the military and police to civilian authority and promotion of trade and anti-narcotics programs. Unfortunately, in 1994 the Clinton administration was unable or unwilling to assign the resources necessary to achieve these goals.

Honduras, once a major aid recipient, had not received military assistance since 1992 and for fiscal year 1995, the only grant it received was $325,000 for military training. The country, however, has $15.2 million in residual military aid from previous fiscal years, of which $5.3 million remained unallocated, restricted by U.S. legislation pending payment of arrears to the International Monetary Fund and other foreign lending institutuions. Human Rights Watch/Americas recommended that the Clinton adminstration re-channel this military aid to the professionalization of the new Directorate of Civilian Investigation (DIC) and other democratic reforms.

Though largely accurate with regard to human rights abuses committed by Honduran officials, the State Department's *Country Report on Human Rights Practices for 1993* for Honduras had little on policy and grossly denied any implicit U.S. involvement in the disappearances of the 1980s. The report alleged that Dr. Valladares "included in his report [*The Facts Speak for Themselves*] unsubstantiated material from news articles from the 1980's which claimed that U.S. advisers...may have known of and tolerated the disappearances." This comment was particularly reprehensible given the wealth of available information, including statements by both Honduran and U.S. officials, documenting the close relationship between the U.S. and Battalion 3-16.

The U.S. Agency for International Development worked closely with the Supreme Court to train and replace incompetent judges and the Inspector General's office to help eliminate corruption. The Immigration and Naturalization Service and Drug Enforcement Agency also offered to advise and assist with the transfer of immigration and anti-narcotics operations to civilian authority. Perhaps most important, in conjunction with other U.S. government agencies, the International Criminal Investigative Training and Assistance Program (ICITAP), administered by the Department of Justice, conducted a series of three-week training sessions for the new DIC detectives.

The U.S. failed to support the Reina administration's reforms at a critical juncture. In addition to the ICITAP seminars, the Honduran government had requested further training and assistance for the new DIC. Had the State Department provided sufficent funding for the DIC it could have helped Honduras seize the unprecedented opportunity to replace the corrupt and abusive DNI with a professional unit under civilian authority.

Likewise, the administration dragged its feet on accountability. In December 1993, Human Rights Commissioner Valladares called on the Clinton administration to declassify documents that could help Honduras identify and prosecute those responsible for the disappearances reported in *The Facts Speak for Themselves*. Despite assurances that it would comply with Valladares's request, the administration delayed declassification of the documents, claiming that the financial burden would be too great.

The Work of
Human Rights Watch/Americas

Human Rights Watch/Americas sought to further the reform efforts of the current administration, while protesting continuing human rights abuses. In conjunction with the Center for Justice and International Law (CEJIL), Human Rights Watch/Americas continued to press the Honduran government to comply with the Inter-American Court on Human Rights's ruling that it pay the full indemnization owed the families of Angel Manfredo Velásquez and Saúl Godínez Cruz.

In July, Human Rights Watch/Americas released the English translation of the Valladares report, *The Facts Speak for Themselves*, published jointly with CEJIL. Human Rights Watch/Americas, in conjunction with Valladares, lobbied the Clinton administration to declassify documents that could help Honduras identify and prosecute those responsible for the disappearances of the 1980s. In addition, a Human Rights Watch/Americas researcher conducted a fact-finding mission to Honduras in September to monitor recent efforts to improve human rights in Honduras.

MEXICO

Human Rights Developments

In 1994, political killings, police abuse, interference with freedom of expression and association, and the widespread impunity of those responsible for these abuses continued to defeat government efforts to improve Mexico's human rights image. In his final year of office, President Carlos Salinas de Gortari was faced with an Indian rebellion in the southern state of Chiapas and the murder of his hand-picked candidate for the presidential succession.

Ordered at first to suppress the rebellion by force, the Mexican army was responsible for serious human rights violations, including extrajudicial executions and torture. The rebel force, the Zapatista Army of National Liberation (EZLN), occupied four towns in the Los Altos region in a surprise action on New Year's Day which coincided with Mexico's entry into the North American Free Trade Agreement (NAFTA). The EZLN issued a communiqué referring to NAFTA as a "death certificate for the Indian peoples of Mexico" and calling for President Salinas's immediate resignation. After twelve days of heavy fighting in which more than 200 people were killed, President Salinas abruptly reversed his policy and declared a unilateral cease-fire. From February 21 to March 2 his specially appointed envoy, Manuel Camacho Solís, held peace negotiations with EZLN leaders in the cathedral of San Cristóbal de las Casas. The talks resulted in the adoption of a thirty-two point package of reform measures which the EZLN presented to their communities; but on June 10, the EZLN announced that the communities had rejected the agreement, refusing to accept the government's proposals for national political reform. As of mid-November, peace negotiations had not resumed, but both the EZLN and the government had expressed interest in maintaining a dialogue.

Despite promises by President Salinas that human rights would be respected, efforts by the Federal Attorney General's office (PGR), and the military prosecutor to investigate alleged human rights abuses by the Mexican army during the twelve-day conflict were woefully insufficient. As of mid-November, no army personnel had been charged with offenses related to the suppression of the uprising. In several cases, investigations into possible army abuses had been closed and the army exonerated without adequate grounds.

A case in point concerned the summary execution on January 2 of five men, believed to be Zapatista soldiers, in the marketplace of Ocosingo. PGR scientists concluded from autopsy findings of four bodies that the victims had died at different times and that three of them had been killed with weapons which the Mexican army did not possess. Later, investigations carried out by forensic scientists from the government's National Human Rights Commission (CNDH) and the nongovernmental organization Physicians for Human Rights revealed that the PGR had autopsied the wrong bodies. The CNDH called on the Ministry of Defense and the PGR to re-investigate the deaths as probable summary executions. However, on April 7, the PGR announced that it had excluded the army from its inquiries, citing information that was both inconclusive and contradictory.

Although no state of emergency was in force limiting individual guarantees, the Mexican army detained scores of suspected rebel sympathizers, virtually all of them Indians, without warrant, held them in excess of the forty-eight-hour period permitted under the constitution, and interrogated them unlawfully on army premises. The ill-treatment to which detainees were subjected was corroborated by the CNDH in a bulletin published in February, and in June the agency said it had received seventy-six denunciations of torture.

Few, if any, of the seventy civilians charged under state or federal law in connection with the conflict appeared to have been guilty of participating in the uprising. Twenty-eight federal prisoners interviewed by Human Rights Watch/Americas on February 13 denied being Zapatistas and said they had been beaten and threatened into signing statements. On March 29 the twenty-one prisoners still in detention began a hunger strike to protest their innocence. Sixteen of them were released on April 18, after the CNDH sent recommendations to the PGR requesting that the charges against them be withdrawn.

President Salinas gave the CNDH a prominent role in monitoring respect for human rights during the conflict. By June 6, when the commission released its annual report, it had made no specific recommendations concerning extrajudicial executions or the abuse of force during the conflict. The sparse and selective information published by the CNDH only heightened a sense that it had passively acquiesced in attempts by the army and the PGR to cover up the abuses.

The CNDH's inability to enforce its recommendations also remained a major difficulty. In January, the CNDH published a report with the results of its investigation of 140 cases of human rights violations allegedly committed against members of the center-left opposition party, the Party of the Democratic Revolution (PRD) under the Salinas presidency. Recommendations were made in sixty-seven cases, including fifty-seven killings. Of these, the CNDH itself acknowledged that only eight recommendations had been implemented completely. The CNDH's effectiveness was further hampered by restrictions on its mandate, which barred it from investigating cases under court jurisdiction. According to figures published by the PRD in June, of 246 killings of PRD members between 1988 and 1994, no arrests had been made in three-fourths of the cases, either because they have been excluded from the CNDH's mandate or because CNDH recommendations had been ignored.

While President Salinas refused to negotiate global political issues directly with the EZLN, the rebel army's demands for political reforms, widely supported across the nation, galvanized new negotiations aimed at improving the conditions in which the August 21 presidential elections would

be held. Within a month of the outbreak, President Salinas appointed Jorge Carpizo, a noted reformer, as minister of government and titular president of the Federal Electoral Institute (IFE) and signed an electoral reform pact with seven opposition parties. The pact included measures for the appointment of electoral authorities by consensus between the political parties; the compilation of a new electoral registration roll subject to external audits; the issuing of photo-identity voting cards; equal access to media campaign coverage; a prohibition on the use of public resources for electioneering purposes; lower limits on campaign spending; and the appointment of a special prosecutor to investigate electoral crimes.

The elections, which were monitored for the first time ever by almost 1,000 international "visitors" as well as a plethora of Mexican nongovernmental organizations, brought the ruling Revolutionary Institutional Party (PRI) back for another six-year term with a 49 percent majority. Most observers agreed that the contest, with a record 78 percent turnout, was more competitive than earlier elections, despite being marred by numerous irregularities. In a sample of 1,758 polling stations conducted by the Civic Alliance, the largest nonpartisan monitoring group, the secrecy of the ballot was violated in 34 percent of the stations, and in 65 percent the names of some accredited voters were omitted from voter lists. Thousands of these citizens were unable to vote due to an insufficient number of ballots in the special booths installed for out-of-town voters, which were the only ones to which they had access. The Civic Alliance also reported widespread pressure on voters and misuse of the indelible ink used to prevent multiple voting. Apart from these election-day abuses, the heavy electronic media bias in favor of the PRI and the ruling party's enormous superiority in campaign resources were enormous obstacles to genuinely fair electoral competition. Despite these evident shortcomings, the elections were not followed by the widespread violence that had been widely predicted.

Assassinations, however, continued to blight Mexican political life. In contrast to previous years, the victims were not only militants of left-wing opposition parties, rural organizers, and social activists but prominent reformists within the ranks of the ruling PRI. They included PRI presidential candidate Luis Donaldo Colosio Murillo, who was murdered on March 23 at the close of a campaign rally in Tijuana, and the party's secretary general, José Francisco Ruiz Massieu, who was shot dead in his car in Mexico City on September 28.

Colosio's assassin, Mario Aburto Martínez, was convicted of murder and sentenced to forty-two years in prison, eight years less than the maximum penalty under Mexican law. At one point prior to the October verdict, Miguel Montes, the special prosecutor responsible for the case, declared that there had been a conspiracy to kill Colosio. When he reversed himself and then resigned in July, his conclusion that Aburto had acted alone was widely disbelieved. Public faith in the official view of the killing was further undermined by the fact that the trial proceedings took place in a federal prison, out of public view. Despite the conviction, investigations reportedly continued.

In the Ruiz Massieu case, the PGR accused a PRI member of the Chamber of Deputies, Manuel Muñoz Rocha, of contracting the killers. The PGR cited testimony from one of Muñoz Rocha's co-conspirators to the effect that Ruiz Massieu was on a list of top officials "condemned to death for supporting reforms to modernize the country politically." Muñoz Rocha, whose whereabouts were unknown, later contacted officials of the PGR to inform them that he had acted under threat from individuals linked to a powerful drug cartel. Links between drug traffickers and government officials had already been denounced in September by a former adviser to Jorge Carpizo, Eduardo Valle, who said in testimony to a multi-party commission in Washington that members of the Gulf Cartel had infiltrated Colosio's security team prior to his assassination.

Numerous incidents of violence and intimidation against PRD militants were reported before and after the elections. On July 29, for example, Antonio Zúñiga Díaz, a Federal District police officer assigned to protect PRD senator Porfirio Muñoz Ledo, was abducted by two men at gunpoint, beaten, and threatened. Muñoz's son Alejandro narrowly avoided the same fate, and the family's home was repeatedly broken into.

The Right to Monitor

The extensive network of Mexican nongovernmental human rights groups played a key monitoring role both in Chiapas and during the elections. While there were few reports of physical attacks on monitors, subtle and not-so-subtle tactics of intimidation and discreditation were extremely common. The Mexican National Network of Civil Organizations documented eighty-six illegal acts against nongovernmental organizations (NGOs) from April to July, ranging from arbitrary detention and surveillance to illegal searches of homes and offices.

Sections of the PRI-controlled press resorted frequently to scandal-mongering reports whose obvious purpose was to discredit church-based human rights and indigenous activist groups by falsely linking them with the Zapatistas. On April 21 the Mexican Jesuits filed a lawsuit against the daily newspaper *Summa*, which had claimed to have leaked intelligence files showing EZLN spokesman Marcos, who has never revealed his face in public, to be a Jesuit priest named Father Jerónimo Hernández. When the Jesuits produced proof to the contrary, the newspaper refused to publish a retraction, but countered with a different story: Marcos was in fact Father Eugenio Maurer, a sixty-six year-old Jesuit who walked with the help of a cane. On May 11, as defendants in the lawsuit were testifying before the Public Ministry, the Jesuits' provincial curia in Mexico City received three telephoned bomb threats. A month later, the Attorney General's office threw out the charges against *Summa*. The newspaper was owned by Televisa, the powerful television consortium known to be close to the PRI. The government remained silent on the accusations despite the reference to official intelligence documents. Similar articles in the magazines *Impacto* and *Novedades*, also citing confidential government information, accused a total of nineteen Chiapas human rights workers, journalists, and local NGO members of having links with the EZLN.

Bishop Samuel Ruiz of San Cristóbal de las Casas, who attended the peace talks as an observer, received frequent death threats during the year, and in June social activists belonging to several nongovernmental groups were subjected to surveillance and harassment by undercover military agents. The attacks included a raid by twenty armed men dressed in black on the Jesuit-run social assistance center for children in Palenque, which was run by Father Jerónimo Hernández.

Intimidation also extended to media workers considered sympathetic to the EZLN or the political opposition. The independent video producer, Canal 6 de Julio, set up in 1988 to provide an alternative to the regular television news fare, had its office broken into three times in January, shortly after it had made a documentary on the Chiapas conflict.

In June there were signs that the Ministry of Government was tightening up on immigration restrictions in order to remove foreign observers from the conflict area in Chiapas. A Peruvian doctor and a French nurse from Médecins du Monde, who had been volunteers at a church clinic in Altamirano, were expelled on a visa technicality, and long delays were being reported whenever foreign visitors had to pass military checkpoints.

U.S. Policy

The Clinton administration was caught off guard by the rebellion in Chiapas. Throughout the conflict, administration officials went out of their way to avoid criticizing the Mexican government, ignoring reports of the Mexican army's involvement in human rights violations. When questioned by the press on these abuses, State Department spokespersons stated for nearly a month that the U.S. Embassy in Mexico had no independent way of confirming the abuses, so was unable to condemn them. When President Salinas changed course and restrained his forces, U.S. officials praised the decision while continuing to avoid acknowledging human rights violations.

On January 25, Assistant Secretary of State Alexander Watson stated that the U.S. had "raised human rights at the very highest level from the outset of the crisis," but explained that "[the inquiry] was preemptive. It was not reacting to information." Despite the Mexican government's record of impunity, Watson stated that he had no reason to think the Mexican government would not investigate all of the allegations. Assistant Secretary of State for Democracy, Human Rights, and Labor John Shattuck was the first U.S. official to confirm that abuses had taken place, stating at a Congressional hearing on February 2 that the allegations, "must be fully and thoroughly investigated so that those responsible can be brought to justice under Mexican law." After that statement, however, Shattuck's department did not make any public statements criticizing the inadequate prosecution efforts undertaken by the government against members of the armed forces who committed abuses during the uprising.

The Clinton administration gave similar unqualified support to the Mexican government's electoral reform measures without publicly expressing any reservations about their adequacy or effectiveness. In addition to praising the reforms, the administration also urged members of Congress not to express reservations. For example, in a July 11, 1994 letter, the State Department's assistant secretary for legislative affairs urged members of Congress not to proceed with a draft resolution that merely "expressed the hope" that "the efforts of the government of Mexico, the major political parties and concerned members of civic society to reform the electoral process will be successful." The State Department argued that the resolution might be counterproductive by offending nationalist sensitivities.

The National Democratic Institute for International Affairs (NDI) and the International Republican Institute (IRI), both funded by the U.S. government, sent a ninety-person international delegation to observe the elections and issued a preliminary statement on their findings, which praised the elections but also contained several serious criticisms. Given the numerous doubts that were raised by national observers and international visitors, including these U.S. delegations, Human Rights Watch/Americas finds it unfortunate that the Clinton administration failed to express any of these concerns in public.

In one positive development, U.S. Ambassador to the Organization of American States (OAS) Harriet Babbitt testified in a July Congressional hearing that fraudulent elections in an OAS member state might constitute a sufficient "interruption" in the state's democratic political process to justify calling a meeting of the OAS Permanent Council, pursuant to OAS Resolution 1080. She later told reporters that this interpretation of Resolution 1080 would not exclude Mexico. Although Babbitt did not specifically refer to the Mexican elections in her written statement, her proposal for OAS review of any future elections marred by fraud would be invaluable.

Mexico received a relatively small amount of security assistance from the U.S., but it did purchase large amounts of U.S. weaponry through governmental and commercial channels. In fiscal year 1994, Mexico acquired an estimated $110 million in arms purchases from private U.S. companies and the government, and its fiscal year 1995 request was higher than for any other Latin American country. The U.S. continued to make or approve arms sales to Mexico, without considering the human rights situation, as required by law.

The Mexican government purchased millions of dollars worth of riot-control vehicles from U.S.-based manufacturers, presumably for post-election protest control, it was reported in April. The armored vehicles purchased featured water cannons and gun ports, with optional features such as side tanks for dyes that could be used to mark protest participants, remote-controlled television systems with recording capabilities, and a hydraulic barricade remover. When asked about the anti-riot equipment in early May, both Assistant Secretary for Inter-American Affairs Alexander Watson and U.S. Ambassador to Mexico James Jones said they had no information about the sales. Although the State Department later advised Human Rights Watch that export licenses were not required from their agency or from the Commerce Department in this case, we believe that administration knowledge of the sales provided an appropriate opportunity to encourage the Mexican government to use the equipment with restraint and in a manner consistent with the rights of peaceful demonstrators.

During the year, labor rights organizations attempted to utilize mechanisms in NAFTA's labor side agreement—one of the agreements negotiated in response to concerns raised by union leaders and others about the effects of the free trade accord—by filing complaints of alleged workers' rights violations in Mexico with the U.S. Department of Labor. After accepting two of the complaints for review, over the protests of Mexican officials and the corporations involved, the Department of Labor refused to pursue the complaints further in October. According to press reports, in defending its determination that the Mexican government had not denied workers the right to organize, the Labor Department conceded that, "The timing of the dismissals appears to coincide with organizing drives at the two plants." The Labor Secretary's decision to halt its inquiry led many rights activists and union leaders to repeat concerns about the weakness of the labor rights complaint mechanism and to question the Clinton administration's commitment to upholding basic labor rights standards. A third complaint was accepted for review and was pending as of mid-November.

The Work of
Human Rights Watch/Americas

For the first six months of the year Human Rights Watch/Americas devoted its resources to the human rights crisis in Chiapas. While supporting President Salinas's pacification efforts, our aim was to promote and publicize the quest for justice and accountability on behalf of the victims of human rights violations and their families. In February we published a report on the conflict, *Mexico: The New Year's Rebellion, Violations of Human Rights and Humanitarian Law during the Armed Revolt in Chiapas, Mexico.* On February 2, Human Rights Watch/Americas' Executive Director testified on the rebellion before the Congressional House Subcommittee on Western Hemisphere Affairs, urging members to push the Mexican government for a full investigation of human rights violations.

Human Rights Watch/Americas worked closely with Physicians for Human Rights (PHR) in undertaking a careful documentation of human rights violations committed by the Mexican army. The results of this investigation were published in December in a joint report titled *Mexico: Waiting for Justice in Chiapas.* This report criticized the investigations conducted by the PGR and the CNDH into extrajudicial executions and arbitrary killings committed by the army and included the results of field investigations conducted by PHR's own forensic anthropologists. It showed, alarmingly, that not a single killing or case of torture had been satisfactorily investigated.

In June a Human Rights Watch/Americas delegation visited Mexico City, and the states of Michoacán, Oaxaca, and Chiapas, to look into violations of political rights in the context of the election campaign. Our report *Mexico at the Cross Roads, Political Rights and the 1994 Presidential and Congressional Elections,* released a week before the election, concluded that despite recent electoral reforms political rights were still not fully or equally exercised in Mexico, and called for the government to introduce additional election-day safeguards, for the special prosecutor for electoral crimes to ensure impartiality in his investigations, and for the independence and security of human rights and election monitors to be strictly safeguarded.

PERU

Human Rights Developments

Although professing to uphold human rights, in practice the Peruvian government continued to treat the issue as well as its proponents with disdain. Among the human rights violations Human Rights Watch/Americas continued to monitor in 1994 were extrajudicial executions, disappearance, rape, torture, and a glaring lack of due process in the special courts set up to convict accused insurgents and drug traffickers. For its part, the Communist Party of Peru—the Shining Path—continued to murder opponents, bomb civilian targets, and threaten those it deemed enemies to its political goals. Although political violence decreased markedly since the beginning of the Shining Path's campaign to seize power in 1980, groups that monitor key indicators continued to register disturbing levels of violence perpetrated by both sides.

Since the April 5, 1992 "self-coup" by which elected president Alberto Fujimori took on dictatorial powers, the structure that encouraged and protected egregious abuses in the 1980s not only remained in place but was significantly reinforced. The government's power continued to rest on a military with unlimited license and a civilian bureaucracy willing to cover up military crimes. While the government attempted to modernize economic and trade policies, on human rights it remained entrenched in a model that considered these rights dispensable.

In 1994, recorded disappearances decreased in comparison to previous years, totalling eight for the first eight months of the year. This dramatic fall from last year's total of 168 was due largely to international pressure and clearly indicated the extent of government control over disappearances. None of the more than 4,000 registered disappearances were being seriously investigated, nor were the perpetrators being prosecuted. Over one-third of the country remained under emergency legislation and the *de facto* control of the military, which continued to violate human rights with impunity.

Military impunity was underscored in April when the army mounted a large-scale operation near Tingo María, Huánuco. In the preceding months, the prosecutor for human rights in the departments of Huánuco and Pasco had documented a series of disappearances, rapes, beatings, and threats by soldiers against the civilian population. After "Operation Aries" concluded, human rights groups documented extrajudicial executions, torture, rape, and the wanton destruction of homes by the army. Thirty-one of the thirty-seven extrajudicial executions recorded between January and October occurred during Operation Aries, according to the Coordinadora Nacional de Derechos Humanos.

Although the army claimed that they targeted Shining Path weapons caches, villagers and journalists who visited the area say that houses were attacked indiscriminately. The dead included the elderly and a two-year-old child. According to a formal report, fifteen soldiers gang-raped and killed a thirteen-year-old girl named Lourdes on April 8. The woman who testified about this incident also told the Coordinadora that soldiers knifed her husband to death and beheaded him. She said six others were also murdered. The woman testified that she was gang-raped but that her life was spared because the troops needed a guide.

Far from taking these reports seriously, the government moved to suppress them by naming as special prosecutor a retired soldier, who failed to visit key sites or direct adequate autopsies. Repeatedly, military authorities accused the International Committee of the Red Cross, denied access to the area, of collaborating with guerrillas. For its part, the pro-government majority in the Democratic Constituent Congress (CCD) passed a motion condemning the Coordinadora for "distributing negative reports about the behavior of the Armed Forces."

In 1994, civil patrols allied with the army continued to be implicated in killings. On February 12, friends of Hugo Zapata Gutiérrez, a teacher near Ulcumayo, Junín, who had been detained by patrol members at his home two months earlier, found his body with other burned remains in a gorge two hours from the village. According to one of the five patrol members accused of killing Zapata, they murdered suspected subversives on orders from the local base commander.

Perhaps the best-known example of government defiance of human rights was the continued cover-up in the "La Cantuta" case, which involved the disappearance of nine students and a professor from the Enrique Guzmán y Valle (La Cantuta) University in July 1992. After the bodies of some of the victims were discovered outside Lima in November 1993, pressure mounted to arrest the military and intelligence officers believed to have planned and carried out the murders. Although the exhumation was a travesty of scientific method, family members managed to identify some remains through clothing, dental work, and belongings, including a set of keys.

Once the bodies were identified, the military and its supporters abruptly stopped denying military involvement and instead rushed to pursue a case in military court. Threatened with a challenge from the civilian court already investigating the case, in February the government pushed through Decree Law 26291. The "Cantuta Law" changed the procedure for determining civilian or military jurisdiction, allowing the Supreme Court's simple majority of pro-Fujimori appointees to vote to send the case to a secret military tribunal. While historically the military has won in such jurisdictional disputes, the new law provided fail-safe insurance.

After a four-day procedure, nine of the eleven men accused were given sentences of between one and twenty years in military prison. Ranking officers believed to have planned and ordered the killings, however, were never charged and remained on active duty. According to subsequent press reports, the convicts, dubbed "Los Cantutos," were enjoying special privileges, including color television, a bar, daily family visits, regular salary payments, cellular telephones, and free run of the prison tennis and indoor soccer courts. The La Cantuta victims' family members enjoyed no such luxuries. After pressing for the return of their loved ones' remains, they were given ragged evaporated milk and computer boxes containing human bones, dirt, and trash.

The Cantuta Law, passed easily by the CCD's pro-Fujimori majority, revealed the lengths to which the highest levels of the Peruvian government would go, in defiance of international condemnation, to protect those implicated in abuses, so long as its victims were labeled enemies of the state. In protest, the Coordinadora withdrew from a dialogue with Peruvian government officials initiated at the request of the U.S. government.

The law also marked the third time that the CCD voted in flagrant violation of the constitution only four months after that document was approved by referendum. Because the judiciary remained weakened by the 1992 coup, which included mass firings of judges and the dissolution of the Constitutional Guarantees Tribunal, there was no legal body with the power to challenge laws that violated the constitution, and open manipulation by the executive continued to be the rule.

Fujimori's manipulation of the judicial system, indeed, made it a principal tool in government repression. Though the number of disappearances fell in 1994, for example, the number of arbitrary detentions skyrocketed. In the twenty months after the terrorism and treason laws were implemented in mid-1992, 7,667 people were arrested. Of that number, 1,219 individuals were sentenced by secret, or "faceless," military and civilian courts, more than double the number sen-tenced for similar crimes over the previous eleven years. Military courts convicted 95 percent of the treason cases brought before them, an indication that in these courts a defendant is guilty until proven innocent.

Many of those charged with terrorism during 1994 were arrested on the uncorroborated testimony of a single individual, called an *arrepentido*, who claimed to have participated in guerrilla activities and agreed to implicate others in exchange for a reduced sentence. After the CCD passed a new law guaranteeing arrepentidos special benefits, authorities began announcing mass surrenders. By mid-1994, 3,095 former members of the Shining Path and 1,044 former members of the Movimiento Revolucionario "Túpac Amaru" (MRTA) had been registered with the office of the special prosecutor for terrorism cases, an astonishing number given that estimates of the armed strength of these groups in previous years had never surpassed 5,000.

A closer look, furthermore, reveals that not a single person charged with terrorism or treason received a fair trial. Trials were conducted in secret by prosecutors, judge, and witnesses whose identities were never revealed; police were permitted to hold defendants for up to thirty days incommunicado, during which prisoners were regularly subjected to torture. Defendants remained in prison until a final verdict was rendered and confirmed by a higher court. In Iquitos, Loreto, 600 detainees staged a hunger strike in September to protest trial delays of up to three years.

Hundreds of innocent Peruvian were trapped by planted evidence, perjury, mistaken identities, personal vendettas, political witch hunts, and even typographical errors in court documents. Typical was the case of the couple Juan Carlos Chuchón Zea and Pelagia Salcedo Pizarro. Internal refugees who fled their Ayacucho village in 1982 because of threats from the Shining Path, they resettled in Lima. Their new life ended on December 11, 1992, when police broke into their house. Without the prosecutor required by law to be present, police beat them, forcing Salcedo to sign a declaration admitting that weapons planted in the home by the police were theirs. Chuchón refused to sign until he was taken to the headquarters of the anti-terrorism police (DINCOTE) and tortured with blows, electric shocks to the genitals, and death threats. Chuchón stated that before concluding their report, DINCOTE agents offered to let him go in exchange for money. Despite illegalities and the documented use of torture in the case, the couple was sentenced to thirty years in prison.

While it is true that some prisoners have regained their freedom after concerted campaigns by families, friends, and human rights groups, many others remained behind bars, forced to prove their innocence under a punitive and often life-threatening prison regime worse than that faced by convicted murderers. To this injustice, government authorities have responded with icy indifference. "Unfortunately, unfair arrests and irregularities...have occurred," agreed Special Prosecutor for Terrorism Cases Daniel Espichan in September. "But one can't cry over spilled milk."

Although a few of the most draconian measures were modified—including one restricting lawyers to representing only one client charged with terrorism or treason at a time and a ban on *habeas corpus* petitions—the essence of the legislation remained fundamentally abusive. While government officials have stated that the faceless court system should be reviewed, the government has taken no action. In October Peru's permanent representative before the OAS called for a modification of the treaties prohibiting an expansion of existing death penalties, heralding the start of a new campaign to impose this sentence, authorized by the new constitution, on Peruvians convicted of treason.

For its part, although much weakened and diminished in geographical scope, the Shining Path continued to violate the laws of war by murdering opponents, bombing civilian targets, and attacking and threatening its critics. After the arrest of Abimael Guzmán and other top leaders, the group apparently split into a faction that supports Guzmán's plan to negotiate a peace and a group of militants still in the field determined to continue their war.

The latter group was considered responsible for the April 16 massacre of eighteen people, including children and the elderly, in the village of Monterrico, Junín. In June, militants also killed David Chacaliaza García, a long-time activist in the Lima shantytown of Huaycán.

In December 1993, guerrillas put a bomb in the doorway of the Center for the Development and Study of Populations (CEPRODEP), a development group that worked with internal refugees in the southern highlands. Three months later, a similar dynamite blast was left at the home of conservative columnist Patricio Ricketts, killing a passerby and injuring Ricketts's daughter. The Shining Path was believed to be responsible for the March 30 bombing of the Yompián mall in Lima, which caused significant damage but no casualties.

The Right to Monitor

Underscoring the government's scorn for human rights was its continued failure to fund or empower the office of the Defensor del Pueblo, a governmental office created under the new constitution to investigate human rights violations. In an indication of the importance the government attaches to human rights, it shut down the office of the special attorney for human rights, though the defensor, its supposed replacement, had not yet been established.

Lawyers who represented the victims of human rights abuses continued to be harassed. On March 28, Heriberto Benítez Rivas, who represented some of the family members connected with the La Cantuta case, complied with a court order requiring him to give testimony on a matter related to the case. Previously, he had received threatening telephone calls from a member of the Judicial Police, who said that he would be arrested if he testified. After his court testimony, Benítez was arrested with an illegal warrant. He was released after spending twenty-four hours in jail.

Also in relation to the La Cantuta case, family members of General Rodolfo Robles, who left the country after publicly confirming details of the disappearance, murder, and army cover-up published in the press, continued to suffer harassment and telephone death threats. Four La Cantuta students who participated in a peaceful march to protest the killings were briefly detained in September.

Journalists were also the targets of threats for their human rights work. Mariano Paliza Mendoza, who hosts "Urgent Action," a radio program sponsored by the Association for Human Rights (APRODEH), which offers air time to human rights activists and the relatives of victims of violations, received several death threats beginning on March 25. The program also suffered persistent electronic interference with the apparent purpose of stopping its transmission.

U.S. Policy

With the urging of influential members of Congress, the U.S. government continued to press Peru on its dismal human rights record, particularly after the government rejected the recommendations on legal reform made by an international commission of jurists. The commission, known as the Goldman Commission for its chair, Robert K. Goldman, was established by the Clinton administration with the acquiescence of the Fujimori government in 1993. Its report analyzed the impact on judicial independence of legal changes imposed after Fujimori's "self-coup" and detailed violations of international legal standards represented by the new faceless courts.

Among the recommendations were that the government end military trials of civilians and any trials in which the defendant does not know the identity of the judge and prosecutor; the establishment of an honor council to review the work of district attorneys and judges and to fill vacancies left after Fujimori's purge of the judiciary; the repeal of the treason law, which violates the rights of civilians not to be tried by military courts; a review of all sentences handed down by military courts in cases of treason: and a revision of the definition of terrorism. which the commission determined was currently too broad and prone to erroneous interpretation.

When the commission traveled to Lima in December 1993 to present its conclusions. Justice Minister Fernando Vega Santa Gadea refused to meet with the members. Rather than address the content of the report. the government attacked the commission as a sign of Yankee interventionism and summarily rejected it.

In a statement released after the Cantuta Law was promulgated, the State Department lamented the regime's interference with judicial independence. However, according to the State Department, the U.S. would be satisfied by a "transparent and impartial trial in either jurisdiction," in essence accepting military courts for trials in human rights cases, one of the principal tools the army has used to protect its members from prosecution.

This mixed message seemed to typify a willingness among some to normalize a relationship damaged by the April 5 coup and human rights violations. Interested in supporting privatization, free trade, and anti-narcotics efforts, they have lobbied to make human rights secondary. Before the Cantuta Law was passed, Assistant Secretary of State for Inter-American Affairs Alexander Watson had signaled to human rights groups his interest in releasing $30 million in balance of payments funding which had been frozen because of the coup. Nonetheless, the funds were not released to the government because of the negative developments noted above.

State Department officials did, however, begin discussions with human rights organizations about the use of some of the suspended funds for support to the judiciary. This plan was modified, however, after Human Rights Watch/Americas and the Washington Office on Latin America together objected to any funding to a judiciary whose independence from the executive branch had not been restored after the 1992 coup. A new plan, using some $16 million of the suspended funds, was later agreed on which avoided our most significant objections. The program avoided balance of payments support, channeled funds instead to specific projects such as the Central Registry of Detainees, the Defensor del Pueblo, and the human rights and legal defense work of several nongovernmental organizations.

Meanwhile, the administration provided $8.4 million in anti-narcotics aid to the police, despite continuing human rights abuses attributed to them, including torture. For fiscal year 1995, the administration requested $18.5 million in "alternative development" assistance and additional police aid. Human Rights Watch/Americas continued strongly to oppose aid to the police so long as its agents continue to torture detainees with impunity.

The drug war assumed a low profile in U.S. policy circles. "Drug czar" Lee P. Brown urged Congress to increase funding to Peru and "find a way to separate our counternarcotics interests in Peru from other foreign policy interests..." In other words, Brown urged the Congress to suspend human rights concerns.

One bright spot was the inauguration in February of the Central Registry of Detainees, whose creation had been made a condition for some U.S. aid in 1991. The registry was intended to track all detentions and thereby deter disappearances. Although its establishment was long delayed, and its implementation limited initially to Lima, the registry and the drop in the reported number of disappearances described above testified to the influence the United States is able to exert over human rights issues in Peru, despite the Fujimori government's nationalistic rhetoric.

The Clinton administration continued to play an important role in defending the work of domestic human rights monitors. After the CCD denounced the Coordinadora for its criticism of Operation Aries, U.S. Ambassador Alvin Adams visited the Coordinadora. Also important, when Assis-

tant Secretary of State Watson visited Lima in January, his delegation's first stop was the Coordinadora office. These symbolic acts of support, as well as the administration's open door policy towards human rights groups, sent an important message to the Fujimori government that their work was important to U.S. policymakers.

The Work of
Human Rights Watch/Americas

Through reports, press releases, frequent communication over specific violations with the U.S. and Peruvian governments, and litigation through the inter-American system of human rights protection, Human Rights Watch/Americas continued to condemn human rights violations and violations of the laws of war by insurgents.

One principle concern of Human Rights Watch/Americas was to focus attention on the deplorable record of the Peruvian justice system. In early 1995, we plan to publish a report that examines the detention of innocent people held on terrorism and treason charges, the impunity with which military and police agents commit human rights violations, and so-called popular trials carried out by the Shining Path. We continued to bring cases to international attention by presenting them to the Inter-American Commission on Human Rights and the Inter-American Court. As noted above, our frequent dialogues with the Clinton administration shaped U.S. aid decisions; our efforts to bring to light Peru's policy of disappearances contributed to their reduction in number. Finally, pressure from Human Rights Watch/Americas on the Fujimori government on behalf of individuals wrongly prosecuted by the faceless courts helped bring about freedom for several of them.

VENEZUELA

Human Rights Developments

In 1992, Venezuela witnessed two military coup attempts; in 1993, President Carlos

Andrés Pérez left office under charges of misappropriating public funds; in 1994, events in Venezuela were perhaps less conspicuously dramatic, but not less serious. Facing the worst economic crisis in its history, marked by high inflation, economic contraction, and the collapse of several major banks, the Venezuelan government suspended six constitutional guarantees in late June, including those protecting fundamental rights to liberty and personal security. The suspension inaugurated a wave of human rights violations, adding to the abuses already occurring throughout the year.

In December 1993, Rafael Caldera, who had previously occupied the presidency from 1969 to 1974, was again elected president. Despite a few promising early measures, Caldera did not squarely confront any of the fundamental human rights problems facing the country, and his mid-1994 suspension of constitutional guarantees did much to exacerbate them.

The single bloodiest event of the year occurred even before Caldera's inauguration, however. On January 3, 1994, a massacre in the Sabaneta prison in Maracaibo left more than a hundred prison inmates dead and scores injured. For about two hours, as prison guards and members of the National Guard stationed at Sabaneta watched, a group of inmates from one section of the prison set fire to cellblocks in another section, and shot or stabbed inmates who managed to escape the inferno. A number of sources interviewed by Human Rights Watch after the attack suspected that the National Guard and prison personnel intentionally delayed restoring order, facilitating the massacre. Whether purposeful or simply negligent, the official failure to act constituted a breach of Venezuela's obligation under international and domestic law to protect prisoners' rights, most importantly, their right to life. ·

Despite the seriousness of the incident, subsequent developments in its judicial investigation discouraged hopes that those responsible would be held accountable for their conduct. Because the judge investigating the case had issued two arrest warrants

against members of the National Guard, out of a total of fifty-four warrants issued, a jurisdictional conflict arose between military and civilian tribunals. In September, the Supreme Court resolved the conflict in favor of military jurisdiction. Under this ruling, not only were the two National Guard members to be tried before a military court, so too were the fifty-two prisoners implicated in the massacre.

Unfortunately, the violence exhibited at Sabaneta, though unique in its severity, was indicative of a general pattern of violence in the Venezuelan prison system. During the first six months of 1994, approximately 400 prisoners died in prison violence. Even though the law clearly provides that prison authorities may be criminally liable for the death of persons under their custodianship, not a single prison official was prosecuted for these killings.

To some extent, those who administered the prisons might have been shielded by the view that the abuses occurring were not their responsibility, but were rather the predictable, even inevitable, result of the state of the prison system. During 1994, there were more than 28,000 prisoners cramped, under deplorable conditions, into a prison network designed to accommodate little more than half that number.

As the prison example illustrates, impunity for human rights violations remained the rule in Venezuela. Much of the responsibility for this state of affairs lay with the judicial system. Civilian courts were plagued by politicization, corruption, inefficiency, and lack of resources; military courts were not impartial and were subject to a high degree of executive control. Unsurprisingly, then, there was no significant progress in several important human rights cases, including one involving the mid-1993 massacre of sixteen members of the Yanomami tribe. In the most notorious past case, in fact, the guilty parties were exonerated by a military tribunal. That case, known as the El Amparo case, involved members of the since-disbanded CEJAP, a special military-police unit, who massacred fourteen fisherman in

1988 near El Amparo in southwestern Venezuela. While extended proceedings continued in the Venezuelan courts, where the case fell under military jurisdiction, an action was begun before the Inter-American Commission on Human Rights (IACHR). On January 15, 1994, the IACHR submitted the case to the Inter-American Court of Human Rights. The court granted Venezuela three months to comply with recommendations made by the commission: specifically, punish the guilty, indemnify the victims, and amend the Code of Military Justice.

Although Venezuela asked for and received an extension of time for compliance, when the extension finally expired in August Venezuela had not complied with any of the Commission's recommendations. Not only had the CEJAP agents not been punished, but on the contrary, they were absolved of all criminal liability by an *ad hoc* military court on August 12. This decision, the fruit of six years of proceedings in the Venezuelan courts, underscored fundamental weaknesses in the Venezuelan system of justice.

New human rights violations involving killings, torture, arbitrary detention, and the use of excessive police force, continued to occur in 1994. The assassination of Ildefonso Carmona, a prominent *campesino* leader, was one of the most notable such incidents. Carmona was shot in the face in front of his wife on November 26, 1993. Before his murder, he had complained before the state legislative assembly and the media that his life was being threatened by members of the Grupo de Tareas 1.2, a special military unit. The crime remained unsolved as of this writing.

In another disturbing incident, three members of the Yupka tribe were killed on February 2, 1994. Reportedly, when women of the tribe tried to block members of the Grupo de Tareas 1.2 from taking wood that they had cut, the military responded by firing indiscriminately. The investigation of this case stalled after March due to a jurisdictional dispute between military and civilian tribunals.

A wave of human rights abuses was introduced by the government's suspension of six basic constitutional guarantees on June 27, 1994. Citing the crisis of the financial system, exchange market instability, and speculation, President Caldera issued a decree suspending the protection against arbitrary searches, the protection against arbitrary arrest, the right of freedom of movement, the right to own private property, the guarantee against expropriation of property without compensation, and the right to freely engage in any legal economic activity. The suspension of guarantees was immediately criticized as unconstitutional: as the Venezuelan Program of Education and Action in Human Rights (PROVEA), a prominent local human rights group, noted, "None of the reasons given by the government demonstrates a threat to the constitutional fabric of the country, the only justification for decreeing restrictions to individual rights." In late July, the Congress rejected the administration's arguments in support of the suspension and voted to reinstate five of the six suspended guarantees.

The following day, President Caldera defied Congress and once again suspended the five restored rights. Equally troubling, he was extremely vague about how long this exceptional circumstance would last, prompting fears that the suspension might be prolonged indefinitely.

Although the government justified the curtailment of constitutional rights as necessary because of the economic crisis—specifically, the grave state of the financial system—it profited from the suspension to take aggressive actions far removed from the economic sphere. After the suspension, the police conducted numerous raids in poor urban areas of Caracas. Along with poor youths—a common target of these raids—social activists, popular leaders, and members of leftist political parties were searched and detained arbitrarily, and often held incommunicado. During the month of July, for example, PROVEA reported that 1,995 persons had been detained in police raids, of which only forty-two had been sought for the commission of crimes. In September, according to Inter Press Service, 1,600 police and military officers carried out an enormous raid of housing projects in a poor urban area west of Caracas, affecting some 10,000 families. Indeed, rather than a focused effort to resolve the economic crisis, it appeared that the suspension of guarantees facilitated an unrestricted fight against crime, urban violence, and social unrest.

The Right to Monitor

Several human rights monitoring and advocacy organizations worked in Venezuela during 1994. Their members generally operated with some degree of government cooperation and without physical danger, although some harassment occurred. In July, for example, PROVEA reported five harassment complaints, three of them from activists of the Red de Apoyo por la Justicia y la Paz, an organization that monitors and promotes human rights in Venezuela. According to a letter that the activists sent to Interior Minister Ramón Escovar Salom, the harassment, which included death threats, occurred after the activists appeared on radio and television programs discussing police and military involvement in human rights violations.

U.S. Policy

Because of its tradition of civilian government and, perhaps more significantly, its position as the second largest supplier of oil to the United States, Venezuela has long been considered an important U.S. ally. As the administration explained in presenting Congress with its security assistance request for fiscal year 1995, "Access to Venezuela's vast petroleum reserves remain[s] vital to our national security." Moreover, Venezuela was the second largest purchaser of U.S. goods in Latin America, and, specifically, the third largest purchaser of U.S. arms. U.S. policy was therefore driven by a strong interest in maintaining good relations with the Venezuelan government.

Nonetheless, in its *Country Reports on Human Rights Practices for 1993*, published in February 1994, the State Department sharply criticized Venezuela's poor human rights record. By contrast, the administration's immediate public reaction to abuses in 1994 was confined to President Clinton's statement, when the incoming Venezuelan ambassador presented his credentials, that the United States expected "an early return of the constitutional guarantees that have been suspended."

Notwithstanding the poor human rights record of the Venezuelan security forces, Venezuela continued to receive U.S. assistance through both the International Military Education and Training (IMET) program, by which military officers are trained in the United States, and the International Narcotics Matters (INM) program. Specifically, Venezuela received $200,000 in IMET assistance in fiscal year 1994, with $250,000 requested for fiscal year 1995. The level of anti-narcotics assistance was somewhat higher: $400,000 in fiscal year 1994 and $500,000 estimated for the following year. Human Rights Watch/Americas remained concerned that this funding had proven ineffective in promoting respect for human rights, one of the stated goals of the assistance programs.

The Work of Human Rights Watch/Americas

In conjunction with the Human Rights Watch Prison Project, we sent a fact-finding mission to Venezuela on January 11, 1994, in the immediate aftermath of the Sabaneta prison massacre. This mission led to the release of a report titled *Prison Massacre in Maracaibo,* which described the tragedy, outlinined our recommendations regarding investigation and prosecution, and urged that conditions at Sabaneta and other prisons be improved so that similar events might be prevented. Unfortunately, our recommendations were disregarded: neither prison conditions nor the problem of impunity was remedied to any discernible extent during 1994. The lack of improvement was especially disturbing given the notoriety of the problem.

Human Rights Watch/Americas also

wrote to President Caldera regarding the suspension of constitutional guarantees and ensuing human rights abuses, the February killing of three members of the Yupka tribe, and the death threats suffered by members of the Red de Apoyo.

HUMAN
RIGHTS
WATCH
/ ASIA

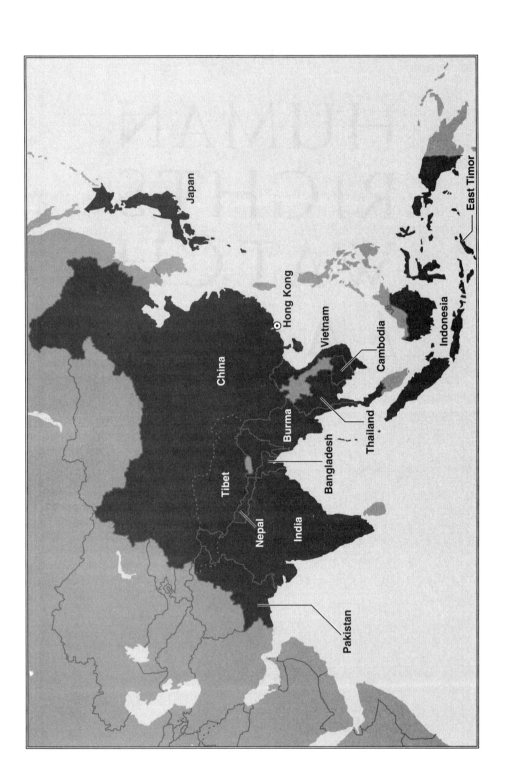

HUMAN RIGHTS WATCH

Japan

Hong Kong

China

Vietnam

Cambodia

East Timor

Indonesia

Thailand

Burma

Bangladesh

Tibet

Nepal

India

Pakistan

HUMAN RIGHTS WATCH/ASIA
OVERVIEW

Human Rights Developments

Asia continued to be a region of impressive economic growth rates and poor human rights, with China the outstanding example of both. If in 1993, in an effort to keep western critics at bay, some of the worst abusers in the region argued that Asia had its own definition of human rights, in 1994, they did not even have to make the argument: criticism eased anyway. One by one, developed countries pursued a policy of "commercial diplomacy," looking to China, Indonesia, India, Vietnam, and even Burma, for investment opportunities and good trade deals. Human rights concerns were inevitably pushed to the sidelines, and repressive governments could feel triumphant. With President Bill Clinton's decision in May to end the linkage between Most Favored Nation (MFN) trading status and human rights in China, use of trade conditionality and other forms of economic leverage seemed, for the moment, a thing of the past.

The problem was that the abuses did not go away—indeed, in some cases, the easing of international pressure seemed to generate more. Developments in China, Indonesia, and India were illustrative.

In China, at least nineteen activists were arrested for peaceful activities between March and December 1994, including Wei Jingsheng, China's most famous prisoner. After serving over fourteen years in prison for having advocated democratic change in China through a series of posters and mimeographed journals, Wei had been released in September 1993 and proceeded almost single-handedly to revive the pro-democracy movement in China. He wrote articles, gave interviews and met diplomats, all of which, according to Chinese authorities, violated the terms of his parole. On February 27, 1994, he met with U.S. Assistant Secretary of State for Democracy, Human Rights and Labor John Shattuck, much to the Chinese government's anger, and in April, he and his

assistant, Tong Yi, were detained. Tong Yi was later tried on a spurious criminal charge; as of mid-November, Wei Jingsheng remained in untried detention in an unknown location.

There were no significant releases of political prisoners between May and mid-November, when eight people were paroled on the eve of President Clinton's meeting with Jiang Zemin at the November 1994 summit meeting of the Asia-Pacific Economic Cooperation (APEC) forum in Jakarta, Indonesia. The paroles were offset, however, by the secret trial of Chinese journalist Gao Yu, who on November 10 was given a six-year sentence for "leaking state secrets" for having written an article based on a copy she had obtained of a secret speech by Chinese President Jiang Zemin. Gao Yu's family was not informed of the trial until after it was over, and she had no legal counsel. She had been arrested in October 1993, one day before she was to leave for the United States to begin a fellowship.

Negotiations over access to Chinese prisons by humanitarian organizations ground to a halt after President Clinton's unconditional renewal of MFN status became certain, and violations of China's own criminal procedure code seemed to increase.

Human rights abuses in Tibet continued, with thirteen monks and nuns arrested in February and March in and around Lhasa, the Tibetan capital, for organizing peaceful protests. In May, Chinese authorities began a campaign to ban the display of photographs of the Dalai Lama.

In Indonesia, where the threat of American trade sanctions because of worker rights violations was effectively ended in February, the government had no hesitation in putting independent labor organizers on trial weeks before President Clinton and his trade representative arrived in Jakarta for an APEC summit. Mochtar Pakpahan, leader of the Prosperous Workers Union of Indonesia, an independent labor union, was sentenced to three years in prison on November 7 on charges of inciting labor unrest in Medan, North Sumatra in April. Mr. Pakpahan was not in Medan at the time of the unrest.

The APEC meeting triggered a series of harsh measures by the Indonesian government to prevent any signs of dissent or unrest. These included curbs on the press, surveillance of human rights activists, harassment of outspoken academics and an anti-crime campaign that resulted in dozens of extrajudicial executions.

In India, deaths in custody in Kashmir took a sharp upward swing after international criticism became more muted. Police abuses continued in Punjab, despite the crushing of the militant Sikh opposition. Indeed, the continuing abuse was a direct legacy of the extrajudicial methods, including many disappearances and executions, used to curb militant violence. Indian officials, particularly at the state level, continued to use special security laws such as the Terrorist and Disruptive Activities act, usually known as TADA, to arrest and detain suspected members of armed opposition groups or members of particular communities. In the state of Gujarat, Muslims were disproportionately arrested under TADA, for example.

Many Asian human rights groups and other nongovernmental organizations (NGOs), from Sri Lanka to Thailand, expressed cynicism over the eagerness of Western governments to buy into the miracle economies of Asia, particularly when they themselves were feeling more heat. In Bangladesh, NGOs came under physical attack from religious extremists, and the government made little effort to investigate or prosecute the perpetrators. In Indonesia, a draconian draft presidential decree on NGOs was threatening to drastically increase government control over their activities and give broad new grounds for dissolution. In China, new state security regulations signed into law in June widened the basis for restricting peaceful dissent and independent organizing.

Intraregional concerns took on a new prominence during the year. This was particularly true of the countries of ASEAN, the Association of Southeast Asian nations: Brunei, Indonesia, Malaysia, the Philippines, Singapore, and Thailand. A theory of "ASEAN solidarity" was propounded to mean that each ASEAN country would try to prevent activities disliked by another from taking place on its soil. Thus, Indonesia bullied first the Philippines, then Malaysia and finally Thailand to stop conferences or demonstrations on East Timor from being held in those countries. The Asia-Pacific Conference on East Timor in Manila went ahead in May, but some foreign participants were denied visas. In July, the Thai government put eleven East Timor activists on a blacklist and deported three others who were in Thailand for a conference on human rights in East Timor and Burma. In the case of the Manila meeting, the Indonesian government used economic sanctions, including canceling joint ventures, to try to halt the conference. In September, Malaysia persuaded Thailand to arrest a religious activist whom it accused of "deviating" from Islam. The man was deported and immediately arrested under Malaysia's abusive Internal Security Act; he was released in November but two of his followers remained in detention. The actions of both the bullying and the bullied governments sparked widespread protests from NGOs in the region.

At the same time that governments of the region were colluding in human rights abuses, they were also having increasing problems with the way neighboring governments treated their own nationals, particularly workers. Labor shortages in the more developed countries of the region exerted a strong pull on workers from poor countries: some 200,000 to 400,000 Burmese, for example, were working in Thailand, while Thai workers went to Taiwan, Korea, and Japan. Indonesians constituted most of the 430,000 legal and 200,000 illegal foreign workers in Malaysia, and Filipina domestic workers could be found in Taiwan, Singapore, Malaysia, and Hong Kong. When Malaysia arrested over 1,000 Filipina maids in March on suspicion of prostitution, the Philippines government was furious. When the Japanese government imprisoned trafficked Thai women as illegal immigrants, Thailand requested that they not be considered criminals and that they be given safe passage home, even though its own officials were actively involved in the trafficking into Thailand of Burmese women and girls. China was upset at the treatment of Chinese workers in a Japanese-owned factory in Dalian, and Korean managers at joint ventures in Indonesia were singled out for criticism by Indonesian labor officials.

Worker rights continued to be one of the major issues for Asia, leading to over 10,000 strikes and work stoppages in China in 1993 by the government's own admission, and to tens of thousands of workers out on the streets of Medan, North Sumatra in April 1994. Wages and working conditions were usually key issues, but so was the freedom to organize to present demands for improvements. Vietnam gave workers the right to strike, but the new labor code denied that right to those in state-owned factories or private firms deemed essential to the economy and security. Many Asian governments were creating a pressure cooker by keeping tight controls on freedom of association and allowing worker grievances to build up.

The Right to Monitor

Human rights monitoring from within the country was not possible in North Korea, Burma or Brunei and extremely restricted in Singapore, China, and Vietnam. In Burma, a former UNICEF employee was sentenced to fifteen years in prison for providing information to foreign embassies and media. Chinese human rights activists were particularly targeted after it became clear that international pressure was evaporating. The best-known of those activists, Wei Jingsheng, was detained on April 1 and remained in custody as of this writing. Elsewhere, human rights organizations were subjected to harassment if they probed too deeply into sensitive subjects, but were able to operate nevertheless. No restrictions were placed on NGOs in Japan or Hong Kong, and there were few restrictions in Thailand.

One positive development in the region was the development of national institutions for human rights monitoring, even when the institutions created were less than fully independent. The Indonesian national human rights commission set up by presidential decree in June 1993 began functioning that December. By the end of 1994, it had proved to be more independent than expected, even if it seemed to be better at dispute arbitration than investigation. It had no power to compel testimony. A slightly stronger commission set up in India proved also to be better than human rights activists feared, and showed a willingness to take on some of the country's most controversial issues, like Kashmir. The human rights commission of the National Assembly in Cambodia was active in investigating complaints and in raising human rights issues related to proposed legislation. A bill to set up a human rights commission was pending in Thailand at the end of the year.

Asian governments made increasing use of the specialized human rights mechanisms of the United Nations. In July, the U.N.'s special rapporteur on summary and arbitrary executions visited East Timor, and the working group on arbitrary detention visited Vietnam for three weeks in November. The special rapporteur on religious intolerance was scheduled to visit China, also in November.

The Role of the
International Community

As noted above, virtually all donor countries rushed to board the economic bandwagon in Asia. The U.S., in particular, lost credibility as a human rights advocate with the delinkage of MFN and human rights in China after two years of strong rhetoric. The "comprehensive engagement" of the United States in China was matched by Australian Foreign Minister Gareth Evans's "principled pragmatism" toward Burma. The European Union, for its part, moved toward "equal partnership" with the countries of ASEAN. In all cases, the move was away from criticism and toward engagement, as if the two were mutually exclusive.

Japan's human rights diplomacy continued to evolve slowly, conditioned largely by overriding economic and political interests. Thus, Tokyo was more energetic in applying its principles for allocating overseas aid (Official Development Assistance or ODA) outside of Asia—for example, in Haiti and Nigeria—than in China or Indonesia.

There were moves in the United States to involve the private sector in human rights protection through the adoption of a voluntary set of principles for corporations. The White House took the lead in formulating those principles after President Clinton made his decision on MFN. But the principles, which were initially expected to relate to companies operating in China, were reportedly broadened to become more generic, and as of November, it was unclear whether the White House formulation would turn American businesses into a more pro-active force on behalf of human rights.

The Work of
Human Rights Watch/Asia

Human Rights Watch/Asia focused on several key countries of the region: Burma, Cambodia, China, Indonesia, Japan and India. Additional research and monitoring took place on Nepal, Pakistan, Hong Kong, Vietnam, South Korea, Thailand and the Philippines.

In terms of thematic issues, political imprisonment, worker rights and the trafficking of women were high priorities, as were human rights abuses associated with internal strife or conflict, such as Kashmir.

Human Rights Watch/Asia issued three book-length reports during the year, including *Detained in China and Tibet,* a 688-page directory of political and religious prisoners in China, the most comprehensive account of arbitrary detention ever published on post-Cultural Revolution China. It also published sixteen short reports, nine of them on China.

In advocacy, particular attention was paid to pressing the U.S. and Japanese gov-ernments to use their leverage in Asia, and to engaging the American corporate sector in a dialogue on human rights, with particular attention to China, Vietnam, and Indonesia. The World Bank and World Bank-chaired donor meetings were also the focus of advocacy efforts, as were major regional meetings, such as the November APEC summit in Jakarta.

In several countries, most notably Cambodia, Human Rights Watch/Asia staff provided critical commentary on proposed laws and directives, pointing out those sections that were inimical to human rights and in some cases, suggesting alternative language.

Human Rights Watch/Asia staff worked closely with NGOs in the region, exchanging information, sharing skills, and undertaking coordinated advocacy efforts where possible. A report issued in December 1993, *A Modern Form of Slavery: Trafficking of Burmese Girls and Women into Brothels in Thailand,* provided an opportunity to work with Thai NGOs in evaluating the book's impact.

BANGLADESH

Human Rights Developments

The Bangladesh government failed to denounce, investigate or punish much of the widespread violence against women, and NGOs, and threats against writers and editors that occurred during the year, all linked to militant Islamic groups.

Some humanitarian agencies alleged that government officials were using threats and physical abuse to persuade thousands of ethnic Rohingya refugees from Arakan state in Burma to return home. The refugees had been living in camps in and around Cox's Bazar since 1991. Most of the returning refugees were interviewed by staff from the United Nations High Commissioner for Refugees (UNHCR), but the intimidation was reported to take place before the interviews. In May, a cyclone hit southern Bangladesh, leaving 100,000 refugees without shelter; in

July, humanitarian NGOs in the camps reported that the Bangladesh authorities were preventing a speedy rebuilding of the camps in order to "encourage" the refugees to return. In talks on August 12, 1994 in Cox's Bazar, the governments of Bangladesh and Burma agreed to a figure of 20,000 repatriations a month and by November, nearly 95,000 refugees had returned.

On June 30, the Jamaat-i-Islami, the country's largest religiously-based political party, called a strike *(hartal)* to demand an end to NGO activities. On that day, a clinic in Zakiganj run by the Bangladesh Women's Health Coalition was burned to the ground and an adjoining NGO's office was badly damaged. The clinic's medical officer, Dr. Sultan, narrowly escaped being burned alive. Arrests were made, but charges were dropped, reportedly after a call from the prime minister's office.

Two of the country's largest NGOs, the Bangladesh Rural Advancement Committee (BRAC) and the Grameen Bank, became particular targets, in part because their efforts to promote the development and empowerment of women and girls were considered "un-Islamic." In January, *fatwas* (edicts) were issued by local *imams* in the Sadar subdistrict of Kishorganj to prevent children from going to BRAC schools. Trees being grown by local women for silk production were cut down at the imams' instigation.

A number of writers and editors came under attack during the year, including Taslima Nasreen, thirty-one, a doctor-turned-writer whose novel *Lajja (Shame)*, a fictional account of a Hindu family's persecution by Muslims following the destruction of the Ayodhya mosque in 1992, was banned in Bangladesh in July 1993. Certain militant religious groups accused Nasreen of blasphemy and called for her execution; threats against her intensified in May 1994 after a Calcutta newspaper quoted her as having called for the Qur'an to be revised. The Bangladesh government issued a warrant for her arrest on June 4 on charges of having violated Section 295(a) of the penal code by acting with "deliberate and malicious intent"

to hurt the religious sentiments of the people of Bangladesh. The Jamaat-i-Islami continued to urge that she be hanged, and on June 10 a leading imam issued a fatwa offering a reward for her assassination. No one was charged in connection with these threats. Nasreen remained in hiding until August 3 when she turned herself in to authorities and was granted bail and leave to travel abroad by the High Court. On August 10, she arrived in Sweden.

The government failed to prosecute many cases of violence against women. As of November, no charges had been brought in the December 1992 murder of Nilufar Rashid. The case was portrayed by human rights organizations as an instance of dowry death, with Nilufar's husband the main suspect. The failure of the police to conduct a thorough investigation led to charges of suppression of evidence by order of Home Minister Abdul Matin Chowdury because of his close relationship with the suspect.

Women in Farhadnagar Union, Begumganj Thana, Chohelgachi Union, Jessore, and Kasba were verbally and physically attacked for allegedly committing adultery *(zina)*. Traditional village councils *(salish)* pronounced sentences ranging from public floggings and stoning, to forced marriage. Punishments were generally more severe in cases that involved pregnancy.

On July 29, in a positive move, Attorney General Aminul Huq warned that the enactment of a "blasphemy law," as advocated by the Jamaat-i-Islami, would constitute a contradiction of fundamental human rights and Islam and foster an atmosphere of religious intolerance and fear. Draft legislation, making acts which "defile" the Qur'an or the name of Prophet Muhammad criminal and punishable by death, had been introduced in 1992. The attorney general's statement emboldened others to speak out against the proposed law, but it remained pending at the end of the year.

Intervention by women's and human rights groups succeeded in getting the government to compensate victims of violence incited by fatwas and to initiate police inquiries and make arrests in some cases.

The Right to Monitor
The Bangladesh government imposed no restrictions on the right to monitor human rights, but the failure to prosecute violence against NGOs cast a pall over human rights work more generally. Father Richard W. Timm, a human rights activist who has worked extensively on land issues, child labor and abuses in the Chittagong Hill Tracts, was denied a visa renewal on December 31, 1993. He had worked in Bangladesh for over forty years, and the denial was believed linked to his human rights activism. He remained in Bangladesh, however, knowing that if he left the country, he would be unable to return.

The Role of the
International Community
Taslima Nasreen's plight drew an outpouring of international concern with quiet offers of asylum and expressions of dismay and outrage from governments around the world. Less attention was paid to the attacks on NGOs.

The international community paid scant attention to the repatriation of ethnic Rohingya refugees to Burma, despite allegations from human rights and humanitarian groups that some Bangladeshi government officials were intimidating them into going back. In late October, a group from the U.S. and British missions in Bangladesh visited the refugee camps at the invitation of the UNHCR. They reported "no evidence of systematic forced repatriation," but said they could not comment on the appropriateness of the program, since they were denied access to the Burma side of the border.

The Work of
Human Rights Watch/Asia
Until July, Human Rights Watch/Asia had restricted its work on Bangladesh to monitoring the situation of the Rohingya refugees from Burma. In July, however, on the eve of the nationwide strike called by Muslim militant groups, it issued a short report on the violence against NGOs, warning that if it were not addressed, human rights problems could worsen. Together with the Human Rights Watch Women's Rights Project, it also worked with members of Congress to raise concern about the case of Taslima Nasreen and gender-related violence in Bangladesh. At the end of the year, Human Rights Watch/Asia was in discussions with the Bangladesh government about a possible mission to the country.

BURMA
(MYANMAR)

Human Rights Developments
The State Law and Order Restoration Council (SLORC), a military body established as a temporary government in Burma after the pro-democracy uprising in 1988, continued to be responsible for forced labor, especially on infrastructure projects; arbitrary detention; torture; and denials of freedom of association, expression, and assembly. Fighting with armed ethnic groups along the Thai and Chinese borders continued to diminish, as the SLORC reached a cease-fire agreement with the Kachin Independence Organization in February and opened talks with others.

Nobel Laureate Aung San Suu Kyi, leader of the democratic opposition, remained under house arrest but for the first time since her detention in July 1989 was permitted to meet with visitors outside her family. On September 21, as the U.N. General Assembly opened in New York, she was allowed out of her house for a televised meeting with the chair and secretary-1 of the SLORC, Senior General Than Shwe and Lieutenant General Khin Nyunt. A second meeting took place on October 28.

Some seventy political prisoners were released during the year under SLORC Order 11/92, though there were no details of those released, and it was likely that at least some had served their full sentences.

The National Convention, the constitutional forum established by the SLORC in January 1993, continued with no clear end in sight. Members of political parties elected in May 1990 made up only 14 percent of the 700 delegates, the rest being hand-picked by the SLORC.

In September, some of the principles on which the constitution would be based were announced. Ethnic nationality was one. Burma is currently divided into seven states, named after the majority ethnic nationality in the area, and seven divisions where Burmans are the majority. Under the new constitution these states and divisions (renamed "regions") would have equal status, and smaller ethnic nationalities which previously had no representation in the legislature would be given self-administered zones or divisions if they made up more than 0.1 percent of the population in any one area. In cases where ethnic nationalities were already represented in a state, they would not be allowed further representation, regardless of the size of their population in other areas. This arrangement could lead to increased ethnic tension and discrimination.

The legislature would have two houses, a House of Representatives and a House of Nationalities. In both houses, representatives from the armed forces, the *Tatmadaw*, would have a quarter of the seats.

Apparently believing that these measures were not sufficient to ensure the military's hold on power, the SLORC created another mechanism of control, the Union Solidarity Development Association (USDA). Formed on September 5, 1993 to provide general assistance to the military and headed by civilian (but ex-military) members of the cabinet, it only became active in 1994. In January, mass USDA rallies were held across the country, which the SLORC claimed were attended by four million people, though western journalists present noted that the numbers were often less than half those claimed. Local residents and civil servants complained of being forced to join the rallies and become members of USDA.

Arrest and harassment of the political opposition continued. At least seven people were arrested in May when they stood to watch two foreigners who held aloft banners calling for the release of Aung San Suu Kyi. It is not known if they were later freed or tried. On July 8 and 11, seven people were arrested for distributing pamphlets calling for the release of Aung San Suu Kyi. Although their names are known, no details were available on their trials or sentences. In September, a former UNICEF employee, Khin Zaw Win, and four members of the National League for Democracy (NLD), the opposition party headed by Aung San Suu Kyi, were arrested for passing "fabricated news" to foreign media and embassies and distributing "documents of expatriate groups." On October 9, Khin Zaw Win was sentenced to fifteen years in prison, and San San Nwe, a well-known writer and NLD member, to ten years. The others were all sentenced to eight years. They were tried under the 1950 Emergency Provisions Act and the 1957 Unlawful Associations Act. Most political prisoners in Burma are held under these two laws.

Following the cease-fire agreement with the Kachin, the SLORC continued to push for similar agreements with other ethnic groups based on the Thai border, aided by pressure from Thai authorities. In May, the Karenni Nationalities Peoples Liberation Front signed an agreement, while a second Karenni faction, the National People's Party, resumed talks in October, having suspended them in January after a SLORC attack on their troops near Loikaw. On October 9, the Shan State National Liberation Army, a small group of ex-Communist Party rebels, also known as the Red Pa-O, signed an agreement.

The New Mon State Party (NMSP) began talks early in the year, but they were suspended in July, following an attack by the Tatmadaw on a Mon refugee camp. At the end of the year the Karen National Union (KNU) remained the only major nationality group with which the SLORC had not begun direct talks.

As these discussions continued, little

fighting was reported around the country, with the notable exception of the Shan state, where the SLORC launched a major offensive against drug warlord Khun Sa at the beginning of the year. In the course of that offensive, refugees arriving in Thailand in May claimed that up to 5,000 people from Keng Tung and Tachilek towns had been seized by the army to work as porters carrying ammunition and other supplies by the Burmese army. In mid-July the SLORC launched air strikes against Khun Sa's troops, in some instances targeting civilian villages alleged to be supporters of Khun Sa.

There was also fighting in Maungdaw Township, northern Arakan, between forces of the Rohingya Solidarity Organization and the Burmese army in late April. The RSO is one of two groups claiming to represent the 270,000 Muslims refugees who fled to Bangladesh in late 1991. The repatriation of these refugees continued through the year, and by November nearly 95,000 had gone back, amid charges that their return was involuntary. Under an agreement between the SLORC and the U.N. High Commissioner for Refugees, nine UNHCR staff arrived in Arakan state in April to oversee their "re-integration" and resettlement. Despite their presence, some refugees returned to Bangladesh claiming that abuses by the military in Arakan state continued.

Forced labor took place on a massive scale across the country. Journalists visiting Burma noted that people, including shackled prisoners, were forced to dredge the moat in Mandalay, Burma's second largest city. In Bassein in southern Burma, 30,000 villagers forced to build a new airport reportedly received no wages, food, or medical supplies, despite a cholera outbreak at the site in June.

The most widely publicized forced labor project was the construction of a railway line from Ye in the Mon State to Tavoy in Tenasserim Division, a distance of 110 miles. Refugees from the project who arrived in Thailand estimated that 50,000 people a day were being forced to work here, using crude tools to clear the forest and scrub-brush and construct high embankments. The SLORC insisted that these projects were undertaken by "volunteers" under a traditional system of *corvée* labor (a form of unpaid labor owed by peasants and serfs to feudal rulers).

The trafficking of women into sex slavery in Thailand and elsewhere in Asia continued to be a major problem. There was also a rise in prostitution inside Burma, as the government-promoted tourism industry tried to attract tourists through promoting the sexuality of young girls and women. In a speech to senior police officers, the secretary-1 of SLORC in March noted, "Illegal activities such as gambling and prostitution [are] on the rise...while brothels and disreputable houses [are] known to enjoy police protection."

The Right to Monitor

There are no indigenous human rights groups in Burma, and the right to form any association in Burma is severely restricted. Individuals who passed on human rights information to journalists or through embassies faced arrest, as in the case of Khin Zaw Win who had assisted the U.N. special rapporteur on Burma in 1992.

The U.N. special rapporteur, Professor Yozo Yokota, on his mission in November 1993 was allowed access to prisoners in detention for the first time, although one man, Dr. Aung Khin Sint, cut short the visit for fear of reprisals later. U.S. Representative Bill Richardson was also allowed to meet with five political prisoners, including Aung San Suu Kyi.

The International Committee of the Red Cross, which has been seeking access to political prisoners in Burma since 1989, continued its negotiations with the SLORC during the year.

The Role of the International Community

The international community continued to express its concern about persistent human rights abuses in Burma. In December 1993, the U.N. General Assembly passed a resolution by consensus urging the SLORC to restore democracy. It also called on the Secretary-General of the United Nations to assist in the implementation of the resolution. In October, talks were held between the secretary-general's office and the Burmese foreign minister.

The countries of ASEAN continued their policy of "constructive engagement" towards Burma, officially inviting the SLORC to the annual ASEAN ministerial meeting in Bangkok in July. Thailand, which sees itself as a center for regional development and already has extensive fishery and other economic deals with Burma, was supported in its overtures to Burma by Singapore, which signed trade and tourism development deals in Burma worth $465 million in 1993. In March the Singaporean prime minister, Goh Chok Tong, became the second head of state to visit Burma since the SLORC took power.

At the opening of the ASEAN meeting in July however, Thai Prime Minister Chuan Leekpai in private meetings with the Burmese foreign minister urged the SLORC to start a dialogue with Aung San Suu Kyi.

Even as ASEAN countries ventured a few mild criticisms of Burma, the west moved away from a policy of isolating the SLORC. Led by Australia and the European Union a new, pro-active policy of "critical dialogue" was adopted, intended to end the western isolation of Burma in favor of direct contact. As part of this new policy, Australian Foreign Minister Gareth Evans met with SLORC officials during the ASEAN meeting, and German, U.S., and U.K. officials went on missions to Rangoon in late October and early November.

On November 8, Japan announced it would be extending $10 million of aid for medical and humanitarian purposes. China continued to play an important role in Burma throughout the year. Arms shipments from China, including naval frigates, were reported in *Jane's Defense Weekly*, and trade between Burma and Yunnan Province alone rose by 26 percent in 1993 to U.S.$228 million, though the total trade between the two countries is estimated to be in the bil-

lions of dollars. China also granted millions of dollars' worth of soft loans, and was helping build new airports in Rangoon and Mandalay, roads from Yunnan to Mandalay, and several other smaller projects. Diplomatic ties were reinforced when China opened a consulate in Mandalay in August.

The U.S. remained the second largest investor after Thailand ($203 million, compared to Thailand's $210 million), despite the pull-out of the Amoco oil company from Burma in 1994. The Clinton administration, while maintaining a ban on any direct aid to SLORC, took the first tentative steps late in 1994 towards opening a dialogue, even as it continued its outspoken condemnation of Burma's human rights violations. However, implementation of an effective policy towards Burma during much of the year was hampered by internal divisions within the administration and the halting, disjointed efforts of a long-delayed White House review of Burma policy. Congress expressed frustration at the delays and made specific recommendations for U.S. actions.

President Clinton ordered a high-level review of Burma policy in mid-1993, but a formal discussion by the National Security Council did not take place until March 1994. A decision was made to endorse ongoing diplomatic efforts at the U.N., to press for appointment of a special envoy by the U.N. Secretary-General, and to continue quiet efforts to encourage restraint by some of Burma's arms suppliers. But decisions were deferred on some of the most controversial issues, such as economic sanctions and the role of U.S. investors, and no new significant policy initiatives were announced. In June, the administration told the House Foreign Affairs Committee that there were no plans to appoint an ambassador to Rangoon (the position has been vacant for four years). Divisions and debate within the government over how to deal with SLORC on the narcotics issue also continued throughout the year.

Despite the policy vacuum, the administration made *ad hoc* decisions in response to certain developments and opportunities. When Congressman Richardson was invited to Burma on February 14 for separate meetings with Khin Nyunt and Aung San Suu Kyi, he carried with him a letter to the Nobel laureate from President Clinton and closely coordinated his visit with the administration. Richardson urged SLORC to begin talks with Aung San Suu Kyi.

While the U.S. objected to Thailand's move to invite Burma to send an observer to the ASEAN post-ministerial conference, it did not try to block the decision. In advance of the ASEAN meeting, fifty-three members of the House and Senate wrote to Secretary of State Warren Christopher, urging the administration to call on ASEAN's member states to use their influence with SLORC to press for specific human rights improvements.

On July 15, the Senate unanimously adopted a resolution on Burma suggesting specific U.S. policy actions, including attempts to urge ASEAN states to join an arms embargo, imposition of a U.N. arms embargo, and steps to prevent Burmese refugees from being forcibly repatriated from Thailand and Bangladesh. The Senate also expressed opposition to "commercial arrangements that only provide financial support for the SLORC" or to sending an ambassador to Rangoon. The House Foreign Affairs Committee approved a similar resolution.

On the fifth anniversary of her house arrest, President Clinton issued a strong statement urging SLORC to release "unconditionally Aung San Suu Kyi and all other remaining prisoners of conscience in Burma." He also called on SLORC to "begin a substantive dialogue" with the Nobel laureate.

In late October, the administration completed its review of Burma policy. Thomas Hubbard, Deputy Assistant Secretary of State for East Asia and Pacific affairs, went to Rangoon on October 30 to present the new policy directly to Khin Nyunt, offering the SLORC "two visions of a future relationship with the U.S., either increased cooperation based on positive movement on human rights, democratization and counternarcotics issues, or increased isolation." He was accompa-

nied by State Department officials from the bureaus of Democracy, Human Rights and Labor, and International Narcotics Matters. The administration insisted the trip did not represent a softening of its position towards SLORC. No immediate progress was announced as a result of the visit, and the delegation was denied access to Aung San Suu Kyi; Burmese officials told Hubbard they would continue talks with her and that they would allow prisons visits by the International Committee of the Red Cross.

The Work of Human Rights Watch/Asia

Human Rights Watch/Asia paid particular attention to advocacy work on Burma during the year, focusing on both bilateral and multilateral channels of pressure. Staff made policy recommendations and provided information on human rights in Burma to U.N. agencies as well as to the U.S., Japanese, European, and other governments, with the aim of continuing international pressure on SLORC to implement key U.N. recommendations and increase protection for Burmese refugees in Bangladesh and Thailand.

At the U.N. Human Rights Commission meeting in Geneva in February and March, Human Rights Watch/Asia joined other human rights organizations in pressing individual government delegations to support a strong resolution on Burma; the resolution was adopted on March 4. With other major American human rights groups, Human Rights Watch/Asia wrote to the U.N. Secretary-General on July 20, the anniversary of Aung San Suu Kyi's house arrest, urging him to use his good offices to assist in bringing about her release.

Human Rights Watch/Asia had meetings with staff of the UNHCR to discuss concerns related to the repatriation of Rohingya refugees from Bangladesh. On the issue of trafficking of Burmese women into Thailand, Human Rights Watch/Asia supported U.S. Congressional efforts to put pressure on the Thai government to enforce its own laws and respect internationally-recognized rights. (*See* the Human Rights

Watch Women's Rights Project section.)

Human Rights Watch/Asia briefed Representative Richardson prior to his visit to Burma in February and on June 29, testified before the House Foreign Affairs Committee (Subcommittee on Asia and the Pacific) on U.S. policy towards Burma. Human Rights Watch/Asia staff was routinely consulted throughout the year by Congressional offices drafting appeals, letters, or resolutions on Burma. In August, they briefed the President's director for national drug policy on human rights concerns and drug trafficking in Burma.

In May, Human Rights Watch/Asia sent a mission to the Thai-Burmese border to interview newly arrived refugees from the Mon State.

CAMBODIA

Human Rights Developments

Cambodia, in the first year of a democratically elected government, faced continued civil war, the dislocation of tens of thousands of civilians, and severe human rights abuses by both the Khmer Rouge and government forces. Local human rights activists and the burgeoning independent press were the targets of official attacks as various elements within the government vied for power. Murders of ethnic Vietnamese continued, and the Cambodian legislature approved an immigration law that failed to resolve the issue of nationality and gave little protection to long-term Vietnamese inhabitants against summary expulsion.

At the same time, there were many signs of significant change, not least the Cambodian government's willingness to acknowledge problems and to cooperate with international human rights and humanitarian bodies. Prison conditions remained poor, but local and international monitors continued to have access, and government officials took steps to relieve overcrowding in one of the worst facilities in Phnom Penh when pressed. The legislature debated and investi-

gated human rights issues, the government sought military reform, and individuals scattered throughout the administration struggled to put in place legal and political means of enforcing accountability.

The political and military events of the year provided a difficult context for human rights progress and institution-building. Although the royalist FUNCINPEC party had won a narrow victory over the Cambodian People's Party in May 1993, it agreed to share leadership of the government after a failed secession attempt led by two CPP hard-liners in June 1993. FUNCINPEC leaders shared key offices with CPP officials at the national and provincial levels, but in practice the CPP retained control of local government as well as the bureaucracy and security apparatus. By the end of 1994, the coalition was showing signs of strain, having weathered another coup attempt by CPP elements and a Cabinet reshuffling that sidelined certain reformers.

The Phnom Penh military and the two non-communist forces integrated their military commands, and by early 1994 the combined forces had knocked the Khmer Rouge out of several logistical bases. While King Sihanouk unsuccessfully tried to end the civil war by negotiating a governmental role for the Khmer Rouge, the new Cambodian army moved against the two largest Khmer Rouge strongholds, Pailin and Anlong Veng. Both campaigns ended disastrously, with the government forces holding the two bases for a month or less before Khmer Rouge guerrillas pushed them out. Although each side's positions returned to roughly where they had been prior to the offensive, the Khmer Rouge built up forces in the north and northwest, declaring Anlong Veng their "capitol," and the security situation deteriorated, with free movement increasingly restricted in this region. Military activity also intensified in the southwest province of Kampot, where Khmer Rouge guerrillas had been kidnapping local Cambodians for ransom over the years. When the Khmer Rouge attacked a train in late July, abducting three Westerners, international attention prompted the government to respond by pouring troops into the area and periodically bombarding it. (The hostages were later killed.)

Although the world had closely followed the repatriation of Cambodians from Thai border camps during the U.N. Peace keeping mission, it largely ignored the war's continuing displacement of Cambodians within Cambodia. Over 50,000 Cambodians fled during the Pailin offensive in 1994; when they returned several months later, many found their homes pillaged and their gardens planted with fresh landmines. On the Khmer Rouge side, between 25,000 and 30,000 persons fled Pailin into Thailand as the government forces advanced. Thailand responded by sealing off access to these persons by all humanitarian organizations (and indeed, even by Thai civil authorities) and forcing them back across the border into a malarial and mined Khmer Rouge zone.

Reports of grave abuses committed by both sides during the fighting were widespread, including allegations that civilian women were raped and prisoners of war summarily executed. The Khmer Rouge used civilians for portering and frequently took civilians hostage, as well as abducting and sometimes killing civilian authorities in areas of conflict. Over eighty wounded government soldiers left behind in the Pailin clinic were reportedly executed by the Khmer Rouge when they recaptured the town. The government engaged in forced conscription and extortion of men at various points of the year, and its troops, ill-disciplined and ill-supplied, plundered territory as often as protecting it, earning the fear and enmity of the local population. Information on Khmer Rouge abuses is sporadic, due to the lack of access to areas under their control; abuses committed by the government's military against civilians are more visible, and have often been extreme.

For example, members of the B-2 military intelligence units in the northwestern provinces, authorized to arrest and interrogate resistance fighters, turned in 1993 and 1994 to abducting civilians, extorting ransom from their families and often murdering the victims. A report by the U.N. Centre for Human Rights, leaked in 1994, estimated the group murdered at least thirty-five individuals between late June and November 1993 and held others captive in secret locations in Battambang City and a remote village called Che K'mau. Some of the victims have never been located and were believed to still be detained; among the others are one man who allegedly died while his captors ate his liver and another who lost a limb and an eye when forced to perform de-mining, according to the report.

Although the crimes of these B-2 units were privately reported to political leaders during the peacekeeping period, the new government was slow to take action. An investigation by the Ministry of Defense corroborated most details of the U.N. Centre's reports, but investigators from the prime ministers' office initially denied the findings. Details of the investigations were then leaked to the press in August, and pressure from within the country and abroad forced the government to continue its inquiry. As of October, First Prime Minister Norodom Ranariddh and Interior Minister You Hokry, both of FUNCINPEC, had suggested that all the abuses had occurred prior to the May 1993 elections, in what appeared to be an attempt to absolve the new government of responsibility. The prime minister's office continued to conduct investigations, inviting the U.N. Centre to participate as an observer. As of this writing, no action had been taken against any of the accused perpetrators, and indeed, one of the accused, jailed for shooting at police at a checkpoint, was released for an alleged lack of evidence.

The Prime Ministers' office was expected to announce its findings in this case by the end of the year. A failure to act decisively against this military intelligence group could undercut one encouraging development: the willingness of provincial prosecutors and courts to refer cases of serious abuse by high military officers to the Ministry of Defense for investigation by the military prosecutor. Some courts had also begun to investigate and try low-ranking military offenders and their relatives. Military police were deployed in some provinces in the latter half of the year, and succeeded to some extent in diminishing abuses by renegade soldiers, but banditry, extortion, and killing by persons in military uniform remained an extremely serious problem.

The public exposure in Cambodia and abroad of military atrocities demonstrated the power of the press and the local human rights movement to mobilize public opinion, and in turn raised the specter of retaliation. An early danger signal was the inadequately investigated death of Tou Chhom Mongkol, Editor-in-Chief of the newspaper *Antarakhum (Intervention)*, on a main city thoroughfare on the night of June 11, following a March 24 grenade attack on the newspaper's office by perpetrators never identified by the police. Suspicions of official retribution were fueled by the paper's articles condemning corruption among government authorities.

The suppression of a second coup attempt on July 3, again attributed to Prince Chakrapong and Sin Song, provided a pretext for the government to rein in the press. Shortly after the coup attempt, the prime minister warned that anyone publishing "inaccurate" information with the aim of provoking "turmoil" would be treated as having committed a crime. Noun Nonn, editor of *Dom Ning Pei Prek (Morning News)* was the first target, arrested on July 8 for an article that suggested high officials in the Ministry of Interior were responsible for the coup. The "law" invoked in his case was a 1992 enactment of the Phnom Penh regime during the peacekeeping period, that forbade publishing "inaccurate" information with "intent to alarm the citizenry" or information "detrimental" to national security. Although Noun Nonn was released from prison in August, charges against him are still pending, and his son is under investigation for an article the newspaper published alleging corruption on the part of the governor of Svay Rieng, who since has been appointed national chief of police. The government also issued warnings it would take legal action to close half a dozen other newspapers that had published articles on the coup or criticisms of senior officials.

Another opportunity to curb the press came in early September. Prime Minister Norodom Ranariddh threatened to expel foreign journalists who "exaggerate," after international newspapers exposed both the atrocities that had been committed by the B-2 units in Battambang, and the denial by the prime minister's office that secret prisons existed.

On September 7, Noun Chan, the editor of the journal *Sam-leng Yuvachun Khmer (The Voice of Khmer Youth)*, was gunned down by two men on a motorcycle as he was driving around one of Phnom Penh's main traffic circles. The newspaper had received written warnings from the Ministry of Information for articles which criticized CPP leaders Hun Sen and Chea Sim, and senior staff members had also received death threats prior to the murder. The newspaper had also criticized FUNCINPEC security officials and controversial business figures. Several human rights organizations, that strongly condemned the slaying themselves received warnings from government officials. Television broadcasters have also been warned not to air the views of critics of government policies.

On the positive side, the Human Rights Commission of Cambodia's National Assembly took an active role in investigating complaints submitted to it and raising human rights issues pertaining to proposed legislation, and after a slow start, the National Assembly increasingly became a forum for genuine discussion of draft laws. The government's proposal to outlaw the Khmer Rouge occasioned hot debate in July in the parliament, which added measures to clarify the definition of forbidden acts and to punish those who use the law to accuse others maliciously. A proposed law on the press was withdrawn from legislative consideration in May following criticism by both foreign and local nongovernmental organizations, including the Khmer Journalists Association.

A new immigration law, however, passed the assembly in August without serious objection, despite the fact it neither defined nationality nor explicitly protected the rights of refugees. The law was widely perceived as facilitating the possible expulsion of ethnic Vietnamese residents of Cambodia, who are estimated to number between 200,000 and 500,000. It empowered the government to summarily expel foreigners who cannot produce proper documentation, and to close areas of the country off to alien residents. Prior to the law's enactment, the Ministry of Interior had inquired whether the United Nations High Commissioner for Refugees (UNHCR) would approve the use of centers it built to house aliens pending deportation. Ethnic Vietnamese in certain parts of the country had also had their identity documents temporarily confiscated by government authorities conducting a rough "census" of aliens.

Attacks against ethnic Vietnamese continued, with reports of at least forty civilians killed and another thirty injured since the beginning of the year in eight separate incidents. Although the Khmer Rouge were suspects in most of the massacres, in at least three of these instances the political identity of the murderers could not be established, although there were some signs that government military may have been involved. In the worst case, thirteen Vietnamese in Peam So village, Sa-ang district Kandal province were murdered in cold blood, among them nine children. Government authorities apprehended but then freed suspects who had confessed, and whose voices were recognized by victims, on the grounds of "lack of evidence." Approximately 5,000 ethnic Vietnamese, some of them with documents proving residency in Cambodia since the 1960s, continued to languish on houseboats in the middle of the Bassac river at Chrey Thom, the Vietnamese-Cambodian border. These people had fled their homes on the Tonle Sap lake in 1993, at the height of a wave of Khmer Rouge attacks against Vietnamese fishing settlements, and have been acknowledged as citizens by neither Vietnam nor Cambodia.

The Right to Monitor

A wide variety of NGOs, including human rights groups, operated in Cambodia, and their efforts in popular education and human rights monitoring were beginning to have an impact, at least gauged by signs of an official backlash against their activities. Mid-year, the interior minister issued a series of new regulations for NGOs, including requirements that they give the authorities lists of their members, reports on their activities, and advance notice of all meetings; officials justified these requirements as necessary for maintaining public order. But authorities in at least two provinces relied on these directives to deny permission to established human rights groups to carry out their activities. Following criticism by human rights organizations and other NGOs, the Ministry of Interior proposed to "clarify" these directives, but no formal repeal or revision of the directives was issued. The CPP minister of interior did explain that existing NGOs do not have to ask permission to conduct educational activities, though they must report them. Following the murder of Noun Chan, NGO leaders in Phnom Penh were also given direct warnings by government officials to tone down their criticism of the government or be shut down. As of this writing, no human rights NGO had yet been closed despite the warnings.

The U.N. Centre for Human Rights opened its first field office in Phnom Penh in late 1993, and the U.N. Secretary-General appointed a special representative for human rights in Cambodia, whose mandate was due to be reviewed in March 1995. Bureaucratic obstacles delayed the transfer of funds to the U.N. center's office for many of its planned technical assistance programs. Yet despite funding problems, the center's small staff performed superbly, providing educational services and legal advice, and investigating military abuses and prison conditions. The U.N.'s special representative, Justice Michael Kirby visited three times since the field office's establishment in late 1993, raising a wide range of human rights concerns with the Cambodian government and publishing comprehensive reports on the human rights situation.

But the superior work in highlighting abuses drew attention to the U.N. Center, and possibly retaliation. In September, the five-year-old daughter of one employee was deliberately abducted and shot in the leg when gunmen waiting in front of the family's home hijacked their car as it arrived. Government investigations had not produced results by November, and there was evidence that the attack may have been retribution against the U.N. center for its role in exposing abuses.

The International Committee of the Red Cross continued to monitor government prisons, but did not have a formal arrangement to monitor prisons operated by the Khmer Rouge. The UNHCR maintained a presence in Cambodia, and field protection staff closely monitored the welfare of those who returned from the border in 1993 and persons newly displaced by the continuing war. The UNHCR was considering plans to close down its field office in Battambang by the end of the year, a move that Human Rights Watch/Asia viewed with concern in light of the continuing prospects for dry season warfare and expulsions of Vietnamese residents under the new immigration law.

The Role of the International Community

Pledges from the international community for Cambodia's development remained strong, but so did concerns about the government's ability to absorb and account for aid, and its political instability. At the March 1994 donors' conference, where a total of $773 million in pledges were confirmed overall, the U.S. pledged $29.4 million for programs under the Agency for International Development (USAID) for fiscal year 1994 and $37 million for fiscal year 1995; it also pledged an additional $6 million for de-mining activities and support.

Ambassador Charles Twining made the U.S. interest in human rights known through gestures such as attending a court hearing in the case of imprisoned editor Noun Nonn, and the embassy on several occasions expressed concern privately over serious human rights violations. USAID funded a range of democracy and human rights programs, including training of Cambodian criminal defenders and technical support for the National Assembly. Among the visitors to the U.S. that Washington sponsored were various legislators and human rights activists, but also Sar Kheng, the CPP minister of interior who is widely perceived as Hun Sen's rival and who later was suspected of complicity in the July coup attempt.

The United States and most other countries approached for military aid remained wary of providing weaponry, but considered other programs to train and professionalize the government's forces. American soldiers trained both the Cambodian Mine Action Center and the Royal Cambodian Armed Forces in de-mining and construction engineering. Australia began an assistance program to the fledgling Cambodian navy, and France began training a military police force that would answer directly to the prime ministers. Indonesia and Malaysia planned to train specialized military units. Countries negotiating to supply military equipment or ammunition to the Cambodian military included North Korea, Singapore, Malaysia and Israel. The Khmer Rouge reportedly still have access to ample military supplies delivered before the 1991 peace accords, and have bought further weaponry on the open market and from Cambodian military forces.

Thailand continued to maintain that the government's policy was to support the elected government, not the Khmer Rouge. However, it opposed arms sales to the Cambodian government on the grounds that it would only delay the prospect of reconciliation and negotiation with the Khmer Rouge, and did not cooperate with Cambodian requests to bar access by Khmer Rouge leaders to Thailand, much less to freeze Khmer Rouge assets or extradite Khmer Rouge leaders under the new Cambodian legislation outlawing the group.

The discovery in December 1993 of a major arms cache in Thailand guarded by Khmer Rouge soldiers, some of whom had just accompanied a delivery to the border, caused a major scandal, and raised the question of whether the Thai military supported logistical aid for the guerrillas. Although no other major instances of arms supply came to light, the Khmer Rouge continued to retreat tactically into Thailand, and on some occasions appeared to attack Cambodian positions from Thai soil. Thailand has maintained an official policy of disarming and repatriating Cambodians who are displaced into Thailand.

The Work of
Human Rights Watch/Asia

Human Rights Watch/Asia continued to broadly assess human rights conditions in this first year of the new Cambodian government, with a particular focus on military abuses, a field in which Cambodian NGOs were less able to safely probe and report. Researchers visited Cambodia in March and August 1994 to conduct field investigations in Phnom Penh and five other provinces.

In March, Human Rights Watch/Asia investigated allegations that secret prisons continued to operate in Battambang province under the direction of military intelligence units. In view of the extreme nature of the abuses and the difficulty in gathering evidence and protecting witnesses, the organization urged international groups based in Cambodia to pursue the inquiry; the U.N. center for Human Rights field office ultimately produced a comprehensive report on the abuses. Human Rights Watch/Asia wrote privately to the prime ministers on July 6, urging that action be taken against the military officials responsible for the abuses in these secret prisons. Human Rights Watch/Asia planned to publish a report in conjunction with the Arms Project of Human Rights Watch at the close of the year on military abuses on the part of both the government and the Khmer Rouge.

The organization also produced a series of public letters to Cambodian executive and parliamentary authorities on human rights problems with proposed laws and directives, including the press law, the immigration law, the law banning the Khmer Rouge, and regulations on the registration and activities of NGOs. It also protested the arrest and imprisonment of editor Noun Nonn in July. Human Rights Watch/Asia staff participated in several conferences assessing the U.N. performance in Cambodia.

CHINA AND TIBET

Human Rights Developments

Human rights in China deteriorated during the year. By the beginning of March, when it became clear that support in the United States for placing human rights conditions on China's receipt of Most Favored Nation (MFN) trade status was fast waning, China began stepping up its moves against dissidents. At least nineteen activists were arrested for peaceful dissent between March and December, and many of them "disappeared" after being taken into custody. The use of repeated short-term arbitrary detentions increased. In April, negotiations with the International Committee of the Red Cross (ICRC) came to a halt and as of early November had not resumed. After President Clinton announced the unconditional renewal of MFN in May, prisoner releases all but ceased, and long-delayed trials of political prisoners began. New security regulations, further restricting the limits of lawful dissent, went into effect in June. At the same time, old patterns of human rights abuses, including torture and beatings in prison and strict curbs on freedom of association, expression, assembly and religion persisted. In Tibet, the treatment of prisoners remained harsh.

Dozens of dissidents were rounded up in Shanghai and Beijing in late February and early March, before or during the visits of senior U.S. officials and the early March meeting of the National People's Congress. Among those detained were Wei Jingsheng, China's most famous political prisoner; his assistant, Tong Yi; most of the leadership of the Shanghai-based Study Group on Human Rights; and the founders of a new organization called the League for the Protection of the Rights of the Working People, including Yuan Hongbing, Liu Nianchun, and Wang Zhongqiu. As of November, Wei Jingsheng remained in detention without formal charges in an undisclosed location under what the government called "residential surveillance." Tong Yi had been charged with a minor criminal offense, four Shanghai activists had been sent to re-education camps for three years, and Liu Nianchun had been released.

Releases of prisoners sentenced in connection with the Tiananmen Square crackdown of June 4, 1989, effectively ended after President Clinton renewed MFN in May. Wang Juntao and Chen Ziming, the "black hands" of the 1989 protests, released in April and May respectively, were the last significant figures to be freed as a result of international pressure, while others, such as veteran pro-democracy activist Ren Wanding and former senior party official Bao Tong, remained in prison. Both of the latter were ill and had been denied access to appropriate medical care. Bao Tong, serving the remainder of a seven-year sentence for "leaking an important state secret" and "counterrevolutionary propaganda and incitement" was due to be released in 1996. Human Rights Watch honored him, *in absentia*, with other international human rights monitors at the Human Rights Watch obsevance of Human Rights Day in December.

Trials and sentencing appeared to be timed to express maximum contempt of Western human rights pressure. Immediately after the decoupling of human rights and MFN, the long-delayed trials began of the so-called Beijing Fifteen, dissidents who were accused of organizing "counterrevolutionary groups." The sentencing of three of the Shanghai activists mentioned above, Bao Ge, Yang Zhou, and Yang Qinheng, took place less than a week after Foreign Minister

Qian Qichen met with President Clinton on October 3.

Several developments underscored the Chinese government's abuse of its own legal procedures. Increasingly, the authorities refused to inform families of the whereabouts of detained dissidents, making several of these cases tantamount to disappearances. Prisoners were kept in detention despite the lack of evidence against them.

Gao Yu, formerly deputy chief editor of the banned newspaper *Economics Weekly*, was tried *in camera* on April 20 and was still in detention in November despite the judge's finding that the evidence against her was insufficient. Trials and sentencing were unaccountably delayed. At least nineteen dissidents in Gansu and Beijing, arrested in May and June 1992, were still being held incommunicado as of October 1994. The "Gansu Four," Liu Wensheng, Liu Baiyu, Gao Changyuan, and Ding Mao, tried and convicted in July 1993, had not been sentenced by the end of the year. The fates of five others indicted with them, and twelve more referred to in the indictment, were still unknown. None of the fifteen tried in Beijing in July 1994 was sentenced by December, to Human Rights Watch/Asia's knowledge.

The use of repeated short-term arbitrary detention was another trend during 1994. For example, in a three-month period starting at the beginning of March, Bao Ge was picked up a total of five times, three of them in connection with visits by foreign dignitaries. Released activists were under constant surveillance. Wang Dan, who in 1989 had been No.1 on the student "most wanted" list, was sent on "vacation" outside Beijing to prevent "disruption" during the visit to Beijing in March of U.S. Secretary of State Warren Christopher.

New security regulations, the *Detailed Rules for the Implementation of the Security Law of the People's Republic of China*, were signed into law by Li Peng on June 4, 1994. They widened the basis for restricting peaceful political dissent and freedom of religion, expression, association, and assembly, by heavily penalizing the "cooperation" of Chinese activists with "hostile" nongovernmental organizations outside China (the definition of hostile was left to the Ministry of Public Security). The regulations also defined speech, including rumors, or writing harmful to state security as "sabotage." Interviewing or contacting certain people or organizations could be construed by Chinese authorities under the new law as a criminal offense.

Persons arrested for political activities were increasingly charged with criminal offenses rather than with "counterrevolution." During 1994, at least seven dissidents were administratively sentenced to two or three-year "re-education through labor" terms on such charges.

Among them were Zhang Lin, a labor organizer, for "hooliganism" on the trumped-up charge of never having registered his marriage; Liu Huanwen, a Christian labor activist, also for "hooliganism"; Qin Yongmin, after meeting with other dissidents to discuss a "Peace Charter," for "disturbing the social order"; and Yan Zhengxue, an avant-garde artist and representative to the People's Congress, for "stealing a bicycle." Tong Yi, who was We Jingsheng's assistant, was charged with forging a seal to a university document, and Bi Yimin was accused of giving "public money" to the families of Wang Juntao and Chen Ziming.

Old patterns of human rights abuse continued into 1994. Qin Yongmin was badly beaten and mutilated in prison in June and July, according to his wife. Zheng Muzheng, an active Protestant proselytizer, was beaten to death the day after he was taken into custody. In both cases, the prisoners' spouses were harassed, interrogated, and threatened with arrest for attempting to seek governmental redress.

New religious regulations, spelling out rigorous conditions and procedures for registering churches went into effect in January. Catholics and Protestants who refused registration continued to be detained, harassed, and fined. Another set of regulations tightened the conditions under which foreigners can worship with their co-religionists.

Curbs on freedom of expression tightened in 1994. In a case viewed as a warning to the Hong Kong media to restrict reporting on human rights, Xi Yang, a reporter for the Hong Kong newspaper, *Ming Bao*, received a twelve-year sentence for writing an article on central bank gold strategies and loan interest rates. The information had not yet been officially released, thus constituting a "state financial secret." Tian Ye, a clerk at the Peoples' Bank implicated in the case, was given a fifteen-year term.

In March, in an effort to limit human rights violations from reaching the international community, China barred Wei Jingsheng from meeting with foreign reporters for three years. When the wife of veteran dissident Xu Wenli tried to talk with foreign reporters after her husband was detained twice within a twenty-four-hour period in early April, police officers forcibly dragged her into her house. Five foreign journalists were held for questioning in the incident. A Dutch journalist, Caroline Straahof, was detained five hours for attempting to visit Liu Nianchun; and some thirty police officers interrogated Nick Driver, Beijing bureau chief of United Press International (UPI), a U.S.-based news agency, and Matt Forney of *Newsweek* after they left Liu's house. Crew members from the National Broadcasting Company (NBC), a U.S. television network, were questioned for several hours after interviewing Wang Dan; a Taiwan reporter was held for trying to interview dissident intellectual Ding Zilin; and Lena Sun of *The Washington Post* was detained for taking pictures of dissidents' graves.

The media crackdown was particularly severe in the run-up to the fifth anniversary of the June 4 crackdown in Beijing. Police interrogated Kathy Chen, a *Wall Street Journal* reporter, for four hours for trying to interview Beijing University students. A South Korean camera operator and his crew were expelled from China for "reporting without permission." A Columbia Broadcasting Service (CBS) crew from the U.S. was prevented from filming in Tiananmen Square and had their video tape confiscated.

Chinese police sent a fax to Beijing hotels on June 2 to switch off Cable News Network (CNN) transmission until after June 6.

Free expression was restricted in other ways. At Beijing universities, even minor symbolic protests to commemorate June 4 were dealt with harshly. When paper money, a traditional means of commemorating the dead, was burned at People's University, all evening students were detained until the culprits could be interrogated and taken away. On March 12, seven film directors were banned from work for illegally participating in a Rotterdam film festival.

The right to free assembly was violated in March when the Chinese government prevented leading dissidents from meeting with Secretary of State Christopher. That same month, security forces in Beijing prevented a group of friends from gathering to mark the fifteenth anniversary of the arrest of We Jingsheng. More than one hundred elderly Chinese protestors were detained for gathering outside the Japanese Embassy in an attempt to deliver a letter to then-Japanese Prime Minister Morihiro Hosokawa demanding compensation for war-related damages.

Human rights abuses in Tibet continued. Despite the unexpected January releases of two Tibetan human rights monitors, Gendun Rinchen and Lobsang Yonten, Tibetan activists continued to receive harsh treatment, and curbs on free expression escalated. As of February, over 200 political prisoners were in TAR No.1 Prison (Drapchi), more than double the number held four years ago. Twenty-year-old Phuntsog Yangki, a nun, died in a police hospital in early June reportedly from lack of medical treatment after Drapchi Prison staff beat her for singing Tibetan independence songs in February during Tibetan New Year. She had been serving a five-year term for a 1992 independence demonstration.

Courts handed down heavy sentences. In late 1993 or early 1994, twelve nuns who allegedly tried to organize a demonstration received sentences of up to seven years. In July, five Tibetans in Pakshoe County in eastern Tibet, received twelve- and fifteen-year terms for "counterrevolutionary" offenses. Police arrested at least thirteen monks and nuns in February and March in Lhasa and Kyimshi (twenty-seven miles south of Lhasa), some for organizing a peaceful poster and leaflet campaign.

The Chinese concern for limiting information flows also applied to Tibet. In March, all units subscribing to cable television channels and owning ground satellite stations were ordered to immediately stop receiving and relaying British Broadcasting Company (BBC) and three Star Television channels, then to reapply to receive foreign programming. In Lhasa, all travel agencies were notified they would be punished if journalists or diplomats journeyed with them.

In May, a renewed crackdown on religious freedom began in Tibet with the apparent aim of discrediting the Dalai Lama as a religious leader. Party members were ordered to remove from their homes all signs of devotion, including any photographs of him. By August, the ban had been extended to government and semi-official agency personnel. At the end of September, police seized all of the Dalai Lama's pictures on display in Lhasa's city markets.

The Right to Monitor
No independent human rights monitoring was permitted in China, and attempts to raise human rights concerns publicly met with severe reprisals. Three members of the Shanghai-based China Study Group on Human Rights were sentenced in early October to three-year "re-education through labor" terms. All three had been subject to repeated detentions, surveillance, and harassment. One of those sentenced, Bao Ge, was picked up just after he had mailed an application to the Ministry of Civil Affairs requesting permission to establish a nationwide organization, the Voice of Human Rights.

Petitioning for adherence to the Universal Declaration of Human Rights brought retribution. Three professors, Xu Liangying, from the Chinese Academy of Social Sciences, and Ding Zilin and Jiang Peikun of People's University, who joined with four other academics, were under virtual house arrest in March and April for sending a human rights appeal to President Jiang Zemin and to the chair of the National People's Congress.

Meanwhile, the government funded and set up a "nongovernmental organization" of its own, the China Society for Human Rights Studies. To date, the statements and publications of this group, which is headed by a former chief of the official New China News Agency, Zhu Muzhi, have been indistinguishable from government policy.

The Role of the International Community

The last vestige of meaningful pressure on China from the international community ended with President Clinton's decision to de-link human rights and Most Favored Nation (MFN) trading status on May 26. The U.S. decision had immediate negative consequences. In addition to the deterioration of human rights documented above, it also signaled the marginalization of human rights on the U.S.-China bilateral agenda, and damaged American credibility on human rights worldwide. The U.S. was the last to abandon a tough human rights stance, as other governments and key trading partners with China had long since given priority to expanding economic ties.

By January 1994, it was clear that while the Clinton administration was deeply divided over the utility of continuing its threat to deny MFN to China if the conditions in the President's May 1993 Executive Order were not met, the forces in favor of jettisoning the MFN-human rights link were strong and growing. Treasury Secretary Lloyd Bensten visited China in late January and hinted that the annual MFN review might be dropped altogether. He also praised China for granting the U.S. Customs Service access to a handful of suspected prison labor sites— part of the administration's ongoing pattern of giving credit to China for token gestures which undermined the prospects for securing genuine human rights improvements.

Assistant Secretary of State for Democ-

racy, Human Rights and Labor John Shattuck met with Chinese officials in Beijing in late February, and infuriated them by also meeting with prominent dissident Wei Jingsheng. Shattuck's message, however, was undercut by a concurrent visit by Undersecretary of Commerce Jeffrey Garten, lobbying in Beijing for U.S. trade deals and publicly extolling the value of the Chinese market for American exporters.

Secretary of State Christopher was the next American official to visit, and despite the detention of Wei Jingsheng and other dissidents prior to his arrival in March, he refused to suspend or delay an ill-timed trip that also coincided with the National People's Congress plenum—a time of domestic tension under the best of circumstances. Christopher did raise human rights issues with Chinese officials. But the visit brought him only public humiliation by the Chinese, a marginally useful agreement on prison labor exports, and Congressional attacks on the credibility and effectiveness of the President's overall policy.

In April, China dispatched a huge trade delegation to the U.S., which signed contracts worth over $11 billion, further eroding Congressional support for the MFN linkage.

By the time President Clinton made a last-ditch appeal on human rights to Vice-Premier Zou Jiahua in the Oval Office on May 3, China was convinced the U.S. was more interested in access to its markets than in human rights improvements, and Zou made no promises. But China did release two prominent dissidents on "medical parole," Wang Juntao and Chen Ziming, as a face-saving gesture to Clinton.

With those releases in hand, Clinton justified his decision to renew MFN and de-link human rights from future annual renewals (still legally required under the Jackson-Vanik amendment of U.S. trade law, making tariff benefits to non-market economies conditional on free emigration) on the most tenuous grounds possible. China, Clinton said, had not made "overall significant progress" as required by his May 1993 executive order, but it had agreed to resolve a dozen emigration cases, signed a new agreement on prison labor, and said it would adhere to the Universal Declaration of Human Rights. He argued that a tough human rights policy was hampering the ability of the U.S. to pursue trade and security interests, citing, among other things, the need for Chinese cooperation on resolving the North Korean crisis. The MFN decision, it should be noted, had no effect whatsoever on China's stance on that issue.

As a sop to Congressional advocates of selective trade sanctions, Clinton imposed a wrist-slapping sanction by banning $200 million worth of annual imports of Chinese weapons and ammunition. (A bill to impose broader sanctions on some $5 billion worth of exports, vigorously opposed by the administration, was defeated in the House of Representatives on August 9 by a vote of 270 to 158.) He also announced an "aggressive" and "vigorous" new human rights policy, including an effort to get U.S. businesses operating in China to adhere to a voluntary set of principles, increased support of broadcasting to China on internal political developments, undefined expanded multilateral efforts on human rights, and support for nongovernmental organizations in China—despite the fact that Chinese NGOs do not exist. This would be part of an "enhanced engagement" strategy designed to erase the stigma of the 1989 crackdown near Tiananmen Square and to remove human rights as an obstacle to improved Sino-American relations.

By year's end it appeared that the new human rights policy was all form and little substance, and there would be no significant political or economic pressure exerted to replace MFN. The administration embarked on an aggressive campaign to expand high-level contacts with China across the board, while keeping the human rights discussion muted. At the G-7 summit meeting in Naples in July, the White House ruled out any discussion of China, thus squandering a key opportunity to develop a multilateral agenda. Commerce Secretary Ron Brown, the first cabinet level official to visit China after the MFN decision, led a delegation of twenty-four American corporate executives in August. They negotiated nearly $6 billion worth of trade deals. Discussion of human rights was relegated to quiet diplomacy, however, and Brown refrained from publicly criticizing detentions that took place during his trip. He was followed by a series of other senior administration officials, including Secretary of Defense William Perry, Energy Secretary Hazel O'Leary, and Export-Import Bank president Ken Brody.

The White House chaired an interagency group to develop so-called voluntary principles for U.S. businesses in China, but no such principles were announced as of November 1994. Meanwhile, legislation was introduced in the House of Representatives outlining a specific code of conduct for U.S. companies in China and requiring regular reports to the State Department. No action was taken by the House on the bill; it was expected to be reintroduced in 1995.

The administration was actively considering dropping two remaining sanctions imposed after the 1989 crackdown: a ban on Overseas Private Investment Corporate loans and insurance to U.S. investors, and suspension of the Trade and Development Administration's export program. It was not clear what, if any, human rights improvements would be secured in exchange.

In October, Chinese officials told the U.S. that they were resuming a "human rights dialogue" with Assistant Secretary Shattuck, broken off by Beijing following Shattuck's meeting with Wei Jingsheng in February, talks with the Voice of America on international broadcasting, and negotiations with the International Committee of the Red Cross over access to prisoners. Although the Clinton administration expressed delight, there was no indication by the time of this writing that any real progress had been made in the three areas.

China lobbied heavily for a visit by President Clinton to Beijing sometime in 1995. During an Oval Office meeting on October 4, he privately raised human rights issues (including cases of individual dissidents) and foreign minister Qian Qichen reiterated an invitation to China first extended by President Jiang Zemin at the 1993 APEC meeting. The White House said "no formal plans" for a visit had been made. President Clinton met with President Jiang Zemin again at the APEC meeting in Jakarta in November.

The administration made no new efforts to exert leverage on China through the World Bank, which continued to give China more funds than any other nation. By the end of June, China received over $3.07 billion, and commitments by the bank to give another $3 billion in fiscal year 1995. The fiscal year 1995 U.S. foreign aid bill requires the U.S. directors at multilateral lending institutions to "use their voice" to promote internationally recognized worker rights. Before the bill was signed, China voiced strong opposition to this provision, which it viewed as a potential threat to its access to multilateral development bank loans. However, it was unclear how vigorously the administration planned to implement the new law with respect to China.

Other governments in Europe and Asia also took steps in 1994 to emphasize their expanding commercial relations with China, while marginalizing or downgrading the importance of human rights. Beijing was thus largely able to deflect effective bilateral or multilateral pressure on human rights through a combination of strategically aimed trade deals and reciprocal exchanges of high-ranking officials.

Anxious to restore relations with Beijing damaged by the sale of jet fighter planes to Taiwan in 1992, French Prime Minister Eduoard Balladur went to China in April. But his visit was marred by the detention of prominent dissidents in Beijing and Shanghai (Xu Wenli, Wang Fuchen, and Bao Ge) just prior to his arrival. The prime minister was further embarrassed by Chinese Foreign Ministry denials that any detentions had taken place. On July 5, the French minister for foreign trade, Gerard Longuet, led a delegation of 125 business people to China and signed deals worth approximately $1 billion. To cap the effort to boost economic relations, President Jiang Zemin was invited to Paris in September. Authorities initially banned protest demonstrations in Marseille and Paris, but ultimately allowed few to take place. Eighteen protesters were arrested. Just hours after signing trade agreements worth $2.5 billion, Jiang Zemin rejected criticism of China's human rights practices on the grounds that stability is a "primordial condition" for economic development. President François Mitterand, according to press accounts, gave Jiang a list of jailed dissidents and discussed human rights.

Even more controversial was Chinese Prime Minister Li Peng's tour of Europe in June and July, which was marked by protest demonstrations and by Li's vehement defense of his decision to crush the pro-democracy demonstrations in 1989. Li toured Austria, Romania, and Germany. The Green Party circumvented a ban on public protests in Vienna and held a protest meeting in parliament, while Austrian officials completed agreements on trade and development projects and Li offered, in exchange, to start a human rights "dialogue" with Austria. Li cut short his week-long visit to Germany after being harassed by protests in several German cities; complaints about China's human rights practices were voiced by various German politicians. Though a public relations disaster, the trip succeeded in further cementing Chinese-German economic relations: Li signed over $3 billion worth of aerospace contracts, for example.

Canada's prime minister, Jean Chrétien, told parliament in June that Ottawa would seek to improve human rights in China through expanded trade, and announced that in November he would be the first Canadian leader to visit China since 1989. China is one of Canada's largest export markets, with bilateral trade of about $4 billion. Accompanied by provincial authorities and business representatives, Chrétien planned to visit Beijing and Shanghai in mid-November en route to the APEC summit meeting.

Australia continued its policy of promoting trade (in 1992-1993, exports to China totaled $2.2 billion), while conducting a human rights "dialogue" through separate channels. Australian Prime Minister Keating and Foreign Minister Gareth Evans actively lobbied the Clinton administration to de-link MFN and human rights. Canberra decided to defer sending a third human rights delegation to China pending a reciprocal delegation from Beijing to investigate Australia's human rights conditions. (Australia had sent human rights delegations to China in 1991 and 1992.) Until such a visit was scheduled, Australia's dialogue was "on hold" as of November 1994.

Japan's prime minister also visited China in March 1994, and Tokyo continued to give Beijing more bilateral aid than any other country.

The Work of
Human Rights Watch/Asia
Human Rights Watch/Asia sought to keep public attention focused on China's abysmal human rights practices by a steady stream of detailed information and to debunk the widely held belief that economic reforms were leading to human rights improvements. It redoubled its efforts to involve the private sector in discussions on human rights and by the end of the year was increasingly turning its attention to issues related to worker rights.

China remained the most important country in Asia for Human Rights Watch/Asia in terms of staff time and resources. In February, it issued the 688-page *Detained in China and Tibet*, a directory of over 1,000 political and religious prisoners and perhaps the most comprehensive report on arbitrary detention ever published on post-Cultural Revolution China. Approximately one report a month was released thereafter, two of them in collaboration with another organization, Human Rights in China. The reports ranged from detailed accounts of prison life and lists of prisoners, to information on religious persecution, to accounts of efforts of dissident intellectuals to raise concerns about the impact of China's economic reforms on society, to documentation on the sale of executed prisoners' organs for medi-

cal transplants.

Human Rights Watch/Asia also issued a steady stream of press releases on U.S. policy toward China and on developments in individual prisoner cases. The Washington director of Human Rights Watch/Asia was repeatedly called upon to testify at Congressional hearings, to brief members of Congress and others traveling to China on human rights developments and to raise concerns about those developments with other governments, including Japan. At the same time, the Hong Kong office remained the center for Human Rights Watch/Asia's investigatory research on China, collecting and analyzing documents and conducting interviews as needed.

Major work went into opening a dialogue with American, and by the end of the year German, corporations involved in China, much of it over the development of a voluntary set of principles to which companies could subscribe in the interests of promoting human rights.

HONG KONG

Human Rights Developments
Hong Kong's fate was thrown into deeper uncertainty during 1994 when Beijing reacted to the adoption of Governor Patten's electoral reforms by resolving to abolish all elected bodies upon its resumption of sovereignty in 1997. The implications for human rights in Hong Kong were ominous, given that elected legislators had become key advocates for stronger protections for civil and human rights. For its part, the government responded reluctantly to their proposals for civil rights measures, anxious not to reignite conflict with Beijing.

Governor Patten, after numerous futile efforts to reconcile China to its proposals for moderate electoral reforms, finally sent the first set of proposals regarding the 1994 District Board elections to the Legislative Council (Legco) in February. Legco approved them, lowering the voting age from twenty-one to eighteen, abolishing appointed seats and reducing the number of popularly elected legislators to one per constituency. In June, legislators approved the government's proposal for the 1995 Legco elections, which for the first time made all sixty seats elected by one or another electoral constituency, although the proposal fell short of recommending direct election by universal franchise for each seat.

Beijing's response was not subtle. The day after the vote, Chinese officials unveiled an electric signboard to count the number of days remaining until Chinese rule, and reiterated threats to dismiss all legislators and reconstitute all representative bodies after the June 30, 1997 handover. In September, just before Hong Kong held elections to district boards under the new law, Beijing formalized its position through a resolution of the Standing Committee of the National People's Congress ordering the termination on July 1, 1997 of all elected positions at the legislative, municipal and district levels. Yet despite the pall cast by these pronouncements, Hong Kong successfully carried off the elections, producing the first district boards where all members were chosen by popular vote. A dark note was the disqualification as a candidate of Lau San-ching, a Hong Kong resident who spent ten years in a Chinese prison because of his attempts to contact Democracy Wall activists. The government, and later the High Court, upheld his disqualification under an ordinance barring criminal convicts and persons who did not reside continuously in Hong Kong for ten years, despite the fact that Lau's "criminal record" and forced sojourn in China were themselves human rights abuses.

As relations with the British administration broke down in 1993 over Governor Patten's electoral reforms, China had unilaterally established the so-called Preliminary Working Committee to prepare for the 1997 transition; in late September 1994, reports circulated that Beijing was also planning to organize a separate Chinese Communist Party committee to supervise the post-1997 Hong Kong administration. Following China's resolution to dissolve the legislature due to be elected in 1995, a subcommittee of the Preliminary Working Committee recommended in October that a "provisional" legislature be chosen by a committee appointed by China until new elections were organized. Each of these developments signaled a departure from the 1984 agreement on the transfer of rule between Britain and China, and each lent credibility to fears that China felt it could alter Hong Kong's legal and political structure with impunity.

Despite this gloomy prospect, human rights activists and legislators pressed for further institutional and legislative reforms to entrench human rights, even while the government dragged its heels, anxious to avoid further confrontation with China. Britain and the Hong Kong government opposed the creation of a human rights commission, despite the explicit endorsement of Legco and the British House of Commons Foreign Affairs Select Committee. Lu Ping, China's senior Hong Kong official, promised that China would disband any such commission, and for good measure reiterated that China felt no obligation to discharge the reporting requirements on human rights to the U.N. as required by the International Covenant on Civil and Political Rights (extended to Hong Kong by Britain) after 1997. The governor officially refused to introduce to Legco a private bill to establish such a commission, proposing instead measures to increase human rights education.

A group of legislators led by Christine Loh proposed a law on free public access to officially held information which China opposed, and Governor Patten refused to support it. Instead, the government began preparing a much narrower set of discretionary administrative measures in the form of a code of practice, and announced plans to submit a law giving individuals the right of access to their personal records held by the government.

The government moved slowly on other legal reforms necessary to bring Hong Kong's colonial legislation into line with its Bill of Rights and the International Covenant on

Civil and Political Rights, and it failed to amend or introduce new provisions in ordinances that concerned censorship, police powers to search for and seize evidence from journalists, sedition, criminal penalties for publication of information relating to investigations of the secretive Independent Commission Against Corruption, or penalties for leaks of government information.

Hong Kong's Basic Law, the so-called constitution for the post-1997 era, stipulates the territory shall prohibit "any act of treason, secession, sedition or subversion" against China or "theft of state secrets." There was strong debate on the need for Hong Kong to reformulate its current laws on treason, sedition, and disclosure of official information, both to bring them into closer conformity with international human rights standards and to ensure they would not expire with the end of British rule, leaving these areas to the discretion of a provisional legislature appointed by Beijing.

The importance of clarifying legal protections for freedom of expression was underscored by China's conviction in 1994 of Xi Yang, a mainland journalist working for the Hong Kong paper *Ming Pao* who received a twelve-year sentence for allegedly stealing "state secrets."

Journalists throughout Hong Kong participated in several demonstrations protesting the trial of Xi Yang, but the incident provided new opportunities for intimidation and self-censorship. Some publications warned writers not to sign petitions on Xi's behalf or run stories on the incident. In May, Beijing temporarily banned ten Hong Kong reporters, all of whom had signed a letter of protest, from entering China. Hong Kong's director of education appeared to be caught in the self-censorship trend when he recommended that two textbook publishers delete references to the Tiananmen massacre; he reversed this position after intervention by Governor Patten.

The year also saw some of the worst official abuses to date against Vietnamese asylum-seekers, although they fell into a long-established pattern of violations asso-

ciated with efforts on the part of the Hong Kong government to forcibly repatriate most of the Vietnamese from the prison-like detention centers in the colony. Early in the year, Vietnamese began peaceful hunger-strikes and demonstrations in the detention centers to protest the regional multilateral decision to approve of deportation of non-refugees. Protests against forcible repatriation, however, had been going on for years. The protests alarmed the Hong Kong government, already concerned by the drop in voluntary repatriation, and on April 7, it launched a massive dawn raid on the Whitehead Detention Centre involving some 1,260 officers in full riot gear, for the purpose of moving 1,055 adults and 421 children to another detention center. In the process, the correctional and police officials fired 557 canisters of tear gas at the confined inmates. Over 300 injuries resulted, including burns on small children who were sprayed at point-blank range, and wounds from unprovoked beatings by the officers.

Under pressure from legislators and human rights groups, the governor ordered an independent inquiry, which documented serious abuses. The report, however, made no recommendations as to who was responsible and declined to question the wisdom of the massive police operation in the first place.

Action to hold officers accountable for the brutalities suffered by the Vietnamese did not take place until September 28, when the government announced it would seek prosecution of three low-ranking officers for the assaults at Whitehead, claiming that evidence was insufficient to take action against others.

During the first week of September, 550 armed officers moved against many of the same Vietnamese to break up another nonviolent demonstration, this time in anticipation of the forced deportation of twenty-one asylum seekers. On this occasion, a private monitoring group was allowed to observe the operation. Teargas was again deployed in large quantities and at close range to dislodge protestors from the roofs of huts. In an eerie repetition of the April incident, the government at first misrepresented the number of Vietnamese injured to be only a handful; newspapers ultimately reported well over two hundred injuries and complaints of maltreatment at the hands of the officers in riot gear. At the deportation, Hong Kong authorities forcibly injected tranquilizers into those Vietnamese who had protested return through suicide attempts, wrapping the men in blankets to get them onto the plane to Hanoi.

The Right to Monitor

At present, Hong Kong offers one of the most hospitable environments for local human rights and civil liberties activists in Asia, and these issues receive increasing attention in the local media. In 1994, the Hong Kong Journalists Association, in conjunction with the London-based group, Article 19, published a sequel to its 1993 report on freedom of expression, and several legislators held public hearings on human rights issues, including the police assault on Whitehead.

To its credit, the government protested China's position that it does not feel obliged to continue reports to the United Nations on human rights in Hong Kong, as presently required under the International Covenant for Civil and Political Rights, to which Britain is a signatory but China is not. The 1984 treaty between Britain and China stipulates that the covenant shall apply to Hong Kong, which would include the covenant's reporting requirement as well.

The government, however, compromised on the public's right to information by opposing visas for two well-known Chinese democracy proponents, Liu Binyan and Ruan Ming, to visit Hong Kong on the fifth anniversary of the Tiananmen massacre. Although the government conceded the need for legislation to allow individuals access to dossiers the government keeps on them, it opposed a private bill to also require government departments to provide basic information on their activities to the public on demand.

Media access to Vietnamese confined in detention centers remained limited to those who had volunteered for repatriation, and regulations enforcing censorship and restriction of printed materials remained in force. Reporters were allowed to observe police raids and deportations from a distance, but not to interview the Vietnamese involved. Although the Hong Kong government permitted four independent observers to monitor the September raid, it did not release police videotapes of the action, nor did Legco seek any independent inquiry into the use of tear gas or force. Lawyers and human rights monitors continued to receive access to Vietnamese clients, albeit on restrictive terms, and nongovernmental development agencies continued to have a presence in the detention centers, although their operations are gradually being phased out. Human Rights Watch/Asia expressed concern that the confined and isolated conditions of detention contributed to the sense of desperation in the camps, and increased the danger of violent confrontation.

The Role of the International Community

In the United States, the Clinton administration maintained a conspicuous silence on virtually all major human rights issues connected to Hong Kong during 1994. The U.S. signaled stronger support for forcible repatriation of non-refugees in the region at the regional conference on the Comprehensive Plan of Action (governing policy towards Vietnamese boat people), which Hong Kong authorities took as an endorsement of their deportation policy. No concern was expressed by the State Department over either the April or September police actions against protesting Vietnamese.

Congress, however, took a more critical view of these events. At the House of Representatives Asia-Pacific Subcommittee hearing in April, members of Congress expressed concern over the use of force by Hong Kong authorities and faulty screening practices that left genuine refugees in danger of forced return. In October, fifty-one members of Congress called on President Clinton to take action in egregious cases of individuals wrongly denied refugee protection.

Congressional interest in democratization and human rights in Hong Kong also found expression in a Senate resolution congratulating Hong Kong for its successful district board elections and urging the government to "make every effort to support the progress of democratic reforms...and to encourage all parties to protect these gains as the 1997 transition approaches."

The Work of Human Rights Watch/Asia

Human Rights Watch/Asia continued to work with local human rights and refugee advocates to bring international attention to abuses in Hong Kong in 1994. It began the year by campaigning for the Congressional Human Rights Caucus to urge Governor Patten to establish a human rights commission.

Following the raid on the Whitehead detention facility in April, Human Rights Watch/Asia expressed dismay to the government over the excessive use of force and resultant injuries, and urged a public inquiry and punishment of responsible officials. At the same time, Human Rights Watch/Asia privately urged the United Nations High Commissioner for Refugees to aggressively monitor such incidents and swiftly and publicly respond to abuses. When the commission of inquiry's report was released in June, Human Rights Watch/Asia voiced disappointment with its failure to assign responsibility for the abuses committed in April. In July, after receiving letters from over a hundred Vietnamese asylum-seekers injured in the raid, Human Rights Watch/Asia urged the Hong Kong secretary of security to pursue vigorously the police inquiry into responsibility for assaults.

INDIA

Human Rights Developments

India attempted to silence international critics of its human rights record during the year by using two radically different tactics. One was wooing foreign investors in India's burgeoning market and stressing the advantages of business over pressure. The second was admitting that some abuses had taken place but insisting that Indian organizations, including a new Human Rights Commission, were well equipped to deal with them. Neither tactic led to major improvements in the human rights situation.

Abuses in the disputed territory of Kashmir continued to mount, particularly deaths of suspected militants in custody. Communal violence remained a problem, with police involvement in Hindu-Muslim clashes in Bangalore in October and discriminatory arrests of Muslims in Gujarat under a controversial law called the Terrorists and Disruptive Activities (TADA) law. The TADA law grants sweeping powers to local authorities to arrest and detain suspects, allows for lengthy pre-trial detentions, and reverses the presumption of innocence.

Two years after communal violence claimed more than 2,000 lives following the December 1992 destruction of a sixteenth century mosque by Hindu nationalists, to Human Rights Watch/Asia's knowledge, no police officer identified as participating in attacks on Muslims had been prosecuted.

In Kashmir, Indian troops continued to execute detainees in custody, kill civilians in reprisal attacks, and burn down neighborhoods and villages as collective punishment of those suspected of supporting the militants. In the first half of 1994, human rights groups in Kashmir recorded more than 200 deaths in custody. The Jammu and Kashmir Bar Association reported fifty summary executions between mid-May and mid-June alone.

On May 9, for example, Border Security Force (BSF) troops arrested and then shot dead three teenage boys in Bandipora: Nisar Ahmad Mir, thirteen, Fayaz Ahmad Bhat, sixteen, and Irshad Ahmad Mir, sixteen. The killings were believed to be in retaliation for an attack five days earlier, in which militants had hurled a grenade at a BSF patrol.

Not a single soldier was prosecuted in a court of law or convicted for the murder or torture of a detainee. Army authorities did, however, make public a number of courts-martial of soldiers accused of rape. On July 29, 1994, two soldiers were sentenced to twelve years in prison after being court-martialed for raping a village woman in Kashmir.

In August, India's junior defense minister admitted that there had been fifty instances of soldiers killing civilians in India since the beginning of the year.

In May, and then again in October, Indian authorities released key Kashmiri opposition leaders from prison. The government then announced that elections would be held within eight months, despite objections by Kashmiri opposition parties who said they would boycott Indian-administered elections. The released prisoners included Yasin Malik, head of the Jammu and Kashmir Liberation Front, Abdul Gani Lone and Syed Ali Shah Gilani of the All Party Hurriyat, and Shabir Ahmed Shah of the People's League. Shah was released on October 14 after four years in detention under the Jammu and Kashmir Public Safety Act.

Militant factions were also responsible for abuses in Kashmir during the year, including the June 1994 kidnapping of two British tourists by a pro-Pakistani militant organization called the Harakatul Ansar (both men were released unharmed); the June 19 assassination of Dr. Qazi Nisar, a well-known religious leader, reportedly by the Hezb-ul Mujahidin, the most powerful of the groups that support accession to Pakistan; and the October kidnappings of three British and one American tourist by Al Hadid, a group Indian authorities said was based in Pakistan and Afghanistan and had links to Harakatul Ansar.

In Punjab, where militant violence had all but ended, police abuses continued, including the disappearance of a prominent human rights lawyer in May. The press was also targeted. On January 11, eight employees of the Punjabi newspaper *Aj Di Awaz*, including the managing editor Gurdeep Singh, were arrested under the TADA law. Ten days before the arrests, Gurdeep Singh had been called to the office of the assistant district police commissioner and ordered to refrain from criticizing state authorities.

The Indian government came under increasing international pressure to answer charges of abuse by Punjab's police force. On September 16, India's Supreme Court ordered a federal inquiry into the disappearance in Punjab of seven members of one family in October 1991. Chief Justice M.N. Venkatachalliah criticized Punjab's police chief, K.P.S. Gill, for inadequate investigation of the case and expressed deep concern for the "safety of the citizenry at the hands of an errant, high-handed and unchecked police force." Gill has been personally identified with many of the most serious abuses of human rights in Punjab.

Communal violence broke out in the southern state of Karnataka in October. Twenty-six people were reportedly killed and more than two hundred injured in the city of Bangalore when Hindus and Muslims clashed over the state government's introduction of Urdu-language news broadcasts. Urdu is spoken mainly by Muslims, a minority in India. According to Bangalore police, at least eight of those killed were shot by police who opened fire on rioters armed with knives and sticks. The violence reportedly began when Muslims threw stones at Hindus protesting the broadcasts. Karnataka's Congress Party-led government accused its chief political rival, the Hindu-nationalist Bharatiya Janata Party (BJP), of organizing the protests, seeking to ignite Hindu-Muslim enmity in advance of state elections. In the wake of the violence, the state government suspended the broadcasts.

Indian counterinsurgency efforts in the northeastern states of Assam and Manipur in 1994 continued to be marked by reports of severe abuses of human rights, including indiscriminate attacks on residential areas, disappearances, extrajudicial killings, and torture of suspected militant sympathizers. In Assam, staged "encounter" killings of young men detained, tortured and executed by the Central Reserve Police Force continued to be reported by human rights organizations and featured in the local press. The apparent torture and extrajudicial execution of five members of the All Assam Student Union in February drew widespread criticism from local activists who submitted the case to the National Human Rights Commission for investigation.

Special security laws, including TADA, the National Security Act and the Armed Forces Special Powers Act, have severely restricted freedom of expression and dissent in the northeast. TADA was used repeatedly in 1994 to silence journalists, including Ajit Kumar Bhuyan, the convener of the human rights organization Manab Adhikar Sangram Samiti (MASS), who was arrested in July. At least ten other journalists in Assam were arrested in the second half of the year.

Northeastern India was also the site of increased insurgent violence in 1994. In Assam, between May and July, clashes between militant members of the Bodo community and Bangladeshi Muslim immigrants led to more than one hundred deaths and the displacement of some 50,000 people. Violence also continued in Manipur between members of the National Socialist Council of Nagaland (NSCN), an ethnically based group fighting for an independent Naga state, and rival Kuki militants. Since May 1993, an estimated 1,000 people have been killed and tens of thousands have been displaced in violence between the two groups, which has been characterized by the destruction of villages and large-scale attacks on Kuki and Naga civilians. In January, the Indian government dissolved the Manipur's state government and imposed president's rule.

In Maharashtra and Madhya Pradesh, peaceful protesters who opposed a World Bank-funded dam on the Narmada river were subjected to arbitrary arrest, illegal detention, beatings, and other forms of physical abuse. These abuses were part of a repressive campaign by the state governments involved to prevent the groups from organizing support for the protests in villages affected by the dam. Nevertheless, protests intensified in a number of villages near the dam site in mid-1994 when officials began to forcibly evict villagers in the submergence zone in anticipation of monsoon flooding.

The Right to Monitor

In Punjab, attacks on human rights monitors continued. On May 12, Sukhwinder Singh Bhatti, a human rights lawyer, was abducted by armed men in plainclothes, thought to be police, as he was traveling by bus from Sangrur to his home village of Badbur in Punjab. The authorities denied that Bhatti was in custody. On June 17 the Punjab and Haryana High Court directed the Central Bureau of Investigation to inquire into his "disappearance," but as of November he had not been traced.

In Assam, as noted above, the journalist Ajit Kumar Bhuyan was arrested and detained in July under TADA after he published an exposé on official corruption. He was accused of inciting the kidnapping of a tax official featured in the article.

In March 1994, the International Committee of the Red Cross was invited to conduct a survey of humanitarian needs in Kashmir. In mid-September, the Indian government agreed to allow the ICRC to provide limited humanitarian assistance in Kashmir. The government also agreed in principle to allow the organization to visit prisons, but the details of the agreement had not been finalized at this writing. At the same time, the government blocked the granting of visas to two Human Rights Watch researchers. In August, Minister of State for External Affairs Salman Khurshid told the press that the government would not consider a request from Human Rights Watch for a research mission.

The first reports of the National Human Rights Commission, established in September 1993, were issued in early 1994 and were more hard-hitting than many had expected. For example, its report on the October 1993 massacre of forty-three civilians in Bijbehara, Kashmir, called for the prosecution of fourteen members of the Border Security Force (BSF). According to the Indian government, a BSF staff inquiry charged four BSF members with excessive use of force, and a separate magesterial inquiry indicted twelve. Court-martial proceedings were initiated against persons named in the inquiries and their commanding officer was placed under a form of house arrest. The Indian authorities have not publicized the proceedings. The Human Rights Commission also requested reports from every state where deaths in custody or custodial rapes occur within twenty-four hours of the incidents, and has acknowledged widespread concern over the abuse of TADA by undertaking a review of the law. On October 7, Indian Home Minister S.B. Chavan denied allegations of abuse under the act and ruled out the possibility that TADA would be repealed.

The Role of the International Community

Pressure on India to improve its human rights record was more muted than in previous years, in part because of a successful campaign by the Indian government to woo critics with business opportunities. In both the United States and Europe, trade increasingly became the cornerstone of bilateral policies toward India. In July, the Council of the European Union approved a comprehensive trade agreement with the Indian government, despite a key article in the agreement asserting that human rights was the basis for cooperation.

Both the United States and Europe backed away from criticism of Indian human rights abuses.

U.S. Policy

In 1993, the Clinton administration had broken with previous administrations in publicly criticizing India's human rights record. Reaction to what was portrayed by Indian leaders as a dramatic change in U.S. policy was swift. In a move apparently designed to persuade the Clinton administration to back off its public stance, Indian officials condemned U.S. criticism as a "tilt" to Pakistan

which would endanger Indo-U.S. relations. The Clinton administration quickly capitulated, and since early 1994 has blunted criticism of India's human rights record, choosing instead to focus on economic relations. That human rights would be relegated to private discussion only was made clear by the new U.S. Ambassador to India, Frank Wisner, in an interview published in the July 15, 1994, issue of the prominent Indian news magazine *India Today*. Ambassador Wisner stated that he believed human rights was an issue governments should discuss privately. In a letter to Human Rights Watch/Asia dated July 21, Assistant Secretary of State Robin Raphel echoed this line, stating that the administration "believe[d] that at this time the most effective way for the U.S. government to influence the Indian government...is through private, rather than public, diplomacy."

The State Department repeatedly gave India credit for measures the government had not even taken. At a hearing before the Senate Appropriations Subcommittee on April 19, Assistant Secretary of State for Democracy, Human Rights and Labor John Shattuck claimed that the administration had "successfully pushed for unfettered access for international human rights and humanitarian organizations to Kashmir." In fact, no international human rights groups were permitted to conduct independent investigations in Kashmir. As previously noted, twice in 1994, India failed to grant visas to Human Rights Watch/Asia researchers.

In April, U.S. Deputy Secretary of State Strobe Talbott made a trip to India his first official visit after assuming office. Talbott and Prime Minister Rao discussed U.S. initiatives to end the nuclear stalemate between India and Pakistan, and Rao accepted an invitation from President Clinton to visit the U.S.

During Prime Minister Rao's visit to the U.S. in May, during which he was given the honor of addressing a joint session of Congress, all mention of human rights was avoided. At a lunch hosted by Vice President Al Gore in honor of Prime Minister Rao's visit, human rights, which had been a major issue between the two countries, was not mentioned.

At the meeting of the U.N. Commission on Human Rights in March, India went to extraordinary lengths, even enlisting the support of such dubious allies as Iran and China, to ensure that a resolution condemning abuses in Kashmir was withdrawn. The U.S. abstained.

E.U. Policy

An agreement of cooperation between India and the European Community, which was approved by the Council of the European Union on June 18, 1994, completely disregarded India's human rights record when it pledged mutual cooperation on trade and investment, "technical, economic and cultural matters," acceleration of India's economic development, and liberalization of imports and exports. Article 1 of the agreement stated, without irony, that "[r]espect for human rights and democratic principles is the basis for the cooperation between the Contracting Parties and for the provisions of this Agreement, and it constitutes an essential element of the Agreement."

The Work of
Human Rights Watch/Asia

Human Rights Watch/Asia broadened its work on India in 1994 to include new projects on the role of political forces in communal violence, the trafficking of Nepali women and girls for prostitution in India, and the relationship between HIV/AIDS and human rights. Human Rights Watch/Asia continued to monitor events in Kashmir, which remained among the most serious human rights situations in Asia, and on Punjab, where despite the cessation of militant violence, police continued to commit abuses and to enjoy impunity for past violations.

Human Rights Watch/Asia sought to sustain international pressure on the Indian government to stop abuses by its forces and prosecute past violations. In May, Human Rights Watch/Asia and Physicians for Human Rights published *Dead Silence: Legacy of Abuses in Punjab*. The report, which documented continuing violations of human rights by Punjab's police force despite the end of militant violence, was released during Prime Minister Rao's visit to the U.S. Conditions documented in the report were raised by members of Congress and the press during his visit.

Human Rights Watch/Asia's work on Kashmir in 1994 focused on the power of international bodies like the U.N., and important trading partners like the U.S., to help or hinder efforts to improve human rights conditions in the region. In August a new report, *Continuing Repression in Kashmir: Abuses Rise as International Pressure on India Eases,* examined the link between an upsurge in violations by Indian forces in Kashmir during the first half of 1994 and decreased international pressure on India to end abuses.

INDONESIA AND EAST TIMOR

Human Rights Developments

Indonesia's policy of "openness," characterized by broadened press freedoms, greater tolerance of demonstrations, increased visibility of nongovernmental organizations, and open discussion of previously taboo subjects, came to an abrupt end during the year with the closing of three well-known news publications in June. The closures, weeks before the Asia-Pacific Economic Cooperation (APEC) summit was to be held in Jakarta, served to draw international attention back to a pattern of abuse that the policy of "openness" had temporarily obscured.

That pattern was characterized by military intervention in virtually all aspects of Indonesian public life and by the arbitrary exercise of authority by President Soeharto, well into his fifth term as president and looking increasingly likely to stay in office for life. More and more, however, the president and senior army officers were at odds, with Soeharto's championing of the powerful minister of research and technology, B.J. Habibie, a major sore point with the military as Habibie increasingly took on defense procurement functions and worked on turning an organization of Muslim intellectuals into a vehicle to build a political base for the president and himself. (The immediate cause of the press closures was a series of articles in one of the banned magazines about Habibie's controversial decision, without the military's knowledge, to purchase thirty-nine ships from the former East German navy.) Neither the military nor the president was accountable to the Indonesian public for their actions, and therein lay one of the key factors in ongoing human rights abuses.

In addition to restrictions on freedom of expression and curbs on dissent, the abuses included denial of worker rights, especially the ability to form independent trade unions; harassment and intimidation of nongovernmental organizations and professional associations; forcible dispersal of peaceful demonstrations and other legitimate exercises of freedom of assembly; arbitrary detention; and torture. In East Timor, violations of fundamental civil rights were particularly severe.

The issue of worker rights came to a head with a massive workers' rally on April 14 and 15 in Medan, North Sumatra, where workers poured into the streets demanding higher wages and the right to organize, and the subsequent trials of its alleged organizers in October and November. The rally was the culmination of months of wildcat strikes and turned into anti-Chinese violence on the second day, with Chinese-owned shops vandalized and one ethnic Chinese businessman reported as killed; although his death was initially reported as a lynching, an autopsy showed that he died of a stroke after his car was set upon by angry workers. The violence appeared to have been instigated by typed flyers distributed by military-backed thugs.

Hundreds of workers and labor organizers were arrested in connection with both the rally and several subsequent strikes in North Sumatra, and they were tried more quickly than usual, apparently to try to defuse worker grievances before the APEC conference. Most workers accused of damaging property were sentenced to relatively lenient terms of three or four months in prison. Independent labor organizers accused of incitement were treated more harshly. Amosi Telaumbanua, the head of the Medan branch of the independent but officially unrecognized labor union called Serikat Buruh Sejahtera Indonesia (SBSI), was sentenced to fifteen months in prison in late October, and SBSI's national head, Mochtar Pakpahan, was expected to get three years—long enough to keep him out of circulation during the national parliamentary elections in 1997. Several other labor organizers, including two activists from Medan named Janes Hutahean and Parlin Manihuruk, were on trial as of early November. Human Rights Watch/Asia believed all those charged with incitement were arrested in violation of their right to freedom of association.

In an effort to dampen domestic and international criticism of worker rights, especially with the threat of American economic sanctions looming large, the Indonesian government announced a series of labor reforms in January and raised the minimum wage. It also entered into an agreement with the International Labor Organization which many local labor activists saw as merely serving to strengthen the government-recognized union.

Freedom of association was also at stake with the drafting of a presidential decree on nongovernmental organizations (NGOs) that would tighten government control of their activities and make it possible for them to be dissolved if they were judged to have engaged in actions detrimental to undefined "national interests." The draft decree was circulated by the Ministry of Home Affairs in February, and as of November, it had not yet been promulgated, although many believed the government was waiting until after the APEC conference to do so. The decree appeared to be aimed at many of the most outspoken human rights and environmental organizations including the Legal Aid Institute and WALHI. The latter, an environmental organization, brought a lawsuit against President Soeharto in September in the Jakarta administrative court, alleging that he had allowed Minister Habibie to take a no-interest loan from funds meant for reforestation in order to support the development of Habibie's aircraft manufacturing company.

The travails of Independent Journalists Association (Aliansi Jurnalis Independen, AJI), were also indicative of controls on freedom of association. Most professional organizations in Indonesia are government-backed or run and have no interest in challenging government policies. The officially-recognized journalists organization, Persatuan Wartawan Indonesia (Indonesian Journalists Association, PWI), was no exception. The closure of two magazines, *Tempo* and *Editor*, and a tabloid newspaper, *DeTik*, on June 21, however, led outraged journalists and editors, many of them from the banned publications, to set up AJI on August 8. In what became known as the Sirna Galih Declaration after the place where it was announced, the journalists rejected "all kinds of interference, intimidation, censorship and media bans which deny freedom of speech and open access to information." The Ministry of Information then began to harass AJI members, saying the organization was not recognized, suggesting to their editors that they be fired and stating that access to important meetings like APEC would be restricted to PWI members. On October 31, Andreas Harsono, a prominent AJI member and journalist from the English-language *Jakarta Post* was fired, on vague charges of misconduct.

Two of the publications closed down in June attempted unsuccessfully to reopen under other names and with a new editorial staff. The editor of *DeTik*, Eros Djarot, tried to publish a look-alike tabloid called *Simponi* on October 3, but it was shut down after one day, in part on the grounds that journalists who were not PWI members were involved in its publication. The staff of *Tempo* loyal to the former editors tried to obtain a new license for a *Tempo* look-alike called *Berita*, but as of November, their chances of doing so looked slim.

Academic freedom became a major issue late in the year with the military interrogation and dismissal respectively of two noted activist professors from a small Christian university, Satya Wacana Christian University, in Salatiga, Central Java. Dr. Arief Budiman, a Harvard-trained sociologist and professor of development studies at the University, was fired, effective October 31, ostensibly for "making unauthorized comments that damaged the good name" of the university. Budiman was outspoken on everything from human rights to political succession in Indonesia to the need for democracy on campus. Dr. George Aditjondro, who holds a PhD in education, was intensively interrogated by police in the central Javanese city of Yogyakarta in October. He was suspected of having insulted governmental authorities for humorous remarks he made about the political power structure in Indonesia during a university seminar on August 11. He had also been repeatedly criticized by officials for his work on East Timor, suggesting that the death toll in the 1991 Dili massacre was far higher than acknowledged.

The government made no effort to investigate, let alone stop, torture by both the military and police, who are also part of the armed forces. One prominent case publicized during the year involved members of one faction of a church dispute in North Sumatra who were severely tortured in the district military command of Tarutung, North Tapanuli, after their arrest on May 12. They were arrested, in violation of their right to freedom of assembly, on suspicion of having conducted a secret meeting to discuss church affairs; a month afterwards, two were still hospitalized as a result of the torture they suffered. Torture was also a major issue at the trial of eight civilians and one military officer accused in the May 1993 slaying of a labor organizer named Marsinah, whose murder became one of the most notorious human rights cases of the decade. At the trials in Surabaya and Sidoarjo, East Java, between March and July 1994, all of the civilians alleged that they had been tortured during the nineteen-day period in October 1993 and that they had been held in incommunicado detention by the intelligence unit of the East Java division of the army.

The army also stepped up an anti-crime campaign that appeared to involve the extrajudicial execution of criminal suspects, when it launched a so-called Operation Clean-Up in April. The Jakarta police commander gave the upcoming APEC conference as one reason for the draconian measures. At least thirteen suspected criminals were shot dead in the first month of the operation.

East Timor, the territory invaded by Indonesia in 1975 and unlawfully annexed as its twenty-seventh province in 1976, continued to be the site of major human rights abuses, as the government tried to prevent any expression of pro-independence sentiment or dissatisfaction with Indonesian administration. At the same time, there were some signs of movement on the question of East Timor's political status. A "reconciliation meeting" took place in England from September 27 to September 29 between East Timorese working with the Indonesian government and East Timorese exiles, who for the most part, however, were not supporters of the largest resistance organization, the Maubere National Resistance Council (CNRM). A CNRM leader, Jose Ramos Horta, met with Indonesian Foreign Minister Ali Alatas in New York on October 7 for further talks, although Indonesia said the talks did not constitute negotiations.

In East Timor itself, tight controls on the freedoms of expression, association and assembly remained in place, and while disappearances and extrajudicial executions were increasingly rare, there was no progress on accounting for past cases. (The U.N. Human Rights Commission's special rapporteur on summary and arbitrary executions visited East Timor at the invitation of the Indonesian government in July.)

Two demonstrations were forcibly broken up by the military. On April 14, a small group of East Timorese held a pro-independence demonstration in front of the hotel in Dili, the capital of East Timor, where a delegation of foreign journalists was staying. They were briefly detained, then released until after the journalists had departed. In early May, eleven young men were arrested in connection with the demonstration, and six were eventually charged and tried. The heaviest sentence was given to Pedro de Fatima, three years and six months for "spreading hatred toward the government of Indonesia."

On July 14, a march of students from the University of East Timor to the local parliament to protest the behavior of Indonesian soldiers and perceived religious insults had just gotten underway when it was forcibly dispersed by the military. The military blamed the students for initiating the violence by throwing stones at security forces, but this account was contradicted by the university's rector, a Javanese named Bratasudarma, who saw developments unfold and said soldiers had led the attack.

Peaceful supporters of independence continued to be arrested. On May 19, an East Timorese theological student named Jose Antonio Neves was arrested in Malang, East Java, while posting a letter from the East Timorese guerrilla leader Konis Santana to supporters attending a conference in Manila. His trial was ongoing in November. Dozens of East Timorese remained in prison for their nonviolent role in organizing or participating in a funeral procession on November 12, 1991, on which Indonesian troops opened fire.

Indonesian sensitivities over East Timor led to an effort to export controls on freedom of expression and assembly to neighboring countries. In May, the Indonesian government tried to stop a conference on East Timor from being held in Manila; after canceling joint venture contracts with Philippine companies and engaging in other heavy-handed tactics, it succeeded in persuading

President Fidel Ramos to ban foreigners from attending the four-day Asia-Pacific Conference on East Timor (APCET). Similar pressure was exerted on Malaysia in June and on Thailand in July to stop meetings or demonstrations in support of East Timor.

The Right to Monitor

Indonesia human rights groups faced routine harassment, and the pending presidential decree on NGOs appeared to be aimed in particular at them. One provision in particular would make it possible for the government to dissolve any nongovernmental organization (NGO) that provided assistance to "foreign parties" in a way that could be considered "damaging to Indonesia's foreign policy." Provision of human rights information to international NGOs might well fall in that category.

Some human rights lawyers were arrested during the year. Maiyasyak Djohan, a lawyer with an organization called the Indonesian Institute for Children's Advocacy (Lembaga Advokasi Anak Indonesia) was arrested in September in connection with the April worker unrest in Medan, apparently because of information given to him during confidential conversations with his clients who had been involved in earlier strikes. He was expected to be tried on charges of incitement in November. A lawyer named Munir from the Legal Aid Institute's Surabaya (East Java) branch was arrested and briefly detained on August 19 in Malang, East Java, for advising workers on how to pursue legal claims for unfair dismissal. He was accused of holding a meeting without a permit. As the summit meeting of the APEC organization approached, human rights activists from the Legal Aid Institute and other organizations found themselves under constant surveillance by military intelligence. On November 12, twenty-nine East Timorese climbed into the American embassy compound in Jakarta, demanding a meeting with President Clinton and the release of resistance leader Xanana Gusmao. Other East Timorese who did not make it into the embassy grounds were arrested; as of mid-November, four were in military custody in Jakarta and the fate of some thirty-six others was unclear.

The Role of the International Community

International concern over worker rights and East Timor was more than matched by the increasing tendencies of developed countries to see Indonesia as an emerging regional power and attractive market. The latter view began to prevail in the United States, after a relatively tough stance on human rights during the Clinton administration's first two years led to increasing pressures from sources ranging from the business community to the Australian government, to take a more "constructive" approach.

The American reversal on labor rights was a case in point. After having given the Indonesian government eight months in July 1993 to improve its labor rights policies or face a cut-off of tariff benefits under the Generalized System of Preferences (GSP) program, the U.S. Trade Representative's office decided in February that the legal reforms announced by the Indonesian government in January were sufficient to warrant a decision to "suspend but not terminate" its review of labor rights practices. The legal reforms in question, however, which included revoking a decree that allowed military intervention in labor disputes; allowing workers to negotiate collective bargaining agreements at the workplace level; restructuring the single government-recognized union; and raising the minimum wage, had little effect in practice on abuses of worker rights. In late August, the USTR's office visited Indonesia to assess worker rights again, and despite the fact that key labor organizers were under arrest in Medan and that military intervention in labor disputes continued to be routine, the Clinton administration showed no signs of reviving the pressure.

Indonesian pressure on the Philippines over the East Timor conference in May provoked especially strong reactions in France, where one of the invitees denied a visa to attend was Danielle Mitterand, wife of the French president. Several delegations of parliamentarians visited East Timor during the year, from Britain, Sweden, New Zealand, and Japan. In November, the Japanese parliamentarians, who had visited in August, urged Prime Minister Murayama to raise the issue of human rights in East Timor during his bilateral meeting with President Soeharto at the APEC conference in Jakarta; they also criticized the use of Japanese development aid to monitor shortwave transmission in East Timor.

Several countries expressed concern about the clashes in July between Indonesian soldiers and East Timorese in Remexio and Dili; on July 18, the European Union issued a declaration calling for respect for human rights, access by international organizations and creation of the conditions that would allow a just, lasting and internationally acceptable solution to the question of East Timor.

The newspaper closures in June generated widespread, but muted, international criticism. Australian Prime Minister Gareth Evans called it "a very disappointing development indeed." The initial American response was to express "regret." A somewhat stronger statement, buried in paragraphs of praise for economic achievements, was included in the U.S. delegation's statement at the annual meeting in July of the Consultative Group on Indonesia (CGI), the countries and international lending institutions that provide Indonesia with development aid.

A debate ensued in both Europe and the United States over arms sales to Indonesia. On June 16, the Senate Foreign Operations Subcommittee, in a report attached to the 1995 foreign aid bill, urged the U.S. government to "carefully consider progress in addressing human rights concerns" prior to approving licenses to sell military equipment. The Clinton administration adopted a new policy on Indonesia in 1994, ceasing both sales and the granting of licenses for export of small arms and other crowd control items. The subcommittee report suggested that certain human rights conditions be met before the sales or licensing was resumed. The administration opposed the proposal, and the Indonesian government said it would rather buy arms elsewhere than accept conditions. But on August 1, Congress went ahead with wording that arms sales and export licensing to Indonesia could take place only if the President could report that the Indonesian government was reducing its military presence in East Timor, complying with the recommendations made by the U.N. Human Rights Commission in a resolution on East Timor in March 1993 and working to advance the U.N. Secretary-General's efforts to resolve the political status of the territory.

As it did in 1993, the American embassy in Jakarta played a useful role in raising concerns over a number of human rights issues that arose during the year, including press freedom, the arrest of labor activists and East Timor.

The Work of Human Rights Watch/Asia

Indonesia remained a priority country for Human Rights Watch/Asia, both in terms of research and advocacy. As with China, the challenge was to keep public attention to human rights high as the desirability of the Indonesian market loomed larger to foreign investors. Worker rights continued to be a primary focus and the subject of two short reports in January and May. Efforts were also made to look at abuses in areas outside Jakarta and Java that were less likely to be covered by the international press.

After a research visit to Indonesia in June, Human Rights Watch/Asia issued a book-length report, *The Limits of Openness: Human Rights in Indonesia and East Timor*, in September, followed by an analysis of the measures Indonesia was taking to prevent any signs of dissent or unrest during the APEC conference. The June visit was also an opportunity to reinforce already close ties with Indonesian NGOs and to discuss priorities, tactics and training with them.

The Washington office of Human Rights

Watch/Asia was central to advocacy efforts, again with a particular focus on workers' rights, maintaining contacts and providing information to the State Department, foreign embassies, the World Bank, and Congressional offices and the business community.

JAPAN

Human Rights Developments

Japan experienced dramatic changes on the domestic political front in 1994, but the impact on foreign policy, specifically in the area of human rights, was negligible. The resignation of Prime Minister Morihiro Hosokawa in April led to the creation of a short-lived minority coalition government headed by Tsutomu Hata; this, in turn, was replaced by a tripartite alliance of political parties, which chose Tomiichi Murayama, chair of the Social Democratic Party, as prime minister on June 29. Murayama came into power pledging a continuation of Japan's existing foreign policy.

Japan's human rights diplomacy continued to be conditioned largely by overriding political and economic interests. On the sensitive question of the participation of Japan's Self-Defense Forces (SDF) in overseas multilateral operations, however, Murayama's party abandoned its traditional opposition, and Japan agreed in August to send SDF medical, engineering and other forces to provide humanitarian assistance to Rwandan refugees in Zaire.

The guiding principles for Japan's foreign aid program—or Official Development Assistance (ODA)—first adopted in 1991, remained in place, including making provision of aid contingent on respect for human rights and progress towards democratization. Sixty percent of ODA was given to Asian governments in 1993 (the last year for which statistics are available), with Indonesia, China, the Philippines, Thailand, and Malaysia among the top ten ODA recipients worldwide. Rather than adopting specific human rights criteria for ODA, the govern-

ment emphasized constructive improvements through "quiet and continuous *démarches*." In a handful of cases, "flagrant violations of human rights," clearly designated as such by the broader international community, might result in cut-off or suspension of economic assistance. In 1994, for example, all aid with the exception of certain humanitarian assistance, remained suspended to Sudan (as of October 1992); to Sierra Leone (as of May 1993); and to Malawi (as of May 1992). As of the military coup in September 1991, ODA to Haiti had been suspended. Following President Aristide's return, ODA was restored in October 1994; Japan also pledged the equivalent of U.S.$14 million to help Haiti settle its arrears to international financial organizations. Assistance to Nigeria was suspended on March 18, 1994, with a public statement calling on the military to transfer political power to a civilian government and publish a timetable for the transition.

The only Asian country where aid flows were directly affected by the ODA human rights guideline was Burma, where economic assistance had been suspended in principle since 1988, with the exception of certain projects of a "humanitarian" nature. In February, following cabinet-level discussions, it was decided to give $50,000 to the Burmese Red Cross and another $180,000 to Médecins sans Frontières. In June, a forty-five-member corporate delegation led by Keidanren (the Federation of Economic Organizations) visited Burma to assess the investment potential and met with top-ranking military leaders and oil industry officials. In November, Japan announced it was extending $10 million in humanitarian and medical aid, and was considering full resumption of ODA.

At the same time, on the diplomatic level, Japan continued to call for the release of imprisoned Burmese opposition leader Aung San Suu Kyi, while welcoming the September 20 meeting between the imprisoned leader and senior military officials. This message was also conveyed in July at the so-called Post-Ministerial Conference of the Association of Southeast Asian Nations

(ASEAN), during a brief meeting between Japan's foreign minister and his Burmese counterpart.

Members of the Diet expressed concern about the human rights situation in Burma and urged action by the Japanese government, in a petition delivered to then-Prime Minister Hata on May 18, 1994, signed by 508 members of parliament.

Aid levels to other major human rights abusers in Asia, however, remained unaffected by the ODA principles on human rights. China, which received $1.05 billion in 1992, was told in 1994 that the next package of ODA loans would be scaled back from five years to three years, but the step appeared to be more a signal of concern about China's growing military budget than about human rights practices. Likewise on India, while Tokyo raised concerns about India's proliferation policies an ODA delegation that visited Delhi in March did not bring up human rights and humanitarian concerns in Kashmir.

In the case of Indonesia, at the annual bilateral donors meeting in July 1994, Japan pledged a record $1.67 billion in ODA in the coming fiscal year, and during the meeting, voiced only very general concerns about the human rights situation. East Timor continued to attract attention from both the foreign ministry and Diet. When an ODA delegation met with President Soeharto in Jakarta in February, there were oblique references made to human rights and East Timor. Five Diet members went to Indonesia in August on a fact-finding mission and publicly called for the withdrawal of Indonesian troops from East Timor.

China presented one of the most difficult challenges to Japan in 1994. Tokyo provoked a sharp backlash from Beijing, including a formal protest from its ambassador in Japan, when it co-sponsored a resolution criticizing China at the 1994 session of the U.N. Human Rights Commission in Geneva. Shortly thereafter, then-Prime Minister Hosokawa went to Beijing immediately following U.S. Secretary of State Warren Christopher in March, at the height of the dispute over Most Favored Nation (MFN) status. While there, he reportedly urged Li Peng to take steps to improve China's human rights record, citing the concern of the international community and the final communiqué of the Vienna U.N. human rights conference in 1993 in particular. But Chinese officials and Hosokawa himself later contradicted these reports, acknowledging that the Japanese prime minister had in fact reinforced Li Peng's assertion that human rights are essentially a Western notion—thus effectively undercutting the MFN pressure from the U.S. at a critical time. The Japanese government welcomed Clinton's decision in May to de-link MFN and human rights.

Tokyo further strengthened its relations with Vietnam during the year, while largely ignoring human rights concerns. ODA to Vietnam was resumed in 1992, and by last year Japan was Hanoi's single largest aid donor, supporting construction of thermal power plants and other major infrastructure projects, and giving aid totaling $523 million in fiscal year 1993. When Prime Minister Murayama visited Vietnam in August 1994, he promised even more aid, but said nothing about human rights—thus wasting Japan's considerable potential for urging both economic and political reforms in Vietnam.

As the foreign ministry explored various means of implementing Japan's evolving human rights policy, it commissioned a study group, convened by the Japan International Cooperation Agency (JICA), to examine the concept of "good governance" and to suggest ways in which Japanese policy might reflect this approach to development assistance. Its study was due to be published at the end of 1994.

Human rights in Japan came into sharper focus during the year with attention to mistreatment of foreign workers, including Asian women trafficked into Japan for prostitution. Prison conditions also came under the scrutiny of international and domestic human rights organizations. (*See* Human Rights Watch Prison Project section.)

Right to Monitor

Human rights groups in Japan faced no legal restrictions.

U.S. Policy

In February 1994, U.S. Assistant Secretary of State for Democracy, Human Rights and Labor, John Shattuck visited Tokyo for talks with his counterparts in the Foreign Ministry. This was the first step in developing a formal means of bilateral cooperation on specific human rights issues. Within the Foreign Ministry, there appeared to be genuine interest in working with the U.S. on human rights problems, while recognizing that Japan's approach and strategy might differ.

Six ranking members of the U.S. Senate, including the chairman of the Foreign Relations Committee, wrote to the Japanese ambassador in March 1994, to express concern about possible resumption of ODA to Burma and to urge Japan's continued support for human rights and civilian rule in Burma.

The Work of
Human Rights Watch/Asia

Human Rights Watch sent four missions to Japan in 1994. The Washington director of Human Rights Watch/Asia visited Tokyo in March and again in November to continue a dialogue with government officials, Diet members, and others on Japan's human rights policies. Also in March, the Women's Rights Project sent a team to begin investigations of the trafficking of women from Southeast Asia in Japan. In July, the Prison Project sent a delegation to assess conditions in Japanese penal institutions, with a report expected in early 1995.

The Human Rights Watch/Asia office in Washington, D.C. maintained regular contacts with the Japanese embassy and exchanged information throughout the year on a range of human rights concerns.

NEPAL

Human Rights Developments

Throughout Nepal in 1994, police continued to be the primary violators of human rights. Abuse occurred in connection with crowd control, during arrests, and in detention. Between May and August 1994, Nepal experienced its most serious period of political unrest since a popular movement led to the reestablishment of multiparty democracy in April 1990. Nationwide strikes and political protests accompanied the dissolution of the country's elected government. Reports followed of large-scale arbitrary arrests and detention and police abuse—including beatings and torture—of opposition supporters, journalists, and street children.

Demonstrations and political rallies continued in the days leading up to the November 15 elections. At least six people were killed in pre-election violence, including two who were shot when police opened fire on stone-throwing demonstrators at an opposition rally on November 3. More than twenty-five others were injured in the shooting.

The state's unwillingness to prosecute police officers guilty of wrongdoing has perpetuated routine custodial abuse and promoted corruption. Several disappearances from police custody were reported in 1994, and at least one prominent disappearance case from 1993 remained unresolved. Beatings and mistreatment in police lockups, attempts by police to extort money from detainees, and the almost systematic fleecing of Tibetan refugees attempting to enter Nepal have been widely reported. Like many Asian nations, Nepal has made little progress in eradicating contemporary forms of slavery such as the trafficking of women and girls for prostitution in India, the sale of children as factory workers, and the unchecked use of bonded labor. The trafficking industry has been sustained by bribes made to police officers and other officials, and by corrupt politicians who profit from the trade.

On May 4, the first of a series of nationwide strikes and demonstrations was called by the United People's Front, an opposition party, to protest the government of Girija Prasad Koirala perceived subservience to India in the wake of an unauthorized raid on houses in Kathmandu by Indian police searching for a criminal. The strike and ensuing demonstrations, which were largely peaceful, led to the arrests of some four hundred people, many of whom were held for more than four days without charge. Among those arrested were more than eighty street children, who have frequently been found at the front of such demonstrations and sometimes throw rocks. According to Child Workers in Nepal (CWIN), a local organization that monitors the rights of children, many of the children who were detained during the May demonstrations complained of beatings and torture by police, said they were not provided with food, blankets or bedding during the two to three days they were detained, and charged that some of them were forced to perform labor for the police.

In July, Nepal's first democratically elected prime minister in three decades, Girija Prasad Koirala, resigned after he failed to receive his party's support on a crucial parliamentary vote. On July 11, King Birendra dissolved Nepal's parliament, called midterm elections for November, and appointed Koirala interim prime minister—a move that led to protests by opposition supporters throughout the country. Between July 20 and 24, human rights workers reported that some 500 people, mainly opposition party supporters, were arrested in connection with political protests. While some demonstrators reportedly engaged in rock throwing or vandalism, many people thought to be potential troublemakers were arrested before the demonstrations as a preventive measure.

The Informal Sector Service Center (INSEC), a prominent Nepali human rights organization, reported that at least three people disappeared from police custody in the first half of 1994. Two were criminal detainees; the third, thirty-two-year-old Triloki Gaud, disappeared on May 17 from a local police post where he had gone to report the theft of a large amount of timber. His mother, who had gone with him, reported that she and her son were both badly beaten by police before she was forcibly ejected from the police station. Her son never returned home.

The well publicized disappearance of Prabhakar Subedi, a twenty-year-old engineering student who disappeared during a demonstration on June 25, 1993, remained unresolved in spite of a 1993 court order directing the police to investigate.

Local human rights organizations continued to raise concerns over unlawful use of force by Nepali police. In January 1994, for example, one person was killed and several injured when police in eastern Nepal opened fire on demonstrators protesting the actions of a police officer who poured boiling water under the skirt of a woman who ran a roadside restaurant. The police officer was suspended pending investigation.

Reports of police corruption and the involvement of politicians in the forcible trafficking of Nepali women and children for prostitution in India persisted in 1994. The Koirala government has made little effort to investigate or prosecute officials accused of links to the industry. Despite laws which provide for prison terms of up to twenty years for the trafficking of persons, the flow of young women and girls to Indian brothels continued unabated, with thousands estimated to be sold every year into conditions akin to slavery, where they are subjected to years of debt-bondage, repeated rapes, and physical assaults.

Human rights organizations in Nepal also raised concerns about the pervasive use of bonded labor in industry and agriculture. But in its March 1994 report to the U.N. on Nepal's compliance with the International Covenant on Civil and Political Rights, the government stated that "No slavery, slave trade or institutions or practices similar to slavery are found in Nepal."

The Right to Monitor
Although human rights organizations enjoyed much greater freedom to operate than

before the democratic government took office, several apparent attempts to silence dissent were reported in 1994. In January, Gopal Siwakoti and Gopal Krishna Siwakoti of the human rights organization INHURED reported receiving a series of anonymous threatening telephone calls after they submitted a petition to the Supreme Court calling for public disclosure of information about the controversial World Bank-funded Arun III hydroelectric project. The petition also called for postponement of the project pending a parliamentary review. On July 22, the office of the Arun Public Commission, another organization critical of the project, was attacked by unknown assailants.

On April 27, the office of the Kathmandu chapter of Amnesty International (AI) was raided by armed men from the Ministry of Finance's revenue investigation department. A Finance Ministry official told the press a team had "visited" the office to investigate the human rights body's financial dealings for tax purposes. Local AI chair Krishna Pahadi said the gunmen had "terrorized" his staff. Eight human right groups in Nepal issued a joint statement on May 1 denouncing the raid.

On July 24 Subodh Pyakurel, a member of the executive committee of the Human Rights Yearbook, a project of INSEC, was among hundreds who were placed in preventive detention in connection with political protests. He was released the following day. Several journalists were also detained.

The Role of the International Community

Nepal is greatly dependent on international aid and on three crucial industries, handmade carpets, tea and tourism. The carpet industry came under intense scrutiny from local human rights groups and the international community in 1994 for its reliance on child labor—including bonded child labor—and its links to the trafficking of girls and women into prostitution in India. A report by the U.S. Department of Labor, published in July 1994, on the use of child labor in American imports supported these findings,

and noted that in 1992 Nepal exported approximately $17 million worth of carpets to the United States. The European Union stopped negotiations concerning possible E.U. aid to the carpet industry due to allegations about the use of bonded child labor.

A report by the United Nations special rapporteur on the sale of children, Vitit Muntabhorn, which was published in January 1994, commented on the trafficking and sale of Nepali children for labor and prostitution, concluding that Nepal's "[l]aw enforcement authorities are often weak, understaffed, undertrained and corrupt..." and that "[t]here is an expansive web of criminality which exploits children and which abuses the open border with India."

The Work of Human Rights Watch/Asia

In March, Human Rights Watch/Asia visited Nepal to renew ties with local human rights groups and to investigate reports of the forcible trafficking of Nepali girls and women to India for prostitution. Meetings and interviews were conducted with women who had been trafficked to India, human rights activists and relief workers who monitor the trade, police, and government officials. A companion mission to India was conducted in August.

In July, Human Rights Watch/Asia wrote to Nepali Home Minister Sher Bahadur Deuba expressing concern over reports of mass arrests, unacknowledged detentions, and torture of political activists. The letter also raised concerns about threats against nongovernmental organizations critical of the Arun dam project.

PAKISTAN

Human Rights Developments

In stark contrast to 1993, when Pakistan experienced four changes in government, in 1994 a coalition led by Prime Minister Benazir Bhutto of the Pakistan People's Party (PPP) held onto its control of the national parliament and the two largest provincial governments, Punjab and Sindh, without significant interference from the president or army. With the political situation thus relatively stable, the government could have addressed the problem of widespread and endemic human rights abuses. It failed to do so, however, and torture, persecution of religious minorities, arbitrary detention, discrimination against women, bonded labor, and other violations of labor rights continued. There were also several reports of extrajudicial executions in the context of violence in Sindh between the government and the Mohajir Qaumi Movement, or MQM, a political party that claims to represent Urdu speakers who fled to Pakistan from India after 1947 and has itself been responsible for serious violations of human rights.

In late April, conflict in Sindh between the MQM and the PPP government flared up. The government's inability to broker a power-sharing arrangement in the region with the MQM, whose primarily urban-based supporters claimed to be underrepresented in the provincial power structure, led to riots in Karachi from April 29 to May 5, leaving thirty-two dead. Police reportedly fired indiscriminately at people in riot-torn neighborhoods. On May 3, police and rangers were reported to have summarily executed five men in two separate incidents in the town of Sukkur, apparently for supposed ties to the MQM.

In October, riots broke out again in Karachi, with some thirty people killed. While much of the violence in Karachi was a direct result of MQM-government conflict, it also involved clashes between Sunni and Shi'a Muslims. The Pakistan government has been complicit in the sectarian violence to the extent that it has routinely failed to denounce, punish or prosecute those involved.

The treatment of religious minorities deteriorated as systematic use was made of the so-called blasphemy law. The blasphemy law makes offenses against Islam, broadly defined, punishable by death and serves as a judicial tool for vengeance in cases of religious, political, social or economic rivalry. While most cases were dismissed, the blasphemy law was also used to incite obscurantist sentiments, which resulted in public violence against the accused. It was also used disproportionately against religious minorities, especially Christians and Ahmadis. In June, in a positive move, the federal cabinet approved a bill to amend the procedure for registering cases of blasphemy. However, after a number of religious parties and the opposition sought to block the proposed amendments, the government deferred its decision to bring the bill before parliament.

Despite the government's stated desire to regulate the use of blasphemy laws, accusations continued to multiply, resulting in attacks on the accused which the police then ignored. On April 5, Manzoor Masih, a Christian on trial under the blasphemy law, was shot and killed after his court hearing in Lahore. The authorities made no concerted effort to find or punish his killers.

Many Muslims have also been prosecuted under the law. While many of the cases do not reach the courts because of the weakness of the evidence against the accused, the public response to accusations can be dangerous. In April, Farooq Sajjad, a practitioner of traditional medicine, was accused and detained near Gujranwalla for allegedly burning a copy of the Qur'an. Soon afterwards, a local mob broke into the police lockup, dragged Sajjad into the streets, and stoned him to death. His corpse was set afire and paraded around town. The police took no action to intervene.

The status of women continued to be neglected by the government. While the government gained media attention during the year for prosecuting Maulvi Mohammad Sharif in a case in which he was charged with inserting electrified iron rods into his wife's vagina, it did not seek to implement legislative reforms to protect women. The Hudood Ordinances, a penal code based on an interpretation of Islamic law which, as applied in Pakistan, explicitly discriminates against women, remain on the statute books. One feature of the Hudood Ordinances is that to secure a conviction for rape, four male Muslim witnesses must testify against the defendant, and if the victim is thought to have accepted the forced intercourse passively, she can be charged and convicted for adultery. Many rape victims thus no longer attempt to prosecute their rapists for fear of prosecution themselves. Such was the case of five women in Larkana who were gang-raped in January and revoked their allegations when they were threatened with prosecution under the Hudood Ordinances.

Abuse of women in custody, 60 percent of whom have been placed in Pakistan jails under the Hudood Ordinances, continued unabated as did the trafficking of women into Pakistan from Bangladesh for purposes of prostitution.

The basic rights of workers in Pakistan continued to be violated as the government failed to respect a number of International Labor Organization (ILO) Conventions to which it is a party including those on freedom of association and the prohibition of forced labor. Pakistan, under Benazir Bhutto, has emphasized economic development over worker rights, allowing multinational corporations and many domestic industries the right to restrict unions. The government did nothing to address the plight of bonded laborers.

Torture continued to be widespread and endemic in Pakistan. Detainees were routinely slapped, beaten with sticks, stripped naked and sexually abused, hung upside down by a rope from the ceiling, and burned with cigarettes. Among case reports were those of men whose genitals were crushed with pliers, and their legs pulled apart until bones were broken or ligaments torn. An official with the Pakistan CIA (a body created to investigate cases which fall outside the purview of the police) publicly stated in February, "Without torture interrogation is impossible."

The Right to Monitor

Human rights groups generally functioned freely in Pakistan during 1994. In late June, amid the controversy surrounding the government's proposal to amend the blasphemy laws, a militant religious group urged "those who love Islam" to kill Asma Jehangir, General Secretary of the Human Rights Commission of Pakistan. She was not harmed.

The Role of the International Community

In June, the ILO and Pakistan signed a memorandum of understanding which, according to the ILO, "will enable the government progressively to prohibit, restrict, and regulate child labor with a view to its ultimate elimination." In exchange for financial and advisory services from the ILO, the government agreed to establish national steering committees, comprising representatives from ministries, employers' groups, and workers' groups, to carry out an action program. The ILO also called on Pakistan to liberate all adult or child bonded laborers, as national legislation had abolished the bonded labor system in March 1992.

U.S. aid to Pakistan, which was canceled under the Pressler Amendment in 1990 as a result of Pakistan's nuclear program, was not restored in 1994. However, the U.S. government sought closer ties, and U.S. Energy Secretary Hazel O'Leary visited Pakistan in September to promote stronger economic links between the countries.

The Work of Human Rights Watch/Asia

Human Rights Watch/Asia testified on the widespread existence of bonded child labor in Pakistan at the U.S. Department of Labor hearings on child labor. The Arms Project of Human Rights Watch released a newsletter documenting the complicity of the Pakistan government in the flow of arms to groups responsible for human rights abuses in Punjab and Kashmir. Human Rights Watch/Asia invited I.A. Rehman, director of the Human Rights Commission of Pakistan (HRCP), to be honored for his work at Human Rights Watch's observance of Human Rights Day in December.

THAILAND

Human Rights Developments

To the extent that Thailand's human rights practices came to international attention at all, the focus was on ill-treatment of refugees and immigrants, police abuses, forced prostitution and worker rights. Thai nongovernmental organizations focused as well on human rights violations associated with land disputes. The Thai government came under fire during the year for succumbing to pressure from its neighbors to restrict freedoms on their behalf. Thus, in July, bowing to pressure from Indonesia, the government withdrew the visas of eleven supporters of East Timor scheduled to attend a conference in Bangkok, and deported two Australians. In early September, at Malaysia's request, Thai police arrested and deported the leader of a Muslim organization, Al-Arqam, and nine of his followers, even though it was clear they faced arrest under Malaysia's draconian Internal Security Act for nothing more than peaceful religious activities. The Thai military also came under criticism for alleged continued support of the Khmer Rouge.

Burmese, Lao, and Cambodian refugees were forcibly repatriated during the year in violation of the principle of *non-refoulement*; Burmese in particular also faced abuse in Thai immigration detention centers. Ethnic minority refugees from Burma continued arriving in large numbers, bringing the refugee population on the Thai-Burmese border to nearly 77,000, up 4,000 from the year before.

Ethnic Mon refugees and migrant workers living in the Loh Loe camp south of Three Pagodas Pass were forced back into Burma in April, to a camp called Halockhani. The camp was also half a day's march from a Burmese military post, and in July, the new camp was attacked by the Burmese army and partly destroyed by fire. Sixteen men were taken away, and the Thai army's division commander responsible for the area acknowledged most of them had been taken to be used as porters. (Forced portering has been a particularly egregious practice of the Burmese military.) Some 6,000 refugees fled back into Thailand to a border checkpoint where they were told they could not stay; the Thai government cut off all supplies of food and medicine, and they were eventually forced to return in September. No journalist was allowed access to them in Thailand.

Days after the refugees were forced back, the state petroleum companies of Thailand and Burma, together with Total (France) and Unocal (U.S.), signed an agreement to build a 240-mile natural gas pipeline to transport gas from offshore oil fields in Burma's Yadana area to the Kanchanaburi district in Thailand. The pipeline would cross through Mon territory and enter Thailand at Nat Ei Daung, only a few miles from Loh Loe, the camp from which the refugees were first evicted.

In similar moves, close economic cooperation between Thailand and Laos, including the opening of the Friendship Bridge in April, was followed by a crackdown on ethnic Hmong refugees whom Laos accused of being anti-government activists. Under the terms of an agreement reached in July 1993 between the United Nations High Commissioner for Refugees (UNHCR) and the governments of Thailand and Laos, some 8,000 ethnic Hmong refugees were repatriated from the drug rehabilitation center at Wat Tham Krabok where they had been living. Thai authorities claimed that the Wat was being used as a refuge for Hmong insurgents. On September 30, the Baan Na Pho refugee camp, which housed 20,000 Hmong, was closed and the residents sent back to Laos. Thai authorities insisted the repatriation was voluntary, but they also warned that those who did not return would be prosecuted under Thai immigration laws. UNHCR was able to interview some but not all of the returnees.

Cambodians faced a similar fate. In March, between 25,000 and 30,000 Cambodians who had fled fighting with the Khmer Rouge were pushed back into a malarial Khmer Rouge zone, to which international humanitarian agencies were barred from access. In April, 3,000 ethnic Karen refugees were denied entry into Thailand, forcing a Karen organization to establish Klay Mu Hta camp on the Burmese side of the Salween river. And in May and June, hundreds of Burmese Shan refugees, fleeing fighting between the Burmese army and drug warlord Khun Sa, were forcibly sent back by Thai authorities in Mae Sai, Chiang Rai Province.

The publication of the Human Rights Watch report *A Modern Form of Slavery: Trafficking of Women and Girls into Brothels in Thailand* in December 1993 added to the domestic and international debate on issue of trafficking of Burmese women and girls into forced prostitution and may have helped spark an initiative for legal reform that was continuing at the end of the year (*see* Human Rights Watch Women's Rights Project section).

In August, Police Major General Darun Sothipan admitted that torture of suspects occurred in police custody. The admission followed numerous reports of police corruption and abuse, including a statement from twenty Taiwanese prisoners that abuses in Thailand's jails were widespread and the trial of seven tourist police officers who had robbed and murdered over thirty Asian tourists in July. Most notorious were the revelations of high-ranking police involvement in the "Saudi jewel case" involving the theft in 1989 of some U.S.$20 million worth in jewels from a Saudi prince by his Thai servant who later fled to Bangkok. Seven police and one civilian went on trial during the year for their role in this case, which had involved seven murders, including the wife and son of a key witness on August 1.

In Parliament, discussions continued on amendments to the constitution to guarantee the civil and political rights of individuals, and a first draft of a bill to establish a national human rights commission.

Worker rights continued to be abused. Following the May 1993 fire at the Kader factory outside Bangkok in which 188 workers died and 469 were injured, workers and activists complained that none of the owners, designers or government safety inspectors were brought to justice. Only one man was arrested in connection with the fire, a guard at the factory who admitted smoking a cigarette on duty. While it was clear that safety procedures at the factory were ignored by both the owners and government inspectors, so that the workers were unable to escape before the entire building collapsed on top of them, there were no plans to prosecute the management or owners of the Kader Company, which produced "Cabbage Patch" dolls.

The Right to Monitor

Most Thai human rights organizations and activists were able to operate without obstruction in Thailand, and many had a cooperative relationship with the government, especially in the areas of trafficking of women and child labor. Bangkok was rapidly becoming the city in mainland East Asia where regional and international human rights organizations felt they could operate most freely, especially as Hong Kong, the other regional hub, became increasingly sensitive to Chinese government concerns.

But several areas of human rights work remained highly sensitive and subject to government monitoring and restrictions: any work related to Burmese refugees or immigrants; activities related to abuses by a neighboring ASEAN country, such as Indonesia; and work that touched on the commercial activities of the Thai military, such as logging.

The Role of the
International Community

The Clinton administration's policy towards Thailand was aimed at further strengthening political, economic and security relations with Prime Minister Chuan's government, while relegating human rights concerns to the margins of discussion. Throughout the year there were signs of strain in the Thai-U.S. relationship though, as Thailand reacted vociferously to U.S. claims of human rights abuses and linkages of foreign aid to Thailand's support of abusive regimes in neighboring Burma and Cambodia. The issues of forced prostitution and trafficking of Burmese women were addressed by the administration as serious violations of women's rights in Thailand.

Arms sales to Thailand remained brisk as Bangkok obtained much of its military equipment from the U.S. Foreign Military Sales (FMS) accounted for the bulk of the transfers in fiscal year 1993: FMS agreements reached $388 million, with another $12 million in commercial transfers. In fiscal year 1995, FMS sales were estimated to total $350 million, which would make Thailand the largest U.S. arms recipient in the East Asia and Pacific region, and sixth in estimated U.S. arms sales globally.

The 1995 fiscal year Foreign Aid Bill contained $875,000 for the International Military Education and Training (IMET) program, which the administration said would provide education focused on civilian control of the military and would help to "institutionalize Thai democracy." Congress attached a provision requiring a report by February 1995 on "the efforts of the Thai Government to impede support for Burmese democracy advocates, exiles and refugees" and Thai support for the Khmer Rouge. The State Department also called in the Thai ambassador to protest the treatment of Mon refugees at Halochani, but when President Clinton met with Thai Prime Minister Chuan Leekpai on October 6 refugee issues were not raised.

In December 1993, the U.S. Trade Representative's office had officially suspended its review, under the annual Generalized System of Preferences (GSP) process, of worker rights abuses in the state sector in Thailand. The suspension was based on a commitment by the Thai government to undertake certain reforms in the State Enterprise Labor Relations Act restricting freedom of association and the right to organize for state enterprise employees, but as of November 1994 those reforms had yet to be implemented.

In July 1994, the U.S. Labor Department published a detailed study of the use of child labor in American imports from countries worldwide titled (*By the Sweat and Toil of Children*). It described Thailand's use of at least four million child workers in the garment, seafood processing, and furniture industries. Thailand is a party to the U.N. Convention on the Rights of the Child, but has not ratified international labor conventions on minimum age for employment.

The Work of
Human Rights Watch/Asia

Following the publication of the report *A Modern Form of Slavery* in December 1993, much of Human Rights Watch/Asia's work in Thailand continued to focus on human rights violations associated with the trafficking of Burmese women into Thailand.

Human Rights Watch/Asia also continued to monitor the treatment of Burmese and other refugees in Thailand. In May, a research mission visited ethnic Mon refugees in Thailand. A report scheduled for publication in December analyzed the reasons why refugees continued to leave Burma and their treatment by Thai authorities.

VIETNAM

Human Rights Developments

Vietnam maintained tight controls on political and religious dissent as economic reform continued, an approach that seemed to heighten internal tensions. The government continued to imprison people for peaceful dissent. Under sustained international pressure, however, it quietly released several dozen political prisoners held on security charges and provided certain others with minimally improved medical care. Conflict between the government and groups within the Buddhist community continued at high pitch, frictions with the Vatican increased, and Protestant evangelical groups suffered heightened repression. Vietnam engaged in discussions of human rights with a number of countries, including the United States, but an Australian delegation canceled a trip after

Vietnam denied a visa to an outspoken member who told the BBC that one purpose of the visit was to investigate human rights issues.

Arbitrary detention remained a major concern. Nguyen Van Ho, a former senior party cadre and founder of an independent Vietnamese military veterans group, was arrested on March 7 for writing and distributing an autobiographical essay, which called for greater freedom, democracy and respect for human rights in Vietnam. He was held incommunicado for three months without trial until his failing health forced authorities to move him to a military hospital in late May. Nguyen Ho was allowed to return home on June 25, but at year's end, remained in extremely poor health and under house arrest.

One of Vietnam's best-known dissidents, Dr. Doan Viet Hoat, was transferred abruptly among three different prisons this year, ending up in Thanh Cam camp, a facility for common criminals in a remote and malarial part of Thanh Hoa province, where he was the only political prisoner. Arrested in November 1990, Dr. Hoat was given a fifteen-year sentence for producing the reformist newsletter *Freedom Forum*.

Dr. Nguyen Dan Que, an endocrinologist whose public call for political reform and respect for human rights earned him a twenty-year prison sentence in 1991, was placed in solitary confinement in August 1993 and was reported to be in poor health. Doan Thanh Liem, a constitutional law specialist, entered the fourth year of a twelve-year term for "counterrevolutionary propaganda" for his association with American businessman Michael Morrow and his writings on constitutional reform. He was reported to be suffering from a serious pulmonary condition.

The government released a number of political prisoners, some of whom had been the subject of international pressure. Tran Vong Quoc was released on June 5 from the Ham Tan prison camp, thirty months before his twelve-year sentence for "attempting to overthrow the government" was to expire. His activities included attempts to report executions and other abuses to human rights groups abroad. Human Rights Watch/Asia also received reports of the early release of several dozen prisoners held on security charges from Ham Tan prison in April and May, but was not able to confirm their identities. Well-known dissident Quach Vinh Nien, who had been imprisoned for sixteen years for publishing newspaper articles critical of the government, was also released early this year and allowed to rejoin his family in Australia.

The government improved medical treatment for some ill prisoners who had been the subject of international pressure. Nguyen Van Thuan, another *Freedom Forum* defendant, suffered a stroke on February 15 at the Ham Tan prison camp. After three days of being denied medical care, Thuan was admitted to a military hospital; at the end of the year, he still faced eventual return to prison.

The government kept a tight rein on a wide range of religious activities and engaged in outright repression of groups deemed reactionary. Tensions with the Unified Buddhist Church (UBC), which has demanded institutional autonomy from the government, led to further protests and arrests. (In at least one case, a Buddhist monk not associated with the UBC was also arrested for his protests against religious repression.)

On August 7, a monk named Venerable Thich Giac Nguyen was taken away in a government car from the Phap Hoa Temple in Ho Chi Minh City after a two-day protest. The Vietnamese government confirmed his arrest, claiming he was arrested for "committing a number of dissident acts," and was being held for questioning. As of mid-November, his family had not received any information from authorities about his location or condition.

Police in Tra Vinh province reportedly arrested two Buddhist nuns at Ngoc Dat pagoda after Venerable Thich Hue Thau, a UBC supporter, immolated himself there on May 28. The nuns had reportedly been arrested when they requested permission to enter the temple to prepare Venerable Thau's remains for burial. As of November, it was not clear whether they were still in detention.

Many Buddhist leaders arrested and tried in 1993 for their involvement in protests remain imprisoned.

A crackdown was reported against ethnic Hmong converts to evangelical Protestant sects in Vietnam's northern provinces of Son La, Lai Chau and Ha Tuyen. Thao A Tong, a thirty-two-year-old local official and Christian convert, was arrested in January for proselytizing in Hong Thu village, Sonh Ho district of Lai Chau province. Additional arrests of Hmong Protestants reportedly took place in Lai Chau and Tuyen Quang provinces in February and April.

Vietnam was able to maintain its tight control over the Catholic church when the Vatican agreed in March to seek approval from the government for all clerical appointments, including those of bishops. On March 17, the Vietnamese Foreign Ministry announced that the Holy See had also agreed not to appoint Bishop Nguyen Van Thuan as deputy to the archbishop of Ho Chi Minh City, and would assign him to a position in Rome. Bishop Thuan, former archbishop of Saigon in 1975 and a nephew of former South Vietnamese President Ngo Dinh Diem, was imprisoned in Vietnam for thirteen years and had been living in exile in Rome since 1992.

Freedom of movement for priests remained restricted, sermons were subject to censorship, and church personnel were kept under close surveillance. At least eleven members of Catholic movements that the government considered reactionary remained imprisoned, They included Father Nguyen Van De other members of the Sacerdotal Maria Movement and the Movement of Humble Souls.

Vietnam continued to apply the death penalty to a wide range of crimes. On August 22, Le Thi Thu Ha, a policewoman from Nam Ha province, was sentenced to death for fraud in accordance with a 1991 amendment to the criminal code which expanded the application of the death penalty to cases of serious fraud and bribery.

Although the media continued to be state-controlled, press coverage of sensitive subjects, such as official corruption, was lively, and the *doi moi* or "renovation" policy allowed a wide range of authors to publish their work. Many other topics remained off-limits, however, such as challenges to the one-party system or criticism of Communist heros.

Elements in the party and government were apprehensive of the social and political impact of western influence in the wake of the lifting of the U.S. trade embargo. Throughout the year articles appeared warning of schemes by both Vietnamese citizens and foreign governments to use the promotion of political pluralism and human rights, identified as "peaceful evolution," to destabilize the Vietnamese state. Citing "technical reasons," Vietnam in March canceled a week-long seminar at which a group of prominent foreign journalists was to provide training for Vietnamese reporters. The *Far Eastern Economic Review* reported that the meeting was canceled by security officials who had launched a campaign against "peaceful evolution" in the press and in meetings around the country at that time.

Vietnam's National Assembly drew up a labor code in June, which for the first time, gave Vietnamese workers the right to strike and prohibited unlawful forced labor. In the six months before its passage, there were eleven strikes in Ho Chi Minh City alone, compared to only twenty reported for all of Vietnam in the previous two years. Under the new labor code, the right to strike does not extend to workers at state-owned industries, or to private firms considered essential to the national economy or security. Additionally, those who organize strikes deemed to be unlawful by the government can be subject to administrative penalties.

The Right to Monitor

The government continued to isolate and punish Vietnamese citizens who criticized its human rights record. Authorities transferred Dr. Doan Viet Hoat five times since

November 1993 to prevent him from issuing public statements about human rights conditions in Vietnam.

Vietnam allowed restricted access to the country by some international human rights and humanitarian agencies. It permitted a three-week visit by the U.N. Human Rights Commission's Working Group on Arbitrary Detention in October, including a prison visit. However, Vietnam drew back from a planned visit by an Australian parliamentary consultative human rights delegation. Australia called off the trip when Vietnam canceled visits to a prison and ethnic minority areas, meetings with several ministries and the Vietnamese writers association, and denied a visa to a delegation member after that member publicly described a primary goal of the mission as investigating human rights.

The United Nations High Commissioner for Refugees (UNHCR) maintained a small staff in Vietnam to monitor the treatment of returned boat people, who now number over 60,000. In at least one case there is concern that an asylum-seeker deported from Hong Kong may have been arrested for political reasons. Nguyen Van Kha, a former student activist in Hanoi, was detained incommunicado after his return in January and faced the death penalty for crimes, including murder, that the government alleges he committed prior to his departure from Vietnam in 1990. Vietnam denied requests by both the UNHCR and the British Embassy for access to Kha and failed to produce a copy of Kha's original arrest warrant.

The Role of the
International Community

Desire to bolster trade and investment with Vietnam tended to push human rights to a low priority for the international community.

The U.S. lifted a nineteen year-old trade embargo against Vietnam on February 3. In doing so, the Clinton administration announced that human rights would continue to be a major element in future relations with Vietnam. But the issue of prisoners of war and those missing in action from the Vietnam War, the so-called POW-MIA issue, continued to dominate all policy discussions, often to the exclusion of human rights issues more broadly.

The U.S. and Vietnam did initiate an official "dialogue" on human rights in which the U.S. raised cases of specific prisoners, and meetings were held in both February and August between State Department officials and Vietnam's U.N. ambassador. Little, however, emerged in the way of tangible results. An agreement was reached in May 1994 between Vietnam and the U.S., in which the State Department was given the right of consular access to American citizens of Vietnamese descent imprisoned in Vietnam. At the end of the year, access had been granted in some, but not all, cases.

The U.S. Congress continued to take a stronger stance in defense of Vietnamese political and religious prisoners than the administration, and members addressed numerous public and private appeals on their behalf to the Vietnamese government. On June 22, twenty-four members of Congress sent a letter to Assistant Secretary of State Winston Lord urging him to raise human rights issues and specific cases during a visit to Hanoi that began on June 28. The letter, which was made public during Lord's visit, drew special attention to the cases of Dr. Doan Viet Hoat, Doan Thanh Liem, *Freedom Forum* member Pham Duc Kham, and Venerable Thich Huyen Quang. According to Vietnamese Deputy Foreign Minister Le Mai, Lord requested information on the well-being of four Vietnamese imprisoned for political offenses during his visit. A concurrent resolution adopted by Congress on October 5 urged the administration to "place a high priority" on seeking the release of all nonviolent political prisoners and urging the government of Vietnam to allow access to its prisons by international humanitarian organizations.

Vietnam agreed on July 23 to the inclusion of a human rights clause as part of a new trade and cooperation pact that it was negotiating with the European Union. As of

November, however, final agreement on the pact was still pending.

Hanoi hosted a number of high-ranking foreign officials in 1994, many of whom raised human rights concerns. Among the visitors were Dutch Foreign Minister Peter Kooijmans, who discussed human rights with his Vietnamese counterpart during a March 10 meeting, and Swedish Prime Minister Carl Bildt, who held a discussion of human rights with Prime Minister Vo Van Kiet on April 7. British Foreign Secretary Douglas Hurd also raised the issue of human rights with Vietnamese leaders during a two-day visit in September, and submitted a list of specific cases. Although Japanese Prime Minister Tomiichi Murayama met with Vietnamese leaders in Hanoi in late August, human rights concerns were conspicuously absent in his discussions. As of the time of Murayama's visit, Japan had pledged a total of approximately $640 million through its Official Development Aid (ODA) program, making it Vietnam's largest foreign aid donor. Japan's ODA program requires the government to "pay full attention" to the human rights situation in recipient countries.

In March, the U.N. Human Rights Commission voted to remove Vietnam from a confidential "1503" procedure under which human rights abuses were being investigated.

The Work of
Human Rights Watch/Asia

Human Rights Watch/Asia continued its efforts to document and publicize political and religious imprisonment while maintaining a dialogue with the Vietnamese government through meetings with officials in the U.S. It also sought to broaden its human rights advocacy by keeping various governments, international organizations and members of the business community apprised of human rights concerns and urging them to press Vietnam for concrete improvements.

Human Rights Watch/Asia provided briefings and case studies to representatives of various foreign governments and international bodies such as the U.N. Working Group on Arbitrary Detention. It also worked closely with U.S. legislators on Vietnam policy. On February 9, it submitted written testimony to the Senate Foreign Relations Committee, urging the Clinton administration to ensure that human rights remain a long-term component of U.S. policy as relations with Vietnam develop. It supported a request by several members of the Senate on February 4 that the administration issue a full report to Congress on the progress of the human rights "dialogue" no later than February 1, 1995.

On March 28, in testimony before the House Subcommittee on Asia and Pacific Affairs, Human Rights Watch/Asia drew special attention to the repression of religious dissent. It encouraged the U.S. to work together with other countries to press Vietnam to allow international organizations, such as the International Committee of the Red Cross, to provide humanitarian services to prisoners and to allow diplomatic observers to attend key political trials.

Human Rights Watch/Asia also released press statements expressing concern over the arrest of Nguyen Van Ho, and the transfer of Dr. Doan Viet Hoat to a remote jungle camp.

HUMAN RIGHTS WATCH /HELSINKI

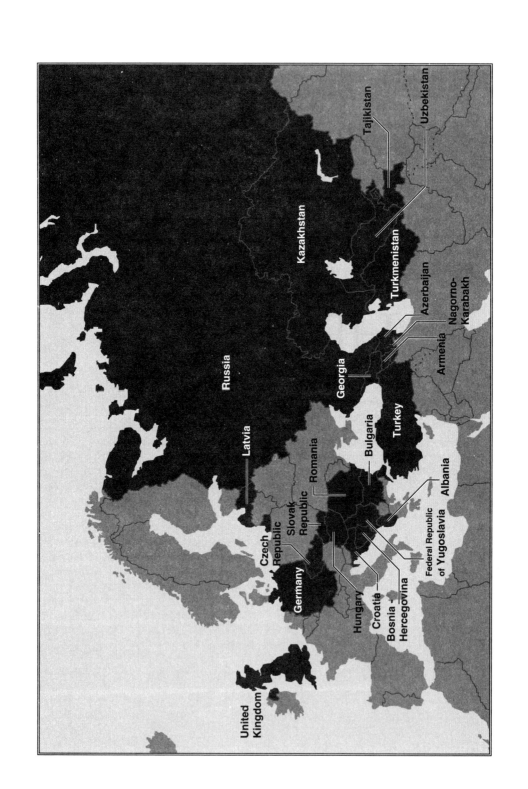

HUMAN RIGHTS WATCH/HELSINKI OVERVIEW

Human Rights Developments

The face of Europe has changed radically in recent years, blurring what was once a clear distinction between East and West. Although the legacy of communism will remain for many years—not so much in the way countries are governed as in the mentality of the people and in their understanding of human rights and the rule of law—the countries of the former Soviet bloc have taken on distinctive personalities no longer defined by geographical spheres of influence. Western Europe has also been profoundly affected by the political and economic aftermath of communism's demise.

In a region once divided between countries with democratic systems and those ruled by communist dictatorships, just about every known form of human rights abuse was found in 1994 in a depressing patchwork with few bright colors. Yet, as difficult as the post-communist transition may be, enough time has passed not only to assess the human rights situation in Europe but to hold all European governments, including the governments of the new states, responsible for their behavior.

The breakup of the Soviet Union, Yugoslavia, and Czechoslovakia, swelled the ranks of the Helsinki signatory countries from thirty-five to fifty-three; the range of abuses in these countries was very wide in the year just past. Among abuses in 1994 were bestial crimes of war; unchecked violence against ethnic minorities, foreigners, refugees, and displaced persons; a growing roster of political prisoners; the beating, harassment, and short-term detention of political oppositionists; restrictions of free speech and assembly; torture in pre-trial detention; political trials; and discriminatory citizenship and residency laws.

"Ethnic cleansing," a new term coined in Croatia and Bosnia-Hercegovina, is a euphemism for savage acts including murder, rape, torture, and looting, aimed at forcing terrified, unwanted minorities to flee their homes. It continued unabated in Bosnia-Hercegovina in 1994, where a war in which civilians were both hostages and targets raged throughout the year. Although abuses were committed by all sides, the vast majority were by Bosnian Serbs. The international community failed to protect even the "safe areas" the United Nations had created, and "ethnic cleansing," which initially was used by the Bosnian Serbs in the fight to attain territory, became even more menacing as it continued in northern Bosnia in areas, now under the firm control of Bosnian Serbs, where no fighting was taking place. The so-called demilitarized zone around Sarajevo did not prevent the continued deaths of innocent civilians as a result of snipers and shelling.

War crimes against civilians also continued, far from the public eye, in Nagorno-Karabakh, where one of the longest conflicts in the region entered its seventh year. Despite a May 1994 cease-fire, there seemed no end in sight for the civilian victims on both sides of the Karabakh war, in which ethnic Armenians, covertly aided from outside by the Armenian government, were fighting the government of Azerbaijan for their independence.

Another conflict in the region, also largely neglected by the outside world, was taking place in eastern Turkey where the Turkish government has long been battling a violent guerrilla group known as the PKK (Workers Party of Kurdistan). The struggle continued to escalate in 1994 in the face of government vows to bring it to an end militarily before the close of the year. Ethnic Kurds were the main victims of the war in southeast Turkey. On the one hand, they were forced by the Turkish military to become "village guards" against the PKK, thereby becoming subject to PKK retribution. On the other hand, they were violently punished by the PKK for any cooperation with the state. The residents of villages who refused to become part of the village guard system became targets of the military, their residents driven from their homes in brutal sweeps. More than 1,000 villages and hamlets in eastern Turkey were reportedly depopulated by the Turkish armed forces; their inhabitants have become internal refugees within Turkey, deprived of homes and means of support. Turkey has imposed a cloud of secrecy over the situation in the east, restricting access by journalists and human rights investigators and suppressing free expression and association in the region. There were numerous reports of torture, deaths in detention, disappearances, and death squad-style assassinations as Turkey pursued its "anti-terrorism" campaign.

Armed conflict also continued in areas of Tajikistan, despite a cease-fire and sporadic peace talks between the government and a cluster of opposition movements. The government held elections in November despite the fact that most opposition leaders remained in exile. Other armed conflicts in the region—in Georgia and Russia's southern regions of North Ossetia and Ingushetia—subsided, albeit uneasily, in 1994.

Suppression of political dissent and free expression was severe in a number of countries, including parts of the former Yugoslavia. Serbia maintained its repressive control of the ethnic Albanian province of Kosovo, where unwarranted arrests, police beatings, political trials and abuse in detention continued. Repression of civil and political rights, although to a lesser extent than in Kosovo, also continued in other parts of Serbia and Montenegro and in Croatia.

Political dissent was also suppressed, to varying degrees, in many parts of the former Soviet Union. In Uzbekistan and Turkmenistan, former communist leaders maintained authoritarian control in a fashion similar to that which prevailed under the communists. Both governments exercised control by enforcing complete censorship of the press, prohibiting free expression and association and keeping dissenters under constant surveillance, which sometimes amounted to virtual house arrest. In Uzbekistan, where there were a number of political trials, the list of political prisoners continued to grow. Georgia, although it tried to show a liberal face to the West, continued to be harsh with political dissenters, who were beaten, harassed or arrested. Torture and forced confessions in pre-trial detention, appalling conditions in places of detention and failure to provide timely access to legal counsel raised deep concerns about the criminal justice system throughout Georgia. In Tajikistan, whose government still holds many political prisoners, there was mistreatment in detention, illegal searches of homes, and violations of due process. In Azerbaijan, state of emergency decrees were aimed at suppressing opposition parties, whose members were beaten and harassed and their demonstrations broken up.

In Russia, there was grave concern about free expression at the beginning of the year because of a crackdown on political dissent and against non-Muscovites in October 1993, following the violent October events at the Russian parliament. Yet considerable freedom of expression was exercised throughout the year. In August 1994, the presidential Human Rights Committee issued a "white paper" dealing with human rights abuses within Russia in 1993, a hard-hitting document that did not spare important political figures such as the powerful mayor of Moscow. Nevertheless, there remained many causes for concern over human rights. President Boris Yeltsin introduced a law allowing arbitrary house searches and detention for thirty days without trial, and other forms of "anti-crime" legislation were used in a discriminatory fashion, especially in Moscow where local authorities continued to pick on dark-skinned people from the Caucasus or Central Asia, beating, fining, and harassing them if they did not have proper residency papers. At the same time, the Russian government continued to express concern about discrimination against the many Russians living elsewhere within the Confederation of Independent States (C.I.S.).

Reports of abysmal prison conditions

in Russia and throughout the C.I.S. and of abuses within the army also continued to surface. Security forces from other C.I.S. states—Tajikistan, Uzbekistan, and Turkmenistan, in particular—persecuted with impunity their dissident nationals who had fled to Russian soil. The fact that little public attempt was made by Russian authorities to curb such operations gave rise to suspicions of widespread collusion among security agencies throughout the C.I.S.

Persecution of foreigners and ethnic minorities was by no means limited to Russia. Xenophobic sentiments gave rise to distressing developments in Europe as a whole. A wave of violence and resentment toward foreigners was in evidence throughout the former communist countries and in Germany and other parts of Western Europe as well. Ethnic minorities, foreigners and asylum-seekers were subject to discrimination and acts of violence often tolerated and sometimes abetted by law enforcement authorities. Roma (Gypsies) were among the most persecuted, especially in Romania and Bulgaria, where entire Roma villages were attacked and burned by non-Roma villagers, while the police did little or nothing to prevent such abuse. Discrimination against Roma and/or foreigners was also reported in Germany, England, and France, as well as in countries of the former communist bloc. In the Czech Republic, Roma were also victimized, and provisions of a new citizenship law seemed aimed at preventing Roma from becoming Czech citizens.

There were efforts to restrict freedom of the press in several of the countries of eastern Europe and the C.I.S. For example, journalists in Albania, Romania, and Slovakia were prosecuted for articles considered insulting to the "state" or to specific government officials. In both Slovakia and Hungary, the governing parties made efforts to manipulate state-controlled media especially during national electoral campaigns. The governments of Tajikistan, Uzbekistan, Turkmenistan, and Azerbaijan continued routinely to censor the media using old, Soviet-era tactics.

There were a few bright spots in the region at the close of 1994: the establishment of a war crimes tribunal for the former Yugoslavia and, with the appointment of a chief prosecutor, the start of serious investigations; a cease-fire and peace talks in Northern Ireland; a cease-fire in the fighting between Muslims and Croats in Bosnia and the establishment of a fragile Muslim-Croat Federation there; the work of the presidential Human Rights Committee in Russia in documenting and publicizing human rights abuses; and the passage of an amended naturalization law in Latvia that omitted quotas. But these isolated occurrences were small solace in a region beset with the ethnic and political antagonisms that characterize the post-communist fallout in Europe.

The Right To Monitor

The freedom that governments provided to indigenous human rights monitoring groups and to visiting human rights groups from abroad was not necessarily a measure of the human rights situation in a country, as it had been in the communist days. Some countries with unsatisfactory human rights practices nevertheless allowed human rights groups to function on their territories. In a sense, this was a tribute to the growing strength of the human rights movement and the moral imperative it brings to human rights monitoring. Repressive governments concerned with their international image sometimes allowed human rights work to be conducted in their countries in order to show the world that they respected human rights. In this way they tried to exploit the efforts of local or foreign monitors.

An example of such manipulation occurred in Georgia, where the government harassed local human rights activists but cooperated with a Human Rights Watch/Helsinki mission. In Turkey, a country that cares greatly about its international image, two effective human rights organizations operated legally, but not without great difficulty. The Human Rights Association, which had numerous branches in the troubled southeast of Turkey, was subjected to official repression and threats from right-wing groups suspected of ties to the government. (Ten members of southeastern branches of the Turkish Human Rights Association have been assassinated in recent years.) A publication of the Human Rights Foundation was seized by the government in November 1994 and charges were brought against two foundation members, including its chairman. On separate occasions, the Turkish government prevented a member of the Amnesty International staff from entering Turkey and, in August, the Turkish military command in the southeast gave no cooperation to a Human Rights Watch/Helsinki mission that was expressly interested in documenting PKK abuses against civilians.

Although the government of Tajikistan grudgingly tolerated outside monitors, no indigenous human rights groups functioned there. The situation was even worse in Uzbekistan and Turkmenistan, where almost all local activists were followed and hounded and in almost all cases prevented from meeting with visiting dignitaries.

Serbia denied access to the U.N. Commission on Human Rights' special rapporteur for the former Yugoslavia and expelled a Conference on Security and Cooperation in Europe (CSCE) mission from Serbia and Montenegro. A representative of Human Rights Watch/Helsinki was detained in Kosovo and was also detained and expelled from Serbian-controlled Bosnia while attempting to do human rights research in both areas.

Elsewhere in the region—in Albania, Armenia, Azerbaijan, Bulgaria, Croatia, the Czech Republic, Germany, Hungary, Kazakhstan, Latvia, Romania, Russia, Slovakia, and the United Kingdom—human rights monitoring was generally unobstructed.

U.S. Policy

With a few exceptions, the Clinton administration's human rights policies with regard to the Helsinki countries were either non-existent, reliant on quiet diplomacy, or, as in the case of Bosnia and the rump Yugo-

slavia, hopelessly weak and inconsistent.

The administration's main focus in Eastern Europe and the newly independent states of the former Soviet Union was, as before, on furthering the development of market economies. The administration seemed to believe that free enterprise would lead to a pluralistic, democratic society and that respect for human rights would come naturally in a democracy. Neither of these assumptions, however, is necessarily true. The administration's commitment to developing market economies actually served at times to undermine human rights by becoming a justification for avoiding forthright criticism of human rights abuses. In Uzbekistan, where Most Favored Nation status was granted unconditionally, the administration missed an opportunity to speak up for human rights compliance; it did so vociferously, however, when activists were detained for trying to meet with a visiting U.S. Senator. Presumably in response to the Armenian lobby in the United States, the U.S. government did not speak out publicly about Armenia's involvement in the Karabakh war, although sanctions remained in place with regard to Azerbaijan, the other party to the war. The U.S. remained mainly silent throughout the year about human rights conditions in places as varied as Bulgaria, the Czech Republic, Georgia, Hungary, Kazakhstan, Northern Ireland, Romania, and Turkmenistan, limiting itself largely to assurances that human rights matters were raised privately in the high-level meetings that were held with the leaders of many of these countries.

U.S. policy in both Russia and Georgia continued to be tailored to support the policies of President Yeltsin and Head of State Eduard Shevardnadze. Russian support of so-called stable governments in the "near abroad," including severe human rights offenders such as Tajikistan, Uzbekistan, and Turkmenistan, may have been a factor in the U.S. government's quiet approach to diplomacy in those places. In bilateral meetings on human rights, John Shattuck, Assistant Secretary of State for Human Rights, Democracy and Labor, and other U.S. officials raised privately some important concerns, such as emigration, abuse of the residence permit system, and anti-Semitism, but continued to avoid other issues such as Russian policies affecting human rights in the "near abroad." Because Kazakhstan signed the nuclear Non-Proliferation Treaty, it received high praise from the U.S., praise which appeared to encompass everything the Kazakh government did while ignoring the human rights problems that were evident in Kazakhstan in the course of the year.

The U.S. State Department's *Country Reports on Human Rights Practices for 1993*, issued in February 1994, continued to offer an informed and realistic view of the human rights situation in most of the countries in the region. Moreover, U.S. embassy personnel in most, if not all, of the countries in the region monitored the human rights situation and worked to improve it. But the information offered in the country reports, largely based on evaluations by the various embassies, seldom seemed to be translated into a meaningful day-to-day policy.

The worst failings of the Clinton administration were revealed in its policies toward Serbia and Bosnia, countries in which the human rights situation demanded attention that could not be deferred. Despite statements early in the year that the U.S. government would not support the lifting of sanctions against the rump Yugoslavia until Serbia agreed to cooperate with the U.N.'s international war crimes tribunal for the former Yugoslavia, the U.S. later went along with the lifting of some sanctions when Serbia agreed to cut off aid to the Bosnian Serbs and to allow observers on the border to verify its actions. Moreover, by November the U.S. was considering the further lifting of sanctions against the rump Yugoslavia if Serbia agreed to give diplomatic recognition to Bosnia and Croatia. The contradiction between the statements and the actions of the U.S. government continued to undermine its credibility. Human Rights Watch/Helsinki urged that the lifting of sanctions against Serbia be conditioned on an improvement of the internal human rights situation in Serbia and on Serbia's cooperation with the international war crimes tribunal, including allowing prosecutors to conduct investigations on its territory and facilitating the extradition of those indicted by the tribunal. It is our belief that the Serbian government should be held accountable for past crimes and not rewarded merely for undoing some of the damage it created.

With regard to Bosnia, the U.S. policy was, on the whole, weak and indecisive. The U.S. failed to protect sufficiently the "safe areas" established by the United Nations; NATO retaliation was minimal and did little to prevent continuing Bosnian Serb abuses. When the "safe area" of Gorazde was under attack, the U.S. vacillated on approving NATO air attacks. It wavered on the question of lifting the arms embargo against Bosnia. It went along with the European peace plan to partition Bosnia after stating firmly that it would protect the territorial integrity of Bosnia. Efforts to address continuing violations by Bosnian Serb forces were virtually non-existent.

To its credit, the U.S. successfully brokered a cease-fire between Muslims and Croats in Bosnia and helped establish a Muslim-Croat federation.

The most positive developments in U.S. human rights policies toward the Helsinki countries occurred with respect to its NATO allies, Turkey and Germany. U.S. officials made several high-level visits to Turkey in 1994, including two by Assistant Secretary of State John Shattuck, whose second visit was to eastern Turkey. Assistant Secretary Shattuck and others visiting Turkey made unprecedentedly forthright public statements about the need to improve the human rights situation in Turkey and the possibility of Turkey losing U.S. aid on human rights grounds. The U.S. Congress also approved a bill making 10 percent of U.S. aid to Turkey conditional on the administration's providing a report on human rights improvements there.

The U.S. Embassy in Berlin was unusually outspoken in publicly criticizing the

German government's response to right-wing extremism, although the State Department moved quickly to distance itself from the embasssy's comments. The U.S. engaged in discussions with the German government on ways in which it could cooperate in combatting "hate crimes."

The Role of the United Nations and European Institutions

The U.N. played an ineffective and uncertain role in the former Yugoslavia in 1994, failing to protect "safe areas" under attack and hastening to lift some sanctions against the rump Yugoslavia despite Serbia's uncertain enforcement of the border blockade with Bosnia. U.N. and NATO officials disagreed on their approach to Bosnian Serb violations of U.N. resolutions protecting human rights: NATO's attempts to penalize such violations were frequently thwarted by U.N. officials who sought accommodation with the Bosnian Serbs. Although the U.N. Security Council mandated the use of force to protect peacekeeping operations, U.N. officials were reluctant to use such force. Instead, the need to protect U.N. peacekeeping forces on Bosnian territory became a reason in itself for not punishing violations of human rights. U.N. peacekeepers did not have the manpower or the official encouragement to prevent the crimes associated with "ethnic cleansing" and often stood by while such abuses took place. In the fall of 1994, attacks against civilian areas in Bosnia were launched from Serbian-controlled parts of Croatia, which were under U.N. supervision and which should have been demilitarized by the U.N. in 1992.

After long delays, the international war crimes tribunal, established by the U.N. to adjudicate war crimes and crimes against humanity in Croatia and Bosnia-Hercegovina, finally got underway in 1994 with the appointment of a chief prosecutor, the start of intensive investigations, and the issuing of indictments.

The Council of Europe played a positive role with regard to Russia's application for membership by spotlighting human rights concerns. In the fall of 1994, experts from the council concluded that Russia did not meet the council's human rights standards. Nonetheless, political pressure for Russia's admission to the council continued.

The CSCE played an active role in Latvia dealing with the issue of citizenship. The United Nations Development Progam and the Council of Europe also weighed in on citizenship issues in Latvia, and each body was to be credited for the eventual passage of a citizenship law that omitted strict naturalization quotas.

The Work of Human Rights Watch/Helsinki

Human Rights Watch/Helsinki continued its efforts to improve the human rights situation in many of the countries it monitored by bringing pressure upon the offending governments directly whenever possible and also through other governments and international bodies that had influence on the countries in question. Our main efforts in this respect involved the U.S. government, the Russian and other national governments, the United Nations, the European Union, the Council of Europe, and the CSCE. Our country specialists went to Brussels to meet with staff members at the European Union, to the Hague to meet with the prosecutorial staff of the international war crimes tribunal, and to Budapest to discuss a range of human rights concerns with delegates to the CSCE Review Conference. In Budapest we spoke at a public forum about problems in Turkey and in Yugoslavia and violence against Roma in Romania and Bulgaria. Throughout the year, we conducted missions to various countries in the region, prepared reports and publicized these reports by holding press conferences, issuing press releases, and trying in every way possible to pressure and/or embarrass the government in question into improving its human rights practices.

Human Rights Watch/Helsinki prepared a detailed critique of the human rights situation in Russia for the Council of Europe, whose parliamentary committee subsequently concluded that Russia's human rights record did not yet conform with council standards. We also called attention to human rights problems in Russia in meetings with the staff of the European Union and with delegates to the CSCE Review Conference in Budapest. Similar points of pressure were used with regard to other C.I.S. countries such as Tajikistan, Uzbekistan, Georgia, Turkmenistan, Armenia, and Azerbaijan. During the visit to the United States by the president of Armenia, we urged President Clinton to pressure the Armenian government about its role in human rights abuses in the Nagorno-Karabakh war. We publicized human rights abuses in Tajikistan and Georgia before the leaders of those countries were to visit New York at the opening of the U.N. General Assembly. We also publicly urged the CSCE and participants at its September seminar in the Uzbekistan capital to pressure the government of Uzbekistan to speak out about abuses, particularly the detention of political prisoners, and thereby earn the international legitimacy implied in hosting the seminar, and we were gratified when five political prisoners were subsequently released. Human Rights Watch/Helsinki also kept up its work of documenting abuse of and discrimination against foreigners in Moscow. We followed the citizenship issue in Latvia and achieved some success from our efforts in Latvia with the firing of the head of the Department of Citizenship and Immigration and the passage of a naturalization law in Latvia that eliminated quotas.

Halfway through the year we stationed a representative in Tajikistan which enabled us to monitor human rights developments there firsthand, to publish information about political prisoners and to monitor pre-election conditions in the country.

We used a two-pronged approach with regard to Bosnia. The first was to continue our detailed monitoring of human rights abuses in Bosnia, where our staff engaged in lengthy missions, interviewing the victims of war crimes in Bosnia. In 1994 we published eight reports detailing war crimes and other abuses in various parts of the former Yugoslavia. Our other major focus in Bosnia included both public and behind-the-scenes efforts to get an appropriate chief prosecutor appointed to the war crimes tribunal for the former Yugoslavia so that work could get underway. Our staff made its detailed files on war crimes available to the prosecutorial staff of the tribunal. It was our belief that the war crimes tribunal, by prosecuting criminals at the highest level, could help dispel the notion of collective ethnic guilt and perhaps avoid future conflicts by placing blame on the individuals responsible for the crimes. With this in mind, we continued to urge that amnesties not be granted to war criminals, especially those at the highest levels, and that witnesses and victims be granted adequate protection by the tribunal.

In addition to our work on war crimes in Bosnia we reported on civil and political rights in Croatia and on repression by the Serbian government in Kosovo.

In 1994 Human Rights Watch/Helsinki focused most of its work in Turkey on the under-reported abuses in the Turkish southeast. We verified reports of depopulated villages by interviewing refugees who had been driven from their homes and publicized our findings in Turkey and elsewhere. We also reported on abuses by the PKK and continued our efforts to gain access to southeastern Turkey in order to investigate such abuses at first hand.

Human Rights Watch/Helsinki kept up its work of documenting violence against Roma. In 1994 we published new reports on attacks on Roma in Bulgaria and Romania and released those reports in Budapest during the CSCE Review Conference there.

In 1994 we conducted thirteen missions and issued twenty-one reports based on research and missions in the field. We also sent seventy-four lengthy letters of protest or inquiry to government officials in fifteen countries; many of the letters ultimately found their way into the pages of the press. Human Rights Watch/Helsinki continued its association with the International Helsinki Federation for Human Rights in 1994 and planned to continue to be represented on its executive committee in 1995.

ALBANIA

Human Rights Developments

Albania has undergone radical change since democratic reforms began in 1990. Still, 1994 was marred by serious human rights abuses directed in particular at the independence of the judiciary, freedom of the press, and the rights of minorities. Police abuse and harassment of the political opposition also remained serious problems.

Throughout the year, there were many examples of political tampering with the courts, as well as trials and investigations that contained violations of both Albanian and international law. Several judges were transferred to lesser posts or fired after passing verdicts in politically sensitive cases. About 200 people received law degrees and were then appointed as judges, prosecutors and investigators in 1994 after attending a six-month legal training course. Most of the students were selected by local chapters of the ruling Democratic Party.

One of the most prominent trials during 1994 was that of Fatos Nano, a member of parliament and leader of the opposition Socialist Party. Mr. Nano was arrested in 1993 on charges of corruption when he served as prime minister of a 1991 transition government. After eight months in detention, Nano was tried and sentenced to twelve years in prison. The proceedings before and during the trial contained many irregularities, suggesting political motives for his conviction and harsh sentence.

Albania is currently run under a series of transitional constitutional laws that establishes the country as a parliamentary democracy with a commitment to international human rights documents. The Chapter on Fundamental Human Rights and Freedoms protects basic civil and political rights, as well as the rights of minorities. On November 6, a popular referendum rejected a complete constitution that would have affirmed these rights, but was criticized for the power it gave the president.

In late 1993, several communist-era articles of the penal code were repealed. However, new amendments were passed that made it a crime to insult or defame publicly the president, parliament or other state organs, putting a chill on peaceful political criticism.

Albanian television and radio were the principal means of communication with the mostly rural population and remained strictly controlled by the Democratic Party. No legislation allowed for private electronic media. There were many independent newspapers and magazines in the country, but they continued to face frequent threats, including high taxes, criminal prosecution and, on occasion, attacks on journalists by unknown assailants.

In October 1993, a new press law was enacted, despite protests from many Albanian journalists and numerous international human rights and journalists' organizations. Although the law recognized the freedom of the press, it also allowed for prior restraint and government confiscation of publications under vague conditions. In addition, violators of the press law were subject to disproportionately high fines. Six journalists were brought to court under the new press law or the penal code for slander or revealing state secrets. All of them were convicted, although four were subsequently pardoned by presidential decree on May 3, 1994, in honor of World Press Freedom Day.

Greek-Albanian relations took a marked turn for the worse during 1994 following a series of violent border incidents. The debate centered on the trial of five Albanian citizens from the Greek minority who were convicted in August to between six and eight years of imprisonment for espionage and the illegal possession of arms. Investigations by a Human Rights Watch/Helsinki representative and reports from international observers confirmed that the defendants were denied basic procedural protections before and during the trial. On the first day of the trial, a crowd of people outside the courtroom was beaten and dispersed by Albanian police, and at least twenty-two people were detained. Albanian and Greek journalists covering the trial complained of continual harassment by the Albanian police.

Greece responded to the trial by expelling about 70,000 Albanian emigrants who had been working in Greece; many complained of brutal treatment by the Greek police. The Greek minority in the south of Albania complained of a strong presence by the Albanian secret police, which contributed to an atmosphere of fear.

Other human rights issues of continuing concern included a high level of police abuse. During the year, a number of people died as a result of police violence, while many others complained of abuse during detention. Disciplinary actions against abusive police were rarely taken.

Human Rights Watch/Helsinki also observed the continual harassment of the political opposition. The government sometimes denied opposition parties permission to hold public meetings. On January 26, in Shkoder, a party activist for the opposition Democratic Alliance, Gjovalin Cekini, was shot to death after a struggle incited by individuals who had disrupted a party meeting. As of early November, police had still failed to identify the murderer. Similarly, although the files of the former secret police (Sigurimi) were supposedly closed and under state control, opponents of the government occasionally found that portions of their files were selectively used against them and published in the pro-governmental newspapers.

Local elections held on May 29 in four districts were marked by procedural irregularities and a high incidence of threat and intimidation primarily directed against opposition candidates. Among other incidents, a large number of unregistered soldiers voted in the village of Zallherr. In other districts, unknown assailants reportedly harassed and, in some cases, assaulted candidates and voters.

The Right to Monitor

Human Rights Watch/Helsinki received no reports during 1994 of human rights groups who were hindered in their monitoring efforts. However, the Society for Democratic Culture, a local political initiative supported by the U.S.-based National Democratic Institute, reported anonymous threats made against its members who were monitoring the local elections in May.

U.S. Policy

The United States has maintained very close relations with the Albanian government since 1991, including high levels of foreign aid and the granting of MFN status in August 1992. Various senior U.S. officials from the State Department, military, and Congress visited Albania during 1994. Military cooperation between the two countries also continued, as U.S. military advisors stationed in the country worked closely with the Albanian Ministry of Defense. On February 23, Albania became a member of NATO's Partnership for Peace.

The State Department's *Country Reports on Human Rights Practices for 1993* praised Albania for the progress it had made toward "establishing a multiparty democracy with legal guarantees for human rights." However, the report appropriately criticized "significant human rights problems," such as police abuse and restrictions on the freedom of press and assembly.

In July, the State Department issued a statement calling on the Albanian government to provide a fair and objective trial for the ethnic Greeks accused of espionage and arms possession (one of the accused also held an American passport).

The Work of
Human Rights Watch/Helsinki

Human Rights Watch/Helsinki concentrated its effort during 1994 on the most egregious human rights abuses, particularly the government's attempts to silence or intimidate its critics. On March 2, Human Rights Watch/Helsinki sent a letter to President Berisha protesting government restrictions on freedom of the press. On September 8, Human Rights Watch/Helsinki criticized the trial of the five ethnic Greeks, and urged President Berisha, among other things, to investigate reports of mistreatment and denial of basic rights.

Human Rights Watch/Helsinki plans to release a short report documenting the condition of the Greek minority in Albania and a comprehensive report on the human rights situation in Albania in the coming months.

ARMENIA

Human Rights Developments

In its seventh year, the conflict over the former Nagorno-Karabakh Autonomous Oblast of Azerbaijan continued in large part to shape human rights developments in Armenia. Forced draft raids were common, and many complained of the increased power of security forces.

During 1994, the country still remained under an Azerbaijani trade embargo that reduced energy and food supplies to the country, forcing the government to reopen the troubled Metzamor nuclear reactor. An estimated percent of the population has left the country. Conscripts were forcibly drafted into the army in raids using press-gang tactics as Armenia continued to send forces including conscripts to fight in Nagorno-Karabakh and in other parts of occupied Azerbaijan.

The year began with the as-yet-unexplained deaths of eight Azerbaijani prisoners of war in a Armenian Defense Ministry prison in January 1994. Other areas of concern included harassment of Hari Krishna temples in Armenia and the allegedly politically-motivated trial of Vahan Avakyan, former deputy of opposition political leader Ashot Manucharyan. Armenia failed to ratify a new constitution during the year, complicating economic and political reforms.

From the beginning of the Karabakh conflict, Armenia provided aid, weapons, and volunteers. According to Karabakh authorities, Armenia was providing upwards of 90 percent of the enclave's yearly budget in the form of interest-free credits. Some analysts believed that payments to Karabakh constituted 7 to 9 percent of Armenia's yearly budget.

Armenian involvement in Karabakh escalated after a December 1993 Azerbaijani offensive. The Republic of Armenia began sending conscripts and regular Army and Interior Ministry troops to fight in Karabakh. In January 1994, several active-duty Armenian Army soldiers were captured near the village of Chaply, Azerbaijan. While Armenia denied involvement in the conflict, in London in February 1994 President Levon Ter-Petrosyan stated that Armenia would intervene militarily if the Karabakh Armenians were faced with "genocide" or "forced deportation." The fighting during this Azerbaijani offensive, which lasted until February 1994, was exceptionally brutal. International aid agencies and foreign governments were concerned at the low number of prisoners of war registered given the scale of fighting.

To bolster the ranks of its army, the Armenia government resorted to press-gang raids to enlist recruits. Draft raids intensified in early spring, after Decree no. 129 was issued, instituting a three-month call-up for men up to age forty-five. Military police would seal off public areas, such as squares, and round up anyone who looked to be draft age. All male Armenian citizens between the ages of twenty-five and forty-five were forbidden to leave the country without special permission. According to a report in the influential German daily *Sueddeutsche Zeitung*, the United Nations High Commissioner for Refugees issued an order by which Armenian draft resisters should be given refugee status.

A particularly troubling human rights development in Armenia in 1994 was the unexplained deaths of the eight Azerbaijani prisoners of war in Yerevan. They were in the custody of the Armenian Ministry of Defense on January 29, 1994, their deaths remained unexplained as of this writing. According to the official version, after an aborted escape attempt in which a guard was killed, eight of the prisoners committed suicide with a pistol in a matter of minutes. The

Armenian government originally issued two different, contradictory explanations of the deaths. An independent forensic pathologist who examined the bodies stated that, "the pattern of injuries of the six individuals who died of gunshot wounds to the head suggest mass execution, but the possibility of a mass suicide cannot be absolutely excluded, however unlikely."

Domestically, there were widespread reports of the harassment and imprisonment of members of the Hari Krishna religious group, who were reportedly threatened and forced to leave various cities where they had gone to disseminate literature. Although these attacks often came from private citizens or from clergy of the Armenian Orthodox Church, the police response was at best perfunctory. On August 28, 1994, an unidentified group raided the main Hari Krishna temple in Yerevan, beating several members. Three days later, the police reportedly arrested sixteen Hari Krishna members.

On May 6, 1994, Vahan Avakyan was arrested by Armenian security forces at Sheremetovo-2 airport in Moscow and taken to Armenia. Avakayn was charged with transporting contraband, illegal weapons possession, and divulging state secrets. According to the Russian newspaper *Utro Rossii*, a multiparty Armenian parliamentary commission found the charges against Avakyan baseless, but nevertheless his case was sent to trial. Many believe Avakyan's trial to be politically-motivated, an attempt to discredit his former chief, opposition politician leader Ashot Manucharyan, former national security adviser to Armenian President Ter-Petrosyan. On October 10, Avakyan was found guilty of divulging state secrets then sentenced in November to five years imprisonment. At the time of this writing, an appeals court was set to review the sentence.

The Right to Monitor
Human Rights Watch/Helsinki was unaware of any interference with human rights monitoring in Armenia, and during an April 1994 mission to Armenia received full government cooperation.

U.S. Policy
While the Clinton adminstration adopted a more balanced approach regarding the conflict in Nagorno-Karabakh (*see* section on Azerbaijan), it has consistently refused to acknowledge publicly Armenia's military involvement there, which is marked by gross human rights abuses by all sides. The Armenia section of the State Department's *Country Reports on Human Rights Practices for 1993*, for example, only mentioned "Armenian support" for the Karabakh Armenian rebels, not the human rights consequences of that support. This official administration silence was most apparent during Armenian President Ter-Petrosyan's official visit in August to Washington, when President Clinton made no public statement concerning Armenian involvement in Karabakh or its consequences for human rights.

Armenia has consistently been the largest per-capita recipient of U.S. aid in the former Soviet Union. Through December 1993, Armenia received $305 million in humanitarian aid and $30 million in technical assistance. In fiscal year 1994, the U.S. Department of Agriculture provided $66 million in food aid, while the U.S. Agency for International Development expected to provide $11 million in food aid for children and post-partum mothers. The United States also allocated about $15 million for the transport of kerosene, kerosene heaters, and containers, while supporting market economy and democratization programs. An estimated $75 million in assistance has been allocated to Armenia for fiscal year 1995.

The Work of Human Rights Watch/Helsinki
In 1994, Human Rights Watch/Helsinki tried to focus attention on Armenian involvement in the war in Nagorno-Karabakh, a conflict beset by human rights abuses. We pressed the U.S. government to withhold all aid, except humanitarian, from all parties engaged in the Nagorno-Karabakh conflict. Human Rights Watch/Helsinki sent an April 1994 mission to Armenia, where we met with government and military officials, po-

litical parties, and the press. We brought widespread attention to the deaths of the eight Azeri prisoners in Yerevan. Throughout the year, we were also in close contact with the Armenian government concerning these deaths. In August 1994, a Human Rights Watch researcher met the Armenian Foreign Minister Vahan Papazyan to discuss this issue. We also criticized the human rights consequences of Armenian military intervention in Nagorno-Karabakh, addressing a letter to President Clinton before his August 1994 meeting with President Ter-Petrosyan, holding a press conference in Moscow, and meeting with European Union officials in Brussels.

AZERBAIJAN

Human Rights Developments

In 1994, as in the preceding year, political chaos, internal revolt, bombings, political assassinations, and battlefield setbacks in the war over Nagorno-Karabakh all took a disastrous toll on the human rights situation in Azerbaijan. The government of Heidar Aliyev continued to intimidate opposition political parties (especially former President Elchibey's Popular Front), harass the press, and prevent political demonstrations. Armenian forces from Karabakh seized more Azeri territory, creating nearly 50,000 Azeri displaced during one brief April 1994 offensive. Over 800,000 Azeri refugees and displaced persons from Armenia, Nagorno-Karabakh, and the Azeri-provinces surrounding Nagorno-Karabakh are still unable to return to their homes, crowding tent cities, public buildings and hotels, or simply squatting along the roadside.

On September 30, gunmen assassinated the deputy speaker of Azerbaijan's parliament, Rasul Guliyev, and President Aliyev's security chief, Shemsi Ragimov.

Shortly thereafter, police units whose members had been charged in the assassinations seized Azerbaijan's general prosecutor, Ali Umarov, and held him hostage,

prompting the October 3 imposition of a sixty-day state of emergency in Baku, Azerbaijan's capital, and a similar decree seven days later in Ganje, Azerbaijan's second largest city. President Aliyev charged that his prime minister, Surat Husseinov, was plotting a coup in Ganje, a replay of the June 1993 coup that brought Aliyev to power. Several ministers were arrested, and Husseinov was stripped of his post and charged with treason.

Among other restrictions, the state of emergency decree banned all rallies and demonstrations, outlawed political parties that "obstruct normalization of the political situation," and expelled non-Baku residents who did not follow "social regulations."

Political life in Azerbaijan and the activity of certain parties especially the Popular Front fell victim to government repression in 1994. There was evidence of illegal searches of opposition parties' headquarters as well as beatings and harassment of their members. A February 28 raid on the Azeri Popular Front headquarters in Baku resulted in the police banning the party. Allegedly weapons were found in the basement of the party headquarters, and Azerbaijan's procurator claimed that the Popular Front had been plotting a coup for March 5. The Popular Front denied the charge. As a result of the raid more than one hundred Popular Front and Musavat Party activists were arrested. On March 29, a Musavat party parliamentarian was beaten by an Aliyev adviser. There were reports that an estimated 450 individuals were fired from government jobs in the first few months of 1994 for their political beliefs.

Political demonstrations, many of them to protest proposed Karabakh peace settlements, also were repressed by security forces. On March 26, a rally to be led by former Popular Front Interior Minister Iskender Hamidov was broken up by police, and several demonstrators and journalists were detained. On May 21, a demonstration by thirteen opposition parties opposed to a would-be Karabakh peace plan was dispersed forcibly by police. At least 125 individuals were arrested, and it was reported that the police detained passersby and those holding opposition newspapers. Parliamentarians Tofik Gassimov, Ibrahim Ibrahimli, Hijran Kerimli, and Tair Kerimli were beaten and detained. On September 10, another demonstration protesting Aliyev's Karabakh policy was disrupted by the police, with a reported 400 injured and seventy-seven detained, including the former Interior Minister Iskender Hamidov.

Free speech also suffered from government repression, prior censorship, and state harassment in 1994, with major papers and television and radio operating under Soviet-era regulations and conditions. On December 6, 1993, military censorship was instituted after a December 2 decree banning publication of independent newspapers was lifted. Opposition publications, like the Popular Front's *Azadlyg*, were severely repressed. The police often raided the office on the pretext of looking for draft evaders: on April 18, for example, police raided *Azadlyg's* office and arrested fifteen individuals allegedly for evading the draft, though several were past draft age. On May 14, security forces again raided *Azadlyg's* headquarters and forced out the staff, which was allowed back in the next day. Other publications or news organizations suffering from government oppression were the Turan news agency, the satirical newspaper *Chasma*, and the National Independence Party of Azerbaijan's *Millat*.

The war over Nagorno-Karabakh entered its seventh year in 1994, with human rights violations such as the abuse and possible execution of prisoners committed by all sides in the conflict. In 1993, Karabakh Armenian forces often with the aid of the Republic of Armenia had seized all Azeri-populated provinces surrounding Nagorno-Karabakh on the south, west, and east and expelled approximately 450,000 Azeris and the destroyed their homes. Two major offensives marked the course of the war in the year covered by this report: a December 1993 Azerbaijani offensive that for the most part failed to regain territory seized in 1993

by Karabakh Armenian forces; and an April 1994 Karabakh Armenian offensive against Terter that resulted in over 50,000 displaced Azeri civilians.

A May 1994 cease-fire was still in effect as of November, which allowed confidence-building measures such as the exchange of prisoners and hostages. On September 7, 1994, the International Committee of the Red Cross facilitated the exchange of three Azeris and three Karabakh Armenians; a week later the Karabakh Armenians released twenty-four Azeri female hostages.

The Right to Monitor

There were no known restrictions on foreign human rights groups in Azerbaijan in 1994, but local human rights groups cited the overall repressive atmosphere as an impediment to their activities.

U.S. Policy

The United States government and embassy in Baku raised human rights issues such as the repression of the press and of political opponents both publicly and in meetings with the Azerbaijani government during 1994. This concern was reflected in the Azerbaijani section of the State Department's *Country Reports for Human Rights Practices for 1993*. At the same time, the Clinton administration sought repeal of Section 907 of the Freedom Support Act, which denies all aid to the Azerbaijani government because of its conduct of the war in Karabakh and its blockade of Armenia. Azerbaijan was the only state in the former Soviet Union to be denied such aid, and the Clinton administration believed this restriction prevented the U.S. from acting as a fair arbiter in the conflict. In early 1994, at the behest of the Clinton administration, Rep. Lee Hamilton, chair of the House Foreign Affairs Committee, introduced legislation that would have repealed the restriction on aid to the Azerbaijani government. The resolution did not pass. Under Section 907, the United States government can channel support to private-volunteer organizations operating in Azerbaijan. As of November, the U.S. had provided 34 million dollars in humanitarian assistance and 2 million in technical aid to private volunteer organizations for disbursement in Azerbaijan. Human Rights Watch/ Helsinki took the position that no aid, other than humanitarian assistance, should be provided to any party in the conflict in Nagorno-Karabakh.

The Work of
Human Rights Watch/Helsinki

While not neglecting its monitoring of domestic human rights developments in Azerbaijan, in 1994 Human Rights Watch/ Helsinki sought to focus international attention on the human rights consequences of the under-reported war in Nagorno-Karabakh. We highlighted involvement in the war by the Republic of Armenia and the consequences of Armenian policy for human rights. In March/April 1994, a researcher for Human Rights Watch/Helsinki visited numerous refugee camps in Azerbaijan to interview displaced from 1993 Karabakh Armenian offensives against Azeri provinces surrounding the Armenian enclave. In August 1994, we called on President Clinton to raise the issue of Armenian military involvement in the conflict during his meeting with Armenian President Ter-Petrosyan.

BOSNIA-
HERCEGOVINA

Human Rights Developments

Abuses against Bosnia's three ethnic groups—Muslims, Serbs, and Croats—continued in late 1993 and early 1994 but the overwhelming majority continued to be perpetrated by Bosnian Serbs. Most of these abuses were associated with "ethnic cleansing," whose main objective is the removal of an ethnic group from a given area through murder, population exchanges, forced displacement, and terrorization. Non-Serbs in northern Bosnia continued to be "cleansed" from their homes by Bosnian Serb authori-

ties, while abuses between Bosnia's Muslims and Croats noticeably decreased after the two groups ended their year-old war. Despite a lull in the fighting in Sarajevo, the city remained under siege by Bosnian Serb forces for much of 1994.

On February 5, a Bosnian Serb mortar attack killed sixty-three people in Sarajevo's open market. By late February, a NATO ultimatum forced Bosnian Serb forces to pull back their weaponry around Sarajevo or place it under U.N. supervision and a weapons exclusion zone was established around the city. As a result, shelling in Sarajevo decreased and a general cease-fire remained in place until mid-year, although snipers continued to kill civilians in the city. By July, however, shelling and sniping increased in Sarajevo, and roads on Mount Igman, which had been open for commercial traffic since February, were once again too treacherous to transit.

In April, the Bosnian Serb army used indiscriminate and disproportionate force in retaliation against Bosnian army provocation in the Gorazde enclave, which had been designated as a "safe area" by the U.N. in 1993. Bosnian Serb forces eventually captured part of the Gorazde enclave and then prevented journalists and some U.N. personnel from entering the area to assess the material damage and loss of civilian life. In response to the Bosnian Serb attack, Muslim forces within Gorazde expelled some Serbs and placed under house arrest others who remained in the enclave. Bosnian Serb forces restricted access to the area throughout the year.

In October, a Bosnian army commando unit killed twenty Bosnian Serb soldiers and military medical personnel on Mount Igman, an area which had been declared a demilitarized zone by the U.N. in 1993. Soon after the attack, Bosnian Serb forces opened fire on a trolley car in Sarajevo, wounding eight civilians. The Bosnian army refused U.N. demands that it withdraw from Mount Igman, saying it would do so only if the U.N. guaranteed the opening of a road through which commercial traffic could enter Sarajevo. As of mid-November, a tunnel under the airport was Sarajevo's primary link with the outside world.

Bosnian Serb forces were responsible for most of the attacks on humanitarian aid convoys throughout 1994. In October, they attacked a U.N. convoy and killed a U.N. driver near Gorazde. Bosnian Serb forces cut utilities to the Bosnian capital in mid-September and prevented opening of the Sarajevo airport in late September by refusing to guarantee the safety of U.N. relief flights.

"Ethnic cleansing" in Bosnian Serb-held areas continued during the early part of 1994 but decreased following international condemnation. However, in July, non-Serbs from the Bosanska Krajina and Bijeljina regions were once again expelled in large numbers and those who remained behind in Serbian-occupied territory were conscripted into work gangs and used as forced labor. Between July and October, more than 10,600 non-Serbs were expelled from northern Bosnia.

The war that raged between the mostly Muslim forces of the Bosnian army and the Bosnian Croat militia (HVO) after mid-1993 ended in late February 1994. On February 28 and March 1, the Bosnian Croats and the Bosnian government reconciled and formed a federation. At the same time, Bosnia and the Republic of Croatia, which supported the Bosnian Croats, also agreed to form a confederation. Following the formation of the federation, human rights abuses in central and southwestern Bosnia-Hercegovina decreased substantially. Despite the arrival of administrators from the European Union in mid-1994, abuses in the Croat-held part of Mostar continued, albeit to a lesser degree than in 1993. More than one-hundred Muslim families were evicted from Mostar after the signing of the Muslim-Croat federation. In an apparent assassination attempt on September 11, HVO soldiers launched a rocket-propelled grenade into the bedroom of Hans Koschnik, the E.U. administrator of Mostar. The Croatian authorities arrested four soldiers and removed the local police chief after the incident, but tensions between Muslims and Croats in the city remained high. Moreover, an ombudsman and court established by the federation to monitor human rights had not begun work as of early November. Repatriation of the displaced had not begun either, because minority populations in parts of the federation were not guaranteed safety.

Despite its past support for the Bosnian Serbs, Serbia closed its border with its Bosnian surrogates in September, following the Bosnian Serbs' refusal to accept an internationally brokered peace plan. One hundred and thirty-five international observers were stationed along the Bosnia-Serbia border and, by mid-October, the Bosnian Serbs generally were denied fuel and military support from Serbia. As of this writing, no violations of international law by either Bosnian army or HVO forces during their latest offensives in the Bihac, Sarajevo or Kupres areas had been reported. However, thousands of Serbs fled the offensive and sought refuge in Serbian-held areas of Croatia and other parts of Bosnian Serb-held territory.

The Right to Monitor

The Bosnian government and Bosnian Croat officials generally did not impede human rights monitoring by domestic and international organizations, but the Bosnian Croats continue to reject U.N. efforts to rectify the eviction of Muslims from their homes in west Mostar.

By contrast, human rights monitoring was severely restricted in Bosnian Serb-held areas. International monitors and much of the international press were banned from entering, or their movements were severely restricted within, Bosnian Serb territory. In August, a Human Rights Watch/Helsinki researcher attempted to interview Serbs who had left or been forced to leave Bosnian government-controlled areas of Sarajevo. Upon her arrival on August 26 in Pale, the headquarters of the Bosnian Serb authorities, the researcher was told by the "state security forces" to leave on the next bus. An advisor to Bosnian Serb leader Radovan Karadzic overruled this order and advised her to stay. The next day, she was again ordered by a plainclothes police officer to leave; the officer also threatened and insulted the researcher and accused her of espionage. Hours later, the officer told her that she was welcome to stay. Finally, forty-eight hours after she had arrived in Pale, the researcher was placed under armed guard in a car and not told where she was being taken. Finally, at 1:00 A.M. she was brought to the border with Serbia and expelled from Bosnian Serb territory.

The Role of the
International Community

U.S. Policy

With the notable exception of brokering a peace between Bosnia's Muslims and Croats, the Clinton administration's policy toward Bosnia was marked by indecision and policy reversals. Having distanced itself from the Bosnia crisis in late 1993, the U.S. reluctantly joined its allies in January 1994 calling on the NATO command to prevent the strangulation of Sarajevo and other U.N.-declared safe areas in Bosnia.

The Clinton administration's major accomplishment in Bosnia during 1994 was the brokering of a peace agreement between Bosnian Croats and Muslims. In late September, the Clinton administration pledged $20 million in non-humanitarian aid to the federation. The aid was intended to rehabilitate housing and infrastructure primarily in central Bosnia. In late October, the U.S. announced that it would send approximately fifteen U.S. military officers to Bosnia to integrate the military alliance between Bosnian government forces and the HVO.

On March 30, Madeline Albright, U.S. representative to the U.N., and Gen. John Shalikashvili, chair of the Joint Chiefs of Staff, visited Sarajevo in a show of support for the Bosnian government. In a speech there, Ambassador Albright supported the sovereignty of Bosnia and announced that the U.S. would donate $10 million to the reconstruction of Sarajevo. The following day, however, the U.S. blocked passage of a

U.N. Security Council resolution authorizing the deployment of 10,000 more peacekeeping troops to Bosnia, citing the financial strain of the U.N. field mission and the potential unwillingness of the U.S. Congress to approve the U.S. share of the bill. The U.S. sponsored instead a compromise resolution which approved an initial deployment of 3,500 peacekeepers and left the deployment of further troops for a later date.

The Clinton administration's vacillations in the face of the Gorazde crisis in April were emblematic of U.S. policy toward Bosnia more generally. As Bosnian Serb forces began a new and vigorous offensive against the Bosnian government-controlled enclave of Gorazde, a U.N.-declared safe area, the Clinton administration faced the familiar situation of attempting to avoid military intervention while, at the same time, risking a potential loss of credibility as further Bosnian Serb abuses went unpunished. On April 3, following the start of the offensive against the encircled Bosnian town, U.S. Secretary of Defense William Perry stated that the U.S. would not use military power to prevent the fall of Gorazde. Perry's statements seemed to jeopardize U.S. peace efforts in Bosnia by sending a "green light" to Bosnian Serb forces to do as they pleased. An embarrassed U.S. tried to provide a different impression of its intentions on April 7, when National Security Adviser Anthony Lake claimed that "neither the president nor any of his senior advisers rules out the use of NATO air power to help stop attacks such as those against Gorazde."

On April 10, as Bosnian Serb troops stood on the verge of overrunning Gorazde, two U.S. jets flying a NATO mission attacked a Serbian command post outside the besieged town. The attack represented not simply the first NATO air strike of the Bosnian war, but the first air strike in NATO history. Bosnian Serb forces briefly halted their offensive, but by the next day they advanced once again. U.S. jets carried out a second mission, this time destroying a Bosnian Serb tank. On the same day, President Clinton announced that NATO would continue to use air power until the advancing forces withdrew from the Gorazde area.

The U.S.'s newfound resolve quickly dissipated. Faced with Russian criticism and dissension within U.N. ranks, NATO did not follow up on its first round of air strikes, even as Serb forces continued their offensive. Finally, on April 17, the Clinton administration announced that it would seek no new air strikes against Serb forces in Bosnia. Three days later, however, the administration endorsed a plan by which NATO would use air power to protect all six U.N.-declared safe areas in Bosnia as weapons-exclusion zones, which NATO had previously established in the Sarajevo area. A version of this plan became NATO policy on April 22.

In a major policy shift, U.S. officials signaled at the same time that they were ready to entertain European proposals gradually to phase out U.N.-imposed sanctions against Serbia in exchange for Serb cooperation in Bosnian talks. Previously, the Clinton administration had opposed any loosening of sanctions against Serbia and its surrogates in Bosnia and Croatia until, among other things, they demonstrated cooperation with the international tribunal established to adjudicate war crimes and crimes against humanity in the former Yugoslavia. Given the continuing assault on Gorazde, the apparent involvement of Yugoslav army troops from Serbia in that attack, and the Serbs' unwillingness to accept the legitimacy of the tribunal, the Clinton administration's new position on easing of sanctions against Serbia was particularly ill-timed.

On April 25, U.S., Russian, and British officials announced the establishment of a "contact group," consisting of representatives from the U.S, the United Kingdom, Russia, Germany, and France, that would seek to broker an end to the Bosnian war. The contact group presented a map giving the Muslim-Croat federation control of 51 percent of Bosnia, and both the Bosnian government and the Bosnian Croats eventually accepted the proposal. Bosnian Serbs rejected the plan because it decreased their control of Bosnia from 70 percent to 49 percent. In light of Bosnian Serb rejection of the plan, Bosnian President Alija Izetbegovic withdrew his government's support for the plan in late July. U.S. support for the contact group's plan marked a departure from its long-articulated support for the territorial integrity of Bosnia. However, Viktor Jakovich, the U.S. Ambassador to Bosnia-Hercegovina, promised U.S. support for "an undivided Sarajevo and for a free and democratic Bosnia-Hercegovina within its internationally recognized borders" at the July 4 opening of the U.S. Embassy in Sarajevo.

The proposed plan focused solely on the territorial division of Bosnia; it offered no protection to minorities, particularly non-Serbs who continued to be persecuted in Bosnian Serb-held areas, nor was the right to repatriation mentioned. Though the contact group repeatedly threatened to adopt severe punitive measures against any party that refused to accept the proposed map, its members were far from united in their desire to punish the Bosnian Serb forces for their rejection of the plan. Indeed, in October, members of the contact group began considering new concessions to the Bosnian Serbs in exchange for their accession to the peace plan. In particular, Russia argued that the plan should be amended to allow the Bosnian Serbs to form a confederation with Serbia proper, as the Bosnians had done earlier in the year with Croatia.

For much of the year, the Clinton administration faced strong pressure from Congress to lift the arms embargo against the Bosnian government and confronted opposition to such action by the E.U. and Russia. Although President Clinton's rhetoric signified his support for lifting the embargo, his public dithering on the issue and his vigorous campaign against Congressional initiatives showed that he was unwilling to differ with the European allies on the issue for much of the year.

On August 11, President Clinton declared that he would urge the U.N. Security Council to lift the arms embargo against the Bosnian government if the Bosnian Serbs failed to accept the contact group's proposal by October 15. Despite E.U. rejection of such a proposal, the U.S. renewed calls for lifting the arms embargo in mid-October, this time saying it would consider lifting the arms embargo unilaterally.

Reportedly under pressure by the U.S., and in light of French and British threats to pull out their troops in Bosnia, Bosnian President Izetbegovic accepted a six-month postponement for lifting the arms embargo. Izetbegovic's statement, made before the U.N. General Assembly on September 27, spared President Clinton the need to confront both the E.U. and the U.S. Congress. In late October, the Clinton administration introduced a resolution at the U.N. to lift the embargo in six months' time unless the Bosnian Serbs accepted the contact group's peace proposal by then. Then, in a decision bound to strain relations with NATO allies, the Clinton administration announced on November 10 that it had directed the U.S. military to stop enforcing the arms embargo against the Bosnian government as of November 12.

In 1994, the U.S. was forthcoming with humanitarian aid for victims of the war in Bosnia. In addition to the $10 million pledged for Sarajevo's resconstruction and $20 million to support the Muslim-Croat federation, the U.S. gave a total of $387 million for humanitarian efforts in Bosnia-Hercegovina in the 1994 fiscal year.

The United Nations and NATO

In 1994, U.N. and NATO officials disagreed on their approach to Bosnian Serb violations of U.N. resolutions and NATO ultimatums: while NATO was generally willing to penalize Bosnian Serb violations, U.N. officials sought to accommodate Bosnian Serb demands.

Though existing Security Council resolutions mandated the use of force to protect peacekeepers and to ensure the delivery of humanitarian aid, military and civilian authorities of the U.N. Protection Force (UNPROFOR) were reluctant to exercise this option. This inaction drew criticism from two commanders of U.N. forces in Bosnia, one of whom was removed and the other resigned. On the occasions that the U.N. did use force, the action was typically marked by short-sightedness and lack of a broad-reaching strategy or goal. As a result, the U.N. suffered a devastating lack of credibility.

On January 19, a week after the NATO alliance had reasserted its willingness to carry out U.N.-requested air strikes, U.N. Secretary-General Bourtros Boutros-Ghali formally announced his opposition to air strikes in Bosnia, arguing that they would endanger the U.N. peacekeeping mission. Around the same time, the international press announced that both Britain and France were seriously considering withdrawing their troops from the U.N. mission in Bosnia.

Following the highly publicized February 5 marketplace massacre in Sarajevo, the international community responded to intense pressure to make good on its previous threats. On February 9, the NATO allies issued an ultimatum to the Bosnian Serb forces, demanding that by February 21 they either withdraw their heavy weaponry at least twenty kilometers from Sarajevo and place it under U.N. control, or face NATO air strikes. The ultimatum represented a bold new step in Western policy toward Bosnia, and, because the threat of military action seemed credible, Bosnian Serb troops complied with NATO's demands.

By May 18, however, the U.N. was admitting to the presence of at least four Serb tanks and ten other heavy weapons within the NATO-declared weapons exclusion zone. Because NATO and the U.N. refused to enforce compliance with the weapons exclusion zone, Bosnian Serb leaders grew increasingly confident in their ability to test the world community's resolve and resumed the siege of Sarajevo by mid-year.

On March 2, two U.S. aircraft under NATO command shot down four Serb jets near Banja Luka in northwestern Bosnia. Though an April 1993 U.N. resolution authorized the enforcement of a "no-fly zone" over Bosnia, the downing of the Serb jet represented the first enforcement after nearly

1,400 reported violations.

According to an April 22 NATO ultimatum, Bosnian Serb forces were ordered to immediately halt their attack on Gorazde, allow the free passage of displaced persons and relief personnel, and withdraw all troops from the town's center. NATO threatened air strikes against Bosnian Serb heavy weaponry and other military targets found within a 12.4-mile radius of Gorazde's center, and later extended the ultimatum to include the remaining U.N.-declared safe areas of Bihac, Srebrenica, Tuzla, and Zepa.

On April 24, when it appeared that Bosnian Serb forces were not complying with NATO demands, then-NATO Secretary-General Manfred Werner asked that the alliance begin conducting air strikes. After the U.N. extended their deadline, the Bosnian Serbs made significant strides in withdrawing its troops from the 1.9- mile zone, and both NATO and U.N. authorities stated that air strikes would not be necessary. NATO and U.N. leaders expressed satisfaction with the withdrawal, but a number of Serbian forces remained within the exclusion zone in violation of NATO's demands.

In July, UNPROFOR forces found themselves under increasing attack by Bosnian Serb militias. On August 5, two U.S. war planes under NATO command bombed a Bosnian Serb antitank vehicle near Sarajevo after Serbian soldiers sneaked into a U.N. weapons collection point and removed heavy guns. In the fourth NATO attack in 1994, NATO war planes strafed and bombed an vacant Bosnian Serb tank near Sarajevo in retaliation for a Serb attack on French U.N. peacekeepers.

In October, Bosnian Serbs attacked a U.N. convoy and killed a U.N. driver, forcing British U.N. soldiers to return fire. The attack lasted two hours, but senior U.N. officials decided not to call for a NATO air strike for logistical reasons.

Throughout 1994, NATO and the U.N. were at odds over the use of force in Bosnia. NATO was more willing to use force when U.N. troops or safe areas were attacked, while the Russians and Lt. Gen. Sir Michael Rose, the commander of U.N. forces in Bosnia, were opposed to expanding the use of force or the role of NATO in the Balkans. On October 27, NATO and the U.N. reached a draft compromise that would allow unannounced air strikes when there is little danger of civilian casualties, and require warnings if the strikes could endanger civilians.

On August 15, South African Judge Richard Goldstone took office as prosecutor to the international war crimes tribunal established by the U.N. to adjudicate war crimes and crimes against humanity in Bosnia and Croatia. The prosecutor's office began investigating specific cases of abuse in 1994 and, on November 8, it issued its first indictment against Dragan Nikolic, the former commander of the Bosnian Serb-run Susica camp. On the same day, the tribunal announced that it would ask Germany to extradite Dusko Tadic, a Serb accused of atrocities in the Omarska detention camp in 1992, who had been arrested in Munich in February. Other suspected war criminals from the former Yugoslavia had been apprehended in Denmark, Switzerland, and Austria by mid-November.

The Work of
Human Rights Watch/Helsinki

Throughout 1994, Human Rights Watch/ Helsinki continued monitoring and reporting on violations of the rules of war in Bosnia, with a view to identifying by name those responsible for such abuses. We also urged international negotiators to address human rights concerns as part of an overall peace settlement.

In April, we reported on, and identified persons responsible for, crimes in the northern Bosnian town of Bosanski Samac. In June, we issued a report about continuing human rights violations in the Banja Luka area and criticized international peace negotiators' disregard for continued "ethnic cleansing." Indeed, on June 28, prior to a meeting of the G-7 leaders (Canada, France, Germany, Italy, Japan, United Kingdom, and United States), Human Rights Watch/ Helsinki issued a press release warning the

G-7 not to endorse the contact group's peace proposal partitioning Bosnia until human rights concerns were made part of an overall peace settlement; we sent a similar letter to President Clinton. In early September, we issued a press release calling on the contact group to use its influence with Bosnian Serb authorities to stop "ethnic cleansing" in Bijeljina and other parts of northern Bosnia. We continued calling on the international community to respond to continued "ethnic cleansing" in northern Bosnia in a November newsletter. In a March letter to Jose Ayala Lasso, U.N. high commissioner for human rights, we suggested improvements in the UNPROFOR mission in Croatia and Bosnia-Hercegovina.

Human Rights Watch/Helsinki sent a mission to Sarajevo in May and June and issued a newsletter in October reporting on past and present human rights violations in the city. In September and October, Human Rights Watch/Helsinki sent a mission to central and southwestern Bosnia to investigate the status of human rights and accountability for past crimes in the Muslim-Croat federation. We met with E.U. administrators of Mostar in the field and in Brussels. Also in the fall, we researched the campaign to "ethnically cleanse" eastern Bosnia of Muslims and to identify persons who planned or perpetrated abuses in the area in 1992.

Throughout the year, Human Rights Watch/Helsinki kept up pressure for the establishment and support of the international tribunal to adjudicate war crimes and crimes against humanity in Bosnia and Croatia. In February, Human Rights Watch/Helsinki issued *The War Crimes Tribunal: One Year Later,* which called for the appointment of a prosecutor to the international war crimes tribunal and for the tribunal to begin its work. We also advocated for proper funding and staffing of the tribunal, and on February 25 sent a letter to U.N. Secretary-General Boutros-Ghali expressing concern over the failure to provide adequate funding. In March, we urged U.N. budgetary bodies to allocate sufficient funds to the tribunal. Prior to and after the appointment of Judge Goldstone,

representatives of Human Rights Watch maintained regular contact with the prosecutor's office and forwarded our documentation to the tribunal's staff.

BULGARIA

Human Rights Developments

The most serious human rights abuses in Bulgaria continued to be directed primarily at ethnic minority groups, and especially Roma (Gypsies), during 1994. Human Rights Watch/Helsinki continued to receive many credible reports of violence against Roma, much of it committed by police officers and private security guards. For example, on August 4, 1994, the police carried out a large-scale raid in the Roma neighborhood in the town of Pazardzhik. As in a similar raid in the same neighborhood in 1992, the police brutalized innocent victims and intentionally damaged the property of Roma. Lyubcho Terziev, a Roma who was arrested during the raid, died while in detention. According to the official death certificate, his death was the result of "cardiovascular insufficiency." However, persons who saw Terziev's body reported that there was evidence he had been beaten on the head and that there were burn marks on his genitals.

In addition to the numerous cases of police and private security guard violence against Roma, in the period covered by this report the phenomenon of mob violence against Roma intensified. During the month of December 1993, the Roma neighborhood of Pobeda in Burgas was attacked on several occasions. In each of the attacks, the perpetrators wore helmets and threw molotov cocktails. On January 10, 1994, six Roma houses in the same neighborhood were set on fire. During that attack, a Roma teenager was also severely beaten and a four-year-old child was badly burned.

On February 25, a Roma soldier robbed and murdered a seventy-year-old ethnic Bulgarian in the town of Dolno Belotintsi. The murderer was arrested about three hours later, but vigilantes took reprisals against the entire ethnic group. That evening, a group of ethnic Bulgarian villagers attacked the homes of Roma living in the village, rounding up and beating many of them. The Roma were then forced to march to the next town, and in the following days, several Roma homes were set on fire or damaged.

On March 26, 1994, approximately fifty skinheads attacked the homes of Roma in the town of Pleven, beating residents and setting one house on fire. Victims' testimonies indicate that the police not only did not intervene to protect them, but actually participated in the beatings.

On October 17, Kiril Yosifov Yordanov, a Roma who had filed a complaint against the police in Pazardzhik for allegedly having beaten him, was again detained with three other Roma and beaten by the police. While the police were looking at Yordanov's passport, they found a telegram from the Human Rights Project about his lawsuit and a notification from the court regarding the date of the next hearing. The officers reportedly then asked Yordanov if he was "the brave guy who is suing us?" The police then started beating him and cursing him. His request to contact his lawyer was denied.

There is substantial evidence that during 1994 Bulgarian police and prosecutors have failed to investigate acts of violence promptly and thoroughly when the victim was Roma. Prosecutors have frequently decided that there was not enough evidence to open a formal investigation in cases where Bulgarian and international human rights organizations had documented substantial evidence of police brutality and misconduct. Frequently the testimony of Roma victims was not even taken or, if taken, was disregarded.

Police abuse and use of excessive force against minorities in general continued to be a serious human rights concern. In addition to the numerous cases of police brutality against Roma discussed above, there were numerous other reports of police abuse, especially directed at racial and ethnic minorities. For example, following the murder of

two policemen by Iranian citizens in December 1993, the Bulgarian police shot and killed four Iranian citizens over the following two weeks. Reports indicated that the police made no effort to arrest the Iranians or to warn them before shooting. An investigation was still underway in early November 1994, with no results to date. In June, representatives from the Movement for Rights and Freedoms also submitted a series of complaints of police brutality against ethnic Turks to the Ministry of the Interior.

The Bulgarian government continued to restrict the free expression and association of certain Bulgarian citizens who identify themselves as ethnic Macedonians during 1994. On April 23, the authorities denied a request by members of United Macedonian Organization Ilinden (OMO Ilinden) for permission to assemble to commemorate the anniversary of the death of Yane Sandanski, a Macedonian leader from the beginning of the twentieth century. (OMO Ilinden has been denied registration by the government because it is considered a separatist organization.)

In addition, efforts to restrict the activities of certain "non-traditional" religious groups intensified during 1994. On February 3, the law governing nonprofit organizations was amended to increase the discretion of the executive branch, which was already quite substantial, to determine which religious groups should be granted legal status. Article 133a of the Law on Persons and the Family, as amended, stated that "nonprofit juridical entities which have religious or related activities or perform religious education should be registered under this chapter after the approval of the Council of Ministers." The law, which entered into force on February 21, did not specify the conditions under which religious organizations could be denied registration. It did not set out the procedure for implementing the law, nor establish an appeals process. Previously registered nonprofit organizations and religious foundations were given three months to re-register. As of the end of July, thirty-nine religious organizations had been denied registration and twenty-three had been re-registered.

Denial of legal status made it impossible for an organization to rent public lecture halls or sign contracts in the name of the organization. An unregistered organization was unable to open a bank account or publish journals or newspapers in the name of the organization and was denied certain tax advantages. The law effectively discriminated against non-traditional religious groups and prevented many of them from functioning as legal entities in Bulgaria.

Attempts to prosecute those accused of abuses during the communist era progressed slowly during 1994. The murder trial of three former guards at the Lovetch labor camp, which had started in 1993, continued. President Zhelev pardoned former Prime Minister Gueorgui Atanasov who, along with the former Minister of Industry Stoyan Ovcharov, was sentenced in 1993 to ten years and nine years of imprisonment respectively for misappropriation of funds. The pardon was due to Mr. Atanasov's poor health.

One encouraging step during the period covered by this report was the National Assembly's adoption of a new National Police Law on December 15, 1993. Among other things, the law, which entered into force on January 1, 1994, removed the police from the jurisdiction of the military courts, such that in the future, all allegations of police misconduct and brutality are now the responsibility of civil prosecutors and investigators.

Although the 1990 moratorium on the death penalty remained in effect during 1994, capital punishment remained legal and Bulgarian courts continued to issue death sentences. In January and February, the parliament discussed legislative initiatives to lift the moratorium, but they were never considered by the plenary hall of the parliament.

The Right to Monitor

Human Rights Watch/Helsinki was not aware of any instance in 1994 in which the government of Bulgaria had hindered human rights monitors in their work.

U.S. Policy

Bulgarian and U.S. officials held several high-level meetings during the year to discuss such issues as the Partnership for Peace initiative and the situation in the Balkans. However, the only significant public comment on human rights developments in Bulgaria were found in the State Department's *Country Reports on Human Rights Practices for 1993.* The section on Bulgaria was, for the most part, accurate and thorough in reporting on the human rights situation there.

The Work of
Human Rights Watch/Helsinki

Human Rights Watch/Helsinki concentrated its efforts during 1994 on encouraging international bodies to play an active role in ensuring that the Bulgarian government took the necessary steps to protect Roma from mob violence and to guarantee that the victims of such violence could obtain adequate remedy. To this end, we documented the Bulgarian government's tolerance for and acquiescence in the violence committed against the Roma minority. In May 1994, Human Rights Watch/Helsinki sent a mission to Bulgaria to investigate recent reports of police brutality and cases of mob violence against Roma. A report on the findings of the mission was released during the Conference on Cooperation and Security in Europe (CSCE) Review conference in Budapest in early November. In addition, Human Rights Watch/Helsinki used the information contained in the report to urge representatives of the various member states of the Council of Europe and the European Union to initiate a dialogue with the government and to insist that concrete steps be taken by the government to address our concerns, targeting especially those countries that have close ties to Bulgaria and may therefore have more influence with the Bulgarian government. In November, Human Rights Watch/Helsinki called on the Council of Europe and the CSCE, among other things, to initiate a dialogue with the Bulgarian government and to insist that the Bulgarian government take concrete steps to address our concerns.

Human Rights Watch/Helsinki also raised with the Bulgarian government a number of other human rights concerns, including restrictions on religious freedoms and the arrests of several Macedonian leaders.

CROATIA

Human Rights Developments

Although there were some human rights improvements in Croatia in 1994, the Croatian government continued to evict persons living in housing formerly owned by the Yugoslav army and to impede the functioning of a free press. To its credit, the Croatian government pressured its surrogates in Bosnia to accept a peace plan between Muslims and Croats in late February, which had a positive effect on human rights in that country. Having already "cleansed" non-Serbs from much of the area under their control, insurgent Serbian forces in Croatia continued to deny water to the civilian population in Croatian government-controlled areas and to impede cooperation with U.N. officials investigating war crimes.

In 1992, the Croatian Defense Ministry had assumed the right of ownership of all property belonging to the Yugoslav army (JNA), including apartments and homes owned by the JNA which housed its personnel. As in 1993, the Defense Ministry continued to forward eviction notices to those who were granted tenancy rights to JNA-owned property after October 1991, usually non-Croatian former JNA personnel or their families. Those evicted were not always granted the opportunity to appeal to an independent entity, such as a civil court. When the court did rule in favor of the person being evicted, the Defense Ministry did not always abide by the court's ruling and often forced people from their homes.

In July, the Croatian Ministry of Culture and Education revoked the tax exempt status of the independent weekly *Feral Tri-bune* despite the fact that such exemptions were normally granted to the print media as a form of public subsidy. Human Rights Watch/Helsinki believes this action was politically motivated because *Feral Tribune* consistently criticized government policies and satirized Croatian government officials, thereby invoking the ire of the Croatian government and conservative members of the ruling Croatian Democratic Union (HDZ). The 50 percent tax on profits that the paper was thus forced to pay, threatened its very existence.

Physical violence against Serbs and their property and mistreatment of Muslim refugees lessened in 1994. Also, some decisions to refuse citizenship to some non-Serbs were reversed, and the *refoulement* of Bosnian refugees decreased. On the other hand, trials of alleged "war criminals" in Croatia continued to suffer from lack of due process. Most trials continued *in absentia*, and those who were physically present for their trials were not always allowed to call witnesses for their defense, or had been mistreated while in police custody. Moreover, the Defense Ministry did little to discipline members of the military police, who were responsible for most abuses in Croatia during the year.

Thirty percent of Croatia remained under the control of Serbian insurgents in 1994. Efforts to open peace negotiations between the Croatian government and the authorities of this area—the self-proclaimed "Republic of Serbian Krajina" (RSK)—produced little result. Serbian authorities in the Obrovac area continued to refuse to supply water to the civilian population in government-controlled areas around Zadar. Bosnian Serb forces shelled the Dubrovnik area intermittently during the summer and Zupanja and Bosnjaci in the fall. Most non-Serbs had long been expelled from Serbian-controlled areas of Croatia, but 1994 saw an influx of Bosnian Muslim and Serb refugees into Serbian-held areas of Croatia. As of mid-November, there were no reports of mistreatment of either the Bosnian Serb or Muslim refugees; indeed, before they fled the

Velika Kladusa area, fleeing Muslim refugees and their leader, Fikret Abdic, advocated cooperation with and were supported, in part, by Serbian officials in Croatia.

The United Nations Protection Force (UNPROFOR) continued to operate with little success in Serbian-controlled areas in Croatia. The UNPROFOR mission was not sufficiently forceful with the Serbian authorities and, as a result, continued to be unable to fulfill its mission. For example, the repatriation of the displaced was part of the U.N.'s mandate in Croatia, yet not one displaced non-Serb was repatriated to Serbian-held areas in 1994. Moreover, the U.N. did little to pressure the insurgent Serbian authorities to resupply water to the civilian population in parts of government-controlled Croatia, despite the fact that the denial of water to civilian populations was contrary to international law. Finally, although the U.N. was to have demilitarized Serbian-controlled areas of Croatia, U.N. forces did nothing to prevent Serbian forces in Croatia from launching attacks against the safe area of Bihac in northwestern Bosnia in late 1994.

The Right to Monitor

Although conservative members of the government and ruling party took issue with positions taken by some human rights groups, the Croatian government generally did not interfere with the activities of domestic or international human rights organizations. The Croatian Helsinki Committee continued its second year of operation, and local human rights groups in Split, Osijek, Rijeka, and Zagreb worked generally unimpeded. Serbian political and cultural groups also continued their human rights activities in Croatia. The Croatian government cooperated with efforts by a U.N. forensic team to exhume the remains of Serbs summarily executed by Croatian soldiers in the Pakrac area in 1991. Amnesty International established a local chapter in 1994, and Human Rights Watch/Helsinki representatives continued to operate within Croatia throughout the year.

Although the U.N. monitored human rights abuses in Serbian-held areas of Croatia, Serbian authorities generally were not willing to cooperate with international human rights groups. In November 1993, authorities in the self-proclaimed RSK continued to prevent a U.N. forensic team from exhuming a mass grave containing the remains of approximately 200 Croats summarily executed in Vukovar, after that city fell to Serbian forces in 1991.

U.S. Policy

U.S. policy toward Croatia was dominated by concern for Croatian government involvement in the war in neighboring Bosnia. The U.S. nonetheless took some action to press the Croatian government to improve its human rights performance at home and brought attention to the need for accountability for crimes committed during the 1991 wars in Croatia and Bosnia.

In January 1994, Madeline Albright, U.S. ambassador to the U.N., visited Croatia. In a strong, important speech delivered at the site of the mass grave in Vukovar, Ambassador Albright stated that the U.S. would oppose lifting sanctions against Serbia unless the authorities in Serbian-held areas of Bosnia and Croatia and the governments of Serbia and Montenegro cooperated with the international war crimes tribunal by permitting unhindered investigation of war crimes and crimes against humanity and by extraditing those indicted for these offenses. But this position was later abandoned; the U.S. agreed to ease U.N.-imposed sanctions against Serbia and Montenegro following the Yugoslav government's isolation of the Bosnian Serbs, despite a lack of progress in cooperation with the tribunal.

To its credit, in early 1994, the U.S. pressured Croatia to withdraw its military and financial support from the Bosnian Croat militia (HVO) in their war against the Muslim-dominated Bosnian Army. During her January visit to Croatia, Ambassador Albright responded to Croatian President Franjo Tudjman's threats to send Croatian troops to Bosnia, warning that any increased Croatian presence there could be met with U.N. sanctions against Croatia.

By early March, the U.S. had brokered a federation between the Bosnian Croats and Muslims, and the governments of Croatia and Bosnia-Hercegovina agreed to form a confederation. Instrumental to the success of these negotiations and the consequent human rights improvements in central and southwestern Bosnia was the role the U.S. played in convincing Croatian President Tudjman to exert his influence with the Bosnian Croat leaders. According to the international media, a particular incentive to President Tudjman was the U.S.'s promise to take a more active role in finding a satisfactory solution to the struggle between the Croatian government and Serbian insurgents in Croatia.

On June 30, Peter Galbraith, U.S. ambassador to Croatia, warned the Croatian government that despite U.S. recognition of Croatia's territorial integrity, the Clinton administration discouraged the forceful reintegration of Croatia's Serbian-occupied territories. Arguing that Croatia did not possess the strength to complete a successful military takeover of the occupied territories, Galbraith urged the Croatian government instead to improve its treatment of Croatia's Serbian minority and create an environment conducive to peaceful negotiation. Galbraith's comments came in the wake of increasing threats on the part of Croatian officials to resort to force should negotiations with Serbian leaders of the self-styled RSK make no progress by the fall.

In October, Ambassador Galbraith, along with representatives from the United Nations, European Union, and Russia, attempted to broker a peace between the Croatian government and Serbian insurgents. The proposed peace plan granted a high degree of autonomy to Croatia's insurgent Serbs if they returned oil wells and farmland to Croatian control and allowed Croats expelled from Serbian-held territory to return to their homes. The plan was unacceptable to both parties.

The Work of Human Rights Watch/Helsinki

In order to monitor and respond to violations of civil and political rights and the rules of war in Croatia and Croat-controlled areas of Bosnia-Hercegovina, Human Rights Watch/Helsinki continued to maintain one or more staff members in Croatia throughout 1994. Staff representatives sustained contacts with human rights activists, government officials and the press in Croatia. Human Rights Watch/Helsinki conducted a mission to Croatia in March and April to investigate the status of the Croatian government's prosecution of alleged war criminals. In September, we sent a letter to the Croatian government protesting continued impediments to freedom of the press. We continued to monitor U.N. operations in Croatia and to lobby for member states' cooperation with the international tribunal established to adjudicate war crimes and crimes against humanity in Bosnia and Croatia.

THE CZECH REPUBLIC

Human Rights Developments

Although the human rights situation in the Czech Republic has improved dramatically in recent years, continuing human rights concerns related in particular to the treatment of Roma (Gypsies) and the increase in skinhead attacks against them during 1994. More generally, tensions over nationality and integration provided the context for legal discrimination against certain non-Czechs. For example, the Law of the Czech National Council on Acquisition and Loss of Citizenship, adopted on January 1, 1993, was amended in 1994 to extend the date for Slovak citizens to apply for Czech citizenship under more favorable conditions than other foreigners until June 30, 1994.

The law provided, *inter alia,* that Slovak nationals can be denied Czech citizenship if they have criminal records dating five years prior to application. Human rights and minority rights groups expressed concern that the law would have a negative impact on the Roma minority, many of whom are Slovak citizens although they may have lived their whole lives on Czech territory. As the U.S. Helsinki Commission pointed out, "The law attaches to past criminal acts new penalties (i.e. loss of citizenship) which were not in existence at the time of the crime, has the impact of discriminating against the Czech Republic's largest minority, and is being implemented in a manner which fails to provide the kinds of administrative law protections" envisioned in human rights documents. It is estimated that approximately 100,000 Slovak citizens, most of whom are Romas, have been left without Czech citizenship as a result of the law. On September 13, the Czech Constitutional Court rejected a challenge to the law on the basis that it was discriminatory.

There continued to be reports of violent attacks on Roma. For example, following the killing of a policeman allegedly by a Roma man on June 19, two Roma houses were set on fire in the town of Bruntal. Many of the attacks were carried out by skinheads. On July 15, skinheads threw Molotov cocktails into the home of a Roma family in Jablonec nad Nisou, severely injuring a young girl and her mother. Some Romas reported that the police were often unwilling to protect citizens of Roma ethnicity.

On April 29, after much controversy, the Czech parliament adopted a law providing for the restitution of Jewish property confiscated by the Nazis during World War II. The government identified for return some 202 synagogues, cemeteries and other community buildings still in the possession of the state or municipalities. Under the new law, Jewish property that was later sold to individuals would not be returned, but financial compensation would be paid by the state.

During 1994 representatives of the Sudetan Germans, who were expelled from Czechoslovakia after World War II, increased pressure on the Czech Republic to provide restitution and repatriation rights. Czech government officials had consistently refused to negotiate with the Sudetan Germans, but during 1994, the German and Austrian governments began to support more vocally the demands of the Sudetan Germans and to suggest that a resolution of their demands might be linked to the Czech Republic's admission into the European Union. International human rights documents prohibit discrimination on the basis of ethnic or national origin and guarantee that all individuals shall receive equal treatment of the law and shall have the right to obtain adequate reparation for damages suffered due to discrimination.

On April 13, the Czech Constitutional Court held that provisions of Article 102 of the criminal code that prohibit defamation of "the government, parliament and the constitutional court" were unconstitutional. Although human rights observers applauded the court's decision, they pointed out that the criminal code still prohibits defamation of the Czech Republic and of the President of the Republic. Petr Cibulka, editor-in-chief of the anti-communist weekly *Uncensored News*, had been charged under these provisions for having made critical remarks about Czech President Vaclav Havel. On March 17, President Havel pardoned Cibulka.

The Right to Monitor
Human Rights Watch/Helsinki was not aware of any attempt by the government of the Czech Republic to impede human rights observers in their monitoring activities.

U.S. Policy
Although United States and Czech officials met frequently during 1994, the only significant comments on human rights in the Czech Republic were found in the State Department's *Country Reports on Human Rights Practices for 1993*. Its section on the Czech Republic was, for the most part, accurate in reporting on the human rights situation and appropriate in tone. However, the report described as "cultural" the "central issue" in the controversy over the provision

in the citizenship law requiring a clean criminal record for a five-year period prior to the application, stating "ethnic Czechs see five years as reasonable, Roma see it as punitive." By doing so, the State Department appeared to be trivializing serious human rights issues raised by the law.

The Work of
Human Rights Watch/Helsinki

Human Rights Watch/Helsinki's primary concern in the Czech Republic continued to be the treatment of the Roma minority and, in particular, the impact that the citizenship law would have on Roma. In September, Human Rights Watch/Helsinki wrote to Minister of the Interior Jan Ruml expressing concern and requesting specific information regarding the impact of the law on the Roma minority.

GEORGIA

Human Rights Developments

The fighting in the western regions of Abkhazia and Megrelia, which had marred Georgia's human rights record in recent years, decreased dramatically in 1994. However, violations of refugee rights, police brutality, abysmal conditions of confinement, and restrictions on peaceful dissent continued to plague this Caucasian country.

After fourteen months of fighting the central government for autonomy, Abkhazian forces took full control of the disputed territory in October 1993, and the warring sides signed the first of a series of U.N.-sponsored peace agreements on December 1. Beginning in June 1994, Russia deployed some 3,000 peacekeepers under the Confederation of Independent States (C.I.S.) banner to de-mine the conflict zone. At the same time, the bloody civil war between supporters and opponents of Head of State Eduard Shevardnadze that had gripped Megrelia and the capital, Tbilisi, since 1991 also tapered off. The parties to the conflict signed a cease-fire agreement in September 1993, former

President Zviad Gamsakhurdia died in December, and anti-Shevardnadze military leader Vakhtang "Loti" Kobalia was sent to jail on murder charges on July 7, 1994.

War criminals from both sides of the Georgia-Abkhazia conflict remained unpunished, however, and Abkhazian diplomatic and armed resistance and the slow pace of peace negotiations prevented almost all of the estimated 250,000 primarily ethnic Georgians driven from Abkhazia from returning home.

Similarly, the central government engaged in a conflict of wills against its detractors. Growing discontent over the country's economic and social deterioration spurred the government to keep a tight grip on society. The government and the Mkhedrioni (Horsemen, a paramilitary group working with the police) harassed, beat and arrested dissidents and nonconformist journalists. They also dispersed several peaceful protest rallies in Tbilisi, including on April 7, 9, 14, and 20, July 9, September 19 and October 11. Torture continued in police lockups and pre-trial investigation centers, most notably in the capital.

Georgia's pre-trial detention centers and prisons were appallingly overcrowded and unsanitary. Facility administrators in Tbilisi blamed empty government coffers for the failure to provide adequate medical care and the inability to feed inmates more than bread. Human Rights Watch considers such conditions severely abusive.

In 1994 the government imprisoned or failed to release dozens of members of the loosely organized opposition in an apparent attempt to silence them. Charges ranged from political crimes such as treason and terrorism to criminal violations, and many suspects faced the death penalty. On May 19, for example, Avtandil Rtskhiladze, a leading supporter of President Gamsakhurdia, went to jail on murder charges; as of this writing, however, the Procuracy (prosecutor's office) was not known to have submitted any evidence against him. In response to criticism of such arrests, Mr. Shevardnadze created a commission in July to investigate whether Georgia kept political prisoners. His appointment of officials exclusively from his own government to serve on the commission raised doubts about the impartiality of the inquiry.

Nineteen opposition members arrested in 1992 for murder and terrorism, among other crimes, came to trial in October 1993, and, despite serious due process violations, they remained on trial throughout 1994. They testified that investigators tortured them into confessing. Sixteen of the defendants faced capital punishment. With only one known exception, the court failed to investigate these serious allegations. Indeed, throughout the trial Judge Mirza Dolidze barred access to counsel, prohibited medical care, and expelled defendants and defense lawyers from the courtroom arbitrarily, ultimately trying five individuals facing the death penalty *in absentia*. Special forces (OMON) reportedly beat one defendant, Viktor Domukhovskii, in his cell on August 13. Soon after Mr. Domukhovskii protested the beating, the judge expelled him and his legal representative from the trial. The Supreme Court and the Collegium of Lawyers (roughly equivalent to a bar association) refused to investigate these gross violations of due process. On the contrary, in June the Collegium disbarred an outspoken defense lawyer in the case, Tengiz Nijeradze.

In March the parliament lifted a two-year moratorium on the death sentence. The Committee for Human Rights and Inter-ethnic Affairs confirmed that executions had taken place, but was unable to confirm how many. It reported in August, however, that the government had approved at least eight acts of clemency in 1994.

Residents enjoyed relatively unrestricted free expression. However, the government's attacks on independent journalists, or failure to condemn such attacks, chilled some critical speech. On March 23, six armed men reportedly beat Zaza Chenguelia, director of the independent TV station Obervisa, at his office so badly that he required hospitalization. Three days later, the station was bombed. On April 9, another bomb exploded at the editorial offices of the independent newspaper *Svobodnaia Gruziia*. On June 14, militia arrested and beat David Khvizhinadze, a Reuters correspondent, as he filmed an opposition rally in Tbilisi, and confiscated his camera.

In 1993, the Procuracy charged Elizbar Javelidze, editor of the independent newspaper *Sakartvelos Samreklo*, with slandering Mr. Shevardnadze for publishing a translation of a critical article from the British journal *Soviet Analyst*. According to Mr. Javelidze's wife, the militia repeatedly searched his home and harassed his family in 1994, forcing him into hiding. One activist with the opposition Helsinki Union claimed that as of June, twenty-five Georgian journalists had lost their jobs because of government pressure.

In at least two broadcasts, the government media grossly distorted coverage of Human Rights Watch's concerns in Georgia; at least one journalists' organization declined to cover the issues at all, citing fear of government reprisals.

In a rare positive development, the government on April 7 agreed to re-register the once illegal newspaper *Tavisupali Sakartvelo*.

The Right to Monitor

Government harassment and the politicization of human rights work reduced the number of active independent monitors in Georgia to a handful.

Over the summer, law enforcement officials twice detained Tbilisi-based activist Giorgi Khoshtaria; on September 19 Deputy Minister of Internal Affairs Chaladze reportedly personally beat him during interrogation. Mr. Khoshtaria reported that the interrogations focused on his defense of political prisoners. The human rights branch of the Helsinki Union reported that the militia arrested members arbitrarily and tapped their telephones. It is unclear whether the harassment was intended to curtail their political or human rights activities.

The governmental Committee on Human Rights met with Human Rights Watch representatives in June and August, held a joint press conference with the organization in August, facilitated some access to prisons, helped collect copies of laws, and promised to correct some minor due process violations in Criminal Case No. 7493810. However, the committee also prevaricated about medical attention to prisoners.

In June government and prison authorities barred a Human Rights Watch representative from speaking with incarcerated defendants. Prison authorities punitively moved one inmate, Zaza Tsiklauri, who was suffering from tuberculosis and the effects of torture, from the hospital where he was interviewed by our representative to an overcrowded detention cell where he received no medical care and later contracted hepatitis from a cellmate. The presiding judge and prison officials refused him medical treatment until relatives and human rights groups joined in protest of his mistreatment; then they returned him to the hospital in September.

United Nations Policy

The U.N. forged difficult peace agreements for Abkhazia, and the officer of the U.N. High Commissioner for Refugees (UNHCR) assisted tens of thousands of displaced persons. U.S. Ambassador to the U.N. Madeleine Albright traveled personally to Tbilisi on September 1 to speed the peace process.

At the same time, the U.N. helped negotiate restrictions on the right to return home. Article 3(c) of the April 4 quadripartite (Georgia, Abkhaz, Russia and U.N.) agreement denied returnees immunity when there were "serious signs" that they had committed a "military offense...a serious criminal offense or earlier participated in military actions and currently belong to armed formations that are preparing for military actions in Abkhazia." No one should be immune to investigation of alleged human rights violations. However, the very real fear of biased prosecution discouraged displaced persons from returning to Abkhazia. The restrictions stipulated in the April agreement are also objectionable since they target a particular group, the overwhelmingly Georgian population that fled Abkhazia.

The U.N. declined to send peacekeepers to Abkhazia pending a political settlement of the conflict. The U.N. had no legal obligation to do so, and its resistance was understandable. However, its lack of participation in the process yielded a dangerous situation for civilians. Partisan bodies such as the Russian army, Georgian Procuracy, and Abkhazian militia and Procuracy were responsible for law enforcement in the wake of the conflict. Since most of the individuals designated to perform law enforcement and prosecutorial duties were either victims of or parties to the conflict, the risk that suspects would not receive a fair trial increased. The U.N. was also slow to muster the military observers it authorized (only 104 out of 136 authorized observers had been deployed as of this writing), and thereby weakened the necessary supervision of regional law enforcement efforts.

The Georgian government and Abkhazian authorities are responsible for investigating suspected violations of the laws of war and trying them fairly. Should they fail to fulfil that obligation, the U.N., as the representative of the international community, should stand ready to prosecute and punish violations of the laws of war in full conformity with international standards.

U.S. Policy

The Clinton administration was responsive to Georgia's humanitarian crisis, sending some $106 million for assistance. It also promoted a broad spectrum of educational programs through the United States Information Agency (USIA) and the United States Agency for International Development (USAID).

However, the U.S. government limited its criticism of Georgia's dismal human rights record almost exclusively to its strong annual State Department *Country Reports on Human Rights Practices for 1993* and the work of its embassy, which raised concerns locally and interceded directly on behalf of victims. Although President Clinton met with

Mr. Shevardnadze in March 1994, he is not known to have raised criticism of Georgia's appalling human rights record. Failure to publicly criticize that record squandered the opportunity to condition the close relations the U.S. has cultivated with Georgia and the relatively extensive aid package it has provided on improvement in its human rights record.

The Work of
Human Rights Watch/Helsinki

Human Rights Watch/Helsinki pursued two goals in Georgia in 1994: to expose violations in the media and in personal meetings with government officials, and thereby to compel government authorities to take action.

Our representatives traveled to Tbilisi in June and August, visited prisons, hospitals and pre-trial detention centers, and raised concerns with government officials. In August, we issued a report about torture in detention and other serious violations, and held press conferences on violations in Moscow and Tbilisi. We also urged Russia and the European Union to condemn violations in Georgia. Our protests resulted in heightened government and media attention to these abuses, decreased harassment of some activists, and medical treatment for inmates.

Throughout the year we demanded that the government and prison officials provide medical care to inmates and stop due process violations. We also urged the Procuracy to review the February 7 murder conviction of Anzor Sharmaidze, who was charged with the 1993 death of C.I.A. agent Fred Woodruff, in light of evidence that Mr. Sharmaidze was tortured into confessing.

GERMANY

Human Rights Developments

Right-wing violence and police brutality against foreigners and non-citizen residents continued to be the primary human rights concern in Germany during 1994. On the positive side, the state's investigatory and judicial response became more forceful and timely. But the police failed to protect foreigners under attack in some cases, and were accused of custodial violence against foreigners in Berlin and elsewhere. Germany's immigration policy also continued to be a matter of serious concern, as reports emerged of the *refoulement* of legitimate asylum-seekers who faced repression once deported or excluded, and of mistreatment and inhumane conditions in detention for foreigners awaiting deportation.

Government statistics indicated that for the first time in four years there had been a decline in the number of violent attacks against non-Germans. This decline was due, in part, to more forceful government measures to combat xenophobic violence, such as the expansion of the number of police and prosecutors trained to investigate and prosecute cases of xenophobic violence. Despite the important change, however, the figures were still significantly higher than prior to 1991. According to the Office for the Protection of the Constitution, between January and October 1994, over 2,000 attacks motivated by xenophobia were reported to the German authorities. According to foreigners' rights groups, a large number of attacks also went unreported.

On May 12, in the eastern city of Magdeburg, a group of approximately 150 skinheads and neo-Nazis attacked asylum-seekers from Africa, chasing them through the streets and into a cafe owned by a Turkish resident, where four of the assailants were then stabbed by Turkish employees. For several hours after the attack, skinheads and neo-Nazis roamed the streets of Magdeburg attacking foreigners. The police were reportedly slow to respond to the violence and, although they arrested forty-nine suspects, all were released that same night save for two who had outstanding arrest warrants related to other crimes. The police claimed that they could not identify any of the assailants, which appeared unlikely. Moreover, the police had failed to prevent the violence in spite of having been warned that a large group of right-wing youths would gather in the town center. Many human rights and foreigners' rights groups in Germany criticized police conduct in this case.

Elsewhere, there did appear to be an overall improvement in the police response to right-wing violence against foreigners as compared to 1992 and 1993. This coexisted, however, with a serious and growing problem of brutality and mistreatment of foreigners and non-German residents by the police themselves. For example, in October the minister of justice for Berlin admitted that forty-six police officers were under investigation for allegedly having mistreated Vietnamese cigarette dealers in that city. Community leaders in Berlin reported numerous allegations by Vietnamese of brutal beatings and sexual harassment—as well as two suspicious deaths—in police custody. Similarly, Hamburg's minister of the interior resigned on September 12 to protest against xenophobia and racism within the Hamburg police force. The next day twenty-seven policemen accused of attacking foreigners were suspended from duty pending the completion of an investigation.

The judiciary appeared to treat cases of violence against non-Germans more seriously than it had in previous years. There were numerous prosecutions of crimes against foreigners, for example, that ended in convictions and comparatively high sentences. For example, in the Magdeburg case discussed above, the four defendants were convicted and sentenced to between two and three-and-one-half years of imprisonment; significantly more than requested by the prosecutor in the case. However, several judges did express sympathy for the xenophobia and right-wing extremism of defendants appearing before them.

There were also numerous efforts during 1994 to prosecute neo-Nazi leaders for a variety of offenses, including incitement to racial hatred and possessing banned right-wing propaganda. For example, Sasha Chaves was convicted of inciting racial hatred for his reported telephone network to announce neo-Nazi meetings and to disperse anti-foreigner propaganda. Charges were also brought against several individuals for continued participation in banned neo-Nazi parties. The federal Ministry of the Interior classified the Republican Party, the largest right-wing party, as "extremist" and ordered its federal security officials to put the party under surveillance. International human rights groups expressed concern that these groups not be singled out solely for exercising their protected right to hold political opinions without interference and to free expression.

Foreigners were not the only victims of right-wing violence during 1994. There were numerous reports of vandalism and destruction of Jewish properties and symbols, including the defacement of Jewish graves with swastikas and anti-Semitic graffiti. On March 25, on the eve of Passover, firebombs ignited the synagogue in Lubeck, a port city in western Germany. Fortunately, several Jewish families who lived in the building were able to escape unharmed. Four young neo-Nazis were arrested in May and charged with the arson attack.

In April the German constitutional court ruled that individuals who spread the "Auschwitz Lie"—propaganda that the Holocaust never happened—would not be protected by freedom of speech and could be prohibited from stating their views publicly. According to one of the justices on the court, "proven untruthful statements do not have the protection of freedom of speech." The court's ruling appeared to restrict unduly the protected right to free speech and expression.

The implementation of the new asylum law that was adopted by the German parliament in May 1993 resulted in a significant decrease in the number of asylum applicants in Germany during 1994. German government officials reported that 62,802 individuals applied for asylum in the first half of 1994, compared to 224,099 in the same period in 1993, indicating a 72 percent decrease. There were many disturbing reports of abuses related to the implementation of the asylum law. Representatives for foreigners' rights reported that the law's expedited procedures had resulted in the *refoulement* of many individuals who had well-founded fears of persecution. They pointed, for example, to cases of deported Kurds who, once back in Turkey, reported they had been mistreated. There were also many credible reports of inhumane conditions in deportation centers. According to a Reuters report, a court in Bremen stated in August that it had found two cases in which asylum seekers were "housed in crowed, unsuitable buildings with inadequate sanitary facilities."

The Right to Monitor

Human Rights Watch/Helsinki has received no information to indicate that human rights observers in Germany were prevented from conducting their investigations and reporting on their findings during 1994.

U.S. Policy

The Clinton administration and the German government maintained close and friendly relations throughout 1994. However, in April, Douglas H. Jones, principal officer in the U.S. Embassy's Berlin office, gave an unusually critical analysis of the German government's response to right-wing extremism. *The Washington Post* reported that Jones delivered a speech in Berlin in April, in which he questioned

> whether it was "psychologically consistent" for the chancellor to assert, as he did last year, that Germany is both friendly to foreigners yet not a country of immigrants. If I were a skinhead, I would take a certain amount of comfort in hearing that Germany is not a country of immigration...That would signal to me that the nearly seven million foreigners who live here legally do not belong here and that I am justified in wanting them out. And to be honest with you, this sentiment is by no means limited to skinheads.

According to reports Jones had not cleared his comments with then-Ambassador Richard Holbrooke. Although Jones's remarks were a forceful commentary on the treatment of foreigners in Germany, the State Department moved quickly to distance itself from them, assuring the German government that Jones had expressed purely personal views.

The U.S. and German governments also discussed ways in which they might coordinate efforts to combat organized crime and specifically "hate crimes" by the radical right. Louis J. Freeh, director of the Federal Bureau of Investigation, held a series of meetings with German government officials in late June, in which he expressed the willingness of U.S. federal law enforcement agencies to assist German prosecutors by providing certain evidence on neo-Nazi publications shipped to Germany from the United States.

The Work of Human Rights Watch/Helsinki

Human Rights Watch/Helsinki focused its efforts during 1994 on continuing to urge the German government to take additional steps to combat abuses against foreigners, whether committed by right-wing groups or by law enforcement officials. This work was part of an ongoing project to combat xenophobia and governmental policies that exacerbate xenophobic sentiments, not only in Germany, but throughout Europe. In Germany, Human Rights Watch/Helsinki conducted a mission in June to evaluate the various measures taken by the German government to combat right-wing violence since our release of a 1992 report on that subject. A report on the findings of that mission and our recommendations will be released in January 1995 at a press conference in Germany.

HUNGARY

Human Rights Developments

Despite improvements in Hungary's human rights situation in recent years, abuses continued to be reported during 1994, including police brutality and restraints on the independence of the press. More generally, during the electoral campaign the then-government attempted to interfer with the broadcast media and to limit political opponents' access to state-owned television and radio.

Human Rights Watch/Helsinki received several reports during 1994 of Hungarian police mistreatment of individuals in custody. For example, on January 19, police officers in the town of Szavasgede reportedly detained and mistreated two men, Jozsef Palinkas and Peter Herman, the latter an activist with the Green Alternative, an environmental organization that had been opposing construction of an incinerator near the town. Both men were seriously injured in detention. In addition, Palinkas was reportedly forced to sign a written statement that implicated Herman in an assault that had allegedly occurred a week earlier; members of Palinkas' family were also forced to give statements that implicated Herman in the assault. All retracted their statements at a later date. Human rights groups expressed concern that the police had fabricated the charges of assault against Peter Herman and his friend in an effort to intimidate him and to interfere with his right to free expression.

After a soccer game in Budapest on June 16, police in the capital reportedly beat fans for no apparent reason. Minister of the Interior Imre Konya expressed shock at the police officers' conduct and ordered an immediate investigation.

The May elections, which resulted in a resounding victory for the Hungarian Socialist Party (HSP), were generally considered free and fair. Although the HSP obtained an absolute majority, it formed a coalition government with the Alliance of Free Democrats, the largest opposition party. During the election campaign, there were allegations of pro-government bias at the state television and radio. In early March, the government dismissed 129 radio journalists from the state-run Hungarian radio. The government denied that the dismissals were motivated by political considerations,

claiming instead that financial restraints had made it necessary to reduce the radio staff. But a statement by then-Acting Director Laszlo Csucs announcing the dismissals suggested otherwise. According to the *Wall Street Journal*, Csucs said, "The roots of Hungarian Radio have always been as a virtual fortress of communist journalists," and accused the programming staff of "smuggl[ing] in their ideological commitments," and "sabotag[ing] my instructions."

These political struggles inside the broadcast media were part of an ongoing "media war" in Hungary. As Human Rights Watch/Helsinki reported in 1993, a moratorium on the privatization of radio and television was imposed by the former communist government in 1989 to prevent the establishment of private radio and television stations until comprehensive legislation on the media could be enacted. However, the political parties and government could not agree on a law to regulate the media and, thus, the moratorium has remained in effect, preventing a diversification of the views that are broadcast. On August 23, 1994, the Hungarian parliament completed work on the draft media law regulating Hungarian television and radio, which was expected to be debated and voted on before the end of the year.

In 1994 Hungary was increasingly confronted with pressures related to migration and refugees, and responded with new legislation. Refugees from other East European countries, as well as from Asia and Africa, either used Hungary as a transit to Germany and other West European countries or, because of the tightening of asylum laws in the west, applied for asylum in Hungary. A comprehensive immigration law went into effect on May 1, establishing a legal framework to regulate the status of foreigners. The new law allowed certain refugees, whose status had previously been unclear, to apply for Hungarian citizenship after three years. The law also provided that no migrant could be kept in a camp for more than five days without a court order, and that those with criminal records being kept in camps should be segregated from the other migrants. However, the law also allowed the police greater powers, for example, to go to foreigners' homes, review their papers, and verify their legal status. The law was criticized by the Council of Europe for violating the European Convention on Human Rights' prohibition against discrimination because it required certain foreigners to undergo testing for AIDS and provided that a positive test can be grounds for denying an asylum application.

The Right to Monitor

Human Rights Watch/Helsinki was not aware of any attempt by the government to impede human rights observers in their investigations and reporting during 1994.

U.S. Policy

During 1994, there were several high-level meetings between the governments of the United States and Hungary, including a meeting in January between then-Prime Minister Peter Boross and President Clinton. These meetings focused on the Partnership for Peace Initiative, which Hungary welcomed but viewed as a stepping-stone to possible future membership in NATO.

The only significant comment on human rights in Hungary was found in the State Department's *Country Reports on Human Rights Practices for 1993*. The country report was generally accurate and comprehensive in its portrayal of the human rights situation in Hungary. For example, the report discussed the specific problems of the Roma minority in Hungary and concluded that "there is still widespread popular prejudice against the Gypsies. Gypsies are generally assumed to be untrustworthy and treated as such, including by police . . ."

The Work of
Human Rights Watch/Helsinki

Human Rights Watch/Helsinki devoted its efforts in Hungary during 1994 to keeping pressure on the government to guarantee equal access to the state-run broadcast media, which were critically important especially during the election campaign. Two

months before the May elections, Human Rights Watch/Helsinki and the Human Rights Watch Free Expression Project sent a letter to then-Prime Minister Peter Boross expressing concern about, among other things, the dismissal of two well-respected independent persons who had been appointed to serve as presidents of, respectively, Hungarian Television and Hungarian Radio, and about what appeared to be political bias in radio and television programming and in government assumption of control over the budgets of these institutions. This effort is part of an ongoing strategy by Human Rights Watch/Helsinki in several East European countries to press for new media legislation that would insulate state radio and television from political control and would allow for the allocation of new franchises on a nondiscriminatory basis.

KAZAKHSTAN

Human Rights Developments

Restrictions on freedom of speech, arrests of conscientious objectors, ethnic discrimination and irregularities in election procedures in 1994 marred Kazakhstan's reputation for having a relatively strong human rights record.

The government made strides toward greater protection of free speech in the fall of 1993 by repealing Article 170-3 of the Kazakhstan Criminal Code. It had invoked this article, which protected the dignity and honor of the president, in 1992 and 1993 to silence peaceful criticism of President Nursultan Nazarbaev. However, the government failed to inform pertinent courts promptly of the decision to repeal Article 170-3. Consequently, one person charged under the article, writer Karishal Asanov, remained on trial until December 27, 1993. The government failed to repeal an analogous law, Article 170-4, which protects the honor and dignity of parliamentarians. As a result, the right to legitimately criticize leading public officials remained at risk.

In early 1994 the independent newspaper *Karavan* printed an article critical of head of the Almaty city administration, Mr. Nurkadilov. Soon after, the government closed the printing shop that published *Karavan*, suspending publication of all of the newspapers that used it. As a result of this pressure, *Karavan* later ceased publication in Kazakhstan.

In the absence of a law providing for alternative military service, the government sentenced eighteen Jehovah's Witnesses in the spring to a year of imprisonment for refusing military induction. All but two received suspended sentences: one unidentified man was reportedly confined to a psychiatric hospital and another, Roman Grechko, began serving a one-year prison term on March 30.

Government concern over ethnic tension and the rise of crime also led to violations of the right to association and peaceful assembly. On March 14-16, state police arrested forty people following clashes between Kazakhs and Russian Cossacks in Topolevka and Pokatilovka. Roughly two weeks later, Petropavlovsk law enforcement authorities briefly detained two leaders of the Russian community on the eve of a pro-Russian rally. On April 12, one of them, Boris Supruniuk, the outspoken chairman of the Russian-Speaking Community of Northern Kazakhstan, was jailed in the capital, where they detained him for forty days and forced him to undergo psychiatric examination. According to an article in the weekly periodical *Novoe Vremia* (No. 22), law enforcement officials offered Mr. Supruniuk his freedom in exchange for a pledge to renounce his political activities.

In December, Justice Ministry Order No. 31 rescinded the registration of all Russian organizations and community groups in Kazakhstan. Leaders of the ethnic Uighur community complained that the government refused the group permission to register.

On May 7, the Ministry of Internal Affairs launched an anti-crime campaign in the capital that allowed the militia to arrest and search individuals arbitrarily. According to the independent Almaty Helsinki Committee, the militia detained 1,500 people on the first day of "Operation Noose (*Petlia*)" alone; 90 percent were released without charges. Later, the militia reportedly carried out similar operations in other parts of Kazakhstan.

On or around May 16, Almaty militia arrested twelve hunger-strikers who were demanding that the current government step down, and imprisoned five of them for fifteen days for alleged violations of social order. In an April 20 statement, Mr. Zhovtis, a local human rights activist, reported that such government harassment had stopped virtually all public demonstrations in Kazakhstan.

Representatives of the Kazakhstan Procuracy and Ministry of Internal Affairs pledged to stop Uzbekistan security forces from harassing Uzbekistan dissidents on Kazakhstan territory. An official from the Kazakhstan Committee on National Security announced that the Committee had deported two Uzbekistan agents from a human rights conference in Almaty in May in protest. Authorities did not, however, stop Uzbekistan security agents during the summer from arresting three members of the Uzbekistan opposition engaged in peaceful activities in Kazakhstan, and forcing them to return to Uzbekistan.

Kazakhstan enforced the death penalty in 1994, although information about the number of times was not available to us as of this writing.

The Right to Monitor

Although the government failed adequately to protect Uzbekistan activists in Kazakhstan, local activists did not report any impediments to their work.

U.S. Policy

The Clinton administration sent a clear message of support to Kazakhstan in 1994. Stressing security initiatives, Vice-President Gore met with President Nazarbaev in December 1993; in Washington President Clinton met with him in February 1994, and Defense

Secretary Perry visited him in Kazakhstan in March. The U.S. also promised to more than triple general aid from $91 million in 1994 to $311 million in 1995. After Kazakhstan signed the nuclear Non-Proliferation Treaty in December 1993, it began to disarm its nuclear warheads with assistance from $85 million allocated by the United States for that purpose and an additional $15 million for defense conversion.

According to a U.S. official quoted on February 13 in *The New York Times*, this aid policy aimed "to show we are good to countries that want to reform." Secretary of State Christopher's conclusion that Kazakhstan was "doing everything right" (*The Washington Post*, October 24, 1993) reflected an unfortunate tendency of the U.S. government to equate acquiescence to U.S. wishes with a satisfactory human rights situation in Kazakhstan. Such a position would ignore the findings of the State Department's own annual report on violations in Kazakhstan, which accurately reported grounds for concern.

The Work of
Human Rights Watch/Helsinki

Our goal in Kazakhstan in 1994 was to gather information on ongoing violations and reinforce contact with the government and local human rights groups. As part of that effort, representatives participated in a human rights conference in May in Almaty.

LATVIA

Human Rights Developments

In 1994, nearly three years after its August 1991 declaration of independence, two major events marked Latvia's democratization process: most Soviet troops left the country after a fifty-one-year occupation; and a naturalization law was passed, enabling some 700,000 non-citizens, roughly 34 percent of the population, to become Latvian citizens over a ten-year period. Adopting a naturalization law was an important step in building

a fully democratic society in which all residents could eventually participate, and the Latvian government took several positive steps with regard to human rights. But there were still setbacks concerning the rights of Latvia's large non-citizen minority and its freedom of expression, especially when non-citizens interacted with the Latvian Department of Citizenship and Immigration. Sometimes human rights setbacks were the fault of local authorities, rather than of the central government.

Latvia's October 1991 Renewal of Citizenship resolution only restored citizenship to those who held Latvian citizenship (or their descendants) prior to the Soviet Union's 1940 invasion and annexation of the country. Consequently, some 700,000 individuals, mostly Russian-speakers who migrated to Latvia after 1940, in effect became stateless persons.

After rejecting an earlier naturalization bill in which strict quotas limited naturalization to some 2,000 non-citizens per year, on August 11, 1994 Latvian President Guntis Ulmanis signed Latvia's Citizenship Law—an amended naturalization bill that omitted quotas. According to this law, which gained the approval of an expert legal group of the Council of Europe, naturalization was set to commence on January 1, 1996 and to proceed in eight steps, with preference given to those born in Latvia. After January 1, 2001, all those born outside of Latvia would be eligible for naturalization. By January 1, 2003, the last group of non-citizens born outside of Latvia would be eligible for naturalization.

Articles 11 and 12 of the law set restrictions and requirements for naturalization. Some of the requirements and restrictions such as a "legal source of income" or "anti-constitutional" activity are rather broad, permitting arbitrariness and abuse in spite of the safeguard that most decisions regarding restricting naturalization must be through "court decree." Requirements for naturalization included a five-year residency in Latvia as of May 4, 1990, a command of Latvian, a legal source of income, and basic knowledge of Latvian history as well as the national anthem. Under the law, certain categories of non-citizens were not granted the right to naturalization. Among others, they include convicted criminals who had received sentences of one year or more, those who had acted "anti-constitutionally" against the Latvian state, individuals who remained members of certain organizations after January 13, 1991, and employees of foreign intelligence services.

Other human rights concerns in Latvia in 1994 also affected the country's non-citizen minority and Soviet past. Although the Latvian government fired the director of the Latvian Department of Citizenship and Immigration, Maris Plavnieks, who grossly abused his office and allowed discrimination against non-citizens, complaints of abuse still plagued the department. According to the Latvian State Minister for Human Rights, Olaf Bruvers, the majority of complaints his office received during 1994 concerned the Latvian Department of Citizenship and Immigration. Human Rights Watch/Helsinki documented at least three cases in which non-citizens with the right to reside in Latvia were denied that right by the department and thus were no longer able to return to and live in the country.

On April 14, 1994, the Ministry of Justice refused to register the Latvian Union of Non-Citizens, ostensibly because the organization was pursuing political activities restricted solely to Latvian citizens, an accusation the Latvian Union of Non-Citizens refuted. On April 28, five deputies of the Saeima (parliament), including then Foreign Minister Georgs Andrejevs, were temporarily suspended from parliament because of accusations that they had collaborated in the past with the KGB. Four of the accused denied any collaboration with Soviet security forces.

Local government, meanwhile, has proved at times to be more restrictive than the central government concerning individual freedoms. In January, Andrejes Rucs, chairman of a local council in Riga, Latvia's capital, ordered the arrest of two Russian army generals. The men were released after the intervention of Latvian President Ulmanis. On September 20, 1994, the Riga City Council passed an ambiguously worded resolution banning several militant Russian-language newspapers. Reform Minister Vita Terauda vowed to overturn the resolution.

In spite of these problems, the Latvian government instituted several human rights measures. In February 1994, the government appointed a state minister for human rights in the Ministry of Justice. On August 12, 1994, former Prime Minister Valdis Birkavs announced a national program for the protection and promotion of human rights on the recommendation of the United Nations Development Program (UNDP). In accord with the UNDP proprosals, as a first step the Latvian government plans to open a human rights institute that will conduct a public information campaign concerning human rights and citizen's rights and also create a review board for individual complaints.

The Right to Monitor

To our knowledge, there was no interference with human rights monitoring in Latvia.

The Role of the International Community

The international community played an active role in Latvia during 1994. An observer mission of the Conference on Security and Cooperation in Europe (CSCE) observer mission based in Riga since late 1993 continued under a double mandate to deal with non-citizen issues and troop withdrawal. In July 1994, a mission from the United Nations Development Office (UNDP) visited Latvia and made several recommendations to the government concerning creation of a national human rights program. Most importantly, the Council of Europe played a crucial role in advising Latvia on its citizenship law, specifically against the inclusion of strict naturalization quotas.

U.S. Policy

On July 6, 1994, President Clinton paid a

state visit to Latvia's capital Riga, where he met with all three Baltic presidents, the first such visit of a U.S. president to a Baltic state. Clinton reiterated U.S. support for Latvia and concern about Russian troop withdrawal, while underscoring the message that "a tolerant and inclusive approach is needed to integrate these groups [minorities] into the political and social life of all the countries." U.S. aid to Latvia during 1994 included funds from a $50-million Baltic American Enterprise Fund, a $10-million Baltic Peacekeeping Force, $4 million to help dismantle Russia's Skrunda radar station, and money to build 5,000 apartments in Russia for retired Russian officers from Latvia and Estonia.

The Latvia section of the State Department's *Country Reports on Human Rights Practice's for 1993*, reported that there were no obstacles to freedom of movement within the country or to foreign travel for citizens and mentioned that non-citizens may need re-entry permits. The country report noted abuses by the Department of Citizenship and Immigration, but failed to mention cases in which individuals with legal right to remain in Latvia were denied that right.

The Work of
Human Rights Watch/Helsinki
Human Rights Watch/Helsinki continued to monitor developments in Latvia to ensure that non-citizen rights were respected. Encouraged by the Latvian Government's response in firing the Director of the Latvian Department of Citizenship and Immigration after the release of an Human Rights Watch/Helsinki report outlining abuses by the department, we remained in contact with the Latvian government concerning its citizenship law, press freedom, and non-citizen rights. In March 1994, we met with several Latvian parliamentarians in Washington, D.C. to discuss these issues.

ROMANIA

Human Rights Developments
Although Romania has made significant progress in its human rights record since the 1989 revolution, serious abuses remain, particularly against minority groups such as the Hungarians and the Roma (Gypsies). The Romanian government has at time attempted to exploit and manipulate ethnic tensions for its own political gains. This has been especially true since the 1992 parliamentary elections when the ruling Party of Social Democracy in Romania (PDSR)failed to obtain an absolute majority. Since that time the PDSR has had to depend on support from the political parties of the far-right and far-left, entering into a coalition with these parties in late 1993, and giving members of the ultranationalist Party of Romanian National Unity portfolios in the government in 1994.

Mob violence against Roma and their inability to obtain adequate redress for such violence continued to be among the most severe human rights abuses in Romania during 1994. Human Rights Watch/Helsinki received frequent reports of attacks by villagers on their Roma neighbors in 1994. For example, despite the arrest of two Roma teenagers who had murdered an ethnic Romanian shepherd on May 26 during a robbery in the village of Racsa in Satu Mare county, an estimated 800 to 1,000 villagers in Racsa went to the Roma quarters on May 28, ransacked all nine houses and then set them on fire. Although three police officers arrived in the village before the last houses were torched, they did not stop the villagers.

In dramatic contrast to most cases, the Racsa authorities conducted a prompt and thorough investigation of the events, resulting in charges against thirty-eight people for a number of crimes, including destruction, theft, and illegal entry into a residence. However, although all nine houses were burned down, no one was charged with the more serious crime of arson, which requires the authorities to prosecute the case even if there are no complaints from the victims.

Romanian authorities have often refused to bring arson charges even when warranted by the facts, intentionally leaving open the possibility that the victims can be pressured to settle or that with enough delay they will lose interest in seeking a legal remedy for their suffering.

The speedy investigations and indictments in the Racsa case were exceptions to the general practices of the police and prosecutorial bodies, which ignore, delay and downplay cases of violence against Roma. Despite pressure from the international community and some assurances from the Romanian government, very few individuals have been prosecuted for the numerous violent crimes against Roma since 1990.

Foot-dragging in such cases has often been blatant. For example, after 170 Roma were forced to flee a violent attack and arson in the town of Hadareni, local prosecutors reported in November 1993 that the criminal investigation had produced sufficient evidence to warrant the arrest and indictment of at least twelve individuals. The investigation was apparently ongoing with regard to others who may have also committed crimes. In May 1994, local prosecutors reiterated that the investigation was near completion and that there was ample evidence to bring charges against fifteen to seventeen individuals. Despite this evidence, no arrests have been made.

Local officials, especially in the Transylvanian town of Cluj, continued to try to provoke ethnic tensions and hostility between the ethnic Hungarian minority and the Romanian majority. In June 1994 the ultra-nationalist mayor of Cluj, Gheorghe Funar, announced the excavation of the center square, which would have required the removal of a statue of King Mathias that had long been a cultural symbol for the Hungarian minority. The excavation attempt was only one of several efforts by Funar to remove all traces of Hungarian history and culture from the city and as such it provoked both fear and a sense of insecurity among the Hungarian minority.

On November 11, 1993, the Romanian Senate approved amendments to the penal code that, if they become law, could seriously restrict freedom of speech and the press. Of particular concern was Article 239, which aimed to protect public officials while exercising their official duties. Under Article 239, the punishment for defamation of a public official would be "a prison term from six months to four years," compared to "one month to one year or a fine" if the victim were a private person. If the victim were the president, or another senior government official, or if the defamatory statements were made by the print or broadcast media, the law would provide for even heavier prison terms. These amendments, which will be considered as part of a revision of the penal code, are expected to be voted on by the Romanian parliament in late 1994 or early 1995.

Several individuals charged under Article 200 of the Romanian penal code for homosexual relations challenged the constitutionality of the law, which provided that "same sex relationships shall be punished by prison from one to five years." In July, following an intense lobbying effort by Romanian and international groups, Romania's constitutional court ruled that the law was unconstitutional to the extent that it "applies to sexual relations between adults of the same sex, freely consummated, not committed in public or not causing public scandal." The court's decision was an improvement for the rights of gay men and lesbians in Romania. However, by preserving criminal prosecution for same-sex relations that "produce a public scandal" the court maintained dangerously vague language that invited arbitrary enforcement. Subsequently, on October 25, the plenum of the Chamber of Deputies voted to maintain the present law's provision that consensual homosexual relations, even if conducted in private, are prohibited. Punishment is imprisonment from one to five years.

On March 24 the government issued Decree no. 120, which pardoned all the members of the former executive committee of the Romanian Communist Party who had been sentenced for abuses committed during the revolution in December 1989. By early November, only one person remained imprisoned for crimes related to the shooting of demonstrators during the 1989 revolution. Some Romanian observers believed that this pardon reflected the government's lack of commitment to prosecute any abuses of the communist era. The decree also reduced the sentences for several ethnic Hungarians who had been convicted of crimes against Romanian police officers during the revolution.

The Right to Monitor
Human Rights Watch/Helsinki was unaware of any instance in which the Romanian government had hindered human rights monitors in their work during the year.

U.S. Policy
Several high-level meetings between representatives of the United States and Romanian governments took place during 1994. For example, in June, the two governments agreed on future cooperation on defense and military issues. However, there were no significant public comments on human rights developments in Romania during 1994 and Human Rights Watch/Helsinki has no specific information regarding the Clinton administration's effort to raise human rights concerns during such meetings.

Human Rights Watch/Helsinki has been especially troubled that the Clinton administration did not publicly denounce the Romanian government for its continued failure to address the serious problem of violence against Roma and the government's continued effort to downplay the ethnic tensions that fuel such violence. What is more, the Clinton administration did not use the important opportunity of reviewing Romania's Most Favored Nation trade status, which had been restored in October 1993, to elicit specific commitments from the government regarding human rights concerns.

The Work of
Human Rights Watch/Helsinki
During 1994, Human Rights Watch/Helsinki devoted most of its efforts to raising international awareness about the failure of the Romanian authorities to protect Roma and their property from ethnic violence, and the pattern of state tolerance for and acquiescence in the violence, as well as to provide the victims of ethnic violence with an adequate legal remedy. In May 1994, Human Rights Watch/Helsinki representatives traveled throughout Romania interviewing not only Roma victims of violence but also local prosecutors and national government representatives responsible for investigating and prosecuting the numerous cases of violence against Roma since 1990. A report based on the mission, including specific recommendations to the Council of Europe, the Conference on Security and Cooperation in Europe (CSCE), and the Romanian government, was released at a press conference in Budapest during the CSCE Review Conference in November. Human Rights Watch/Helsinki representatives also met with many government delegates attending the Budapest conference to urge the international community to demand specific remedial steps from the Romanian government.

We continued to raise our concerns regarding human rights issues in Romania with the Council of Europe and in a series of communications with representatives of the Romanian government. Human Rights Watch/Helsinki campaigned actively against, among other issues, restrictive amendments to the Romanian penal code that would have a chilling effect on freedom of the press in Romania. Human Rights Watch/Helsinki criticized these amendments in a protest letter that was addressed to members of the Senate and Chamber of Deputies, as well as the government. We also informed representatives of the Council of Europe about our concerns and encouraged them to address these matters during official meetings with the Romanian government in late March. Human Rights Watch/Helsinki monitored issues of freedom of the press and issued a report in April documenting a number of serious violations of international law.

RUSSIA

Human Rights Developments

Russia presented a contradictory record in 1994. Intransigent problems overshadowed symbolic and legislative progress. The gravest concerns included appalling prison conditions, abuses of military draftees in the Russian armed forces, restrictions on movement, and state-sponsored ethnic and gender discrimination.

In reportedly free and fair elections on December 12, 1993, Russia adopted a new constitution enshrining human rights protections. The parliament drafted a law creating the post of a human rights ombudsman. The human rights committee that President Boris Yeltsin created in November 1993 issued a highly critical report on the government's human rights record in 1993, in what was intended to be the first of a series of such annual reports.

During the same time period, however, President Yeltsin legalized some violations of civil liberties in the name of crime prevention. He authorized arbitrary house searches and detention for up to thirty days without charges—human rights abuses akin to those widely criticized under Soviet rule. In October a group of experts appointed by the parliamentary assembly of the Council of Europe concluded that "the Russian Federation does not (yet) fulfil the condition 'of the enjoyment by all persons within its jurisdiction of human rights and fundamental freedoms'," and thus fell short of standards enshrined in the European Convention on Human Rights.

Despite some government restrictions, Russians enjoyed considerable freedom of speech. The Presidential Human Rights Committee's report also did not shy from criticism of specific government figures, such as influential Moscow Mayor Yuri Luzhkov. Strong investigative reporting by the independent media and human rights groups kept violations from being completely ignored.

However, on December 22, 1993, President Yeltsin took direct control of Russian state mass media, and four days later brought two news agencies, ITAR-TASS and RIA Novosti, back under government control after a short-lived independence. The October 17 suitcase-bomb murder of a *Moskovskii Komsomolets* investigative reporter, twenty-seven-year-old Dmitri Kholodov, who was about to present his findings to parliament on illegal arms sales, was a horrifying development. President Yeltsin promised a thorough investigation, one which will be closely watched by the international community.

Two watershed court rulings upheld fundamental civil liberties this year. In June a court awarded scientist Vil Mirzaianov compensation (approximately $15,000) from the Federal Intelligence Service—the ostensible successor to the KGB—and the General Procurator's Office for psychological damages suffered when he was wrongly imprisoned in 1993 and 1994 for allegedly disclosing state secrets.

In August, a court also overturned the travel ban that had prevented Dr. Mirzaianov from leaving Russia. According to the independent civil rights group Movement Without Frontiers, the decision gave hope to an estimated 6,200 individuals who have been denied, on security grounds, the right to leave the country by the Russian government. According to Movement Without Frontiers, the government commission created to review such cases confirmed that 95 percent of the decisions in the 120 appeals they reviewed were "arbitrary."

At then end of August, Russia, the security giant of the former communist bloc, withdrew the last of its troops from Estonia, Germany, and Latvia, dismantling the instrument of fear that had terrorized these areas for decades. At the same time, abuses continued both by the military against civilians in the C.I.S. and within the military's own ranks. Elements of Russia's armed forces that had attacked civilians and committed other serious violations of the laws of war during conflicts in 1992 and 1993 in the "near abroad," including Moldova, Tajikistan and Georgia, remained unidentified and unpunished in 1994. There were almost no reports in 1994 of fresh abuse by Russian forces in the "near abroad."

The North Caucasus, an ethnically mixed area of the Russian Federation north of Georgia and Azerbaijan, remained an area of upheaval in 1994. Since the November 1992 "six-day war" in North Ossetia's Prigorodnyi region between Ingush and Ossetians, ethnic relations have settled into a uneasy peace, with the majority of the more than 47,000 Ingush expelled from their homes in North Ossetia unable to return. After the fighting, bands of Ossetians wantonly destroyed Ingush homes and property with little interference from either Russian or North Ossetian authorities. In neighboring Chechnya, which proclaimed independence from the Russian Federation in November 1991, bloody fighting erupted in late summer 1994 as opposition groups with purported Russian support battled the Dudayev government.

Little progress has been achieved in restoring normalcy to the Prigorodnyi region despite the fact that large areas of both Ingushetiya and North Ossetia remain under state of emergency decree, ruled from Vladikavkaz by a temporary administration under a Moscow-appointed governor, Vladimir Lozovoi. Russian Interior Ministry troops patrol the area and have set up command posts in most villages in the Prigorodnyi region. But few Ingush have been able to return to their homes, despite these security measures and a December 1993 presidential decree ordering their return to four villages of the Prigorodnyi region. Few have been brought to justice for crimes committed during the fighting in November 1992, and efforts to disarm paramilitary groups have progressed slowly. The Russian government has also been slow to release funds earmarked for reconstruction of destroyed homes, gas lines, electricity and water systems, sewers, and public buildings.

According to the independent Moscow-based human rights group Foundation of the Rights of the Mother, some 4,000-5,000 draftees in the Russian armed forces died annually in the 1990's, some beaten to death during hazing (*dedovshchina*), and others reportedly driven to suicide because of degrading and harsh conditions. In a July 14 article in *Izvestia,* the Russian Defense Ministry acknowledged the phenomenon, although its figures were significantly lower: that 5 percent (twenty-five people) of the total deaths in the Russian armed forces for January through June 1994 (518 people) were victims of hazing, 8 percent (forty-two people) were murdered, and 27 percent (140 people) committed suicide.

Public and government acknowledgment that Russian penal facilities were dangerously overcrowded, unsanitary, and rife with physical and mental mistreatment of inmates increased in 1994. At the invitation of the Russian government, the United Nations Special Rapporteur on Torture conducted an investigation of detention conditions in June. The Russian government also reversed a seventy-year ban on prison work by the International Committee of the Red Cross.

So far, however, these steps have done almost nothing to improve widespread misery in the facilities. On August 1, some 3,000 inmates launched a mass hunger strike in pre-trial detention center No. 1 in Ekaterinburg, and in September over one hundred inmates in Moscow's notorious Butyrki facility did the same. Both groups were protesting severe overcrowding and lack of adequate medical attention.

Russia's record on protection of minority rights was also checkered, and favored protection of Russians over other ethnic groups. In August, the Duma, or parliament, finalized a draft law to protect the rights of Russian-speakers living in the republics of the former USSR, and the Foreign Ministry pressured other nations in the Commonwealth of Independent States to grant dual citizenship rights among other measures it claimed would protect minority rights.

The government did not equally protect the rights of minorities within Russia proper, however. Following the bloody failed coup in Moscow on October 3-4, 1993, Moscow

Mayor Yuri Luzhkov issued Ordinance No. 1122, which allowed Moscow police to stop thousands of individuals on the street or to enter their homes, to check their identification and vehicles, and to levy heavy fines and otherwise intimidate those who cannot prove they are legal residents of the capital. In practice, almost all of those detained were dark-skinned or otherwise thought to be non-Muscovites.

Thus, the decree turned into an instrument for government-sponsored racism. In addition, Mayor Luzhkov's November 15, 1993 decree required non-Russian citizens to register their whereabouts with the Ministry of Internal Affairs within one day of arriving in the capital and to pay the equivalent of U.S. $1 per day to remain there (the average monthly salary in Moscow at the time of the passage of the act was about U.S. $100). The regulation became tantamount to extortion, and was enforced disproportionately against refugees and minorities.

In early September 1994, the immigration control agency was empowered to conduct interrogations, check vehicles, confiscate unacceptable identification papers, and order the Ministry of Internal Affairs to forcibly expel individuals who refused to leave Russia voluntarily. The southern region of Krasnodar, a major refugee processing center, imposed particularly strict restrictions, severely limiting non-ethnic Russians' ability to obtain residence permits (*propiskas*) or even stay temporarily in the region. The legitimate need to fight crime in the Russian capital spawned legislation allowing legal infringement of fundamental civil rights. Presidential Decree No. 1226 concerning "immediate measures for the protection of the population against banditry and other manifestations of organized crime" authorized local law enforcement agencies to search homes and vehicles without a warrant, use information gained illegally as evidence at trial, and hold individuals in detention for up to thirty days without charges. The director of Counterintelligence Services stated that he was "in favor of the violation of human rights if the person is a bandit or criminal." In a largely ceremonial vote, the Duma rejected the decree by a rate of 279 to 10 on human rights grounds, but President Yeltsin ultimately adopted it on June 14.

A Human Rights Watch Women's Rights Project investigation in March revealed that the government offered jobs on a gender-specific basis and failed to treat reports of violence against women as a law enforcement problem, relegating it instead to "domestic" problems.

There were numerous incidents of security forces from other parts of the C.I.S. committing abuses on Russian territory during the year covered in this report. On November 5, 1993, men believed to be from the Uzbekistan security service beat three activists in their Moscow apartments; one of them was beaten again on the street in March 1994. Otakhon Latifi, chairman of the Coordinating Center of Democratic Forces in Tajikistan and an outspoken leader of the opposition in exile, was similarly attacked on August 4 in front of his Moscow apartment. Yet another vicious Moscow street attack on October 4 left Turkmenistan opposition leader Murad Esenov with broken bones and head contusions. Three other members of the Turkmenistan opposition reported that Turkmenistan security servicemen watched their Moscow homes following the suspicious death of another opposition leader on July 2 in the Turkmenistan capital. Desultory Russian investigations were unsuccessful as of this writing, suggesting that the Russian government lacked the will to confront fellow C.I.S. intelligence forces about violations.

The Right to Monitor

Monitors, both domestic and international, worked unimpeded in all areas of investigation except in one penal investigation. In April, Human Rights Watch requested permission from the Minister of Internal Affairs to investigate conditions in several Russian pre-trial detention centers, to follow up the organization's study of Russian penal facilities in 1991. Two months later, the Ministry rejected the proposed work as "undesirable" since the Duma was currently doing similar work, and in July rejected an appeal without elaboration.

The Role of the International Community

Council of Europe Policy

The Council of Europe actively reviewed Russia's compliance with council standards in preparation for rendering a decision on admitting Russia as a member state. The delegations made human rights their centerpiece issue. The council sent teams of independent experts and Parliamentary Assembly representatives to gather information, including conducting first-hand prison visits, and met with government officials and governmental and non-governmental human rights groups.

In October, experts appointed by the Council concluded that Russia did not yet meet council standards. Nonetheless, the investigation and deliberation process continued, raising concern that the October expert report may not be the final word in the decision-making process. Political pressure to grant Russia membership in order to win political and economic compliance jeopardized broad and sufficiently serious consideration of the experts' concerns.

U.S. Policy

U.S. officials repeatedly raised human rights concerns with their Russian counterparts in 1994. Presidents Yeltsin and Clinton met in January and September 1994, reaffirmed commitments to human rights protection, and ultimately paved the way for expanded U.S. investment in Russia. U.S. obligations under all assistance programs totalled a staggering $3.6 billion in 1994, including useful programs on the rule of law and administration of justice. Assistant Secretary of State for Democracy, Human Rights and Labor John Shattuck traveled to Moscow in March and July, received documentation of violations from human rights organizations, and raised human rights concerns.

U.S. officials were known to have touched on issues of restrictions on emigration, abuse of the residence permit system and violations of minority rights, particularly anti-semitism. The scope of issues known to have been raised was narrower than the actual situation warranted, however. Specifically, the U.S. talking points on human rights apparently gave short shrift to the appalling conditions in prisons, government-sponsored gender discrimination, abuse of conscripts in the armed forces, and the need to identify and prosecute individuals in the army who violated the laws of war in Abkhazia (Georgia), Moldova, and Tajikistan. The limited scope of issues raised is surprising since the section on Russia from the U.S. State Department's *Country Reports on Human Rights Practices for 1993* did portray a much broader spectrum of abuse in Russia.

U.S. Federal Bureau of Investigation chief Louis J. Freeh visited Russia in July and voiced concern about the need to protect human rights. Later actions undermined this message, however. Mr. Freeh stated that the U.S. had "also" suspended civil rights in times of emergencies. The F.B.I. also signed an agreement on cooperation with Russia's intelligence services, and opened an office in Moscow to assist in crime-fighting efforts. There is hope that the U.S. side will integrate human rights training into its program. Until then, however, it runs the risk of sending a message that the U.S. is willing to work within the framework of President Yeltsin's abusive anti-crime law.

In early September, the U.S. began nine-day joint military training exercises with Russian counterparts in Totskoe, Russia, with an eye toward peacekeeping. Despite these highly visible and expensive efforts, no concern was known to have been raised by the U.S. military about the Russian armed forces' failure to discipline those in its ranks who had committed serious violations, including killing civilians, during operations in the "near abroad."

The Work of
Human Rights Watch/Helsinki

Human Rights Watch/Helsinki attempted to change Russia's human rights behavior by documenting and publicizing its findings about various abuses in the press and in meetings with Russian officials. We actively documented abuses the Russian government either sponsored or failed to condemn, and monitored trials and conducted investigations in Ingushetiya and North Ossetia, St. Petersburg, and Moscow. We also sought to influence Moscow through third-party pressure, by alerting members of the U.S. government and the Council of Europe to such abuses.

In a November 1993 letter and subsequent report, we challenged President Yeltsin to refute evidence that some Russian troops participated in gross abuse of civilians in Moldova, Georgia, and Tajikistan. In letters to the government and interviews with the media, we protested Mayor Luzhkov's ordinances restricting the rights of non-Muscovites, and elicited a promise from his office in a letter of June 15 that "the principle of unlimited freedom of movement and a rejection of the residence permit (propiska) will definitely be realized in Moscow and Russia." We also urged the Russian and U.S. governments to protect fourteen political refugees from Central Asia, at risk of persecution in Moscow, and facilitate the immediate issuance of proper documentation to allow them to remain in Moscow. We took advantage of Russia's influence throughout the C.I.S., holding six press conferences and issuing more than twenty press releases in Moscow concerning violations throughout the region.

We informed the international community about violations in Russia and recommended specific action. In July, we met with and submitted information to U.S. Assistant Secretary of State John Shattuck for this purpose. As the Council of Europe reviewed Russia's application for membership, Human Rights Watch/Helsinki recommended conditioning membership on improvements in its human rights record. We also met with

members of the European Union in Moscow and Brussels, and regularly briefed embassies in Moscow. Human Rights Watch/Helsinki expanded its work by monitoring trials in and around Moscow in which we objected to the charges on principle or feared miscarriage of justice. The positive results of the trials we monitored illustrated vividly the efficacy of such efforts in both averting due process violations and unjust decisions, and raising consciousness among defendants and legal workers, including judges, about the need for human rights protection.

Throughout the winter, we monitored and issued protests about the closed trial of scientist Vil Mirzaianov, accused of disclosing state secrets. Dr. Mirzaianov was ultimately cleared of all charges and awarded damages. We criticized the government for bringing charges of "war mongering" against Yeltsin critic Vladimir Zhirinovsky, suggesting the charges were brought to silence and discredit him. In June and July, we attended the trial of two demonstrators accused of "hooliganism" for burning photos of President Yeltsin, and we disseminated information about the case to the media. The defendants were given the minimum sentence, a nominal fine. Throughout 1994, representatives of Human Rights Watch/Helsinki attended numerous trials of refugees facing eviction from their temporary shelters in Moscow in accordance with municipal ordinances. In September, a representative attended the Moscow trial of eleven men who had been held for up to five years in appalling conditions awaiting trial. All but three were cleared of all charges and immediately released on September 30.

Human Rights Watch/Helsinki also promoted the work of independent human rights organizations. In August we conducted two joint fact-finding missions—to Georgia and southern Russia—with the Moscow-based group Memorial and held one joint press conference on our findings. On July 9 we organized a meeting at our Moscow office between leading members of the human rights community in Moscow and U.S. Assistant Secretary of State John Shattuck.

THE SLOVAK REPUBLIC

Human Rights Developments

During 1994 the nature of human rights abuses in the Slovak Republic corresponded to the shifts in political power. Government efforts to interfere with the independence of the press and to place restrictions on the rights of ethnic minorities, in particular the ethnic Hungarian minority, subsided substantially during the six months prior to the September 31 elections.

On March 11, the government of Vladimir Meciar was defeated by a no-confidence vote and a coalition government was formed by Jozef Moravcik, former Slovak foreign minister. Then, in parliamentary elections held on September 31 and October 1, Meciar's Movement for a Democratic Slovakia (MDS) won almost 35 percent of the vote, making it the decisive winner. By early November, Meciar, in coalition with the Slovak National Party and several other small parties, had not been able to form a new government.

Although election observers did not report any significant irregularities on election day, voters in some precincts, including Vladimir Meciar himself, were unable to vote on the first day of the elections because their names did not appear on the election lists. The electoral commission was apparently able to resolve the problem by allowing individuals to vote if they fulfilled other criteria set out by the law. There were also complaints that Slovak Television, which is state-run, was biased in its reporting during the election campaign. The Council of Slovak Television concluded that Slovak Television had not given the political parties equal access to television airtime and that the reporting on political events and the campaign had been biased.

Controversy over the media had long preceded the election campaign. For nearly two years the Meciar government had been intolerant of press criticism, tending to view such criticism as slanderous attacks on the Slovak state. As early as 1992, Slovak government officials had become preoccupied with what they viewed as the failure of the press to tell the "truth" about the Slovak Republic and its government, and they initiated a series of steps intended to subjugate the media to the government's own political interests. For example, on January 25, 1994, Andrej Hrico, editor-in-chief of the independent newspaper *Domino efekt*, was charged with defamation under Article 103 of the penal code for having published a reader's letter critical of several political leaders, including then-Prime Minister Meciar and President Kovac. Hrico was interrogated by the police on several occasions during 1994. His case was still pending in November.

Tensions between Slovaks and the ethnic Hungarian minority ran high during the first half of 1994. The Meciar government repeatedly refused to approve legislation that was of particular concern to the Hungarian minority and that had been recommended by the Council of Europe when it approved the Slovak Republic's membership in October 1993. By contrast, the Moravcik government took steps that reduced tensions during the summer and fall of 1994. For example, on May 3 the interim government adopted legislation allowing members of minority groups to spell their names in a manner consistent with their own language and traditions. On May 10 the interim government also approved a new law allowing approximately 600 towns and villages with minority populations of 20 percent or more to post bilingual road signs. What is more, the outgoing cabinet of Jozef Moravcik established a new governmental agency to combat racism, xenophobia, and anti-Semitism. This agency fulfilled another recommendation made by the Council of Europe in 1993.

The Right to Monitor

Human Rights Watch/Helsinki was not aware of any interference in the work of human rights monitors by the government of the Slovak Republic.

U.S. Policy

Immediately prior to the elections, on September 16, President Clinton sent a letter to then-Prime Minister Moravcik expressing the interest of the U.S. in continued progress in the Slovak Republic's transition to democracy. This letter was widely viewed in the Slovak Republic as indicating U.S. support for the Moravcik government in the upcoming elections.

The only other significant comment on human rights in the Slovak Republic was found in the State Department's *Country Reports on Human Rights Practices for 1993.* The country report was generally comprehensive in its discussion of the human rights issues in the Slovak Republic. However, the report failed to discuss adequately the nationalist and anti-minority sentiments given expression by the Meciar government and their impact on human rights policies. For example, the report failed to discuss in any detail the statements made by then-Prime Minister Meciar in September 1993 that it was necessary to curtail family allowances that encourage "widespread reproduction" because Gypsies are having children who are "mentally and socially unadaptable."

The Work of
Human Rights Watch/Helsinki

Human Rights Watch/Helsinki closely monitored developments regarding restrictions on the press in the Slovak Republic, particularly in the months leading up to the September electoral campaign. In June, we issued a report documenting a series of governmental abuses related to the press that had occurred during the previous two years. Human Rights Watch/Helsinki called on the interim government of Jozef Moravcik to disassociate itself from the media policies of its predecessor in order to create an environment in which the independent press could flourish. Specifically, the report stated:

> It is not enough that the new government leaders, prior to coming to power, criticized the Meciar government for its efforts to control

and intimidate journalists who were critical of its policies. The new government, which is itself likely to become the focus of increased press scrutiny, must also resist the temptation to resort to such methods against its own opponents in the press.

Human Rights Watch/Helsinki also continued to monitor closely the treatment of the Roma and Hungarian ethnic minorities, as well as efforts by the Slovak government to address serious problems of discrimination on the basis of race and ethnicity.

TAJIKISTAN

Human Rights Developments

Two years after the end of the Tajik civil war, which resulted in the deaths of an estimated 20,000 to 50,000 people and the displacement of more than 500,000 residents, the situation in Tajikistan remained tense and unstable. Thoroughly undemocratic conditions during the 1994 presidential elections bore testimony to the abysmal state of civil and political rights in Tajikistan. In addition, the Tajik government continued to detain political prisoners, stifle the press, and allow mistreatment in detention. Also, it responded inadequately to the harassment and violence against Tajik refugees returning from Afghanistan.

Due to its strategic location, bordering on Afghanistan, Uzbekistan, and Kyrgyzstan, and the strong influence of Russia, the resolution of the conflict in Tajikistan had broad international implications. In December 1992 the present government, deriving from the communist era, defeated the "opposition," composed of a wide range of democratic, nationalist, cultural revivalist, and Islamist parties. Armed struggle continued along the Tajik-Afghan border between armed factions of the opposition based in Afghanistan and Russian border troops assigned to guard the border.

In March, the government and the opposition entered into U.N.-sponsored peace negotiations, aimed at achieving national reconciliation and resolving the refugee problem. On July 20, the Supreme Soviet voted to hold presidential elections and a popular referendum on a new draft constitution on September 25. As a result of international pressure, particularly from the U.N., Uzbekistan, and Russia, both the elections and referendum were postponed until November 6. Shortly thereafter, on September 17, the government and the opposition signed a cease-fire and agreed to release political prisoners and prisoners of war within one month. Two deadlines passed, however, with no prisoners released. Finally, on November 13, the opposition released twenty-seven prisoners of war, in exchange for twenty-seven prisoners released by the government (four had actually been released earlier). The presidential election, which was won by Emomali Rahmonov, chair of the Supreme Soviet, was preceded by an unfair electoral campaign and conducted in a climate of fear, intimidation, and fraud. International organizations such as the United Nations and the Conference on Security and Cooperation in Europe (CSCE) refused to send official monitors to the election.

Although there was a significant decline in the number of summary executions, political disappearances and murders, civil and political rights continued to be violated in Tajikistan. At least two individuals died during detention, one of whom had been among the prisoners scheduled to be released pursuant to the September 17 agreement. Human Rights Watch/Helsinki received frequent reports of mistreatment during detention and illegal searches of homes, as well as violations of the due process rights of detainees, including the right to legal counsel, the right to a fair and public hearing by an impartial tribunal and the right to be tried without undue delay.

In addition, even after the November 13 prisoner release, the government continued to hold scores of political prisoners, despite a lack of compelling evidence of criminal activity. Many of these prisoners had been detained without trial since early 1993 because of having exercised their right to legitimate, nonviolent dissent. The authorities also continued to pursue a sweeping criminal case against the leaders of the various opposition parties and movements.

The major newspapers in the country remained under government control, and a February 21 decree suspended the activities of the independent media. In August, at least four individuals were detained and mistreated for alleged distribution of *Charoghi Ruz*, an independent newspaper published in Moscow.

The repatriation of refugees from Afghanistan continued successfully, with the assistance of the United Nations High Commissioner for Refugees (UNHCR). The UNHCR estimated that by November 1994, nearly 26,500 of the estimated 60,000 refugees who had fled to northern Afghanistan had returned through UNHCR-assisted repatriations, and many thousands of others had returned on their own. Precise figures for the number of refugees remaining in Afghanistan or other countries were unavailable.

Returning refugees whose origins were from the Pamir or Gharm regions of Tajikistan—regions associated with the opposition—continued to experience security problems in areas of Khatlon province in southern Tajikistan. At least twelve returning refugees were killed in Khatlon, and beatings and threats against refugees were even more common. Although the number of such incidents declined significantly as compared with the previous year, incidents that were reported to the authorities were inadequately investigated. In and around Dushanbe, residents of predominantly Gharmi and Pamiri neighborhoods were harassed, threatened and routinely subjected to illegal house searches by officials from the Ministries of Internal Affairs and Security. In a number of cases, these individuals were detained and beaten, and at least one person died during detention.

Another targeted group were the Uzbeks

living in the Panj region who, during the course of a disarmament campaign, were subjected to illegal house searches and harassed, detained and beaten by forces of the Ministry of Internal Affairs, often simply to extract information regarding other individuals suspected of possessing arms. A number of Uzbeks reportedly fled the region as a result of these abuses. In heavily Uzbek regions such as Shahrtuz and Kabodian, however, where Uzbeks occupy positions of control in the local government and police, there was evidence of mistreatment of returning Tajik refugees by Uzbeks. In two separate incidents in March and July, hundreds of Uzbeks attacked Tajik returnees, causing scores of serious injuries.

Members of other minority groups, such as Russians, Jews, and Germans, continued to emigrate in large numbers. However, most of these departures were related to the general political and economic instability in the country, and not to acts of violence or discrimination aimed at these groups. Attacks on the 3,000-member Afghan community of Tajikistan also decreased, although there were still numerous cases of Afghans who were beaten or threatened, and in which the government failed to conduct satisfactory investigations.

The Right to Monitor

No indigenous monitoring group operated in Tajikistan during 1994; most rights activists had been forced into emigration. A small international community has functioned there, including several U.N. agencies, the International Committee of the Red Cross (ICRC) and the CSCE, and during 1994 Human Rights Watch/Helsinki stationed a representative in Dushanbe for the express purpose of conducting human rights work. Although the government of Tajikistan did not interfere with the work of Human Rights Watch/Helsinki, it did not provide significant cooperation. We received no response to numerous protest letters addressed to government officials and, despite repeated requests, were never accorded permission to visit political prisoners. Moreover, we were often unable to obtain even basic factual information from authorities, and senior officials repeatedly expressed outrage that international organizations were "wasting their time worrying about fundamentalists, criminals and murderers." The ICRC continued to be denied universal access to prisoners. The Tajikistan mission of the CSCE also reported dissatisfaction with the lack of cooperation and, at times, hostile attitude shown by the General Procuracy, or prosecutor's office. However, the government cooperated, for the most part, with the UNHCR in the repatriation and reintegration of Tajik refugees.

The Role of the International Community

United States Policy

When officials of the U.S. Department of State met with Abdujalil Samadov, chair of the Council of Ministers, in March, and with Emomali Rahmonov, chair of the Supreme Soviet, in October, human rights concerns were privately raised. On September 22, the House Foreign Affairs Subcommittee on Europe and the Middle East held hearings on Tajikistan and included its human rights record. At this meeting, administration spokesman Joseph Presel, in answers to questions from members of Congress, frankly acknowledged serious abuses of human rights by the Tajik authorities, though his characterization of the upcoming November elections was more optimistic than necessary. He repeatedly stated that the elections would not live up to the standard of elections in Switzerland or the U.S., without attempting to convey the degree to which the Tajik elections fail to come close to even the most minimal international standards. While the State Department never spoke out publicly regarding the human rights situation in Tajikistan or the undemocratic conditions surrounding the presidential elections, the U.S. Embassy in Tajikistan did take the initiative in raising human rights concerns at all levels of the government and intervening on behalf of victims of violations.

U.S. leverage with the Tajik authorities was somewhat limited, given that American aid was almost exclusively humanitarian and delivered through nongovernmental organizations. The U.S. provided $16 million in emergency humanitarian assistance to Tajikistan, and the United States Agency for International Development (USAID) funded a $1.3 million technical assistance program for training in fields including human rights. On the other hand, the United States could use its extensive influence with Russian President Boris Yeltsin, and urge that the Russian government demand a stop to violations by Tajik authorities, over whom Russia wields enormous influence. However, when President Yeltsin visited the U.S. in September 1994, State Department officials indicated privately that the issue of Tajikistan was not even on the agenda.

Russian Federation Policy
In addition to providing significant humanitarian and economic assistance, Russia continued its heavy military involvement in Tajikistan. Approximately 7,000 troops of the 201st Motorized Rifle Division made up the vast majority of the Commonwealth of Independent States (C.I.S.) peacekeeping forces in Tajikistan. Despite their peacekeeping mandate, many sources alleged that these forces were actually involved in the hostilities. In addition, approximately 17,000 border troops under Russian command continued to guard the Tajik-Afghan border and were involved in regular clashes with the armed opposition.

Russia sought to justify its strong military presence by citing a need to curb "Islamic insurgency," although Russian border troops were reportedly responsible at times for provoking incidents along the border. On the other hand, Russia supported efforts toward national reconciliation and pressured Tajikistan to postpone the presidential elections until there could be broader political participation. Once the elections had been postponed, however, the Russian position became far more complacent, despite remaining flaws in the election process and continued violations of human rights by the Tajik government. Russia also sought to safeguard the rights of ethnic Russians in Tajikistan.

Policy of the Republic of Uzbekistan
Uzbekistan continued to demonstrate its influence in Tajikistan by controlling the Tajik-Uzbek border and blocking the import of goods, automobile and passenger rail transportation, and even the repatriation of refugees from Afghanistan. Uzbekistan exerted pressure on the Tajik government to postpone elections, but its policy was guided by a desire to influence politics, not human rights.

United Nations Policy
The United Nations, particularly the Secretary-General's special envoy to Tajikistan, Ramiro Piriz-Ballon, was instrumental in arranging peace negotiations between the government and the opposition. U.N. mediation also played an important role in the subsequent postponement of the elections and the agreement of the parties to sign the September 17 cease-fire agreement. The United Nations Mission of Observers to Tajikistan (UNMOT) was active in coordinating the U.N.'s peacemaking initiatives and observing the military and security situation in the country. UNMOT also worked towards an improvement in human rights but, despite its visibility in the country, kept a low public profile in this respect, opting to discuss human rights issues privately with authorities. The UNHCR played a critical role in protecting the human rights of returning refugees and internally displaced persons.

The Work of Human Rights Watch/Helsinki
Human Rights Watch/Helsinki established an office in Tajikistan in April 1994. In light of the grave human rights violations committed by all parties to the conflict during the civil war and by the Tajik government, in particular, immediately thereafter, our goal was to monitor the post-war transition pe-

riod and urge those governments with interests in Tajikistan to condition economic and military assistance on an improvement in the government's human rights record. Human Rights Watch/Helsinki also sought to inform both the Tajik government and the international community of the conditions necessary to ensure that presidential elections could be considered free and democratic. In addition, we intervened regularly before the General Procuracy and the Ministries of Internal Affairs and Security on behalf of individuals who had experienced human rights violations, and briefed multilateral organizations, nongovernmental organizations, and journalists on the current situation in the country.

In September, Human Rights Watch/Helsinki testified on human rights in Tajikistan before the House Foreign Affairs Subcommittee on Europe and the Middle East. Two newsletters released in October dealt with, respectively, political prisoners and the general human rights situation on the eve of Tajikistan's presidential elections. Throughout 1994 we issued twelve press releases and letters of protest concerning, among other things, deaths in detention, continued detainment of political prisoners. and undemocratic elections conditions.

TURKEY

Human Rights Developments

The human rights situation in Turkey continued to deteriorate in 1994, in large part due to the government's heavy-handed response to an escalation of the conflict in southeastern Turkey. The government restricted freedom of expression and association, especially of groups voicing opposition to government policy in the southeast or toward Turkey's large Kurdish minority. Political freedom also was limited. In March 1994, the Turkish parliament lifted the parliamentary immunity of eight deputies, six of whom were deputies from the Kurdish-based Democracy Party (DEP). In June, Turkey's

Constitutional Court banned the Democracy Party and stripped immunity from the remainder of its deputies, though a new Kurdish-based party, the Peoples' Democracy Party (HADEP), was formed in its place. Eventually eight parliamentarians whose immunity had been removed, seven from DEP and one independent, were charged with treason and separatism, allegedly for collaboration with the banned PKK, a violent guerrilla group. Torture in pre-trial police detention, death-squad style assassinations with alleged links to security forces, and violent police house raids in which alleged suspects are killed all continued in 1994.

The Turkish government's ten-year battle with the Kurdistan Workers Party [PKK] reached new heights of violence in 1994. Of the 13,000 civilians and soldiers estimated to have been killed between 1984 and 1994, half died in the past two years. Both security forces and the PKK continued to violate basic human rights of the civilian population in the southeast, with police targeting those suspected of collaborating with the PKK, and the PKK in turn striking at those whom it considered state supporters, such as teachers, civil servants, and village guards.

As in 1993, security forces in southeastern Turkey increasingly conducted intensive, large-scale counterinsurgency campaigns to eliminate the PKK's logistical base of support. Such operations resulted in hundreds of thousands of displaced Kurdish villagers in 1993-1994. [The total number of civilians displaced from the southeast during the decade of the conflict was estimated at a staggering two million.] Security forces often burned down the homes and evicted people from villages that refused to enter the village guard system. The village guard system was instituted in late 1985 in an attempt to arm villagers, enabling them to defend themselves against PKK pressure. Village guards, however, have been implicated in numerous human rights abuses, and in turn the PKK has targeted them and their families. Arbitrary detention and torture often accompanied security forces' raids on villages. Former Chief of Turkish General Staff Dogan Gures has termed this the "go hungry and surrender strategy," while the state minister for Human Rights, Azimet Koyluoglu, referred to it as "state terrorism".

The PKK, on the other hand, brutally punished any cooperation with the state. At its March 1994 Third National Conference, PKK leadership declared that, "all economic, political, military, social and cultural organizations, institutions, formations—and those who serve them—have become targets." The PKK interfered with local elections in March 1994 and vowed to kill candidates in December 4 by-elections. Attacks were often launched against villages that had entered the village guard system. During such raids, PKK members often killed both guards and their families. During a raid on January 22, 1994, against two villages in Mardin province, the PKK killed four village guards, six children, and nine women. The PKK routinely committed such abuses as summary execution, hostage-taking, indiscriminate shooting, bombings, and the destruction of civil property in an effort to force the population to sever contact with state authorities or officials. Teachers were a prime target: in September-October 1994 the group murdered fourteen educators. Bombs were often placed in tourist areas, and travelers to the southeast were sometimes kidnapped by the PKK.

Freedom of expression suffered greatly in 1994. Intended to replace articles of the penal code outlawing communism, Kurdish separatism, and fundamentalism, the 1991 Anti-Terror Law especially Article 8 prohibiting "separatist propaganda" was widely applied to punish debate and expression concerning Turkey's Kurdish minority and the war in the southeast. Article 8 forbade all forms of expression, "regardless of method, intention, and ideas," that would damage the "indivisible unity" of the Turkish state. Some estimated that half of the cases in State Security Courts (DGM) were charged under Article 8. Despite some government attempts to amend the law to make it less restrictive, no changes have been made as of this writing.

In May 1994 the Turkish government introduced a democratization package that among other things would have amended the restrictive 1982 constitution to allow political participation by labor unions, academics, and students, but as of November the measure had still not been passed by the Turkish parliament.

While the mainstream press in Turkey was not greatly affected by Article 8 or other press restrictions during the year under review here, numerous intellectuals, journalists, and writers were jailed and the publications for which they wrote banned under its provisions or under other restrictive legislation. In December 1993, police raided the Istanbul headquarters of the pro-Kurdish *Ozgur Gundem* (*Free Agenda*) and arrested thirteen editors and writers. The government charged that weapons, ammunition, and identification cards from dead Turkish soldiers were found in the building. In April 1994, *Ozgur Gundem* was closed down by the government for publishing "separatist propaganda" and later reopened under a new corporation and with a new name, *Ozgur Ulke* (*Free Country*). In June 1994, the thirteen *Ozgur Gundem* staffers arrested in December were put on trial, either for alleged PKK membership or for aiding the PKK. In June 1994, Dr. Haluk Gerger, founder of the Turkish Human Rights Association, was imprisoned for fifteen months under Article 8; in September, another three years were added to his sentence for refusing to pay a fine equal to roughly U.S. $295. In July, Recep Marasli was arrested on charges of "separatist propaganda" for a televised speech he gave in 1993 advocating broader Kurdish rights. Small leftist or pro-Kurdish journals, such as *Emegin Bayragi* (*Worker's Banner*), *Alinteri*, *Kizil Bayrak* (*Red Banner*), and *Gercek* (*Real*), suffered either seizure of editions, arrests of journalists and editors, or harassment.

A great blow to political freedom in Turkey came with banning of the Kurdish-based Democracy Party and the subsequent trial of seven of its parliamentary representatives and one independent. In March 1994 eight parliamentarians, six from Democracy Party, one independent, and one from the Islamist Welfare Party (Refah Partisi or RP), were stripped of their parliamentary immunity. Hatip Dicle, Ahmet Turk, Orhan Dogan, Sirri Sakik, and Leyla Zana of the Democracy Party, and independent Mahmut Alinak were charged under Article 125 of the Turkish penal code for treason, a crime that carries the death penalty. In July 1994, the Turkish Constitutional Court banned the Democracy Party, and consequently all remaining members lost their immunity. Some fled abroad, while an additional two, Selim Sadak and Sedat Yurttas, were arrested and charged with treason. The trials of the seven DEP parliamentarians and independent Mahmut Alinak continued in Ankara's State Security Court at this writing.

While the decision to lift the immunity of the parliamentarians came from the Turkish parliament, most observers believe the action was motivated by then-Chief of the Turkish General Staff Dogan Gures, who complained that "terrorists" were sitting in parliament, and thus constitutes punishment for speech, rather than for any action committed. None of the deputies was charged with acts of violence or terrorism, rather they seemed to have been punished for speeches they had made abroad or at DEP gatherings, in parliament or for interviews they gave. Only one of the deputies, Orhan Dogan, was charged for an action he allegedly took: giving shelter to five PKK members and helping one of them obtain medical attention.

On September 20, 1994, the Turkish government announced that by-elections would be held on December 4, to fill twenty-two seats left vacant by the banning of the Democracy Party and by the deaths or resignations of other parliamentarians. At the time of this writing, the by-elections were tentatively rescheduled for December 18. According to the government's decision, all former DEP deputies including those on trial would be allowed to stand for election and, if victorious, could regain parliamentary immunity and the charges against would be dropped.

Conditions for electioneering for either HADEP or former DEP deputies would be limited, however, both by government harassment and death-squad assassinations of HADEP workers, and by the fact that large numbers of their likely supporters in the southeast had either migrated or been forcibly displaced from their rural homes by fighting and were no longer registered to vote. On October 14, Turkey's Supreme Electoral Board refused to update voter rolls to allow migrants to vote. On November 3, citing "negative and anti-democratic conditions," HADEP decided not to participate in by-elections. Repression directed against HADEP also played a factor, with reports that phones were bugged and organizers followed, often detained, and even killed. On October 3, 1994, two HADEP members, Rebih Cabuk and Sefer Cef, were assassinated in the town of Yuregir, Adana province, and a companion seriously wounded. Five days earlier, in the same town, one of HADEP's executive members, Salih Sabuttekin, was gunned down. Finally, on November 16, the Turkish Constitutional Court ordered voting rolls to be updated, and on November 17, Nihat Yauuz, head of the Supreme Electoral Board, cancelled the elections.

Such death squad-style assassinations and suspicious disappearances have plagued Turkey the past few years, especially in the southeast, increasing to new levels in 1994. Either the victim was killed by unidentified assailants with a single shot to the head, or he was detained by security forces, who then alleged that the individual detained earlier was released and was no longer in custody. Victims included suspected PKK sympathizers, HADEP and DEP organizers, journalists especially of pro-Kurdish publications, and trade union activists. Sometimes the victim's body was discovered days later by the side of the road, or he simply disappeared. The assassins were suspected of having unofficial links with security forces.

Often the police simply did not investigate the crime seriously.

In June 1994, however, thirty-five members of the Menzil faction of Hizbollah were charged with twenty-five death squad-style executions, and a month later thirteen members of the Ilim faction of Hizbollah, a group opposed to Menzil, were charged by authorities with fourteen such killings. Many believe the charges stem from killings the two factions carried out against each other.

Torture and suspicious death in pre-trial detention and house raids in which deadly force is used continued in 1994. "Falaka" (beatings on the soles of feet), the application of electric shock, and beatings with truncheons in police lockup were widespread abuses. According to the Turkish Human Rights Foundation's *File of Torture* (*Iskence Dosyasi*), fourteen people died under suspicious circumstances in pre-trial detention in the first eight months of 1994, and 387 individuals were tortured in the first seven months of the year including 117 females and sixteen children. There were also a reported twelve rapes in detention in 1994. House raids, especially against violent, extreme leftist groups like Dev Sol (Revolutionary Left), often result in the deaths of the house's occupants even though no return fire was reported.

For their part, violent leftist groups like Dev Sol continued their activities in Turkey in 1994, targeting military and security members, judges and prosecutors, and government officials, including those retired. On September 29, 1994, Dev-Sol militants, for example, assassinated former Justice Minister Mehmet Topac.

The Right to Monitor

In Turkey, the main monitoring group is the Human Rights Association (Insan Haklari Dernigi, or IHD), a decentralized, membership-based group with forty branches. The Human Rights Foundation, (Insan Haklari Vakfi, or IHV), set up by the Human Rights Association but now independent, runs a human rights documentation center and publishes a yearly journal, a daily news summary, as well as thematic monographs. Both organizations operate legally.

While the IHV operated largely free of government interference, in October the Ankara State Security Court confiscated the IHV publication *File of Torture* and considered bringing charges under Article 8 against the author of the work and the chair of the IHV. In 1994, many of the human rights associations, especially those in the southeast, faced government repression and threats from right-wing groups. In the past two-and-one-half years, ten association officials or members have been killed, three of whom died in 1994. Branches of the association were often raided, with documents seized and members detained and reportedly tortured. On May 1, for example, police raided the Iskenderun association and briefly detained its chair, Sadullah Caglar.

In several instances, the associations were closed down for a period of time. In September, moreover, the Adana Human Rights Association was ordered closed indefinitely. According to Akin Birdal, chair of the Turkish Human Rights Association, many of the associations in southeastern Turkey, especially those in Hakkari, Siirt, Agri, Mardin, Sirnak, Tunceli, and Batman, were no longer able to operate normally because of severe harassment and repression. On September 22, chair of the Tunceli Human Rights Association, Ekber Kaya, was detained by police.

Often human rights association members were harassed for their publications. In July, Kutahya branch President Seydi Bayram was sentenced to twenty months in prison for press statements he made in 1993, and in October, a trial was launched against the executive leadership of the human rights association for a book it had published, *A Section from the Burnt Down Villages*, (*Yakilan Koylerden Bir Kesit*). Both cases were brought under Article 8 of the Anti-Terror Law.

A drastic decrease in access to southeastern Turkey for both journalists and foreign human rights monitors complicated human rights monitors. While travel was allowed to Diyarbakir, attempts to enter the countryside were either strictly monitored or blocked, often with a short detention resulting. The government usually justified such actions by stating the need to protect the individuals in question from the PKK. Toward the end of 1994, the Foreign Ministry instituted stricter controls on entry into Northern Iraq: official humanitarian organizations and international bodies would be allowed in, while journalists and nongovernmental groups would face a strict application process. In October, Amnesty International's Turkey researcher was refused a Turkish entry visa on grounds of his alleged contacts with the PKK, a charge the London-based group completely denied.

U.S. Policy

In 1994, the Clinton administration consistently raised human rights issues with the Turkish government, a dialogue underscored through two high-profile trips by Assistant Secretary of State for Democracy, Human Rights, and Labor John Shattuck and one by former Assistant Secretary of State for European Affairs Steven Oxman.

The administration advised Turkey that it must not sacrifice human rights in its legitimate fight against the PKK. In March 1994, Oxman said he favored "civil and social" solutions to the conflict in the southeast between security forces and the PKK. During an October 25, press conference in Ankara, Shattuck stated that human rights and democracy were "very much" the focal point of Turkish-U.S. relations. Shattuck warned, "The United States has laws that make very clear that the use of military assistance to violate human rights of any individuals or civilians is particularly prohibited....That has been made very clear to the Turkish officials." Shattuck reportedly told Turks that they stood to lose "millions" in military aid if the human rights situation did not improve. Turkish Foreign Minister Soysal, however, rejected such pressure and stated that Turkey would diversify its arms procurement.

The Clinton administration had hith-erto been reluctant to condition U.S. military aid to Turkey on human rights performance. The "millions" Shattuck mentioned refered to the 10 percent of U.S. military assistance to Turkey for fiscal year 1995 that Congress had withheld pending an administration report on Turkey's human rights practices and Cyprus negotiations. In fiscal year 1994, Turkey received $405 million in military credits at an interest rate of 5 percent and $120 million in Economic Support Funds. For fiscal year 1995, the administration proposed giving Turkey $450 million in military credits, but Congress reduced this to $364.5 million and then withheld 10 percent of it as mentioned. Turkey remained the third largest recipient of U.S. military aid after Israel and Egypt.

Surplus U.S. weapons are still being delivered to Turkey, and according to the Congressional Research Service, the agreements under which they are transferred to Turkey allow their use for internal security purposes. In 1993, Turkey received from the U.S. main battle tanks, howitzers, armored personnel carriers, attack helicopters, and anti-ship missiles. In 1994, Turkey purchased an estimated $1.8 billion in weapons from the U.S. and plans to acquire $1.3 billion in weapons in 1995, making it the second largest purchaser of U.S. weapons during both years.

The executive branch's policy of supplying Turkey with extensive military equipment, much of which might be used in a counterinsurgency campaign in southeastern Turkey marked by human rights abuses, undermined the administration's welcome policy of increased candor about rights abuses. In 1994 this new candor was demonstrated by the Shattuck visits and by excellent human rights reporting in the section on Turkey in the State Department's *Country Reports on Human Rights Practice for 1993.*

The Work of
Human Rights Watch/Helsinki

In 1994, Human Rights Watch/Helsinki kept pressure on Turkish government officials directly and also pressed the U.S. government, the Conference on Security and Cooperation in Europe (CSCE), and the European Union to use their influence to bring about human rights improvements in Turkey. We focused on three issues: the war in the southeast and its consequences; the banning of the Kurdish-based Democracy Party; and PKK violations of the laws of war. In April 1994, a Human Rights Watch/Helsinki mission went to Turkey to investigate the stripping of parliamentary immunity and jailing of parliamentarians. We met with government officials, DEP members and parliamentarians, politicians, and human rights activists. The Turkish government, however, refused our request to meet with the jailed deputies. In August and September 1994, another Human Rights Watch/Helsinki mission to Turkey investigated the forced displacement of civilians by government security forces. During that mission Human Rights Watch/Helsinki also wanted to investigate PKK violations in southeastern Turkey: although the Turkish Foreign Ministry encouraged the idea, the Emergency Rule Governor's Office in Diyarbakir did not allow the mission to proceed.

Human Rights Watch/Helsinki publications for 1994 included *Turkey: 21 Deaths in Detention* and *Turkey: Forced Displacement of Ethnic Kurds From Southeastern Turkey*, based on our August-September 1994 mission. The Human Rights Watch Women's Rights Project released *State Control of Women's Virginity in Turkey*, based on a 1993 mission. Human Rights Watch/Helsinki also regularly published articles and issued letters and press releases condemning abuses by the Turkish government and the PKK.

TURKMENISTAN

Human Rights Developments

Continued government repression brought a virtual end to what little remained of free speech in Turkmenistan this year. The January 15 referendum gave an implausible 99.9 percent approval to President Saparmurad Niyazov's guaranteed presidency, which is to continue without elections until 2004. More dissidents fled the country under threat of arrest and continued harassment, the handful of dissidents remaining in Turkmenistan were all but silent, and no protest rallies took place. Reportedly, the government also enforced the death penalty widely to inhibit nonconformist behavior, although exact data have not become internationally available.

On December 28, 1993, a court in the capital, Ashgabat, sentenced dissident Karadzha Karadzhaev to three years of imprisonment on what were believed to be fabricated charges of slander, malfeasance in office and embezzlement. The court then released him under an October 1993 presidential amnesty, following four months of imprisonment. Mr. Karadzhaev later emigrated to Ukraine fearing further persecution. On July 2, Momma Seiitmurad, one of the leaders of Turkmenistan's moribund opposition, died under suspicious circumstances in Ashgabat. Opposition leaders cited the government hospital's refusal to conduct an autopsy as evidence that it was a political killing. Not only dissidents in Ashgabat but dissidents who had fled to Moscow reported that security agents intensified surveillance of their homes immediately following the death. The beating of outspoken dissident and Radio Liberty correspondent Murad Esenov on October 4 on a Moscow street further fueled suspicion that the Turkmenistan government was involved even in Moscow in the persecution of its critics.

The government gave high-profile attention to the enforcement of the death sentence, ostensibly as part of an anti-crime campaign. State television—the only television—broadcast at least one execution. Official statistics concerning the number of executions in 1994 were unavailable, but reliable and confidential sources reported that the number was higher than in the recent past. In addition, one resident, Orazguly Khanov, told Human Rights Watch that on June 8 a court in the capital executed his son for murder, for which he claims the procurator framed him in exchange for a bribe. The

Procuracy declined to comment on the case. However, reported violations of due process and mistreatment of the family, raise suspicion about the fair conduct of the trial. The elder Mr. Khanov reported that the court barred both him and witnesses to the crime from attending the trial. In a grim reminder of Soviet practice, the prison did not inform the family of the execution. Mr. Khanov reported that when his family went to the Procuracy on July 3 to confirm rumors of the death, authorities detained them, including small children, without charges for seven hours.

State censorship reduced local media to government mouthpieces, and the government blamed funding shortages for the nearly complete absence of information from abroad. In September, the government subsumed *Edebiiat ve sungat*, the newspaper of the Writer's Union, under presidential control and closed the newspaper *Subbota*, according to one journalist to punish their insufficient praise of President Niyazov.

Efforts to correct years of discrimination against ethnic Turkmen resulted in discrimination against non-Turkmen instead in 1994. Job advertisements in newspapers requested applications only from ethnic Turkmen. The government also refused to register the Russian-speaking community organization with no explanation.

The Right to Monitor
Economic limitations and fear of government reprisals made human rights reporting possible only from outside the country. Some local victims and activists preferred to travel to Moscow at great expense to convey information about abuse rather than to risk reprisals for reporting from within the country. Even outside of Turkmenistan, security forces were believed to have harassed monitors in Moscow this year.

No foreign monitors were known to have attempted an investigation in Turkmenistan this year.

U.S. Policy
According to the State Department, U.S. representatives raised human rights concerns at every meeting it held with Turkmenistan counterparts this year. The administration also identified grave human rights concerns in the section on Turkmenistan of the State Department's *Country Reports on Human Rights Practices for 1993*. Among other things, the State Department concluded that "Turkmen authorities severely restricted civil and political liberties." However, the U.S. government's failure to condemn these abuses publicly outside the scope of the annual report gave the impression that it was neglecting the country's appalling repression of elementary human freedoms.

The Work of
Human Rights Watch/Helsinki
Our goal this year was to gather accurate information about developments in this closed society. We did not conduct a site investigation because local activists indicated they feared reprisals for speaking with us. We did, however, promote the concerns of Turkmenistan's Russian-speaking community by arranging meetings between its leaders and concerned individuals in the Russian Foreign Ministry.

UNITED KINGDOM

Human Rights Developments
The leading human rights development of 1994 was the August 31 cease-fire announcement by the paramilitary Irish Republican Army (IRA) in Northern Ireland, followed six weeks later by a similar announcement from their loyalist counterparts—the Ulster Freedom Fighters (UFF) and the Ulster Volunteer Force (UVF). This was the first bilateral cease-fire aimed toward long-term peace since the long-simmering "Troubles" erupted into armed conflict in 1969. Among the more than 3,300 people killed in the long conflict were fifty-eight killed between January and October 1994 (fifty-two civilians,

three police officers and three British soldiers). In 1994, murders by loyalist paramilitaries (thirty-three) outnumbered those by republicans (twenty-four) for the third straight year. Security forces killed one person in 1994 in disputed circumstances.

On October 21, Prime Minister John Major accepted the cease-fire as genuine and offered to hold talks with Sinn Fein, the political arm of the IRA, before the end of 1994. Major simultaneously announced the opening of roads between Northern Ireland and the Irish Republic and a partial lifting of the exclusion order that had prevented dozens of presumed terrorists from entering other parts of Britain; earlier, he had lifted the much-criticized five-year-old broadcasting ban against proscribed groups (see below). Most significantly, Major stated Britain's intent to remove British soldiers from Northern Ireland eventually and turn over policing to an entirely civilian force.

Despite these positive developments, grave human rights concerns remained in Northern Ireland and other parts of the United Kingdom. In Northern Ireland, a cluster of "emergency" legal provisions continued to restrict severely the due process rights of detainees and criminal defendants. Among these, the 1973 Emergency Provisions Act removed the right to trial by jury for a broad range of serious criminal charges, including murder, manslaughter, rioting, and robbery. Still in effect in late 1994, it also permitted the use of uncorroborated confessions, which were relied on in nearly 90 percent of all prosecutions for alleged terrorist offenses; over the years, numerous allegations of coercion had surfaced in connection with the extraction of confessions. The right to silence, a crucial component of the right against self-incrimination, had been eviscerated by the 1988 Criminal Evidence Order, which allowed judges to "draw adverse inferences" from a suspect's refusal to answer questions. Finally, the 1974 Prevention of Terrorism Act allowed suspects to be held seven days without charge. During the first forty-eight hours, detainees could be interrogated without access to a lawyer. Because less than 25 percent of those detained under the PTA have been charged later with criminal offenses, it had long appeared that PTA detention and interrogation powers were frequently used to search for information rather than investigate specific crimes.

In January 1994, the first annual report of the independent commissioner for the holding centres, Sir Louis Blom-Cooper, was released. Blom-Cooper, who was appointed in late 1992 amid growing criticism of the holding centres in Northern Ireland and reports of ill-treatment of detainees, reported many of the same concerns previously raised by Human Rights Watch/Helsinki and others. These included substandard physical conditions in the holding centres, a need for audio and video recording of interrogations to guard against impermissible coercion, and a need for prompt access to legal advice. Unfortunately, Blom-Cooper's proposed solution for quick legal advice—creation of a state-run in-house solicitor scheme—would severely restrict detainees' right to choice of counsel and right to attorney-client confidentiality. His laudable proposal for electronic monitoring of interrogation sessions was opposed by the secretary of state to Northern Ireland, Sir Patrick Mayhew. The presence of juveniles in the holding centres—thirty-seven were detained in 1993—was not investigated by Blom-Cooper, despite international law forbidding the detention of juveniles together with adults.

The failure of normal policing in troubled areas of Belfast contributed to the phenomenon of "alternative policing" by the IRA and, to a lesser extent, the Ulster Defense Association (UDA). During 1994, under this system of summary punishment and intimidation, people believed to be guilty of common crimes, including many juveniles, were subjected to banishment from Northern Ireland, brutal beatings, and "kneecappings," or punishment shootings of knees and other joints. There is no semblance of due process in this procedure. Punishment beatings and shootings continued after the August cease-fire.

Curbs on free expression continued in the United Kingdom, which has no Bill of Rights or other written protection for free speech. The Official Secrets Act criminalizes disclosure of vast categories of state information, thereby screening large portions of government conduct from public scrutiny. There is no explicit protection for peaceful assembly, and the Public Order Act of 1986 grants the police power to restrict or ban public gatherings.

The government lifted the 1988 broadcasting ban that had prevented the airing of the voices of members of Sinn Fein or proscribed Northern Ireland paramilitary groups. This development, while positive, highlighted the need for laws fully protecting British media from government interference.

Overcrowding in prisons continued to raise human rights concerns in England and Wales. In Northern Ireland, prisoners rioted in July at the Crumlin Road jail to protest unsanitary conditions and severe overcrowding. About 200 prisoners were subsequently transferred. Hunger strikes and protests by those who remained were reportedly met by threats and excessive violence by prison authorities.

The Right to Monitor
International and domestic human rights activists exerted a vigorous and visible presence in Northern Ireland, and for the most part operated free from government interference or intimidation. One disturbing exception to this in 1994 was a statement made in the House of Commons by Member of Parliament Douglas Trimble, who accused three men, including "one of the Finucane brothers," of being "well-known IRA godfathers." This was considered to be a reference to Martin Finucane, who runs the Patrick Finucane Center for Human Rights and Social Change. Patrick Finucane, Martin's brother, a well-known and respected civil rights and criminal defense lawyer, was killed in 1989, three weeks after a speaker in Parliament accused unspecified solicitors of being "unduly sympathetic to the cause of the IRA." Many other defense attorneys in Northern Ireland have been threatened and harassed for their work on behalf of those accused of terrorist actions. Given this background, Trimble's remarks presented a clear danger to the safety of Martin Finucane.

U.S. Policy
The State Departments's *Country Reports on Human Rights Practices for 1993* in the section on the United Kingdom noted many ongoing human rights concerns, including British policy on the use of lethal force, threats to and intimidation of Northern Ireland defense attorneys, harassment of civilians by Northern Ireland security forces, restrictions on due process, and substandard conditions in prisons and holding centres. Despite these observations, the Clinton administration remained silent on the issue of human rights in the United Kingdom.

The United States offered vocal support for the Northern Ireland peace process and, according to many observers, played an extremely useful role in brokering peace. In fiscal year 1994, as in previous years, Congress appropriated $20 million to the International Fund for Ireland, which "promotes peace and reconciliation through economic progress." In November 1994, the administration announced its intention to secure a "peace dividend" of an additional $10 million, and to expand the role of the National Endowment for Democracy, the United States Information Agency and the U.S. Agency for International Development in Northern Ireland.

After repeated denials in 1993, the Clinton administration granted Sinn Fein President Gerry Adams a two-day visa to the U.S. in February 1994. Adams was given a visa again in October, following the IRA cease-fire announcement; while in the U.S. Adams met with senior State Department officials, marking the first official contact between the United States government and Sinn Fein. Human Rights Watch/Helsinki had criticized the earlier visa denials, arguing that they violated Adams' right to free expression.

The Work of
Human Rights Watch/Helsinki

In 1994, Human Rights Watch/Helsinki helped support the work of local human rights activists by issuing reports and otherwise bringing international attention to the human rights situation in Northern Ireland. In March, Human Rights Watch/Helsinki released a newsletter highlighting continuing human rights abuses, including the use of plastic bullets for crowd control, harassment by security forces, and allegations of collusion between security forces and loyalist paramilitaries. In April, Human Rights Watch/Helsinki wrote to British government officials to express concern regarding the heavy militarization of Crossmaglen, a small town near the Irish border. The militarization of Crossmaglen remained a concern at year's end, as reports of excessive radiation levels, caused by the heavy concentration of military surveillance equipment along the border, and corresponding illnesses and deaths were confirmed by medical researchers.

In June and again in September, Human Rights Watch/Helsinki met with the independent commissioner for the holding centres and offered a critique of his first annual report. Our concerns, spelled out in a detailed letter and shared with Northern Ireland human rights activists, focused on protecting detainees' right to counsel.

In October, the newly formed Children's Rights Project of Human Rights Watch reported to the United Nations Committee on the Rights of the Child regarding the abuse of children in Northern Ireland. The report, drawing on groundwork laid by Human Rights Watch/Helsinki, reported on the abuse of children in the criminal justice system, street harassment of children by security forces, and abuse of children by paramilitary organizations on both sides of the conflict.

UZBEKISTAN

Human Rights Developments

Uzbekistan retained its repressive grip on civil and political freedoms in 1994. The government arrested, beat, bombed and followed members of the Erk Democratic Party and Birlik Popular Movement, as well as Islamic leaders and human rights activists. Local and foreign media were restricted, journalists who criticized the government were beaten, and repression intensified against persons associated with *Erk*, the Erk party's outlawed publication. The government continued to refuse to register opposition groups, including Erk and Birlik.

However, the government's efforts to mask the political nature of its crackdown on the opposition suggested its growing sensitivity to criticism. Previously, security forces arrested most dissidents for political crimes such as treason and slandering the president. In 1994, however, the government increasingly lodged purely criminal charges, such as assault, embezzlement, and illegal possession of narcotics and weapons. Such charges portrayed opposition members as dangerous to Uzbekistan society rather than as political figures. The only substantive improvement in an otherwise bleak year was that the government did not seriously harass any local or foreign activists during the three-day Conference on Security and Cooperation (CSCE) in Europe seminar on democratic principles, which it hosted in September.

Unrelenting government harassment polarized the opposition during 1994, muffling local activists and radicalizing some in exile. Some activists called for cooperation with the government. In alarmingly familiar Soviet style, at least five leading opposition figures, all victims of past government repression (Uktam Bek-Mukhammedov, Shukhrat Ismatullaev, Abdunabi Abdiev, Abdulkhai Abdumavlonov, and Khamidulla Nurmukhammedov), publicly condemned their "mistakes" and resigned from political life. Abdunabi Abdiev's capitulation followed his release from prison in September; soon after his apologetic article was published, his brother Abdurauf was also freed from prison, strongly suggesting a link between his self-criticism and his brother's release.

In September, Human Rights Watch documented seventeen possible political prisoners in Uzbekistan. Of them, at least four had been arrested on charges of illegal weapons possession. On November 27, 1993, authorities arrested Birlik activists Akhmadkhon Turakhonboi-oghli and Nosyr Zakirov in Namangan, citing the discovery of a single hand grenade in each home. On February 22, 1994, law enforcement officials in Bukhara searched the house of Erk activist Nasrullo Saidov and reportedly found a single hand grenade in his child's room wrapped in a T-shirt. Witnesses asserted that the officials fanned out into all rooms of the house at the same time and planted the grenade during the search. On October 13, the Ministry of Internal Affairs arrested Erk, Birlik and Islamic movement activist Dadakhan Khasan in Ferghana after allegedly finding several rounds of ammunition in his car.

In August, Human Rights Watch/Helsinki learned that the Procuracy brought additional charges—of willfully disobeying the prison administration—against political prisoner Pulatjon Akhunov, who is serving a four-and-a-half-year sentence for narcotics possession and assaulting a guard. According to relatives who spoke with Mr. Akhunov, the prison administration frequently threw him into solitary confinement and otherwise punished him arbitrarily, although beatings reportedly ceased this year, and barred his lawyer from the prison. Human Rights Watch/Helsinki believes all charges against Mr. Akhunov were fabricated to ensure his silence.

Men wielding clubs and knives—believed to be paid by the government—assaulted numerous other outspoken leaders of the opposition during the period covered by this report, often threatening them to cease criticism of the Uzbekistan government. On December 7, 1993, on the eve of a human rights conference in Kyrgyzstan, men armed with knives reportedly broke into the Tashkent home of Mamura Usmanova, leader of the Birlik women's organization Tumaris, beat her and her husband, and took personal property. On May 17, 1994, a bomb exploded at the Tashkent home of Khamidulla Nurmukhamedov, a secretary of the Erk Central Committee. Two female journalists and the male interpreter of a foreign correspondent, all of whom requested anonymity, reported that the Tashkent militia beat and harassed them during 1994 because they had participated in interviews with dissidents.

Uzbekistan security forces also stepped up persecution of activists outside of Uzbekistan, most egregiously in Kazakhstan and Russia. On June 17-18, Uzbekistan law enforcement agents captured Murad Dzhuraev, former deputy of Uzbekistan's Supreme Soviet and former chair of the district council in Mubarek, Kashkadaria region, and Erkin Ashurov, an Erk member, in their apartment in the capital of Kazakhstan. They forced them to return to Uzbekistan, where they were imprisoned, it is believed, for their association with *Erk* newspaper. Uzbekistan officials also forcibly repatriated Birlik activist Vasila Inoiatova and a traveling companion from Kazakhstan in May.

Likewise, in Russia, on November 5, 1993, a gang reportedly beat Albert Musin, Iadgor Obid, and Abdurashid Sharif, political refugees from Uzbekistan and active correspondents, in their Moscow apartment and confiscated materials concerning their activities. On March 5, 1994, several men reportedly stopped the elderly Mr. Obid on a Moscow street, asked whether he was the Iadgor Obid who worked for Radio Liberty, and beat him. To date, the Russian government has failed to condemn these attacks publicly or to apprehend suspects.

Government censorship controlled the media as strictly as state-paid thugs controlled outspoken journalists. Only one Russian newspaper reportedly reached Uzbekistan this year, and it was censored. In apparent fear that its censorship practices would be exposed, the government barred Prof. William Fierman, a U.S. scholar, from leaving the Tashkent airport when he arrived in January to gather information about the national media.

The most obvious attack on the media was the banning of the newspaper *Erk* on November 13, 1993, and the sentencing of editor-in-chief Ibragim Khakkulov, two of his deputies and the newspaper's accountant to two years of imprisonment for alleged abuse of office and financial violations. When the newspaper continued to be published outside of Uzbekistan and distributed clandestinely within the country, the government launched a widespread crackdown. Dozens of *Erk* distributors were arrested between late February and June 1994, particularly in the Kashkadaria region, and in early September in Khwarazm province. Khamidulla Nurmukhamedov, secretary of the Erk party's Central Committee; Gabnazar Koshanov, secretary of the Urgench branch of Erk; and activists Negmat Akhmedov and Abdunabi and Abdurauf Abdiev were all imprisoned during this period. Individuals close to the cases reported that their interrogations centered on association with *Erk*, although charges were not known to have been lodged against any of them.

The government continued to abuse the fifteen-day limit to "administrative arrest" (detention without charges) allowed by law to silence dissent. In May, law enforcement officials detained activists Mikhail Ardzinov, Tolib Iaqubov and Vasila Inoiatova, tried them *in absentia* while they were in custody and convicted them to between seven and fifteen days for "hooliganism," preventing their participation in an international human rights conference. Dr. Iaqubov reported a new and bizarre twist to punitive detention this year. In the past, he and other dissidents were held in foul police lockups or pre-trial detention cells. He reported that in June, however, law enforcement officers drove him and at least four others to separate mountain resorts and offered to feed them while they waited out the visit of a U.S. senator in the capital.

Dissidents reported that surveillance was so heavy it was "useless" to attempt to engage in any but the most mundane public activities. A Tashkent activist reported that five cars continually surrounded the home of Birlik co-chair Shukhrat Ismatullaev, even though he had renounced political life; Vasila Inoiatova was apparently shadowed by no less than ten men at a time.

On July 1, the International Commercial Arbitrating Court in Russia found groundless an Uzbekistan court's 1993 ruling that former vice-president and current opponent of President Islam Karimov, Shukhrullo Mirsaidov, pay the equivalent of U.S. $5 million in restitution for alleged abuse of office. The decision gave credence to Mr. Mirsaidov's assertions that the charges were political fabrications.

The government continued to punish and intimidate prominent activists by harassing their relatives. On March 7, Maqsud Bekdzhan, the brother of Muhammad Solih, chairman of the Erk party, was arrested; Amnesty International received information in May that he had been released. Not long before that, reportedly false allegations of malfeasance by housing officials in Tashkent drove Mr. Bekdzhan and other close relatives from the city. Sherali Ruzimuradov, an eighteen-year-old student, Erk member, and brother of Erk leader Iusuf Ruzimuradov, was arrested on charges of illegal arms possession on June 1 in Karshi, after Iusuf escaped the custody of Uzbekistan security agents in Kazakhstan, where they had taken him against his will to force him to disclose the names of individuals there involved in distributing the newspaper *Erk*. Sherali had been detained and fined in April for possession of a book written by Erk chairman Muhammad Solih. It is broadly believed that Sherali Ruzimuradov was arrested to punish his more active brother and to extract incriminating evidence against him.

According to the office of the United Nations High Commissioner for Refugees (UNHCR) in Tashkent, beginning roughly in the spring, the Uzbekistan militia detained and deported some refugees from Afghanistan. Exact statistics were not available. However, a UNHCR spokesperson reported in October that in a representative case, Uzbekistan authorities had held one family, including six children, in detention for twenty days, seized their UNHCR refugee certification and on September 24 had deported them to Afghanistan.

The Right to Monitor

Human rights activism remained extremely risky during 1994. Local monitors reported that security agents followed them and otherwise restricted their activities. Punishment of three Moscow-based activists was more brutal, as noted above. As previously, the government refused to register the country's only independent human rights group, the Human Rights Society of Uzbekistan. Moreover, the Foreign Ministry continued using visa restrictions as a pretext to prevent outside observers from entering the country. It thwarted a scheduled December 1993 visit by former Soviet dissident Yuri Orlov and a January 1994 trip by U.S. citizen William Fierman, an expert on media.

These patterns were interrupted in September, however, for the CSCE conference in Tashkent. The government not only did not detain dissidents, it allowed activists Jamol Mirsaidov and Vasila Inoiatova to address the conference without known repercussions. It also issued visas to all foreign participants. In a particularly hopeful sign, representatives of Amnesty International reported that they conducted work in Tashkent for about one week almost unmolested following the conference.

The Role of the International Community

U.S. Policy

The United States' almost solo efforts to condemn abuses in Uzbekistan appeared to wane in 1994. Vice-President Gore's whirlwind one-day visit at the end of 1993 gave the government ill-deserved recognition without substantive rebuke, missing a critical opportunity to publicize the ample information on violations in the State Department's *Country Reports on Human Rights Practices for 1993*. In Jaunary, the unconditional granting of Most Favored Nation status in January squandered another opportunity to press for improvements.

As in the past, U.S. criticism was clearest when abuse involved representatives of its own government. Uzbekistan law enforcement officials detained at least six leading Tashkent dissidents in June until Sen. Arlen Spector left the capital. According to *The Washington Post* of June 4, Senator Spector publicly denounced the "deliberate pattern" of violations of civil rights in Uzbekistan and, in an open letter to President Karimov, stated that "the denial of normal contacts between individuals of our two countries creates a serious obstacle to closer relations."

Kazakhstan Policy

At an international human rights conference in May, the deputy procurator general of Kazakhstan acknowledged that Uzbekistan security forces were engaged in surveillance at the conference, and sent two of them home to indicate the government's displeasure. However, Kazakhstan authorities turned a blind eye to other, more abusive activities. They did not prevent Uzbekistan law enforcement agents from arresting and forcing dissident Vasila Inoiatova and her traveling companion to return to Uzbekistan from Kazakhstan in May, or Murad Dzhuraev and Erkin Ashurov to return in June, suggesting that Kazakhstan law enforcement bodies may actually have deliberately facilitated this abuse of fundamental civil rights.

The Work of Human Rights Watch/Helsinki

Human Rights Watch/Helsinki is dedicated to documenting and exposing violations in Uzbekistan in order to improve government behavior. In 1994 we gave particular attention to the existence and abuse of prisoners of conscience, and the need to protect political refugees outside Uzbekistan.

We wrote to the government and its parliamentary human rights commission about instances of abuse, such as a letter in May condemning the arrests of dissidents on their way to a human rights conference, and a summary of abuse, including a list of possible political prisoners, in September. We held two well-attended press conferences in Moscow about ongoing violations, one jointly with the Society for the Promotion of Human Rights in Central Asia, to maintain public pressure, and participated in the CSCE conference in September. There we urged fellow participants to strengthen international condemnation of Uzbekistan's appalling record.

Human Rights Watch/Helsinki urged the Russian authorities to register some ten Moscow-based dissidents from Uzbekistan, and pressed them to repeal local ordinances that jeopardized such newcomers to Moscow. We also assisted political refugees seeking asylum outside the Commonwealth of Independent States.

FEDERAL REPUBLIC OF YUGOSLAVIA

Human Rights Developments

Throughout 1994, human rights conditions continued to deteriorate in the rump Yugoslavia, now renamed the Federal Republic of Yugoslavia (FRY) and comprising Serbia and Montenegro. Although paramilitary violence against Hungarians and Croats subsided somewhat, continuing oppression against Sandzak Muslims and Kosovo Albanians continued throughout the year, directly contradicting Serbian President Slobodan Milosevic's remarks that "in Serbia there is no policy of ethnic discrimination." The Yugoslav government also failed to investigate and prosecute abuses by armed civilians and paramilitary squads.

Police raids on homes and marketplaces occurred frequently in Kosovo; heavily armed Serbian police officers patrolled the streets, creating a state of terror. Albanians were arbitrarily arrested, interrogated and subjected to torture and cruel, inhumane and degrading treatment in detention. Their political trials were marked by violations of the rights of the accused, including denial of the right to counsel and denial of the right to a fair and open public hearing by a competent, independent tribunal without unreasonable delay.

In late 1993 and early 1994, police violence increased in Sandzak, a heavily Muslim-populated region straddling Serbia and Montenegro. Police there used the same tactics as their counterparts in Kosovo: raids on homes, arrests and beatings as part of ostensible searches for illegal weapons. During these searches, police beat Muslim men with rifle butts and clubs over their entire bodies and heads. After such severe ill-treatment, many victims were unable to walk. When villagers had no guns to surrender, the police threatened them with further beatings unless they delivered weapons by a certain date. Police thus coerced Muslims into selling their meager property to buy guns to turn over, in the hope that they would be spared additional abuse. Although such attacks subsided by mid-1994, reports of police violence continued to be received from Sandzak throughout the year.

Also, in late 1993 and early 1994, Serbian authorities clamped down on the predominantly Muslim Party of Democratic Action (SDA), arresting dozens of its activists. Some of the defendants were taken to Serb-controlled territory in Bosnia-Hercegovina, where they were tortured until they signed "confessions" stating they had planned an armed rebellion. For weeks, even though prisoners had serious wounds from the beatings, the authorities refused to grant them access to either defense counsel or medical treatment. By October, the defendants had been tried, found guilty and sentenced to prison terms ranging from one to six years. Between mid-1992 and late 1993, more than fifty Muslims from Sandzak were murdered or went missing. Their leaders have been silenced, hundreds have been displaced, and thousands have fled the country. Through these repressive practices, the Yugoslav authorities have effectively crushed the Sandzak Muslims' participation and future voice in Yugoslav politics.

While Yugoslav authorities continued their repression in Sandzak, from late 1992 to mid-1993, Bosnian Serb forces too abducted and disappeared Sandzak Muslims travelling through Bosnian Serb territory. Yugoslav authorities showed little will to identify or arrest the perpetrators of these abuses despite pledges by numerous senior Serbian officials, including President Milosevic, to bring to justice those responsible for the abductions and disappearances. Only one man, a Belgrade resident named Milan Lukic, was arrested in connection with the disappearances. In early 1994, Lukic was "extradited" to the Bosnian Serb authorities but he was not taken into custody in Bosnian Serb-held territory.

The Serbian government launched a campaign against the free press in April, targeting foreign journalists, and independent domestic media. Foreign correspondents accused of spreading "anti-Serb propaganda" were stripped of their accreditation, while others found it increasingly difficult to obtain entry visas. The Belgrade office of the U.S.-based humanitarian Soros Foundation was also included in this campaign, as the Serbian authorities opposed the foundation's support for the independent media. On April 17, state television broadcast a twenty-five-minute attack on the Soros Foundation, with the government-controlled press following suit; the tone of the report was also clearly anti-Semitic.

In 1994, President Milosevic sought to exonerate himself and his government of any blame for atrocities perpetrated against non-Serbs in Croatia and Bosnia-Hercegovina. Rather, he blamed individual extremists and the Bosnian Serbs for such crimes. In an interview with a U.S. magazine published in June, President Milosevic stated, "Serbs have not started this war [in Bosnia-Hercegovina]. In fact, Serbia is not even at war. Bosnia is." Two weeks after the article was published, a district court in the town of Sabac in Serbia, indicted a citizen of Serbia—Dusan Vuckovic—on war crimes charges, including killing sixteen Muslims near the northeastern Bosnian town of Zvornik in June 1992, as well as raping a Muslim woman in the Serbian town of Loznica in July 1992. This was the first time a war crimes act was officially recognized by the Serbian authorities but it was widely regarded as a show trial within Serbia. The trial was scheduled to begin on November 21.

In October, the chief prosecutor for the international tribunal established to adjudicate war crimes and crimes against humanity in the former Yugoslavia visited Belgrade but failed to obtain the full cooperation of the Yugoslav authorities. Instead, the rump Yugoslav government stated that it regarded the tribunal "as an act of discrimination." At most, the government stated that it would consider appointing officials within the FRY's Public Prosecutor's Office to facilitate cooperation between governmental and nongovernmental organizations and the tribunal's prosecutor.

The Right to Monitor

Although local human rights groups were allowed to function in the rump Yugoslavia, international monitors were denied access to the country, or prevented from investigating human rights abuses there. In November 1993, police detained and interrogated a Human Rights Watch/Helsinki representative in Kosovo because she had been monitoring a trial of Albanians. In July 1994, Yugoslav officials rejected the efforts of the special rapporteur for the United Nations Human Rights Commission, Tadeusz Mazowiecki, to send a mission to Yugoslavia, as they found his work "one-sided, full of prejudice and above all politicized."

The Role of the
International Community

European Union, Russian, and U.N. Policy

Economic sanctions imposed on the rump Yugoslavia continued to be grossly violated: a July 6 Reuters article reported that "some 1,000 trucks, including some carrying oil, cross the border [with Macedonia] every week ... So much fuel is coming in that as a fire safety measure, Belgrade authorities are setting up semi-official petrol markets to move smugglers' canisters and oil drums from impromptu sales points on city roadsides." Other news sources reported that private vehicles brought some twenty tons of fuel into Serbia every day through Bulgaria.

On August 4, President Milosevic announced that Yugoslavia was cutting all political and economic ties with the Bosnian Serbs because of their rejection of the latest international peace plan for Bosnia-Hercegovina. Despite a failed attempt to seal the Bosnia-Serbia border in 1993 and continued resistance by the Serbian government throughout 1994, on September 14 President Milosevic finally consented to the stationing of approximately 140 international civilian observers along Serbia's 375-mile land and river border with Bosnia instead of the 1,500-2,000 troops originally envisaged. International negotiators accepted President Milosevic's demands that the observers not be called monitors and not include military officers as originally planned. The observers also depended on drivers and interpreters supplied by the Yugoslav authorities. Inspections were to be carried out in warehouses rather than at border crossings, and observers were not given the authority to inspect suspect trucks, which suggested that they could act only with the consent of Yugoslav police and customs officials.

The enforcement of the border blockade remained in dispute after international observers were deployed. In early October, the U.S. and German press reported massive cross-border commercial traffic, including black-market fuel and light weaponry. U.S.

Secretary of Defense William Perry said on September 30 that the Bosnian Serbs were still receiving weapons or other equipment from across the Drina river, but Lord David Owen, the European Union's peace negotiator for the former Yugoslavia, reported to the U.N. in early October that "controls of the border have been adequate." Meanwhile, hundreds of helicopter flights were reported over Bosnia in mid-September and early October; fifty-five flights took place on Saturday, October 8 alone. After U.N. officials said the flights might be a Yugoslav army effort to resupply Bosnian Serb forces, the flights reportedly stopped.

Despite the early failures and uncertain enforcement of the border blockade, on October 23 the U.N. Security Council approved a resolution partially lifting economic and cultural sanctions against the government of rump Yugoslavia, thus rewarding President Milosevic for his pledge to seal the border. The resolution was to remain in effect for one hundred days, unless U.N. Secretary-General Boutros Boutros-Ghali found that arms were once again being transported across the border.

U.S. Policy

The Clinton administration paid some attention to continuing abuses in the rump Yugoslavia in 1994, particularly Kosovo, but it also acquiesced to European pressure to reward the Milosevic government for its alleged rupture of relations with the Bosnian Serbs. Little attention was paid to the human rights record of the Yugoslav authorities or the Serbian government's past support for "ethnic cleansing" in Croatia and Bosnia.

Initially against lifting sanctions, the U.S. in late August and early September supported easing U.N. sanctions against Yugoslavia. The U.S. moved to support further efforts to lift sanctions if President Milosevic granted diplomatic recognition to Croatia and Bosnia-Hercegovina. This position contradicted statements made by Madeline Albright, U.S. ambassador to the U.N., in late 1993 and in January, when she stated that the U.S. would oppose lifting sanctions against any state that did not cooperate with the investigations and prosecutions of the international tribunal by freely permitting investigation of war crimes and crimes against humanity and by extraditing those indicted for offenses. Because the Yugoslav government continued to question the legitimacy of the tribunal and had failed to cooperate with it, and because the human rights situation within the rump Yugoslavia had not improved, Human Rights Watch/Helsinki considered the U.S. change of position extremely unfortunate.

The Work of
Human Rights Watch/Helsinki

Because of the lack of an international human rights presence in the rump Yugoslavia, Human Rights Watch/Helsinki continued to maintain one or more staff members there throughout 1994 in order to monitor human rights in the rump Yugoslavia and Serbian-controlled areas of Bosnia and Croatia.

Throughout the year, staff researchers investigated human rights violations in Serbia proper, Kosovo, and Sandzak. In February, Human Rights Watch/Helsinki issued a protest letter calling on Yugoslav Defense Minister Pavle Bulatovic to cease activities related to recruiting Serbian refugees from Bosnia and Croatia to serve in the Bosnian

Serb army. In March 1994, *Open Wounds: Human Rights Abuses in Kosovo* was published, a report that documented escalating human rights abuses of Albanians by Serbian authorities. On May 6, *Human Rights Abuses of Non-Serbs in Kosovo, Sandzak and Vojvodina* reported on human rights abuses against non-Serbs in these provinces of Yugoslavia. At the request of Tadeusz Mazowiecki, the special rapporteur for the United Nations Human Rights Commission, on September 1 Human Rights Watch/Helsinki submitted a lengthy letter reporting human rights abuses in rump Yugoslavia.

Human Rights Watch/Helsinki also protested against restrictions on freedom of the press and the right to monitor in 1994. On April 14, in a letter to the prime minister and information minister of Yugoslavia, Human Rights Watch/Helsinki protested the revocation of press credentials to foreign journalists.

Human Rights Watch/Helsinki investigated the state of domestic war crimes trials and advocated that the easing of sanctions against the rump Yugoslavia be conditioned on the Serbian authorities' demonstrated cooperation with the international tribunal established to adjudicate war crimes and crimes against humanity in the former Yugoslavia.

HUMAN
RIGHTS
WATCH
/MIDDLE EAST

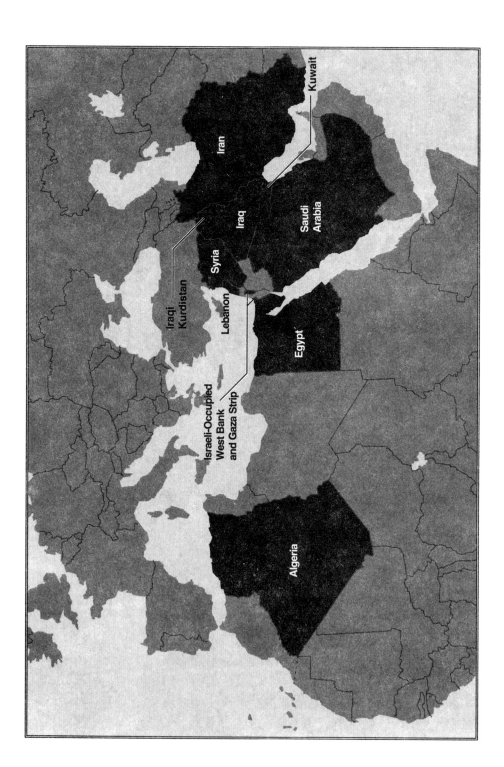

HUMAN RIGHTS WATCH/MIDDLE EAST OVERVIEW

Human Rights Developments

The Arab-Israeli peace process dominated the news of the Middle East, but ongoing domestic political conflicts between governments and opposition groups—mainly Islamist—had a far greater impact on human rights conditions in 1994.

The year demonstrated the danger of viewing improvements in the promotion and protection of human rights as merely the end results of a peace process. Human rights issues were crucial concerns at all stages. As states, like Syria, entered the peace process, they were reminded that improving their international image was no substitute for improving their human rights record. Courageous peace treaties and international agreements demanded complementary measures to introduce similarly sweeping changes in national legal systems to protect individual rights.

The rapid and dramatic international developments—including the implementation of the Israel-PLO accords, the signing of the Jordan-Israel peace treaty, and other openings in the Arab-Israeli relations—diverted attention from the internal problems of the countries involved, exposing deep rooted abusive government practices. As old and seemingly unsolvable international disputes moved toward resolution, internal political conflicts—some unrelated to the international issues—heated up; as shown by the chaos in Algeria, the civil war in Yemen, clashes in Israel and the occupied territories, and Islamist-government conflicts throughout the region.

Fueled by a combination of domestic and internal grievances and united by a religious ideology, Islamist opposition groups challenged established governments in practically every country in the Middle East, including conservative Saudi Arabia. Their goal was essentially the same, a radical transformation of society based on a return to the fundamentals of Islam and the establishment of Islamic states. But their methods varied, depending in large part on the policies and practices of the governments which they opposed. In Jordan, where the government displayed relative tolerance, the Islamic party took a moderate approach. In other countries, most notably Egypt and Algeria, some Islamist groups resorted to violent action, that was often indiscriminate.

In Algeria, the government and Islamist opposition groups remained locked in an escalating ideological and military struggle in which virtually no member of the population was safe—amidst death threats, mass arrests, reprisal killings, gun battles in the streets, summary executions, and a campaign of random violence and sabotage against public property. Over 4,000 persons had been killed in Algeria since 1992, many of them unarmed civilians.

In Egypt, conditions continued to deteriorate, with acts of political violence carried out by Islamist groups that violate international humanitarian standards, including deliberate attacks on foreign and Egyptian civilians. The security apparatus resorted to arbitrary arrest, incommunicado detention, torture, the use of excessive force, and possible extrajudicial execution. Harassment and intimidation by security forces affected not only families of suspected Islamist militants, but lawyers, journalists, and human rights advocates, contributing to a climate of fear and repression.

In Israel and the occupied territories, Palestinians and Jewish militants opposed to the peace process staged several attacks on civilians. In February, a Jewish settler opened fire in a crowded mosque in Hebron, killing twenty-nine worshippers. And in October, a Palestinian suicide bombing of a commuter bus in downtown Tel Aviv killed twenty-two people. Israeli forces in the occupied territories, in the name of protecting security, carried out arbitrary arrests, tortured prisoners, used excessive force against demonstrators, and sometimes shot deliberately to kill when there was no immediate threat to their own or others' lives. They committed these violations with virtual impunity.

Even the nonviolent Islamist opposition in Saudi Arabia was subjected to a heavy handed crackdown of arbitrary arrests, incommunicado detention, torture and ill-treatment in prison.

In battles against armed insurgents, or as a means to stifle the emergence of any political opposition, governments maintained emergency measures that restricted rights. Emergency laws have been in force in Egypt since 1981, and were extended 1994 for three more years. Hafez Asad continues to rule Syria under a state of emergency, first imposed in 1963.

Emergency measures in Algeria, Egypt, Syria, Kuwait, and the Israeli-occupied West Bank and Gaza Strip included extensive arrest and detention powers and the use of courts of exception that fell well short of meeting international fair trial standards. These tribunals failed to provide adequate due process, including legal representation; they routinely dismissed claims of torture, even when there is clear evidence of it. In some cases there was no appeals process; the decision of the court is final. In Algeria the identity of the special court judges was kept secret. The "justice" of these courts was so compromised that they were little more than a legal facade for the rapid and high-volume processing of security and political prisoners. In Algeria, 3,000 Islamists were tried in special courts in 1994.

The sentences handed down by the state security courts were often harsh: lengthy prison terms and the death penalty. In Egypt and Kuwait, death sentences were handed down and executions carried out. Five Iraqis and one Kuwaiti were sentenced to death for plotting to assassinate former President Bush during his visit to Kuwait.

Lebanon limited a defendant's rights and abbreviated the legal process as it made more liberal use of special military courts to try civilians accused of nonviolent crimes. The state security court in Syria disregarded due process guarantees and continued to sentence members of opposition political parties to lengthy prison terms. Defendants in Iran's Revolutionary Court were routinely held in incommunicado pre-trial detention and denied access to legal counsel.

Harsh sentences were not limited to these special courts. Regular courts in Saudi Arabia sentenced to death more than thirty people convicted of drug trafficking. They were beheaded in 1994. Their trials did not come close to meeting international fair trial standards. The government of Yemen, in an apparent effort to demonstrate its control after emerging victorious from a civil war, ordered the execution of eleven common criminals who had been convicted several years earlier under dubious trial procedures.

In many cases, detainees' rights were violated long before they were brought before courts. In Kuwait, Palestinians and Bedoons (nomadic people indigenous to Kuwait but denied citizenship) were arrested arbitrarily in large numbers. The largest mass arrest in Saudi Arabia's recent history sent hundreds of Islamist opponents to prison in 1994. In Lebanon, scores of people were arrested on the basis of political affiliation, or after expressing criticism of the Lebanese or Syrian government. The newly established Palestinian Authority, under pressure to respond to a wave of attacks on Israelis, arrested hundreds of Gazans on the basis of their suspected political affiliation. Egypt's security forces practiced a particularly ruthless form of arbitrary arrest—taking hostage family members of fugitive security suspects to pressure suspects to turn themselves in.

When political conflicts intensified, human rights abuses often mounted. Detainees—often the same people caught up in random sweeps—were often abused. Torture was practiced in nearly every country monitored this past year. Eradication requires work at two levels: enforcement of existing domestic laws that prohibit torture, and revision of legislation and directives that explicitly prescribes abuse: such as laws stipulating flogging in Saudi Arabia, amputation and branding in Iraq, and guidelines, approved by Israel's cabinet, for using "moderate physical pressure" in the interrogation of security suspects.

Keenly aware of what the political leadership required or tolerated, most security forces in the Middle East—including intelligence services, police, and army—violated fundamental human rights with impunity. In Egypt, torture by security forces continued unabated, with no signs that the government had the political will to identify and prosecute vigorously the abusers. The death in custody of a thirty-year-old Islamist lawyer in Cairo was one of the region's high-profile cases in 1994. Israeli forces systematically and severely abused Palestinians held for interrogation. Although dismissed by the government as isolated cases, Human Rights Watch concluded in a 1994 report that the abuses constituted a pattern that could only persist with government acquiescence.

The escalating political conflicts in several countries—most notably, Egypt and Algeria—engulfed and polarized societies, leaving little room for those who refused to take sides. Human rights monitors, lawyers, journalists, writers and artists found themselves targeted by either the government or its opponents, and in some cases by both.

In Egypt the government detained outspoken lawyers, harassed editors and journalists from opposition newspapers, and blocked the distribution of a report by a local human rights organization. In Algeria, sixteen journalists were murdered in the first ten months of the year by gunmen who in most cases went unidentified, but who appeared to be supporters of one of several clandestine Islamist groups. The president of one of the two main human rights leagues was killed by unknown assailants in June. In October, the eighty-three-year-old Egyptian writer and Nobel laureate Naguib Mahfouz was stabbed, in Cairo, in an attack widely believed to have been carried out by Islamist extremists. Iran maintained its call for the death of author Salman Rushdie and held incommunicado the prominent writer Ali Akbar Saidi-Sirjani. Defying intimidation, 134 Iranian writers courageously signed an open letter criticizing the government's "anti-democratic practices."

The human rights picture included some bright spots. The implementation of, and movement toward, peace agreements raised hopes for an environment more favorable to protecting human rights. Arab states began to open diplomatic or trade relations with Israel, in some cases tacitly acknowledging an end to the state of war they had so often used in the past to justify violating the rights of their own citizens.

The implementation of the Israeli-PLO Declaration of Principles led to the withdrawal of Israeli troops in May from population centers in Gaza and Jericho. The Palestinian Authority took over the administration of internal security and government services. Although it is too early to identify systematic patterns in the human rights record of the new authority several incidents, including a death under torture and the mid-November clash between police and demonstrators that left fifteen dead and more than eleven wounded, raise serious concerns. Before the November incident, the levels of violence, arrests and restrictions on movement within the Gaza Strip had dropped sharply since May.

For the vast majority of the West Bank, still under Israeli military occupation with no significant presence of the Palestinian Self-Rule Authority, the human rights picture remained largely unchanged: Israeli troops continued to arrest hundreds of Palestinians every month, use excessive force against demonstrators and others, torture and ill-treat suspects under interrogation, and impose comprehensive curfews and other measures that amounted to collective punishments.

The massacre by an Israeli settler of worshippers in a Hebron mosque in February immediately drew attention to militant Israeli groups, and highlighted the need to address human rights issues related to the status of Jewish settlements and government tolerance of settler violence in the occupied territories.

Still waiting for the fruits of a peace process, a large portion of south Lebanon remained under Israeli occupation. Israel continued to violate international humanitarian law in this zone by indiscriminately shelling and bombing civilian areas, ostensibly targeting guerrilla bases. Hizballa, the sizable militia that Lebanon and Syria permit to operate in Lebanon, also violated humanitarian norms by indiscriminately firing rockets into northern Israel and Israeli-occupied south Lebanon, causing civilian casualties.

Gulf War after-shocks continued to bring human rights abuses. Hundreds of Kuwaiti citizens who disappeared during the Iraqi occupation remained unaccounted for. The Kuwaiti government maintained pressure on Bedoons, Palestinians, and individuals and groups suspected of harboring pro-Iraqi sympathies. Kuwait maintained its ban on political parties and took steps to close down over fifty human rights groups and other nongovernmental organizations.

The Iraqi government's treatment of its Shi'a population, part of which rose up in rebellion at the close of the Gulf War, stands out as the region's gravest example of violence and repression against an ethnic or religious group. Human Rights Watch received, but was unable to confirm, reports of mass executions of Shi'a in southern Iraq. The government continued to drain the southern marshlands, threatening the environment, livelihood, and security of hundreds of thousands of Shi'a Marsh Arabs who live there.

There was a deterioration of human rights conditions in Iraqi Kurdistan, which, under allied forces protection, remained outside Baghdad's control. In addition to the hardship caused by the Baghdad regime's continuing internal blockade of the north, clashes between the two main Kurdish political groups left hundreds of fighters and civilians dead or wounded.

Ethnic and religious conflict, one of the major human rights problems in the world today, simmered in a number of Middle East countries. In Iran, where religious minorities continued to suffer from state-sanctioned discrimination, three Christian clerics were killed under suspicious circumstances. In Saudi Arabia, non-Sunni Muslims faced discrimination and non-Muslims were strictly forbidden to practice their religion in public. Copts, which the Egyptian government has adamantly refused to recognize as a minority, were subjected to state-sanctioned discrimination and political violence from suspected Islamist militants.

Along with minorities, foreign workers faced discrimination by the state and ill-treatment by their employers. In Saudi Arabia alone there were five million foreign workers. There, as in most Middle East countries, local labor laws did not adequately protect them. Furthermore, authorities failed to apply relevant criminal laws to protect foreigners.

In September, women from the Middle East joined forces with women from around the world at the U.N. International Conference on Population and Development, hosted by the Egyptian government. In Cairo, women activists called for increased respect for women's human rights as a key to their reproductive health and to population planning. Governments at the conference responded by adopting a program of action that emphasized the importance of respecting women's rights in population programs.

In general, however, governments in the region took few steps to end violations of women's human rights. In Saudi Arabia the government enforced discrimination in employment and restrictions on women's freedom of movement. In Kuwait women were still denied the right to vote, or run for office. Also in Kuwait, foreign female domestic workers—mainly Filipina and Sri Lankan—were doubly vulnerable as women and foreign workers. About two thousand women fled from their employers in 1994, charging them with abuses ranging from withholding wages to physical assault and rape. Kuwait's criminal and labor laws offered little or not protection.

Women in Algeria were increasingly the victims of violence by Islamist groups, often in the name of religion, that targeted them as women. In Iran, despite some advances in access to education and in some professions, women were forced to live under increasingly arbitrary restrictions in their day to day activities. Two women were reportedly stoned to death for adultery.

After the unification of north and south Yemen in 1990, the country had enjoyed a relative opening to freedom of expression and association. A free and fair parliamentary election—with universal suffrage—was held in April 1993. But in May, a civil war erupted that brought rights abuses during seventy days of fighting. The government prevailed, but its actions during and after the war were a significant setback for human rights.

Human Rights Watch sent a mission to both northern and southern regions of the country in July and identified rights abuses by both parties to the conflict. Northern government forces killed and injured hundreds of civilians by indiscriminately shelling the city of Aden. They also deliberately damaged a water pumping station, cutting off Aden's water supply and leaving the city and suburbs practically without water for weeks. Separatist forces fired Scud rockets at northern cities and injured and killed civilians. Their attack on government military positions in the immediate vicinity of a Somali refugee camp injured and killed scores of refugees. Both sides arbitrarily detained people without charges and mistreated hundreds of civilians during the conflict.

When the fighting was over, first separatists and then government forces engaged in and tolerated extensive looting and vandalism in Aden. The victorious government of General Ali Abdullah Saleh continued to detain several hundred people despite the lifting of the state of emergency on July 27 and the declaration of a general amnesty. The death penalty, which had not been carried out for years, was abruptly used against five common criminals and upheld for nine others. Participants in a conference were arrested and beaten before being released. Printing companies, already disabled by vandalism, were warned not to publish opposition newspapers.

The Right to Monitor

Obstacles to human rights monitoring in the Middle East ranged from intimidation and fear in Lebanon, direct government interference in Egypt, banning by law in Kuwait and Saudi Arabia, long-term imprisonment in Syria, and assassination in Algeria. In June, the President of the Algerian League of Human Rights, Yucef Fathallah, was assassinated by unknown assailants. As the need for local monitoring increased, human rights activism in the Middle East became increasingly difficult and dangerous.

The governments of several countries (Egypt, Israel and the Occupied Territories, Tunisia, Morocco, Algeria, and Lebanon) tolerated human rights organizations, although at times they restricted and interfered with them.

Moncef Marzouqi, former president of the Tunisian League for Human Rights, was imprisoned for four months. Egyptian security forces blocked the distribution of the annual report of the Egyptian Organization for Human Rights, and interfered with its investigators as they conducted field work.

Human rights organizations in the Israeli-occupied territories were generally allowed to operate and carry on their activities, although some Palestinian human rights workers were restricted or detained. In the Palestinian self-rule areas of Gaza and Jericho, human rights activists were allowed to work freely.

In Syria, Iraq, Iran, Kuwait, Libya, and Saudi Arabia, independent human rights organizations were prohibited from operating openly. The only recourse for activists was to move underground or work in exile.

Even exile did not guarantee safety. Former Libyan diplomat Mansour Kikhia, who disappeared from his Cairo hotel in December 1993, remains missing. Kikhia, a lawyer and prominent member of the Libyan political opposition, was a founding member of the Arab Organization for Human Rights and served on its board of directors.

While continuing its ban on local human rights groups, Syria improved its cooperation with international human rights organizations. Although scores of political prisoners were released in 1994, eleven human rights activists remained in prison, ten of them sentenced to terms of five to ten years.

Kuwait allowed visits by international human rights organizations in 1994, but refused to grant licenses to several local human rights groups and then proceeded to close them down because they were unlicensed. The organizations' attempts to carry on human rights work openly, in spite of the ban, were blocked.

U.S. Policy

U.S. policy in the Middle East in 1994 was framed around several long-standing strategic imperatives: maintaining a commitment to Israel's security and well-being; facilitating the Arab-Israeli peace process; promoting U.S. commercial interests; maintaining pressure on Iraq and the isolation of Iran; and the defense of Kuwait and Saudi Arabia. Human Rights considerations were secondary, at best. In each of these areas, however, there were opportunities—and obligations—to press for improvement in the protection and promotion of human rights.

The Clinton administration had, at its inception, signalled that there would be greater emphasis on human rights in the conduct of U.S. policy toward the Middle East. Robert H. Pelletreau, Assistant Secretary of State for Near Eastern Affairs, said that one of the U.S. government's priorities for the region was "promoting more open political and economic systems, and respect for human rights and the rule of law." While such pronouncements were fairly common, public policy actions were rare. And although the State Department generally reported faithfully and carefully on human rights conditions and abuses, these reports were not consistently factored into foreign policy decisions.

A key factor in determining the potential for U.S. action on human rights issues was tangible influence. The U.S. found itself without much influence in countries such as Iran, Algeria, and Yemen. In others

—Egypt, Kuwait, Saudi Arabia, the Israel-Occupied Territories, and Syria—the U.S. had significant opportunities to have an impact on human rights conditions.

The U.S. claimed to have only limited influence over the region's worst human rights disaster, Algeria. But, ironically, along with this diplomatic distance came a degree of helpful objectivity. Unlike France—intimately involved and influential—which felt it had to uncritically support the government, the U.S. was able to take a more neutral and principled position. To its credit, the U.S. criticized both the government and opposition groups for human rights abuses and called on both sides to negotiate.

At the other end of the influence spectrum was Israel, recipient of $3 billion in U.S. foreign assistance in 1994 and beneficiary of consistent U.S. commitments to its security and military superiority in the region. The U.S. maintained its silence on Israel's human rights abuses in the occupied territories and, even more disturbing, refused to articulate at critical junctures what had been long-standing U.S. policy positions on settlements and the status of Jerusalem, two thorny issues slated for future negotiations between Israel and the PLO.

The U.S. was generally reluctant to criticize publicly Egypt's human rights record, given its close relationship, an annual aid package of $2 billion, and the fact that it was fighting against an Islamist opposition. The exception came when Assistant Secretary of State for Democracy, Human Rights and Labor John Shattuck mentioned in a Cairo press conference his concerns about human rights violations. And, in a display of support for a local human rights group, Shattuck visited the offices of the Egyptian Organization of Human Rights and publicly praised its work.

In the case of Syria, President Clinton had opportunities in both Geneva and Damascus in 1994 to raise human rights issues. He might have done so in private. The only issue related to human rights that the U.S. publicly raised was the question of Syrian support for terrorism.

In the Gulf region, U.S. policy included the staunch maintenance of sanctions and no-fly zones in Iraq, the isolation of Iran, and defense of Kuwait and Saudi Arabia—put to a test in October when Iraq moved troops near the Kuwaiti border.

After military and strategic issues, economic agreements appeared to be of paramount concern in the Gulf. In Kuwait, the U.S. placed far more importance on increasing American business than improving human rights. Bilateral military agreements with Saudi Arabia accomplished both strategic and commercial objectives. As the largest foreign investor in Saudi Arabia, the U.S. had significant leverage and an obligation to raise human rights issues, but generally chose not to do so, at least publicly.

The U.S. did not consistently appreciate the importance of human rights to the Arab-Israeli peace process. For example, soon after the signing of the Israel-PLO Declaration of Principles, the U.S., as well as other governments, sought ways to show Palestinians in the occupied territories "immediate tangible benefits" of the agreement. Rather than pressing for human rights improvements, the U.S. focused its efforts on economic development.

Jobs and infrastructure development were important, but when Secretary of State Warren Christopher stated in October, "Palestinians greatest need is economic development," and again when U.S. officials attributed the November violence in Gaza to poverty, the U.S. appeared to overlook the human rights dimension of this critical transition period in the West Bank and Gaza Strip.

If the promise of peace—to create an environment in which human rights are better protected—is realized, then the U.S. will have made an enormous contribution as a facilitator. But, persistent attention to human rights is needed to achieve this goal. Human Rights Watch realizes that there is more to peace negotiations than public statements and deals between competing authorities. There may be sound tactical reasons for dealing privately with some issues—including human rights concerns—in the course of negotiations. But it is the role of objective third parties to ensure that fundamental human rights issues are not squashed under the weight of a stronger negotiating party, or shoved aside by the momentum of a peace process.

The Work of
Human Rights Watch/Middle East

Human Rights Watch approached its overall goals of promoting and protecting human rights in the Middle East by monitoring human rights conditions and practices; supporting local human rights efforts; and bringing pressure for improvements through reporting and sharing concerns with governments, media, policymakers and colleagues. Nine countries, reviewed in detail below, were strategically selected for concentrated research in 1994. This does not suggest that abuses did not exist in other countries.

A report on violations of freedom of religious belief and expression of Egypt's Christian minority was slated for publication at the end of the year. Field research in Egypt also documented the security forces' practice of taking hostage the family members of suspects. The report will be released in December.

Consistent with our commitment to promote accountability, Human Rights Watch continued to coordinate an effort to bring before the International Court of Justice a case of genocide against Iraq for its massacre of Kurds in 1988. And in December, it will publish a report on the Iranian government's assassination campaign against political dissidents abroad.

Based on research on eighteen metric tons of Iraqi government documents seized by Kurdish rebel parties after the Gulf War, Human Rights Watch published *Bureaucracy of Repression: The Iraqi government in its Own words.*

A mission to Yemen in the aftermath of the civil war to study human rights and humanitarian law issues related to the conduct of the war and during the period immediately following the war, resulted in a report, *Human Rights in Yemen During and*

After the War, was published in October.

Stressing the central role of human rights in the peace process, Human Rights Watch published a 316-page report in June based on field research in the West Bank and Gaza Strip entitled *Torture and Ill-Treatment: Israel's Interrogation of Palestinians from the Occupied Territories.* As Israel and the PLO proceeded to implement the accords, Human Rights Watch/Middle East focused its research and monitoring on the newly established self-rule areas of Gaza and Jericho, while maintaining coverage of the West Bank, as well. A report on the self-rule areas will be released in December.

A study of Israeli settler violence and state-sponsored discrimination in the occupied territories will be published along with a chapter on the Lebanese civil war in a study of communal violence worldwide.

In the course of its research and investigations, Human Rights Watch representatives traveled to Egypt, Kuwait, Israel and the occupied territories, Syria, and Lebanon in 1994.

As a rapid response to problems ranging from the detention of human rights activists to a death in custody, to the disappearance of a writer, Human Rights Watch/Middle East sent approximately fifty open letters to fifteen Middle Eastern governments expressing its concerns and lodging protests.

In the course of the year Human Rights Watch/Middle East provided extensive information to journalists working on human rights issues in nearly all countries in the Middle East.

ALGERIA

Human Rights Developments

The conflict between security forces and the Islamist insurgency grew far bloodier in 1994. Civilians playing no part in the armed conflict lived amidst growing terror and lawlessness.

Radical Islamist groups made good on death threats to a lengthening list of men and women and categories of persons accused of support for the regime or behavior contrary to Islam. Even the relatives of such persons were considered fair game.

Security forces sustained hundreds of casualties at the hands of Islamist groups, and responded with increasing brutality. They targeted not only armed rebels, but also the relatives of Islamists, suspected sympathizers, and, more generally, the local population of areas where armed groups were active.

Estimates of the number of persons killed between 1992 and September 1994 ranged between 4,000 and 30,000. In August, the government put the number at 10,000, a number that was more than double any previous official tally. Such figures cannot be confirmed, since reliable and detailed information of this kind is almost impossible to come by. No independent news or human rights organization has compiled an accurate tally of killings or been able to determine responsibility for the vast number of killings that went unclaimed by any party.

The conflict forced ordinary citizens into deadly dilemmas. They often could not tell whether the uniformed men at their door or at a checkpoint were bona fide police or Islamists in disguise, preparing an ambush. If their car was stolen by militants, and they reported the theft, they feared reprisals. But if they instead remained silent and the car was then used in a guerrilla operation, they risked accusations of complicity.

Islamists claimed responsibility for some killings and, on the basis of their threats and their clandestine publications, were the probable perpetrators of many that went unclaimed. But the authenticity of claims of responsibility could not always be verified. Most of the civilians killed during the conflict were not prominent political, intellectual or cultural figures, but ordinary men and women killed for causes that remained obscure.

Women encountered special risks. Islamist groups engaged in a campaign of threats, invective, and physical assaults that frightened many women who wished to hold jobs outside the home, move about freely, or wear Western clothes in public.

There were cases in which women appeared to have been targeted for defying these pressures. For example, an unveiled young woman was shot dead at a bus stop in the Islamist stronghold of Meftah on February 28. The attack was attributed to Islamists, but, like so many of the murders that took place during the year, it went unclaimed and the motive could not be confirmed.

While women felt the dangers and pressures to varying degrees, many shared a sense that the government was failing to protect them from Islamist intimidation and violence.

The current turmoil in Algeria stems from the halting of elections in January 1992 and the replacement of the president by the military-dominated "High State Council" (HSC). These steps were taken to block the Islamic Salvation Front (Front Islamique du Salut, or FIS) from capturing a majority in parliament after its strong showing in the first round of voting. In February 1992, the HSC declared a state of emergency that is still in effect, banned the FIS and cracked down on its members. The HSC was succeeded by Liamine Zeroual, who was appointed president in January 1994. Zeroual, like the HSC, presented himself as a caretaker authority, and has promised presidential elections in 1995.

Since the cancellation of elections, a well-armed movement seeking Islamist rule has waged war against the regime. (Armed attacks by Islamists were before then an isolated phenomenon.) Composed of various groups whose tactics and objectives diverge in some respects, the insurgency established strongholds that the security forces contested only in massive operations.

Relations between the FIS and the armed groups were nebulous. FIS leaders were in prison, underground or in exile after 1992, and unable to convene and articulate definitive platforms or positions. This was not changed, at least initially, by the transfer from prison to house arrest in September of FIS chief Abbasi Madani and deputy chief Ali Belhadj. Party figures, however, continued to issue statements, both in exile and from hiding inside Algeria, that gave some indication of party thinking.

The two prominent armed groups were the AIS (Armé Islamique du Salut), considered the Islamic Salvation Front's armed wing, and the more radical GIA (Groupe Islamique Armé). Both violated fundamental norms of humanitarian law by targeting civilians in addition to security forces. During 1994, the FIS took steps to distance itself from some of the attacks on civilians, but did so in a halting and inconsistent way, and in any event failed to stop the carnage.

The GIA opposed "any dialogue, truce or reconciliation" with the regime. It issued death threats against broad categories of people including journalists, women who did not wear headscarves, foreigners who did not leave Algeria, butchers who did not lower their prices during the holy month of Ramadhan, proprietors of cinemas, and vendors of such "forbidden" products as musical cassettes, French newspapers, and tobacco. It claimed responsibility for a wave of car bombings in October, and for the bombs that killed three in a June 29 demonstration in Algiers.

The GIA also declared war on the public school system. In August it ordered the closure of all high schools and universities and declared that elementary and middle schools could remain open only if they: segregated students by gender; eliminated the teaching of music, French, and, for girls, physical education; and required headscarves for women staff and students past the age of puberty.

The sabotage began in the fall. An official tally on October 6 stated that 610 schools had been vandalized since the beginning of the summer, many of them completely destroyed. Several educators, from elementary schoolteachers to university rectors, were assassinated.

The Armée Islamiqe du Salut did not spare civilians either, although it condemned certain GIA tactics such as the assault on education. In August, it claimed responsibility for abducting a newspaper editor and then releasing him with a warning that the AIS had drawn up a death list of journalists who were "accomplices of the regime."

As a political party with aspirations to govern Algeria, the FIS had a strong moral obligation to condemn atrocities committed by Islamist forces. The initial, belated steps it took in this direction were disappointing. In February, Anouar Haddam, president of the FIS parliamentary delegation in exile, who had justified the slaying of some prominent intellectuals during 1993, took a step away from this deplorable practice when he urged "everyone to renounce the violence against Algerians—civilian or military—and foreigners who are not directing or taking direct part in security operations involving the use of force."

The FIS did not consistently project this message, however. It failed, for example, to condemn the August 3 killing of five French citizens, including three embassy guards, for which the GIA had claimed responsibility. Nor did it dissociate itself from the AIS's announcement of a "death list" of journalists.

No security threat or atrocity for which the insurgency was responsible could justify the methods used by the security forces. They killed many of their victims not during armed clashes but after they had been captured or incapcitated. State repression thrived in an atmosphere of impunity. The government, to Human Rights Watch/Middle East's knowledge, never provided details of a case in which a security force member was punished for human rights abuses. An Amnesty International report on Algeria contained testimony of relatives of persons who had been executed after being detained by the security forces. Human Rights Watch/Middle East interviewed a surgeon at an Algiers hospital who said security forces brought in Islamists who had been wounded in clashes for emergency care. The security forces gave false names for the patients and, after initial care was administered, transferred them to a military hospital. Some of the patients he treated were never again seen alive, the surgeon said, even though their injuries were not life-threatening.

Several deadly reprisal raids were carried out against residents of neighborhoods in which security forces had been ambushed. In Blida, paratroopers went from door to door rounding up youths on March 20, the day after six members of the security forces had been killed. The corpses of fourteen of those arrested were found on the streets the following morning, Le Monde reported. Reprisals rates were sometimes carried out in death-squad-like operations by groups wearing civilian clothes. Death threats were issued against Islamists in the name of shadowy anti-Islamist groups. The links between these activities and the security forces were not clear. Authorities denied any connection to death-squad activity, but failed to condemn it and did not announce the arrest of anyone implicated in the killing of Islamists outside of clashes.

Many Islamists received anomymous death threats. A university instructor interviewed by HRW went into hiding and then fled abroad after receiving an unsigned written threat accompanied by a bullet. He said that many such threats had been delivered to pro-FIS intellectuals and persons who, like himself, had run as FIS candidates in the elections.

Torture under interrogation was common for persons detained on suspicion of participating in, or having information about, the armed opposition. Methods included various forms of beatings and forcing bound detainees to drink large quantities of dirty water.

More than 3,000 suspected Islamists were tried during 1994 in "Special Courts" set up by a 1992 anti-terrorism decree. Special Court judges routinely dismissed the claims of defendants that their confessions had been extracted under torture. They ignored violations of legal safeguards against mistreatment, such as the twelve-day limit on incommunicado detention in "terrorism" cases and the right of detainees to independent medical examinations.

The Special Courts have pronounced over 500 death sentences since their inception, most of them in absentia. However, none has been carried since 1993.

About 350 men were being held in administrative detention in September, according to the semi-official National Human Rights Monitoring Body. Some of those detained had been held without charge since early 1992.

Sixteen journalists were assassinated in the first ten months of 1994—more than in any other country during the same period. The murders usually went unclaimed, although they followed numerous threats from Islamist groups. The victims worked for both independent and state media; they were not necessarily prominent or known for anti-Islamist views. The terror drove many journalists to go into semi-hiding. Another 200 fled the country, the daily *El-Watan* reported.

Since the cancellation of legislative elections, Algerians have been ruled by an unelected head of state, and without a parliament. Most of the FIS members they had elected to local offices in 1990 were ousted by the national authorities. Thus, in 1994, Algerians spent another year deprived of their basic right "to take part in the conduct of public affairs, directly or through freely chosen representatives" as written in Article 25 of the International Covenant on Civil and Political Rights.

The Right to Monitor

While there are few formal strictures on human rights work, solid reporting about abuses was a casualty of the wanton violence that made fieldwork life-threatening and terrorized potential sources into silence. In June, unknown assailants murdered Youcef Fathallah, president of the Algerian League of Human Rights and a critic of both government and opposition abuses. The assassination campaign against journalists dissuaded many reporters from conducting field investigations; and prompted the exodus of most of the locally based international press. Many physicians and lawyers refused to correspond or converse openly with foreign journalists or organizations, fearing reprisals.

Foreign Minister Mohamed Saleh Dembri told the press in June that international human rights organizations were welcome to visit. In September, Amnesty International carried out a mission. But the International Committee of the Red Cross continued to be prevented from visiting administrative detainees in desert camps.

The Role of the International Community

U.S. Policy

During 1994, the United States continued to support the Algerian government through large commodity credit and loan guarantee programs. On the critical issue of debt relief, the U.S. went along with efforts to ease the government's crippling short-term obligations. Although the Clinton administration kept a certain distance from the regime, and State Department officials spoke frankly about human rights abuses, there was no effort to link U.S. credits, loan guarantees, or support for debt relief to a commitment by the government of Algeria to curtail rights abuses.

The U.S. has no direct assistance programs for Algeria, other than a $50,000 International Military Education Training grant. No senior U.S. official publicly traveled to Algeria during 1994. No public displays of warm relations accompanied visits to the State Department by Algeria's foreign minister.

The main U.S. programs benefiting Algeria are Department of Agriculture loan guarantees, via the Commodity Credit Corporation (CCC), to purchase U.S. farm products; and Export-Import guarantees for private bank loans to U.S. firms doing business in Algeria. Algeria is one of the largest customers of the CCC, receiving $550 million in credits during 1994.

The U.S. also supported World Bank loans to Algeria as well as debt relief provided by the International Monetary Fund as part of a structural adjustment program.

Despite prodding from France to become more involved, the Clinton administration viewed the Algeria crisis as of secondary importance in the Middle East, far behind developments in the Arab-Israeli conflict and the Persian Gulf.

Expressions of concern over the political situation in Algeria focused on the need to broaden political participation. Washington took a more nuanced view of the Islamist opposition than did Paris, attempting to distinguish between groups that favored the targeting of civilians and those that did not.

President Clinton made one of his rare public comments on Algeria at the G-7 conference of Western leaders in July. The U.S., he said, "supports the Algerian government in its attempts to halt terrorism...and hopes still to help it find a way to take into consideration legitimate opposition forces, so that a democracy, or at least a functioning government can exist in order to reduce the level of violence and destruction."

The section on Algeria in the State Department's *Country Reports on Human Rights Practices for 1993* surveys the range of governmental and opposition abuses, although its cautious tone bespeaks the difficulty that Embassy staff faced in collecting first-hand information. State Department officials used appearances before Congress as occasions to reiterate the concerns expressed in the *Country Reports*. On March 22, Acting Assistant Secretary for Near Eastern Affairs Mark R. Parris, filling in for Assistant Secretary Robert H. Pelletreau, raised allegations of torture in testimony before the House, along with concerns about administrative detentions and the Special Courts.

Pelletreau spoke forcefully in testimony before the House on September 28. He began by urging Islamist political figures to dissociate themselves from violence. "At the same time," he said, "excesses by government security forces, in their efforts to contain the insurgency, continue. We are disturbed by reports of extra-judicial killings, torture, [and] detention without trial."

Although unwilling to impose any form of financial penalty on Algeria for its record of gross abuses, the U.S. has made its dissatisfaction known on human rights.

French Policy

France actively supported the Algerian regime by extending financial credits and lobbying creditors to ease that nation's crushing debt burden. While the government claimed that these steps were aimed at benefiting "the people, and not this or that government," in the words of Minister of European Affairs Alain Lamassoure in December 1993, French policy bespoke a clear determination to bolster the regime against the insurgents. This translated into a double standard on human rights.

The French government pursued a policy based on the assumption that an Islamist victory would, as Foreign Minister Alain Juppé put it on April 15, mean "the arrival of an extremist regime, anti-France, anti-European, anti-West...[that] would threaten the balance throughout the region." Juppé made clear that this description applied to the FIS. Foremost among French concerns were that an Islamist victory would destablize North Africa and provoke a wave of refugees to France.

France's generous support for Algeria gave it standing, if it had chosen to use it, to press for an end to abuses committed by government forces, despite the sensitivities surrounding relations between Algeria and its former colonizer. France is Algeria's leading public creditor, having provided it with credits for purchases totalling $1.2 billion in 1993 and again in 1994. Algeria is the third leading beneficiary of credit guarantees furnished by France's state export credit agency, COFACE. France was also the key player in mobilizing the European Union and the Paris Club grouping of creditor nations to provide Algeria with desperately needed debt relief, following Algeria's signing in April of a standby agreement with the International Monetary Fund.

France was always quick to condemn the violence committed by armed opposition groups, especially when French citizens were targeted. It responded also by detaining suspected Islamist activists in France, expelling some of them and banning several militant Islamist publications. But French officials only rarely, and in a passing manner, called attention to the gross violations committed by the Algerian government, despite growing evidence that security forces were engaging in reprisal killings and systematic torture. Never was a suggestion made, at least publicly, that French aid and advocacy on behalf of Algeria should be linked to the government making efforts to curtail human rights abuses.

France did grow sensitive, however, to criticism that its policy was one-sided. On August 11, Foreign Minister Juppé declared, "What right do observers have to accuse France of unconditionally supporting the Algerian authorities?" France, he pointed out, had been saying all along that "the solution to the Algerian situation cannot be an exclusively security one. It must include a political dimension....When conditions permit, the Algerian people must be able to express themselves."

But in the context of active French support for aid to Algeria at a time of worsening human rights abuses, these kinds of mild statements did not dispel the impression that France was unwilling to speak out on the human rights record of the regime, or to link continued French support to improvements.

The Work of
Human Rights Watch/Middle East

Human Rights Watch/Middle East pursued three principal objectives. First, it condemned the killing of civilians and of persons in custody committed by Islamist groups. It urged FIS leaders to condemn publicly and unequivocally these attacks, and to do everything within their power to halt these violations of basic humanitarian norms.

Second, Human Rights Watch/Middle East sought to complement the widely disseminated reports on killings by Islamist groups with information about the grave abuses committed by government forces.

Finally, Human Rights Watch/Middle East urged Algeria's creditors to use the process of deliberation over loans, credits, and debt relief for Algeria as a forum for raising the government's dismal human rights record.

In January, Human Rights Watch/ Middle East released in Paris *Human Rights Abuses in Algeria: No One is Spared.* The report focused on Special Court trials, restrictions on the media, the killing of civilians by opposition groups, and the need for a more active human rights policy toward Algeria on the part of Western nations. The report, which was well covered by the French media, was sent, with cover letters, to European foreign ministries, E.U. and French parliamentarians, and international lending institutions.

Human Rights Watch/Middle East continued the advocacy in February, when it urged E.U. foreign ministers meeting with their Algerian counterpart to link aid to a commitment from Algeria to curb human rights violations.

Human Rights Watch/Middle East briefed journalists on Algeria, and urged them to keep pressing FIS spokesmen in exile on that party's views on the violence being carried out by Islamists. Apparently in response to this pressure, FIS spokespersons in exile made increasing, though still inadequate, efforts to condemn attacks on civilians.

EGYPT

Human Rights Developments

Egypt faced continued political violence and a deteriorating human rights situation in 1994. Military wings of underground Islamist opposition groups carried out acts of violence against members of security forces, Egyptian civilians, and foreigners. The security apparatus committed abuses with impunity. Increasingly, deadly force was used in encounters with suspected militants, and in some cases it appeared that security forces may have carried out extrajudicial executions.

In other developments, lawyers and journalists were detained, and human rights monitors harassed. There was no visible progress in the official investigation of the suspicious death in custody in April of thirty-year-old lawyer Abdel Harith Madani. Military courts handed down death sentences to civilians convicted of security offenses, and executions were carried out swiftly. Peaceful protests were forcibly, and sometimes violently, dispersed by riot police.

The country has been ruled under emergency law since October 1981. In April, the state of emergency was extended until May 31, 1997, and Prime Minister 'Atif Sidqi cited political violence as the justification: "There is a need to maintain the state of emergency in view of the regrettable terrorist acts in the country, including attacks on tourists, assassination of officials, bombing of banks, and the treacherous killing of innocent civilians, police officers and police commanders." Such violence was indeed a reason for concern in 1994.

With utter disregard for the minimum standards set forth in international humanitarian law, the Islamic Group—the clandestine militant organization that advocates the creation of an Islamic state in Egypt—continued to target civilians for murder. On September 27, two Egyptians and a German tourist were killed in the Red Sea resort of Hurghada, when gunmen opened fire with automatic weapons in a busy marketplace. The Islamic Group took responsibility, stating that the attack by one of its military brigades represented "the opening of a new front against the Egyptian regime." It warned "foreigners, especially tourists, not to come to Egypt in the immediate future." The group issued claims of responsibility for other actions during the year, such as attacks on cruise boats, trains and other vehicles, which caused the death and injury of both Egyptians and foreigners. On October 14, eighty-three-year-old Nobel laureate Naguib Mahfouz was stabbed by an assailant in Cairo. Although no organization claimed responsibility for this attack, clerical censorship of Mahfouz's novel *The Sons of Gaballawi*—banned since 1959 because Egypt's Muslim religious authorities continue to deem the work blasphemous—made the writer a target for Islamist extremists. In 1989, Sheikh Omar Abdel Rahman—the spiritual leader of the Islamic Group now awaiting trial in the U.S. on a twenty-count conspiracy indictment involving the bombing of the World Trade Center and plans for other acts of violence—declared that Mahfouz should be killed unless he repented for writing the book.

Members of the Christian minority also continued to fall victim to apparent political violence. On March 11, two Coptic priests and three Egyptians were killed when gunmen opened fire at the gates of the historic Muharraq monastery, north of Assyut in Upper (southern) Egypt. Police officials blamed Islamist extremists, although no organization claimed responsibility (which is typical when Christians have been targeted and killed in Egypt). Father Bakhmious, a priest at the monastery, told the Egyptian weekly *Rose al-Youssef* that one week prior to the incident police had been alerted that an anonymous telephone caller warned the abbot of an attack. Father Bakhmious said that increased security measures were not taken, noting that protection had only been provided to tourists who visited the monastery. Christians have long complained about the inaction of police and security forces in the face of threats, intimidation and violence.

Human Rights Watch/Middle East condemns such acts of violence in the strongest terms. The deliberate targeting of civilians violates one of the basic principles of international humanitarian law, which prohibits indiscriminate attacks against the civilian population. But human rights abuses by one party in a situation of internal unrest, no matter how egregious, can never be used to justify violations by another party. Acts of murder and attempted murder by armed opposition groups do not give the Mubarak government a license to abandon the human rights standards that it has pledged to uphold under Egyptian and international law.

Egyptian security forces, particularly

State Security Investigation (SSI), the internal-security agency attached to the Ministry of Interior, continued to operate in a lawless manner, with arbitrary arrest, incommunicado detention, and torture of suspects during interrogation the norm. These forces did not stop the practice of intimidating and detaining the relatives—including women. children and the elderly—of Islamist militants wanted by authorities on suspicion of carrying out violence. Threats and detention were also used to intimidate those with information about gross human rights abuses, and to discourage relatives of victims of abuse from pursuing complaints or speaking to the media and investigators from human rights organizations. The intended effect of these tactics was often achieved. In June and July. Human Rights Watch/Middle East representatives witnessed the overwhelming sense of fear—and in some cases, terror—that gripped family members in Upper (southern) Egypt. ensuring their silence or refusal to speak on the record.

The continuing practice of incommunicado detention provides security forces with a virtual blank check to torture suspects with impunity to extract confessions and information. Prosecutors have systematically failed to investigate vigorously the allegations of torture of suspected Islamist militants and to bring charges against SSI officers. The death in custody of thirty-year-old Islamist defense lawyer Abdel Harith Madani in April focused attention on the practice of torture in Egypt. Actions by authorities following Madani's death, including the detention and intimidation of members of his family, only raised additional suspicions of a government cover-up. The lack of progress to date in the official investigation of the death, which Prosecutor General Raga'a el-Arabi conceded in May was "criminal," is further proof that senior Egyptian officials lack the political will to identify and hold accountable security forces personnel who order and carry out acts of torture.

On the night of April 26, Madani was taken from his Cairo law office by SSI officers, following a two-hour search of the pre-

mises. The next day, Madani was dead, but, inexplicably, authorities did not notify the family until the morning of May 7, over one week later. Human Rights Watch/Middle East learned that while attorneys from the powerful Cairo Bar Association were negotiating with Prosecutor General el-Arabi on May 7-8 for a second autopsy by independent forensic pathologists (to ascertain Madani's cause of death, believed to be from torture) security forces were pressuring members of the Madani family in Cairo to accept custody of the body quickly and bury it. An uncle and two cousins were detained on May 7 at the Waraq police station, released, then re-detained in the evening, held for several hours. and again released. "They were told that if they would not accept the body, it would be buried in an unknown place," a lawyer in close contact with the family told Human Rights Watch/Middle East. On May 8. one of the cousins was arrested again, held for six hours, and subjected to what one lawyer described as "severe pressure." The cousin then informed the bar association that the family had decided to take the body. "He would not say what the pressures were," the lawyer said, "but he asked us to understand [his position]."

The body, delivered to the family in a sealed coffin, was brought under police guard to Madani's home village of Mat'ana in Upper Egypt. Following the burial, security forces guarded the grave and placed family members in the village under surveillance. Local security operatives used intimidation and threats to discourage relatives from speaking with international human rights monitors and foreign journalists in June and July.

Minister of Interior Hassan el-Alfi claimed on May 14 that Madani died in custody from a fatal asthma attack, although family members and close friends told Human Rights Watch/Middle East that the young lawyer had been in excellent health and suffered from no particular ailments. The official autopsy report has not yet been made public. although Cairo Bar Association head Abdel Aziz Muhammed told the press on June 28 that Egyptian Bar Association chairman Ahmad al-Khawajah had learned from authorities that the post-mortem examination of Madani's body by state doctors documented "seventeen injury marks." Additional information was not provided, and lawyers and human rights groups were unable to obtain authorization for a second independent autopsy.

Since 1990, security forces have been accused of carrying out summary executions of suspected militants, including Dr. Alaa Mohei al-Din, the spokesperson for the Islamic Group who was shot and killed in Cairo in September 1990 under suspicious circumstances. Beginning in February 1994, a series of operations by security forces generated charges that the Ministry of Interior had embarked upon a policy of "shoot-to-kill" in retaliation for its own heavy losses in the ongoing battle with armed militants. In February alone, two separate raids in Cairo left ten suspected "terrorists" dead. At least three of the victims were summarily executed, according to eyewitnesses. Also in February, six suspected militants were killed in one operation in Upper Egypt; local lawyers claim that three of them were in custody at the time, brought to the scene, and summarily executed.

On February 14, three men were shot dead in the Zeinhom section of Cairo in what the government Middle East News Agency (MENA) described as "a good preemptive strike" by security forces against terrorists. But the testimony of neighborhood residents suggested that the men may have been victims of extrajudicial execution. Residents told investigators from the Egyptian Organization for Human Rights (EOHR) that they first heard screams and then saw a large number of men in plainclothes holding four people. Three of the four were moved into a truck, and the residents then heard shooting coming from inside the vehicle. "According to eyewitnesses," EOHR reported on February 20, "the bodies of the victims were moved out on to the street where a machinegun and some bombs were placed beside the bodies."

Local lawyers told Human Rights Watch/Middle East that three persons in custody had been summarily executed on March 21, when six suspected Islamist militants—three of them teenagers—were shot to death in a cemetery during a dawn raid in Balayza village west of Abu Tig in Upper Egypt. The killings occurred several hours after five policemen, including two high-ranking officers, died in an ambush by the Islamic Group near Abu Tig. The semiofficial government daily al-Ahram described the Balayza killings as an immediate act of revenge for the deaths of the five policemen: "Before the blood of the martyrs, the innocent victims of blind terrorism, had turned cold, swift retribution was delivered on the vampires of darkness." Such language lends support to theories that security forces have summarily executed suspects already in detention to avenge the killings of fellow officers.

The father of Muhammed Ra'fit Tawfiq al-Naqrashi, one of the Balayza victims, claimed that his son had been in custody at the Abu Tig police station prior to his death, and that he had visited him there. The father provided this information to the local prosecutor, who neglected to include it in his report about the killings, according to EOHR. One SSI officer—believed by local residents to have been involved in the killings—later prevented an EOHR investigator from discussing the case with family members and the prosecutor.

The police explained to EOHR that al-Naqrashi and two other detainees, also victims, had revealed that armed members of the Islamic Group were in the area and that the detainees accompanied security forces to the hiding place. A gunbattle erupted, according to the police version, and the three detainees and three other suspected militants were killed. It remains to be explained by authorities how detainees in custody of the heavily armed police force that approached the hideout could have been so poorly protected and killed.

Civilians accused of involvement in violent security offenses continued to be tried by three-judge Supreme Military Courts.

The courts' lack of independence and due process flaws, including the absence of the right to appeal verdicts to a higher tribunal in violation of international fair trial standards, were exacerbated by defendants' allegations of torture and sentences of capital punishment. As of November 9, 1994, fifty-eight death sentences had been handed down since President Hosni Mubarak began to move cases to the military courts in October 1992. Forty-one of the condemned men had been put to death, the largest number of executions in recent Egyptian history.

Continuing the pattern of surveillance, harassment, and detention of Egyptian lawyers who support the Islamist political trend, attorneys who represented militants before the military courts were themselves detained in 1994. Montasser al-Zayyat, a leading defense attorney who has been outspoken in his criticism of torture and other abuses against Islamists and their families, has been detained since May 17. He is under investigation by the state security prosecutor for membership in an illegal organization seeking to undermine the constitution, spreading false information against the interests of the state, and having contact with terrorists. According to EOHR and lawyers interviewed by Human Rights Watch/Middle East, the prosecutor's questioning of Zayyat is based solely upon his home and office telephone conversations with clients, Egyptian and foreign journalists, and human rights organizations, that were recorded by authorities since June 6, 1993. One lawyer who attended the early investigation sessions told Human Rights Watch/Middle East in July that prosecutors were concerned about Zayyat's "meetings with the media, communicating with international and local human rights organizations, and his speeches in defense of political cases." On October 4, Zayyat's detention was extended for forty-five days.

On September 18, lawyers Ibrahim Nasr and Hussein Gaber, who had managed Zayyat's Cairo law office since his arrest, were detained. They were accused by the state security prosecutor of having contact with fugitive Tharwat Salah Shehata.

(Shehata, along with three others, was condemned to death *in absentia* by the Supreme Military Court in Cairo on March 17 for involvement in the attempted assassination of Prime Minister Sidqi in November 1993. An additional five defendants, all of them in custody, were sentenced to death in the same trial and hanged on May 3.) After Nasr's arrest, he was first held at SSI headquarters in Cairo and interrogated. When he was seen by lawyers who attended his session with the prosecutor on October 1, there were obvious blindfold marks on his face and he looked weak. Nasr informed the prosecutor that he had been tortured, but was not examined by state forensic medical doctors until November 1.

The government continued to backslide on freedom of expression. State security prosecutors in 1994 detained journalists and editors from the opposition press and questioned them about articles that were critical of the government. In one controversial case, journalist Abdel Sattar Abu Hussein, a writer on military affairs for *al-Sha'b*, the twice-weekly newspaper of the opposition Labor Party, who reported on alleged corruption involving the Egyptian military, was tried before a military court and sentenced to one year in prison with hard labor on April 30. He was convicted of "publishing news related to the armed forces without prior permission," the government news agency MENA reported. The "news" in this case concerned Egypt's joint military exercises with other countries; the story was confirmed by the Ministry of Defense and published in two semi-official Egyptian newspapers less than two weeks after Abu Hussein's piece appeared in June 1993. The journalist's prison term was later reduced to three months.

During the year authorities prevented students, political activists, lawyers, and workers and their families from exercising the right to peaceful assembly. In March, following the massacre of Palestinians at the mosque in Hebron, Egyptian authorities deployed riot police to break up protest demonstrations. On May 17, security forces blocked hundreds of attorneys who had assembled at the headquarters of the bar association in Cairo from marching peacefully to the presidential palace to protest the death in detention of Abdel Harith Madani. Twenty-seven lawyers were arrested; the next day, another ten lawyers, including three officers of the Cairo Bar Association, were detained and charged with inciting the demonstration. On October 2, four people were killed and dozens injured in the industrial city of Kafr el-Dawwar in the Nile Delta, where some of the 23,000 workers at the huge, state-owned textile factory had days earlier begun a peaceful sit-in to protest unfair actions by management. Anti-riot forces were deployed around the factory and in the adjacent residential quarters on September 30. Security forces on October 2 attempted to disperse relatives who had gathered near the factory and to prevent them from bringing food to the workers. Tensions escalated, and police fired tear gas, rubber bullets and buckshot into the factory and at the crowds, and then stormed a nearby residential area. "A large amount of buckshot was fired indiscriminately," EOHR reported on October 6. It later documented nine cases—including that of an eleven-year-old girl—of serious injury from buckshot in one or both eyes. After the violence, over seventy workers and their relatives were arrested.

The Right to Monitor

Egyptian authorities tolerated—but sometimes interfered with—the activities of locally based and international human rights organizations. EOHR continues to operate without official legal status and thus remains subject to arbitrary closure at any time. In October, the Ministry of Interior banned the Egyptian branch of Amnesty International from holding two days of scheduled meetings in Cairo.

Senior government officials continue to deny that the state commits human rights violations, and have accused rights monitors of harming Egypt's image and providing moral support to "terrorists." Interior Minister el-Alfi stated that "calls for the protection of human rights are out of place in Egypt" and "that those who make such calls are encouraged by foreign quarters," MENA reported on June 13. EOHR officials have expressed concern about an overly broad provision in the penal code, Article 80(d), which specifies prison terms of up to five years for any Egyptian who has intentionally published or written information, news, reports or "malicious rumors" concerning the internal conditions of the country that could weaken Egypt's financial stability, reputation or image. The same penalties apply to anyone who in any way has undertaken any activity that harms Egypt's interests. EOHR had been warned through informal official channels that authorities could use these provisions against the organization.

Over the last year, state security agents interfered with the work of EOHR investigators in Upper Egypt, and twice in Cairo took action to block the dissemination of its reports. EOHR reported in December 1993 that SSI had pressured several printing houses to obstruct the timely publication of its report *A Crime Without Punishment: Torture in Egypt*. At one company, SSI officers remained on the premises to prevent the book from being printed. The report was eventually published, although SSI blocked a second report in 1994. EOHR reported in September that security authorities had orally informed publishers Akhbar al-Youm and al-Akhbar that the organization's report on human rights conditions in Egypt in 1993—a paperback book released at a press conference in Cairo in July 1994—could not be distributed and sold inside the country. The same publishers had distributed two earlier EOHR reports on human rights. In another serious development, the Ministry of Interior banned two meetings scheduled for October 28-29 in Cairo by the Egyptian branch of Amnesty International, which comprises some 300 members organized in over thirty local groups. The Ministry of Interior told the branch's secretary general that the reason for the action was the group's lack of official legal status.

For the second consecutive year, the

movements of Human Rights Watch/Middle East representatives were closely monitored by security forces in Upper Egypt. In June, continuous surveillance by agents in plainclothes—on foot and on the roads in a variety of unmarked vehicles—hampered the delegation's ability to interview families and lawyers and collect information about alleged abuses. Human Rights Watch/Middle East was forced to curb its activities and contacts so as not to place unprotected individuals at risk of harassment or other punitive actions by security forces. On June 23, Human Rights Watch/Middle East sent a letter of protest to President Mubarak about the surveillance, and provided details in a memorandum delivered on June 29 to the Ministry of Interior. On July 8, SSI officers in Mallawi, north of Assyut, attempted to detain for questioning the Egyptian interpreter accompanying Human Rights Watch/Middle East in Upper Egypt. This incident occurred immediately after the delegation had watched armed plainclothes and uniformed security forces raid a mosque used by the Islamic Group, remove a large quantity of materials from the building, and cart it away in waiting vehicles.

In July, the Ministry of Foreign Affairs refused to provide Human Rights Watch/Middle East representatives access to senior government officials in Cairo, despite repeated written requests for such meetings since May. The ministry also did not permit visits to prisons; requests had been made to inspect the new maximum-security facility (known as *al-Aqrab*, or the scorpion) opened in May 1993 in the Tora prison complex near Cairo, where conditions and treatment were said to be appalling. Prison authorities had banned all visits by families and lawyers since December 1993, despite an April 1994 ruling by the administrative court that found the open-ended ban on visits unjustifiable.

U.S. Policy

Despite persistent patterns of human rights abuse, Egypt remains the recipient of the second-largest package of U.S. military and economic assistance in the world, after Is-rael. The Mubarak government's reliance on annual U.S. aid of $1.3 billion, from the Foreign Military Financing Program, and $814 million in Economic Support Funds offers enormous potential for the Clinton administration to press for specific human rights improvements, such as low-cost steps to prevent incommunicado detention and demonstrable progress on official investigations of suspicious deaths in custody. But other foreign policy considerations continue to override human rights and—to the best of Human Rights Watch/Middle East's knowledge—no measurable performance criteria have been laid down for Egyptian authorities.

"Egypt needs and deserves our continuing support," Assistant Secretary of State for Near Eastern Affairs Robert H. Pelletreau, the former U.S. Ambassador to Egypt, told the Middle East subcommittee of the House Foreign Affairs Committee on March 1, emphasizing the Mubarak government's domestic problems and its backing of U.S. foreign policy. "Despite difficult economic problems at home and an ongoing confrontation with Islamic extremists, President Mubarak has been immensely helpful in advancing the [Arab-Israeli] peace process. He has also supported enhancement of stability in the gulf and has rigorously enforced international sanctions against Iraq and Libya."

National security advisor Anthony Lake noted in an article in *The Washington Post* on July 24 that "the stability of friendly Arab countries" is in U.S. interests. Citing "Islamic extremism" as a threat to the future of the Middle East, Lake put forth the case for a lead U.S. role in "helping to form a community of like-minded regional states that share our goals of free markets, broad democratic values and controls on proliferation of weapons of mass destruction." With one important exception, Clinton administration officials maintained a conspicuous silence over the last year about the long-term threat to Egypt's stability posed by the deteriorating human rights situation, and did little to stress publicly the incompatibility of democratic values with continued erosion of the rule of law.

In December 1993, Assistant Secretary of State for Democracy, Human Rights, and Labor John Shattuck visited Egypt for three days. At a press conference in Cairo on December 4, Secretary Shattuck criticized the Mubarak government's performance. "[T]here is evidence of torture, some extrajudicial killings, incommunicado detentions and some constraints on freedom of expression," he said, adding that "violations of human rights are neither lawful nor effective in combatting political violence." He refrained, however, from linking the continued practice of torture either to high-level established policy or to the consistent failure of authorities to investigate torture complaints made by security detainees and to prosecute the officers responsible for abuses. Instead, he stated that the office of the public prosecutor gave him "a strong commitment that all allegations of torture would be fully investigated and that appropriate action will be taken."

Secretary Shattuck should have known that the proffered commitment carried no special significance; similar assurances have been offered in the past, with no discernible effect, as the Clinton Administration itself has recognized. Two months after Secretary Shattuck's comment, the State Department's *Country Reports on Human rights Practices for 1993* stated—accurately—that torture is systematically practiced by police and security forces in Egypt, and that "the Government does not adequately investigate torture complaints in cases involving detainees in political or religious cases. There is no public record that offending officers in such cases are punished, thus suggesting that the Government tacitly condones the mistreatment of those it considers to be opponents." Commendably, Secretary Shattuck did meet with EOHR during his mission, and at the press conference publicly acknowledged the importance of the role of EOHR and other nongovernmental organizations in Egyptian civil society.

The Work of
Human Rights Watch/Middle East

Initiatives on Egypt during the year were guided by three objectives: to support and publicize the work of Egyptian human rights organizations; to monitor and report on state policies and practices that have an impact on human rights and the rule of law; and to communicate concerns to Egyptian government officials, the media, and policymakers in the U.S. and the European Union.

Human Rights Watch/Middle East protested and publicized the harassment of EOHR (December 1993 and September 1994); possible excessive use of lethal force by security forces (March); detention of lawyers without charge or trial (April); the death in custody of Abdel Harith Madani (May); the lack of information about investigations of deaths in detention from 1991 to 1993 (May); violations of freedom of expression (September); and the torture and detention of children (October). Of seven letters of protest sent by Human Rights Watch/Middle East to various Egyptian government officials between March and October, not one was acknowledged in writing.

In June and July, Human Rights Watch/Middle East conducted a four-week fact-finding mission to examine security forces practices, Madani's death in detention, and the crackdown on lawyers. On June 14, during this mission, SSI arrested five defense and human rights lawyers in Cairo. Human Rights Watch/Middle East representatives collected information and issued a press release the following day. Citing the state's continuing attempts to harass and intimidate lawyers, Human Rights Watch/Middle East called on President Mubarak to release immediately all lawyers detained or charged for the exercise of their right to free expression and free association. On July 5, the prosecutor general ordered the five lawyers released.

Human Rights Watch/Middle East issued reports about the intimidation and detention of family members by security forces, and violations of freedom of religious belief and expression of the Christian minority.

IRAN

Human Rights Developments

The human rights situation in Iran showed no improvement in 1994. A picture emerged of new obstacles to the rule of law, a marked worsening in the situation of religious minorities, heightened enforcement of intrusive restrictions on every day life, limitations on basic freedoms of expression, thought, opinion and the press, and discrimination against women. The government generally excluded independent human rights monitors.

The cumulative effect of the erosion of human rights in Iran was reflected in March in a resolution of the U.N. Commission on Human Rights condemning Iran's violations of human rights. Its wording was strong, particularly with reference to Iran's failure, for the third consecutive year, to grant access to the U.N. Special Representative on the Human Rights Situation in Iran. The resolution expressed "deep concern at the high number of executions, cases of torture and cruel, inhuman or degrading treatment and punishment."

In August 1994 the U.N. Sub-Commission on Prevention of Discrimination and Protection of Minorities denounced widespread violations of human rights by the Iranian government including "arbitrary and summary executions, arbitrary arrests and imprisonment, unexplained disappearances, the absence of guarantees essential for the protection of the right to a fair trial." The Sub-Commission regretted the refusal of the Iranian government to implement existing agreements for delegates of the International Committee of the Red Cross (ICRC) to visit Iranian prisons.

In a population of sixty-two million, Iran's religious minorities include 3.5 million Sunni Muslims, 350,000 followers of the Bahai faith, 80,000 Christians and 30,000 Jews. Tens of thousands of Christians, Jews and Bahais have fled Iran in the past fifteen years. During 1994 the government mounted a fierce campaign against the small Christian minority. Churches have been shut down, scores of young Christians—many of them converts from Islam—have been imprisoned and tortured, especially in the cities of Gorgan and Kermanshah. Three leading Evangelical Christians were killed in suspicious circumstances. In January, Bishop Haik Hovasepian Mehr, who had come to international prominence leading a campaign for the release of Pastor Mehdi Dibaj, was murdered. Mehdi Dibaj, who converted from Islam to Christianity about forty-five years ago, had been imprisoned in Sari, northeastern Iran, from 1983 to 1994. In late June, another evangelical minister, Tateos Michaelian was shot and killed. He was acting chair of the Council of Protestant Ministers in Iran, a post he assumed following the murder of Bishop Hovasepian Mehr. Pastor Mehdi Dibaj was killed a week later in early July.

There was no evidence of a thorough official investigation into the killings, and Christian sources held the government responsible for the deaths. Iranian officials claim that evangelical churches have political agendas besides worship.

There was also no let up in the persecution of the Bahai minority, which is not recognized as a religion under the Constitution of the Islamic Republic and is referred to as a heretical sect.

In February a judge released two Muslims who had killed a Bahai citing a religious authority to the effect that Bahai blood may be shed with impunity. The judge based his ruling on the late Ayatollah Khomeini's *fatwa* (edict) that a Muslim will not be killed for killing an apostate.

According to Amnesty International, Haji Mohammad Ziaie, a Sunni Muslim leader from Bandar-Abbas, known to be critical of government policies, was found dead in suspicious circumstances in July. He had been summoned for interrogation by security forces in Laar, Fars province on July 15, and he was never been seen alive again.

These incidents appear to illustrate the growing strength of militant forces within the Islamic leadership. The persecution of religious minorities, which received widespread media attention in the West, worked directly against the interests of others in the government who had hoped to normalize relations with the West.

One of the few remaining public voices of dissent in Iran appeared to have been silenced with the detention in Tehran in March of Ali Akbar Saidi-Sirjani. His associate, Mohammad Sadeq Said, a poet, whose pen-name is Niazi-Kermani, was also arrested. The arrest of Saidi-Sirjani, a prolific writer, further narrowed the scope of expression in the Islamic Republic.

Since 1989, the authorities have imposed a complete ban on all of Saidi-Sirjani's seventeen volumes of essays and social commentary. The writer responded to this muzzling by circulating open letters to the authorities, courageously denouncing censorship and the lack of freedom in Iran.

A month after his arrest the authorities produced an alleged confession they attributed to Saidi-Sirjani, of a wide range of crimes "conspiring to defame the Islamic regime and its founders." He also purported to have confessed to being a homosexual (a criminal offense in Iran punishable by death), as well as to gambling, drinking, and smoking opium. At the end of the year Mr. Saidi-Sirjani's status was unclear.

Iran's news media, too, suffered strict controls and editors and journalists faced arbitrary arrest and imprisonment. For example, in April, Abbas Abdi, edito- in-chief of the newspaper *Salam*, and a frequent critic of President Rafsanjani's policies, was released after serving ten months of a one year sentence on payment of a bond.

In June, the Press Council, a government appointed body, announced the withdrawal of the right of publication of a magazine, *Havades*, which it deemed "obscene and empty."

In an episode that has chilled freedom of expression worldwide, Salman Rushdie and all associated with the publication and translation of his novel, *The Satanic Verses*, remained under the express threat of assassination on the authority of the Iranian state. In June, Ayatollah Meshkini—head of the eighty-two member Assembly of Experts, which appoints the leader—endorsed the principle that one *fatwa* (edict) can be challenged by another, thus opening the door for Ayatollah Khamenei to revoke the death sentence on Rushdie. In a public sermon, Ayatollah Meshkini said "if even a religious leader issues a fatwa, and [the current leader] issues a ruling, the latter takes precedence." Yet Khamenei, despite his title as Iran's supreme spiritual leader, remains a junior religious figure relative to Khomeini. For conservative Muslims, any countervailing fatwa he may issue on the Rushdie case would be unlikely to gain mass support. In addition President Rafsanjani in his interview with *Le Figaro*, in September, said "there is no question of pardon in Rushdie's case, because the fatwa was pronounced against him. One cannot reverse this. It is not in the interests of the West to protect someone who has insulted a billion Muslims."

A bill on banning the use of television satellite reception equipment passed through the parliament in September, but is not yet law. Before the bill passed, the Head of the Judiciary announced that judges may order the removal of satellite dishes in order to halt the spread of "corruption." Ayatollah Yazdi justified the immediate removal of the offending dishes by saying that "in the view of Islamic judges, satellite programs come under the category of spreading corruption." Yazdi's opinion appeared to short-circuit the parliamentary process, and opened the door for the security forces to enter houses by force to remove dishes with no basis in law for these actions.

There were conflicting signals for women in Iran, and increasing arbitrary harassment. In December 1993, the government lifted all restrictions on what women can study in the nation's universities. On the other hand, single women were still banned from traveling abroad to study.

In April parliament ratified a bill concerning the selection of judges enabling qualified women to work as assessors in administrative tribunals, and in other low-level judicial positions. This was the first time since 1979 that women were permitted by law to work as judges of any kind.

Such small advances for women had to be weighed against a constant barrage of arbitrary restrictions. For example, in June the police issued a statement condemning women's smiles as something which could arouse corruption in men. In September, the daily newspaper *Jomhuri-e-Islami* reported on a meeting of officials in which the Minister of the Interior had called for no toleration of non-compliance with the Islamic dress code (*Bad Hejabe*). He also condemned women who ride motorcycles with men as disrespectful of Islamic principles.

Public discontent over economic and other conditions led to riots in Iranian cities. Serious public demonstrations, leading to violent confrontations between demonstrators and the security forces, took place in Tehran, Zahedan, Qom, Qazvin, Tabriz, Najafabad and many other cities.

In March, people in Tehran clashed with security forces who had been ordered to suppress all public manifestations of the traditional "fire-day" observances which mark the Iranian new year. Leader of the Islamic Republic, Ayatollah Khamenei, condemned such manifestations as "atheist celebrations." According to journalist Safa Ha'eri, a secret official report recorded eleven dead and more than five hundred wounded in the clashes.

In August, in Tabriz, the capital of Iranian Azerbaijan, hundreds of angry demonstrators were arrested and some were reported killed in protests after the *Basij* (militia) attacked young women who had mixed with young men at the end of a soccer match. The government's interpretation of Islamic rules forbid social mixing of men and women.

According to *Middle East International*, Qazvin, an industrial town 150 kilometers west of the capital, was the scene of social unrest and virtual insurrection in August. After the rejection by parliament of a bill to promote the status of the surrounding district to a province, thousands of Qazvinis poured into the streets of the city to show their frustration. The peaceful demonstration deteriorated into violent confrontations as soon as non-native security forces were rushed to the scene with orders to open fire to disperse demonstrators. At least thirty people were killed, 400 wounded and over 1,000 arrested. Putting down the riot in Qazvin, turned out to be one act of repression too many for some members of Iran's army. Four generals who claimed to be speaking on behalf of the whole of the armed forces including the *Pasdaran* (Revolutionary Guards), which are generally considered more loyal to the Islamic leadership, warned the political leadership that the army could "no longer remain silent" while the country was threatened by "aggression from outside and disintegration from within."

Nevertheless, in November Associated Press reported that the parliament passed a bill authorizing law enforcement officers to shoot and kill demonstrators "to restore law and order at times of unrest."

In June a bomb explosion killed twenty-six and injured scores of other pilgrims at Iran's holiest shrine in Mashhad. This was the most shocking incident in a year of widespread social unrest, and came as yet another sign of spreading discontent. No group claimed responsibility, but in the politically charged atmosphere conspiracy theories were rampant.

Closer cooperation between the governments of Iran and Turkey, in security measures targeting opposition groups from both countries, threatened the security of thousands of Iranian refugees and asylum-seekers in Turkey. Iranians who were recognized as refugees by the office of the United Nations High Commission for Refugees (UNHCR), and some whose cases were pending, were forcibly returned by the Turkish authorities to Iran, even though many of them risked serious human rights violations in Iran. For its part, in March the Iranian government handed over four alleged members of the separatist Kurdistan Working Party (PKK) to stand trial in Turkey, where torture of political prisoners is endemic. Other

PKK supporters were attacked or harassed by the Iranian authorities.

Another group of Iranians at risk in Turkey were refugees who had been registered by UNHCR in Iraq, but who had moved to Turkey looking for better living conditions. Some of these refugees feared persecution in Iraq as Kurds or as former members of the Iranian opposition group, the People's Mojahedin Organization of Iran (PMOI), based in Iraq. UNHCR refers to such cases as "irregular movements" and encourages them to return to Iraq despite the risk of persecution there as well as in their native Iran.

Iran's Kurdish minority continued to suffer persecution inside and outside the country. In April, two villages in Iraq sheltering displaced Iranian Kurds were virtually destroyed by Iranian shelling. According to the Democratic Party of Iranian Kurdistan (PDKI), in October the Iranian government activated plans, dating from 1975, to depopulate the border region with Iraq. Inhabitants of six villages in Piranshahr region, part of Western Azerbaijan province in Iran, were ordered to evacuate. Members of Kurdish opposition groups were assassinated in attacks attributed to the Iranian government by Kurdish sources. In January Taha Kerminch, a refugee, was killed in Turkey. A leader of the PDKI was assassinated on August 4, in Baghdad.

Opponents of the Iranian government living abroad continued to fear attack by Iranian government agents active in Turkey and throughout Europe. In November, the trial began in Paris of the accused killers of former Prime Minister Shahpour Bakhtiar. The three defendants, all with links to the Iranian government, went on trial for the August 1991 murder. Despite the more than sixty murders of Iranian dissidents abroad, this is only one of the few times an assassination case has been tried. In most of the other cases the suspected assassins either escaped arrest or were permitted to return to Iran by western governments fearing reprisals against their interests or their nationals by the Iranian government.

In any country, the law, upheld by a strong impartial court system is the basis of human rights protection. After six years of discussion, a law reorganizing the court system passed the parliament in August. It is envisaged that this system will be implemented gradually within a five-year period. In places where the new General Courts (*Dadgahayeh Aam*) are established, existing structures of revolutionary courts, penal courts, and other courts will be dissolved. However, in places where the new system is not implemented, the old systems still pertain. This means that different parts of the country will have widely varying court structures; defendants accused of the same crimes will not necessarily be tried before the same type of court or enjoy the same procedural safeguards.

For example, the new law provides for the abrogation of the function of the prosecutor. In the new General Courts, the judge acts as both investigator and judge. Among the major objectives of this new law is to expedite the legal process. This means that the two-phase study of a case, first by an investigating magistrate and then by a trial judge, will be reduced to a single phase. This will shorten the time needed for cases to pass through the system at the expense of the rights of the defendant. A right of appeal to a higher court is not clearly established in the law, and in some cases it is explicitly ruled out, further contravening international fair trial standards to which Iran is a party. In support of the new law Ayatollah Yazdi, the Head of the Judiciary, asserted that giving powers of investigation to the judge is more consistent with Islamic Law.

Another special characteristic of the new law is that power over the judiciary, and the appointment of judges in particular, is concentrated in the hands of the Head of the Judiciary. No reference is made in the law to regulations governing the qualifications required by those serving as judges, thus opening the door for unqualified but compliant judges to be appointed at the discretion of the Head of the Judiciary. The concentration of such wide powers in the hands of one man works against the independence of the judiciary, and to the detriment of the rule of law.

Despite continuing efforts by the Head of the Judiciary to promote judicial reform, the workings of the judicial system continued to be capricious. Basic fair trial safeguards have long been absent, particularly in political trials, which take place before revolutionary courts. Defendants in such trials have no access to legal counsel and are held in indefinite incommunicado pre-trial detention.

In an incident that highlighted the contradictions at the heart of the task of judicial reform in a theocracy, Ayatollah Yazdi traveled to the province of Khuzestan, in May, to negotiate with local tribal leaders and government officials "to put an end to practices contrary to religious and civil law." Ayatollah Yazdi in particular drew attention to the practice of fathers who murder their own daughters but go unpunished because, under Islamic Law, they "own the blood." Ayatollah Yazdi condemned "honor crimes"—crimes committed on the pretext of defending family honor—saying, "although the Lord of the Universe has given the right to the owner of blood, he has also given the right to the government."

Incidents of corporal punishments which violate international human rights standards were also reported. According to the daily newspaper *Abrar*, in Gilan province seven thieves were punished in one day by amputation of the four fingers of their right hands in accordance with the penal code. Human Rights Watch/Middle East received reports of two cases of women stoned to death for adultery, one in Evin Prison, Tehran in February, the other in Qom in March. In May an American woman was given eighty lashes in public for alleged "prostitution."

If the Head of the Judiciary was able to reassess traditional interpretations of Islamic Law in Khuzestan, he could have acted to prevent such abusive punishments. President Rafsanjani has been quoted on a number of occasions in the international press expressing his disapproval of such practices, and in September, he told *Le Figaro*, evi-

dently in error, that the punishment of stoning no longer took place in the Islamic Republic. If the government asserts that it has a right to legislate against practices which some defend as condoned by Islamic law, such as honor crimes, then its arguments that Islam is an immutable system preventing compliance with international norms lose consistency.

The Right to Monitor

Iran remained hostile to both internal and external human rights monitors. No independent international human rights organization was given access to the country during the course of the year, and would-be Iranian monitors faced severe problems. Opposition political activity is also severely curtailed. The Freedom Movement headed by former Prime Minister Mehdi Bazargan applied for a permit as political party more than ten years ago, and still is waiting for an official response from the government. Other parties have also met with no success in achieving registration. Similarly, the Association of Writers has been unable to reopen despite public requests from leading writers. The Bar Association, was taken over by the government in 1980. Lawyers have been seeking for many years to elect a new leadership, but the government has not permitted free elections to be held.

Although parliamentary deputy Said Rajaie Khorassani was able to establish a Parliamentary Human Rights Committee, its activities have yet to show any signs of independent monitoring of, or comment on, the human rights situation.

Criticism of the government did emerge from inside Iran. For example, in May, Darioush Forouhar, the leader of the National Party of Iran, and a former minister in the Bazargan Cabinet, criticized the government and asked for democratic reform, a call that was echoed in September by prominent retired general, Azizollah Amir Rahimi. In October a group of 134 renowned writers and poets wrote an open letter to the government criticizing "anti-democratic practices" such as restrictions on freedom of expression, and harassment and persecution of writers.

The Role of the
International Community

U.S. Policy

Although U.S. officials made reference to Iran's poor human rights record with some frequency, and described it as "the world's most significant state sponsor of terrorism", bilateral trade between Iran and the United States continued to grow. U.S. law forbids the direct import of Iranian exports, including oil. However. as U.S. oil companies purchased Iranian crude oil on the international market, the volume of U.S.-Iran trade in 1994 reached $5 billion. The U.S. became Iran's chief trade partner. The Clinton administration consolidated its policy of "Dual Containment"—seeking to isolate the political influence in the region of the Baghdad and Tehran regimes. For example, President Clinton said in August, "The two key obstacles of [peace] are Iraq and Iran and the radical groups they continue to support."

Secretary of State Warren Christopher said in May, "Iran is an outlaw country, and deserves to be treated with containment and isolation." But this isolation did not extend to trade, where Christopher said the U.S. "cannot expect to end trade with them." In August Christopher blamed Iran for bombings in Argentina and London. He used the occasion to pressure Russia to hold back arms sales, and he was critical of other states that maintained close trade and financial ties with Iran.

The U.S. pressure on its allies to limit ties with Iran could be seen at the World Bank. This year, there was no World Bank loan to Iran, largely due to U.S. pressure. At the G-7 meeting in July, Russia, France and Germany joined the U.S. in condemning Iran as a "sponsor of international terrorism." These nations are four out of Iran's top five trading partners.

The European Community

European governments were more concilia-tory in their statements and actions towards the Iranian government. For example, the Swiss authorities requested the extradition of the two suspects wanted in connection with the 1990 assassination, near Geneva, of prominent opposition leader, Kazem Rajavi. but in January the French government returned the suspects to Iran.

President Francois Mitterand of France met in Paris with Iranian Deputy Foreign Minister Mahmoud Vaezi in June, his first meeting with an Iranian official since the assassination in Paris of former Prime Minister Shahpour Bakhtiar. In a move out of step with U.S. efforts to curb Iranian access to credit, France, Germany, Japan, and the Netherlands began to reschedule Iran's short and medium term debts.   There was continuing tension in the Iran-British relationship, partly because of the Rushdie affair. The British government formally complained to the Iranian government, who it also alleged had sought to hire the Irish Republican Army to carry out contract killings against targeted opposition figures in Europe.

The Work of
Human Rights Watch/Middle East

Human Rights Watch/Middle East played a leading role in reporting on the suspicious deaths of Evangelical Christian leaders. In February, it made the first of a series of requests to send observers to attend the trial of those accused of carrying out these killings, and to be kept informed of the progress of the investigations. No reply was received.

Human Rights Watch/Middle East protested on a number of occasions the imprisonment of Ali Akbar Saidi-Sirjani and sought information about his case, including the circumstances leading to his confession, and his access to legal counsel. At the end of the year Human Rights Watch/Middle East was seeking information about his current whereabouts. We received no reply.

At the invitation of the General Prosecutor, international journalists visited Tehran's Evin prison in April. Human Rights Watch/Middle East welcomed the access granted to the international press and sought permission to send a delegation to carry out a study of Iran's prison system. No reply was received.

Human Rights Watch/Middle East monitored the situation of Iranian refugees in Turkey, making a number of interventions to the Turkish government on behalf of refugees threatened with deportation. In March Human Rights Watch/Middle East presented its concerns about refugee protection in Turkey to UNHCR officials in Geneva.

Following press reports of torture and ill-treatment of prisoners by the Iranian opposition group PMOI, and the receipt of complaints from former PMOI members, in October Human Rights Watch/Middle East wrote to their leader in Iraq, requesting access to detention facilities within PMOI bases in Iraq.

Throughout the year Human Rights Watch/Middle East maintained contact with a broad range of activists, scholars, and concerned individuals inside and outside Iran. It participated in conferences on human rights issues, and gave interviews to the U.S. and international press on these and other human rights issues.

IRAQ AND IRAQI KURDISTAN

Human Rights Developments

The government of Saddam Hussein continued to rely upon police, military and intelligence agencies to control and intimidate the general populace. Pervasive violations of human rights included torture, executions and disappearances, and arbitrary detention. Through these various means of abuse, the government repressed ethnic groups and stifled freedom of expression and association.

After the Gulf War, the U.N. Security Council's Resolution 687 of April 3, 1991 required Iraq to eliminate all its weapons of mass destruction and to recognize Kuwait's sovereignty and borders. Two days later, in Resolution 688, the Security Council expressed great concern about "the repression of the Iraqi civilian population in many parts of Iraq" and called on the government to take steps to end the repression. Iraq maintained that it had fully complied with Resolution 687 and that the sanctions that limited the sale of oil and the importation of goods should be lifted.

Rolf Ekeus, the U.N. envoy in charge of dismantling and monitoring weapons systems, acknowledged that the Iraqi government had grown more cooperative and essentially complied with the provisions regarding weapons monitoring under Resolution 687. He still proposed a six month probationary period of monitoring, to begin in October 1994, before the Security Council lifts the sanctions.

Before U.N. discussions regarding the renewal of sanctions were held in October, the government sent over 50,000 troops to within twelve miles of the Kuwaiti border. Within a week, however, the Iraqi forces had largely withdrawn from their positions near Kuwait. On November 10, Hussein issued a decree accepting the "sovereignty of the State of Kuwait, its territorial integrity and political independence."

Iraq argued that sanctions violated human rights by starving its citizens. In October, Deputy Prime Minister Tariq Aziz said that the sanctions and the embargo were "a process of vengeance, a process aimed at depriving the people of Iraq...of the simplest constituents of human life." Iraq avoided widespread hunger, however, distributing monthly food rations that provided 70 percent of the average daily caloric requirements. Hyperinflation, however, made supplementing the rations difficult for many. In September, the Iraqi government announced that it was cutting the food rations in half. Iraq refused to make a one-time sale of $1.6 billion in oil, as authorized by Security Council Resolutions 706 and 712, to pay for essential civilian food and medical needs, because it rejected the U.N.'s conditions by which the expenditure would be monitored and controlled.

As the economic situation worsened, the regime employed new measures of repression to bolster its position and power. In May, Hussein assumed the Prime Minister's position. Following the formation of a new Cabinet, he appointed three deputy prime ministers (Tariq Aziz, the former Foreign Minister, Vice President Taha Yasin Ramadan, and Muhammad Hamzah al-Zubaydi). Several members of Hussein's family also received cabinet positions in a further consolidation of power.

Following the cabinet reshuffle and ostensibly in response to increasing crime, the Iraqi government issued several new decrees introducing cruel and extreme punishments said to be based on Islamic law, *Shari'a*, for a range of crimes.

First-time offenders convicted of stealing cars and other property valued over five thousand dinars (approximately $15 U.S.) are to have their right hand amputated and an "X" tattooed on their forehead. A second conviction would result in another amputation. The penalty for forging official government documents is amputation of the right hand or life imprisonment. Deserters from the military are to have their earlobes amputated and their foreheads tattooed. If a person had a weapon during the commission of a crime or a death occured during the commission of the crime, the person is liable to the death penalty. A death sentence will also be handed down if the person committing the crime is a member of the armed forces, the security service or a government employee. Conviction for smuggling Iraqi antiquities too, was made punishable by death.

Iraqi courts moved promptly to sentence people under the new decrees; an Iraqi government official told Human Rights Watch/Middle East that in the first months after their introduction several hundred convicts had suffered the amputation of limbs and earlobes and been branded. Opposition groups and fleeing soldiers estimate the number is much higher. The Iraqi government explained that these penalties were "an im-provement" upon the previous policy of executing deserters.

News reports suggested that the government enacted these punishments to relieve prison overcrowding and the costs of caring for prisoners. According to the *Times* (London), riots ensued in September to protest the ear amputations. In the southern city of Amarah, angry crowds stormed Ba'ath Party offices and cut off the ears of several Ba'ath Party officials. Moreover, the *Times* indicated that a man in Nasiriyeh later killed the doctor who performed the amputation on his hand in an incident highlighting the public's rising frustration. Iraqi doctors who opposed the amputations were warned not to protest.

The government also began a crackdown against money changers in the spring. Under a new law issued in June, conviction for currency speculation, too, carries a punishment of hand amputation. Amnesty International reported that on March 26 five money changers were executed for currency speculation at Abu Ghraib Prison outside Baghdad.

During the Iraqi occupation of Kuwait, thousands of Kuwaitis were taken as captives to Iraq. After the war, over 7,000 were repatriated, and the Hussein regime maintains that as of January 1992 all Kuwaitis held in Iraq had been released, but hundreds who have yet to be accounted for were last seen in Iraqi custody. The Kuwaiti government claims that 625 Kuwaitis are still being held by Iraq. Recent Iraqi exiles continue to report gross human rights violations at the Radwaniya military camp situated west of Baghdad. Hussein Sharastani, head of the Gulf War Victims organization, reported that Iraqi exiles fleeing to Iran charge that the Iraqi regime executed two thousand prisoners early in the year, mostly Shi'a, who have been detained since the failed 1991 uprising in southern Iraq. Sharastani said that although many of the victims were buried in mass graves, the regime delivered hundreds of bodies for family burials in the first quarter of 1994 in order to further intimidate the Shi'a. Independent confirmation could not be obtained since Iraq does not permit human rights monitoring and the few journalists who visit the country are severely restricted.

On April 12, Iraqi opposition figure Taleb al-Suheil, a leader of the London-based Free Iraqi Council and a principal actor in an attempt to oust Hussein from power last year, was assassinated in Beirut. Within hours of the assassination, Lebanese authorities arrested several diplomats from the Iraqi Embassy, two of whom allegedly confessed that the Baghdad office of *Mukhabarat,* the Iraqi foreign intelligence service, ordered the assassination. Lebanese security personnel also arrested Ali Darweesh, the Iraqi Consul, and Hadi Hassan as they attempted to board a plane to Amman. Lebanese authorities claimed Darweesh planned the assassination while Hassan actually shot al-Suheil.

On April 3, Lissy Schmidt, a German reporter and Aziz Qadar, her Kurdish bodyguard, were driving on the road between Sulemaniyeh and Penjwin in the Kurdish controlled region near the Iranian border when they were killed by gunmen with automatic weapons. Kurdish authorities arrested Zaki Said Abbas and Ismail Muhammad Mustafa. They allegedly confessed to the murder as well as other attacks against foreigners in Iraqi Kurdistan. They maintained that *Mukhabarat* had recruited them and offered them at least $3,000 for every foreigner killed. The two men also claimed that their relatives were held hostage by *Mukhabarat* until they carried out such attacks.

In two separate incidents in March and April, U.N. guards were wounded by gunfire in Iraqi Kurdistan. In March, two Swedish journalists were seriously injured in a car bomb explosion near Aqrah in northern Iraq.

Western journalists reported in June that Hussein allegedly extrajudicially executed three senior army officials in a political purge. The victims were all from the el-Douri family and had served within Hussein's circle of close advisors.

The state employs a policy of discrimination and repression against ethnic minorities; in addition to Arabs, Iraq has populations of Kurds, Turkomen, Yazidis, and Armenians. Its population is also religiously diverse. Sunni Muslims dominate the present government, despite a Shi'a Muslim majority. Moreover, there are minority communities of Assyrian and Chaldean Christians and Jews. Government policy forbids citizens from classifying themselves as members of any ethnic group except Arab or Kurd. Furthermore, in a campaign of Arabization, government demographers frequently coerced non-Kurdish people to identify themselves as Arabs. This policy was also applied to groups like the Yazidis who consider themselves Kurdish, although practicing their own religion, unlike the Kurds, who are Sunni Muslims.

Although Shi'a Muslims constitute approximately 55 percent of the Iraqi population, the ruling Baath party has generally excluded them from any role in the government. Since the Shi'a uprisings after the Gulf War, Hussein's military forces have waged an aggressive campaign against the Shi'a in southern Iraq, including the Marsh Arabs, Shi'a Muslims who have traditionally lived in the marshy area of southern Iraq. By diverting the major rivers, the government is draining the marsh region and destroying the environment that is essential to the economy and culture of the Marsh Arabs.

Among the government documents seized by Kurdish rebels after the Gulf War was a 1989 document entitled "Plan of Action for the Marshes." It declares that "security operations (such as poisoning, explosions and the burning of houses) must be conducted against the subversives." The plan further describes measures to destroy local village life. "The principle of economic blockade must be applied to the villages and areas in which subversives are operating." This blockade calls for "withdrawal of all food supply agencies;... a ban on the sale of fish;... the severest of measures against persons who smuggle foodstuffs;... [and] prohibiting goods traffic from entering those villages and areas." Lastly, the plan required the region to be drained in order to facilitate controlling the population and building roads in the area.

The government maintains that the massive marsh draining operation is actually a development project to create new agricultural land. In February, the *MacNeil/Lehrer Newshour* reported that Hussein described the operations in the marsh region firstly as an issue of national security: "[t]he opposition in our country, it was no longer a local opposition but an international opposition. It calls for it to be subject to execution and to torture. In accordance with the law, we say he who collaborates with a foreign party is sentenced to death."

The Right to Monitor

Private citizens, individually or collectively, can monitor or disseminate information about government violations of human rights only at extreme personal peril in Iraq and access to international human rights monitors is closed. Laws punish harshly those who "insult or demean" any government or Ba'ath Party institutions, subjecting them to arrest, detention, imprisonment, and even the death penalty. As a result, Iraqi human rights organizations are either located abroad or, since October 1991, operate in the Kurdish-controlled enclave.

Iraqi exiles monitor human rights developments primarily from Tehran, Damascus, and London. The Iraqi National Congress, a London-based coalition of opposition parties; the Documental Center on Human Rights in Iraq, affiliated with the Supreme Assembly of the Islamic Revolution in Iraq; the Organization for Human Rights in Iraq, a private London-based group; and Gulf War Victims, a private relief organization located in Tehran, were principal sources of information about human rights violations. The last three organizations focus on the rights of the Iraqi Shi'a. Various international human rights organizations, including Human Rights Watch/Middle East as well as the U.N. Commission on Human Rights have repeatedly called on Iraq to permit human rights monitoring to determine whether Iraq was complying with Resolu-

tion 688.

The Role of the International Community

U.S. Policy

The United States has maintained a strong stance against lifting the U.N. sanctions despite growing pressure from several countries. In March, Assistant Secretary of State for Near Eastern Affairs Robert Pelletreau told the House Foreign Affairs Committee that lifting the embargo hinged on Iraqi compliance with Security Council resolutions and not the removal of Hussein.

In October, Chief U.S. Delegate to the U.N., Ambassador Madeleine K. Albright, called for expanding the conditions for lifting of sanctions to include compliance with human rights requirements under Resolution 688. Observers noted that from both a legal and practical perspective changing compliance conditions at this late stage could discourage compliance.

The U.S. military maintained its "no-fly" zones above the 36th parallel and below the 32nd parallel. In October, the U.S. sent approximately 50,000 troops to counter the Iraqi troop buildup near the Kuwaiti border.

The Clinton administration gave periodic reports to Congress during the year on the situation in Iraq, including human rights conditions. President Clinton cited Iraq's refusal to sell oil pursuant to Resolutions 706 and 712, in arguing that Iraq bears full responsibility for the suffering of its citizens, since the income would buy food, medicine and other essential goods to meet civilian needs. President Clinton also asserted that the Hussein regime continued to repress the civilian population and to deprive them of humanitarian assistance, among other means through a total blockade of Iraqi Kurdistan and the military attack on the Marsh Arabs. He expressed concerns about Iraqi chemical weapons capabilities and highlighted Iraq's failure to cooperate in the location and release of Kuwaitis detained during the Gulf War.

In September, Central Intelligence

Agency Director James Woolsey asserted that Iraq "is still hiding Scud missiles, chemical munitions and its entire biological-weapons warfare program." He claimed that "Iraq is accelerating construction of deep underground shelters and tunnels to produce and store weapons of mass destruction."

U.N. Policy

The U.N. Human Rights Commission issued a report listing numerous human rights violations, condemning the Hussein regime for creating "an all-pervasive order of repression and oppression which is sustained by broad-based discrimination and widespread terror." Nigel Rodley, the Special Rapporteur on Torture to the Commission on Human Rights, submitted a report discussing torture and cruel or inhuman punishment which named several Iraqis who allegedly died in detention from torture.

On February 25, Special Rapporteur on Human Rights in Iraq Max Van der Stoel issued a report on the human rights situation in Iraq, accusing Hussein and his cousin, Defense Minister Ali Hassan al-Majid of committing crimes against humanity. It states that Iraqi military and security forces routinely cause people to disappear, arbitrarily detain individuals, and commit torture. They commit executions in an extrajudicial, summary or arbitrary manner. He discussed a system of collective punishment, whereby civilians are routinely detained and held responsible for the crimes and activities of their family members.

Rolf Ekeus, head of the U.N. Special Commission for weapons monitoring in Iraq, issued a report on October 7 stating that Iraqi cooperation and declarations had improved but fell short of full compliance with Resolution 687. The Commission anticipated installing all monitoring devices by the end of 1994.

E.U. Policy

On May 8, the Council of Ministers issued a statement calling for prompt and full Iraqi implementation of all Security Council resolutions as a prerequisite for the establishment of peace and security in the region. It stressed that Iraq must fully comply "with Resolution 687 concerning the immediate release of all Kuwaiti and other POWs and detainees held by Iraq, Iraq's weapons of mass destruction, and Iraq's payment of full compensation for the losses and damages caused by her aggression against the State of Kuwait." Furthermore, the European Union expressed concern regarding "the continued repression and sufferings of the entire Iraqi population, for which the Iraqi regime bears sole responsibility." In December 1993, the European Parliament issued a resolution condemning continued attacks against the Marsh Arabs and linked lifting sanctions to the end of these abuses.

The Work of Human Rights Watch/Middle East

Human Rights Watch/Middle East focused on the examination of Iraqi government documents captured in Iraqi Kurdistan in March 1991, during the uprising against the Hussein regime. In January, the organization published its second report on these documents, *Bureaucracy of Repression: The Iraqi Government in Its Own Words.* The report offers a unique look into the inner workings of a sophisticated, one-party police state responsible for over twenty-five years of systematic repression of Iraq's Kurds. These documents, from the files of the General Security Directorate and other government agencies, corroborate eyewitness testimony and forensic evidence gathered by Human Rights Watch in Iraqi Kurdistan regarding the 1988 genocidal campaign against the Kurds. The extraordinarily brutal methods of control practiced against the Kurds in the past are still official policy—part of the governmental arsenal that continues to be used against other groups branded as dissidents, such as the southern Marsh Arabs. Among the abuses brought to light by the documents published in the report are Baghdad's long-standing policy of "Arabizing" Kurdish-populated regions of northern Iraq; the carte blanche given to security forces to carry out extrajudicial executions; and the measures

Hussein took in 1991 to restore control over Iraq.

In a five-page letter dated October 18, the Iraqi government responded to several key issues discussed in *Bureaucracy of Repression*. The main arguments are summarized as follows: Iraq's military actions were in response to a hostile insurgency by Kurdish rebels assisting Iranian forces; reports that the Iraqi military used chemical weapons against the Kurds are erroneous; Kurdish rebels inserted forged documents among the genuine ones. The documents project is part of a wider effort by Human Rights Watch to provide evidence that Iraq's *Anfal* campaign against its population of rural Kurds amounted to genocide. On the basis of the evidence contained in the eighteen tons of documents and two years of field research, Human Rights Watch is fully convinced that the *Anfal* campaign breached the 1951 Convention on the Prevention and Punishment of the Crime of Genocide, to which Iraq is a party. Thus, the organization is urging governments to bring a case under the Convention against the Government of Iraq at the International Court of Justice.

IRAQI KURDISTAN
Human Rights Developments
Human rights conditions in the Kurdish controlled region deteriorated during 1994. Extrajudicial executions reportedly occurred during fighting between the Islamic Movement in Kurdistan and Patriotic Union of Kurdistan (PUK) in December 1993 as well as between the Kurdistan Democratic Party (KDP) and the Socialist Party. Both sides are believed to be responsible for killing outside of combat, although the PUK's Washington representative Barham Salih denied this charge in January.

Fighting broke out between the PUK and the KDP in May and spread quickly throughout the region. In KDP heartlands, PUK offices were surrounded and their members and soldiers were arrested and disarmed. The PUK took similar actions in their territory. The hostilities resulted in violations of the laws of war, including sum-

marily executing persons held in custody. A fragile cease-fire was declared after a week of fighting which left hundreds of *peshmerga*—Kurdish rebel fighters—and civilians dead. PUK peshmerga allegedly opened fire on a crowd mourning the death of a KDP commander on June 13 killing twelve people. Several cease-fire agreements were reached and breached shortly thereafter. The head of the Iraqi National Congress Ahmed Chalabi mediated talks between the two Kurdish leaders in June.

The Right to Monitor
The Kurdish regional authorities have generally been open to foreign human rights monitoring. Many Western nongovernmental organizations have conducted missions to Iraqi Kurdistan, although these visits have become more dangerous with the recent attacks on foreigners by Iraqi agents in the region. The politicization of Kurdish life based on the split between the PUK and the KDP hinders some investigation efforts.

Amnesty International investigated alleged abuses during the fighting in December between PUK and the Islamic Movement in Kurdistan. It documented abuses committed by both sides with photographic and medical evidence.

U.S. Policy
The United States has been careful to call for limited autonomy in the Kurdish area without promoting independence for the Kurdish region. The maintenance of the Combined Task Force/Operation Provide Comfort has remained central to U.S. policy toward Iraqi Kurdistan. The military mission provides a shield over the areas of Iraq north of the 36th parallel. Aircraft patrolling the region enforcing the "no-fly" zone as well as a small allied liaison force at Zakho depend entirely on the Turkish government for base support and logistics. Turkey has become increasingly less cooperative with the U.N. sanctions over both Iraq and its operations with regard to the Kurdish region. It wishes to resume trade with Iraq and is wary of iniatives that grant the Iraqi Kurds autonomy, fearing that

it would serve as a potential catalyst for autonomy demands by Turkish Kurds.

In January, the U.S. expressed grave concern over allegations of extrajudicial executions by the PUK in discussions with the PUK's Washington representative.

The Work of
Human Rights Watch/Middle East

Human Rights Watch/Middle East was in correspondence with Kurdish leaders throughout the year expressing concern over human rights abuses during the fighting between factions, especially summary executions of prisoners. The organization emphasized the need to adhere to the laws of war.

In a December 17, 1993 letter to Massoud Barzani, the organization questioned the KDP's involvement in an attack with gunfire on a large crowd of peaceful demonstrators outside the KDP headquarters building in Suleimaniyeh on December 13. A letter was sent on May 17, 1994 to Massoud Barzani, Jalal Talabani, and Abullah Rasoul, Prime Minister of the Kurdistan Regional Government, discussing the fighting. The letter highlighted international legal obligations under international humanitarian law, including the protection of civilian populations from harm during military operations as well as the prohibition on indiscriminate attacks under the 1949 Geneva Conventions.

Iraq's Crime of Genocide: The Anfal Campaign Against the Kurds, based on previously published reports by Human Rights Watch/Middle East, will be co-published with Yale University Press in early 1995.

ISRAELI-OCCUPIED WEST BANK AND GAZA STRIP

Human Rights Developments

This section is divided into two parts. The first concerns the areas under Israeli occupation with no concessions to Palestinian control (apart from limited responsibility in education, tourism and social welfare). These areas included all of the West Bank and Gaza Strip through May 1994, and, from May onward, only the West Bank excluding Jericho, an area with a combined population of about one million. The second covers the areas where, beginning in May, partial self-rule was implemented, namely the Gaza Strip and greater Jericho, with some 800,000 inhabitants.

Human Rights Developments
In the Areas Not Under Palestinian Partial Self-Rule

The peace process under way between the government of Israel and the Palestine Liberation Organization (PLO) dominated political developments in the West Bank and the Gaza Strip during 1994. In May, the first step was taken to transfer responsibilities to an interim Palestinian Authority (PA) as envisioned in the September 1993 Israeli-PLO Declaration of Principles. Israeli troops withdrew from population centers throughout the Gaza Strip and the West Bank town of Jericho, and the PA took over internal security and governmental services inside these areas. In August, the two sides reached an agreement in principle on transferring responsibilities over several civilian sectors throughout the occupied territories, excluding East Jerusalem. (Human Rights Watch/Middle East considers the parts of Jerusalem captured in 1967 to be occupied territory. However, since Israel unilaterally annexed these areas and applies to them its domestic law, the human rights situation there differs from the rest of the West Bank and is not covered in this report.)

The applicable legal framework for Israel's treatment of the Palestinian population includes the Hague Regulations of 1907, the Fourth Geneva Convention of 1949, and broad portions of international human rights law. Israel's government has, in defiance of a broad international consensus, never recognized the *de jure* applicability of the Fourth Geneva Convention.

During 1994, Palestinians under Israeli direct rule continued to experience widespread abuses, including killings through the excessive use of force, torture, arbitrary arrests, and long-lasting curfews over wide areas. They also were subjected to strict and arbitrary controls on movement, which impeded their ability to earn a living, study at universities, obtain goods and services, and otherwise conduct their everyday lives.

The level of certain abuses, including killings by the security forces, declined compared to previous years. No Palestinians were deported during the first ten months of 1994, and scores who had been deported in the past were permitted to return. No houses were demolished as a security-related sanction.

These trends accompanied a decline in the level of everyday violence in the occupied territories. The fervor of the early *intifada*, or uprising, had cooled for Palestinians, although it was easily reignited. The Israeli security forces also entered Palestinian population centers less frequently than in past years, thereby reducing the opportunities for violent clashes that so often ended in unarmed Palestinians being shot dead by soldiers.

Palestinians also suffered at the hands of Israeli settlers, who are licensed to bear arms by the state. Settlers continued to use unjustifiable force against Palestinians with little risk of experiencing the harsh response that the military authorities reserved for Palestinian attacks on Israelis.

Militant Palestinian groups were also responsible for grave abuses. Between January and October, forty-nine Palestinians were murdered by other Palestinians on suspicion of collaborating with the Israeli authorities, according to an Associated Press tally. The rate of such killings in the past had been higher.

The Islamist Hamas movement claimed responsibility for a number of attacks on Israelis. These included bombings in April directed at civilians in the Israeli towns of Hadera and Afula, killing twelve people and an October 19 suicide bombing of a civilian bus in Tel Aviv that killed twenty-three persons, including the bomber. Earlier in October Hamas militants took a soldier hostage and then apparently killed him during a failed rescue operation. All of these acts violated basic humanitarian principles that prohibit the targeting of civilians and acts of violence against any person who is in custody.

The peace process brought about the release of over 5,000 prisoners between October 1993 and October 1994, halving the number of Palestinians in Israeli prisons. In negotiating releases with the PLO, Israel said priority would be given to prisoners who did not "have blood on their hands." However, as of early November, some of the prisoners still being held had not been convicted of or charged with any violent offense. And, as in previous years, hundreds of West Bank Palestinians were arrested each month by the Israeli security forces.

The majority of Palestinian prisoners were held in detention facilities inside Israel, in violation of Article 76 of Geneva Convention IV, which forbids the occupying power to transfer prisoners out of the occupied lands. One consequence of this policy was that relatives and lawyers faced difficulties in visiting prisoners because of restrictions on entering Israel.

Many detainees were subjected to torture or ill-treatment at the hands of their interrogators. They underwent some combination of beatings, shackling, confinement for prolonged periods in painful positions, hooding, sleep deprivation, denial of access to a toilet, and other forms of humiliation.

The abuse is systematic, and not limited to persons suspected of committing grave acts of violence. Many who are mistreated are not themselves suspected of serious offenses, but rather are picked up and interrogated for the purpose of obtaining information about acquaintances.

There were 163 Palestinians in administrative detention (internment without charge or trial) as of August 3, 1994, according to official figures. This number indicated the continuing overall decline in the resort to this measure, but obscured a surge that put the number of administrative detainees over 400 in May as a result of a crackdown on Islamists following two bombing attacks inside Israel. Geneva Convention IV permits the use of administrative detention only as an exceptional measure.

Between January and October, Israeli security forces killed 102 Palestinians, including fourteen aged sixteen or under. Many of these killings occurred in situations where the soldier's resort to lethal force could not be justified in terms of an imminent danger facing the soldier or others. As Human Rights Watch/Middle East has pointed out in its reports, both the Israel Defense Forces' permissive open-fire orders (especially with regard to shooting at fleeing suspects) and its failure to vigorously punish breaches of these norms contribute to this phenomenon.

Israeli special forces continued to carry out undercover operations, mainly in the pursuit of fugitive militants. While these units often succeeded in arresting the persons being sought, they also killed a number of persons, sometimes in what appeared to be shoot-to-kill operations.

For example, on May 31, two men were shot dead as they got off a bus near Jerusalem. Eyewitnesses said the men were shot without warning by members of an undercover unit, who continued to fire into their bodies as they lay on the ground. Security sources said one of the men was wanted in connection with the killing of an undercover agent, and the other in connection with membership in Hamas. But at the time they were killed, they were posing no threat to others,

according to the witnesses.

The mass murder committed at the Ibrahimi mosque in Hebron on February 25 forced the issue of settler violence to center stage. Early that morning, settler and reserve soldier Baruch Goldstein, armed with an army-issued automatic rifle, entered the shrine and fired indiscriminately on worshippers, killing twenty-nine and wounding scores more.

The government-appointed commission of inquiry into the massacre concluded in June that Goldstein had acted alone. But the testimony before the commission revealed that settler violence did not occur in a vacuum. Soldiers and officers testified to conflicting instructions on handling settlers, with several asserting that the standing orders were never to fire at a settler, even if he or she was unjustifiably endangering lives.

Embarrassed, the Israel Defense Forces (IDF) promptly "clarified" the orders, stating that the procedures for responding to life-threatening situations applied whether the perpetrators were Jews or Palestinians. A communiqué from the Israeli Cabinet affirmed that the government "is solely responsible...for the security of all inhabitants, both Jewish and Arab" of the occupied territories, and "will continue to act to prevent harm to Jews and Arabs."

Israeli security and judicial authorities have long practiced a double standard, moving forcefully to prevent and punish acts of violence perpetrated by Palestinians against Israelis, but acting leniently when armed settlers shot at Palestinians, launched vigilante raids in villages and refugee camps, or harassed motorists. Palestinian suspects are tried in military courts, while settlers, should they be charged, face judgment in civil courts, where they enjoy greater due-process rights.

These points were made in a March 1994 study by B'Tselem that assessed the Israeli judicial system's handling of the sixty-two cases in which Palestinians were killed by Israeli civilians (nearly all of them settlers) between 1988 and 1992. In at least forty-nine cases, B'Tselem found, the perpetrator was not in mortal danger. Yet among these cases, only one resulted in a murder conviction and one in a manslaughter conviction.

In responding to Palestinian unrest following the Hebron massacre, the IDF displayed some of its most abusive practices. When protests broke out, troops suppressed them forcibly, killing twenty-one Palestinians during the six days following the massacre.

Three-quarters of the population of the occupied territories was placed under a curfew lasting four to five days after the massacre. In addition, authorities imposed a strict closure of the West Bank and Gaza Strip, preventing Palestinians from entering Israel or East Jerusalem. As in the past, settlers were exempted from both measures.

Hebron's 100,000 inhabitants remained under a round-the-clock curfew for more than a month, with infrequent breaks. Employment, commerce, school, and medical services were all severely disrupted for Palestinian residents of the Hebron region, as the Palestine Human Rights Information Center documented in a May report.

The IDF spokesman said the post-massacre closure and curfews were imposed owing to the "valid security considerations" of "prevent[ing] massive disturbances, and the risk to human life, and to reduce friction between Jews and Arabs." However, these disruptive measures were carried out on a wholly disproportionate scale. They constituted a collective punishment of nearly two million Palestinians for a crime committed by a Jewish settler.

In responding to demands to rein in settler violence Israel took unprecedented measures against settler militants. It banned two militant organizations and applied military orders, rather than domestic law, to administratively detain six men. But administrative measures against a handful of individuals known for their advocacy of violence, in violation of their rights to due process are no substitute for a committed and consistent policy of preventing, investigating, and prosecuting all acts of violence.

After a month of difficult negotiations after the massacre, Israel and the PLO agreed to a three-month, 160-person multinational monitoring presence in Hebron whose purpose was to create "a feeling of security among Palestinians" by "promoting stability and in monitoring and reporting the efforts to restore normal life." The Temporary International Presence in Hebron (TIPH) represented the first time that Israel had consented to the insertion of a multinational force in the occupied territories.

However, the mandate of the TIPH was weak. It sought to protect rights by its mere presence on the ground, its offer of good offices, and by filing reports to a joint Israeli-Palestinian committee and to donor governments. (It did not make these reports public.) It was not given police powers or any other means of physically intervening to halt abuses, mobilizing international opinion, or enlisting third-party intervention. The TIPH was hobbled further by the absence of any reference in its mandate to applicable humanitarian and human rights law.

Many human rights advocates hope that future agreements on international observers—envisioned in general terms in the Declaration of Principles — will assure a protection role more substantive than the one performed by the TIPH.

Regulatory controls on various aspects of Palestinian life by the occupying power are an often underestimated form of abusive conduct. The opaque, inconsistent and time-wasting procedures Palestinians endure when seeking permits and authorizations seriously impede the exercise of freedom of movement and other rights. Moreover, they affect nearly the entire Palestinian population and not only those suspected of resistance activities.

Israel's internal intelligence agency, the General Security Service (GSS), routinely reviews applications to travel abroad or to obtain permission to enter Israel and East Jerusalem. As B'Tselem pointed out in a September 1994 report, "Unlike a conventional civilian authority, the GSS does not operate according to uniform, reasonable, and open criteria. Its considerations are secret and it is under no obligation to explain its decisions, endowing it with immense power, which it frequently uses arbitrarily."

The most wide-reaching bureaucratic controls are over the movement of Palestinians into Israel and East Jerusalem. Because the latter was unilaterally annexed in 1967, all Palestinians who are not registered as Jerusalem residents are required to obtain permits in order to enter the city.

These controls have tightened in response to violent attacks inside Israel carried out by residents of the occupied territories. Now, Palestinians wishing to enter Israel and East Jerusalem must obtain hard-to-get temporary permits. Many categories of persons, such as those with security records, are usually refused.

Obstacles to travel affect not only Palestinians who work in Israel and East Jerusalem, but also those who need to cross Israel when traveling between the West Bank and Gaza Strip. The Gaza Strip is not a self-sufficient entity; cut off from Israel and the West Bank, Gazans are deprived of access to certain essential services such as comprehensive health care facilities, foreign consulates, and a broad range of higher education institutions.

Immediately after the Hebron massacre, Israel closed the occupied territories and cancelled all valid permits. Most men who had jobs in Israel found themselves unemployed for months with no compensation. (Few alternative jobs are available in the occupied territories, owing in large part to Israeli policies that stunted economic development in these areas.)

The post-Hebron closure was lifted very gradually beginning in March. Prime Minister Rabin pointed out in August that, according to a defense establishment study, none of the political killings inside Israel since the March 1993 closure had been committed by workers holding permits. A new closure was nevertheless imposed in October in response to a series of attacks inside Israel claimed by Hamas and carried out by residents of the occupied territories.

Israel, like all countries, has the right to restrict entry at its borders, and is permitted by humanitarian law to restrict the movement of the population under its occupation. However, Israel is obliged to weigh these prerogatives against the obligation to attend to the occupied population's legitimate daily needs, some of which require enjoying freedom of movement.

Human Rights Developments In the Areas under Palestinian Partial Self-Rule

An unprecedented legal situation in the West Bank and Gaza Strip has emerged from the Israeli-PLO peace process. The Palestinian Authority has assumed control over Jericho and much of the Gaza Strip, yet it lacks essential elements of sovereignty. Israel, meanwhile, no longer exercises full nor exclusive control over these areas, yet its impact on daily life remains significant.

Both Israel and the PA bear responsibility for protecting the human rights of the residents of the self-rule areas. Israel's legal responsibilities as occupying power have not ended, even if its contact with the protected population has diminished.

As for the Palestinian Authority, it is not a state government and therefore cannot formally accede to human rights treaties. Nevertheless, it is bound by humanitarian norms and customary human rights law. The Geneva Convention IV affirms that the protection it provides toward a population under occupation cannot be compromised by any interim agreement, short of a definitive political solution, that is reached between the occupying power and other authorities.

While Gazans celebrated the withdrawal of Israeli troops from most of the Gaza Strip, they were soon reminded how utterly dependent their economic and community life remained on Israeli decisions, particularly with regard to their freedom to travel into and out of the Strip. Israeli control over the population of the self-rule areas was also evident in the continued incarceration, as of early November, of over one thousand residents of the self-rule areas, nearly all charged with or convicted of "security" offenses.

In its first half year in office, the Palestinian Authority had a mixed record on human rights. For most Palestinians in the self-rule areas, the replacement of Israeli troops by Palestinian forces in population centers marked a substantial improvement in their safety and freedom. There were no more daily casualties in clashes with troops, and no more nighttime curfew. The number of persons imprisoned for periods longer than a few days dropped sharply.

At the same time, the Palestinian Authority took a number of troubling steps, including hundreds of arbitrary arrests, the temporary banning of the only critical daily newspaper, and directives restricting political gatherings. The first violent clashes between the Palestinian police and demonstrators erupted on November 18. The toll of at least fifteen dead and hundreds wounded raised troubling questions about the committment and ability of the police to use non-lethal means in confronting unarmed protestors.

Despite widespread confusion over what laws and regulations were in effect, the Palestinian Authority failed to anchor the conduct of its agencies and security forces in the rule of law. Security forces in Gaza, for example, routinely carried out arrests without warrants, without explaining the reasons for the arrest, and without informing families of the whereabouts of the person taken into custody.

Some of the problems could be attributed to the extraordinary difficulties that the Palestinian Authority faced in assuming responsibilities over a restive population in the wake of a twenty-seven-year occupation. The Palestinian Authority commenced governing without adequate funding and with substantial limits on its powers, pursuant to the Israeli-PLO agreements. Its security forces lacked the experience, training and equipment that might have helped to promote respect for human rights in their conduct.

None of these shortcomings, however, could not excuse the violations of fundamental rights that occurred, such as the use of violence against detainees under interrogation, and the closure of *an-Nahar* newspaper because its views offended the PLO.

Arbitrary arrests generally took the form of round-ups of supporters of a particular opposition movement shortly after an attack on Israeli targets claimed by or attributed to that group. Hundreds of alleged supporters of Hamas, Islamic Jihad, and the Democratic Front for the Liberation of Palestine were rounded up in this fashion beginning in August. Most of those arrested were never charged, and were released within three weeks. The handling of these detainees and the way they were questioned suggested that persons were being detained on the basis of their suspected political affiliations rather on solid evidence linking them to specific criminal acts.

There was no pattern of physical abuse of opposition group members and supporters while in detention. However, these sweeps formed a dangerous precedent. Even the Palestinian Justice Minister, Freih abu Medein, acknowledged to the *Los Angeles Times* in September, "Mass arrests are political arrests, and they are against the law. To make an arrest, you must have evidence and go to a specific address and detain a specific person. You can't just sweep through a mosque and pick up those you find."

Beatings and harsher conditions were experienced by some suspects detained on suspicion of collaborating with the Israeli authorities. One such suspect, Farid Jarbou`. died under torture in July. Authorities quickly acknowledged that he had died under torture, and three security-force members were charged in connection with causing the death. But other collaboration suspects arrested in May and June complained to their lawyers and to visitors that they too had been beaten.

In July, the Palestinian Authority took a laudable step toward promoting accountability by authorizing the International Committee of the Red Cross to conduct regular visits to all persons detained by the Palestinian Authority.

The PA's record has been mixed with regard to freedom of expression, assembly and association. The gravest attack on press freedom came on July 28, when PA Chair Yasir Arafat banned the only critical daily newspaper, the Jerusalem-based *an-Nahar*. The pretext provided was that the paper's license had expired, but the legal basis of the licensing requirement was never made clear. Instead, the ban was widely seen as an act of displeasure with *an-Nahar*'s sympathies for Jordan's King Hussein at the expense of Arafat. *An-Nahar* resumed publication on September 5, with a distinctly more pro-PLO line than before.

At the same time, there has been no systematic effort by the Palestinian Authority to suppress the diverse and vibrant political life in the self-rule areas. Permits have been issued to independent and opposition figures to launch new papers in the Gaza Strip. And while the Gaza police chief in September banned unauthorized political gatherings in Gaza's four largest meeting halls, opposition political organizations continued to hold meetings, rallies, and demonstrations without police interference; human rights organizations documented and publicized abuses without harassment, and criticism of the authorities was heard from a variety of quarters.

By the end of October, one of the most important rights of Palestinians, the right to take part in public affairs through the free election of representatives, had yet to be realized. With Israeli-PLO negotiations bogged down over the modalities of Palestinian elections, the Palestinian Authority remained entirely an unelected body. This made it vulnerable to charges from Palestinian critics that its authority derived entirely from the Israeli occupation authorities.

The Right To Monitor

Human rights work was generally permitted. A variety of organizations conducted monitoring and produced highly critical reports with minimal interference from the authorities.

However, restrictions on movement affecting much of the Palestinian population also impeded the work of Palestinian rights workers. Monitors and journalists based in Gaza or the West Bank were constantly forced to miss work-related appointments in Jerusalem because of closures and permit problems. Because of curfews, checkpoints, and other restrictions, field workers had great difficulty documenting the aftermath of the Hebron massacre in and around that city.

Israeli and foreign journalists were able to work with only occasional hindrance from soldiers on the ground or the military censors. Palestinian journalists faced more difficulty moving about, and have sometimes been assaulted by soldiers. Human rights reporting by the Palestinian media was subject to significant Israeli censorship.

The International Committee of the Red Cross (ICRC) and the United Nations Relief and Works Agency both maintained representatives in the field whose responsibilities included monitoring human rights conditions (but not making public their findings). They carried passes that generally enable them to reach trouble spots without hindrance. The ICRC was permitted by the Israeli authorities to visit all Palestinians arrested for security reasons within fourteen days of their arrest.

Human Rights Watch/Middle East was invited to visit Israeli prisons during 1994, but declined the invitation because the IDF, in contrast to the Israel Prison Service, had stipulated that conversations with inmates would have to take place in the presence of IDF escorts.

A number of human rights workers were subjected to administrative sanctions. Al-Haq field worker Zahi Jaradat was prevented from traveling in August to attend a human rights seminar in Cyprus. Al-Haq paralegal Sha'wan Jabarin was held in administrative detention from March until May and again under a six-month order commencing in June. Israel's Ministry of Justice asserted that "Jabarin has never been detained for his work with al-Haq....In addition to his open activities in al-Haq, Jabarin has been for many years a senior member of the Popular Front for the Liberation of Palestine. a terrorist organization..." Similarly, the Ministry of Justice stated that the administrative detention for five months of lawyer Faraj al-Ghoul, director of the Gaza-based organization House of Right and Law, was due not to his professional work but to his being a "senior activist" in Hamas. In the absence of specific charges or trials, the official claims that these detentions had nothing to do with human rights work could only be met with skepticism.

In the Palestinian self-rule areas, the Palestinian authorities allowed human rights organizations to work freely. They collected information, criticized violations committed by the Palestinian Authority, and met with Palestinian officials. However, unlike the ICRC, which obtained PLO approval to conduct regular visits to all detainees in Palestinian hands, no independent Palestinian organizations obtained authorization to conduct regular prison visits, although some were able to conduct ad hoc visits.

In 1994, a group of prominent Palestinians formed the Independent Commission for the Rights of the Citizen, pursuant to a vow by Yasir Arafat to charter an independent human rights ombudsman agency. The Commission, which is independently funded and chaired by Dr. Hanan Ashrawi, received complaints and made interventions with the Palestinian authorities, mostly in private. Although Dr. Ashrawi occasionally publicly criticized violations by the Palestinian Authority, the Commission adhered to its declared preference for attempting to discourage abuses through direct and private contacts with the authorities.

U.S. Policy

The U.S., the leading third-party player in the Middle East, has actively promoted the peace process in the region. It is also Israel's largest benefactor, with a military and economic aid program exceeding $3 billion a year.

The Clinton administration insisted that maintaining U.S. aid to Israel was essential to achieving peace. Deputy Assistant Secretary of State Dan Kurtzer stated on April 13 that President Clinton had "reaffirmed his commitment to work with Congress to maintain our present levels of assistance to Israel" and "to maintain and enhance Israel's qualitative military edge over any likely combination of aggressors. The security of Israel must not be in doubt if the peace process is to succeed."

After Israel and the PLO signed the Declaration of Principles in 1993, the U.S. pledged $500 million in assistance over five years to the West Bank and Gaza Strip, a huge jump from previous years. The stated objective was to provide Palestinians with quick rewards from the peace process.

Israel's poor human rights record in the occupied territories has never been a focus of U.S. policy. No administration has publicly suggested that aid should be conditioned on improvements in Israel's treatment of Palestinians. The U.S. approach to human rights problems has been, almost invariably, to treat them as subordinate to the quest for peace: variously as symptoms of the lack of peace, as irritants to negotiations, or as candidates for confidence-building measures.

The relationship between peace and human rights is indeed complex. Achieving progress toward peace can brighten the human rights outlook, while stigmatizing abusive governments can upset delicate negotiations. But neglect of human rights can also derail peace moves. Abuses can erode public support for the process, fuel the cycle of violence, and undermine the prospects for a stable, democratic authority in the West Bank and Gaza Strip. Third parties do not necessarily serve the goal of a stable peace by placing faith in whatever is agreed upon by a weak and unelected Palestinian negotiating team and a far stronger Israeli side.

During 1994, as the peace process was producing tangible changes on the ground, the Clinton administration pursued to its logical conclusion the policy of subordinating human rights to the peace process. The administration remained virtually silent on Israeli human rights abuses, despite its clear grasp of their gravity, as shown in the generally sound section in the 1993 State Department's *Country Reports on Human*

Rights Practices for 1993.

Whenever an issue with human rights dimensions was slated for negotiations between Israel and the PLO, the U.S. adopted a hands-off approach in public, stating that the issue was a matter for discussion between the parties. The U.S. even backtracked on issues on which it had, in the past, taken at least partially principled positions, including settlements, the status of Jerusalem, and the rights of refugees. And when new issues arose, such as the presence of a multinational observer force, the U.S. missed opportunities to advocate principled positions, declaring that whatever the two sides okayed would also be fine with Washington.

This approach was pursued at the United Nations, where Ambassador Madeleine K. Albright wrote in July to member nations urging them to adopt a policy in the General Assembly such that "Resolution language that refers to 'final status' issues of the peace process should be dropped on the grounds that such issues are now under negotiation by the parties themselves....Key final status subjects include refugees, settlements, territorial sovereignty and the status of Jerusalem."

The U.S. position would have been less objectionable if Israel had frozen its activities in these realms pending negotiations. But new settlement activity, especially in and around annexed East Jerusalem, was changing facts on the ground, while Washington obligingly remained silent on these "final-status" issues.

The U.S. was quick to deplore the Hebron massacre, as it was to condemn attacks on Israeli civilians by militant Palestinians. But at the United Nations, the U.S. invoked the peace process to oppose a resolution on the massacre that referred to East Jerusalem as occupied territory and that endorsed "the need to provide protection and security for the Palestinian people."

On March 18, Resolution 280 passed only after the Security Council had accepted a U.S. demand for a paragraph-by-paragraph vote. Alone among the fifteen Council members, the U.S. abstained on the passages regarding international protection and Jerusalem. Although the U.S. had in the past approved resolutions referring to East Jerusalem as occupied territory, this was no longer desirable. Ambassador Albright explained, because the city's final status was now a matter for bilateral talks.

U.S. efforts during the post-massacre crisis focused not on promoting effective protection mechanisms or compliance with human rights and humanitarian law, but rather on finding a package acceptable to Israel that would coax the PLO back to the negotiating table. Palestinian human rights organizations reported being asked at the time by U.S. diplomats to suggest the "minimum price" sought by Palestinians in terms of protection that would ensure the PLO's return to the talks.

In the view of Human Rights Watch/Middle East, the U.S. should use its standing as Israel's most generous backer and staunchest ally to promote respect for human rights and humanitarian law in the territories, including, when necessary, through publicly criticizing abusive practices. Such a policy will help rather than hinder the prospects for peace.

With regard to the Palestinian Authority, the U.S. has to its credit pledged to increase aid programs aimed at promoting the rule of law in the self-rule areas. It has endorsed free and fair elections as vital to Palestinian self-rule. But while senior officials publicly urged Palestinian authorities to establish fiscal accountability and prevent attacks on Israelis, they were more circumspect toward the human rights of Palestinians in the self-rule areas. Initial missteps by the Palestinian Authority, including the first death in detention and the banning of *an-Nahar* daily, occasioned no public comment by senior officials.

Secretary of State Warren Christopher, in Jerusalem in October during the crisis over the kidnapping by Hamas of an Israeli soldier, echoed Prime Minister Rabin's incorrect assertion that the hostage was being held in the self-rule areas. He was also widely reported to have endorsed the Israeli assertion that Arafat was directly responsible for solving the crisis. Christopher's statements came at a time when Palestinian security forces were carrying out their most indiscriminate round-up of suspected opposition figures to date. In their timing and content, Christopher's comments gave the impression that the U.S. condoned the mass arbitrary arrests in the self-rule areas.

The Work of
Human Rights Watch/Middle East

With the peace process and transfer of authority dominating the news, Human Rights Watch/Middle East worked both to cover the evolving situation and to re-direct attention toward abuses that continued unabated.

In keeping with its focus on abuses involving violence, Human Rights Watch/ Middle East released a report in June on Israel's torture of Palestinians under interrogation. The inclusion of testimonies of persons who had been tortured since the signing of the Declaration of Principles showed that the peace process had not done away with the problem of torture. Press interest in the report was enhanced by releasing it just as Israel television was airing a major documentary on the same subject. Following the report's release, Human Rights Watch/ Middle East worked to engage the world medical community in the issue of the complicity of Israeli prison doctors in abusive interrogations.

After the Hebron massacre, Human Rights Watch/Middle East visited the West Bank to research settler violence. A study of the issue is included in the forthcoming Human Rights Watch report on communal violence around the world.

With regard to the Palestinian self-rule areas, Human Rights Watch/Middle East visited the Gaza Strip in June, September and October to assess human rights conditions. Human Rights Watch/Middle East wrote letters to the Palestinian Authority regarding the first death in detention and the banning of *an-Nahar* newspaper, and met with both civil and security officials to discuss Human Rights Watch/Middle East's

preliminary findings and concerns. And in December, Human Rights Watch/Middle East issued a report on human rights conditions in the self-rule areas, documenting both Israel and Palestinian violations and making recommendations to both parties.

Human Rights Watch/Middle East also issued statements and wrote open letters to Israeli authorities in response to a number of specific cases and incidents throughout the year. In April, we wrote to the Hamas organization to demand a halt to attacks targeting Israeli civilians. This demand was repeated in a statement, issued in English and Arabic, condemning the suicide bomb attack on a crowded bus in Tel Aviv in October.

KUWAIT

Human Rights Developments

There was no change in the government's policy to pressure the Bedoons, Kuwait's longtime native residents, to leave the country. Asian maids remained without legal protection from abusive employers. Early promises to give women and naturalized citizens the right to vote were not fulfilled and dissolved human rights organizations were not permitted to reopen. The State Security Court handed down death penalties and other harsh punishments in proceedings falling far short of international standards for fair trials. Torture and ill-treatment continued to be reported.

Renewed Iraqi threats against Kuwait were cited in 1994 by Kuwaiti officials as justifications for continued human rights abuses and delays in dealing with past violations. Those tensions and Iraq's refusal to assist in locating missing Kuwaitis contributed to a hostile atmosphere for groups suspected as a whole to hold Iraqi sympathies, including the Bedoon and Palestinian communities, leading to renewed pressure on the two groups to leave the country; they were denied freedom of movement, employment, and education for their children.

With few exceptions, the authorities

failed to account for the hundreds of extrajudicial executions, disappearances, and torture cases that took place during the post-liberation martial-law period (February through June 1991). In the first case of its kind, however, a Kuwaiti government official was tried for abuses during the martial-law period; in December 1993, Jaber al-Omairi, a Ministry of Interior official, was sentenced to life in prison for killing Ismael Farhat, a Lebanese citizen, and his son Osama, and the attempted murder of Naimat Farhat, his daughter. In June an appeals court reduced his sentence to fifteen years, citing as a mitigating circumstance what it believed had been al-Omairi's motives—the desire to avenge Iraqi atrocities. Although members of the Farhat family in fact supported the Kuwaiti resistance to the occupation, the courts appeared to make light of the serious crimes which the defendant—and other Kuwaitis—committed in the name of vengeance against foreign residents of Kuwait shortly after the end of the war.

In August, police officers accused of torturing Sudanese prisoner Ahmad Mubarak Badawi in 1992 were arrested and charged with aggravated assault. Other than these two notable exceptions, none of the officials implicated in extradjudicial executions, disappearances or the torture of hundreds of prisoners have been brought to justice. In both the Farhat and Badawi cases, it took years of concerted efforts by local and international human rights organizations, and those of U.S. officials and Kuwaiti parliament members—in addition to extensive media coverage—to bring those responsible to justice. In most other cases Kuwaiti officials expressed doubts that any further investigations of post-liberation abuses would take place.

During 1994, continuing a process begun immediately after liberation, the State Security Court tried scores of Iraqis, Palestinians, and Bedoons charged with collaboration with the Iraqi occupying forces. Although the procedures followed in their trials were an improvement over those of the 1991 martial-law courts, serious shortcomings remained, including the use of confessions obtained through torture, the denial of legal counsel of the defendants' own choosing and a limited right of appeal. Collaboration was defined by the prosecution to include many forms of minor association with the occupiers, under the broadly worded State Security Law of 1970. Assertions made by many defendants that they had been coerced into cooperating with the Iraqi occupation authorities were not accepted in mitigation.

During 1994, the Court of Cassation reduced to long periods of imprisonment eleven death sentences imposed in 1993 by the State Security Court for collaboration. Most other judgments were upheld, despite often credible charges of torture at the hands of investigative authorities; the evidence of torture in the case of ten Palestinians, convicted on charges of supporting the occupation as members of the Arab Liberation Front, was disregarded even when court-appointed physicians documented defendants' injuries.

On June 4, the State Security Court sentenced five Iraqis and one Kuwaiti to death for plotting to kill former U.S. President George Bush during his April 1993 trip to Kuwait. Eight others were sentenced in the same case to prison terms ranging between six months and twelve years. On October 16, the Court of Cassation held its first session to review the case against nine of the defendants. The petition of the other five's convictions was denied, because their sentences were less than three years. Several defendants recanted their earlier confessions, which they said had been obtained through the use of torture. Three defendants, Ali Khudair, Wali al-Ghazali, and Ra'ad al-Asadi told the court that they made their confessions after they had been subjected to torture. Although most of the accused faced the death penalty; all but one of the fourteen defendants were denied legal counsel until their first court appearances.

During 1994, hundreds of foreign residents and Bedoons were administratively detained without charge or trial in the Talha

Deportation Prison and then given a choice between leaving voluntarily or remaining in the overcrowded makeshift detention facility indefinitely. Some had been held since the end of the war, including many who were stateless or refugees. The promise made by the Prime Minister in June 1993 to improve conditions and relocate Talha inmates after some of its residents went on a hunger strike went largely unfulfilled, despite urging from the National Assembly's human rights committee.

The Kuwaiti government employed a range of actions to induce Iraqi, Palestinian, and Bedoon residents to leave the country. Measures of intimidation included arbitrary arrest and detention, torture and ill-treatment of prisoners, unlawful searches, heavy fines, threats, public humiliation, and the denial of employment. Having succeeded in reducing the nearly 400,000-strong Palestinian community to about 33,000, the Kuwaiti government has sought to achieve similar results with the Bedoon community. During the year, it escalated pressure on the Bedoons to secure citizenship elsewhere if they wanted to remain in Kuwait lawfully. Most Bedoons are long-term residents of Kuwait who were born there and have lived there all their lives, but are not officially deemed to qualify for Kuwaiti citizenship. Government figures estimated the community size in 1994 at about 125,000, down from a prewar estimate of over 250,000.

Accused as a group of aiding the Iraqi occupying forces, Bedoons were targeted for retribution, although many had in fact resisted the Iraqis and been killed by the Iraqi occupiers for acts of resistance. Since liberation, Bedoons have been prevented from sending their children to government schools and threatened with expulsion from the only country they have ever known. All those employed by the government were dismissed from their jobs. The military and the police, which before the invasion were largely composed of Bedoons, rehired only a small fraction of their prewar employees—depriving the community of its chief source of income. In 1994, Bedoons found outside the remaining Bedoon slums were detained and pressured to leave the country in exchange for the government dropping the charges of illegal residence. The government remained opposed to reopening the citizenship application process to give Bedoons an opportunity to make their claims.

Many of the Palestinians still in Kuwait are stateless refugees who came originally from the Gaza Strip, but are not allowed by Israel to return. During 1994 in Kuwait, most Gazans were harassed, threatened with imprisonment, denied employment and education, or subjected to fines for every day they stayed in Kuwait.

Another vulnerable group of foreign residents subjected to violent mistreatment was the nearly 200,000 Asian maids, mainly from the Philippines, Sri Lanka, India, and Bangladesh. They are expressly excluded from the protection of labor legislation, and in practice also left at the mercy of their private employers with regard to violent abuse. Hundreds of abused Asian expatriates sought refuge in their respective embassies, charging their employers with rape, physical assault or unlawful confinement, as well as withholding wages. In 1994, about two thousand runaway maids sought shelter in foreign embassies, notably those of the Philippines, where 250 runaways sheltered in October, and Sri Lanka, with 120 in the same month. Abuses by employers recorded in 1994 included cases of murder, rape and other sexual abuse, beatings, confinement, and passport confiscation. Most were not investigated and only two abusive employers were known to have been prosecuted during the year.

The Dasma Police Station, used to detain maids pending their deportation or the resolution of their claims, became extremely overcrowded during 1994, with an average population of 300 maids. In December 1993, a Human Rights Watch investigator found credible evidence of physical and sexual abuse by Dasma guards. Kuwaiti law requires maids who complain about their employers to either stay with their employers until the conflict is resolved or be detained.

Most of those complaining who were not in embassy shelters were detained until their cases were resolved, which may take months, leading many maids to drop their complaints and accept repatriation.

In 1994, the Kuwaiti government reiterated its ban on political parties and took steps to enforce a 1985 moratorium on the formation of new private associations, including human rights groups. On April 21, Shaikh Sabah al-Ahmad, First Deputy Prime Minister and Minister of Foreign Affairs told KUNA, the official news agency, that Kuwait did not have political parties and none would be allowed there. The government also enforced its 1993 decision to close down over fifty unlicensed private organizations, including six human rights groups. The authorities prevented the unauthorized groups from holding public functions or advertising their activities.

In 1994, earlier hopes of enfranchising women and naturalized citizens were not realized. However, the Parliament took action to give the right to vote to male children of naturalized males, provided that they were born after their fathers were naturalized. If implemented, the change is expected to add about 25,000 voters. The enlarged electorate would still be only 16 percent of all citizens, who themselves represent less than 40 percent of the total population.

The Right to Monitor

The right to monitor was dealt a severe blow with the closure in August 1993 of all human rights groups in Kuwait, including the Kuwaiti Association to Defend War Victims (KADWV) and Kuwaiti Association for Human Rights (Kuwait's branch of the Cairo-based Arab Organization for Human Rights). Established immediately after the Gulf War, KADWV had been the main local human rights group. The Kuwaiti government, which never formally recognized the organization's legal existence, ordered KADWV and the other human rights and humanitarian groups to close down, because they had not been licensed.

Although the order was directed at all unlicensed organizations, government officials cited only human rights and humanitarian organizations and singled out KADWV for criticism. Groups that attempted to defy the ban in 1994 were threatened with the use of force if they held public meetings or conducted public activities. Newspapers were barred from publishing advertisements for the dissolved organizations, and licensed groups were ordered not to host activities by the banned organizations. An attempt in March by KADWV and the Kuwaiti Association for Human Rights to hold a symposium on human rights was scuttled by the Ministry of Social Affairs. In May, the government ordered the eviction of KADWV, the League of Families of POWs and the Missing, the Popular Committee for Solidarity with POWs and the Missing and the Amnesty International's Kuwait group from the public building they had occupied since 1991. Nevertheless, KADWV continued to work privately, as have some of the other banned groups, albeit in a much reduced capacity.

Included in the government's ban were four other human rights and humanitarian groups: Mutual Assistance Fund for the Families of the Martyrs and POWs, Pro-Democracy Committee, Supporters of Single-Citizenship Committee, and Women Married to Non-Kuwaitis Support Association.

In 1994, the Kuwaiti government allowed visits by several international human rights groups, but rarely provided information required by these groups to conduct their research. Most non-Kuwaiti lawyers who volunteered to travel to Kuwait to represent those accused of state security offenses or to assist victims of abuse were not granted entry visas by Kuwaiti embassies. The few who were able to secure visas were not permitted to represent their clients in court.

U.S. Policy

Since the end of the 1991 Gulf War, the U.S. has been the main force protecting Kuwait from renewed Iraqi attack and Kuwait's chief arms supplier. Under a 1991 military agreement, the U.S. maintained a substantial naval presence nearby and held frequent U.S.-Kuwaiti maneuvers. These exercises amount to a semi-permanent presence in light of their frequency, their duration and the large number of troops involved. The U.S. has prepositioned a large amount of war materiel in Kuwait and integrated Kuwaiti facilities with those of the U.S. In October, when Iraq amassed a reported 70,000 Republican Guards near the Kuwaiti border, the U.S. demonstrated its commitment to Kuwait by dispatching tens of thousands of troops to the region and threatening to take military action against Iraq unless Iraq withdrew its troops far from the border.

Senior U.S. officials who visited Kuwait during 1994, including President Bill Clinton, Secretary of State Warren Christopher and Secretary of Defense William Perry cited the defense of Kuwait as a key part of the U.S. strategy for the defense of the Arabian Peninsula.

In statements before the House Subcommittee on Europe and the Middle East in March and October, Robert H. Pelletreau, Assistant Secretary of State for Near Eastern Affairs, listed as one of the U.S. priorities in the region "promoting more open political and economic systems, and respect for human rights and the rule of law." There was little evidence of the administration's efforts towards achieving that priority, other than occasional statements that human rights were raised with Kuwaiti officials in private meetings. One potentially effective method was pursued in 1994 by the Overseas Private Investment Corporation. OPIC withheld approval of insurance for investment in a petrochemical project in Kuwait until the State Department engaged in a high level dialogue with the Kuwaiti government regarding the treatment of Asian maids. OPIC also decided to condition additional insurance on achieving progress in the field of workers' rights.

In addition to military ties, commercial interest appeared to dominate the bilateral relationship. In March, Secretary Pelletreau emphasized the need to ensure unimpeded access, at reasonable prices, to the Gulf's vast petroleum resources and "fair access for American business to commercial opportunities in the region." In June, he told the Congress that, "Since the liberation of Kuwait, American companies have won over $5 billion in reconstruction contracts constituting 50 percent of all the contracts that were awarded. The U.S. Government, our Embassy, our officials in Washington and members of our cabinet have been active in supporting the bids of U.S. contractors....I can assure you that I will be personally engaged in this effort as will our Embassy in Kuwait and other members of the administration." In October, Secretary Pelletreau told Congress, "From President Clinton down, this Administration has made crystal clear its view that supporting American business overseas would be at the heart of our foreign policy interests...Our embassies have been active...in the Gulf helping American business to secure, for instance, over 500 construction contracts in Kuwait worth approximately five billion dollars and a 98 million dollar contract to dredge a channel in Doha."

There were no comparable declarations on human rights. In fact, there was rarely public criticism of the human rights practices of the Kuwaiti government other than the cataloguing of human rights abuses in the State Department's *Country Reports on Human Rights Practices for 1993*.

On specific issues, such as the trial of those accused of plotting to assassinate former President Bush, administration officials expressed their satisfaction with the Kuwaiti record. In June, Secretary Pelletreau defended the trial and praised the "vibrant and growing" role of Kuwait's parliament—an elite all-male body—and made no reference to, for example, previous assurances by U.S. officials that the government had pledged that Kuwait would expand its electorate to include women. The reticence to raise human rights issues is particularly disappointing given Kuwait's near-complete reliance on the U.S. to protect it from external threats.

thus giving the U.S. a unique opportunity as well as a greater obligation to press for improvement in human rights.

The Work of
Human Rights Watch/Middle East

In 1994, Human Rights Watch/Middle East focused on advocacy to improve the observance of human rights in Kuwait, engaging in substantive discussions with Kuwaiti officials and following up previous published reports. A mission sent to Kuwait in December 1993 and January 1994 investigated the conditions of the Bedoons and raised other human rights concerns with officials, including the ban on local human rights groups and the plight of Asian maids.

A Human Rights Watch/Middle East representative observed trials before the State Security Court and the first trial ever of a government official accused of human rights violations in *Kuwait v. al-Omairi*, a case in which Human Rights Watch/Middle East had been instrumental since 1991. Human Rights Watch/Middle East sent letters to Kuwaiti officials urging them to rescind orders preventing human rights and humanitarian groups from continuing their activities.

Human Rights Watch/Middle East sent letters to Kuwaiti officials regarding the mistreatment of Asian maids. It also raised the issue with the Overseas Private Insurance Corporation. OPIC decided to withhold its approval of insurance for investment in Kuwait until the State Department conducted a high level dialogue with Kuwaiti officials on workers' rights. In addition, Human Rights Watch/Middle East worked closely with U.S. Justice Department attorneys who successfully prosecuted a Kuwaiti employer, living in the U.S., charged with holding his Sri Lankan maid in servitude in violation of the Thirteenth Amendment of the U.S. Constitution.

LEBANON

Human Rights Developments

The year was marked by an intensified arrest campaign against government opponents, especially suspected supporters of the banned Lebanese Forces and the ousted General Michel Aoun. The government increased its reliance on military courts to try civilians accused of offenses considered harmful to national security, often in proceedings falling far short of internationally recognized standards for fair trials. In 1994, the government banned all private radio and television stations from broadcasting news bulletins or political programs. Under the pretext of maintaining civil peace, the government jailed protesters and prosecuted reporters and publishers who wrote or aired materials deemed harmful to "civil harmony."

In addition to the Lebanese government, other forces in Lebanon also committed violations of human rights and humanitarian law, including Syria's Military Intelligence, Israel and its ally the South Lebanon Army, the Iranian-supported organization Hizballa, and the Lebanese Forces, a Maronite militia.

After a bomb exploded on February 27 in the Church of Our Lady of Deliverance killing eleven worshippers and injuring about forty, the authorities moved swiftly against the Lebanese Forces, whose loyalists were blamed by the government for the church bombing and a spate of violent acts that preceded it. The political wing of the group was dissolved by executive order, although evidence of its responsibility for the blast was not determined by the courts. Scores of its supporters were arrested and detained, often without due process of law.

Under Lebanese law, those arrested must be released or referred to the Public Prosecutor's office within twenty-four hours of their arrest. This rule was frequently violated, with detainees held incommunicado without charge for weeks or longer. Access to lawyers improved during 1994, as defense lawyers—both Lebanese and foreign—were more aggressive in their efforts to represent prisoners charged with politically motivated crimes. However, lawyers complained of delayed access to clients detained by the military until after confessions were extracted from them by use of force. No private conferences with lawyers were allowed in most cases.

Human Rights Watch confirmed reports of torture and ill-treatment of those detained by Military Intelligence and held in the Ministry of Defense detention facilities. On April 21, Fawzi al-Rasi, from the Lebanese Forces, died after suffering a heart attack while being questioned at the Ministry of Defense, according to an official statement. His family's request for an independent autopsy was rejected. Other detainees were beaten to extract confessions. In July, the military prosecutor rejected a request by a team of international medical experts to examine defendants before the military court who alleged that they had been tortured and forced to sign confessions of guilt. Two physicians from the International Federation for Human Rights and SOS Torture traveled to Beirut but were not allowed to meet with or examine Magi Karam, Gabi Karam, Jeanette Haddad, George Haddad, Chirbil Deeb, Mohamad Sakr, Josef al-Anjam, or Ali al-Bazzal, all on trial before military courts. The defendants were subsequently convicted without consideration of their charges of ill-treatment.

Several suspected supporters of General Aoun were arrested after they had attended a conference held in Paris in June. In speeches before the conference, the ousted general and his supporters criticized the Syrian presence in Lebanon.

The government increased its reliance on military courts to try civilians accused of state security offenses, including the distribution of leaflets critical of the Lebanese government or of Syria. Procedures before the military courts were abbreviated and the rights of defense were circumscribed. Military prosecutors and judges were military officers, with little or no legal training, who were appointed and dismissed by the Minis-

ter of Defense and had no tenure or guarantee of independence.

The government continued to selectively prosecute individuals for crimes committed during the civil war period—most of which were included in a 1991 amnesty law covering the 1975-1991 period. While members of the current cabinet implicated in serious crimes from that period were not questioned, almost all of those prosecuted in 1994 for crimes prior to the 1991 law were members or supporters of the Lebanese Forces or other opposition groups.

In March, the government escalated its campaign against the media by banning private broadcasters from airing news or political programming or commentary. During the year, the government pressured private stations to cease operation, with the government-owned LTV continuing to take legal action against private companies for infringing on its monopoly over television, scheduled to continue until 2012.

In February, a Beirut court acquitted two executives and two journalists from the privately owned ICN television network, which had been shut in April 1993. Henri Sfeir, the owner, Farid Sulaiman, an executive, and news editors Antoine Qustantin and Tony Shamiyya had been charged with fomenting civil strife, a crime under Lebanese law. In May, George Louis Bashir and Youesf Hanna al-Huwaik, two journalists from al-Diyar daily, were indicted under civil war-era Decree 104 for allegedly reporting false news related to Maronite Patriarch Nasralla Sfeir's visit to Australia.

The General Directorate of Public Security (GDPS), the national police force, exercised control over all non-periodical publications, including leaflets and press releases. All such publications were required to be submitted to the police for approval before being distributed. The same rules applied to books, plays and films. In September, Hikmat Deeb, Lina Ghraib, Najla Selim, Fadi Abu-Shaqra, Jean Aoun, Huda Yameen, Mona Shakibyan, Michel Alfteriados, Qizhiya Qurqumaz, Alftari Anastassiou and others were arrested for printing and distributing wall posters protesting a September 17 government-sponsored rally in downtown Beirut.

In addition to the Lebanese government, other forces in Lebanon committed violations of human rights and humanitarian law. Syria's 35,000 troops were deployed mainly in the Beqa' valley, where Iran's Revolutionary Guards are also stationed. Israel and its ally the South Lebanon Army control a self-declared security zone along the Lebanese-Israeli border. The pro-Iranian Hizballa has considerable territorial control in parts of the south and the southern suburbs of Beirut. Until it was dissolved in March, the Lebanese Forces had control over parts of the Metn and Kisrawan districts, north of Beirut.

Under the terms of the September 1991 Syrian-Lebanese agreement, Lebanese officials consulted regularly with commanders of Syrian forces in Lebanon over most security matters, whether involving Syrian nationals or others. Officers of Syrian Military Intelligence were active at the Beirut International Airport and other Lebanese ports of entry, detaining or interrogating Syrian government opponents before permitting them to enter or leave the country. Human Rights Watch/Middle East also received reports of arrests of Lebanese citizens and Palestinian residents by Syrian forces in Lebanon.

Israel and the Israeli-sponsored South Lebanon Army (SLA) were responsible for serious human rights violations in Lebanon during the year. Shelling and air raids by Israel and its allies on southern Lebanese villages and towns, while always ostensibly directed against guerrilla bases, produced a heavy toll of civilian casualties. For example, on August 4, an Israeli jet fired a missile into a residential building in the southern village of Deir Zahrani, killing six and wounding eleven, all civilians. Israel apologized for what it said was a mistake, but according to a Reuters dispatch, Uri Lubrani, the Israeli coordinator for southern Lebanon, said, "[T]hings like this apparently cannot be avoided because when you chop down trees...sometimes chips fly and

this is one of them." On October 19 and 20, Israel and its allied SLA gunners shelled two towns in southern Lebanon, killing seven people and wounding four. All but one—a Lebanese soldier—were civilians.

Israel continued to hold an undisclosed number of Lebanese detainees without charge or trial. Other Lebanese prisoners were held in Israeli prisons beyond the expiration of sentences handed down by Israeli military courts, in "administrative detention" without charge or trial under British Mandate-era emergency regulations. Some of these prisoners had been abducted by Israeli forces from their villages in Lebanon, as happened in May when Israeli commandos seized the Shi`a activist Mustafa Dirani from his home in the Beqa`, reportedly because they believed that he had information on Israeli soldiers missing in action.

The SLA also engaged in the indiscriminate shelling of villages adjacent to the area it controls, the forced conscription of young men, and a policy of arbitrary arrest, lengthy incommunicado detention and torture of suspected opponents held in the notorious al-Khiam prison it controls with Israeli support. In 1994, about 200 detainees were being held in al-Khiam without charge or trial and without access to family or lawyers. The International Committee of the Red Cross continued to be denied access to these detainees.

The Iranian-supported Hizballa, whose forces are supplemented by Iranian Revolutionary Guards, is the only major militia beside the SLA that has not been disarmed by the Lebanese government. It, too, was implicated in abuses, including summary executions, abductions, and beatings. In February, a Hizballa ad hoc tribunal summarily imposed the death penalty on Hassan Awwadha, a sixteen-year-old murder suspect, who was immediately executed with a bullet to the head. Also in 1994, assailants believed connected with Hizballa murdered a Lebanese actor believed to have performed in a pornographic film. In light of the foreign support it enjoys and the significant bloc of parliamentarians from Hizballa in the Chamber of Deputies, the government appeared reluctant to curb abuses by Hizballa loyalists.

Ostensibly aiming to pressure Israel to abandon the Lebanese border area it controls, Hizballa also engaged in 1994 in indiscriminate shelling of northern Israel and areas of southern Lebanon under SLA control, causing extensive damage and casualties among noncombatants.

Elements in the Lebanese Forces, the largest Maronite militia and a major opposition force, were implicated in attacks on civilians, including the bombing on February 27 of the Church of Our Lady of Deliverance, in which eleven worshippers were killed and over forty injured. In contrast with most other abuses, the government swiftly moved against the Lebanese Forces and their supporters suspected of taking part in violence.

The Right to Monitor

There was no prohibition in law of human rights work in Lebanon, but local human rights groups and individual activists reported that fear of Lebanese and Syrian intelligence services curbed their activities. The military prosecutor's office repeatedly summoned Dr. Muhamad Mugraby, a prominent human rights lawyer, to question him about statements he made before the military court in defense of his clients. Government officials contended that elements of Mugraby's statements were punishable under the penal code because they were harmful to Lebanon's foreign policy. A media campaign against Mugraby was believed inspired by government officials, after Mugraby voiced—during a June meeting in Paris attended by Aoun loyalists—criticism of the Syrian presence in Lebanon and the Hrawi/Hariri government.

In September, Hikmat Deeb, active in the Foundation for Humanitarian and Human Rights, was arrested with others and charged with taking part in the printing and distribution of flyers and posters critical of the government.

Among the established groups inside Lebanon were the Lebanese Association for Human Rights, the Foundation for Human and Humanitarian Rights, and the Lebanese Lawyers Association. Outside Lebanon, the Lebanese League for Human Rights was especially active in France and Belgium. Humanitarian and academic organizations reported regularly on issues related to human rights in Lebanon. Among the Beirut-based groups were the Lebanese NGO Forum and the Movement of the Handicapped and Youth for Human Rights and Peace. *The Lebanon Report*, published monthly by the Lebanese Center for Policy Studies, a research institution in Beirut, provided information related to human rights.

U.S. Policy

After a meeting in late September between Secretary of State Warren Christopher and Faris Bouez, his Lebanese counterpart, the U.S. voiced strong support for "Lebanese independence, sovereignty, and territorial integrity." Throughout 1994, U.S. officials appeared concerned primarily with bolstering the Lebanese government and armed forces, and ensuring Lebanon's active participation in the regional peace process. No concern was voiced publicly by officials when the Lebanese government waged an abusive campaign against its opponents in the spring or over the drastic steps taken to further muzzle the media.

While the Clinton administration maintained the travel restrictions imposed by previous administrations on U.S. citizens wishing to travel to Lebanon, it lifted in 1993 an eight-year old ban on the sale of lethal weapons to Lebanon and increased its assistance level. The U.S. approved the sale of 175 M-113A2 armored personnel carriers, out of which 106 were received by July 1994, and funded a training program for the Lebanese military.

Although U.S. economic aid remained relatively small—nine million dollars in fiscal 1994—it had a high multiplier effect; Washington persuaded U.S. allies and multilateral institutions to continue the previous year's record levels of economic aid that made Lebanon, on a per capita basis, the second largest recipient of foreign aid in the Middle East, next only to Israel. According to U.S. officials, President Clinton personally communicated with a number of Arab and European heads of state to encourage their support and assistance to Lebanon. Partly at U.S. urging, the World Bank extended a three-year $2.4 billion aid package for a reconstruction program that was part of a $13 billion expenditure planned by the Lebanese government. U.S. allies, including Saudi Arabia, Kuwait, Qatar, Italy, and Germany, provided the bulk of aid to Lebanon in 1994.

The U.S. and its allies' expressions of support for the Lebanese government were not accompanied by public expressions of concern over the serious human rights violations committed by the Hrawi/Hariri government. To the contrary, foreign aid extended by Kuwait and Saudi Arabia was believed to be implicitly conditioned on the Lebanese government's curbing of media criticism of the two governments.

When asked in June about the Israeli commandos' kidnapping of the Shi'a activist Mustafa Dirani, Robert H. Pelletreau, Assistant Secretary of State for Near Eastern Affairs, told the House Subcommittee on Europe and the Middle East that the U.S. did not condemn the action "because it represents a number of complicated issues in our own system." Although, according to Secretary Pelletreau the U.S. had brokered an agreement between Hizballa and Israel under which the two sides were not to fire at civilian targets, the U.S. rarely condemned the frequent violations of this agreement.

The Work of
Human Rights Watch/Middle East
There were two points of special focus to Human Rights Watch/Middle East's work during 1994: Lebanese government attacks on freedom of expression and the treatment of detainees arrested by military intelligence and tried before military courts.

In March, Human Rights Watch/Middle East protested the Lebanese government's decision to ban private radio and television stations from airing news and political commentaries. In June and July, a Human Rights Watch/Middle East consultant visited Lebanon to investigate recent restrictions on freedom of expression and association. The results of her research are planned for publication in 1995, intended to coincide with preparations for the presidential election scheduled for September 1995 and the parliamentary elections scheduled for 1996.

In 1994 Human Rights Watch/Middle East protested unfair trials by military courts, including their failure to address claims of torture and ill treatment, and refusal to permit independent international physicians to examine defendants who reported being coerced into confessing their guilt.

In October, Human Rights Watch/Middle East supported the efforts of U.S. senators on behalf of eight Lebanese detained for allegedly printing and distributing materials critical of the Lebanese and Syrian governments. All eight were released on bail shortly after the three senators issued a letter protesting their arrest.

SAUDI ARABIA

Human Rights Developments
In 1994 Saudi Arabia witnessed the largest roundup in recent history of opposition activists and a new low in the dismal human rights record of the Kingdom. Arbitrary arrest, detention without trial and ill-treatment of prisoners remained the norm during the year, especially for those accused of political offenses. Several hundred Islamist opponents are known to have been arbitrarily arrested and detained without trial. Scores of drug traffickers were executed, usually by beheading, after summary trials. The ban on free speech, assembly and association was strictly enforced; violators were jailed, deported, banned from travel or dismissed from their government positions. Restrictions on the employment and movement of women were strictly observed, and

harassment of non-Muslims and discrimination against the Shi'a continued unabated.

In response to criticism abroad of the Kingdom's human rights record, the government orchestrated a campaign in the media it controls against human rights principles, which were dismissed as anti-Islamic, Western values. Criticism of human rights abuses in the country was occasionally described as part of "Zionist intrigue of the Israel lobby."

The most significant development in 1994 was the government's crackdown on peaceful dissent by Islamist groups, the largest in recent history. In a campaign begun in April but intensified in September, several hundred religious opponents of the government were arrested. In almost all cases, the arrests and accompanying searches were conducted without warrants and suspects were held without charge or trial. None of the detainees were allowed visits by legal counsel and most, for long periods after arrest, were denied family visits.

According to official statements, about one hundred and fifty of the Islamist detainees were suspected supporters of Shaikh Salman al-Audah and Shaikh Safar al-Hawali, both university professors and religious leaders who had been banned from speaking in public and dismissed from their academic posts in September 1993. Those detained also included founders and supporters of the banned Committee to Defend Legitimate Rights (CDLR), established in May 1993 by Islamist jurists and professors. During May and June 1994, in an attempt to apply pressure and extract information, the government arrested relatives of CDLR spokesman Dr. Muhammed al-Mas'ari after he had fled the country and re-established the committee in London in April 1994. Others detained included religious leaders who signed a June 1994 statement critical of Saudi Arabia's reported support of Southern Yemeni separatists. Although no formal charges were filed against any of the detainees, government statements cited their public speaking in defiance of previous bans and "fomenting dissension and civil strife." Salman al-Audah's book *Kissinger's Promise* was cited

in an official statement as evidence of subversion, as were audiocassettes and handbills distributed clandestinely, in defiance of government regulations.

Soon after the Islamist-inspired CDLR resumed its activities in exile in April 1994, the Directorate of General Investigations (DGI), the secret police known as *al-Mabahith*, began a campaign against all suspected Islamist opposition sympathizers, spokesmen and their family members. The campaign intensified during the summer, when prominent Islamists signed a strongly-worded statement, which was distributed widely, criticizing Saudi involvement in the Yemeni conflict. And on September 12, after Islamists pressured the government into boycotting the U.N. Conference on Population and Development, prominent leaders al-Audah and al-Hawali were arrested with a number of their followers. During the next weeks public protests were held in defiance of the government ban and hundreds more were arrested. By mid-November, the arrest campaign was still under way, with the arrest of many religious teachers, university professors, and others suspected of sympathy with the Islamist opposition.

In February, King Fahd ordered that Usama Bin Ladin, a prosperous businessman who helped finance the *mujahideen* of Afghanistan, be stripped of his Saudi citizenship and have his assets inside the country frozen. Scores of Bin Ladin's followers were detained without charges and most of the foreigners among them were summarily deported.

This crackdown on peaceful dissent belied the promises made by the government when the Basic Law of Government was adopted in March 1992. Although the law was hailed then by Saudi and United States officials as heralding a new era of respect for basic rights, the Saudi government's actions since its adoption proved that such hopes were premature.

In 1994, a government-appointed committee to investigate the violent events of March 1993 at the Rafha refugee camp exonerated camp officials of any wrongdoing. A confrontation there had resulted in the death of at least eight Iraqi refugees and three Saudi government employees and the injury of over 140 refugees. The uprising at the camp, located near the Iraqi-Saudi border, was triggered by the refusal of Saudi authorities to permit family members fleeing Iraq to join their relatives in the camp. To disperse the demonstrators, guards opened fire, killing one, after which refugees apparently set the camp administrative building on fire, resulting in the death of three civilian employees. When security forces subsequently opened fire to disperse the crowds and facilitate the extinguishing of the fire, eight more protesters were killed and hundreds were detained. Many of the detained are known to have been tortured, in an apparent attempt by the authorities to identify those who organized the protest.

Human Rights Watch/Middle East confirmed other reports during 1994 of torture and ill-treatment of detainees during interrogation by the secret police and the religious police. To compel prisoners to provide information they were frequently subjected to electric shock, falaqa (beating on the soles of the feet) and flogging with bamboo sticks. Ill-treatment included prolonged incommunicado detention, sleep deprivation, threats, and insults. Visits by family members or lawyers were often denied for long periods.

In an apparent response to a rise in drug use and other crimes, scores of drug smugglers—almost all foreigners—were beheaded during the first nine months of 1994 after proceedings that fell far short of international standards for fair trials. Most were not represented by lawyers at the trials or assisted in preparing their defense. In 1994, there was a marked increase in the application of corporal punishment, including flogging for a variety of crimes and amputations for theft. On one day in October, five Sudanese nationals had their right hands amputated as a penalty for theft.

Under the Imprisonment and Detention Law No. 31 of 1978 and its 1982 bylaws, issued by the Minister of Interior, detainees may be held indefinitely without trial or judicial review. Although families were often able to find out informally if one of their members had been detained, rarely was there formal notification. This problem applied equally to foreigners arrested in Saudi Arabia, many of whom had no family in Saudi Arabia to notice that they were missing. Saudi authorities did not notify foreign missions of the arrest of their nationals and declined to sign international or bilateral consular agreements mandating such notification or allowing immediate access by foreign consulates.

It was equally rare for a detainee to be informed of the charges against him or her. Saudi law permits interrogation of detainees without the benefit of counsel, and the use of force to elicit confessions was commonplace in the Saudi security system. The law explicitly sanctions flogging, indefinite solitary confinement, and deprivation of family visits, as methods for disciplining prisoners.

Foreigners, estimated officially at about five million (27 percent of the population), faced special hardships, including a ban on travel within the country or abroad without written permission from their employers. Hundreds of foreigners accused of violating the stringent visa regulations by overstaying their residency permits or changing their employers were being held in crowded, substandard deportation facilities throughout the Kingdom. Most were subsequently expelled without judicial review. Since regulations required that aliens secure clearance from their former employers before being permitted to leave the country, many were kept in deportation facilities awaiting these clearances.

Human rights abuses were facilitated by the absence of an independent judiciary and the lack of scrutiny by an elected representative body or a free press. The royal family's concentration of power and the absence of a free press or parliament left government officials and members of the royal family immune to criticism and free to take advantage of their positions. In 1994, there were several reports of unpunished abuse by members of the royal family, including murder and beatings of ordinary citizens and foreign residents. No one has been charged with the murder in 1993 of two men on the estate of Prince Mish'al, King Fahd's brother.

In December 1993, the Consultative Council held its first meeting since it was appointed by King Fahd in the preceding August. Almost all of the sixty-one members of the new council were government loyalists, the majority of them longtime government employees. According to the Consultative Council Bylaws issued in August by King Fahd, the Council's members retain their positions in the executive branch while serving their terms in the Consultative Council. By virtue of its mandate, composition and bylaws, the Council did not appear likely to provide a forum for significant political participation or act as a check on human rights abuses. Although all of the Council's meetings—after the inaugural meeting— have been secret, Human Rights Watch/ Middle East learned that the Council did not take any independent decisions; in at least one case, a decision was taken without debate in support of the government's plan to raise utility prices. Few officials were instructed by King Fahd to brief the council in private sessions, and no members are known to have questioned government policy in these sessions.

In 1994, buoyed by widespread dissatisfaction with the government's financial and foreign policies, Islamists intensified their public criticism of the government. In mosque sermons, books, leaflets and audiocassettes, they criticized corruption and favoritism and called for more political participation. Islamist spokesmen also sought greater autonomy for Islamic preachers, including freedom of expression, as well as an end to arbitrary arrests and searches. To combat this criticism, the government enforced its strict ban on public speaking, assembly, and association; in addition to arresting hundreds of Islamists, it dismissed many from their teaching jobs and banned many others from travel. It also introduced measures to tighten its control over the flow

of information in and out of the country. In several statements issued by the Ministry of Interior, the government warned citizens and residents against publicly criticizing the state's "internal, foreign, financial, media or other policies," or "communicating with anyone outside the country, or any activist inside the country, by telephone or fax." The ban included religious sermons, university lectures and the distribution or ownership of hostile writings or audiocassettes.

The government owns and operates all radio and television stations in the Kingdom, and it keeps the privately owned local press on a very short leash, preventing criticism of government policies. Foreign publications, including daily newspapers and weekly magazines, were barred from the country in 1994 for publishing such views. Although the ban on foreign journalists was slightly relaxed in October, most visa applications submitted during 1994 by journalists from major U.S. and British news organizations were turned down.

During 1994, the government expanded its considerable influence over major regional and international news organizations. Royal family members and their close associates had purchased key news organizations during the preceding few years, including United Press International; *al-Hayat*, a major daily in the Middle East; and MBC, a London-based satellite television network. The Ministry of Information signed an agreement with Radio Monte Carlo's Middle East Division, a major source of news in the Kingdom, to highlight positive elements of government policy. In November 1993, MBC acquired the Arab Network of America (ANA), previously a private radio and television cable network with services in most U.S. metropolitan areas. In the months after it changed owners, ANA cancelled, suspended or censored several programs deemed critical of Saudi Arabia. Also during 1994, the British Broadcasting Corporation (BBC) announced plans to start an Arabic television service with the financial backing of a member of the Saudi royal family, whose company will have exclusive rights to retransmit the program to Saudi Arabia.

In March, a royal decree banned television satellite dishes, imposing a fine equivalent to U.S. $26,667 for possessing and $133,333 for importing the equipment. In June, in an apparent response to broadcast criticism of the government, the Ministry of Interior gave those who already owned dishes a month to re-export or otherwise dispose of them before imposing the fines. Also in March, another decree ordered the scrambling of television signals coming into the country. Foreign networks were instructed to transmit their signals to a central relay station owned by the Ministry of Information, which had the exclusive right to provide television programming "suitable for Saudi religious and social values."

The Right to Monitor

Since monitoring human rights violations is considered by the government as political activity, Saudi Arabian law and practice strictly prohibited such an undertaking. Associations of any kind wishing to report on human rights violations in the Kingdom had to work either clandestinely inside the country, at the risk of arrests, or operate outside the Kingdom. In 1994, the ability to monitor human rights abuses in Saudi Arabia was handicapped by the shutdown in the previous year of groups reporting abuses and the arrests of activists attempting to monitor violations.

However, new opposition groups established in 1994 outside the Kingdom provided a steady stream of news and commentary on violations of the rights of dissidents and government opponents. Since April, the banned Committee for the Defense of Legitimate Rights, a mainstream Islamist opposition group, has resumed its activities from London, publishing regular reports on arrests of Islamist activists. In May, the Advice and Reformation Committee was established in London, representing a more hardline Islamist faction led by Usama bin Ladin, a Saudi businessman known for his support of radical groups in the region.

In May, Muhamed al-Khilewi, a senior diplomat at the Saudi Arabian U.N. mission in New York, sought political asylum in the U.S. accusing the Saudi government of corruption and widespread human rights violations. Al-Khilewi, who was granted asylum in August, announced that he would establish an opposition group with an emphasis on human rights advocacy. Ahmed al-Zaharni, a vice consul in Houston, Texas, sought political asylum in the United Kingdom. accusing Saudi officials of plans to harm him following the publication of his book on Saudi foreign policy.

By the end of the summer, the Reform Movement, the main Shi'a opposition group, had suspended all its activities outside Saudi Arabia, in exchange for promises made by the government to improve conditions for the Shi'a minority. Before they were suspended, the movement's activities had included the publication of a magazine in Arabic and another in English, and the distribution of human rights information by groups affiliated with the movement. During the year, the Holy Shrines Center, run by a smaller Shi'a opposition group continued to issue occasional reports on violations of the rights of the Shi'a minority.

No human rights organizations were permitted to visit Saudi Arabia in 1994. As in the past, requests for information and inquiries made by Human Rights Watch/ Middle East during the year on specific incidents of human rights violations went unanswered. By mid-November, there had been no response to our request to discuss sending a Human Rights Watch/Middle East mission to Saudi Arabia.

U.S. Policy

By virtue of an important strategic relationship with Saudi Arabia spanning over fifty years, the United States is uniquely well-placed to help curb human rights abuses in Saudi Arabia. Although the Clinton election campaign had cited Saudi Arabia as a target for human rights attention, the Clinton administration largely failed to criticize publicly Saudi violations, and occasionally praised the Kingdom's rulers. Apparently subordinating human rights principles to strategic and commercial interests, the increased level of military and commercial activity during the year was not accompanied by public candor in assessing the human rights record of Saudi Arabia. During the year, when senior administration officials, including President Clinton and the secretaries of State, Defense, Commerce and Treasury, as well as Mack McLarty, White House Counselor and former chief of staff, visited Saudi Arabia, they refrained from voicing any concern over human rights violations. Their reticence may have reflected the mistaken belief that promotion of human rights and participatory democracy in the Kingdom would have a deleterious effect on other important interests.

U.S. commitment to the defense of Saudi Arabia is a key goal of U.S. foreign policy that the Clinton administration emphasized from the beginning of its term and repeated several times during 1994. This commitment was demonstrated through a permanent U.S. military presence offshore near Saudi Arabia, and the large number of U.S. military advisers with the Saudi military, in addition to pre-positioning of large stocks of weapons for use against threats to Saudi Arabia. When in October Iraq again threatened Kuwait, the U.S.-Saudi military alliance quickly responded by dispatching U.S. troops to the region using Saudi military facilities and pre-positioned armament.

The bilateral military arrangements included the sale of sophisticated weapons, scheduled for delivery throughout the remainder of the decade, with Saudi Arabia accounting for 30 percent of total U.S. military sales. In addition to military hardware, Saudi Arabia in 1994 awarded two major contracts to U.S. aircraft and telecommunications companies, after intensive lobbying by senior administration officials, including President Clinton, Lloyd Bentsen, Secretary of the Treasury, and Ron Brown, Secretary of Commerce, who traveled to Saudi Arabia for that purpose. A $6 billion contract was awarded to Boeing Company and the McDonnell-Douglas Corporation for civil-

ian jetliners for Saudia, the government-owned carrier. American Telephone & Telegraph won an estimated $4 billion contract to expand the telephone network. According to an October 25 *Wall Street Journal* article. 80 percent of the funding for the Boeing-McDonnell deal was being arranged on favorable terms by the U.S. Export-Import Bank. U.S. firms in general increased their investments in Saudi Arabia, making the U.S. by far the major foreign investor in the Kingdom, increasing the U.S. share from 25.3 percent in 1993 to 35.6 percent this year, according to an October 27 UPI dispatch.

In testimony before Congress in March, June, and October, Robert H. Pelletreau, Assistant Secretary of State for Near Eastern Affairs, repeated administration proclamations about the need to promote "more open political systems, and respect for human rights and the rule of law" as one of the administration's priorities. Despite widespread popular dissatisfaction in Saudi Arabia and the fact that the Saudi government has outlawed elections and popular representation for over thirty years, Secretary Pelletreau told Congress in written answer to members' questions submitted in June, "The U.S. believes that the Government of Saudi Arabia continues to enjoy the support of the overwhelming majority of Saudi citizens." The Secretary did not cite any evidence to support his conclusion.

Nevertheless, in 1994, the U.S. government for the first time in recent history publicly expressed some qualified concern over human rights developments in Saudi Arabia, although it refrained from describing them as violations. On September 29, weeks after mass arrests had taken place in Saudi Arabia, Christine Shelly, State Department Spokesperson, answered a reporter's question about the U.S. position on the Saudi government's arrest of 110 opponents, which had been acknowledged by Saudi authorities three days earlier. Ms. Shelly said, "We're aware of the fact that 110 Muslim militants have been arrested. It's a situation that we continue to monitor. Saudi authorities have indicated that these arrests were made on the basis of evidence that they had, that the individuals involved were seeking to disrupt internal security." (The evidence the Saudi official announcement had cited were leaflets and audiocassettes critical of the government, and a book on U.S. policy in the Gulf written by the central figure among those arrested). Ms. Shelly further stated that, "human rights and rule of law issues, of course, are an important part of our ongoing dialogue with the Saudis. We do have—the United States does have serious concerns about the human rights situation in Saudi Arabia." When asked whether the arrests fell under "the heading of human rights concerns," Ms. Shelly said it was premature to classify them as such. "I think that the activity in question is something that we made a notation of in our human rights report, and we are also aware of what their particular regulations are regarding actions that they take in response to disruptions that they perceive to their internal security...and I think it's premature at this point to make that kind of a characterization." According to a November 4 *New York Times* article, administration officials later apologized to the Saudi government for Ms. Shelly's implication that the U.S. was concerned about the arrests.

The Work of
Human Rights Watch/Middle East

In 1994, despite the Saudi government's failure to approve Human Rights Watch/ Middle East's request for an official mission to the Kingdom, the organization continued its close monitoring of human rights conditions and advocacy on behalf of victims of abuse in Saudi Arabia.

Through letters to the government and the media, Human Rights Watch/Middle East protested the harassment of peaceful Islamist dissidents and the U.S. government's silence. It supported the asylum application of a Saudi diplomat who protested his government's abuses and the royal family monopoly of power. (He was granted asylum in the U.S. in August.) Previously,

Human Rights Watch/Middle East had played a key role in efforts to persuade the Canadian government to grant asylum to a Saudi feminist. The successful effort resulted in an overhaul of the Canadian Immigration and Refugee Board's guidelines widening the scope of the definition of women refugees.

In 1994, for the second year in a row, in an effort supported by Human Rights Watch/ Middle East, the House Judiciary Committee adopted an amendment to the Foreign Sovereign Immunities Act making it easier for U.S. citizens to seek legal remedies in the U.S. for human rights abuses committed abroad. The amendment was partly in response to the 1993 Supreme Court decision in *Saudi Arabia v. Nelson*, in which Human Rights Watch/Middle East had acted as *amicus curiae* in support of Scott Nelson, who was suing the Saudi government for torture and arbitrary arrest during his employment with a Saudi government agency.

SYRIA

Human Rights Developments

The government of President Hafez al-Asad did not dismantle repressive laws and institutions, and gave no visible sign that the state was prepared to tolerate open criticism of its policies and practices by granting legal status to now-banned opposition political parties and human rights groups. The state of emergency, imposed in 1963, remained in effect, suspending constitutional rights and granting broad powers of detention without charge to security services. There was evidence of prolonged incommunicado detention of individuals subjected to arbitrary arrest. Trials of members of the political opposition continued before the security court, and lengthy sentences were handed down. Freedom of expression, association, and assembly existed only as theoretical rights in the Syrian constitution. As in past years, criticism of President Hafez al-Asad and the powerful security apparatus was strictly off-limits.

Fourteen activists from the Committees for the Defense of Democratic Freedoms and Human Rights in Syria (CDF)—the independent group organized in 1989 by lawyers, physicians, engineers, journalists, writers, and students who were forced to work clandestinely inside the country—were imprisoned for most of 1994. Despite the release of four of them during the year, eleven were still behind bars as of early November, ten of them serving sentences ranging from five to ten years. The intimidating effect of the deliberate crippling of CDF—which began with a wave of arrests in late 1991—hampered in-depth monitoring of the human rights situation and, for the third consecutive year, complicated the collection and flow of information. "Human rights groups fail to understand that we must preserve the stability of the country," Minister of State for Foreign Affairs Nasir Qaddour told Human Rights Watch/Middle East in Damascus in October, "and in doing so, we have to limit rights." He justified the continuing state of emergency with these words: "We are in a state of war. We have Iraq to the east and Israel to the south, occupying the Golan [Heights]."

Prolonged incommunicado detention, a practice that facilitates torture, continued in 1994. Early in the year, it became known that thirty-four-year-old Lebanese citizen Dani Mansourati died in detention from torture and ill-treatment at the Damascus headquarters of Air Force Intelligence, which is known for its covert operations in foreign countries. He had been held incommunicado since his arrest in May 1992 in Damascus by Military Intelligence, the security force that plays an important role in Lebanon.

Eleven relatives and friends of the late General Salah Jadid—the Ba'ath Party strongman arrested after the 1970 coup who remained in detention without charge until his death in August 1993—were held in incommunicado detention until their release on July 3. Six of the relatives were students ranging in age from seventeen to thirty-one years old, and another was a thirty-year-old university lecturer. They and four friends of the family, including a dentist, a businessman, an engineer, and a retired army officer, had all been arrested between August 23 and August 29, 1993, following Jadid's death, and taken to an unknown location. On June 20, the Syrian Embassy in London replied to Amnesty International appeals about the case. "[N]o one was arrested or detained because of being a relative or friend of the late Salah Jadid," the Embassy wrote. "Furthermore, the Syrian Arab Republic laws and regulations do not give authority to anyone to arrest or detain any citizen because of his or her blood relation, colour, opinion, religion, or language." The government did not deny that the individuals were in official custody, but it provided no information about why they were detained or where they were being held incommunicado.

In September, the Supreme State Security Court, whose decisions cannot be appealed to a higher tribunal, handed down judgments in the ongoing trials of suspected members or supporters of banned political parties. CDF reported that fifty-six members of the Party for Communist Action and the Communist Party/Political Bureau—another banned opposition group—were sentenced to prison terms of up to fifteen years. The harsh sentences send a strong message that the government remains firm in its policy of denying freedom of association to opposition political groups. Syrian officials told Human Rights Watch/Middle East in October that 275 defendants had been tried before the security court since 1992.

On the positive side, there were releases in 1994 of scores of political prisoners and four CDF activists. Five long-term prisoners were released in 1994: Ahmad Swaidani, Mustafa Rustom, Haditha Murad in February, and Adel Nouaisseh and Dhafi Jouma'ni later in the year. All five had been held without charge or trial: Swaidani since 1969, and the others since the early 1970s. These releases reduced the number of Syria's longest-serving political prisoners to seven. Muhammed 'Id Ashshawi, Fawzi Rida, and Abdel Hamid Muqdad have been detained without charge for over two decades. Khalil Brayez, Mahmud Fayyadh, Jalal el-Din Mirhij, and Mustafa Fallah—who were tried and sentenced in 1971 to fifteen-year prison terms—remained detained despite the expiry of their sentences. Such uninterrupted detention for an extraordinarily long period, and the advanced age of these prisoners, raise serious humanitarian concerns; human rights groups expressed concern during the year about the poor health of Muhammed 'Id Ashshawi, Fawzi Rida, and Mahmud Fayyadh. After almost a quarter of a century, the continued detention of these men appears to be wholly arbitrary and they should be released.

Beginning at the end of April, over eighty detainees were freed, including Ahmad Hasso, a CDF activist who had been imprisoned since early 1992. An additional twenty prisoners were released in September and October, CDF announced on October 24. Three of them were CDF members Jihad Khazem, Ibrahim Habib, and Najib Ata Layqa, all of whom had been detained since early 1992. Others included Adel Nouaisseh, a member of the ruling Ba'ath Party's National Revolutionary Command Council held without charge since his arrest in 1972, and Nihad Nahhas, one of the founders of the banned Party for Communist Action (PCA). Jordanian Dhafi Jouma'ni, a member of the National Command detained since 1970, was released on October 30.

Steps were taken to lift long-standing restrictions on freedom of movement for members of Syria's small Jewish community in advance of the meeting in Geneva in January between President Clinton and President Asad. By late December 1993, authorities had reportedly issued 550 exit permissions to 900 Jews that had until then been unable to obtain these documents. Human Rights Watch/Middle East received information from sources in Syria that in early January about thirty permissions were being issued daily. At the end of February, Syria's deputy chief rabbi Yousef Jajati announced that all members of the community had received exit visas. Damascus-based Western diplomats told Human Rights Watch/Middle East in October that the issue of the Syrian Jews had been "resolved."

The Right to Monitor

The state does not permit its citizens the right to carry out human rights monitoring and reporting. The continued imprisonment of eleven CDF activists serves as a powerful reminder that rights advocacy will be dealt with harshly by authorities. Ten of the CDF members were convicted by the state security court in 1992 in proceedings that fell short of international fair-trial standards. Their human rights work led them to be charged under the emergency law with membership in an illegal organization (CDF), the dissemination of false information, and undermining the state by distributing leaflets critical of the government. In October, Minister of State for Foreign Affairs Nasir Qaddur told Human Rights Watch/Middle East that the CDF activists were "communists calling for the violent overthrow of the state." Their names and prison sentences are: writer Nizar Nayouf (ten years); lawyer Aktham Nouaisseh, the CDF spokesperson in Syria (nine years); jurist Afif Mizher and university lecturer Muhammed Ali Habib (nine years); Bassam al-Shaykh (eight years); and Thabet Murad, Jadi' Nawfal, Ya'qub Musa, Hassan Ali and Hussam Salama (all five years). Several times during the year, CDF called attention to the poor health of Aktham Nouaisseh, who suffers from glaucoma, glomerulonephritis, and partial paralysis due to beating during interrogation following his arrest in December 1991. Nouaisseh was moved from Sednaya prison on August 18 to a hospital, where he remained until August 21. During this time, according to CDF, the lawyer did not receive medical treatment for the glaucoma.

The state's harsh measures against locally-based rights advocates contrasted with government officials' receptivity during the year to international human rights organizations. In October, a delegation from Amnesty International conducted a mission, and senior officials, including Minister of Interior Muhammed Harba, Minister of Justice Abdallah Talba, and Minister of State for Foreign Affairs Nasir Qadur, met with a Human Rights Watch/Middle East representative in Damascus. The organization urged the government to match its dialogue with international human rights organizations with a radical overturning of its restrictions on domestic organizations, and to end the persecution of domestic nongovernmental groups, notably CDF. We said that imprisoned human rights monitors should be freed, and independent rights organization should, in accordance with Syrian law, be granted legal status. Such groups should be permitted to collect and disseminate information freely, and carry out other peaceful activities—including networking with other regional and international nongovernmental organizations—without the fear of state retaliation against members and supporters.

U.S. Policy

The Clinton administration's policy issues with Syria included human rights, although efforts to broker a peace agreement with Israel clearly remained the overriding goal. The Syrian government signalled a desire for an improved political and economic relationship with the U.S., and continuous contact during the year between senior Clinton administration officials and their Syrian counterparts—to facilitate progress on the Israel-Syria track—provided numerous opportunities to pursue this goal.

Improvement of Syria's human rights record was one of the three issues identified by the U.S. as key to an improved bilateral relationship. The U.S. also said it looked for signs that the Asad government was curbing the drug trade that originates in the Syrian-controlled Beka' Valley of Lebanon, and clamping down on Hizballa, the militia armed by Iran that has indiscriminately shelled settlements in northern Israel from positions in southern Lebanon, and other groups implicated in international terrorism. The Clinton administration has identified open political systems and greater respect for human rights and the rule of law as among its priorities in the region. But if the ongoing U.S.-Syria dialogue included in-depth discussion of these issues, nudging from the American side was applied privately. Human Rights Watch/Middle East is aware of no public statement by the Clinton administration officials during the year that called the Syrian government to task for specific abuses such as arbitrary arrest, incommunicado detention, torture, and long-term imprisonment of human rights monitors.

President Clinton met with President Asad twice during 1994—in Geneva in January, and in Damascus in October. Both occasions presented the U.S. with a major opportunity to put forth concerns about Syria's human rights record, but the subject was not broached publicly.

The only references to human rights at the January 16 meeting in Geneva were couched in extremely vague language. At the joint press conference following the meeting, President Asad noted that over the last year he and President Clinton had had "a number of exchanges and telephone communications." President Clinton confirmed this close contact, stating that "from the outset of our administration, I have engaged President Asad in a regular correspondence by telephone and letter." At the meeting that day, President Clinton said that they discussed "the state of relations between the U.S. and Syria" and "agreed on the desirability of improving them. Accordingly, we've instructed the secretary of state and the Syrian foreign minister to establish a mechanism to address these issues in detail and openly." President Clinton explained in generalities one of the stumbling blocks to closer relations, the Asad government's harboring of groups that carry out cross-border political violence: "Well, as we have made clear, we have had differences over the years with Syria over a number of issues, including our differences over questions relating to certain groups—the PKK [the Workers' Party of Kurdistan that carries out guerrilla activity in southeast Turkey], the Hezbollah, the Jabril group and others—other issues. We talked about these differences for about an hour today without any view toward trying to resolve them." National Security Advisor Anthony Lake returned to this issue in a speech about U.S. policy toward Syria at the Washington Institute on May 17. He articulated the concern of the Clinton administration that Syria's "alliance with Iran and its support for rejectionist groups have given the forces of extremism a vital base in the Middle East." Following the bombing of a commuter bus in Tel Aviv on October 19, the State Department said that U.S. Ambassador Christopher Ross was instructed to pressure Syrian officials—with whom he met on October 19 in Damascus—to restrict the activities of Hamas, the militant Palestinian group that claimed responsibility for the attack.

President Clinton visited Damascus on October 27 as part of a six-state Middle East tour and conferred with President Asad for over three hours. He made clear, in his public remarks that day, that the purpose of the meeting was "to add new energy" to U.S. efforts to broker a comprehensive peace between Israel and Syria. As in January, Syria's human rights performance was not on the agenda, and President Clinton was criticized for visiting a state that remained on the U.S. list of countries that sponsor international terrorism. It was reported by *The New York Times* on October 28 that President Clinton had not raised the issue. In the press conference following the meeting, President Asad denied that Syria supported terrorism, and stated: "We did not discuss terrorism as a separate title....[T]his was not one of the topics on the agenda in my discussion with President Clinton, and we are discussing what is more important, and our concern and focus was on the peace process."

When it was announced on October 21 that President Clinton's Middle East tour would include Syria, senior administration officials told *The New York Times* that they hoped that President Asad would issue a strong public statement against terrorism while President Clinton was in Damascus. At a press conference in Jerusalem on October 27, President Clinton publicly reproached the Syrian leader for not doing so: "I regret that President Asad did not take the opportunity to say in public what he said to me in private about his deep regret about the loss of innocent lives and particularly the bus bombing [in Tel Aviv]."

The Clinton administration in 1994 never raised publicly the issue of Syria's continuing detention of the CDF human rights monitors. Early in the year, State Department Acting Assistant Secretary for Near Eastern Affairs Mark R. Parris informed Human Rights Watch in a letter that the case of the CDF monitors has been "followed closely" and that the U.S. ambassador in Damascus "has raised their case with the Syrians and made clear our views." Referring to the Geneva meeting, he added that "human rights issues were indeed raised," although "the focus was on the broad issues rather than individual cases."

Following a meeting with President Asad in Damascus on May 1, Secretary of State Warren Christopher said that he had received "some encouraging responses," *The New York Times* reported on May 2, to his request that a senior U.S. official be permitted to visit Syria to investigate human rights. But the State Department later confirmed to Human Rights Watch/Middle East that the expected mission by Assistant Secretary of State for Democracy, Human Rights, and Labor John Shattuck had not been scheduled as of November 1.

The Work of
Human Rights Watch/Middle East

Human Rights Watch/Middle East worked during the year to press the Syrian government to remove obstacles to the scrutiny of its human rights performance by international and domestic monitors. We sought to obtain a commitment from the government to permit human rights fact-finding inside the country without fear of arrest. We also identified and utilized opportunities for publicizing the continued imprisonment of the CDF monitors, and appealed to the U.S. and other governments to press for their release.

The Clinton-Asad meeting in Geneva in January presented avenues for advocacy on the CDF case. In December, Human Rights Watch/Middle East wrote to President Clinton, recommending that he raise the issue of the imprisoned monitors with President Asad and press for their immediate, unconditional release. In advance of the meeting, we released this letter to the press, and wrote an opinion piece on the subject that appeared in the *Christian Science Monitor*. We also organized fifteen U.S., Arab, and European nongovernmental organizations to press the issue of the CDF monitors with Clinton administration officials prior to the meeting. In February, we distributed the package used in the campaign to European Union ambassadors in Damascus, urging that the CDF case be raised in meetings with Syrian government representatives and that persistent diplomatic pressure be applied to effect the immediate and unconditional release of the rights activists. Following the campaign, four CDF monitors were released. Throughout the year, contact was maintained with officials at the Syrian Embassy in Washington, D.C., to pursue the request by Human Rights Watch/Middle East—first made in November 1993—for permission to conduct a fact-finding mission. The executive director of Human Rights Watch/Middle East traveled to Damascus in October to discuss directly with senior government officials the plan for a mission. They gave assurances that the government would facilitate the mission, including prison visits and observation of state security court trials. But as of November 18, we had not received word that the delegation would be permitted to carry out its planned November visit.

HUMAN
RIGHTS
WATCH

UNITED STATES

In 1994, Human Rights Watch documented serious human rights abuses in the United States, centered on three important themes: U.S. compliance with international human rights treaties; law enforcement-related abuses, including torture and beatings by U.S. Border patrol agents, mistreatment of prisoners in maximum security facilities, and involvement of physicians in executions; and freedom of association, travel, and debate.

U.S. Compliance with the ICCPR

After a delay of more than a quarter century, on September 8, 1992 the United States became a party to the International Covenant on Civil and Political Rights (ICCPR). Under the terms of the ICCPR, the United States had one year from the date of ratification to file a report on its compliance with covenant provisions. In anticipation of that report, in December 1993 Human Rights Watch and the American Civil Liberties Union (ACLU) issued a 216-page report on the U.S. human rights record titled *Human Rights Violations in the United States*.

The report found significant shortcomings in the U.S. record, from the summary repatriation of Haitian boat people to the brutal treatment of prisoners. In these and other cases, the ICCPR could offer greater protection against human rights abuses than the current interpretation of U.S. law. However, the Bush administration, through a series of reservations, declarations and understandings had nullified every provision of the treaty that it believed would have granted expanded rights to Americans. The ACLU and Human Rights Watch called on the Clinton administration to allow Americans to invoke the protection of the covenant in U.S. courts.

In October 1994, the United States made public its report on compliance with ICCPR guarantees. As a follow-up to the December 1993 report, Human Rights Watch and the ACLU evaluated the U.S. report, criticizing it for reserving candor for abuses that were largely in the past while remaining vague or silent about ongoing human rights violations. The U.S. report primarily recited constitutional and statutory provisions, a technique for avoiding serious human rights scrutiny that the U.N. Human Rights Committee criticized.

Human Rights Watch and the ACLU provided an update of substantive areas in which the groups had previously found that the U.S. human rights record fell short of international standards:

Prison Conditions

By forcing prisoners to live in extremely overcrowded conditions and punishing prisoners at "supermaximum security" facilities, the United States routinely violated Article 10 of the ICCPR, which requires that all prisoners and detainees "be treated with humanity and with respect to the inherent dignity of the human person." The anti-discrimination requirement of Article 26 was violated by the unequal treatment of women prisoners, who received fewer recreational, vocational, and educational opportunities than their male counterparts. The crime bill passed by Congress in August would aggravate many problems that U.S. prisoners already faced in penal custody.

Immigrants and Refugees

The interdiction and summary repatriation of Haitian boat people was a flagrant violation of Article 12, which states that "[e]veryone shall be free to leave any country, including his own." In June, the Clinton administration ended its policy of interdicting and returning Haitians without any inquiry into the likelihood that they would face persecution upon return. After a brief period of shipboard screening, the administration settled on a policy of safe haven, which provided for intercepted Haitians to be taken to the Guantanamo Bay naval base in Cuba, where they were detained in a military camp or sent on to refugee camps in third countries.

The September 1994 agreement with

the Cuban government, in which Cuba agreed to prevent its citizens from departing by sea in exchange for a U.S. increase in the number of available visas, appeared to violate Article 12 because of U.S. insistence that Cuba prevent its citizens from leaving their own country.

Human rights abuses by Border Patrol agents of the Immigration and Naturalization Service violated Article 7 (the right to be free from torture or cruel, inhuman or degrading treatment) and Article 9(1) (the right to liberty and security of the person).

The Death Penalty

Article 6 of the ICCPR favors but does not require the abolition of the death penalty. It also limits the circumstances in which the death penalty may be imposed: arbitrary deprivation of life is forbidden, as is the execution of juveniles; furthermore, the death penalty may be imposed "only for the most serious crimes." The United States entered a reservation to the ICCPR that allowed it to use capital punishment to the extent permitted under the U.S. Constitution. But for this reservation, the U.S. would have been in violation of all of the above conditions of Article 6.

The new U.S. crime bill authorized the death penalty for sixty offenses including crimes that did not involve murder such as drug trafficking and certain attempted murders by "drug kingpins." Congress also rejected efforts to create a federal right to be free from racial discrimination in state and federal death penalty cases. As of July 20, there were 2,870 people on death row. As of August 3, there had been 249 executions. The thirty-eight executions carried out in 1993 represented the highest yearly rate since the resumption of capital punishment in 1976; 56 percent of those executed were white; 38 percent African-American, and 4 percent Native American.

Police Brutality

Police abuse in the United States was one of the nation's most pressing human rights issues. The persistent use of excessive force, often exacerbated by racism, violated the Article 7 prohibition on "cruel, inhuman and degrading treatment or punishment" and the prohibition in Articles 2 and 26 against discrimination. The United States further violated Article 2 by failing to take "the necessary steps" to ensure respect for these basic rights.

The new crime bill increases protection against police brutality by permitting the Attorney General to institute a civil action upon reasonable cause to believe that a governmental authority or agent is abusing the rights of juveniles in custody. The legislation also provides for the collection of data about the use of excessive force by police officers nationwide.

The 1993 report also examined U.S. practices in the areas of race and sex discrimination, language rights, religious liberty, and free expression.

Human Rights Watch pressed Congress to enact legislation overturning the restrictive reservations, declarations and understandings that the U.S. had attached, and providing U.S. litigants with the opportunity to invoke the ICCPR in American courts.

Border Violence

In 1994, Human Rights Watch conducted a third investigation of human rights abuses committed along the U.S.-Mexico border by the Border Patrol of the Immigration and Naturalization Service (INS). As a follow-up to 1992 and 1993 reports that documented serious physical abuse and mistreatment, in July 1994 Human Rights Watch visited the San Diego-Tijuana border area in California and the Tucson-Nogales border area in Arizona. In addition to updating information regarding previously documented cases, Human Rights Watch received testimony regarding sixteen new cases of alleged Border Patrol or Customs abuses, including unjustified shootings, sexual assault, and severe beatings. Human Rights Watch examined Border Patrol procedures for training agents, receiving and handling complaints of abuse, disciplining and tracking problem agents, and holding agents accountable for follow-through on investigations of abuse.

Human Rights Watch found that attempts to address concerns raised in previous reports were insufficient and, to the extent changes were implemented at all, unsuccessful. The organization continued to press for Congressional passage of the Immigration Enforcement Review Commission Act, which would create independent civilian review of the INS.

Prisoners' Rights

The Human Rights Watch Prison Project continued to monitor the treatment of prisoners in the United States. In response to news that the United States might negotiate with Cuba for the possible repatriation of Cubans being detained in United States prisons since their arrival in the Mariel boat-lift in 1980, Human Rights Watch wrote to Attorney General Janet Reno in September 1994 to urge fair treatment for the detainees. Because of evidence that Mariel Cuban detainees were denied due process rights in INS detention proceedings, Human Rights Watch opposed repatriation of detained Mariel Cubans without a hearing to determine whether the Cubans should instead be released into American society.

The Human Rights Watch Prison Project continued to request access to the Westville, Indiana Maximum Control Complex (MCC). The project had received reports over the previous two years of human rights abuses in the MCC, including physical brutality and unacceptable living conditions. In April 1994, the Prison Project demanded an independent inquiry of abuses that had been reported, and reiterated its request to conduct an on-site investigation. In September, the Westville MCC denied access, writing, "There will be no inspection. Correctional facilities have not been created, nor do they function, for the purpose of having special interest groups 'inspect' them for whatever specific cause that group may champion." The Indiana Department of Correction (IDOC) was the only jurisdiction under the U.S. authorities, aside from Puerto Rico, that

had refused Human Rights Watch access to a correctional facility.

In a letter urging the IDOC to grant the Prison Project access to the Westville MCC, the Interfaith Prisoners of Conscience Project wrote that the U.N. Standard Minimum Rules for the Treatment of Prisoners and the International Covenant on Civil and Political Rights "are not 'specific issues' championed by 'special interest groups', but human rights standards established by the international community that apply to correctional facilities everywhere in the world." The facility's refusal had generated widespread negative publicity, and the Prison Project, along with civil rights groups and religious leaders, continued to press for access.

The Prison Project collaborated with the Women's Rights Project to conduct a year-long investigation into abuses against women incarcerated in state prisons across the United States. A report based on that research was planned for release in 1995.

Death Penalty

In March 1994, Human Rights Watch, the American College of Physicians, the National Coalition to Abolish the Death Penalty, and Physicians for Human Rights released an 80-page report titled *Breach of Trust: Physician Participation in Executions in the United States.* In addition to the federal government and the U.S. military, thirty-seven states had death penalty statutes. Methods of execution reviewed in the report included lethal injection, electrocution, the gas chamber, hanging, and the firing squad. The United States was the only country in the world using lethal injection as an execution method, which had brought renewed attention to the issue of medical participation in executions.

The report documented continued physician involvement in executions in violation of ethical and professional codes of conduct and American Medical Association (AMA) and World Medical Association (WMA) policies. Physician involvement was often mandated by state law and specified in departmental regulations about execution procedures. Even when state laws were vague about requiring physician participation, research indicated that in practice, physicians were often directly involved in the execution process. The report provided legal and ethical analyses of the issues involved, and made recommendations designed to ensure that U.S. laws would not require physicians to violate professional ethics.

The clash between death penalty law and medical ethics reached the federal level when the U.S. Justice Department proposed new rules for federal executions. The rules proposed use of lethal injections and mandated that at least one physician attend the execution and pronounce death. Medical professionals vigorously opposed the rule. As a result, in early 1993 the Justice Department eliminated the requirement that a physician be present and that physicians be required to pronounce death. Although the new regulation allowed medical professionals to decline to participate in executions on the basis of national ethics, the rules did not prohibit physician participation.

The relevant statutes of the thirty-six states with the death penalty mentioned the presence of a physician in all but two cases. Some statutes were in direct conflict with the AMA ethical standards. Twenty-three states required that a physician "determine" or "pronounce" death. Twenty-eight state statutes or regulations required that a physician "shall" or "must" be present at the execution. Within each state, the Department of Corrections usually designed its own set of regulations for conducting executions. These regulations were frequently difficult to obtain, and were confidential in some states. The regulations translated the usually vague language of the state statute into specific assignments for physicians involved in executions. The report gave a state-by-state analysis of regulations, detailing the participation of physicians in procedures such as inspecting equipment, supervising a heart monitor fitted to the condemned inmate, administering the lethal injection, and witnessing the execution to ensure that death was induced.

Although the regulations left no doubt about physicians' role in the execution process, they did not reliably describe the extent of actual physician involvement. The report provided information from interviews conducted with witnesses to recent executions in Mississippi, Virginia, Alabama, Georgia, Indiana, Nevada, and South Carolina.

Mississippi
According to a former warden, prison staff medical technicians would attach two EKG monitors and two stethoscopes to the prisoner's chest in an isolation cell a few paces from the gas chamber. Two physicians, who would sit behind the gas chamber out of view of the official witnesses, would monitor the EKG and stethoscopes. They were local doctors who volunteered for the task and were not paid. The doctors advised the warden when the prisoner had expired.

Virginia
According to a criminologist who witnessed three executions, a physician employed by the Department of Corrections would await completion of the execution in a small conference room directly off the execution chamber. After the electric chair was turned off, there was a three minute "cooling period." The doctor would enter the chamber, place a stethoscope to the inmate's chest, and pronounce that the inmate had expired.

South Carolina
In 1991, Donald Gaskins attempted suicide about sixteen hours before his scheduled execution. Gaskins used a razor blade to slit his wrists and elbows. He passed out from loss of blood, and was found unconscious about an hour later. A physician was called in to treat Mr. Gaskins, and he stitched the inmates's wounds tightly, restricting movement of the arms. Gaskins remained unconscious, strapped down on a gurney in the cell. The doctor was in and out, periodically checking on his condition. Just before the execution, Mr. Gaskins regained consciousness. He was escorted to the electric chair and executed.

The report also documented instances in which physicians who work for correctional health systems have suffered consequences for refusing to participate in executions.

In the wake of the report, Human Rights Watch worked with physicians' and human rights groups to press for changes in the laws and regulations of all death penalty states to incorporate AMA guidelines on physician participation and urged state medical boards, which were responsible for licensure and discipline, to define physician participation as unethical conduct and to take appropriate action against physicians who violated ethical standards.

Restriction of Free Expression in Miami's Cuban Exile Community

Human Rights Watch continued to monitor free expression in Miami by documenting instances of harassment and intimidation against members of the Cuban exile community in Miami, Florida who express moderate political views on Castro or relations with Cuba. Since its original report, in 1992, which linked anti-communist forces in the exile community to acts of violence against their more moderate compatriots, Human Rights Watch has noted some improvements in free expression in Miami, particularly with regard to direct U.S. government involvement or complicity in repressive activities. Overall, however, the atmosphere for unpopular political speech remained marked by fear and danger. This danger became manifest in late April 1994, following a conference in Havana on "The Nation and Emigration." Miami residents who attended the conference returned home to find themselves besieged by death threats, bomb threats, verbal assaults, acts of violence, and economic retaliation.

The hatred against those who favored dialogue with Cuba was fed by a few powerful local Spanish radio stations, in particular Radio Mambi, Radio CMQ, and La Cubanisima. Radio stations identified conference participants by name and referred to them derogatorily, sponsored listener-participation programs in which callers were permitted to defame conference participants, and invited listeners to vote as to which participants deserved to have an "act of repudiation" carried out against them.

Conference participants who had been victims of attack were generally satisfied with the response of local and federal law enforcement agents, but no arrests were made in connection with any of the violent incidents or threats reported.

While the lack of evidence of direct government involvement in suppressing certain viewpoints was a significant improvement since the 1992 report, Human Rights Watch stepped up its calls on state, local and federal officials to take affirmative action to protect those who exercised their First Amendment rights to freedom of opinion and expression.

Right to Travel

Human Rights Watch continued to advocate for the right to travel. Restrictions on travel violated the right to free speech as embodied in the First Amendment of the United States Constitution and Article 19 of the ICCPR. The right of Americans to travel abroad was critical to their ability to participate fully in public debate on foreign policy and international security matters.

Human Rights Watch urged adoption of the Free Trade in Ideas Act of 1994, passed by Congress in May, which included a non-binding resolution that travel for educational, religious, cultural or humanitarian purposes or for public performances or exhibitions should not be restricted. It also prohibited the banning of travel under any future embargoes.

After the passage of the act, the administration began conducting a policy review for the purpose of implementing the Congressional resolution. In late August, however, this salutary trend was reversed in response to the Cuban refugee crisis. In direct opposition to the protections advocated in the Free Trade in Ideas Act, the administration barred family visits to Cuba except in dire emergencies, excluded free-lance journalists and documentary filmmakers, and banned travel for public performances or exhibitions. In the wake of this reversal, Human Rights Watch reiterated its call for the Clinton administration to lift the ban on travel by U.S. citizens to Cuba.

Ratification of Treaties

During 1994, Human Rights Watch wrote to the Senate Foreign Relations Committee to support ratification of two important international conventions, the Convention on the Elimination of All Forms of Discrimination Against Women (CEDAW) and the International Convention on the Elimination of All Forms of Racial Discrimination (CERD). Human Rights Watch also provided recommendations regarding the Clinton administration's proposed reservations to the conventions. Human Rights Watch urged the Foreign Relations Committee to reject the administration's proposed understanding that implementation of the conventions would be divided among federal, state and local governments, because the understanding could be interpreted to limit federal responsibility for the conduct of state, and local governments. The committee was also advised to reject declarations that would enable the U.S. to decide on a case-by-case basis whether to submit to the jurisdiction of the International Court of Justice concerning disputes over interpretation of the conventions. Finally, Human Rights Watch urged the committee to amend the reservations providing that private discriminatory conduct would be regulated only as mandated by the U.S. Constitution and law.

THE ARMS PROJECT

The Human Rights Watch Arms Project was established in September 1992 with a grant from the Rockefeller Foundation. Its purpose is to monitor and seek to prevent transfers of weapons, military assistance and training to regimes or groups that commit gross violations of internationally recognized human rights or the laws of war. In addition, the Arms Project seeks to promote freedom of expression and freedom of information about arms and arms transfers worldwide.

In the two years of its existence, the Human Rights Watch Arms Project has carved out a unique niche for itself in the world of nongovernmental organizations. We have done so by designing a program that incorporates the strengths of both the human rights community and the arms control community. From the former, we borrow investigative and legal-analytical skills; from the latter, weapons trade expertise. Our unique contribution lies in our effort to highlight the link between, on the one hand, violations of human rights and the laws of war and, on the other, the legal and moral responsibility of governments for these violations through their supply of weapons to abusive regimes and non-state actors. The Arms Project is therefore a human rights undertaking that seeks to prevent the physical means of human rights abuse from reaching the hands of known abusers. It seeks accountability from both suppliers and recipients of weapons for the human rights consequences of their transfer.

Two distinguishing features of the Arms Project since its inception have been its commitment to field research and its emphasis on the trade in small arms and other less-than-major weapons. Most casualties in modern conflicts are civilians who are killed or maimed by small arms and light weapons, like landmines, light mortars, rocket-propelled grenades, and automatic rifles.

The Arms Project's field research attempts to connect the documented abuse of weapons in the field to their supply. Thus, field research undertaken by the Arms Project begins with the demand side of weapons transfers—their use and abuse—and works from there to the supply side. By focusing on abuse, the Arms Project is able to bring to bear the traditional tools of the human rights movement: international denunciation and stigmatization for the violation of international standards. This emphasis on field research makes the Human Rights Watch Arms Project nearly unique among groups researching arms transfers, which generally emphasize research among government and other public documents. Because transfers of less-than-major weapons have not been tracked in the way that major weapons are, field research has been the best way of investigating this trade.

An area of continued special consideration are weapons which as a class are, or in the view of the Arms Project should be, prohibited by the laws of war. These are weapons that by their very nature are indiscriminate weapons. The Arms Project has identified in this area chemical or biological weapons and antipersonnel landmines. The Arms Project has sought to eliminate these weapons under the laws of war, without consideration of the human rights record of the country or group possessing them.

Field Research

During the Arms Project's second year, missions were sent to Lebanon, Israel, Cambodia and Angola. In the meantime, several research projects initiated during the first year were completed or are nearing completion. These missions/projects included the following:

Rwanda

In January 1994, the Arms Project published a 64-page report, *Arming Rwanda: The Arms Trade and Human Rights Abuses in the Rwandan War*. The publication of this previously unknown information on French, South African, Egyptian, and Ugandan involvement in the Rwandan war put tremendous pressures on those governments to halt their military assistance to both sides in the conflict—the government of Rwanda and the Rwanda Patriotic Front. The report, while reproducing secret documentation on plans for the Hutu militias, became a primary source of information in the massive coverage of previously-ignored Rwanda that fol-

lowed the Hutu government's genocidal campaign. The report contributed greatly to the pressures on France to assure the U.N. that its post-genocide military intervention would be strictly humanitarian in nature.

Mozambique

In the spring of 1994, the Arms Project published a 136-page book, *Landmines in Mozambique*. It describes the types of mines that have been laid in Mozambique, the human cost these mines have exacted, and the mine clearance activities that have been undertaken by the United Nations and non-governmental organizations. The report caused the Mozambican government, its RENAMO opponents, and the U.N. to justify their lack of effort to address the landmine crisis in Mozambique, thereby putting pressure on all sides to improve their performance in this regard.

India/Pakistan

In September 1994, the Arms Project issued a 59-page report, *Arms and Abuses in Indian Punjab and Kashmir*. This report focuses on the arms flow from the U.S.-orchestrated "Afghan pipeline" in Pakistan to militants fighting separatist wars in Kashmir and the Punjab in India. These weapons have been used to commit numerous, serious violations of humanitarian law, including direct attacks on unarmed civilians, indiscriminate attacks, summary executions, rape, hostage-taking, threats to commit bodily harm, and the use of religious sites for military purposes.

Angola

In May-June 1994, a researcher from Human Rights Watch/Africa traveled to Angola on behalf of the Arms Project to investigate arms flows into Angola and violations of the laws of war by both the government and the National Union for the Total Independence of Angola (UNITA) forces since the September 1992 elections. The mission also involved research in Zambia, South Africa and Zimbabwe. In a 176-page book issued on November 15, 1994, *Arms Trade and Violations of the Laws of War Since the 1992*

Elections, the Arms Project concluded that Angola's "forgotten war," fueled by a steady supply of weapons to both sides, has claimed an estimated 100,000 civilian lives since September 1992, and that both the government and the UNITA rebels are responsible for an appalling range of violations of the laws of war. Several countries have supplied weapons or provided other forms of military assistance to the two parties to this conflict, including Russia, Brazil, North Korea, Spain, Portugal, Bulgaria, the Czech Republic, Ukraine, Uzbekistan, South Africa, Zaire, Namibia, and the United States.

Israel/Lebanon

In October and November 1993, the Arms Project undertook missions to Lebanon and Israel to investigate violations of the laws of war and illegal use of weaponry by all parties during the fighting that took place in July 1993. The Arms Project concluded that there is extensive evidence of indiscriminate attacks by Israeli forces against the population of southern Lebanon, as well as by guerrillas affiliated with the Hezbollah movement against Israeli civilians. Many of the weapons systems deployed by Israel in the conflict were of American manufacture, and their use by Israel suggests, in addition to possible violations of U.S. law, the difficulty the U.S. faces in controlling the use of weapons transferred to "friendly" governments.

Cambodia

In collaboration with Human Rights Watch/ Asia, the Arms Project sent a researcher to Cambodia and Thailand in February-March 1994, and again in August 1994, to investigate violations of the laws of war in the fighting between the Cambodian government and the Khmer Rouge. The pattern of fighting in Cambodia, typified by mortar bombardment and mine-laying more than by direct engagement, has always taken a heavy toll on civilians. The researcher also examined the transfer of weapons, military aid, and other services by Thailand, which has a long history of military and logistical support to the Khmer Rouge, as well as by

Indonesia and other governments to both parties.

Georgia/Abkhazia

The Arms Project and Human Rights Watch/ Helsinki sent a mission to Abkhazia in 1993 to study violations of the laws of war and abuses of weaponry during the conflict between Georgian and Abkhazian forces there. In particular, the mission documented indiscriminate attacks, mass hostage-taking, and forced relocation of population groups based on their ethnicity by both sides, and took a close look at the role played by Russian forces in the war.

Antipersonnel Landmines

The Human Rights Watch Arms Project was at the forefront of the rapidly growing international anti-landmines movement as a member of the "Steering Committee" of the International Campaign to Ban Landmines. The ban is now endorsed by nearly two hundred NGOs, as well as by the ICRC, UNICEF, UNHCR, and the U.N. Secretary-General. Editorials endorsing the ban have appeared in *The New York Times*, the *Economist*, and many other newspapers and magazines. The U.S. government has also accorded landmines a high priority: On September 26, 1994, President Clinton in a speech to the U.N. General Assembly announced for the first time that the U.S. intends to seek the eventual elimination of antipersonnel landmines.

In 1994, the Arms Project continued work on a comprehensive data base on the production, stockpiling, and trade of landmines. The results of this work, along with the entire data base, are scheduled to be published in early 1995. The staff of the Arms Project also published a number of articles and presented several papers on landmines during the past year. In 1994, the Arms Project closely monitored a series of U.N. Experts Meetings held in Geneva in preparation for the 1995 Review Conference for the 1980 Landmine Protocol.

Data Base and
Documentary Research

The Arms Project continued documentary research on the arms trade as it concerns human rights abusers, with a focus on the trade in light weapons and small arms. In doing so, we made extensive use of the Freedom of Information Act. A computerized data base was established and target countries were identified. During the coming year, the Arms Project intends to begin data entry. The significance of this data base is that it will provide information not previously available that may act as a catalyst for mobilizing public opinion around the transfer and use of particular weapons systems.

THE CHILDREN'S RIGHTS PROJECT

The Human Rights Watch Children's Rights Project was created in April 1994 to work with Human Rights Watch's regional divisions and projects to monitor and campaign patterns and problems of human rights abuse that uniquely affect children—and for which unique campaigning initiatives are required.

The project came into being from a recognition that children are victims of patterns of human rights abuses that are often primarily consequences of their status as children. These abuses pose special challenges for human rights research and campaigning that are not met by the conventional work either of traditional children's welfare groups or traditional human rights organizations. The Human Rights Watch Children's Rights Project was devised to fill a special niche in global campaigning for children by applying an effective research and action methodology to urgent rights matters that are uniquely children's issues.

Children are particularly vulnerable to abuse; they are neither as physically or as psychologically mature as adults. This vulnerability means that treatment that would be harsh to adults, as in a situation of imprisonment, can represent life-threatening ill-treatment to a child—or a life-stunting denial of a child's opportunity to develop physically, emotionally and intellectually. The deliberate killing of children, too, whether through a process of law in which a child is executed as if an adult, or through extrajudicial execution by state agents or with state acquiescence, poses further challenges. The Human Rights Watch Children's Rights Project seeks to meet these challenges by researching the facts of abuse and campaigning for the vulnerability of children always to be taken into account.

Children, particularly children on their own, are also more vulnerable to exploitation then adults. Children are not small adults, but may be forced to play adult roles—as bonded laborers, as child soldiers, or as prostitute chattels to which authorities turn a blind eye. The vulnerability—and availability—of children may be taken advantage of in ways that limit their freedom and exploit their labor or their bodies in ways that endanger their futures and their very lives. The Human Rights Watch Children's Rights Project focused on situations in which agents of authority are party to such situations.

When children are seen by government at any level to represent a social or political threat, their condition of vulnerability is far greater than that of adults who are similarly marginalized. Children may in fact be petty thieves, particularly if forced to live in the streets with no one to care for them. Children may also be drawn into clandestine guerrilla movements; children are the primary recruits of some revolutionary organizations. Children, if suspected of petty theft or as collaborators of a political underground, may be seen as "disposable." Their vulnerability is exacerbated when they lack the protection of a family, or when their families as a whole may be under threat. When adults are regularly the victims of extrajudicial execution, "disappearance," and torture, children cut off from the remedies and resources of adult society may present particularly easy targets for elimination.

The Human Rights Watch Children's

Rights Project was established to deal with cases in which abuses occur because special attention is not given to the particular needs of children, as in the incarceration of children with adults or in otherwise inadequate custodial conditions; cases in which children are subjected to torture or forms of corporal punishment while in custody; and situations in which children are used and abused, by the state or a de facto authority or with their acquiescence, as child soldiers, as bonded laborers, or in another capacity in which the child is forced into servitude at the expense of his or her childhood.

International law has recognized that children should be treated differently from adults because they are especially susceptible to abuse and often lack the physical or mental maturity to protect themselves. The United Nations Convention on the Rights of the Child, in effect since 1990, provides a powerful set of safeguards for children. Unfortunately, many of the 167 states that have ratified or acceded to the convention and agreed to abide by its provisions have failed to alter long-standing patterns of abuse. Safeguards for children incorporated in other international human rights agreements and standards are ignored as well.

The Work of the Children's Rights Project

During 1994 the Human Right's Watch Children's Rights Project, working with the organization's regional divisions, carried out three fact-finding missions: to Liberia to investigate the use of children as soldiers; to Jamaica to investigate the conditions of children detained with adults in adult police lockups; and to Northern Ireland to investigate the abuse of children by security forces and armed opposition groups. In addition, the Children's Rights Project cooperated with other Human Rights Watch divisions in several missions and reports. It invited Peter Volmink, a South African lawyer and assessor in the criminal courts and regional director of Street Law (an organization which educates children and adults of their human rights), to be honored for his work at Human

Right Watch's obsevance of Human Rights Day in December.

Child Soldiers

International law currently sets at fifteen the minimum age at which children can take part in armed conflict (Protocols I and II to the Geneva Conventions of 1949, and the United Nations Convention on the Rights of the Child). In many countries around the world children under fifteen are used as fighters in violation of these conventions. Tens of thousands of these children, some as young as eight or nine, are forcibly recruited to fight in savage conflicts or join rebel groups because the children believe there is no other way to survive. These young children are sometimes used as fighters by governments, but more often by armed opposition groups.

In July, Human Rights Watch adopted a policy opposing the participation of children under the age of eighteen in armed conflict. That policy grew out of our work in Liberia and Sudan.

Liberia

With Human Rights Watch/Africa, the Human Rights Watch Children's Rights Project carried out a fact-finding mission to Liberia in April to look into the use of children as soldiers in the civil war that has been raging since 1990. We interviewed thirty-one former child soldiers, child care and social workers, lawyers, human rights activists, and U.N. and UNICEF personnel, as well as officials from the transitional government and warring factions.

Although international law forbids the use of children under fifteen as soldiers, we found that thousands of children under fifteen, many as young as ten years old, were used by rebel forces, including the National Patriotic Front of Liberia (NPFL) and the United Liberian Movement for Democracy in Liberia (ULIMO). Thousands of children were killed or wounded; others were forcibly conscripted by warring factions—separated from their families against their wills. But most joined the rebel forces "voluntarily"—in order to survive, or to avenge parents' deaths, or to provide food for their families. Some had seen their parents killed—sometimes beheaded before their eyes. Children were forced to take part in the killing, wounding or rape of civilians. Reintegrating these children into their own communities is a task of immense difficulty.

A report that detailed our conclusions and recommendations, *Easy Prey: Child Soldiers in Liberia*, was released in September. BBC Focus on Africa, BBC World Service, National Public Radio, and Voice of America ran radio interviews, and the report received wide press coverage.

Sudan

In June 1994 Human Rights Watch/Africa released a major report entitled *Sudan: Civilian Devastation.* (*See* Human Rights Watch/Africa section.) One chapter dealt with child soldiers and other vulnerable children. It described the situation of many thousands of children in Sudan who had been taken by rebel groups to be used as soldiers or held in reserve as possible fighters in the eleven-year conflict.

Boys as young as eleven were recruited to fight. No one knows the exact number of children who were forced to fight, but the number is in the thousands. Hundreds of these children have been killed or grievously wounded. Others have died of starvation or disease. Many have been subjected to severe beatings and all have lived in deplorable conditions. Rehabilitating these children and reintegrating them into their communities is an immense and daunting task.

In November, the Children's Rights Project and Human Rights Watch/Africa released a report based on the June 1994 report, entitled *The Lost Boys: Child Soldiers and Unaccompanied Boys in Southern Sudan.* The report focuses on the use of child soldiers by the rebel Sudan People's Liberation Army (SPLA). The report was intended to maximize the impact of Human Rights Watch's findings on the special vulnerability and plight of children in the Sudan by directing attention specifically to their exploitation in the conflict. The report will reach an audience with particular concern for the defense of children and be of use in working with international groups on the issue.

The reports on Liberia and Sudan served as the beginning of our effort to campaign to end the use of children as soldiers. We will work with international children's organizations and others to focus international attention on the issue. A United Nations task force has begun work on a two-year study of children in armed conflict, with which we will cooperate.

In addition, a U.N. Working Group began meeting in October to draft an optional protocol to the U.N. Convention on the Rights of the Child that would raise the minimum age at which children can take part in armed conflict from fifteen to eighteen. The Human Rights Watch Children's Rights Project has provided information to that working group, including our reports on Liberia and Sudan. We are working with a large coalition of NGOs pressing the international community to take steps to raise the minimum age.

Children in the Criminal Justice System

In the past, the regional divisions of Human Rights Watch have issued reports on abuses of children in the criminal justice system: *"Nothing Unusual": The Torture of Children in Turkey* (Helsinki Watch, 1992), and *Children in Northern Ireland: Abused by Security Forces and Paramilitaries* (Helsinki Watch, 1992). The Human Rights Watch Children's Rights Project is building on those efforts, focusing on ways in which children are particularly vulnerable to abuse.

The United Nations Convention on the Rights of the Child, the International Covenant on Civil and Political Rights, the Standard Minimum Rules for the Administration of Justice, the U.N. Rules for the Protection of Juveniles Deprived of their Liberty, the U.N. Guidelines for the Prevention of Juvenile Delinquency, and the Standard Minimum Rules for the Treatment of Prisoners provide both broad and specific protections for children. Among other provisions, these agreements and standards require that detained or imprisoned children be held separately from adults, that incarceration be used only as a last resort, and that children be detained in humane conditions. They also forbid the use of torture, inhumane and degrading treatment of children by security forces. They recognize that children are not just "small adults," but require special consideration because of their physical and mental immaturity.

Jamaica

In June 1994, the Human Rights Watch Children's Rights Project, in conjunction with Human Rights Watch/Americas, conducted a mission to Jamaica to investigate allegations of the illegal detention of children in police lockups with adults. We found that children as young as nine and ten were detained in life-threatening conditions in police lockups, sometimes in the same cells as adults charged with serious crimes. Our conversations with more than forty children detained in lockups revealed that the criminal justice system in Jamaica falls far short of international standards as they concern children. These findings were submitted in a report to the United Nations Committee on the Rights of the Child to be used when the committee conducts hearings in January 1995 on Jamaica's compliance with the United Nations Convention on the Rights of the Child. We testified at hearings of the committee in Geneva in October 1994 to highlight Jamaica's ill-treatment of children in lockups. Our findings and recommendations were also released in a report in October 1994, *Jamaica: Children Improperly Detained in Police Lockups*. The report was distributed to Jamaican authorities, the international community, the media and the public. It was widely covered by Jamaican media.

Children detained in lockups told the Children's Rights Project that they had been held for long periods in police cells. One fifteen-year-old boy stated that he had been detained in Halfway Tree Lockup for over forty-two days. The children—some in cells with adults—were held in appalling conditions. Children reported that they were subjected to physical and verbal abuse by police and sometimes denied medical attention. A boy who said that he suffers from severe asthma told us that "police licked [beat] me when I was arrested. I asked to see a doctor, but they won't let me. My chest hurts and I am wheezing." Other children showed us visible wounds from attacks. A lawyer who represents children told us that "police often terrorize children into submission." For many children in Jamaica, the laws that protect them in theory are disregarded in practice.

At Halfway Tree Lockup, inmates urinated into the hallway and raw sewage seeped directly into the sleeping area of the children's cell. Sanitation facilities at the lockups did not function and overflowed with fecal matter. The lockups did not provide children with bedding or blankets and in some lockups there were no beds. Insect infestation was rampant. Children at both lockups visited told us that the food was usually spoiled or inadequate and that requests for drinking water were often ignored. Most children had not been permitted to bathe since they were brought to the lockups. As a child's lawyer told us, "Jamaica has a facade of a juvenile justice system, but in practice, children are treated like criminals."

The Jamaican government allowed the Human Rights Watch Children's Rights Project full access to the lockups, but its response to recommendations concerning the detention of children in lockups was half-hearted. During our mission to Jamaica, the police commissioner acknowledged that children are often detained in lockups in violation of international and Jamaican law, but told us that "there is nothing the police can do." In correspondence following the visit, the police commissioner's office argued that children are detained in lockups because facilities designed to detain children are overcrowded. However, the Jamaican authorities could take immediate steps to improve the situation of children held in the squalor of the lockups. Many of these remedies. such as the provision of functioning sanitation facilities, clean cells, and edible food. could be accomplished at little or no expense. For Jamaica to ignore the most basic rights of its youngest citizens is shameful. A few of the children we met in the lockups were subsequently released on bail, but generally the conditions in the lockups remained the same.

The strategy used by the Children's Right Project with Jamaica was to publicize the fact that children were detained with adults in dreadful conditions in violation of international and Jamaican law, to pressure the Jamaican government to end these abuses. and to collaborate with local groups like the Jamaican Coalition on the Rights of the Child. After our visit, the coalition took on the plight of children in lockups and mobilized further actions to ensure that the situation was addressed with urgency. With the help of the Human Rights Watch Children's Rights Project, the coalition produced and distributed flyers to children and parents that explained children's rights when arrested. They also met with government authorities responsible for detained children and assisted in the distribution of the Children's Rights Project report. In October, the coalition held a youth conference at which children discussed juvenile justice and showed a film on children's rights that was provided by the Human Rights Watch International Film Festival.

Internationally, our strategy was to provide information to the U.N. Committee on the Rights of the Child for its use in questioning the government of Jamaica in January 1995 concerning conditions for children in Jamaica, and to work with international children's groups toward remedying the situation.

Northern Ireland

In June the Human Rights Watch Children's Rights Project, in cooperation with Human Rights Watch/Helsinki, conducted a fact-finding mission to Northern Ireland. The mission interviewed children, parents, lawyers. human rights activists, religious leaders. government officials, and others.

Children under eighteen have suffered greatly as a result of the conflict in Northern Ireland; of the more than 3,100 people who have lost their lives since 1969 in political violence connected with "The Troubles," many have been children. Moreover, children are caught between two powerful forces, the government's security forces and the paramilitary groups—the "republicans," notably the Irish Republican Army (IRA) which is predominantly Catholic and fought for a united Ireland, and the "loyalists," primarily the Ulster Freedom Fighters (UFF) and the Ulster Volunteer Force (UVF), who support continued union with the United Kingdom and are overwhelmingly Protestant. Children are the particular focus of abuse by both sides of the paramilitary divide. and suffer disproportionately abusive treatment by the security forces that puts older children in the same class as adults.

We found that children below the age of eighteen in Northern Ireland were improperly detained in adult interrogation and remand centers; were physically and mentally abused in Castlereagh Holding Centre; were tricked, threatened and pressured by police during interrogation; were denied immediate access to solicitors; were not brought promptly before judges; were deprived of the right to silence; were liable to conviction on the basis of confessions obtained by improper means; and were physically and mentally abused and harassed on the street by the Royal Ulster Constabulary (the RUC, the Northern Ireland police) and by the British Army. The abuse was not confined to Catholic children; Protestant children were abused as well.

Paramilitary groups, both loyalist and republican, victimized children and young people in what they characterized as alternatives to the criminal justice sytem in their respective communities. Young people accused of such crimes as "joyriding" in stolen cars are subjected to arbitrary, cruel and life-threatening punishments including "kneecappings" (shootings), severe beatings, and expulsions from Northern Ireland.

The Children's Rights Project submitted a report on our findings to the United Nations Committee on the Rights of the Child, and addressed the committee in Geneva in October to present our conclusions and recommendations. Our information will be used by the committee to question the government of the United Kingdom formally in January 1995.

Our strategy in Northern Ireland is to document and publicize the abuses against children committed by both security forces and paramilitary groups, to work with local human rights groups to effect change, and to work with the Northern Ireland Office to attempt to persuade officials to end the offenses. In the past, the British government has responded somewhat to international pressure, taking steps, for example, to curb physical abuse of children during interrogation. However, the government has not put into place our recommendations, such as allowing children immediate access to solicitors, that would help to end such abuses permanently.

After our June mission, we looked into the situation of children since the declaring of a cease-fire by republicans and loyalists and found that the abuses continue. We have continued to receive allegations of mistreatment of children during interrogation, of street harassment of children by police (in some areas, residents allege that such harassment has worsened), and of "punishment" beatings of children by both republican and loyalist paramilitary groups.

In December we issued with Human Rights Watch/Helsinki a report entitled *After the Cease-fire: Children's Rights Still Violated in Northern Ireland.*

Colombia
In November, a report entitled *Generation Under Fire: Children and Violence in Colombia* was released by Human Rights Watch/Americas and the Human Rights Watch Children's Rights Project. The fact-finding mission on which the report is based was conducted by Human Rights Watch/

Americas in July.

The report discloses that murder of children has reached epidemic proportions in Colombia; 2,190 children were murdered in 1993—a rate eight times as high as the rate for murders of children in the United States, and with the added element of explicit complicity by state agents in many of the killings. Most of the killings are politically motivated only in the sense that they are intended to eliminate—through murder— children who are seen as social irritants. A significant number are carried out by agents of the state. Police have reportedly taken part in hundreds of killings of children since 1980, including the so-called social cleansing murders of "disposable" street children. Government forces that are pledged to maintain order and that are not directly involved in the killings tolerate the killings of children, fail to intervene when others break the law, and neglect to investigate most of the murders.

Most murderers of children go unpunished. Of the 2,190 murders of children in 1993, only twelve cases have resulted in trials. Police officers continue to be implicated in the murders of children, and investigations rarely result in more than dismissal for the implicated officers. Government promises to restrain the police have yet to bring results.

The report was translated into Spanish and released at press conferences in Bogotá and Medellín in November. We will work closely with local NGOs who will distribute our report and work on the problem with us.

Our strategy with regard to the killings of street children is to publicize and bring international attention to this pattern of abuse and to the government's evasion of accountability. Within the United Nations, the report was sent to the Committee on the Rights of the Child, which will be reviewing Colombia's record in October 1995. We have also sent the report and written to both the U.N. Special Rapporteur on summary or arbitrary executions and the Special Rapporteur on torture, urging both to take action. In addition, we are working with international children's groups and with

UNICEF to urge the international community to bring pressure to bear on the Colombian government to stop these killings and to bring to justice those responsible for the killings that have taken place.

U.S. Policy

One hundred sixty-seven nations have ratified or acceded to the United Nations Convention on the Rights of the Child. The United States is one of only a handful of countries that have taken no action; the Clinton administration is considering signing the convention.

Human Rights Watch supports the signing and ratification of the convention, and will urge the administration and members of Congress to do so.

THE FREE EXPRESSION PROJECT

The Free Expression Project, formerly the Fund for Free Expression, works with the other divisions of Human Rights Watch to examine and investigate abuse to free expression rights throughout the world. This work takes the form of country reports—usually undertaken with Human Rights Watch regional divisions—and thematic reports which seek to stress the connection between freedom of expression and other global social problems. The project also sends protest letters and coordinates legal work and legislative testimony. In addition, the project administers grants to persecuted writers from the estates of American writers Lillian Hellman and Dashiell Hammett, and manages the work of two casework committees, the Committee for International Academic Freedom and Filmwatch.

In 1994, the project undertook two important initiatives to demonstrate that censorship is not the solution to problems of discrimination against women and racial minorities.

In February, a report was issued on the applications of the Canadian Supreme Court decision in *R. v. Butler* which adopted the view that sexually explicit material may degrade women and harm society. Inspired by U.S. anti-pornography activists Catherine MacKinnon and Andrea Dworkin, the ruling aimed to promote gender equality. Instead, the results show that it has been used to confiscate, prosecute, and destroy lesbian and gay publications.

The case originated in Winnepeg where Butler, the operator of an adult video store, was charged and convicted of selling obscene material. The Canadian Supreme Court review found that even though the Canadian Charter protects obscene material, obscenity can be subjected to a "reasonable limit" because of its potential to harm women.

Canadian customs agents have used the ruling to condemn consensual sex between gay men, prosecute a lesbian magazine, and delay delivery of feminist books, videos and journals. Several groups are challenging the constitutionality of Customs' censorship practices. The suit claims that the power of prior restraint violates the Canadian Charter's guarantee of free expression rights and that by targeting gay and lesbian materials Customs is violating the Charter guaranteed right to equality.

The Free Expression Project report demonstrates that censorship is not the answer. Canada's experience shows that laws that permit censorship of sexual expression, while ostensibly aimed at the serious harm caused by violence and discrimination against women, are likely to be directed against people who are already marginalized and discriminated against.

The report served two important purposes. First, because laws along the lines of the Butler decision are being seriously considered by many jurisdictions in the United States, it served to show how they can be applied in ways that are unintended by their sponsors. Second, it lent the support of Human Rights Watch to a broad array of Canadian civil liberties, writers and gay and lesbian activists and organizations who view the Butler decision and its aftermath as a leading threat to freedom of expression in their country.

In March, the Project filed a friend of the court brief supporting Danish journalist Jens Olaf Jersild's appeal to the European Court of Human Rights, asking the Court to reverse a Danish court's decision to convict Jersild of abetting dissemination of hate speech for airing a television interview with a youth gang of racist skinheads. The brief was cited during oral argument by both Jersild's counsel and members of the Court. The decision handed down in September found that "news reporting based on interviews ... constitutes one of the most important means whereby the press is able to play its vital role" in a democratic society. In a 12-7 decision, the Court concluded that Jersild's television program had no racist purpose and ordered his conviction overturned. The Jersild decision is a major free speech victory affirming the primacy of the European Convention on Human Rights over laws of member states.

In addition to these two initiatives, the project joined with Human Rights Watch/ Americas to use the occasion of the Inter-American Press Association Hemisphere Conference on Freedom of Speech in Mexico City, to present a Human Rights Watch report on the persistence in the region of laws used to silence criticism and dissent. The report described three forms of censorship which have been codified in domestic law— desacato, defamation and anti-terrorism laws—and detailed their use in Argentina, Cuba and Chile. The report urged repeal of all desacato laws (which prohibit speech that insults, ridicules or offends the head of state or other national institutions); reform of defamation statues to place the burden of proof on the plaintiffs and require that public officials show that the defendant acted with reckless disregard for the truth; and restoration of due process rights including the right to a public trial, time restrictions on pretrial detention and a mechanism for challenging detention prior to trial. Largely due to Hu-

man Rights Watch efforts in Mexico City, the declaration issued by the Hemisphere Conference—since signed by a number of heads of state in the region—included a strong plank opposing penalties against the press for truthful reporting.

The Free Expression Project wrote letters protesting to the Indonesian government over the closing of three newsmagazines; expressing concern about confiscation of books in Suriname; on behalf of Taslima Nasrin, the Bangladeshi writer who was in hiding and under death threat from Muslim fundamentalists; and for Saidi Sirjani, a prominent Iranian essayist who "disappeared."

Elsewhere in the *Human Rights Watch World Report 1995* are accounts of other work by the Free Expression Project. In collaboration with Human Rights Watch/ Helsinki, the project investigated and protested the Hungarian government's interference with personnel and programming at the state-run broadcast media. With Human Rights Watch/Middle East, it reported on government restrictions on freedom of the press in Egypt.

The United States section describes the Free Expression Project's follow-up coverage of repression of moderate voices in Miami's Cuban exile community, including the use of violence and intimidation to silence those who advocate dialogue with Castro; and project letters to the Treasury Department urging removal of U.S. restrictions on travel to Cuba.

Hellman-Hammett Funds

The Free Expression Project administers a program of annual grants to writers all around the world who are in financial need as a result of political persecution. First established in 1989, the program is funded by the estates of writers Lillian Hellman and Dashiell Hammett who stipulated in their wills that their legacies should be used to help persecuted writers of fiction, nonfiction and poetry. The grants are awarded every spring after nominations have been reviewed by a five-person selection committee composed of members of the Free Expression Project advisory committee. Throughout the year, the selection committee makes smaller grants to politically persecuted writers who need emergency funds to leave their countries, or for medical or legal aid.

In addition to offering financial assistance, the grants highlight individual cases, helping focus attention on repression and censorship around the world. In some instances, however, Human Rights Watch is asked to withhold the names of recipients because of the dangerous circumstances in which they and their families are living.

The 1994 Hellman-Hammett recipients, a diverse group of thirty journalists, novelists and poets from 17 countries, received grants totaling approximately $175,000. Among those whose cases can be safely publicized are: Dodojon Atovullo, a Tajikistani journalist who fled to Russia because paramilitary groups were stalking him for publishing an independent newsweekly; Hwang Suk-Young, a South Korean novelist who was convicted of espionage for accepting a fee from North Korea for the right to make a movie of one of his novels; William M. Mandel, an author of books on the Soviet Union who is still hampered by his 1953 refusal to name names to the Senate Internal Security Subcommittee; Taslima Nasrin, the Bangladeshi poet and novelist who fled to Sweden under death threat by fundamentalists who claim her feminist views are anti-Islam; Shahrunush Parsipur, an Iranian novelist whose books about the challenges women face in Iran have been unofficially banned since 1989; Nguyen Chi Thien, a dissident Vietnamese poet who spent the majority of his life in prison for writing poems critical of the communist regime; and Wu Xuecan, a Chinese journalist and essayist who was imprisoned for his role in the 1989 Democracy Movement and insists that he was wrongly convicted.

Ten emergency grants, averaging $2,000, were given to writers from China, Algeria, Croatia, Cuba, Sudan, and Turkey.

Committee for International Academic Freedom

The Committee for International Academic Freedom acts on behalf of professors, teachers and students around the world when they are harassed or imprisoned for exercising their rights of free expression and inquiry and when their work is censored or universities are closed for political reasons. The Committee sends cables and letters to appropriate government authorities and publicizes the cases of abuse in the U.S. academic community.

In 1994, the Committee wrote about situations in China, Ethiopia, Indonesia, and Peru. The letters protested the arrest, beating and removal from her job of a noted Chinese professor of ethics; urged the end of harassment to two professors for their efforts to help the victims of Tiananmen Square violence; inquired about the Ethiopian government's interference in academic affairs at Addis Ababa University and the detention without charge of the University's former president; protested the dismissal and harassment of Indonesian professors who were targeted for speaking out against the government; protested the arrest and detention of a Peruvian university economist for his advocacy of greater freedom for trade union activity.

The Committee is composed of twenty-three university presidents and scholars and co-chaired by Jonathan Fanton of the New School for Social Research, Hanna Holborn Gray of the University of Chicago, Vartan Gregorian of Brown University and Charles Young of the University of California at Los Angeles.

THE PRISON PROJECT

The Human Rights Watch Prison Project was formed in 1987 to focus international attention on prison conditions worldwide. Drawing on the expertise of the regional divisions of Human Rights Watch, the Prison Project investigates conditions for sentenced prisoners, pre-trial detainees, and those held in police lockups. The Prison Project is distinctive in the international human rights field in that it examines conditions for all prisoners, not simply those held for political reasons.

In addition to pressing for improvement in prison conditions in particular countries, the Prison Project seeks to place the problem of prison conditions on the international human rights agenda. We believe that a government's claim to respect human rights should be assessed not only by the political freedoms it allows but also by how it treats its prisoners, including those not held for political reasons. Our experience has repeatedly shown that a number of democratic countries that are rarely or never a focus of human rights scrutiny are in fact guilty of serious human rights violations within their prisons.

The Prison Project has a self-imposed set of rules for prison visits: investigators undertake visits only when they, not the authorities, can choose the institutions to be visited; when the investigators can be confident that they will be allowed to talk privately with inmates of their choice; and when the investigators can gain access to the entire facility to be examined. These rules are adopted to avoid being shown model prisons or the most presentable parts of institutions. When access on such terms is not possible, reporting is based on interviews with former prisoners, prisoners on furlough, relatives of inmates, lawyers, prison experts and prison staff, and on documentary evidence. The Prison Project uses the U.N. Standard Minimum Rules for the Treatment of Prisoners as the chief guideline by which to assess prison conditions in each country. Prison investigations are usually conducted by teams composed of a member of the Prison Project's staff or advisory committee and a member of a Human Rights Watch regional division's staff with expertise on the country in question. Occasionally, the Prison Project invites an outside expert to participate in an investigation.

The Prison Project's findings, published as reports of Human Rights Watch, are released to the public and the press, both in the United States and in the country in question, and sent to the government of that country. Whenever possible, the report is also published in translation. In addition, the Prison Project conducts advocacy both in the country in question and before international bodies, striving to eliminate human rights violations within prisons.

In previous years, the Prison Project conducted studies and published reports on prison conditions in Brazil, Czechoslovakia, Egypt, India, Indonesia, Israel and the Occupied Territories, Jamaica, Mexico, Poland, Romania, the former Soviet Union, Spain, Turkey, United Kingdom, and the United States (including Puerto Rico, with a separate newsletter published).

The Enforcement of Standards

The U.N. Standard Minimum Rules for the Treatment of Prisoners is the most widely known and accepted document regulating prison conditions. Unfortunately, these standards, although known to prison administrators virtually all over the world, are seldom fully enforced. Based on extensive research over the years, the Prison Project concluded in the 1993 *Human Rights Watch Global Report on Prisons* that the great majority of the millions of persons who are imprisoned worldwide at any given moment, and of the tens of millions who spend at least part of the year behind bars, are confined in conditions of filth and corruption, without adequate food or medical care, with little or nothing to do, and in circumstances in which violence—from other inmates, their keepers, or both—is a constant threat. Despite international declarations, treaties and standards forbidding such conditions, this state of affairs is tolerated even in countries that are more or less respectful of human rights, because prisons, by their nature, are out of sight, and because prisoners, by definition, are outcasts. To strengthen the enforcement of standards, the Prison Project has continued to advocate creating a U.N. human rights mechanism to inspect prisons and to strengthen the mechanism for enforcement of standards and the prevention of abuses.

The Prison Project participated in the 1994 session of the Working Group on the Optional Protocol to the Convention against Torture, convened by the U.N. Commission on Human Rights to devise a universal system of visits to places of detention. Despite its reservations regarding the confidentiality of that system, the Prison Project has endorsed the effort and has been striving to ensure its maximum effectiveness. It has also worked to defeat efforts by some member states to water down the provisions of the system.

In February, in a statement before the U.N. Commission on Human Rights, The Prison Project highlighted the plight of common prisoners and the urgent need for improvements in this area. And throughout 1994, the Prison Project maintained contacts with the other U.N. bodies that concern themselves with prison matters. A Prison Project representative attended a preparatory meeting for the Ninth United Nations Congress on the Treatment of Offenders, and sent a statement to the meeting of the U.N. Commission on Crime Prevention and the Treatment of Offenders, in both cases urging the commission to make the improvement of prison conditions worldwide and monitoring the implementation of standards by member states a priority in its work. Several times during the year, the Prison Project communicated with the office of the U.N. Special Rapporteur on Torture, providing information and urging the rapporteur to take steps in particular instances. The Prison Project also wrote to the U.N. High Commissioner on Human Rights, who had indicated his interest in prison matters, to include prison-related issues in his contacts with governments, and in particular to raise them with the government of Venezuela.

Human Rights Watch has continued to press the U.S. government to promote improvements in prison conditions internationally. It has urged U.S. representatives to the U.N. Commission on Crime Prevention and

the Treatment of Offenders to support and strengthen the human rights component of the U.N.'s work related to prisons. On March 15, in its testimony before the House Foreign Affairs Committee on the foreign aid reform, The Prison Project recommended that the U.S. government (1) improve its reporting on prison conditions in the Department of State's annual *Country Reports on Human Rights Practices for 1993*; (2) stop the recent trend of shifting the focus of the U.N. Commission on Crime Prevention and Criminal Justice from the treatment of prisoners to activities related to international crime and drug trafficking; and, (3) support and strengthen the work of the U.N. Criminal Justice Branch. The Prison Project also cautioned against direct U.S. assistance for prisons and instead advocated channelling such aid through the U.N. Commission on Crime Prevention.

Since 1993, the Prison Project has participated in an international effort by representatives of about a dozen nongovernmental and intergovernmental organizations to strengthen standards regarding prison conditions; the goal is to make these standards more effective in safeguarding the human rights of detainees. A representative of the Prison Project was invited to join a drafting group charged with preparing a human rights guide to the main universal standards that apply to the field of criminal justice. The draft of the document was discussed at a meeting of over one hundred prisoner rights activists and representatives of national prison administrations from countries around the world that was held in November 1994 in The Hague. The final version of the document is to be presented during the Ninth U.N. Congress on Crime Prevention and the Treatment of Offenders that will be held in Tunis in April 1995.

Training

The Prison Project has played a leading role in developing methodology for prison investigations for researchers of all the divisions of Human Rights Watch. A project representative has conducted periodic training sessions for the staff members on interviewing techniques within a prison context as well as on the particular concerns that arise when working with witnesses who are imprisoned.

The Prison Project's director was invited to Geneva in May to conduct a training session during an International Committee of the Red Cross seminar for field staff members of the Detention Division of that organization.

Fact-Finding

The Prison Project continued its fact-finding work and the publication of country-specific reports on prison conditions throughout 1994.

In January, a report on prison conditions in Zaire was published jointly with Human Rights Watch/Africa. Based on an investigation in 1993 that involved visits to several prisons and detention camps, as well as police jails, we described a system in a state of deep crisis, with an extremely high mortality rate, malnutrition leading to occasional cases of starvation and rampant abuses that include a widespread use of torture.

In February, a report on South African prisons was released simultaneously in the U.S. and in South Africa. The study was based on research conducted in 1992 and 1993 by representatives of the Prison Project and Human Rights Watch/Africa. The report noted that despite significant reforms in the prison system since the beginning of political changes in that country, many aspects of prison life remained unchanged since the years of official *apartheid*. The report concluded that many of the needed changes in the South African prison system could be accomplished through policy changes rather than significant investments, and offered a list of specific recommendations.

In March, Human Rights Watch, jointly with the American College of Physicians, the National Coalition to Abolish the Death Penalty and Physicians for Human Rights, issued a report on physician participation in capital punishment in the U.S. The report, titled *"Breach of Trust: Physician Participation in Executions in the United States"* generated significant press attention, with dozens of stories published in newspapers throughout the country, and provoked a discussion in national media on the ethical implications of the participation of the medical profession in judicial killings.

In July, representatives of the Prison Project and Human Rights Watch/Asia conducted an investigation of prison conditions in Japan. Members of the delegation were unable to obtain unrestricted access to prisons. After a series of meetings with the authorities, the Japanese government offered visits to institutions it selected, without the right to interview prisoners, with no possibility to take measurements and under conditions in which the prison authorities would choose the parts of the institution to show to the delegation. Following the institutional rule, the delegation declined this offer and collected information based on interviews with former prisoners, with relatives of current prisoners, clergy, prisoner support group members, and lawyers handling current or recent prison litigation cases, as well as information provided to us by government officials. The Prison Project conducted interviews in Tokyo, Kobe, Osaka, Niigata and Asahikawa. A report will be published in early 1995.

U.S. Prison Issues

For several years, the Prison Project has been involved in issues related to U.S. prisons. The Prison Project continued monitoring conditions for U.S. prisoners in 1994, with particular focus on the proliferation of super-maximum security institutions (or "maxi-maxis"), a problem to which the Prison Project first called attention in its 1991 report on prison conditions in the U.S. In 1994 the Prison Project contacted all state correctional departments to determine which states used what particular forms of super-maximum security institutions. The results of this informal survey are being used by a group of grass roots organizations in establishing a nation-wide "maxi-maxi" monitoring network.

One of the most serious concerns for Human Rights Watch regarding the above issue, has been the situation at a maxi-maxi facility in the state of Indiana. The Prison Project has received distressing reports of abuses since 1991, and has communicated its concerns several times to the Indiana Corrections Commissioner. Since 1993, the project has repeatedly asked to be allowed to inspect the institution. The project's 1994 effort was boosted by a letter from a group of Indiana's political and religious leaders, urging the state administration to admit an inspection by Human Rights Watch. As of this writing, the Commissioner of Corrections has persistently refused to grant his permission for such a visit. On several occasions during the past year, the Prison Project also sent communications to federal officials, raising issues of concern within U.S. prisons.

Upon the public release of the first-ever United States government's report on the country's compliance with the International Covenant on Civil and Political Rights (ICCPR), in October, Human Rights Watch and the American Civil Liberties Union issued a statement criticizing the report and pointing to the main areas in which the U.S. violates the provisions of the covenant. The ICCPR, which includes important safeguards of relevance to prison conditions, was ratified by the United States in June 1992. It provides an extremely valuable tool for establishing accountability for prison abuse. Because in important respects the United States falls short of international standards relevant to prisons, we believe that scrutiny under these standards, and in light of international practices, can be particularly effective.

With international standards, including the ICCPR in mind, the Prison Project jointly with the Human Rights Watch Women's Rights Project has conducted a year-long study of sexual abuse of women in U.S. prisons. Investigators interviewed witnesses, including prisoners, former prisoners, prisoner rights advocates, lawyers and government officials in five states. A report is scheduled to be published in early 1995.

The Human Rights Watch Prison Project joined with the Human Rights Watch Women's Rights Project in inviting Deborah LaBelle, an attorney working on behalf of women abused in prisons in the U.S., to be honored for her work at Human Rights Watch's observance of Human Rights Day in December.

Emergency-type Missions

The Prison Project has over the years sent emergency-type missions following instances of extremely serious prison disturbances. In our experience, the time right after a prison disturbance, especially a bloody one, is often the moment when the most serious human rights violations are likely to occur. By sending a delegation under such circumstances, the Prison Project strives to protect the survivors by publicizing the events both locally and internationally and by raising human rights concerns over the aftermath of a prison disturbance. In January, a representative of Prison Project traveled to Maracaibo, Venezuela, following a prison massacre there in which more than 100 prisoners lost their lives. The Prison Project's visit, that received wide media attention in Venezuela, included interviews with survivors, relatives of prisoners, prison authorities and meetings with elected officials both on national and state level. A newsletter based on this mission was published in February.

Follow-up on Earlier Work

In 1991, the Prison Project—together with Helsinki Watch, the precursor to Human Rights Watch/Helsinki—conducted an in-depth investigation of prisons and pre-trial detention centers in the Russian Federation. Reports of abuse similar to that documented under the Soviet government continued to surface frequently during the years following independence, and in the spring of 1994 Human Rights Watch/Helsinki and the Prison Project initiated a follow-up investigation into the notorious pre-trial detention centers to maintain pressure on government officials to improve conditions. In June 1994, the Ministry of Internal Affairs, which oversees

Russia's penal system, rejected our request for access as "undesirable" since a parliamentary commission would be conducting similar work through 1995. In July it rejected an appeal without explanation. The Human Rights Watch Moscow-based staff is currently collecting testimony from individuals recently released from two pre-trial detention centers in Moscow, which will serve as the basis for a report due out in early 1995.

In Brazil, the Prison Project followed closely the judicial proceedings related to two prison tragedies—one in 1989, the other in 1992—in the aftermath of which the Prison Project sent investigators and worked on publicizing the events both in Brazil and internationally. In the 1989 case of the death of eighteen prisoners in the Police Jail 42 in Sao Paulo, one of the officials indicted was acquitted by a jury in an August trial. More than twenty-five defendants have not yet been tried in this case. Witnesses have been heard in the trials of the 120 military policemen indicted after the 1992 massacre in the Sao Paulo Casa de Dentencao that left 111 prisoners dead. The prosecutor in the case, Dr. Estela Kuhlman, has been receiving death threats for over a year. Human Rights Watch publicized this fact in a press conference held in Sao Paulo in September.

THE WOMEN'S RIGHTS PROJECT

The Women's Rights Project of Human Rights Watch was established in 1990 to work in conjunction with Human Rights Watch's regional divisions to monitor violence against women and discrimination on the basis of sex that is either committed or tolerated by governments. The project grew out of Human Rights Watch's recognition of the epidemic proportions of violence and gender discrimination around the world and of the past failure of human rights organizations, and the international community, to hold governments accountable for abuses of women's basic human rights. The project monitors the performance of specific countries in securing and protecting women's human rights, highlights individual cases of international significance, and serves as a link between women's rights and human rights communities at both national and international levels.

Women's Human Rights Developments

This section does not evaluate progress in women's human rights throughout the world, but describes developments in countries most closely monitored by the Project in 1994: Thailand, Turkey, Haiti, Botswana, Former Yugoslavia, and Kenya.

Thailand

In December 1993, the Women's Rights Project and Human Rights Watch/Asia released *A Modern Form of Slavery: Trafficking of Burmese Women and Girls into Thai Brothels*. The report documented the active participation of Thai police and immigration officials in every stage of trafficking operations. Those operations continued largely unchanged throughout 1994. To date, not a single police officer has been criminally punished for complicity in trafficking or forced prostitution. Burmese women and girls interviewed for the report also alleged that Burmese border guards frequently accept bribes to allow traffickers to pass unhindered with their victims.

In addition to official involvement in forced prostitution, the report also criticized Thai police raids that generally result in the discriminatory arrest of women and girls, while owners, pimps, clients and police collaborators go free. Burmese women and girls who are thus "rescued" through police raids are routinely detained as illegal immigrants rather than protected as trafficking victims. Most are held in immigration detention centers and penal reform institutions under appalling conditions that fail to comply with international standards and Thai law, and that violate the detainees' due process rights. There have also been credible reports that immigration detention officials have, with impunity, themselves sexually and physically abused Burmese women and girls in custody, and tested them for the AIDS virus without their informed consent.

A Modern Form of Slavery generated intense international criticism of the Thai government's failure to control in any meaningful way the problem of trafficking and forced prostitution. In response, the Thai government is undertaking several steps of questionable use. First, the police have stepped up raids on brothels. According to a press report, the Thai Interior Ministry announced to the Thai Cabinet that the police had conducted nearly 3,000 raids on brothels and arrested over 3,400 people on prostitution charges between February and April 1994. All of those arrested were reportedly sent to occupational training centers, suggesting that women and girls, rather than the mostly male intermediaries, continue to be the primary target of the official crackdown on the illegal sex industry.

Second, in July 1994, Thailand's Cabinet of Ministers approved draft legislation to reform the anti-prostitution law to increase prison sentences and fines against convicted recruiters, brothel owners and managers, pimps and those who detain women for prostitution. The new law, which is currently being deliberated in Parliament, would also provide for the first time criminal penalties against clients, with the severity of the sentence varying according to the age of the victim. However, as women's rights activists in Thailand have repeatedly noted, the problem is not with the letter of the law, but rather with lack of enforcement.

The failure of the Thai police to respond effectively to forced prostitution was again highlighted on July 16, 1994 by the death of a fifteen-year-old girl in the Hat Yai police station in Songkhla province. The girl committed suicide after allegedly escaping from a brothel to seek help from the police. A Thai Interior Ministry committee that in-vestigated her death concluded that the Hat Yai police had been derelict in their protection duties.

Following widespread media coverage of the suicide, the Thai government established a special police unit in August 1994 to eradicate prostitution of anyone under eighteen years old. The potential effectiveness of this unit remains to be seen, given the unwillingness and inability of the police to discipline their own thus far.

Turkey

In June 1994, the Women's Rights Project released a report on the Turkish government's use of forced gynecological exams to control women's virginity. The report, "A Matter of Power: State Control of Women's Virginity in Turkey," revealed how police agents force Turkish female political detainees and common criminal suspects to undergo gynecological examinations for the purpose of determining the status of their hymens. State officials, who place no similar emphasis on male virginity, have also subjected female hospital patients, state dormitory residents and women applying for government jobs to such exams. They also perform virginity exams instigated by private individuals.

Despite pledges to address this problem, the Turkish government has, to our knowledge, taken no steps to end its involvement in forced virginity exams. On the contrary, we receive reports that this practice is continuing.

Haiti

In July 1994, Human Rights Watch/Americas and the Women's Rights Project, together with the National Coalition for Haitian Refugees (NCHR), released *Rape in Haiti: A Weapon of Terror*. The report documents the use of rape and physical assault, with impunity, as political weapons against women by Haitian soldiers, police and their armed civilian auxiliaries (known as *attachés*). These agents of the Cédras regime committed rape to punish and intimidate women believed to support then-exiled President Jean-Bertrand Aristide, and to punish them for their actual or imputed political beliefs and the activities of their male relatives.

The greatest number of rapes documented by Human Rights Watch and NCHR were attributable to *attachés*, followed by police and soldiers. To a lesser extent, *zenglendos* (bands of armed thugs) also attacked women, sometimes in random acts of violence, but usually with the tacit protection of the military and police. Regardless of who the assailants were, they almost always plundered and robbed the victim's home and assaulted other family members, in addition to raping and assaulting women.

In an August 1993 incident, a group of *attachés*, armed police and armed soldiers broke into the home of a Port-au-Prince woman, looking for her father-in-law, a known Aristide supporter. In addition to attempting to rape the woman, the intruders shot and killed her twenty-three-month-old daughter, and sexually molested her cousin.

In another case, in 1992, a woman was raped by a policeman when a group of soldiers and police broke down the door to her house searching for her husband, a member of the National Front for Change and Democracy. The armed men accused the husband of distributing pro-Aristide materials, destroyed the house probing for corroborating evidence, and accused the family of being *lavalas* (a reference to the broad-based popular movement that elected Aristide). When the husband returned during this incident, they took him to a local police station where he was brutally beaten, tortured, and interrogated before being released without charge the next morning.

Agents of the de facto military regime also harassed and intimidated women's rights organizations. All women's rights groups that we interviewed reported a dramatic drop in membership, which they attributed to fear of reprisal for being associated with any popular organization. Their fear was not without basis. The headquarters of one women's rights group in Port-au-Prince was burned down. The leader of another such organization received a call threatening rape

from a man who identified himself as aligned with the military authorities.

The military regime's response to increasing allegations of rape was virtual silence. It neither publicly denounced rape committed by its agents nor punished those responsible. The absence of official accountability left women with little hope of legal redress and deepened their reluctance to report sexual and physical abuse. To our knowledge, the Haitian criminal justice system, then under the de facto control of the military, has not investigated a single incidence of rape by state agents.

Botswana

In September, the Women's Rights Project and Human Rights Watch/Africa released "Second Class Citizens: Discrimination Against Women Under Botswana's Citizenship Act." The report condemned the Botswana government—often cited as one of the most successful democracies in Africa—for discriminating against women in its Citizenship Act. It further accused the Botswana government of undermining the rule of law and independence of the judiciary by continuing to enforce this law in defiance of a ruling by the country's highest court that a part of it is unconstitutional on grounds of sex discrimination.

Ruling in the 1992 landmark case *Attorney General v. Unity Dow*, a judge on the Court of Appeal, Botswana's highest court, wrote: "The language of [section 4 of the Citizenship Act] is extremely clear and the effect is incontrovertible, namely that whilst the offspring of a Botswana man acquires his citizenship if the child is born in wedlock, such an offspring of a Botswana woman similarly born does not acquire such citizenship. A more discriminatory provision can hardly be found."

Despite Unity Dow's court victory, the Botswana government has denied her application for Botswana passports for her children by Nathan Dow, her American husband. Nor has the Botswana government made any other effort to implement the court's decision or to amend the discriminatory sections of the Citizenship Act.

By denying citizenship to children of Botswana women married to foreign men, the Citizenship Act also potentially violates the right of women in this category to travel freely abroad because they can do so only by leaving their children behind. The act may also interfere with Botswana women's, but not Botswana men's, right to freedom of marriage, since the resultant complications may dissuade women from marrying the man of their choice, should he be a foreigner.

Former Yugoslavia

Despite worldwide outrage over and condemnation of the rape and sexual mistreatment of women in the former Yugoslavia, Human Rights Watch continues to receive reports of violent rape and other forms of sexual assault inflicted upon civilian women by soldiers. A recent case reported by Human Rights Watch/Helsinki shows that rapists still abuse with impunity and, sometimes, with the consent of their military officers. L.D., a sixty-seven-year-old Muslim man and his Serbian wife, were forced to live in the basement of a house occupied by a Serbian military police officer. One night during the summer of 1994, three young men entered the basement, after passing through the upstairs entrance to the house, and forced L.D. to watch as they raped his wife. After thirty minutes, the officer living upstairs came and told them to stop. The young men then spent an hour drinking with the officer. L.D. and his wife reported the rape to the police, but the prosecutor's office later dropped the charges saying they had no basis.

The Women's Rights Project worked to ensure that the U.N.'s international tribunal to prosecute war crimes in the former Yugoslavia would deal with sexual assault fully and fairly. To this end, we urged that the prosecutor's office hire individuals with experience trying sex crimes; that forced pregnancy be prosecuted as a war crime; and that adequate resources be allocated for the protection and support of survivors of sexual assault who will supply evidence.

Kenya

In 1994, the Women's Rights Project conducted a follow-up mission to the refugee camps in Kenya's North East Province, to assess changes in the security situation of Somali refugee women, after the release of our 1993 report *Seeking Refuge, Finding Terror.* It had documented the Kenyan government's indifference to cases of sexual abuse, notably rape, against Somali refugee women in the Kenyan camps. It had further revealed that from January through August 1993, 192 rapes were reported to the United Nations High Commissioner for Refugees (UNHCR), which administers the Kenyan camps. The report had also found that refugee girls and women were frequently attacked at night by unknown armed bandits, or when they went to the outskirts of the camp to herd goats or collect firewood. These bandits increasingly joined forces with former Somali military men, or fighters from the various warring factions who launched raids across the Kenya-Somali border.

To a lesser extent, refugee women also reported attacks by Kenyan police officers posted in the area who were responsible for seven of the reported rape cases. The UNHCR estimated that registered cases amounted to only one-tenth the number of actual rapes occurring in the camps, at the hands of either bandits, warring parties or local police.

The Kenyan government's initial response to the report was to accuse Somali refugee women of fabricating the rape claims to "attract sympathy and give the government negative publicity." However, relief officials, including the UNHCR, launched a donor drive to seek international funding to address the situation. In 1994, the UNHCR received funding from the U.S., Canada, the Netherlands, Sweden, Japan and the European Economic Community (now the European Union). The money was spent both on prevention measures and on creating services for women once they had been attacked.

In a follow-up mission to the Kenyan camps in September, the Women's Rights Project found that the monthly incidence of rape among the Somali women living there had decreased from double-digit numbers to a handful. The Kenyan government had significantly increased both the number of police and security patrols in and around the camps. The UNHCR had adopted many of the recommendations contained in our 1993 report by improving the design of the refugee camps to promote greater physical safety and by increasing the number of staff in the camps to deal specifically with rape victims. In addition, a local nongovernmental organization, the women's lawyer organization FIDA, had placed one staff member in the camps to assist women in seeking legal redress where possible.

The September 1994 mission also found, however, that although the number of night-time attacks had decreased, women continued to be vulnerable when they left the camp to fetch firewood or to herd goats. Since young girls are often sent out to perform these tasks, they constitute a large proportion of the recent rape victims. As of late 1994 Kenyan police officers continued to be unable or unwilling to investigate and prosecute rape claims effectively, including some by alleged police assailants.

Other Missions

During 1994, the Women's Rights Project conducted five missions, in Russia, Brazil, Japan, Nigeria and the United States. Reports on these missions are forthcoming in 1995.

In March, we documented state discrimination against women in Russia. Our investigation revealed that women in Russia face widespread employment discrimination; public sector employers have fired women workers in disproportionate numbers and refuse to employ women because of their sex. When women challenge such discrimination, they either are ignored by their employers and by state agencies responsible for enforcing anti-discrimination laws, or are told outright that priority should be given to men seeking jobs.

Russian law enforcement agencies and police have also denied women equal protection of the law by refusing to investigate or to prosecute violence against women, particularly domestic violence and rape. In some instances, police discouraged women from filing charges of rape and have even harassed women who do file charges in an attempt to have the complaint withdrawn.

As part of our ongoing efforts to document trafficking in women and girls, the Women's Rights Project did research in Brazil and Japan. In April, together with Human Rights Watch/Asia, we began to investigate abuses against Southeast Asian women in the Japanese sex industry.

In June, we gathered information on the trafficking in Brazil, focusing on the Amazon and Northeast regions. Our research there found that the Brazilian government has largely turned a blind eye to the exploitation of prostitution, including large-scale prostitution of girls and female adolescents. Furthermore, members of the Brazilian police forces have been implicated in abuses against women and girls forced into prostitution, particularly in the goldmining areas of the Amazon.

In July and October/November, the Women's Rights Project and Human Rights Watch/Africa sent teams to research abuses against widows and discriminatory inheritance laws in southern Nigeria, and abuses against child brides in the north. Finally, in conjunction with the Prison Project, we conducted a year-long investigation of violence against women incarcerated in state prisons in the United States.

International Response

This year's work on women's human rights at the international level built on the momentum created by the 1993 World Conference on Human Rights. At that historic meeting, member states of the United Nations pledged to integrate women's rights into all U.N. human rights activities. The Women's Rights Project sought to ensure that governments lived up to that pledge. Thus, at the meeting of the U.N. Human Rights Commission in February 1994, the Women's Rights Project urged the commission to end the international community's lamentable tradition of indifference and inaction regarding the fundamental rights of women and to take steps to protect women against violence and other forms of human rights violations.

To this end, we joined our colleagues in the international movement for women's rights in calling for the appointment of a U.N. special rapporteur on violence against women. At the same time, we emphasized the need for all special rapporteurs and working groups of the commission to report systematically on human rights violations affecting women.

In April 1994, the Human Rights Commission appointed the first Special Rapporteur on Violence Against Women, Radhika Coomaraswamy. She has begun to gather information on violence against women, including its causes and consequences; to name countries where women's rights abuses occur; to recommend steps to end such abuse, and to push the U.N. to act on her recommendations.

In July, the Women's Rights Project joined representatives of nongovernmental organizations from around the world in a meeting with the special rapporteur to discuss the nature and extent of her mandate. The meeting explored ways that women's rights advocates can support the efforts of the special rapporteur to identify and characterize abuse of women's human rights and to recommend measures designed to eliminate violence against women and its causes.

At the regional level, the Inter-American Commission on Human Rights this year appointed a special rapporteur, Claudio Grossman, to assess member states' observance of human rights norms that protect the individual rights and freedoms of women. This special rapporteur will examine domestic laws that are blatantly discriminatory as well as those that are applied in ways that inhibit women's full and equal enjoyment of their human rights.

Aside from creating these offices, the international community also sought in 1994 to integrate women's human rights into a series of other U.N. conferences and prepa-

ratory meetings. At the International Conference on Population and Development, governments adopted a program of action that underscored the importance of women's equality to population programs. The gathered nations also affirmed a loosely-defined concept of "reproductive rights," and roundly condemned the use of violence, coercion or discrimination in family planning programs.

Similarly, women's human rights have been a priority focus of regional preparations for the U.N.'s Fourth World Conference on Women, to be held in China in September 1995. The Latin American and Caribbean governments drafted a regional platform of action that supported increased efforts to monitor and combat violence against women committed by both state and private actors, and to improve the level of women's political participation. The Women's Rights Project urged the U.S. official delegation to call for the reform of national laws that codify rape and other sexual assault as crimes against "honor" rather than violations of bodily integrity.

European and North American governments focused on the need to strengthen respect for women's human rights in the context of the profound economic and political changes occurring in Europe. The project urged the U.S. and other governments to stress that women's human rights are universal, indivisible and inalienable.

U.S. Policy

The Clinton administration made many welcome public statements in support of women's human rights in 1994. It demonstrated a willingness to respond to reports of abuses against women, and to Congressional and public advocacy on behalf of women's human rights. However, the administration was generally slow to act on its own initiative to take tough action to stigmatize individual governments that committed or condoned violations of women's human rights, until such abuses against women were placed squarely in the public spotlight by others.

The administration's general reluctance to take the lead to hold abusive governments to account is disappointing, given the improved reporting on violations of women's human rights in the State Department's *Country Reports on Human Rights Practices for 1993.* Although some problems remained, the 1993 report was more comprehensive both with regard to the types of abuses discussed and the countries in which gender-related abuses were documented.

U.S. policy toward abuse against women in Haiti is a case where the administration was initially dismissive of allegations of abuse against women, only to shift its position following public pressure. Throughout early 1994, the U.S. Embassy in Port-au-Prince chose to ignore or discount reports of human rights abuse, including politically motivated rape. Rather than vigorously and publicly denouncing these serious abuses, U.S. officials at the embassy in Port-au-Prince instead challenged the veracity of the reports and sent out a cable in April dismissing the increase in claims of rape as a "sudden epidemic" and "suspicious." One U.S. Immigration and Naturalization Service officer in Port-au-Prince commented that "...[rape] must be true in some cases, but women have a tendency to blame the worst person they can think of to justify why it happened."

After the release in July of our report, "Rape in Haiti," William L. Swing, U.S. Ambassador to Haiti, acknowledged that the embassy had made "factual errors" in its prior human rights reporting. Expressing "sorrow at the dramatic increase in rape as another form of political violence," he said that the embassy had stepped up human rights monitoring in the outlying areas of Haiti, and had begun roundtable discussions with local human rights groups.

That same month, Congress added its voice on behalf of women in Haiti. In the House of Representatives, Cong. Carrie P. Meek sponsored a resolution condemning the rape of Haitian women and girls by the military and their allies as a form of political persecution, and underscored the need to provide refugees with fair asylum hearings, consistent with international standards.

Another issue where public pressure was needed to move the administration to action was sex trafficking and forced prostitution, particularly in Thailand. Following widespread press coverage of this problem, the State Department, to its credit, quickly developed a more active policy to combat trafficking in women and girls. According to Assistant Secretary of State for Democracy, Human Rights and Labor John Shattuck, the U.S. is raising this issue in bilateral dialogues with senior Thai officials; screening the human rights records of candidates for U.S.-sponsored military and police training; supporting AIDS awareness programs in Thai brothels by the Peace Corps; and promoting AIDS awareness and alternative employment programs through the Peace Corps.

However, as 1994 ended, the U.S. government still lacked clear vetting procedures to ensure that weapons and equipment provided or sold by the U.S. to the Thai police were kept out of the hands of police officials who may be complicit in trafficking and forced prostitution.

The executive branch response has largely addressed prevention of trafficking and forced prostitution. The State Department should also emphasize the need to hold Thai police and immigration officials accountable for abuses against Burmese women and girls. Representative Louise Slaughter and sixty other members of Congress introduced a resolution that highlighted this recommendation. So did the Congressional Working Group on Women's Human Rights, in a May 1994 letter to the Thai Prime Minister. The Senate Appropriations Committee has also directed the Clinton administration to submit a report on efforts taken by the Thai government to control sex trafficking.

Congress also took the lead in vigorously responding to sexual abuse elsewhere. In October 1993, appalled by reports of rape and sexual abuse against Somali refugee women in Kenya, members of Congress pressed the U.S. State Department to take remedial action. The following month, the

State Department Refugee Bureau responded with an allocation of $250,000 to the United Nations High Commissioner for Refugees for a special program to assist the survivors of sexual violence in Kenyan camps. This program, enhanced Kenyan police presence in the camps, and has significantly reduced the number of rapes reported during the first nine months of 1994. Unfortunately, the Kenyan government's record of impunity for alleged rapists has continued. The U.S. could and should use the leverage created by its security relationship with Kenya government to press for the rigorous and thorough investigation and prosecutive of alleged rapists.

The Clinton administration also began to address women's rights violations in Turkey during 1994. In an August visit to Turkey, Assistant Secretary of State John Shattuck arranged to meet with Turkish opponents of virginity exams to discuss ways to combat torture and ill-treatment in that country's prisons. This was a welcome effort that should be continued. Two months earlier, the Senate Foreign Relations Committee had noted persistent reports of human rights abuses in Turkey, including forced virginity exams by police, and had called on the administration to pursue these reports with the Turkish government.

The place where the administration mounted the most spirited defense of women's human rights was at September's International Conference on Population and Development, which drew intense international attention. The U.S. delegation to the conference strongly promoted the idea that women's empowerment is central to the goal of population control. It also condemned the use of violence, coercion and discrimination in family planning programs, and advocated the right of women to information regarding contraception and to contraceptive technology.

Concerns regarding the executive branch's inconsistent record on women's human rights led Congress to call for the appointment of a State Department senior advisor who would seek to ensure the full integration of women's human rights into U.S. foreign policy. In November, the State Department designated Gracia Hillman, formerly with the League of Women Voters, as coordinator for international women's affairs to the Office of the Under Secretary for Global Affairs, Timothy Wirth.

While the appointment is important, it is unfortunate that the State Department seems very likely to expand the mandate of the coordinator beyond women's human rights to include population and other issues, contrary to Congressional advice. The Global Affairs office is responsible for population, refugees, environment, terrorism, and a host of other global issues, including human rights. In the administration's first two years, Under Secretary Wirth focused almost exclusively on areas other than human rights, while largely failing to integrate women's human rights into U.S. foreign policy. To dilute the new coordinator's responsibilities—by including areas already concerned by other Global Affairs staff—represents, effectively, a retreat from Secretary of State Warren Christopher's pledge at the 1993 World Conference on Human Rights to make women's human rights "a moral imperative."

Aside from working with the administration, members of Congress also championed human rights by writing directly to foreign heads of state. In November 1993, prompted by the Women's Rights Project, members of the House of Representatives wrote to then-Prime Minister Morihiro Hosokawa of Japan, urging him to ensure justice for the "comfort women" who were forced into prostitution in Japanese military brothels during World War II. Among other things, members of Congress urged Japan to extend official apologies and to pay compensation to the victims. This July, the Japanese government announced plans to commit about $1 billion for an "exchange program for peace and friendship" to compensate for war crimes. However, advocates for the victims have faulted the plan for failing to acknowledge squarely the Japanese government's responsibility to the individual women.

In early 1994, members of Congress joined together to form the bipartisan Congressional Working Group on International Women's Human Rights. Co-chaired by Sen. Patty Murray and Reps. Jan Meyers and Joe Moakley, the working group sends urgent letters in support of women who are at imminent risk of abuse, or who require international support in their search for justice for past abuse. In the first ten months of 1994, the working group wrote to the governments of Peru, Bangladesh, Kenya, Mauritius, and Thailand to protest state-sponsored or state-tolerated violence and intimidation against women, and to call for immediate investigations.

Unfortunately, the credibility of the U.S. as an advocate for women's human rights around the world suffered a setback during the closing days of the 103rd Congress. Due to opposition from most Republican members of the Senate Foreign Relations Committee, the full Senate failed to deliberate U.S. ratification of the Convention on the Elimination of All Forms of Discrimination Against Women (CEDAW). As a result, the U.S. in October entered the Europe and North America regional preparatory meeting for next year's Fourth World Conference on Women as the only industrialized nation that had not committed itself to the internationally recognized standards of sexual equality enumerated in CEDAW.

The Work of the
Women's Rights Project

As in previous years, our advocacy work in 1994 addressed those specific violations of women's fundamental rights that we have documented. In addition, we have also sought to strengthen U.S., regional and international mechanisms for ensuring full accountability for women's human rights more generally.

The Women's Rights Project continued to work with U.S. policymakers to ensure that the U.N.'s international tribunal to prosecute war crimes in the former Yugoslavia would deal with sexual assault fully and

fairly.

In meetings with senior State Department officials, we pressed the U.S. to endorse the appointment of prosecutors with experience trying sex crimes to the chief prosecutor's office. We further urged the U.N. to allocate funds to the unit established by the tribunal to provide protection, counseling and support to victims and witnesses of war crimes, including sexual assault. The Women's Rights Project and other groups have also advocated the prosecution of forced impregnation as a war crime. During the summer of 1994, U.S. officials indicated that forced impregnation was "highly likely" to be prosecuted as inhuman treatment. If this happened, it would be a significant precedent in the history of international law.

In early 1994, the judges of the international tribunal promulgated rules of evidence for trying war crimes committed in the former Yugoslavia. Human Rights Watch submitted comments on the rules, and the Women's Rights Project suggested amendments to the rule of evidence concerning sexual assault cases. We urged the judges to adopt specific standards regarding the admissibility of irrelevant and prejudicial evidence. Our proposed revision, adopted in part, aimed to protect against the introduction of sex stereotypes intended to impugn the credibility of the victim, and to maintain the integrity of the proceedings.

In March, the Women's Rights Project appeared before the House Subcommittee on International Security, International Organizations and Human Rights in a hearing that was largely inspired by our report *A Modern Form of Slavery: The Trafficking of Burmese Women and Girls into Thai Brothels*. The project made specific recommendations to the U.S. and Thai governments for ending abuses against Burmese trafficking victims in Thailand.

Together with Human Rights Watch/Asia, we also ensured that trafficking for prostitution purposes was integrated into Congressional concerns about human rights in Burma more generally. In July, the U.S. House of Representatives and Senate adopted separate resolutions marking the fifth anniversary of the house arrest of Aung San Suu Kyi, leader of Burma's pro-democracy movement. Both resolutions condemned sex trafficking as one of many human rights abuses occurring in Burma.

The growing importance of trade and investment over bilateral aid has led the project to seek ways to integrate women's human rights into U.S. policy regarding these issues. Thus, after learning that the Overseas Private Investment Corporation (OPIC) had received requests for financing from several corporations for investment in Kuwait, we wrote to the president of OPIC to request that it investigate human rights abuses against Asian domestic workers there. We further advocated that OPIC work with the U.S. Embassy in Kuwait to press Kuwaiti authorities to end such abuse. Specifically, we called on OPIC to urge the Kuwaiti government to (1) amend the private sector labor law to include domestic servants within its protections; (2) stop and punish employers who confiscate their employees' passports; (3) devote more resources and support to the government office established to investigate and respond to problems associated with foreign workers; and (4) monitor the practices of agencies recruiting foreign workers. In response, the OPIC president stated in October that her agency's support of investment and future loans in Kuwait would be predicated on continued progress in protecting worker rights, including extending protections to domestic workers. OPIC took the further initiative of encouraging U.S. State Department officials to meet with Kuwaiti representatives, resulting in assurances from the Kuwaiti government that it would permit, among other things, a visit by the International Labor Organization in November 1994.

The Women's Rights Project also worked through several channels to publicize and ensure accountability for forced virginity examinations in Turkey. In early 1995, the U.S. Agency for International Development will be supporting a two-week training for doctors in Turkey on recognizing the signs of torture and ill-treatment. We called for the training to address directly the use of forced virginity exams as a form of ill-treatment and harassment. The training should instruct Turkish doctors in the strongest terms that, instead of accepting involuntary virginity exams as a routine practice, they should not perform them at all. Additionally, the project received an agreement in principle from U.S. State Department officials to denounce forced virginity exams when reporting on human rights generally in Turkey.

The problem of forced virginity control is also part of our overall effort to make women's human rights a foreign policy priority for European governments. We distributed our report to country representatives at the European Parliament and to members of the Council of Europe's Committee for the Prevention of Torture, which has long denounced torture and ill-treatment in Turkish prisons but has never taken up the problem of forced virginity exams.

Human Rights Watch's representative in Brussels met with members of the torture prevention committee to urge them to include women's human rights, in particular forced virginity exams, in their work on human rights in Turkey. In August 1994, Human Rights Watch wrote to European Commission President Jacques Delors, calling on the European Union to condemn the practice as a human rights abuse. The president's deputy head of office responded in October that the E.U. will urge Turkish officials to take measures to ensure the respect of women's rights and dignity.

The Council of Europe was particularly responsive to human rights violations in Russia. In the fall of 1994, the council considered the Russian Federation's application for membership. Human Rights Watch submitted to the council documentation on ongoing human rights violations in Russia, including state discrimination against women and its failure to investigate crimes of violence against women. We recommended that the council attach human rights conditions to Russia's membership in order to ensure greater compliance with international human rights standards. A council group of experts concluded in October that Russia's unresolved human rights problems rendered it unfit for membership at that time.

In September, the Women's Rights Project contributed the results of our rape investigation in Haiti to a petition to the Inter-American Commission on Human Rights. Coordinated by the Harvard Law School Immigration and Refugee Clinic and Sommerville Legal Services, the petition called on the commission to investigate thoroughly allegations of gender-based abuse in Haiti, and to recognize rape by government agents as a common form of torture there.

Regarding the future role of the U.S. in Haiti, the Women's Rights Project has maintained that any U.S.-sponsored training for the new Haitian police must include women's human rights. We have further pressed Clinton administration officials to urge the Aristide government to include women in the new police force.

Besides country-specific advocacy initiatives, the Women's Rights Project continued to integrate women's human rights into work on human rights more generally. In April, the Project testified in April before the House Foreign Operations Subcommittee on U.S. foreign policy on women's human rights. We commended the State Department's improved efforts to document violations of women's rights, but criticized the U.S. government's frequent reluctance to press for accountability through bilateral and multilateral policy.

In part because of this record, we worked closely with members of both the House and Senate to seek the appointment of a senior advisor on women's human rights within the State Department. The State Department Authorization Bill for 1994 and 1995, as well as the Senate's 1995 Foreign Appropriations Bill, provide for such an appointee. As noted above, the State Department has named Gracia Hillman as coordinator for international women's affairs, but with an overly broad mandate that we believe is likely to hamper her ability to serve as a strong and consistent internal advocate for women's human rights in particular.

In September, the project submitted written testimony to the Senate Foreign Relations Committee to support U.S. ratification of the Convention on the Elimination of All Forms of Discrimination Against Women (CEDAW). While we criticized some of the ways in which the administration proposed to limit U.S. obligations under this treaty, we concluded that the U.S. should nonetheless ratify expeditiously.

The documentary work of the Women's Rights Project has revealed that many women become refugees in order to escape gender-based persecution. Often these women are subject to further persecution as female refugees. Yet, current U.S. refugee law does not explicitly recognize gender-related persecution. Thus, women seeking asylum in the United States due to their well-founded fear of such persecution may be presumptively denied safe haven because the basis of their claims is not acknowledged by U.S. law.

Among other efforts to ensure that women refugees receive fair review of their asylum claims, we participated in the preparation of Guidelines for Women's Asylum Claims that were submitted to the Immigration and Naturalization Service in April 1994. The proposed guidelines explain how sex-specific forms of violence such as rape may constitute persecution, and how women may be targeted for persecution because of their gender. The INS has expressed its strong interest in the guidelines as well as in training asylum officers to improve their ability to consider women's claims fully and fairly.

Finally, the Women's Rights Project has sought to ameliorate the negative impact of gender violence and sex discrimination on women's ability to participate in economic and social spheres. We worked with the Congressional Caucus on Women's Issues on a March 1994 Congressional letter to the chairman of the House Committee on Foreign Affairs. In the letter, members of Congress urged the chairman to support as a central goal of any U.S. foreign aid reform effort "the economic, political, and social empowerment of women, rooted in respect for their fundamental human rights."

Human Rights Watch wrote separately to the director of the U.S. Agency for International Development, Brian Atwood, to suggest ways in which U.S. bilateral assistance can better advance U.S. human rights policy. Among other things, Human Rights Watch urged him to endorse broadening the definition of gross violations of internationally recognized human rights under U.S. law to include systematic official discrimination on the basis of sex.

In conjunction with a coalition of U.S. organizations concerned with worker rights, the Women's Rights Project called for reform of the U.S. Generalized System of Preferences (GSP). The GSP framework allows designated developing countries to export certain products to the U.S. on a duty-free basis, provided they take steps to protect five specific internationally recognized worker rights. The project has advocated the amendment of GSP legislation to include sex discrimination in the workplace as one of the violations of worker rights that GSP beneficiary countries must seek to eliminate. Although the GSP reform bill, sponsored by Rep. George Brown, failed to pass in 1994, we will continue this effort during the next Congress.

HUMAN RIGHTS WATCH INTERNATIONAL FILM FESTIVAL

The Human Rights Watch International Film Festival was created to advance public education on human rights issues and concerns using the unique medium of film. Each year, the Human Rights Watch International Film Festival exhibits the finest human rights films and videos in commercial and archival theaters in the U.S. and on television and in film festivals in cities around the world in an attempt to promote expanded public awareness about human rights issues.

In selecting films for the festival, Human Rights Watch concentrates equally on artistic merit and human rights content. The festival encourages filmmakers around the world to address human rights subject matter in their work and presents films and videos from both new and established international human rights filmmakers. Each year, the festival's programming committee screens more than 600 films and videos to create a program which represents the widest number of countries and issues. Once a film is nominated for a place in the program, staff of the relevant division of Human Rights Watch also view it to confirm accuracy in the portrayal of human rights concerns.

The Human Rights Watch International Film Festival was established in 1988, in part to mark the tenth anniversary of the founding of what has become Human Rights Watch. After a hiatus of three years, it was resumed in 1991 and has since been presented annually. The festival's full run opens each year in New York, but increasingly portions of the festival have been presented elsewhere in the U.S. and abroad, a reflection of both the national scope of the festival and the increasingly global appeal that the project has generated.

The 1994 festival season opened in New York in May. Seventy films and videos (of which forty-eight were premieres) from more than thirty countries were presented over a two-week period, on two screens in a Manhattan theater. The festival presented both feature films and documentaries as well as works-in-progress, short films and animation.

Each year the festival opens its New York run with an opening night fundraising celebration. In conjunction with the opening night festivities the festival annually awards a prize in the name of cinematographer and director Nestor Almendros, who was a cherished friend of the festival. The award, which includes a cash prize of $5,000, goes to a deserving filmmaker in recognition of his or her contributions to human rights. The 1994 recipient was Haitian director Raoul Peck whose work over the years has included "Lumumba" and "The Man By the Shore", a feature film about oppression in Papa Doc's Haiti.

Highlights of the 1994 festival program schedule included a retrospective of the work of renowned feminist director Margarethe von Trotta, customized daytime programming for high-school audiences accompanied by panel discussions on related human rights themes, a weekend of films from and about Sarajevo, and the complete works of Britain's Black Audio Film Collective . Filmmakers and representatives from Human Rights Watch and other human rights organizations attended the screenings and held question and answer sessions following each show.

After its successful two-week run in New York, the festival traveled on to Los Angeles where, following the opening night gala, the festival ran for seven days featuring over thirty films from around the world. As of mid-November, segments from the festival program had appeared in film festivals in Boston, Seattle, Olympia, Portland, East Hampton, Berkeley and Palm Springs in the U.S. and overseas in Vienna, Venice, Hong Kong and Sarajevo. For the first time, the festival was invited to participate in the Bogotá Film Festival, and plans were currently underway for showcases in Florence, Sienna and Lucca in the spring of 1995. Selected Human Rights Watch films would also travel to thirteen cities in Eastern Europe including Warsaw, Sophia, Tallinn, St. Petersburg, Bratislava, Bucharest, Prague, Tirana and Vilnius as part of a collaborative project with The Open Society Institute over the winter months of 1994 and 1995.

In October, the Film Society of Lincoln Center agreed to present the New York run of the Human Rights Watch International Film Festival for 1995.

CONGRESSIONAL CASEWORK

Human Rights Watch continued to work closely with three casework groups composed of members of Congress - the Congressional Friends of Human Rights Monitors, the Congressional Committee to Support Writers and Journalists, and the Congressional Working Group on International Women's Human Rights. All three groups are bipartisan and bicameral. Human Rights Watch initiated the formation of these groups to enable concerned members of Congress to write letters to governments that commit or condone violations against human rights monitors, writers and journalists, or gender based abuses of women. Human Rights Watch supplies the groups with information about appropriate cases of concern; the groups, in turn, determine which cases they would like to pursue.

The goals of the congressional casework groups are three-fold. Most important, their letters and faxes help to pressure governments to end their persecution of human rights monitors, writers and journalists, and women, abuses which are either committed or routinely tolerated by governments. Second, members of the congressional groups are informed about these important incidents of violence and intimidation. Finally, copies of letters are sent to both U.S. ambassadors in the relevant countries, to inform them about cases of concern, and to local press from the countries in question so that they in turn can bring additional attention to human rights violations.

The Congressional Friends of Human Rights Monitors

The Congressional Friends of Human Rights Monitors, which was formed in 1983, was composed of thirty-four senators and 119 members of the House of Representatives. The five members of the steering committee for the group were Sen. Dave Durenberger, Sen. James Jeffords, Sen. Daniel Patrick Moynihan, Rep. Tony Hall and Rep.

Constance A. Morella.

In 1994, the committee's primary focus was on writing urgent action letters about time-sensitive cases of death threats, attacks, and unwarranted arrests of human rights monitors. Letters from the groups describing these concerns were transmitted via fax to relevant government officials.

In Guatemala, the Congressional Friends wrote letters to President de Léon Carpio expressing concern over attacks and acts of intimidation against several activists. A January letter noted that human rights activist Mario Polanco, from the Mutual Support Group (Grupo de Apoyo Mutuo, GAM), was seriously injured when he was attacked by armed men after leaving a human rights demonstration. In addition, other activists from GAM and the Council of Ethnic Communities human rights group (Consejo de Comunidades Etnicas Runujel Junam, CERJ) received death threats and threatening phone calls. In a follow up letter in June, the Congressional Friends reiterated their concern over the ongoing harassment of monitors in Guatemala. This letter placed particular emphasis on the death threats against members of the Chel Human Rights Commission and the threats and accusations against activists from the widows' human rights group, Coordinadora Nacional de Viudas de Guatemala (CONAVIGUA). The Congressional Friends requested that the government carry out an investigation into the attack on Mario Polanco and bring those responsible to justice. The group also urged that every effort be made to see that those found responsible for the death threats and acts of intimidation against the other activists were held accountable for their actions. Harassment of human rights activists in Guatemala continues, but recent reports indicate that the level of intimidation against the activists specifically named by the Congressional Friends in their letters may have declined.

In Rwanda last March, the Congressional Friends wrote to then-President Juvenal Habyarimana expressing concern over attacks against two prominent human rights activists. The letter noted that activist André Katabarwa was gravely injured in a grenade attack while activist Monique Mujawamariya was repeatedly harassed by militia members of the MRND political party; on one occasion she was threatened with knives and on another, while she was driving, her car was stoned and the windows were smashed. The Congressional Friends called on the Rwandan government to conduct investigations into the attack against Katabarwa as well as the threats and attacks against Mujawamariya. The group also urged that those found responsible be prosecuted to the fullest extent of the law. Monique Mujawamariya continued to be targeted because of her human rights activism until her escape from Rwanda last April, soon after the onset of the genocide campaign.

The Congressional Friends wrote to Brazilian officials in March to express its concern over the death threats against several Catholic priests working on human rights issues. The priests had long been active with the church-based human rights group Comissão Pastoral da Terra (CPT) and had been threatened on a number of occasions because of their human rights activities. The Congressional Friends urged the government of Brazil to investigate the death threats against them and to hold accountable those found responsible for issuing the threats. The group also expressed its concern for the physical security of these activists; a few weeks after the letter was transmitted, Father Ricardo Rezende was provided police protection by the government. Threats against human rights activists continued, however, and in late spring, the names of three Catholic priests and a town councillor promoting human rights were included on a "hit-list" of people under threat of being killed. When the Congressional Friends group learned that the activists were in danger because of their work to defend the rights of peasants, it sent another letter to the Brazilian government. It again requested protection for these activists, and reiterated the necessity for a full scale investigation and prosecution of those found responsible for threatening their work.

In Burma, the Congressional Friends wrote to the Foreign Minister on behalf of five National League for Democracy (NLD) activists who were arrested after providing information to foreign officials and the international media about human rights conditions. The Congressional Friends noted to the Burmese government that the activists had engaged in legitimate human rights work and urged the government to drop the charges against them and release them from jail. The group also conveyed its concern over the physical safety of these activists while in solitary confinement. None of the activists were subject to torture, though all five were convicted on political charges and sentenced to from seven to fifteen year's imprisonment. The Congressional Friends wrote again to the Burmese Foreign Minister in October, conveying serious concern over the convictions of these activists, particularly in light of the minister's recent U.N. speech confirming the Burmese government's commitment to uphold the standards enshrined in the Universal Declaration of Human Rights. The group urged the Burmese government to reconsider the conviction of these activists and to commute their sentences.

In Cuba, the Congressional Friends expressed concern over the conviction of Cuban Committee for Human Rights (CCDH) leader Rodolfo González González. The letter indicated that González had been arrested, tried, and convicted after transmitting reports on human rights violations to the special observer of the United Nations Commission on Human Rights. The Congressional group viewed the seven year sentence González faced as particularly severe and expressed its belief that he was targeted because of his participation in legitimate, peaceful human rights activities. The Congressional Friends urged the Cuban government to release him from prison immediately and unconditionally.

Another arrest about which the Congressional Friends expressed concern was that of Tunisian human rights lawyer Mohammed Nejib Hosni. The letter to President Ben Ali noted that Hosni was well known for his human rights advocacy both in Tunisia and abroad, and in addition to his arrest had been subjected to police surveillance and harassment for over a year. Considering that Hosni was arrested on civil charges, his pre-trial detention without a court date and six-week confinement without access to lawyers was highly irregular. The Congressional Friends expressed its concern that the charges may have been filed in an attempt to discourage Hosni from continuing his human rights activities and urged the Tunisian government to release him from prison immediately and unconditionally.

In Georgia, the Congressional Friends wrote to condemn the abuses against Tbilisi-based human rights worker Giorgi Khostaria. It noted several incidents in which Khostaria, who at the time was working as the defense lawyer in a high-profile death penalty case, was subjected to beatings, illegal arrest, and harassment by the government's militia. In one incident he was forcibly taken by officers to the militia station where he was interrogated, beaten, and later released without charges. Khostaria continued suffering from injuries after the attack. The Congressional Friends urged the government to investigate the harassment and abuse, and to prosecute those found responsible. It also requested that the government make every effort to ensure that those working for human rights in Georgia may carry out their activities unimpeded.

The Congressional Committee to Support Writers and Journalists

The Congressional Committee to Support Writers and Journalists was formed in 1988 and is composed of sixteen senators and seventy-six representatives. The members of the steering committee were Sen. William Cohen, Sen. Bob Graham, Rep. Jim Leach, and Rep. John Lewis.

During the year, the Committee condemned murders, attacks, and arbitrary arrests of writers and journalists, as well as acts of censorship against reporters and publications.

In South Africa, the Committee denounced the January killing of photographer Abdul Shariff during an attack in which assailants opened fire on African National Congress leaders. Two other reporters, Charles Moikanyang and Anthea Warner, were shot and wounded as well. The Committee expressed its serious concern that South African police had not been available in the township of Katlehong to protect journalists during what had been an official visit. Following an international outcry over this incident, the South African government appointed an official commission of inquiry. The Congressional Committee urged the government to note the findings of the investigation and prosecute fully those found responsible.

In Mexico, the Committee expressed serious concern after news editor Jorge Martín Dorantes was shot to death by unknown assailants in June. Because there were suspicions that Dorantes may have been targeted because of his investigative reports on controversial issues involving local officials, the Committee urged the government to conduct a thorough and impartial investigation. It also requested that the findings of the investigation be made public and that those found responsible be held accountable.

In Bangladesh, the Committee conveyed its concern over official attempts to censor and silence the press by criminalizing views considered to be religiously insensitive. The writer Taslima Nasreen was criminally charged after making a statement deemed insulting to Islam, and editors from the newspaper *Janakantha* were similiarly charged and arrested after publishing an editorial based on their interpretation of the Qu'ran. In addition, religious leaders held public, and at times violent, rallies denouncing these writers. During some demonstrations, protesters called for Nasreen's death. The Congressional Committee called on the government of Bangladesh to condemn publicly threats of violence against the writers and to prosecute those found responsible for issuing death threats. Finally, the Committee urged the government to drop the charges which appear to stem solely from the writers attempts to express their views.

The Committee also wrote to Cuban authorities after several foreign journalists were held up by armed men in April. The journalists had been en route to interview a political dissident when the assailants, who identified themselves as police, ordered them out of their car and robbed them of $50,000 worth of video equipment. The Committee called the theft an act of intimidation against journalists in Cuba and urged the authorities to take all necessary measures to investigate the incident and see that the journalists' belongings were returned.

In Indonesia, a letter to several officials denounced the June revocation of publishing licenses for three highly respected news publications. The closures followed coverage in each periodical of controversies surrounding government officials. The Committee protested the government's order and noted that hundreds of workers would meanwhile lose their jobs. It stated that the license revocations stemmed from legitimate reporting and therefore urged the government to rescind the closure orders immediately and without condition.

In Mauritania, the Committee again wrote to express its concern over attempts to silence views critical of government policy. On several occasions, publication of the newspaper *Le Calame* was suspended and issues were seized by the government. The newspaper's publisher said that one of the confiscated editions contained critical remarks about a government appointee, as well as condemnations of a discriminatory government action against an ethnic minority. The Committee urged the government to cease efforts to block publication of the newspaper and to ensure that all seized copies were returned to the newsstands and made available for public review. The Committee urged the government to allow future editions of the paper to be published and distributed without interference.

The Congressional Committee expressed concerns in Israel and the occupied territories over attacks against the press in

Jericho, the West Bank, and the Gaza Strip by Israeli Defense Force (IDF) soldiers. In two separate incidents foreign reporters were shot with rubber bullets. On another occasion, soldiers beat a Palestinian cameraman on his way home from work, after he showed them his press credentials. The Congressional Committee also reported that soldiers entered the home of a Palestinian camerawoman, assaulted a journalist with her, ransacked her house, and tried forcibly to confiscate her camera. The Committee urged investigations into these attacks and requested that those found responsible be held accountable for their actions. It also urged that every effort be made to guarantee the safety of journalists as they carried out their legitimate activities.

The highly publicized arrests of two Kenyan journalists who were found guilty of criticizing a high court decision in an article, was addressed in an appeal for their release by the Congressional Committee. The Committee denounced the charges, the due process violations of the journalists' trial, and their incarceration in a detention camp known for its ill-treatment of prisoners. The Congressional Committee wrote that Bedan Mbugua and David Makali had been "unfairly tried and convicted based on the expression of their views." It urged the government to reverse the conviction and release the two journalists immediately and unconditionally.

In Korea, the Committee protested the imprisonment of Park Chi-Kwan, an editor charged under the National Security Law for publishing and carrying a North Korean novel. Following police searches of his home and office, in which computer diskettes and 200 copies of the novel were confiscated, Park was incarcerated. The committee expressed concern that, in the case of Park, the National Security Law had been interpreted to justify the restriction of the non-violent expression of his views. It urged the government to drop the charges against him and release him from prison.

Finally, in Pakistan, the Congressional Committee wrote of its concern over the charges of blasphemy against five Ahmadi journalists. It noted that journalists in the Ahmadiyya community were frequently prosecuted for the expression of their religious views, and that these writers faced long sentences if convicted. The Congressional Committee contended that the journalists' right to express their views was protected by the internationally recognized right of free expression. It urged the Pakistani government to drop all charges against the journalists immediately and unconditionally.

The Congressional Working Group on International Women's Human Rights

The Congressional Working Group on International Women's Human Rights, which was formed in April 1994, was composed of eighteen Senators and thirty-three members of the House of Representatives. It was created to promote accountability for violations of women's rights worldwide. The three members of the steering committee for the group were Sen. Patty Murray, Rep. Jan Meyers and Rep. Joe Moakley.

In 1994, the Working Group denounced violations of women's human rights in five countries.

In May, the Working Group wrote to the Prime Minister of Thailand regarding the illegal trafficking of Burmese women and girls into Thailand for forced prostitution. The Working Group called on the Thai government to investigate and prosecute rigorously allegations of Thai police involvement in trafficking and forced prostitution. The letter also expressed concern over discriminatory police raids on brothels that trigger further violations of the rights of the Burmese women and girls by Thai government agents. The Working Group urged the Thai government to implement a comprehensive program to protect the thousands of Burmese women and girls who are currently in Thai brothels and to prevent continued trade in human beings across Thai borders.

In Peru, the Working Group expressed its deep concern over the arbitrary detention of community activist Santosa Layme Bejar by members of the anti-terrorism branch of the police. The letter noted that at least 200 people who have been arrested under Peru's anti-terrorism laws were falsely charged. The Working Group urged the government to release Bejar; to ensure the humane treatment of all those who are detained; and to grant access to visits by family members and legal counsel.

In Bangladesh, the Working Group questioned the legitimacy of criminal charges that the government filed against feminist author Taslima Nasreen. Its letter also noted the public death threats against Nasreen by religious extremists and the government's failure to denounce publicly such threats. The Working Group urged the President of Bangladesh to uphold the right to freedom of expression by investigating and prosecuting those who advocate violence against Nasreen for her feminist views. In addition, the government was also urged to rescind the warrant for Nasreen's arrest.

In July, the Working Group wrote to the Kenyan Government regarding a armed police crack down against a peaceful meeting of the Kenya League of Women Voters. The letter called the actions of the police a violation of the fundamental rights to security of the person, freedom of speech and association, equal protection of the law and due process. The Working Group urged the government to investigate fully the incident and to ensure that police and other officials who were involved are held to account.

In Mauritius, the Working Group protested the repeated calls for violence against feminist writer Lindsey Collen by religious extremists. The Government of Mauritius not only failed to condemn such intimidation, but instead fueled harassment against her by calling her book *Rape of Sita* blasphemous and an outrage to public morality. Subsequently, the government banned Collen's book. The Working Group urged the Mauritian government to guarantee Collen's right to freedom of expression by lifting the ban on her book; to condemn the campaign of intimidation by religious extremists; and to investigate and prosecute those responsible.

MISSIONS

Human Rights Watch/Africa

January-February/ South Africa: Followed up previous work by investigating violence in Natal and abuses of freedom in Bophuthatswana.

January-February/ Burundi: Investigated massive human rights abuses as a part of an international commission.

March/ Ethiopia: Investigated issues of accountability for human rights violations by officials of the previous regime, and questions of freedom of association and press under the present government.

April-May/ Liberia: Conducted a fact-finding mission to investigate the use of child soldiers by the warring factions in Liberia for a joint project with the Children's Rights Project. The mission also investigated the human rights abuses associated with the ongoing fighting, especially involving the Liberian Peace Council.

May-June/ Angola: Conducted a joint mission with the Arms Project. This was the first visit by Human Rights Watch into UNITA (National Union for the Total Independence of Angola) zones.

July-August/ Nigeria: Investigated human rights abuses directed against women, focusing on widows in the south, as part of a joint project with the Women's Rights Project.

September/South Africa: Followed up information from the May-June mission to Angola.

September/Kenya: Investigated progress made by the UNHCR in the North East Province since the 1993 issue of a report on rape of Somali refugees.

October-November/Nigeria: Investigated human rights abuses directed against women, documenting abuses against child brides in the north, as a part of a joint project with the Women's Rights Project.

Human Rights Watch/Americas

January/ El Salvador: Investigated the status of human rights and death squad killings prior to the March 1994 elections.

February/ Nicaragua: Evaluated the work of the Tri-partite Commission on political violence in Nicaragua.

February/ Haiti: Investigated increasingly widespread human rights violations, including a rise in the use of terror tactics such as rape by state agents, and to study internal displacement and refugee flight.

February/ Mexico: Investigated violations of the laws of war during the Chiapas uprising.

March/ Guatemala: Gathered material for a report on the first year of the government of President De Leòn Carpio. Spanish translation was released in September.

March/ Brazil: Researched violence against indigenous communities, particularly the Wapixana and Macuxi peoples in the Raposa Serra do Sol indigenous area and the Northern Roraima state.

June/ Colombia: Investigated reports of political violence against children. Report released in November.

June/ Peru: Performed advocacy work on several outstanding cases of human rights abuses via meetings with government officials and national press.

June/ Mexico: Investigated political rights as they pertained to the up and coming national election.

June/ Miami: Investigated incidents of violent harassment and intimidation against moderate Cuban-Americans in the wake of their participation in a Havana conference in April.

July/ Peru: Investigated special courts set up to try treason and terrorist cases, as well as "popular trials" carried out by the Shining Path.

July/ U.S.-Mexico Border: Investigated new cases of human rights abuses committed by U.S. Border Patrols and examined efforts by the INS to improve the complaint, review and disciplinary procedures intended to hold abusive agents accountable.

August-September/ Brazil: Updated information concerning cases pending before the Inter-American Commission on Human Rights of the OAS and updated information on violence against children and adolescents.

September-October/ Haiti: Raised the profile of issues related to accountability for human rights violations, with particular emphasis on the scope and content of an amnesty law under consideration in the first weeks of the U.S.-led armed intervention. Investigated the formation of an interim police force and plans to establish a new national civilian police. Monitored the efforts of the multinational force to disarm and dismantle paramilitary groupings.

November/ Guatemala: Attended the exhumation of remains of a disappearance victim, at the request of the family, and pressed the government to resolve that and other disappearance cases.

Human Rights Watch/Asia

February-March/ Nepal: Investigated reports of forced trafficking of Nepalese women and girls into brothels in India. Interviewed trafficking victims who had managed to return home, police and government officials; met with lawyers and human rights workers.

March/ Cambodia: Investigated foreign support for the Khmer Rouge, violations of the laws of war and military abuses, including allegations that secret prisons continued to operate in Battambang province under the direction of military intelligence units.

March/ Japan: Continued dialogue with government officials, Diet members, and others on Japan's human rights policies.

March/ Japan: (with the Women's Rights Project) Began an investigation of the trafficking of women from Southeast Asia in Japan.

May-June/ Thailand: Visited ethnic Mon refugees in Thailand. A report scheduled for publication in late November analyzed the reasons why refugees continued to leave Burma and their treatment by Thai authorities.

May-June/ India: Researched role of political forces in communal conflict in Bombay and Gujarat.

June/ Indonesia: Visited East Java, West Java and Kalimantan to investigate human rights abuses research and discuss advocacy strategies with NGOs.

July/ Japan: (with the Prison Project) Sent a delegation to assess conditions in Japanese penal institutions. Report expected in early 1995.

July-August/ India: Visited Delhi, Bombay and Bangalore to continue investigation of forced trafficking of Nepalese women and girls into brothels in India.

. August/Cambodia: Assessed new laws and regulations pertaining to immigration, control of the press and NGOs, and the government's willingness to investigate and punish military abuses.

July-December/ India: Began a long-term project to research the relationship between human rights and HIV/AIDS in India.

November/ Japan: Met with Japanese officials to discuss Japan's human rights policies as Asia's largest donor nation.

Human Rights Watch/Helsinki

March-April/ Serbia and Croatia: Investigated the trials of alleged war criminals.

March-April/ Armenia, Azerbaijan and Nagorno-Karabakh: Investigated laws of war violations in the Nagorno-Karabakh conflict.

March/ Moscow and Tajikistan: Opened the Human Rights Watch/ Helsinki office in Dushanbe, Tajikistan. The Tajikistan office officially opened on April 1, 1994.

April/ Turkey: Investigated the cause of the Democracy Party (DEP) parliamentarians who had been stripped of their immunity and were being charged with sedition.

May/ Romania and Bulgaria: Investigated mob violence and police brutality against Roma, as well as the response of investigatory and prosecutorial bodies.

May/ Kazakhastan: Participated in an international human rights conference.

May-June/ Bosnia-Herzegovina: In-vestigated rules of war violations in eastern Bosnia and Sarajevo.

June/ Georgia: Documented civil and political violations.

August/ Georgia: Monitored a trial, held a press conference and released the report *Torture and Gross Violations of Due Process in Georgia,* based on the trial.

August/ Russia: (Ingushetia, North Ossetia) Investigated rules of war violations in the conflict between North Ossetia and Ingushetia in the North Caucus region of Russia.

September/Turkey: Investigated fighting between the Kurdistan Workers Party (PKK) and the Turkish government, and forced civilian displacement in Southeast Turkey.

August-October/ Bosnia-Herzegovina: Investigated rules of war violations in eastern Bosnia and the status of human rights and accountability for past crimes in the Muslim/ Croat federation.

September/ Uzbekistan: Participated in a Conference on Security and Cooperation in Europe (CSCE) seminar.

Human Rights Watch/Middle East

December/ United Arab Emirates: Participated in a one-day symposium organized by the Cultural Foundation of Abu-Dhabi on Universal Human Rights and Cultural Relevance in the Middle East.

December-January/ Kuwait: Observed trials before the State Security Court, to investigate conditions of the Bedoons; followed up on the fate of local human rights groups and the plight of Asian maids; and discussed the above issues with government officials and members of Parliament.

January/ Jordon: Participated in a one-week program arranged by the Geneva-based International Commission of Jurists for human rights groups in the Middle East.

March/ Israel and the Occupied Territories: Interviewed Palestinian ex-detainees on their experience under interrogation, and investigated the government's response to settler violence in occupied territories.

April/ Paris: Met with Syrian human

rights advocates.

June/ Israel and the Occupied Territories: Released Torture and Illtreatment reort. began investigating human rights in the Palestinian self-rule areas.

June-July/ Egypt: Investigated security forces practices; government crackdown on lawyers and the death-in-custody of lawyer Abel Harith Madani.

August/ Sweden: Participated in the Fifth Congress of the International Federation of Iranian Refugees and Immigrants Council.

September/ Israel and the Occupied Territories: Attended a conference on human rights enforcement and continued investigation of human rights in the Palestinian self-rule areas.

October/ Israel and the Occupied Territories: Met with local human rights organizations.

October/ Syria: Met with Syrian government officials to discuss human rights concerns and a fact-finding mission by Human Rights Watch/ Middle East.

The Arms Project

February-March and August/ Cambodia: Investigated violations of the laws of war in the fighting between the Cambodian government and the Khmer Rouge; uncovered evidence of the transfer of weapons, military aid and other services by Thailand, Indonesia and other governments to both parties.

May-June/ Angola: Investigated arms flows into Angola and violations of the laws of war by both the government and UNITA (National Union for the Total Independence of Angola) forces since the September 1992 elections.

The Children's Rights Project

April/ Liberia: (with Human Rights Watch/ Africa) Investigated the use of children as soldiers in the ongoing conflict.

June/ Jamaica: (in cooperation with Human Rights Watch/ Americas) Investigated the conditions in which children are held in detention with adults.

June/ Northern Ireland: (in cooperation with Human Rights Watch/ Helsinki) Investigated the abuse of children by security forces and paramilitaries.

October/ Geneva: Presented reports on Jamaica and Northern Ireland to the United Nations Committee on the Rights of the Child.

November/ Colombia: (with Human Rights Watch/ Americas) Held press conferences in Bogotá and Medellin to release report on the killing of street children.

The Prison Project

January/ Venezuela: Conducted an emergency mission following a prison massacre in Maracaibo.

February and April/ United States: (with Human Rights Watch/ Women's Rights Project) Interviewed victims of sexual abuse in prisons in Georgia and New York for a study of sexual abuse in US prisons.

February/ The Hague: Worked on a guide to prison standards.

February/ Vienna: Attended a preparatory meeting for the Ninth UN Congress on Crime and the Treatment of Offenders.

February/ Geneva: Presented Human Rights Watch oral intervention before a Commission on Human Rights.

May/ Geneva: Gave a presentation at the invitation of the ICRC at their teaching seminar for Detention Division field coordinators.

July/ Japan: Conducted a two-week fact finding mission of Japanese penal institutions, with a report expected in early 1995.

October/ Geneva: Participated in the UN Working Group on the Draft Optional Protocol to the Convention Against Torture.

November/ the Hague: Participated in an international conference on prisons.

The Women's Rights Project

February/ Haiti: Examined the use of rape and sexual assault as political weapons under the Cédras regime.

March/ Russia: Documented employment discrimination against women and domestic violence.

April/ Japan: Researched trafficking and forced prostitution of Southeast Asian women and girls.

June/ Brazil: Gathered information on trafficking and forced prostitution of Brazilian women.

August and October/ Nigeria: Investigated abuses against widows and child brides.

September/ Kenya: Conducted a follow-up mission on rape and sexual abuse of Somali refugee women.

Year long/ United States: Investigated sexual and physical abuse of incarcerated women in US prisons.

1994 Publications

To order any of the following titles, please call our Publications Department at (212) 986-1980 and ask for the most recent publications catalog.

Human Rights Watch/Africa

Angola
Angola: Arms Trade and Violations of the Laws of War Since the 1992 Elections, 11/94, 176 pp.

Botswana
Second Class Citizens: Discrimination Against Women Under Botswana's Citizenship Act, 9/94, 20 pp.

General
Human Rights in Africa and U.S. Policy, 7/94, 37 pp.

Kenya
Multipartyism Betrayed in Kenya: Continuing Rural Violence and Restrictions on Freedom of Speech and Assembly, 7/94, 33 pp.

Liberia
Easy Prey: Child Soldiers in Liberia, 9/94, 88 pp.

Mauritania
Mauritania's Campaign of Terror: State-Sponsored Repression of Black Africans, 4/94, 168 pp.

Mozambique
Landmines in Mozambique, 3/94, 136 pp.

Nigeria
"The Dawn of a New Dark Age": Human Rights Abuses Rampant as Nigerian Military Declares Absolute Power, 10/94, 20 pp.

Rwanda
Arming Rwanda: The Arms Trade and Human Rights Abuses in the Rwandan War, 1/94, 64 pp.
Genocide in Rwanda: April-May 1994, 5/94, 13 pp.

South Africa
Prison Conditions in South Africa, 2/94, 136 pp.
Impunity for Human Rights Abuses in Two Homelands: Reports on KwaZulu and Bophuthatswana, 3/94, 23 pp.

Sudan
Civilian Devastation: Abuses by All Parties in the War in Southern Sudan, 6/94, 296 pp.
"In the Name of God": Repression Continues in Northern Sudan, 11/94, 40 pp.
The Lost Boys: Child Soldiers and Unaccompanied Boys in Southern Sudan, 11/94, 25 pp.

Zaire
Prison Condtions in Zaire, 1/94, 72 pp.

Human Rights Watch/Americas

Brazil
Final Justice: Police and Death Squad Homicides of Adolescents in Brazil, 2/94, 160 pp.
Violence Against the Macuxi and Wapixana Indians in Raposa Serra do Sol and Northern Roraima from 1988 to 1994, 6/94, 30 pp.

Chile
Unsettled Business: Human Rights in Chile at the Start of the Frei Presidency. 5/94. 36 pp.

Colombia
Generation Under Fire: Children and Violence in Colombia, 11/94, 104 pp.

Cuba
Stifling Dissent in the Midst of Crisis. 2/94. 18 pp.
Repression, the Exodus of August 1994. and the U.S. Response. 10/94. 19 pp.

El Salvador
Darkening Horizons: Human Rights on the Eve of the March 1994 Elections. 3/94. 20 pp.

Guatemala
Human Rights in Guatemala during President De Leon Carpio's First Year. 6/94. 160 pp.

Haiti
Terror Prevails in Haiti: Human Rights Violations and Failed Diplomacy, 4/94. 46 pp.
Rape in Haiti: A Weapon of Terror. 7/94. 28 pp.
Fugitives from Injustice: The Crisis of Internal Displacement in Haiti, 8/94, 31 pp.

Honduras
The Facts Speak for Themselves: The Preliminary Report on Disappearances of the National Commissioner for the Protection of Human Rights in Honduras, 7/94, 296 pp.

Jamaica
Children Improperly Detained in Police Lockups, 10/94, 17 pp.

Mexico
The New Year's Rebellion: Violations of Human Rights and Humanitarian Law during the Armed Revolt in Chiapas, Mexico, 3/94, 29 pp.
Mexico at the Crossroads: Political Rights and the 1994 Presidential and Congressional Elections. 8/94. 24 pp.

Nicaragua
Separating Facts from Fiction: The Work of the Tripartite Commission in Nicaragua. 10/94. 28 pp.

United States
Dangerous Dialogue Revisited: Threats to Freedom of Expression Continue in Miami's Cuban Exile Community. 11/94. 9 pp.

Venezuela
Prison Massacre in Maracaibo. 2/94. 8 pp.

Human Rights Watch/Asia

China
Detained in China and Tibet: A Directory of Political and Religious Prisoners. 2/94. 688 pp.
New Arrests Linked to Worker Rights in China, 3/94. 17 pp.
No Progress on Human Rights in China: Update No. 1 to Detained in China and Tibet. 5/94, 46 pp.
The Price of Obscurity in China: Revelations About Prisoners Arrested After June 4. 1989, 5/94, 51 pp.
Persecution of a Protestant Sect in China. 6/94, 22 pp.
Pressure off, China Targets Activists. 7/94. 28 pp.
Organ Procurement and Judicial Execution in China, 8/94, 42 pp.
Use of Criminal Charges Against Political Dissidents, 10/94, 22 pp.

General
Human Rights in the APEC Region. 11/94. 36 pp.

India
Dead Silence: The Legacy of Abuses in Punjab; 5/94, 112 pp.
Continuing Repression in Kashmir: Abuses Rise as International Pressure on India Eases. 8/94, 23 pp.
Arms and Abuses in Indian Punjab and Kash-

mir, 9/94, 59 pp.

Indonesia
New Developments on Labor Rights, 1/94, 8 pp.
The Medan Demonstrations and Beyond, 5/94, 13 pp.
The Limits of Openness: Human Rights in Indonesia and East Timor, 9/94, 152 pp.
Tightening Up in Indonesia Before the APEC Summit, 10/94, 21 pp.

Human Rights Watch/Helsinki

Bulgaria
Increasing Violence Against Roma in Bulgaria, 11/94, 32 pp.

Bosnia-Hercegovina
War Crimes in Bosnia-Hercegovina: Bosanski Samac, 4/94, 19 pp.
War Crimes in Bosnia-Hercegovina: U.N. Cease-Fire Won't Help Banja Luka, 6/94, 38 pp.
Bosnia-Hercegovina: Sarajevo, 10/94, 31 pp.
Bosnia-Hercegovina: "Ethnic Cleansing" Continues in Northern Bosnia, 11/94, 36 pp.

Georgia
Torture and Gross Violations of Due Process in Georgia: An Analysis of Criminal Case No. 7493810, 8/94, 20 pp.

Greece
The Macedonians of Greece: Denying Ethnic Identity, 5/94, 88 pp.

Kosovo
Open Wounds: Human Rights Abuses in Kosovo, 3/94, 168 pp.

Romania
Restrictions on Freedom of the Press in Romania, 6/94, 15 pp.
Lynch Law: Violence Against Roma in Romania, 11/94, 41 pp.

Serbia and Montenegro
Human Rights Abuses of Non-Serbs in Kosovo, Sandzak & Vojvodina, 5/94, 11 pp.

Slovak Republic
Restrictions on Press Freedom in the Slovak Republic, 6/94, 24 pp.

Tajikistan
Political Prisoners in Tajikistan, 10/94, 10 pp.
Human Rights in Tajikistan on the Eve of Presidential Elections, 10/94, 13 pp.

Turkey
Twenty-One Deaths in Detention in 1993, 1/94, 6 pp.
A Matter of Power: State Control of Women's Virginity in Turkey, 6/94, 38 pp.
Forced Displacement of Ethnic Kurds From Southeastern Turkey, 10/94, 27 pp.

United Kingdom
Continued Abuses by All Sides in Northern Ireland, 3/94, 10 pp.

Former Yugoslav Republic of Macedonia
Human Rights in the Former Yugoslav Republic of Macedonia, 1/94, 19 pp.

Former Yugoslavia
The War Crimes Tribunal: One Year Later, 2/94, 25 pp.

Human Rights Watch/Middle East

Algeria
Human Rights Abuses in Algeria: No One is Spared, 1/94, 74 pp.

Egypt
Violations of Freedom of Religious Belief and Expression of the Christian Minority, 11/94, 39 pp.

Iraq
Bureaucracy of Repression: The Iraqi Government in Its Own Words, 2/94, 166 pp.

Israeli-Occupied Territories

Torture and Ill-Treatment: Israel's Interrogation of Palestinians from the Occupied Territories, 6/94, 336 pp.

Yemen

Human Rights in Yemen During and After the 1994 War, 10/94, 31 pp.

Human Rights Watch

United States

Human Rights Violations in the U.S.: A Report on U.S. Compliance with the International Covenant on Civil and Political Rights, 1/94, 216 pp.

Breach of Trust: Physician Participation in Executions in the United States, 3/94, 88 pp.

Arms Project

Angola

Angola: Arms Trade and Violations of the Laws of War Since the 1992 Elections, 11/94, 176 pp.

India

Arms and Abuses in Indian Punjab and Kashmir, 9/94, 59 pp.

Mozambique

Landmines in Mozambique, 3/94, 136 pp.

Rwanda

Arming Rwanda: The Arms Trade and Human Rights Abuses in the Rwandan War, 1/94, 64 pp.

Children's Rights Project

Colombia

Generation Under Fire: Children and Violence in Colombia, 11/94, 104 pp.

Jamaica

Children Improperly Detained in Police Lockups, 10/94, 17 pp.

Liberia

Easy Prey: Child Soldiers in Liberia, 9/94, 88 pp.

Sudan

The Lost Boys: Child Soldiers and Unaccompanied Boys in Southern Sudan, 11/94, 25 pp.

United Kingdom

After the Cease-Fire: Children's Rights Still Violated in Northern Ireland, 12/94, 26 pp.

Free Expression Project

Canada

A Ruling Inspired by U.S. Anti-Pornography Activists is Used to Restrict Lesbian and Gay Publications in Canada, 2/94, 11 pp.

General

Persecuted, Banned, Censored and Jailed Writers Receive Grants: 30 Writers from 17 Countries Recognized by Lillian Hellman/Dashiell Hammett Funds, 5/94, 4 pp.

United States

Dangerous Dialogue Revisited: Threats to Freedom of Expression Continue in Miami's Cuban Exile Community, 11/94, 9 pp.

Prison Project

South Africa

Prison Conditions in South Africa, 2/94, 136 pp.

Venezuela

Prison Massacre in Maracaibo, 2/94, 8 pp.

Zaire

Prison Conditions in Zaire, 1/94, 72 pp.

Women's Rights Project

Botswana
Second Class Citizens: Discrimination Against Women Under Botswana's Citizenship Act, 9/94, 20 pp.

Haiti
Rape in Haiti: A Weapon of Terror, 7/94, 28 pp.

Turkey
A Matter of Power: State Control of Women's Virginity in Turkey, 6/94, 38 pp.

STAFF AND COMMITTEES

Human Rights Watch

Staff
Executive: Kenneth Roth, Executive Director; Gara LaMarche, Associate Director; Sandra Necchi, Executive Assistant; Lydda Ragasa, Associate. **Program**: Cynthia Brown, Program Director; Michael McClintock, Deputy Program Director; Juan E. Méndez, General Counsel; Jemera Rone, Counsel; Richard Dicker, Associate Counsel; Farhad Karim, Research Associate; Nandi Rodrigo, Associate; Marti Weithman, Associate. **Advocacy**: Holly Burkhalter, Advocacy Director; Lotte Leicht, Brussels Office Director; Joanna Weschler, United Nations Representative; Allyson Collins, Research Associate; Loren K. Miller, Associate. **Communications:** Susan Osnos, Communications Director; Robert Kimzey, Publications Director; Suzanne Guthrie, Publications Manager; Virginia Muller, Librarian; Lenny Thomas, Production Manager; Fitzroy Hepkins, Mail Manager; Liz Reynoso, Communications Associate; Sobeira Genao, Publications Assistant; Kathleen Desvallons, Publications Intern. **Development**: Ann Johnson, Development Director; Desiree A. Colly, Regional Development Director; Jamie Fellner, Foundations Relations Director; Danielle Probst, Assistant Regional Director of Development; Rachel Weintraub, Special Events Director; Jennifer Lavenhar, Special Events Associate; Jenifyr Lux, Development Associate; Wendy Worthington, Associate. **Finance and Administration:** Derrick Wong, Director; Barbara Guglielmo, Controller; Walid Ayoub, Systems Administrator; Anderson Allen, Office Manager, Washington; Laura McCormick, Office Manager, New York; Urmi Shah, Office Manager, London; Isabelle Tin-Aung, Office Manager, Brussels; Byron Isaacs, Bookkeeper; Del Martinez, Receptionist; Michaela Harrison, Receptionist. **Film Festival:** Hamilton Fish, Director; Bruni Nurres, Programmer; Heather Harding, Coordintor. **Fellowship Recipients:** Mark Girouard, Henry R. Luce Fellow; Joanne Mariner, Orville Schell Fellow; Brian Owsley, Leonard Sandler Fellow; Melissa Crow, Sophie Silberberg Fellow; Ann Beeson, Bradford Wiley Fellow.

Board of Directors
Robert L. Bernstein, Chair; Adrian W. DeWind, Vice Chair; Roland Algrant; Lisa Anderson; Peter D. Bell; Alice L. Brown; William Carmichael; Dorothy Cullman; Irene Diamond; Edith Everett; Jonathan Fanton; Alan Finberg; Jack Greenberg; Alice H. Henkin; Harold Hongju Koh; Stephen L. Kass; Marina Pinto Kaufman; Alexander MacGregor; Josh Mailman; Jane Olson; Peter Osnos; Kathleen Peratis; Bruce Rabb; Orville Schell; Gary G. Sick; Malcolm Smith; Nahid Toubia; Maureen White; Rosalind C. Whitehead.

Human Rights Watch/Africa

Staff
Abdullahi An-Nai'm, Executive Director; Janet Fleischman, Washington Representative; Karen Sorensen, Research Associate; Alex Vines, Research Associate; Berhane Woldegabriel, Research Associate; Alison L. DesForges, Consultant; Bronwen Manby, Consultant; Kimberly Mazyck, Associate.

Advisory Committee

William Carmichael, Chair; Alice L. Brown, Vice Chair; Roland Algrant; Robert L. Bernstein; Julius L. Chambers; Michael Clough; Roberta Cohen; Carol Corillon; Alison L. DesForges; Adrian W. DeWind; Thomas M. Franck; Gail M. Gerhart; Jack Greenberg; Alice H. Henkin; Robert Joffe; Richard A. Joseph; Thomas Karis; Russell Karp; Stephen L. Kass; John A. Marcum; Gay McDougall; Toni Morrison; Barrington Parker, III; James C. N. Paul; Robert Preiskel; Norman Redlich; Randall Robinson; Sidney S. Rosdeitcher; Howard P. Venable; Claude E. Welch, Jr.; Aristide R. Zolberg.

Human Rights Watch/Americas

Staff

José-Miguel Vivanco, Executive Director; Anne Manuel, Deputy Director; Sebastian Brett, Research Associate; James Cavallaro, Brazil Representative; Robin Kirk, Research Associate; Gretta Tovar-Sienbentritt, Research Associate; Lee Tucker, Staff Attorney; Rafael de la Dehesa, Consultant; Stephen Crandall, Associate; Vanessa Jiménez, Associate; Tuhin Roy, Associate.

Advisory Committee

Peter D. Bell, Chair; Stephen L. Kass, Vice Chair; Marina Kaufman, Vice Chair; Roland Algrant; Robert L. Bernstein; Albert Bildner; Paul Chevigny; Dorothy Cullman; Peter W. Davidson; Patricia Derian; Adrian W. DeWind; Stanley Engelstein; Tom J. Farer; Alejandro Garro; Wendy Gimbel; John S. Gitlitz; Robert K. Goldman; James Goldston; Jack Greenberg; Wade J. Henderson; Alice H. Henkin; Russell Karp; Margaret A. Lang; Robert S. Lawrence, MD; J. Rolando Matalon; Jocelyn McCalla; Theodor Meron; David E. Nachman; John B. Oakes; Victor Penchaszadeh; Clara A. "Zazi" Pope; Bruce Rabb; Jeanne Richman; Tina Rosenberg; Jean-Marie Simon; Sanford Solender; George Soros; Alfred Stepan; Rose Styron; Jorge Valls.

Human Rights Watch/Asia

Staff

Sidney Jones, Executive Director; Mike Jendrzejczyk, Washington Director; Robin Munro, Hong Kong Director; Patricia Gossman, Research Associate; Jeannine Guthrie, Research Associate; Zunetta Liddell, Research Associate; Dinah PoKempner, Research Associate; Aung Myo Ming, Consultant; Mickey Spiegel, Consultant; Diana Tai-Feng Cheng, Associate; Jennifer Hyman, Associate.

Advisory Committee

Orville Schell, Vice Chair; Floyd Abrams; Maureen Aung-Thwin; Edward J. Baker; Harry Barnes; Robert L. Bernstein; Julie Brill; Jerome A. Cohen; Adrian W. DeWind; Clarence Dias; Delores A. Donovan; Adrienne Germain; Merle Goldman; Deborah M. Greenberg; Charles Halpern; David Hawk; Paul Hoffman; Sharon Hom; Rounaq Jahan; Virginia Leary; Daniel Lev; Perry Link; Rt. Rev. Paul Moore, Jr.; Andrew Nathan; Victoria Riskin; Sheila Rothman; Barnett Rubin; James Scott; Ivan Shapiro; Judith Shapiro; Nadine Strossen; Maya Wiley.

Human Rights Watch/Helsinki

Staff

Jeri Laber, Executive Director; Holly Cartner, Deputy Director; Erika Dailey, Research Associate; Rachel Denber, Research Associate; Ivana Nizich, Research Associate; Christopher Panico, Research Associate; Fatemah Ziai, Research Associate; Vlatka Miheli, Consultant; Zeljka Marki, Consultant; Anne Kuper, Associate; Ivan Lupis, Associate; Alexander Petrov, Associate.

Advisory Committee

Jonathan Fanton, Chair; Alice H. Henkin, Vice Chair; Roland Algrant; Robert L. Bernstein; Charles Biblowit; Martin Blumenthal; Roberta Cohen; Lori Damrosch; Istvan Deak; Adrian W. DeWind; Fr. Robert Drinan; Stanley Engelstein; Alan R. Finberg; Ellen Futter; Willard Gaylin, MD; Michael Gellert; John Glusman; Paul Goble; Robert

K. Goldman; Jack Greenberg; Rita E. Hauser; Robert James; Rhoda Karpatkin; Stephen L. Kass; Bentley Kassal; Marina Pinto Kaufman; Joanne Landy; Margaret A. Lang; Leon Levy; Wendy Luers; Theodor Meron; Deborah Milenkovitch; Toni Morrison; John B. Oakes; Herbert Okun; Jane Olson; Yuri Orlov; Srdja Popovic; Bruce Rabb; Peter Reddaway; Stuart Robinowitz; John G. Ryden; Herman Schwartz; Stanley K. Sheinbaum; Jerome J. Shestack; George Soros; Susan Weber Soros; Michael Sovern; Fritz Stern; Svetlana Stone; Rose Styron; Liv Ullman; Gregory Wallance; Rosalind Whitehead; Jerome R. Wiesner; William D. Zabel.

Human Rights Watch/Middle East
Staff
Christopher E. George, Executive Director; Eric Goldstein, Research Director; Aziz Abu-Hamad, Associate Director; Virginia N. Sherry, Associate Director; Joost Hiltermann, Iraqi Documents Project Director; Shorsh Resool, Iraqi Documents Project Researcher; Joel Campagna, Consultant; Elahé S. Hicks, Consultant; Suzanne Howard, Associate.

Advisory Committee
Gary G. Sick, Chair; Lisa Anderson, Vice Chair; Bruce Rabb, Vice Chair; Shaul Bakhash; M. Cherif Bassiouni; Hyman Bookbinder; Paul Chevigny; Helena Cobban; Patricia Derian; Stanley Engelstein; Edith Everett; Mansour Farhang; Robert K. Goldman; Rita E. Hauser; Reverend J. Bryan Hehir; Edy Kaufman; Marina Pinto Kaufman; Samir Khalaf; Judith Kipper; Pnina Lahav; Ann M. Lesch; Richard Maass; Stephen P. Marks; Philip Mattar; David K. Shipler; Sanford Solender; Shibley Telhami; Sir Brian Urquhart; Napoleon B. Williams, Jr..

Human Rights Watch Arms Project
Staff
Joost R. Hiltermann, Director; Steve Goose, Program Director; Kathleen Bleakley, Associate.

Advisory Committee
Morton Abramowitz; Nicole Ball; Frank Blackaby; Frederick C. Cuny; Ahmed H. Esa; Gustavo Gorriti; Bill Green; Di Hua; Jo Husbands; Frederick J. Knecht; Edward J. Laurance; Vincent McGee; Aryeh Neier; Janne E. Nolan; Andrew J. Pierre; David Rieff; Kumar Rupesinghe; John Ryle; Mohamed M. Sahnoun; Gary G. Sick; Thomas Winship.

Human Rights Watch Children's Rights Project
Staff
Lois Whitman, Director; Michelle India Baird, Counsel; Mina Samuels, Consultant; Raquel Hyde, Associate.

Advisory Committee
Sanford J. Fox, Lisa Hedley, Alan Levine, Dr. Hadassah Brooks Morgan, Dr. Elena Nightingale, Marta Santos Pais, Robert G. Schwartz, Mark I. Soler, William L. Taylor, Geraldine Van Bueren.

Human Rights Watch Free Expression Project
Staff
Gara LaMarche, Director; Marcia Allina, Program Associate; Lydda Ragasa, Associate.

Advisory Committee
Roland Algrant, Chair; Peter Osnos, Vice Chair; Alice Arlen; Robert L. Bernstein; Tom A. Bernstein; Hortense Calisher; Geoffrey Cowan; Dorothy Cullman; Patricia Derian; Adrian W. DeWind; Irene Diamond; E. L. Doctorow; Norman Dorsen; Alan R. Finberg; Frances FitzGerald; Jack Greenberg; Vartan Gregorian; S. Miller Harris; Alice H. Henkin; Pam Hill; Joseph Hofheimer; Lawrence Hughes; Ellen Hume; Mark Kaplan; Stephen L. Kass; William Koshland; Judith F. Krug; Anthony Lewis; William Loverd; Wendy Luers; John Macrae, III; Kati Marton; Michael Massing; Nancy Meiselas; Arthur Miller; Rt. Rev. Paul Moore, Jr.; Toni Morrison; Aryeh Neier; Bruce Rabb; Geoffrey Cobb Ryan; John G. Ryden; Steven

R. Shapiro; Jerome Shestack; Nadine Strossen; Rose Styron; John Updike; Luisa Valenzuela; Nicholas A. Veliotes; Kurt Vonnegut, Jr.; Deborah Wiley; Roger Wilkins; Wendy Wolf.

Human Rights Watch Prison Project

Staff

Joanna Weschler, Director; Marti Weithman, Associate.

Advisory Committee

Herman Schwartz, Chair; Nan Aron; Vivian Berger; Haywood Burns; Alejandro Garro; William Hellerstein; Edward Koren; Sheldon Krantz; The Hon. Morris Lasker; Benjamin Malcolm; Diane Orentlicher; Norman Rosenberg; David Rothman; Clarence Sundram.

Human Rights Watch
Women's Rights Project

Staff

Dorothy Q. Thomas, Director; Sarah Lai, Research Associate; LaShawn Jefferson, Research Associate; Regan Ralph, Staff Attorney; Deborah Blatt, Consultant; Binaifer Nowrojee, Consultant; Evelyn Miah, Associate.

Advisory Committee

Kathleen Peratis, Chair; Nahid Toubia, Vice Chair; Mahnaz Afkhami; Helen Bernstein; Alice Brown; Charlotte Bunch; Rhonda Copelon; Patricia Derian; Joan Dunlop; Mallika Dutt; Martha Fineman; Claire Flom; Adrienne Germain; Leslie Glass; Lisa Hedley; Zhu Hong; Stephen Isaacs; Helene Kaplan; Marina Pinto Kaufman; Wangari Maathai; Joyce Mends-Cole; Marysa Navarro-Aranguren; Susan Peterson; Celina Romany; Margaret Schuler; Jeane Sindab.

Human Rights Watch
California Advisory Committee

Stanley K. Sheinbaum, Honorary Chair; Mike Farrell, Co-Chair; Jane Olson, Co-Chair; Raquel Ackerman; Rabbi Leonard Beerman; Alan Gleitsman; Danny Glover; Paul Hoffman; Barry Kemp; Donna LaBonte; Daniel Levy; Lynda Palevsky; Lucille Polachek; Clara A. "Zazi" Pope; Tracy Rice; Vicki Riskin Rintels; Cheri Rosche; Pippa Scott; Hon. Phillip R. Trimble; Joan Willens; Dianne Wittenberg.